Scriptural Catholicism

(pardon the redundancy)

Steven L. Kellmeyer

"A welcome addition to my library..."
- **Patrick Madrid,** Editor-in-Chief of *Envoy* Magazine and editor of *Surprised By Truth.*

"I highly recommend this very thorough compilation of biblical data on Catholic beliefs, not only for Catholics who wish to know how to defend their faith biblically, but for non-Catholics who insist on asking the question, "Show me where in Scripture it teaches that ...?!" Mr. Kellmeyer's brief commentaries and explanations of Catholic perspectives on issues like the authority of Scripture and Tradition are also very sensitively and accurately written. This resource should prove to be a very helpful companion to other apologetic resources, such as William Jurgen's *Faith of the Early Fathers.*"
- **Marcus C. Grodi**, Director, The Coming Home Network Interntional

"Sola Scriptura" was a theological novelty when it first appeared at the time of the Protestant Reformation; its more extreme form in contemporary Fundamentalism is even more of an anomaly. That said, Steven Kellmeyer has done an admirable job of buttressing every major doctrine and practice of Catholicism not only with individual Scripture quotes but with the entire sense of Sacred Scripture." - **Reverend Peter Stravinskas**, Editor, *The Catholic Answer*

Steven Kellmeyer's *Scriptural Catholicism* is an extremely useful compendium of a huge assortment of biblical data showing the Bible to be what the apostles understood it to be: the written aspect of the Sacred Tradition which is nothing other than the Catholic Faith. A superb resource for any Catholic student of Scripture! - **Mark Shea**, author of *By What Authority?*

ABOUT THE AUTHOR

Steven Kellmeyer completed his M.A. in theology with catechetics emphasis at Franciscan University, Steubenville, Ohio in May, 1999. He is broadly educated, with an A.A.S. in medical laboratory technology, a B.A. in computer science, and an M.A. in modern European history. In addition to his lectures on apologetic and pro-life issues, he has published articles with *This Rock, Envoy, Lay Witness, The Catholic Answer, Hands-On Apologetics, Social Justice Review* and Human Life International. His first book, *The Scriptural Roots of Catholicism,* is an apologetics textbook which provides full-text Scriptural references and commentary for nearly seventy essential doctrines of the Catholic Faith, along with essays on how the canon of Scripture was established, a short history of Scripture translations, and a discussion of the New Testament use of the deuterocanonical books. He and his wife and children in Plano, Texas.

Explanation of the the Book Cover

The cover painting, Raphael's *Holy Family,* was chosen for several reasons. It is, of course, a uniquely beautiful work which provides an intimate portrait of Jesus, Mary, Joseph, John the Baptist, and St. Elizabeth. Further, Raphael demonstrates a distinctively Catholic style by including each one of us in the Holy Family in depicting the persons of the nameless man and woman through which every human being is made present. Yet the work is distinctive in another way. Raphael completed the painting in 1518, the same year in which an Augustinian priest named Martin Luther was first called before an ecclesial court and asked to explain his writings. Raphael's painting is, therefore, the last pristine image from the age of Christendom to demonstrate the complete Catholic teaching - God's Holy Family is our ultimate destiny.

Steven L. Kellmeyer

Scriptural Catholicism

(pardon the redundancy)

Vigil Press   Plano, TX

Scripture quotations are used from the Revised Standard Version of the Bible, copyright 1946, 1952, and 1971 by the Division of Christian Education of the National Council of the Churches of Christ in the USA. Used by permission.

Excerpts from the English translation of *The Roman Missal* © 1973, International Committee on English in the Liturgy, Inc. All rights reserved.

How To Contact the Author
For information on speaking engagements or
to obtain additional copies of this book,
contact:

Bridegroom Press
2901 Country Place Dr.
Plano, TX 75075

E-mail: info@bridegroompress.com
Phone : 972-758-9209

Web Sites:
BridegroomPress.com

All rights reserved. No part of this publication may be reproduced, stored, in a retrieval system, or transmitted in any form or by any means, electronic, mechanical, photocopying, recording, or otherwise, without the prior permission of the copyright owner.

Cover: Raphael, *The Holy Family*, 1518.

Copyright 1998

ISBN 1-60104-066-0
ISBN-13: 978-1-60104-066-4
Printed in the U.S.A.

FOREWORD

Welcome to Scriptural Catholicism. This book began as a personal list of jotted down notes intended to help me remember the chapter and verse for various apologetics arguments. It became an electronic document, then a Web site, and finally, after promptings from satisfied Internet users, this book. The book retains indications of its Web site origins - the underlinings you see in the text aren't random, they reflect hypertext Web links in the original documents, both to other locations on my Web site and to other sites throughout the Web.

My purpose has always been to provide an easily-referenced index to the Scriptural underpinnings of Catholic doctrine and dogma, with a minimum of exegesis. I have combed through numerous catechetical, apologetics and doctrinal resources to bring together in a single resource the vast majority of the Scriptural references which have historically been used in the defense of Church teaching. This list is by no means complete, but it is a solid start. I strongly recommend further study in the provided list of references. All but two Scripture quotations are from the *Revised Standard Version*. All errors are my own. That having been said, I have only one confession to make.

This is a crippled book. I have deliberately omitted nearly all references to the practice and witness of the earliest Christians, the Fathers of the Church, men like Ignatius, Irenaeus, John Chrysostom, Augustine, and hundreds of others who fought heresy, often suffering torture and death for Jesus Christ. Instead of having the three strong legs of Sacred Scripture, Sacred Tradition, and the Sacred Magisterium, each providing witness to the other, this work balances precariously on one leg - Scripture alone. I have done this because many, many devout believers in Christ simply refuse any authority other than Scripture. We must meet people where they are. However, if any reader of this book begins to entertain the slightest doubt about the validity of using Scripture as the sole or final authority, you are strongly urged to read the lives and witnesses of the earliest Christians. See how they lived, what they believed. If this book is being used to discuss (not fight over) a subject with one of our separated brethren, I urge you to research that subject in the Fathers, so that you are prepared with such witnesses when your brother is ready to listen to them. Passages in the book which bear the addendum "Early Christians comment on XXX" indicate a subject which is strongly attested to by the earliest Christian writers. For examples of such witness, I highly recommend *Faith of the Early Fathers* by William Jurgens, Liturgical Press, 1970. It is a three-volume work, it is still in print, and most libraries should have a copy. It uses the writings of the Fathers and groups them topically - this book's format is loosely based on it.

References to the *Catechism of the Catholic Church* can be found in nearly every section of the book. These references are not exhaustive by any means - they provide an initial guide only. I have included the Litany to Jesus in the Womb of Mary, not because I expect you to pray it (though I hope you do), but because it is one of the most straightforward explanations I have found to explain why Mary is so important to Jesus Christ, and therefore, to us.

Steven Kellmeyer
January 17, 1998
Feast of St. Anthony of the Desert

Table of Contents

The Litany to Jesus in the Womb of Mary 1
God and Covenant 2
The Story 3
THE TRIUNE GOD 7
The Trinity 8
The Holy Spirit is God 13
   Procession of the Spirit 13
Jesus Christ: Fully Human and Fully Divine 14
   Mary, Mother of God 15
Equality of the Three Persons 21
CREATION AS SACRAMENT 22
SCRIPTURE 26
The Relationship between Holy Scripture and the Holy Church 27
Excerpts from: The Dogmatic Constitution on Divine Liturgy 27
   How Scripture Should be Read 29
The Church's Interpretation of Scripture 31
The Canon of Scripture 33
   The Evidence of Ancient Texts 33
   Proving the Bible and the Church Trustworthy 33
   Scripture Translations 34
   How the Canon was Established 35
   New Testament Deuterocanonical Passages 39
   Excerpts from the Old Testament Deuterocanonical books 40
Private Interpretation of Scripture 46
Sola Scriptura 49
   Tough Questions about Scripture 54
THE CHURCH 58
One 59
Holy 64
Catholic 67
Apostolic 69
The Mystical Body 74
The Communion of Saints 77
   Christ is the One Mediator 79
   Relics of Saints 83
Church Authority and Infallibility 85
   Development of Doctrine 90
Papal Authority 93
   The Rock 93
   The Keys 95
   The Shepherd 96
Tradition 99
The Mass - Christ's One Sacrifice 103
SACRAMENTS 113
The Love of Christ 114
Sacramental Principles 117

Table of Contents

Holy Matrimony 120
    Divorce 126
    Birth Control 127
    Abortion 131
Baptism 136
    Types for Baptism 136
    Establishment of Baptism 138
    Marriage to the Bridegroom 140
    Regenerative Baptism 142
    Necessary for Salvation 143
    Immersion 144
    Infant Baptism 146
Confirmation 148
Holy Orders 149
    Women's Ordination 150
    Call No Man "Father" 151
    Celibacy 152
The Eucharist 155
    Types for the Eucharist 155
    The Establishment of the Eucharist 160
    The Eucharist in the Early Church 166
Reconciliation: Reunion with the Church 171
Anointing of the Sick 175
Divinization 175
SACRAMENTALS 179
Blessings 180
Images 181
Holy Water 184
Ashes and Incense 188
SALVATION 189
Salvation Through Faith and Works 190
    Works of the Law 194
    Imputed Righteousness 198
Once Saved, Always Saved 200
Mortal and Venial Sin 204
Redemptive Suffering 206
Temporal Consequences of Sin 209
Purgatory 210
Indulgences 214
Hell 216
Heaven 218
MARY 221
Mary, the Sinless New Eve 223
Mary, Ark of the Covenant 227
Mary, Perpetual Virgin 228
    Brothers of Christ 229

Table of Contents

Mary, Queen of Heaven ... 232
Mary, Our Mother ... 235
Maternal Mediation ... 238
The Assumption of Mary ... 240
The Virtues of Mary ... 241
Martin Luther on Mary and Marian Veneration ... 243
PRAYER ... 245
The Sign of the Cross ... 246
Repetitious Prayer ... 247
    Litany ... 248
The Hail Mary ... 249
The Rosary ... 249
The Sub Tuum Praesidium ... 250
Memorare ... 251
Hail Holy Queen ... 252
Liturgy of the Hours ... 253
Our Father ... 254
    First Petition ... 256
    Second Petition ... 256
    Third Petition ... 257
    Fourth Petition ... 257
    Fifth Petition ... 258
    Sixth Petition ... 259
    Seventh Petition ... 260
GLOSSARY ... 262
RESOURCES ... 263
How To Contact the Author ... 264
Web Sites ... 264
Notes ... 264

The Litany to Jesus in the Womb of Mary

Respond to each invocation with "Have mercy on us."

Jesus, knit so wonderfully in the womb of Mary,
Jesus, conceived by the Holy Spirit in the womb of Mary,
Jesus, uniquely human from the moment of conception in the womb of Mary,
Jesus, present at creation, created in the womb of Mary,
Jesus, word made flesh, taking on a human body in the womb of Mary,
Jesus, revealed by the Father, concealed in the womb of Mary
Jesus, subject to human development in the womb of Mary,
Jesus, whose Precious Blood first flowed through tiny arteries and veins in the womb of Mary,
Jesus, hidden nine months in the womb of Mary,
Jesus, begotten by God, nourished by the substance and blood of His Most Holy Mother in the womb of Mary,
Jesus, leaping from eternity into time, in the womb of Mary,
Jesus, revealing with His Father and the Holy Spirit all wisdom and knowledge to His Most Holy Mother, in the womb of Mary,
Jesus, aware of His role as Redeemer in the womb of Mary,
Jesus, Sanctifier of His Precursor from the womb of Mary,
Jesus, Eternal Word, Divine Child, embraced by the Father, in the womb of Mary,
Jesus, raising His Mother to the heights of sanctification, in the womb of Mary,
Jesus, everlasting delight of heaven, in the womb of Mary,
Jesus, manifesting His Incarnation to His Holy Mother, in the womb of Mary,
Jesus, adored and contemplated by His Mother in the sanctuary of her womb,
Jesus, before whom the angels prostrated themselves, in the womb of Mary,
Jesus, in whom the very angels beheld the humanity of the Infant God and the union of the two natures of the Word in the virginal womb of Mary,
Jesus, our protector and savior, asleep in the inviolable womb of Mary,
Jesus, whose Holy Limbs first budded in the womb of Mary,
Jesus, whose Godhead the world cannot contain, weighing only a few grams in the womb of Mary,
Jesus, Divine Immensity, once measuring only tenths of an inch in the womb of Mary,
Jesus, Sacrificial Lamb, Docile Infant in the womb of Mary,
Jesus, who was to suffer the agony and passion of death, accepting the human capacity for pain and grief, in the womb of Mary,
Jesus, foretelling His Eucharistic Presence, in the womb of Mary,

Jesus, Lamb of God in the womb of Mary -- Spare us, O Lord.
Jesus, Holy Innocent in the womb of Mary -- Graciously hear us, O Lord.
Jesus, Son of God and Messiah in the womb of Mary -- Have mercy on us, O Lord.

God and Covenant

A covenant is more than a simple contract. Where a contract is simply the exchange of goods for services, a covenant is the joining of two separate lives into one. When a covenant is formed between two people, they truly become one body - each is flesh of the other's flesh, and bone of the other's bone, each freely chooses to permanently join self to the other. Covenants create living relationships. Covenants create families.

When Adam and Eve were created, they were children of God, created in the image and likeness of God. Likewise, they were joined to each other in covenantal union, flesh of one flesh, and bone of one bone. All were one family. However, through sin, Adam and Eve died to God. Through their covenantal choice, the patrimony of life was taken from all of their descendants as well - all died to Him. The children of God were no more.

God remedied this by creating a new family, the Chosen People. God chose the People by establishing a covenant with Abraham, a descendant of Adam. Through the free choice of Abraham, the People chose to establish a covenant with God. This establishment of the Old Covenant, which gave the Chosen People their title and their role in salvation history, also made Abraham and his descendants the family, the children, of the living God. By establishing His family on earth, God could bring His only begotten Son into the history of creation, making Him, through them, truly part of His family on earth.

God chose Mary to bear His Son. Mary, freely chose to bear the Son of God. This decision brought the salvational covenant plan of the Father to its fullness. By the marriage covenant established between Mary and the Holy Spirit, Jesus Christ became the First-Born of the family of Man. As the Bridegroom who is the only Son of the Father, He marries the Bride without spot or wrinkle, the Church, who thereby becomes the household of the living God, joined as One Body with Jesus Christ. Through the extended family formed by this marriage, which is the New Covenant, all mankind is brought to salvation. All who are baptized into the death of Jesus Christ are literally raised up and made part of the One Body of Jesus Christ, who is the Bride, the Church.

The history of salvation is thus a history of God's family, for God acts only through family relationships. God saves all mankind by extending to every one of us the invitation to marry into His family. By this marriage, which we call baptism, we are washed, sealed, made clean and pure, and are thereby truly made children of the living God. When we die to Him through mortal sin, His sacraments of forgiveness and grace, administered by and through the Bride who is His Body, anoint us and bring us back to life within the Body of Christ. Just as the prodigal son was adorned upon his return by the father, and just as Jesus ministered to those in need before His crucifixion, so He ministers to those in need after His crucifixion, through His Body, through His sacraments. Every sacrament is intended to constantly strengthen, purify, and re-purify us, raising the dead to life through baptism and confession, strengthening us through confirmation, healing us through the anointing of the sick, ministering to us through Holy Orders, making us fruitful through marriage, and feeding us with His own Body in the Eucharist so that we always be one Body with Him. All who are of the Body of Christ are our sisters and brothers, they are our family. Whether they be here present, undergoing purification so that they may enter heaven, or in heaven, each member of the family is alive in Christ, and is honored in Christ, for he who honors a member of the covenant honors Jesus Christ, who established the New Covenant and who completes the family of God.

The Story

In the beginning was God. He is self-sufficient, perfectly complete in the family of Persons who are the Trinity, Father, Son, Holy Spirit, each totally pouring themselves out to the others. God does not need anyone or anything else, and nothing else exists, because God is the Original Essence, the Original Being. But, out of His superabundant love, He chooses to create. And in this creation, He has a plan.

He creates angels, gives them vast knowledge and power, and gives them freedom. Why? Because He wanted to. He doesn't create out of need. He creates out of love. All that exists He holds in existence from moment to moment, holding them in His mind. The freedom He gives His creatures, the angels, is abused by some of them. The moment each angel is brought into existence, each can choose to love God or not. Each knows perfectly well the full outcome of its choice from the first instance of its existence, and each chooses freely. Most choose to love. Some choose not to love. That is the fall of the angels.

Then Time began, for He also created the rest of the universe and us. We are unique in a special way. We are neither completely spirit, as the angels are, nor completely material, as the animals are. We are indissolubly both spirit and material being. Together, spirit and material being form our human nature. Our spirit-soul holds our bodies together and keeps those bodies working in their inter-related parts. We are made to participate, body and soul, in His divine life. We are made to be loved for all Eternity. That has been the plan from the beginning. God always intended to establish His family on earth, a kingdom of priests mediating His grace and His light to the world. He gave us freedom, just as He gave the angels freedom. Unlike the angels, we are not given a vast intellect. God created us to trust in Him. While we were not capable of understanding the full implications of our choice, either for good or ill, we had presentiments and warnings.

This is the Chain of Being - God creates on every level. Thus, He creates beings with full knowledge of their own destiny from the moment of their existence (angels), He creates beings which grow into knowledge of their own destiny (men), beings with a purely spiritual existence (angels), beings with an unbreakable unity of spirit and material existence (men), and beings with a purely material existence (everything else), having varying degrees of purely natural knowledge (apes down to non-sentient things like rocks).

Within men, there are also gradations of knowledge. Some men are given a great knowledge and love of God and never lose it. Others are given only a partial knowledge of God which they must build up painfully with His help. Others still are given very little knowledge of Him, and must struggle on without a full sense of love. To each who is given a different burden, God gives different gifts. In order to know God as God wants us to know Him, we must have not just natural knowledge, but supernatural knowledge, Divine Revelation. Such knowledge can only be a free gift from God - it cannot be discovered by man. This Divine Revelation is available only through Scripture and the sacramental life of the Church.

Thus, even someone who has not ever heard the Gospel may be saved, as long as their lack of knowledge derives from the terrible cross of an invincible ignorance and does not derive from a conscious decision to reject God, a conscious decision not to love. God gives to each sufficient knowledge and grace to improve themselves before Him, to learn to love, to learn about Him. Each is called to love God and neighbor more than they do now. No one who condemns themselves through their rejection of Love will be able to say to God, "You didn't give me enough help to know You," but each may know God in a lesser or greater way, according to the gifts they were given. Insofar as each responds well to His gifts, each may be saved.

In Adam, we were given the choice to share in Eternal Love and Eternal Life. Adam refused the gift of divine, eternal Love, both as a result of temptation from the evil angels who had refused that same Love and just out of poor choice on our part. Since God existed out of time, and we exist in time, He knew what we would do, and the very act which brought the created universe into existence, the universe which we were supposed to rule and guard, also brought into existence His plan for our salvation from sin and our divinization.

Thus, as soon as the Fall happened, God promised Adam that salvation would come. Over the course of time after Adam's fall, He gradually revealed Himself to fallen man, and gathered together the people necessary for the plan to take root and grow. He gave us prophecies, He gave us promises, He made covenant with us, He taught us how to be a family, the assembly of the Lord. Down through the long corridors of the ages, He let us know what was going to happen by revealing a bit, letting us absorb it, revealing a bit more, letting us absorb it, over and over, each time revealing a bit more of who He is, building up the links of our salvation for us in the people of the earth, people like Noah, Abraham, Moses, David, and the lives of each of us on the earth, lives like yours. He prepared for Himself and for us a community of persons, for He intended to do an extraordinary thing.

In the fullness of time, the fullness of revelation was prepared. He prepared a place for Himself, a place in which He would begin the final, the total revelation. He had revealed His word through the patriarchs and the prophets of old, now He prepared to enter creation not just in a place, but through a person, through the person of Mary. Because He respects free will always, He gave her complete freedom, a freedom as complete as Adam's, and asked if she would agree to His plan. She agreed, in a free choice just like Adam's, to His love and His plan. At the instant of her "fiat," He clothed Himself in humanity, infinite power telescoped into a fertilized egg, taking His human nature from the mother He created for Himself and instantly uniting His eternally pre-existing divine nature to His same Person newly formed in the womb. In that instant, He also united Himself in a mysterious way to every human being who ever has or ever will live. This unity allowed Him to take on our sins, and allows us to become part of His Body, part of God's Family, if we choose to cooperate with His gift. Slowly he grew, was born, grew more, learned, lived, loved. Over the course of thirty-three years, He revealed Himself to a few chosen men and women. This is the central mystery - why would God do this? Why would Infinite Power limit Himself by taking on human nature? Who is man to merit it?

It is insanity, from a human point of view.

It happened.

First they knew Him as a man like them. Then they knew Him as a teacher, a unique teacher who taught with complete authority and called twelve men out of obscurity, teaching in ways and doing things unlike any teacher that Israel had ever seen. He did things they didn't understand, He said things they couldn't comprehend. After each dispute with the learned, each miraculous cure, the same question returned: "Where did he learn to do and say these things? Where did this man come from?" No one knew. But He was not only their teacher. They learned to love Him as they had loved no one else. At the end, He became their friend.

But those who could not bring themselves to love Him also could not bring themselves to let Him walk among them. He was put to death. He knew it would happen from the beginning. He had prepared His friends for it. He was ready.

He rose from death.

His closest friends didn't believe it. Despite all the reports, the women, the disciples, even the witness of Apostles could not convince the last holdout. Each one knew. They knew that no man could rise from the dead. Then He appeared to them. He brought the fruits of His love with Him - redemption, salvation, the opportunity to choose Eternal love forever. He had already established a Church to be His family on earth, to dispense the mystery of salvation to men, to be the kingdom of God, to be the Body of Christ. In the forty days following His resurrection, He taught the men He had picked, the men He had clothed with special power, as they had never before been taught. He completed their preparation. They were made ready to take their places in His Body, His Church. This Body, born on the Cross, came of age on Pentecost. Fifty days after He rose from the dead, fifty days after His Body was torn and crucified, His body, the body of salvation, conceived in the womb of Mary and nurtured by Him over the next thirty-three years, given birth on the Cross, announced Her place in the world when the Spirit came down in tongues of fire upon Her members. United to His Son's Bride, His Body, new sons and daughters of the Most High were added every day. God saves through family. The family of God began to grow.

This growing family, the one Church He established, spread the Word about the God who is Love, the God who suffers for us, the God who saves. In time, she wrote the last pieces of the millenia-long story down, acting under the guidance of God. Even as she wrote, God continued to reveal aspects of Himself to the Apostles through the work of the Third Person of the Trinity, the Holy Spirit. Finally, John, the last living Apostle, died, and with his death, God's work of self-revelation was complete. There remained only two tasks: teaching the truth to all who would hear, and giving all human beings a chance to become a part of the Body of Christ, the Church.

The earliest Christians are called the Fathers of the Church, because they were taught by divinely inspired Apostles, and were often themselves apostles, placed in that office by the Holy Spirit, acting through the Body of Christ. They used their teachers' wisdom and the inspiration of the Spirit to plumb the depths of God's Word, bringing back truly incredible insights into the nature of God. The age of Christendom dawned, an age when a whole civilization, covering more territory than even the mighty Roman Empire of old, spoke with one heart, moved with one being, loved with one love, all directed towards God. Throughout it all, God provided apostles, whom we call bishops, to guide and teach us and saints to witness to us. Eventually, disputes arose and the unity was fractured, but God continued to provide bishops and saints to guide us back to unity. That process continued and continues in the councils of the Church and the work of individual hands. Unity will again be attained, for God's Body will suffer only so long.

In every age, at every moment in history, He supplies His Church, His Body, with the nutrients it needs, sacraments, grace, living examples of love, holy men and women who feed the poor, clothe the naked, care for the sick, instruct the uninformed, who show forth His love. Mother Theresa was just the latest in a long line. He asks each of us to be an example of Eternal love to every person we meet. He asks you to be an example of Eternal love. He loves people through you. That is what it means to be part of His family. At every moment of your life, you choose to be part of His family, His Church, or you choose to reject His family and His love. This choice is rooted in how you love others, how you love Him. This choice to love is not a one-time experience, but a continuum of choice, every moment, every second. We are free. We can reject Him up to the very last, if we desire. We can turn and repent at the very last. God is never far from us, He is always near, pouring out love upon us so that we might choose Him, because God is love, and He can do nothing other than to love us.

He will come again. He will judge each of us by how well we loved, whether we loved Him first, most, best, and whether we allowed Him to use us to love the people around us. If we have loved others well, we will be brought into the heavenly Jerusalem and an eternal life bathed in the consuming fire of Love. That is heaven. If we have chosen not to love, we have chosen an eternity apart from Him, apart from Love. That eternity will be spent with those who chose not love, but hate. That is hell. It is our choice.

This is the story of Scripture.

This is how it works.

This is the story it tells.

There are many details that have been omitted here, many names, many living proofs of His love. Each lifetime of history has its prophets, its saints, the living examples of love who are God's beacons to you and to me, His light shining forth from their eyes, His touch in their caress. Scripture is complete, but it is only the beginning of the story.

THE TRIUNE GOD

2 Corinthians 13:14
The grace of the Lord Jesus Christ
and
the love of God
and
the fellowship of the Holy Spirit
be with you all.

Matthew 28:19
Go, therefore and make disciples of all nations,
baptizing them
in the name
of the Father
and of the Son
and of the Holy Spirit.

The Trinity

The Scripture passages for much of The Trinity, The Holy Spirit is God, Equality, *and* Procession *comes from* Scripture by Topic.

God is a communion of persons, a family whose life is love. He is pure Being, existing from all eternity, both infinitely transcendant, unlimited, unchanging, greater than all His works. He is also infinitely immanent, intimately involved in the existence and life of every creature, most especially with us human persons. In God we live, we move, we have our being. We are meant to abandon ourselves to Him.

The One God is Three Persons in One Divine substance, having one intellect, and one will. Within the Godhead, the Person of the Father is unbegotten and does not proceed from any other Person. However, the Father eternally pours Himself out, eternally begetting the Son. The Holy Spirit, the eternal and complete outpouring of love between Father and Son, eternally proceeds from the Father and (or through) the Son. The procession of the Son from the Father gives two relations: the relations of paternity and filiation. The procession of the Holy Spirit from the Father through the Son also gives two relations: the relations of active spiration (the Father and Son actively spirate the Spirit) and passive spiration (the Spirit is passively spirated). Active spiration is opposed to passive spiration, but is not opposed to paternity and filiation, thus there are three opposing relations and three Persons. God is, therefore, one in indivisible Substance, containing Two Processions, between Three Persons, having Four Relations.

The Father pours Himself out and subsists wholly in the Son and the Father pours Himself out and subsists wholly in the Spirit. The Son and the Spirit each pour themselves out in like manner, subsisting wholly in each other and wholly in the Father. This is the inner life of Trinitarian love. Truth, Beauty, and Goodness all reveal the nature of that life, the mindset of God. This knowledge, available only through the revelation brought to us by Jesus Christ, is part of the inner life of God. (CCC 198-301).

The Father is the Creator (CCC 279,302), the Son is our Redeemer (CCC 599) and the Holy Spirit is our Sanctifier, preparing men, manifesting God, and establishing communion between us (CCC 737). God always intended to share His life with us, so He established a way for that to happen. It is accomplished through the work of the liturgy.

Current misunderstandings: Some self-professed "Christian" sects, deny the Trinitarian nature of God, Three Persons, One God.

Deut 6:4-5 "Hear, O Israel: The Lord our God is one Lord; ⁵ and you shall love the Lord your God with all your heart, and with all your soul, and with all your might.

God is clearly one. However...

Gen 1:26 Then God said, "Let us make man in our image, after our likeness..."

Gen 3:22 Then the Lord God said, "Behold, the man has become like one of us, knowing good and evil; and now, lest he put forth his hand and take also of the tree of life, and eat, and live for ever"—

Gen 11:7 "Come, let us go down, and there confuse their language, that they may not understand one another's speech."

God is also a plurality in some sense.

Gen 1:27 So God created man in his own image, in the image of God he created him; male and female he created them.

For...

Gen 2:18 ...the Lord God said, "It is not good that the man should be alone; I will make a helper fit for him."

God is one. God is Good, complete in Himself. Man is made in the image and likeness of God. However, when man is alone, it is not good. If it is not good for the creature made in the image and likeness of God to be alone, then God is somehow not alone. But God, by definition, lacks nothing, and did not need to create. Therefore, God must be a plurality. It is interesting to note that the word "Paraclete" may also be translated "helper."

Gen 18:1 And the Lord appeared to him by the oaks of Mamre, as he sat at the door of his tent in the heat of the day. ² He lifted up his eyes and looked, and behold, three men stood in front of him. When he saw them, he ran from the tent door to meet them, and bowed himself to the earth, ³ and said, "My lord, if I have found favor in your sight, do not pass by your servant..."

Abraham sees three persons, but addresses them as one Lord.

Is 6:3 And one called to another and said: "Holy, holy, holy is the Lord of hosts; the whole earth is full of his glory."

Rev 4:8 And the four living creatures, each of them with six wings, are full of eyes all round and within, and day and night they never cease to sing,
"Holy, holy, holy, is the Lord God Almighty,
who was and is and is to come!"

The angels recognize the holiness of each Person of the One God.

Ex 20:1-11 And God spoke all these words, saying, ² "I am the Lord your God, who brought you out of the land of Egypt, out of the house of bondage.
    ³ "You shall have no other gods before me.
    ⁴ "You shall not make for yourself a graven image, or any likeness of anything that is in heaven above, or that is in the earth beneath, or that is in the water under the earth; ⁵ you shall not bow down to them or serve them; for I the Lord your God am a jealous God, visiting the iniquity of the fathers upon the children to the third and the fourth generation of those who hate me, ⁶ but showing steadfast love to thousands of those who love me and keep my commandments.
    ⁷ "You shall not take the name of the Lord your God in vain; for the Lord will not hold him guiltless who takes his name in vain.
    ⁸ "Remember the sabbath day, to keep it holy. ⁹ Six days you shall labor, and do all your work; ¹⁰ but the seventh day is a sabbath to the Lord your God; in it you shall not do any work, you, or your son, or your daughter, your manservant, or your maidservant, or your cattle, or the sojourner who is within your gates; ¹¹ for in six days the Lord made heaven and earth, the sea, and all that is in them, and rested the seventh day; therefore the Lord blessed the sabbath day and hallowed it.

Likewise, the Ten Commandments echo the Triune aspect of God, for both here and in Deut 5:6ff, the first three commands deal with honoring God, while the remaining seven witness God's work in creation by outlining our relations with our fellow man.

Prov 8:22 The Lord created me at the beginning of his work, the first of his acts of old.

Sir 24:3-21 "I came forth from the mouth of the Most High,
and covered the earth like a mist. ⁴ I dwelt in high places,
and my throne was in a pillar of cloud. ⁵ Alone I have made the circuit of the vault of heaven
and have walked in the depths of the abyss. ⁶ In the waves of the sea, in the whole earth,
and in every people and nation I have gotten a possession. ⁷ Among all these I sought a resting place;
I sought in whose territory I might lodge. ⁸ "Then the Creator of all things gave me a commandment,
and the one who created me assigned a place for my tent.
And he said, 'Make your dwelling in Jacob,
and in Israel receive your inheritance.' ⁹ From eternity, in the beginning, he created me,
and for eternity I shall not cease to exist. ¹⁰ In the holy tabernacle I ministered before him,
and so I was established in Zion. ¹¹ In the beloved city likewise he gave me a resting place,
and in Jerusalem was my dominion. ¹² So I took root in an honored people,
in the portion of the Lord, who is their inheritance. ¹³ "I grew tall like a cedar in Lebanon,
and like a cypress on the heights of Hermon. ¹⁴ I grew tall like a palm tree in En-gedi,
and like rose plants in Jericho;
like a beautiful olive tree in the field,
and like a plane tree I grew tall. ¹⁵ Like cassia and camel's thorn I gave forth the aroma of spices,
and like choice myrrh I spread a pleasant odor,
like galbanum, onycha, and stacte,
and like the fragrance of frankincense in the tabernacle. ¹⁶ Like a terebinth I spread out my branches,
and my branches are glorious and graceful. ¹⁷ Like a vine I caused loveliness to bud,
and my blossoms became glorious and abundant fruit. ¹⁹ "Come to me, you who desire me,
and eat your fill of my produce. ²⁰ For the remembrance of me is sweeter than honey,
and my inheritance sweeter than the honeycomb. ²¹ Those who eat me will hunger for more,
and those who drink me will thirst for more.

The Second Person of the Trinity is the uncreated, eternally-begotten Son of the Father, yet the passages above seem to indicate He was created, not co-eternal with the Father. Because God writes about divine realities in the finite words of men, Scripture often speaks of the ways of God in terms of limited human understanding, not Divine Being. Thus, though God is love and can do nothing but love, Scripture speaks of God's "hatred" or His "taking away" His love. In fact, God does not remove His love from any person, rather, we who are suffering the effects of sin in this world experience in ourselves the lack of love God receives from mankind. Similarly, Scripture speaks of the "creation" of the Second Person of the Trinity not because He is created, but because there are few good ways to emphasize in human words the real distinctions between the Three co-eternal Persons of the Trinity.

Jn 1:1 In the beginning was the Word, and the Word was with God, and the Word was God.

As can be seen from the Gospel of John, knowing Jesus personally helps us find the necessary words.

Mt 3:16-17 And when Jesus was baptized, he went up immediately from the water, and behold, the heavens were opened and he saw the Spirit of God descending like a dove, and alighting on him; [17] and lo, a voice from heaven, saying, "This is my beloved Son, with whom I am well pleased."

Mt 28:19 Go therefore and make disciples of all nations, baptizing them in the name of the Father and of the Son and of the Holy Spirit,

Scripture asserts we should baptize in "the name" but then gives THREE names, not one.

Lk 1:35 And the angel said to her, "The Holy Spirit will come upon you, and the power of the Most High will overshadow you; therefore the child to be born will be called holy, the Son of God.

Jn 14:16,26 And I will pray the Father, and he will give you another Counselor, to be with you for ever,... But the Counselor, the Holy Spirit, whom the Father will send in my name, he will teach you all things, and bring to your remembrance all that I have said to you.

Jn 15:26 But when the Counselor comes, whom I shall send to you from the Father, even the Spirit of truth, who proceeds from the Father, he will bear witness to me...

Acts 2:33 Being therefore exalted at the right hand of God, and having received from the Father the promise of the Holy Spirit, he has poured out this which you see and hear.

2 Cor 13:14 The grace of the Lord Jesus Christ and the love of God and the fellowship of the Holy Spirit be with you all. .

Gal 4:6-7 And because you are sons, God has sent the Spirit of his Son into our hearts, crying, "Abba! Father!" [7] So through God you are no longer a slave but a son, and if a son then an heir.

Eph 2:18 for through him we both have access in one Spirit to the Father.

Eph 3:14-17 For this reason I bow my knees before the Father, [15] from whom every family in heaven and on earth is named, [16] that according to the riches of his glory he may grant you to be strengthened with might through his Spirit in the inner man, [17] and that Christ may dwell in your hearts through faith; that you, being rooted and grounded in love,

1 Jn 4:13-14 By this we know that we abide in him and he in us, because he has given us of his own Spirit. [14] And we have seen and testify that the Father has sent his Son as the Savior of the world.

God alone is truth. The Spirit must be God. The coming of the Holy Spirit is also foreshadowed in the Old Testament...

Jude 20-21 But you, beloved, build yourselves up on your most holy faith; pray in the Holy Spirit; [21] keep yourselves in the love of God; wait for the mercy of our Lord Jesus Christ unto eternal life.

Ezek 3:12,14 Then the Spirit lifted me up, and as the glory of the LORD arose from its place, I heard behind me the sound of a great earthquake...[14] The Spirit lifted me up and took me away, and I went in bitterness in the heat of my spirit, the hand of the LORD being strong upon me;

Ezek 36:26 A new heart I will give you, and a new spirit I will put within you; and I will take out of your flesh the heart of stone and give you a heart of flesh.

Joel 2:28-32 "And it shall come to pass afterward, that I will pour out my spirit on all flesh; your sons and your daughters shall prophesy, your old men shall dream dreams, and your young men shall see visions. [29] Even upon the menservants and maidservants

in those days, I will pour out my spirit.
³⁰ "And I will give portents in the heavens and on the earth, blood and fire and columns of smoke. ³¹ The sun shall be turned to darkness, and the moon to blood, before the great and terrible day of the LORD comes. ³² And it shall come to pass that all who call upon the name of the LORD shall be delivered; for in Mount Zion and in Jerusalem there shall be those who escape, as the LORD has said, and among the survivors shall be those whom the LORD calls.

The Father is only revealed through the Son.

Lk 10:22 All things have been delivered to me by my Father; and no one knows who the Son is except the Father, or who the Father is except the Son and any one to whom the Son chooses to reveal him.

Mk 1:11 and a voice came from heaven, "Thou art my beloved Son; with thee I am well pleased."

Christ is God's Son.

Jn 10:30 "I and the Father are one."

Is 62:4-5 You shall no more be termed Forsaken, and your land shall no more be termed Desolate; but you shall be called My delight is in her, and your land Married; for the LORD delights in you, and your land shall be married. ⁵ For as a young man marries a virgin, so shall your sons marry you, and as the bridegroom rejoices over the bride, so shall your God rejoice over you.

Only Christ was called the Bridegroom.

Mt 9:15 And Jesus said to them, "Can the wedding guests mourn as long as the bridegroom is with them? The days will come, when the bridegroom is taken away from them, and then they will fast.

In the Old Testament, the terms "spouse" and "shepherd" (Ezekial 34) were strictly divine, yet Matthew refers to Christ as the Bridegroom, and John 10 speaks of Christ as the shepherd.

Lk 5:20-21 ²⁰ And when he saw their faith he said, "Man, your sins are forgiven you." ²¹ And the scribes and the Pharisees began to question, saying, "Who is this that speaks blasphemies? Who can forgive sins but God only?"

Christ forgives sin...

Mk 2:5-7 And when Jesus saw their faith, he said to the paralytic, "My son, your sins are forgiven." ⁶ Now some of the scribes were sitting there, questioning in their hearts, ⁷ "Why does this man speak thus? It is blasphemy! Who can forgive sins but God alone?"

...and forgives on his own authority.

Mt 5:17 "Think not that I have come to abolish the law and the prophets; I have come not to abolish them but to fulfil them.

He perfects and completes the Law.

Mt 12:8 For the Son of man is lord of the sabbath.

Mk 3:1-6 Again he entered the synagogue, and a man was there who had a withered hand. ² And they watched him, to see whether he would heal him on the sabbath, so that they might accuse him. ³ And he said to the man who had the withered hand, "Come here." ⁴ And he said to them, "Is it lawful on the sabbath to do good or to do harm, to save life or to kill?" But they were silent. ⁵ And he looked around at them with anger, grieved at their hardness of heart, and said to the man, "Stretch out your hand." He stretched it out, and his hand was restored. ⁶ The Pharisees went out, and immediately held counsel with the Herodi-ans against him, how to destroy him.

He is Lord of the Sabbath...

Mt 25:31 "When the Son of man comes in his glory, and all the angels with him, then he will sit on his glorious throne.

Rom 2:16 on that day when, according to my gospel, God judges the secrets of men by Christ Jesus.

He is supreme judge of all men...

Mt 11:27 All things have been delivered to me by my Father; and no one knows the Son except the Father, and no one knows the Father except the Son and any one to whom the Son chooses to reveal him.

He has unique, intimate, knowledge of the Father, and the Father reciprocates it...

Rom 9:5 to them belong the patriarchs, and of their race, according to the flesh, is the Christ, who is God over all, blessed for ever. Amen.

Tit 2:13 awaiting our blessed hope, the appearing of the glory of our great God and Savior Jesus Christ...

Paul calls Christ God...

2 Pet 1:1 Simeon Peter, a servant and apostle of Jesus Christ, To those who have obtained a faith of equal standing with ours in the righteousness of our God and Savior Jesus Christ...

So does Peter.

Jn 14:16, 26 And I will pray the Father, and he will give you another Counselor, to be with you for ever,... But the Counselor, the Holy Spirit, whom the Father will send in my name, he will teach you all things, and bring to your remembrance all that I have said to you

The Holy Spirit teaches all Christ taught.

Jn 16:13-15 When the Spirit of truth comes, he will guide you into all the truth; for he will not speak on his own authority, but whatever he hears he will speak, and he will declare to you the things that are to come. [14] He will glorify me, for he will take what is mine and declare it to you. [15] All that the Father has is mine; therefore I said that he will take what is mine and declare it to you.

The Spirit speaks and announces..

Gal 2:17 But if, in our endeavor to be justified in Christ, we ourselves were found to be sinners, is Christ then an agent of sin? Certainly not!

Christ justifies us...

1 Cor 6:11 And such were some of you. But you were washed, you were sanctified, you were justified in the name of the Lord Jesus Christ and in the Spirit of our God.

The Spirit justifies us...

1 Cor 1:2 To the church of God which is at Corinth, to those sanctified in Christ Jesus, called to be saints together with all those who in every place call on the name of our Lord Jesus Christ, both their Lord and ours...

Jesus sanctifies us...

Rom 15:16 to be a minister of Christ Jesus to the Gentiles in the priestly service of the gospel of God, so that the offering of the Gentiles may be acceptable, sanctified by the Holy Spirit.

The Spirit sanctifies us...

Eph 1:13 In him you also, who have heard the word of truth, the gospel of your salvation, and have believed in him, were sealed with the promised Holy Spirit,

Jesus seals us...

Eph 4:30 And do not grieve the Holy Spirit of God, in whom you were sealed for the day of redemption.

The Holy Spirit seals us...

Gal 4:4-6 But when the time had fully come, God sent forth his Son, born of woman, born under the law, [5] to redeem those who were under the law, so that we might receive adoption as sons. [6] And because you are sons, God has sent the Spirit of his Son into our hearts, crying, "Abba! Father!"

God sent the pre-existent Son into the world...

Rom 8:15-16 For you did not receive the spirit of slavery to fall back into fear, but you have received the spirit of sonship. When we cry, "Abba! Father!" [16] it is the Spirit himself bearing witness with our spirit that we are children of God,

God sent the pre-existent Spirit into the world.

The Holy Spirit is God

The Holy Spirit is the Lord and the Giver of Life, He is a Person, the Third Person of the Trinity. He is the Protector and Guarantor of the Church who animates the Church and her people. We who are believers must have a relationship with Him; we obtain this relationship, the indwelling of His life, through the sacraments, which come to us through the liturgy. He is the source of our hope, our advocate, our anchor, our defender, and our sanctifier (CCC 243-248).

Acts 5:3-4 But Peter said, "Ananias, why has Satan filled your heart to lie to the Holy Spirit and to keep back part of the proceeds of the land? ⁴ While it remained unsold, did it not remain your own? And after it was sold, was it not at your disposal? How is it that you have contrived this deed in your heart? You have not lied to men but to God."

Peter asserts that lying to the Holy Spirit is lying to God.

1 Jn 5:6-9 This is he who came by water and blood, Jesus Christ, not with the water only but with the water and the blood. ⁷ And the Spirit is the witness, because the Spirit is the truth. ⁸ There are three witnesses, the Spirit, the water, and the blood; and these three agree. ⁹ If we receive the testimony of men, the testimony of God is greater; for this is the testimony of God that he has borne witness to his Son.

John says the Holy Spirit is God.

1 Cor 3:16-17 Do you not know that you are God's temple and that God's Spirit dwells in you? ¹⁷ If any one destroys God's temple, God will destroy him. For God's temple is holy, and that temple you are.

1 Cor 6:19-20 Do you not know that your body is a temple of the Holy Spirit within you, which you have from God? You are not your own; ²⁰ you were bought with a price. So glorify God in your body.

1 Corinthians also says the Holy Spirit is God.

2 Pet 1:21 because no prophecy ever came by the impulse of man, but men moved by the Holy Spirit spoke from God.

Heb 1:1 In many and various ways God spoke of old to our fathers by the prophets...
Heb 3:7-11 Therefore, as the Holy Spirit says,
"Today, when you hear his voice, ⁸ do not harden your hearts as in the rebellion,
on the day of testing in the wilderness, ⁹ where your fathers put me to the test
and saw my works for forty years. ¹⁰ Therefore I was provoked with that generation,
and said, 'They always go astray in their hearts; they have not known my ways.' ¹¹ As I swore in my wrath,
'They shall never enter my rest.'"

Heb 10:15-17 And the Holy Spirit also bears witness to us; for after saying, ¹⁶ "This is the covenant that I will make with them
after those days, says the Lord:
I will put my laws on their hearts,
and write them on their minds," ¹⁷ then he adds,
"I will remember their sins and their misdeeds no more."

The Holy Spirit's witness is the witness of the Lord. It was He whom the Israelites put to the test. It is He who makes covenant, putting the law in our hearts and forgiving our sins.

Acts 20:28 Take heed to yourselves and to all the flock, in which the Holy Spirit has made you overseers, to care for the church of God which he obtained with the blood of his own Son.

Procession of the Spirit

The Holy Spirit proceeds from the Father and from (or through) the Son. Since the Father is perfect and the Son images the Father perfectly in everything, the Son must also spirate the Spirit, just as the Father does. (CCC 246-248)

Current misunderstandings: Some (albeit not all) Eastern Orthodox Christians assert that the Holy Spirit proceeds from the Father only.

Jn 14:26 But the Counselor, the Holy Spirit, whom the Father will send in my name, he will teach you all things, and bring to your remembrance all that I have said to you.

Jn 15:26 But when the Counselor comes, whom I shall send to you from the Father, even the Spirit of truth, who proceeds from the Father, he will bear witness to me;

The argument is sometimes made that only the Father processes the Spirit from all eternity. They say Jesus merely sends the Spirit on His temporal mission, that is, Jesus only sends the Spirit into the world, Jesus does not take part in the eternal procession of the Spirit. However...

Jn 5:19 Jesus said to them, "Truly, truly, I say to you, the Son can do nothing of his own accord, but only what he sees the Father doing; for whatever he does, that the Son does likewise."

Jesus does all and only what the Father does. The Father spirates the Spirit, therefore Jesus also spirates the Spirit. John 15:26 is not restrictive - the Spirit proceeds from the Father, but He does not proceed only from the Father.

Jn 16:14 He will glorify me, for he will take what is mine and declare it to you.

Jn 20:22 And when he had said this, he breathed on them, and said to them, "Receive the Holy Spirit..."

Rom 8:9 But you are not in the flesh, you are in the Spirit, if in fact the Spirit of God dwells in you. Any one who does not have the Spirit of Christ does not belong to him.

Jn 16:14-15 He will glorify me, for he will take what is mine and declare it to you. [15] All that the Father has is mine; therefore I said that he will take what is mine and declare it to you.

Truth cannot contradict truth. While some passages in the Trinity section may seem to imply the Holy Spirit proceeds from the Father alone, such a reading ignores the passages given above.

Jesus Christ:
Fully Human and Fully Divine

Much of the Scripture and exegesis for this section comes from "Jesus Christ is not God - the JW argument," by Tim Staples, Envoy Magazine, Premier Issue, pp 21-23, and "Christ's Divinity Proved by the JW Bible," Joel S. Peters, This Rock, December 1996, pp. 18-25.

"For to join the mortal and the eternal, and think they can agree and work together, is folly. For what things are more differing or more distinct betwixt themselves, and more opposed, than the mortal and the immortal and eternal, joined together in order to undergo cruel storms?"
— *Lucretius*

God answered the objection with a single Word.

Jesus Christ was, from the first moment of His conception, one Person with two complete natures, a fully human nature completely free from all taint of sin, and the fully Divine nature in which resides the Godhead. Christ was truly generated and born by a human mother through the power of the Holy Spirit descending upon her from God the Father. In this way, the one divine Person united Himself, both in Will and Intellect, to a complete human nature, that is, Jesus has a human body, human will, human intellect, and human soul. Jesus Christ is both fully God and fully man at the same time and in the same person, two complete natures united substantially together in hypostatic union, each nature possessing its own will and its own mode of operation, the human will in free and full harmony with, and in subordination to, the Divine Will (CCC 422-486).

He Incarnated in order to save us from our sins, to show us how much God loves us, to give us a model, showing us how to live, and to enable us to participate in the divine life (CCC 457-460). Jesus is the icon of the Father (Phil 2:5-11) who continues to be present to us in the Eucharist, the priesthood, and the Church. He redeems us through the single event of the Paschal mystery, which is His Passion, Death, Resurrection, and Ascension, the still point of the turning world. Through this four-fold event, Death is conquered, and our sanctification is complete. He will come again to judge the living and the dead. The authority Christ has to do this rules in our lives right now - at His second coming there will be no second chance.

Current misunderstandings: Many Christians assert some diminishing in the Divinity or the humanity of Jesus Christ. The variations on these interpretations are legion - Jesus is not really God, but a lesser, created being (e.g., an archangel), Jesus is two persons in one body, Jesus is both man and God, but only the man died on the cross, while God did not, etc.

Mary, Mother of God

It is impossible to speak of the full humanity or the full divinity of Christ without simultaneously speaking of the motherhood of Mary. Because we know Christ is fully human, like us in all things but sin, we know Mary is truly His mother. Because Jesus is fully divine, we know Mary is the mother of God. The Council of Ephesus (431 A.D.) gave her this title in order to help people understand who Jesus Christ truly is.

Lk 1:31, 35 And behold, you will conceive in your womb and bear a son, and you shall call his name Jesus.... And the angel said to her,
"The Holy Spirit will come upon you, and the power of the Most High will overshadow you; therefore the child to be born will be called holy, the Son of God.

The above verses have been used to argue Mary was Mother of God only in the sense that she carried Jesus in her womb, they say Mary's ovum was not used in the creation of the God-Man, Jesus Christ, but that the Holy Spirit conceived Him without any part or share in the humanity of his mother, Mary. Yet...

Rom 1:3-4 concerning his Son, who was descended from David according to the flesh [4] and designated Son of God in power according to the Spirit of holiness by his resurrection from the dead, Jesus Christ our Lord,

Rev 22:16 "I Jesus have sent my angel to you with this testimony for the churches. I am the root and the offspring of David, the bright morning star."

Scripture states that Jesus is a true descendant of David.

Gen 3:15 I will put enmity between you and the woman,
and between your seed and her seed;
he shall bruise your head,
and you shall bruise his heel."

This is the only occurrence of the phrase "her seed" in all of Scripture. It is a reference to the coming of the Messiah and to the special role a <u>woman</u> will play in the redemption of mankind. Scripture confirms that Mary's ovum was used.

Elizabeth confirms that Mary is the Mother of God when she says:

Lk 1:43 And why is this granted me, that the mother of my Lord should come to me?

Jesus' human nature came to Him through the humanity of His mother, herself created specially by God. Jesus is one Person with two natures. Mary had nothing to do with Jesus' divine nature - the second Person of the Trinity pre-exists all creation. However, she gave Him His human nature - He is like men in all things but sin, and men draw their human nature from their parents. Jesus' biological parent is Mary. Jesus is one Person. Mothers only give birth to persons, not natures, not bodies. We call our parents "mother" and "father" even though they did not give us our immortal soul. Though they gave us only our created body, our human nature, yet God made us a person from the instant of our conception, so our mother is truly our mother, she gave birth to a person, and our father is truly our father, he helped create a person.

1 Cor 3:9 We are God's co-workers...

Eph 3:14-15 For this reason I bow my knees before the Father, [15] from whom every family in heaven and on earth is named...

God works through us - just as our very existence depends upon God, our true parenthood depends upon and derives from the eternal Fatherhood of God. Mary is truly the mother of the Person of Jesus, for she gave birth to the Person of Jesus, even though she didn't give Him His human soul or His immortal divinity, but only His human nature and created body.

Gal 3:16 Now the promises were made to Abraham and to his offspring. It does not say, "And to offsprings," referring to many; but, referring to one, "And to your offspring," which is Christ.

Gal 4:4 But when the time had fully come, God sent forth his Son, born of woman, born under the law...

1 Tim 2:5-6 For there is one God, and there is one mediator between God and men, the man Christ Jesus, [6] who gave himself as a ransom for all, the testimony to which was borne at the proper time.

Jesus is both fully man and fully God.

Jn 20:17 Jesus said to her, "Do not hold me, for I have not yet ascended to the Father; but go to my brethren and say to them, I am ascending to my Father and your Father, to my God and your God."

As a man, God is His God. He worships Him, prays to Him, and needs Him in His life, just as we do. His human soul cries out to God just as ours do. However, Jesus always distinguishes between the disciples' relationship to God and His own relationship to God when He refers to God. Christ is human. But He is also Divine.

Phil 2:6 who, though he was in the form of God, did not count equality with God a thing to be grasped,

Jn 14:28 You heard me say to you, 'I go away, and I will come to you.' If you loved me, you would have rejoiced, because I go to the Father; for the Father is greater than I.

The Father is "greater" than the incarnate Christ because Christ's humanity is a creation, and in His humanity He is subordinate to the Father, though in His divinity, He is equal to, and of the same divine substance as, the Father.

Heb 2:9 But we see Jesus, who for a little while was made lower than the angels, crowned with glory and honor because of the suffering of death, so that by the grace of God he might taste death for every one.

Jn 1:18 No one has ever seen God; the only Son, who is in the bosom of the Father, he has made him known.

Mt 11:11 Truly, I say to you, among those born of women there has risen no one greater than John the Baptist; yet he who is least in the kingdom of heaven is greater than he.

If John is greater than anyone born of woman, does this mean John does not have a human nature? Does it mean that those residing in heaven, who are greater than John, have a different nature? If John the Baptist is the greatest man to ever live, does that mean John the Baptist was greater than Jesus, superior to Him by nature? Clearly not. Thus, there is no difficulty in saying that the Person of God the Father is superior in His divine nature to the human nature of God the Son.

Jn 17:3 Now, this is eternal life, that they should know you, the only true God, and the one whom you sent, Jesus Christ.

Rom 9:5 to them belong the patriarchs, and of their race, according to the flesh, is the Christ, who is God over all, blessed forever. Amen.

One God in Three Persons - this is in perfect harmony with Catholic doctrine.

Is 9:6 For to us a child is born, to us a son is given; and the government will be upon his shoulder, and his name will be called "Wonderful Counselor, Mighty God, Everlasting Father, Prince of Peace."

Psalm 22:28 All the ends of the earth shall remember
    and turn to the LORD;
        and all the families of the nations
shall worship before him.

Mt 1:22-23 All this took place to fulfil what the Lord had spoken by the prophet: [23] "Behold, a virgin shall conceive and bear a son,
and his name shall be called Emmanuel" (which means, God with us)

Paul asserts two things simultaneously about Christ:

Gal 1:12 For I did not receive it from man, nor was I taught it, but it came through a revelation of Jesus Christ.

Paul asserts Christ is not a human being...

1 Tim 2:5-6 For there is one God, and there is one mediator between God and men, the man Christ Jesus, [6] who gave himself as a ransom for all, the testimony to which was borne at the proper time.

... and that Christ is a human being. If Scripture is the word of God, nothing but truth, then both statements must be true. Is Christ an angel? Paul doesn't think so:

Heb 1:1-8 In many and various ways God spoke of old to our fathers by the prophets; [2] but in these last days he has spoken to us by a Son, whom he appointed the heir of all things, through whom also he created the world. [3] He reflects the glory of God and bears the very stamp of his nature, upholding the universe by his word of power. When he had made purification for sins, he sat down at the right hand of the Majesty on high, ⁴ having become as much superior to angels as the name he has obtained is more excellent than theirs.

⁵ For to what angel did God ever say,
"Thou art my Son, today I have begotten thee"? Or again, "I will be to him a father, and he shall be to me a son"? ⁶ And again, when he brings the first-born into the world, he says, "Let all God's angels worship him." ⁷ Of the angels he says,
"Who makes his angels winds, and his servants flames of fire."

⁸ But of the Son he says,
"Thy throne, O God, is for ever and ever,
the righteous scepter is the scepter of thy kingdom.

Paul asserts that the Father calls the Son God.

Heb 1:9-13 Thou hast loved righteousness and hated lawlessness;
therefore God, thy God, has anointed thee
with the oil of gladness beyond thy comrades." ¹⁰ And,
"Thou, Lord, didst found the earth in the beginning,
and the heavens are the work of thy hands; ¹¹ they will perish, but thou remainest;
they will all grow old like a garment, ¹² like a mantle thou wilt roll them up,
and they will be changed.
But thou art the same,
and thy years will never end." ¹³ But to what angel has he ever said,
"Sit at my right hand,
till I make thy enemies
a stool for thy feet"?

In this series of rhetorical questions, Paul makes clear that Christ was much more than an angel.

Tit 2:13 awaiting our blessed hope, the appearing of the glory of our great God and Savior Jesus Christ,

The only thing left is - God.

Psalm 2:7 I will tell of the decree of the LORD: He said to me, "You are my son, today I have begotten you.

Psalm 110:1-3 The LORD says to my lord:
"Sit at my right hand,
till I make your enemies your footstool."
² The LORD sends forth from Zion
your mighty scepter.
Rule in the midst of your foes!
³ Your people will offer themselves freely
on the day you lead your host
upon the holy mountains.

From the womb of the morning
like dew your youth will come to you.

Is 35:4-6 Say to those who are of a fearful heart, "Be strong, fear not! Behold, your God will come with vengeance, with the recompense of God. He will come and save you." ⁵ Then the eyes of the blind shall be opened, and the ears of the deaf unstopped; ⁶ then shall the lame man leap like a hart, and the tongue of the dumb sing for joy. For waters shall break forth in the wilderness, and streams in the desert;

Mt 11:2-6 Now when John heard in prison about the deeds of the Christ, he sent word by his disciples ³ and said to him, "Are you he who is to come, or shall we look for another?" ⁴ And Jesus answered them, "Go and tell John what you hear and see: ⁵ the blind receive their sight and the lame walk, lepers are cleansed and the deaf hear, and the dead are raised up, and the poor have good news preached to them. ⁶ And blessed is he who takes no offense at me."

John knew who Christ was - he had proclaimed Him the Lamb of God, and he saw the Spirit descend on Him (John 1:29-33). John sent his disciples to ask Christ this question in order to make his own disciples realize that Christ was fulfilling the prophecy of Isaiah 35 - Christ is God.

Jer 23:5 "Behold, the days are coming, says the LORD, when I will raise up for David a righteous Branch, and he shall reign as king and deal wisely, and shall execute justice and righteousness in the land. ⁶ In his days Judah will be saved, and Israel will dwell securely. And this is the name by which he will be called: 'The LORD is our righteousness.'

Mt 16:16 Simon Peter replied, "You are the Christ, the Son of the living God."

Col 1:15-19 He is the image of the invisible God, the first-born of all creation; ¹⁶ for in him all things were created, in heaven and on earth, visible and invisible, whether thrones or dominions or principalities or authorities—all things were created through him and for him. ¹⁷ He is before all things, and in him all things hold together. ¹⁸ He is the head of the body, the church; he is the beginning, the first-born from the dead, that in everything he might be pre-eminent. ¹⁹ For in him all the fulness of God was pleased to dwell,

If Christ was created by God and all things were created through Christ, then Scripture is wrong -

Christ did not create all things, since He did not create Himself. Since Scripture cannot be wrong, Christ must be uncreated and thus, God.

Jn 3:16 For God so loved the world that he gave his only Son, that whoever believes in him should not perish but have eternal life.

Jn 5:18 This was why the Jews sought all the more to kill him, because he not only broke the sabbath but also called God his Father, making himself equal with God.

Jn 14:1 "Let not your hearts be troubled; believe in God, believe also in me"

Jn 10:28-30 and I give them eternal life, and they shall never perish, and no one shall snatch them out of my hand. ²⁹ My Father, who has given them to me, is greater than all, and no one is able to snatch them out of the Father's hand. ³⁰ I and the Father are one."

Jn 16:14-15 He will glorify me, for he will take what is mine and declare it to you. ¹⁵ All that the Father has is mine; therefore I said that he will take what is mine and declare it to you.

Heb 3:4-6 Yet Jesus has been counted worthy of as much more glory than Moses as the builder of a house has more honor than the house. ⁴ (For every house is built by some one, but the builder of all things is God.) ⁵ Now Moses was faithful in all God's house as a servant, to testify to the things that were to be spoken later, ⁶ but Christ was faithful over God's house as a son. And we are his house if we hold fast our confidence and pride in our hope.

Rom 9:5 to them belong the patriarchs, and of their race, according to the flesh, is the Christ, who is God over all, blessed for ever. Amen.

1 Jn 5:7-8 And the Spirit is the witness, because the Spirit is the truth. ⁸ There are three witnesses, the Spirit, the water, and the blood; and these three agree..

Rev 17:14 they will make war on the Lamb, and the Lamb will conquer them, for he is Lord of lords and King of kings, and those with him are called and chosen and faithful."

Col 2:9 For in him the whole fulness of deity dwells bodily,

1 Jn 5:20 And we know that the Son of God has come and has given us understanding, to know him who is true; and we are in him who is true, in his Son Jesus Christ. This is the true God and eternal life.

Jn 1:1 In the beginning was the Word, and the Word was with God, and the Word was God.

Jehovah's Witnesses will argue that the correct translation should be "the word was a god." In charity, one may only say this is an extremely poor translation of the Greek, a translation so poor that any professor of Greek would flunk the student who gave him or her such a translation. However, if it were correct (it isn't), that means worshipping Jesus is idolatry.

Ex 20:3 You shall have no other gods before me.

If Christ were only "a god," but not God, then He must be a false God.

Ex 3:14 God said to Moses, "I AM WHO I AM." And he said, "Say this to the people of Israel, 'I AM has sent me to you.'"

This is God's name - I AM.

Deut 13:7-11 some of the gods of the peoples that are round about you, whether near you or far off from you, from the one end of the earth to the other, ⁸ you shall not yield to him or listen to him, nor shall your eye pity him, nor shall you spare him, nor shall you conceal him; ⁹ but you shall kill him; your hand shall be first against him to put him to death, and afterwards the hand of all the people. ¹⁰ You shall stone him to death with stones, because he sought to draw you away from the LORD your God, who brought you out of the land of Egypt, out of the house of bondage. ¹¹ And all Israel shall hear, and fear, and never again do any such wickedness as this among you.

God commanded idolaters and blasphemers to be stoned.

Jn 8:33 The Jews answered him, "We stone you for no good work, but for blasphemy; because you, being a man, make yourself God."

Jn 8:58-59 Jesus said to them, "Truly, truly, I say to you, before Abraham was, I am." ⁵⁹ So they took up stones to throw at him; but Jesus hid himself, and went out of the temple.

The Jews clearly thought Jesus was proclaiming himself to be God. So did other people. People who met Christ gave Him homage as they did God.

Mt 2:11 And going into the house they saw the child with Mary his mother, and they fell down and worshiped him. Then, opening their treasures, they offered him gifts, gold and frankincense and myrrh.

Jn 9:38 He said, "Lord, I believe"; and he worshiped him.

Mt 28:9 And behold, Jesus met them and said, "Hail!" And they came up and took hold of his feet and worshiped him.

Jn 18:4-6 Then Jesus, knowing all that was to befall him, came forward and said to them, "Whom do you seek?" ⁵ They answered him, "Jesus of Nazareth." Jesus said to them, "I am he." Judas, who betrayed him, was standing with them. ⁶ When he said to them, "I am he," they drew back and fell to the ground.

They fell to the ground because Christ called Himself by the divine name God revealed to Moses.

Jn 20:28-29 Thomas answered him, "My Lord and my God!" ²⁹ Jesus said to him, "Have you believed because you have seen me? Blessed are those who have not seen and yet believe."

Some argue that Thomas was not referring to Christ when he said "my God!" rather he was speaking to God. If so, Thomas engages in blasphemy by taking the name of God in vain.

Rev 4:9-11 And whenever the living creatures give glory and honor and thanks to him who is seated on the throne, who lives for ever and ever, ¹⁰ the twenty-four elders fall down before him who is seated on the throne and worship him who lives for ever and ever; they cast their crowns before the throne, singing, ¹¹ "Worthy art thou, our Lord and God,
to receive glory and honor and power,
for thou didst create all things,
and by thy will they existed and were created."

Rev 5:6-7,12-14 And between the throne and the four living creatures and among the elders, I saw a Lamb standing, as though it had been slain, with seven horns and with seven eyes, which are the seven spirits of God sent out into all the earth; ⁷ and he went and took the scroll from the right hand of him who was seated on the throne..... saying with a loud voice, "Worthy is the Lamb who was slain, to receive power and wealth and wisdom and might and honor and glory and blessing!" ¹³ And I heard every creature in heaven and on earth and under the earth and in the sea, and all therein, saying, "To him who sits upon the throne and to the Lamb be blessing and honor and glory and might for ever and ever!" ¹⁴ And the four living creatures said, "Amen!" and the elders fell down and worshiped.

The angels in heaven give the same homage to the Lamb "in the midst of the throne" who is Christ as they give to the One who is seated on the throne.

Rev 7:11 And all the angels stood round the throne and round the elders and the four living creatures, and they fell on their faces before the throne and worshiped God...

People in heaven and on earth fell down and worshipped Jesus as God.

Zech 3:1 Then he showed me Joshua the high priest standing before the angel of the LORD, and Satan standing at his right hand to accuse him. ² And the LORD said to Satan, "The LORD rebuke you, O Satan! The LORD who has chosen Jerusalem rebuke you! Is not this a brand plucked from the fire?"

Jude 1:9 But when the archangel Michael, contending with the devil, disputed about the body of Moses, he did not presume to pronounce a reviling judgment upon him, but said, "The Lord rebuke you."

Even angels cannot rebuke Satan and his demons (not even the archangel Michael) - only God can.

Mt 17:17-18 And Jesus answered, "O faithless and perverse generation, how long am I to be with you? How long am I to bear with you? Bring him here to me." ¹⁸ And Jesus rebuked him, and the demon came out of him, and the boy was cured instantly.

Mk 1:25-27 But Jesus rebuked him, saying, "Be silent, and come out of him!" ²⁶ And the unclean spirit, convulsing him and crying with a loud voice, came out of him. ²⁷ And they were all amazed, so that they questioned among themselves, saying, "What is this? A new teaching! With authority he commands even the unclean spirits, and they obey him."

Mk 9:25-27 And when Jesus saw that a crowd came running together, he rebuked the unclean spirit, saying to it, "You dumb and deaf spirit, I command you, come out of him, and never enter him again." ²⁶ And after crying out and convulsing him terribly, it came out, and the boy was like a corpse; so that most of them said, "He is dead." ²⁷ But Jesus took him by the hand and lifted him up, and he arose.

Lk 4:33-36 And in the synagogue there was a man who had the spirit of an unclean demon; and he cried out with a loud voice, ³⁴ "Ah! What have you to do with us, Jesus of Nazareth? Have you come to destroy us? I know who you are, the Holy One of God." ³⁵ But Jesus rebuked him, saying, "Be silent, and come out of him!" And when the demon had thrown him down in the midst, he came out of him, having done him no harm. ³⁶ And they were all amazed and said to one another, "What is this word? For with authority and power he commands the unclean spirits, and they come out."

Lk 4:40-41 Now when the sun was setting, all those who had any that were sick with various diseases brought them to him; and he laid his hands on every one of them and healed them. ⁴¹ And demons also came out of many, crying, "You are the Son of God!" But he rebuked them, and would not allow them to speak, because they knew that he was the Christ.

Lk 9:42 While he was coming, the demon tore him and convulsed him. But Jesus rebuked the unclean spirit, and healed the boy, and gave him back to his father.

Lk 13:32 And he said to them, "Go and tell that fox, 'Behold, I cast out demons and perform cures today and tomorrow, and the third day I finish my course.

1 Jn 1:1-4 That which was from the beginning, which we have heard, which we have seen with our eyes, which we have looked upon and touched with our hands, concerning the word of life— ² the life was made manifest, and we saw it, and testify to it, and proclaim to you the eternal life which was with the Father and was made manifest to us— ³ that which we have seen and heard we proclaim also to you, so that you may have fellowship with us; and our fellowship is with the Father and with his Son Jesus Christ. ⁴ And we are writing this that our joy may be complete.

Only Christ rebuked on His own authority. The angels invoked God. When the Apostles cast out demons, they did not rebuke, rather they invoked Christ's name, despite the fact that Christ had given them authority to cast out unclean spirits (Matthew 10:1, Mark 6:7, Luke 9:1). Both the Apostles and the angels know that only God has the power to directly cast Satan out.

Acts 16:16-18 As we were going to the place of prayer, we were met by a slave girl who had a spirit of divination and brought her owners much gain by soothsaying. ¹⁷ She followed Paul and us, crying, "These men are servants of the Most High God, who proclaim to you the way of salvation." ¹⁸ And this she did for many days. But Paul was annoyed, and turned and said to the spirit, "I charge you in the name of Jesus Christ to come out of her." And it came out that very hour.

Acts 19:13-15 Then some of the itinerant Jewish exorcists undertook to pronounce the name of the Lord Jesus over those who had evil spirits, saying, "I adjure you by the Jesus whom Paul preaches." ¹⁴ Seven sons of a Jewish high priest named Sceva were doing this. ¹⁵ But the evil spirit answered them, "Jesus I know, and Paul I know; but who are you?"

Lk 10:17 The seventy returned with joy, saying, "Lord, even the demons are subject to us in your name!"

Heb 1:6 And again, when he brings the first-born into the world, he says, "Let all God's angels worship him."

Rev 21:5-6 And he who sat upon the throne said, "Behold, I make all things new." Also he said, "Write this, for these words are trustworthy and true." ⁶ And he said to me, "It is done! I am the Alpha and the Omega, the beginning and the end. To the thirsty I will give from the fountain of the water of life without payment.

Rev 22:13,16 I am the Alpha and the Omega, the first and the last, the beginning and the end..... "I Jesus have sent my angel to you with this testimony for the churches. I am the root and the offspring of David, the bright morning star.

Jesus and God are both the Alpha and the Omega.

Jn 1:1-3 In the beginning was the Word, and the Word was with God, and the Word was God. ² He was in the beginning with God; ³ all things were made through him, and without him was not anything made that was made.

All created things were created through Christ. But if Christ Himself were created, then He would have had to create Himself, which is logically impossible.

Col 1:15 He is the image of the invisible God, the first-born of all creation...

This does not indicate that Christ was created first, but that He has preeminence, a title given by a father to a son. Isaac, Jacob, and Ephraim received the blessing of the first-born, although none of them were first-born. Nowhere does Scripture say that Jesus created everything except Himself. It says He created everything. Period.

Is 44:24 Thus says the LORD, your Redeemer, who formed you from the womb: "I am the LORD, who made all things, who stretched out the heavens alone, who spread out the earth—Who was with me?

Here God says He did it all by Himself. If Christ created all things, why doesn't it say "we"?

Jn 17:3 And this is eternal life, that they know thee the only true God, and Jesus Christ whom thou hast sent.

Gen 1:1 In the beginning God created the heavens and the earth.

If Christ created heaven and earth, then Christ is God.

Acts 20:28 Take heed to yourselves and to all the flock, in which the Holy Spirit has made you overseers, to care for the church of God which he obtained with his own blood.

The only person who shed his blood to acquire the Church was Jesus Christ. Note that this passage does NOT say "the blood of His own son." The Greek reads "periepoiesat dia tou haimatos tou idiou." The word son, "huios," does not appear. Since only Christ shed His blood for the Church, Christ must be God.

Early Christians' comments on Christ's Divinity

Jn 7:16 So Jesus answered them, "My teaching is not mine, but his who sent me..."

Mt 10:19-20 When they deliver you up, do not be anxious how you are to speak or what you are to say; for what you are to say will be given to you in that hour; [20] for it is not you who speak, but the Spirit of your Father speaking through you.

The Spirit teaches with His own teaching, but it is identical to Christ's.

Rom 8:16 it is the Spirit himself bearing witness with our spirit that we are children of God...

1 Cor 12:4-6 Now there are varieties of gifts, but the same Spirit; [5] and there are varieties of service, but the same Lord; [6] and there are varieties of working, but it is the same God who inspires them all in every one.

Ezek 11:19-20 And I will give them one heart, and put a new spirit within them; I will take the stony heart out of their flesh and give them a heart of flesh, [20] that they may walk in my statutes and keep my ordinances and obey them; and they shall be my people, and I will be their God.

Equality of the Three Persons

The Three Persons of the Godhead are co-equal and co-eternal. (CCC 253-260)

CREATION AS SACRAMENT

God did not have to create. He loved so much, so fully, so freely, that He desired to create, and freely willed all creation into existence. The key of love opened the hand of God, and the universe came into being. Even before God began to form the created universe out of nothing, He had a plan. He created human beings in His image, the crown jewel of creation; in our creative power and in our ability to imitate Christ's suffering we image Him in a way that even the angels envy. From the beginning He intended to bring all men to Himself. All of history is the fulfillment of this plan. God has always passionately desired us, His creatures, to share His Wisdom, His Truth, His Goodness, His Beauty and partake of His Glory. Even now, despite the Fall, man participates in God's creative work, we are stewards of creation. Even now, in a certain way, God depends on us to create, yet He does not abandon us to ourselves. He upholds and sustains us at every moment. The Providence of God conquers all: the evil introduced into the world by our sin is neither fundamental nor definitive. Every part of the Christian message is an answer to the question of evil. God provided the answer before He began to create. With Him, this is possible, because God writes the world like men write words. The New Creation in Christ was foreshadowed in the very description of Creation, envisaged from the beginning by God. (CCC 280, 293, 295, 296-298, 309, 356-357).

Current misunderstandings: Sola scriptura *Christians have lost most, if not all, of the aspects of sacramental theology. Because of this loss, their understanding of creation is impoverished. If faith alone is sufficient for salvation, then no creature is necessary for salvation. Therefore, nothing created can save us. They forget the Body of Christ is created, and it saves us.*

The following exegesis of Jeremiah 33, Genesis 6, and Genesis 9 is an extremely short summary of research on early Jewish commentaries on Genesis presented by Dr. Scott Hahn in lecture at Franciscan University, Steubenville, Ohio.

Jer 33:20-22 Thus says the LORD: If you can break my covenant with the day and my covenant with the night, so that day and night will not come at their appointed time, [21] then also my covenant with David my servant may be broken, so that he shall not have a son to reign on his throne, and my covenant with the Levitical priests my ministers. [22] As the host of heaven cannot be numbered and the sands of the sea cannot be measured, so I will multiply the descendants of David my servant, and the Levitical priests who minister to me."

God has a covenant with creation. It is a covenant as strong and meaningful as the covenant with Abraham, with Isaac, with Jacob, and with David. This covenant with creation can also be seen in Genesis, in which God brought forth all of creation in seven days. The Hebrew word for "covenant" also means "to seven oneself." The covenant with Noah (Genesis 6 and 9) was not a new covenant, but rather a renewal of that original covenant with creation, the covenant made through the created representative of all creation, Adam, completed on the seventh day, the Sabbath.

Gen 1:1-2 In the beginning God created the heavens and the earth. [2] The earth was without form and void, and darkness was upon the face of the deep; and the Spirit of God was moving over the face of the waters.

Mt 3:16 And when Jesus was baptized, he went up immediately from the water, and behold, the heavens were opened and he saw the Spirit of God descending like a dove, and alighting on him...

The Spirit of God moved over the waters at the beginning of the first creation and at the beginning of the New Creation...

Gen 2:6-7 but a mist went up from the earth and watered the whole face of the ground— then the LORD God formed man of dust from the ground, and breathed into his nostrils the breath of life; and man became a living being.

Jn 20:21-23 Jesus said to them again, "Peace be with you. As the Father has sent me, even so I send you." [22] And when he had said this, he breathed on them, and said to them, "Receive the Holy Spirit. [23] If you forgive the sins of any, they are forgiven; if you retain the sins of any, they are retained."

... while the breath of God gave life to man at the first creation and the forgiveness of sins to His Bride, the Church, at the New Creation.

Jn 9:6-7 As he said this, he spat on the ground and made clay of the spittle and anointed the man's eyes with the clay, [7] saying to him, "Go, wash in the pool of Siloam" (which means Sent). So he went and washed and came back seeing.

God works in the clay of the earth at the first creation and at the New Creation, healing man and sending him forth to do His work. The sacraments are how God honors His covenant with creation - He uses the things of the created world in order to bestow graces and blessings upon all of creation. This is the essence of the Incarnation. Each of the seven sacraments is an aspect of the Incarnation, each bestows grace upon us in Christ Jesus, as a result of His coming into the world and His sacrifice on the Cross. In this way, the Incarnation reverberates down through the ages.

Gen 2:19-25 So the LORD God caused a deep sleep to fall upon the man, and while he slept took one of his ribs and closed up its place with flesh; 22 and the rib which the LORD God had taken from the man he made into a woman and brought her to the man. 23 Then the man said,
"This at last is bone of my bones
and flesh of my flesh;
she shall be called Woman,
because she was taken out of Man." 24 Therefore a man leaves his father and his mother and cleaves to his wife, and they become one flesh. 25 And the man and his wife were both naked, and were not ashamed.

The unity of man and woman, bridegroom and bride, is present from the beginning. In an earthly manner, Adam and Eve prefigure the One who is to come, the Bridegroom, and the Bride He would save for His Own Name's sake, uniting Her to Himself so the two would become one.

Eph 5:31-33 "For this reason a man shall leave his father and mother and be joined to his wife, and the two shall become one flesh." 32 This mystery is a profound one, and I am saying that it refers to Christ and the church; 33 however, let each one of you love his wife as himself, and let the wife see that she respects her husband.

Every sacrament is a mystery, each images an aspect of the marriage of the Bridegroom with His Bride...

Gal 6:15-16 For neither circumcision counts for anything, nor uncircumcision, but a new creation. 16 Peace and mercy be upon all who walk by this rule, upon the Israel of God.

1 Cor 10:1-4,6 I want you to know, brethren, that our fathers were all under the cloud, and all passed through the sea, 2 and all were baptized into Moses in the cloud and in the sea, 3 and all ate the same supernatural food 4 and all drank the same supernatural drink. For they drank from the supernatural Rock which followed them, and the Rock was Christ... Now these things are warnings for us, not to desire evil as they did.

From the very first verse of Genesis, the sacraments were prefigured in the Old Testament; pre-eminent among these figures were the figures of Baptism (the Wedding) and the Eucharist (the Consummation, the Wedding Feast). The Hebrews mis-used the sacramental types given to them and were punished.

1 Cor 10:7-11 Do not be idolaters as some of them were; as it is written, "The people sat down to eat and drink and rose up to dance." 8 We must not indulge in immorality as some of them did, and twenty-three thousand fell in a single day. 9 We must not put the Lord to the test, as some of them did and were destroyed by serpents; 10 nor grumble, as some of them did and were destroyed by the Destroyer. 11 Now these things happened to them as a warning, but they were written down for our instruction, upon whom the end of the ages has come...

How much more culpable are we who live with sacramental grace available to us, but do not use them or actively mis-use them? God acts through creation in order to save us, His creatures, by using signs of the created world to pour grace into our souls.

The New Creation is described by John:

Jn 1:1, 14, 26, 29, 35, 43, 2:1 In the beginning was the Word, and the Word was with God, and the Word was God. ...and the Word became flesh and dwelt among us [day one]... John answered them, "I baptize with water; but among you stands one whom you do not know,"... The next day [day two] he saw Jesus coming toward him, and said, "Behold, the Lamb of God, who takes away the sin of the world!... The next day [day three] again John was standing with two of his disciples;... The next day [day four] Jesus decided to go to Galilee. And he found Philip and said to him, "Follow me.".... On the third day [day seven] there was a marriage at Cana in Galilee,...

The wedding takes place on the seventh day after John's Gospel begins, the third day after the previous four days had been completed. This marriage account does not give us the names of the couple being wed, it gives us the names of the Bridegroom, Jesus, and the Bride, Mary, the New Adam and the New Eve at the New Creation, a wedding.

Jn 2:3-6 When the wine failed, the mother of Jesus said to him, "They have no wine." ⁴ And Jesus said to her, "O woman, what have you to do with me? My hour has not yet come." ⁵ His mother said to the servants, "Do whatever he tells you." ⁶ Now six stone jars were standing there, for the Jewish rites of purification, each holding twenty or thirty gallons.

The waters of Creation were set apart and new life brought forth. These stone jars contained water for ritual washing....

Num 19:11-12 "He who touches the dead body of any person shall be unclean seven days; ¹² he shall cleanse himself with the water on the third day and on the seventh day, and so be clean; but if he does not cleanse himself on the third day and on the seventh day, he will not become clean.

...water called "baptismoi." In order to be clean, ritual washing with this water had to be performed on the third day and on the seventh day. According to John 2:1, Christ's first public miracle, which relied on "baptismoi," happened on both the third day AND the seventh day.

Deut 32:14 Curds from the herd, and milk from the flock,
with fat of lambs and rams,
herds of Bashan and goats,
with the finest of the wheat—
and of the blood of the grape you drank wine.

Christ's hour washes away impurity, sets the waters apart, transforms them into a gift of finest wine, which is the blood of the grape, all at the bidding of His mother. This beginning of His public ministry is intimately linked to His "hour" yet to come. Where else does Christ speak of His hour?

Jn 4:23 But the hour is coming, and now is, when the true worshipers will worship the Father in spirit and truth, for such the Father seeks to worship him.

The next use of the word is when He talks to the Samaritan woman at the well. Abraham, Isaac, and Moses all find their wives at wells. The word used for "husband" here is "ba'al" - the word a concubine uses to address the man who keeps her. A wife would say not "ba'al," but "adonai." The word "ba'al" also means "lord," "master," and "god."

Hos 2:16 "And in that day, says the LORD, you will call me, 'My husband,' and no longer will you call me, 'My Baal.'

But that isn't all we know of Christ's hour...

Jn 5:25 "Truly, truly, I say to you, the hour is coming, and now is, when the dead will hear the voice of the Son of God, and those who hear will live."

Jn 12:23-24 And Jesus answered them, "The hour has come for the Son of man to be glorified. ²⁴ Truly, truly, I say to you, unless a grain of wheat falls into the earth and dies, it remains alone; but if it dies, it bears much fruit.

Christ specifically links His "hour" with the baptismoi, with marriage, with resurrection, with wine, and with the "fruit" of the wheat, which is bread. Through these things, men will come to worship "in spirit and truth." Christ's hour is the hour of the New Creation.

Jn 9:1-7 As he passed by, he saw a man blind from his birth. ² And his disciples asked him, "Rabbi, who sinned, this man or his parents, that he was born blind?" ³ Jesus answered, "It was not that this man sinned, or his parents, but that the works of God might be made manifest in him. ⁴ We must work the works of him who sent me, while it is day; night comes, when no one can work. ⁵ As long as I am in the world, I am the light of the world." ⁶ As he said this, he spat on the ground and made clay of the spittle and anointed the man's eyes with the clay, ⁷ saying to him, "Go, wash in the pool of Siloam" (which means Sent). So he went and washed and came back seeing.

God heals by working the clay with the water that wells forth from within Himself. Jesus again makes present the story of creation to heal the blind man of his loss. After this baptismal creation image restores and makes the man whole, He SENDS the man, who will witness to Him despite fierce opposition. But note carefully what Jesus says: "WE must work the works of Him who sent me..." We share in God's work. We have a share in God's covenant with creation, a share in His self-donation within and through creation.

Heb 9:2,9-10 For a tent was prepared, the outer one, in which were the lampstand and the table and the bread of the Presence; it is called the Holy Place.... (which is symbolic for the present age). According to this arrangement, gifts and sacrifices are offered which cannot perfect the conscience of the worshiper, [10] but deal only with food and drink and various ablutions, regulations for the body imposed until the time of reformation.

Paul, in describing the Old Law, says the prescriptions of the Old Law, being merely "a symbol of the present time," affected the flesh only. He implies the New Law will perfect the conscience of the worshipper as the Old Law did not. Paul's epistles speak of a new washing, baptism, and a new food and drink, the Body and Blood of the Lord, in the new order.

2 Cor 1:21 But it is God who establishes us with you in Christ, and has commissioned us...

The work of the sacraments are the work of God through Christ. They are a human act only in a sense similar to saying the writing of Scripture is a human act.

Jn 6:57 ff "As the living Father sent me, and I live because of the Father, so he who eats me will live because of me. [58] This is the bread which came down from heaven, not such as the fathers ate and died; he who eats this bread will live for ever."

Acts 2:37-39 "Now when they heard this they were cut to the heart, and said to Peter and the rest of the apostles, "Brethren, what shall we do?" [38] And Peter said to them, "Repent, and be baptized every one of you in the name of Jesus Christ for the forgiveness of your sins; and you shall receive the gift of the Holy Spirit. [39] For the promise is to you and to your children and to all that are far off, every one whom the Lord our God calls to him.""

Acts 19:5 On hearing this, they were baptized in the name of the Lord Jesus.

Acts 8:17 Then they laid their hands on them and they received the Holy Spirit.

1 Pet 3:18-21 For Christ also died for sins once for all, the righteous for the unrighteous, that he might bring us to God, being put to death in the flesh but made alive in the spirit; [19] in which he went and preached to the spirits in prison, [20] who formerly did not obey, when God's patience waited in the days of Noah, during the building of the ark, in which a few, that is, eight persons, were saved through water. [21] Baptism, which corresponds to this, now saves you, not as a removal of dirt from the body but as an appeal to God for a clear conscience, through the resurrection of Jesus Christ,...

1 Pet 1:3-4 Blessed be the God and Father of our Lord Jesus Christ! By his great mercy we have been born anew to a living hope through the resurrection of Jesus Christ from the dead, [4] and to an inheritance which is imperishable, undefiled, and unfading, kept in heaven for you,...

2 Pet 1:3-4 His divine power has granted to us all things that pertain to life and godliness, through the knowledge of him who called us to his own glory and excellence, [4] by which he has granted to us his precious and very great promises, that through these you may escape from the corruption that is in the world because of passion, and become partakers of the divine nature.

The sacraments allow us to share in the divine nature. Christ united Divinity with the creature whom God gave dominion over the physical world, man. Now, through the things of the created world, men can be united with the divinity of Him who saves us.

Through the shadow of the first Creation and the fulfillment of the New Creation, through the Passion, Death, Resurrection, and Ascension of His Son, God has shown Himself and given Himself to all mankind. He has definitively answered the questions regarding the meaning and purpose of life. He has made Himself and His plan abundantly clear. He has revealed all the truths we need. God has delivered His Word through both the sacraments and through oral and written means, always through human mediation. Divine Revelation is summed up and personified in Jesus: He is the Way, the Truth, and the Life. The divine participation in and full knowledge of God is brought to us through and by His Body, the Church.

SCRIPTURE

"For the words of God,
expressed in human language,
have been made like human discourse,
just as the word of the eternal Father,
when He took to Himself the flesh of human weakness,
was in every way made like men."
The Dogmatic Constitution on Divine Liturgy,
Vatican Council II

Romans 16:25-26
...according to my gospel
and the preaching of Jesus Christ,
according to the
revelation of the mystery
which was kept secret for long ages
but is now disclosed and
through the prophetic writings
is made known to all nations,
according to the command of the eternal God,
to bring about the obedience of faith...

Ephesians 3:9-10
...to make all men see what is
the plan of the mystery
hidden for ages in God who created all things;
that through the church
the manifold wisdom of God
might now be made known
to the principalities and powers in the heavenly places.

The Relationship between Holy Scripture and the Holy Church

God is the source of all truth. Jesus Christ is God. Jesus Christ is also the Bridegroom. The Church Christ founded is the Bride. Bride and Bridegroom are joined in sacramental marriage - the two become one flesh. What God has joined, no man may break asunder. Thus, the Church is the Body of Christ, and Christ is the Head of the Body - the source, the foundation, the living principle of His Body. Since the Church is the Body of Christ, the Church is the pillar and foundation of truth, in the same way that Christ is the pillar and foundation of truth. The word of God that is Holy Scripture is the wedding gift given by the Bridegroom to the Bride. Under the tender guidance of the Bridegroom, Scripture was written by the Bride, it was bound together by the Bride, and it is cherished by the Bride. The Bride alone truly understands the gift of love which the Bridegroom has given Her.

We obtain salvation through Jesus Christ alone, through His Body alone, hung on the Cross, resurrected from death, and living vibrantly in the Church. Salvation comes only through being joined to Christ, through becoming part of the Body of Christ. We are joined into the Body of Christ through the sacraments, which are the special charisms of the Bride given her by the Bridegroom. Through these sacraments, the healing ointments of grace administered by Christ through His Body to we who are ill, Christ brings us into union with Himself, making us truly sons and daughters of God. We are joined to the Godhead by virtue of Jesus Christ, His Body, Himself. He feeds us with His own Body, for He is the only true source of life. Thus, Jesus Christ truly is with us until the end of the world, healing the sick, forgiving sinners, and setting captives free.

The Catholic Church uses the phrase "Body of Christ" in three mystically interchangeable, absolutely literal, ways - the Body of Christ who walked in Galilee two millenia ago, touching and healing sinners, the Body of Christ who is the Church, the Bride without spot or blemish, and the Body of Christ who is the Eucharist, the resurrected Body, Blood, Soul, and Divinity of Jesus Christ present in the sacrament of the altar, Him alone, pure and undefiled. The Body of Christ acts through the created world, allowing the grace of God to touch, cleanse, and sanctify all creation, so that it may truly be called "very good." The more you meditate on the three ways in which we can speak of the Body of Christ, the more you will understand what it means to be a Christian.

As the verses leading this section indicate, Scripture is crucial revelation, but the plan revealed by Scripture can be known only through the Church. Indeed, that is why Christ established the Church, to reveal the structure and plan of salvation. Scripture, like the sacraments, makes God present in a created and tangible way, intelligible to men. Catholics understand Scripture to be the revelation of Jesus Christ, venerated just as His Body, because, like that crucified, glorified Body, Scripture reveals who Christ is. The Church reveals the wisdom of God, the plan of God, the Christ in action who is revealed in Scripture. In order to appreciate the Catholic view of Scripture, it is useful to read what the Church teaches in regards to Scripture. (CCC 101-141)

Current misunderstandings: Those who treat Scripture as the only true source of authority are not fully able to appreciate the plan of God, seeing only a single plane of holiness in existence, God. Because they do not accept Apostolic authority, they accept neither a sacramental view of the world, nor the Catholic understanding of the hierarchy of sacred things. In rejecting this heirarchy of sacredness, which extends like a ladder from God to entice men to approach Him, a unique appreciation of the sacred place of Scripture is lost.

Excerpts from:
The Dogmatic Constitution on Divine Revelation,
The Vatican II document
known as *Dei Verbum*.

11. Those divinely revealed realities which are contained and presented in Sacred Scripture have been committed to writing under the inspiration of the Holy Spirit.... In composing the sacred books, God chose men and while employed by Him they made use of their powers and abilities, so that with Him acting in them and through them, they, as true authors, consigned to writing everything and only those things which He wanted.

Therefore, since everything asserted by the inspired authors or sacred writers must be held to be asserted by the Holy Spirit, it follows that the books of Scripture must be acknowledged as teaching solidly, faithfully and without error that truth which God wanted put into sacred writings for the sake of salvation. Therefore "all Scripture is divinely inspired and has its use for teaching the truth and refuting error, for reformation of manners and discipline in right living, so that the man who belongs to God may be efficient and equipped for good work of every kind" (2 Tim. 3:16-17, Greek text).

12. However, since God speaks in Sacred Scripture through men in human fashion, ... attention should be given, among other things, to "literary forms." For truth is set forth and expressed differently in texts which are variously historical, prophetic, poetic, or of other forms of discourse.... But, since Holy Scripture must be read and interpreted in the sacred spirit in which it was written, no less serious attention must be given to the content and unity of the whole of Scripture if the meaning of the sacred texts is to be correctly worked out...

13. In Sacred Scripture... the words of God, expressed in human language, have been made like human discourse, just as the word of the eternal Father, when He took to Himself the flesh of human weakness, was in every way made like men.

14. ...The plan of salvation foretold by the sacred authors, recounted and explained by them, is found as the true word of God in the books of the Old Testament: these books, therefore, written under divine inspiration, remain permanently valuable. "For all that was written for our instruction, so that by steadfastness and the encouragement of the Scriptures we might have hope" (Rom. 15:4).

15. The principal purpose to which the plan of the old covenant was directed was to prepare for the coming of Christ, the redeemer of all and of the messianic kingdom, to announce this coming by prophecy (see Luke 24:44; John 5:39; 1 Peter 1:10), and to indicate its meaning through various types (see 1 Cor. 10:12)....

16. God, the inspirer and author of both Testaments, wisely arranged that the New Testament be hidden in the Old and the Old be made manifest in the New. For, though Christ established the new covenant in His blood (see Luke 22:20; 1 Cor. 11:25), still the books of the Old Testament with all their parts, caught up into the proclamation of the Gospel, acquire and show forth their full meaning in the New Testament (see Matt. 5:17; Luke 24:27; Rom. 16:25-26; 2 Cor. 4:6) and in turn shed light on it and explain it.

18. It is common knowledge that among all the Scriptures, even those of the New Testament, the Gospels have a special preeminence, and rightly so, for they are the principal witness for the life and teaching of the incarnate Word, our savior....

19. ...after the Ascension of the Lord the Apostles handed on to their hearers what He had said and done... The sacred authors wrote the four Gospels, selecting some things from the many which had been handed on by word of mouth or in writing, reducing some of them to a synthesis, explaining some things in view of the situation of their churches and preserving the form of proclamation but always in such fashion that they told us the honest truth about Jesus. For their intention in writing was that either from their own memory and recollections, or from the witness of those who "themselves from the beginning were eyewitnesses and ministers of the Word" we might know "the truth" concerning those matters about which we have been instructed (see Luke 1:2-4).

21. The Church has always venerated the divine Scriptures just as she venerates the body of the Lord, since, especially in the sacred liturgy, she unceasingly receives and offers to the faithful the bread of life from the table both of God's word and of Christ's body. She has always maintained them, and continues to do so, together with sacred tradition, as the supreme rule of faith, since, as inspired by God and committed once and for all to writing, they impart the word of God Himself without change, and make the voice of the Holy Spirit resound in the words of the prophets and Apostles. Therefore, like the Christian religion itself, all the preaching of the Church must be nourished and regulated by Sacred Scripture. For in the sacred books, the Father who is in heaven meets His children with great love and speaks with them; and the force and power in the word of God is so great that it stands as the support and energy of the Church, the strength of faith for her sons, the food of the soul, the pure and everlasting source of spiritual life. Consequently these words are perfectly applicable to Sacred Scripture: "For the word of God is living and active" (Heb. 4:12) and "it has power to build you up and give you your heritage among all those who are sanctified" (Acts 20:32; see 1 Thess. 2:13).

25. Therefore, all the clergy must hold fast to the Sacred Scriptures through diligent sacred reading and careful study, especially the priests of Christ and others, such as deacons and catechists who are legitimately active in the ministry of the word. This is to be done so that none of them will become "an empty preacher of the word of God outwardly, who is not a listener to it inwardly" since they must share the

abundant wealth of the divine word with the faithful committed to them, especially in the sacred liturgy. The sacred synod also earnestly and especially urges all the Christian faithful, especially Religious, to learn by frequent reading of the divine Scriptures the "excellent knowledge of Jesus Christ" (Phil. 3:8). "For ignorance of the Scriptures is ignorance of Christ."...

26. ...Just as the life of the Church is strengthened through more frequent celebration of the Eucharistic mystery, similarly we may hope for a new stimulus for the life of the Spirit from a growing reverence for the word of God, which "lasts forever" (Is. 40:8; see 1 Peter 1:23-25).

How Scripture Should be Read

Scripture, like Christ, has a two-fold nature; the literal sense and the three-fold spiritual sense. The Old Testament is properly interpreted in light of the New, with the literal meaning of the New bringing out the three-fold spiritual sense of the Old. The literal sense is the meaning conveyed by the words of Scripture, discovered through exegesis and sound interpretation. All other senses of Sacred Scripture are based on the literal. This literal sense, while accurately describing what took place, simultaneously points us to:

- *the allegorical sense, which is the literal sense of the Old Testament that signified a foreshadowing or type fulfilled by Christ in the New Testament, through faith - it reveals the doctrine which is to be believed;*
- *the moral or tropological sense, which is the literal sense of the Old Testament recorded for our instruction, which moves the Christian to act justly in the life of the Church, in love - it reveals the application to the individual of what ought to be done;*
- *the anagogical sense, which is the literal sense of the Old Testament leading us towards and being fulfilled in heaven, attainable through Christ in hope, the last end for Whom we all were made.*

Ultimately, we are not people of the Book, but people of the Word. Christ completes, perfects, fulfills the Old Testament, He opens our minds to understand Scripture.

Mt 13:34-35 All this Jesus said to the crowds in parables; indeed, he said nothing to them without a parable. [35] This was to fulfil what was spoken by the prophet:
"I will open my mouth in parables,
I will utter what has been hidden since the foundation of the world."

God writes the world like men write words.

Prov 1:5-6 the wise man also may hear and increase in learning,
and the man of understanding acquire skill, [6] to understand a proverb and a figure,
the words of the wise and their riddles.

Wis 11:15-16 In return for their foolish and wicked thoughts,
which led them astray to worship irrational serpents and worthless animals,
thou didst send upon them a multitude of irrational creatures to punish them, [16] that they might learn that one is punished by the very things by which he sins.

Rom 5:15 Yet death reigned from Adam to Moses, even over those whose sins were not like the transgression of Adam, who was a type of the one who was to come.

Jn 10:6 This figure Jesus used with them, but they did not understand what he was saying to them.

Jn 16:25 "I have said this to you in figures; the hour is coming when I shall no longer speak to you in figures but tell you plainly of the Father."

All that happened to the peoples of the Old Testament was a foretaste, a prefigurement, a shadow of Jesus Christ. Scripture must be read in all four senses to understand Jesus.

Jn 16:29-30 His disciples said, "Ah, now you are speaking plainly, not in any figure! [30] Now we know that you know all things, and need none to question you; by this we believe that you came from God."

The New Testament is the radical perfection of the Old, fulfilling ALL that the Old prophesied, through word and through deed, while the Old Testament provides the context for understanding exactly what God meant to reveal when He acted in the New Testament. Paul refers to this mutal enrichment constantly in his epistles:

Heb 8:5 They serve a copy and shadow of the heavenly sanctuary; for when Moses was about to erect the tent, he was instructed by God, saying, "See that you make everything according to the pattern which was shown you on the mountain."

Heb 9:24 For Christ has entered, not into a sanctuary made with hands, a copy of the true one, but into heaven itself, now to appear in the presence of God on our behalf.

Heb 10:1 For since the law has but a shadow of the good things to come instead of the true form of these realities, it can never, by the same sacrifices which are continually offered year after year, make perfect those who draw near.

In fact, Hebrews is essentially one long typological interpretation of an Old Testament reality. THIS is how we should read Scripture:

1 Cor 10:1-11 I want you to know, brethren, that our fathers were all under the cloud, and all passed through the sea, ² and all were baptized into Moses in the cloud and in the sea, ³ and all ate the same supernatural food ⁴ and all drank the same supernatural drink. For they drank from the supernatural Rock which followed them, and the Rock was Christ. ⁵ Nevertheless with most of them God was not pleased; for they were overthrown in the wilderness.
⁶ Now these things are warnings for us, not to desire evil as they did. ⁷ Do not be idolaters as some of them were; as it is written, "The people sat down to eat and drink and rose up to dance." ⁸ We must not indulge in immorality as some of them did, and twenty-three thousand fell in a single day. ⁹ We must not put the Lord to the test, as some of them did and were destroyed by serpents; ¹⁰ nor grumble, as some of them did and were destroyed by the Destroyer. ¹¹ Now these things happened to them as a warning, but they were written down for our instruction, upon whom the end of the ages has come.

Gal 4:24 Now, this is an allegory: these women are two covenants. One is from Mount Sinai, bearing children for slavery; she is Hagar. ²⁵ Now Hagar is Mount Sainai in Arabia; she corresponds to the present Jerusalem, for she is in slavery with her children. ²⁶ But the Jerusalem above is free, and she is our mother. ²⁷ For it is written,
"Rejoice, O barren one that dost not bear;
Break forth and shout, thou who art not in travail;
for the desolate hath more children than she who hath a husband."
²⁸ Now we, brethren, like Isaac, are children of promise.

This was how ALL the Apostles read the Old Testament:

2 Pet 2:6 if by turning the cities of Sodom and Gomorrah to ashes he condemned them to extinction and made them an example to those who were to be ungodly...

James 5:10 As an example of suffering and patience, brethren, take the prophets who spoke in the name of the Lord.

Jude 7 just as Sodom and Gomorrah and the surrounding cities, which likewise acted immorally and indulged in unnatural lust, serve as an example by undergoing a punishment of eternal fire.

What lay hidden before the foundation of the world in Scripture was revealed in God's Word.

Mt 4:14 the people who sat in darkness
have seen a great light,
and for those who sat in the region and shadow of death
light has dawned."

Col 2:16-17 Therefore let no one pass judgment on you in questions of food and drink or with regard to a festival or a new moon or a sabbath. ¹⁷ These are only a shadow of what is to come; but the substance belongs to Christ.

Lk 1:78-79 through the tender mercy of our God, when the day shall dawn upon us from on high ⁷⁹ to give light to those who sit in darkness and in the shadow of death,
to guide our feet into the way of peace."

The Church's Interpretation of Scripture

The Church has officially defined the interpretation for several passages of Scripture, but most people, Catholic or no, don't realize it. When they do know this is the case, even a well-informed Catholic cannot normally tell you which passages were authoritatively interpreted or what those interpretations were. What follows are all the authoratative interpretations the Church has made of Scripture, taken from Heinrich Denzinger's Sources of Catholic Dogma, *nos. 789, 858, 874, 913, 926, 949, 1822. Remember that the word "anathema" does not mean "condemned to hell," it means "formally excommunicated," and is used in explicit statements of what the Church most emphatically does not believe. Remember also that the authoritative interpretations of these passages do not deny the possibility of additional, non-contradictory interpretations. It means only that the referenced passages certainly carry the defined meanings. Some also ask why the Church does not formally define the meaning and interpretation of every line of Scripture. The Church teaches what is necessary for understanding - what She says needs to be said, nor is any teaching more than is needful. Just as it will take an eternity to plumb the infinite depths of God, so would it take an eternity to plumb the depths of His Word. These passages were defined against pernicous heresies. Every heresy is traceable to a mis-understanding of some combinatinon of these passages.*

Rom 5:12 - Council of Trent, June 17, 1546, "Decree on Original Sin," section 2.
If anyone asserts that the transgression of Adam has harmed him alone and not his posterity, and that the sanctity and justice, received from God, which he lost, he has lost for himself alone and not for us also; or that he having been defiled by the sin of disobedience has transfused only death "and the punishments of the body into the whole human race, but not sin also, which is the death of the soul," let him be anathema, since he contradicts the Apostle who says: "By one man sin entered into the world, and by sin death, and so death passed upon all men, in whom all have sinned. [Rom 5:12]"

Jn 3:5 - Council of Trent, March 3, 1547, "Canons on the Sacrament of Baptism," canon 2.
If anyone shall say that real and natural water is not necessary for baptism, and on that account those words of our Lord Jesus Christ: "Unless a man be born again of water and the Holy Spirit [John 3:5]" are distorted into some sort of metaphor: let him be anathema.

Mt 26:26 ff; Mk 14:22 ff; Lk 22:19 ff; 1 Cor 11:23 ff - Council of Trent, October 11, 1551, "The Real Presence of our Lord Jesus Christ in the Most Holy Sacrament of the Eucharist," chapter 1
First of all the holy Synod teaches and openly and simply professes that in the nourishing sacrament of the Holy Eucharist after the consecration of the bread and wine our Lord Jesus Christ, true God and man, is truly, really, and substantially [canon 1] contained under the species of those sensible things. For these things are not mutally contradictory, that our Saviour Himself is always seated at the right hand of the Father in heaven according to the natural mode of existing, and yet that in many other places sacramentally He is present to us in His own substance by that manner of existence which, althogh we can scarcely express it in words, yet we can, however, by our understanding illuminated by faith, conceive to be possible to God, and which we ought most steadfastly to believe. For thus all our forefathers, as many as were in the true Church of Christ, who have discussed this most holy sacrament, have most openly professed that our Redeemer instituted this so wonderful a sacrament at the Last Supper, when after the blessing of the bread and wine He testified in clear and definite words that He gave them His own body and His own blood; and those words which are recorded [Matthew 26:26ff; Mark 14:22; Luke 22:19ff] by the holy Evangelists, and afterwards repeated by St. Paul [1 Cor 11:23 ff], since they contain within themselves that proper and very clear meaning in which they were understood by the Fathers, it is a most disgraceful thing for some contentious and wicked men to distort into fictitious and imaginary figures of speech, by which the real nature of the flesh and blood of Christ is denied, contrary to the universal sense of the Church, which, recognizing with an ever grateful and recollecting mind this most excellent benefit of Christ, as the pillar and ground of truth [1 Tim 3:15], has detested these falsehoods, devised by impious men, as satanical.

Jn 20:22 ff - Council of Trent, October 25, 1551, "Canons on the Sacrament of Penance," canon 3
If anyone says that those words of the Lord Savior: "Receive ye the Holy Ghost; whose sins you shall forgive, they are forgiven them; and whose sins ye shall retain, they are retained [John 20:22ff]," are not to be understood of the power of remitting and retaining sins in the sacrament of penance, as the Catholic Church has always understood from the

beginning, but, contrary to the institution of this sacrament, distorts them to an authority for preaching the Gospel: let him be anathema.

James 5:14 - Council of Trent, October 25, 1551, "Canons on Anointing of the Sick," canon 1

If anyone says that anointing of the sick is not truly and properly a sacrament instituted by our Lord Jesus Christ [cf. Mark 6:13], and promulgated by blessed James the Apostle [James 5:14], but is only a rite accepted by the Fathers, or a human fiction: let him be anathema.

Lk 22:19, 1 Cor 11:24 - Council of Trent, September 17, 1562 "Canons on the Most Holy Sacrifice of the Mass," canon 2

If anyone says that by these words: "Do this for a commemoration of me [Luke 22:19; 1 Cor. 11:24], Christ did not make the apostles priest, or did not ordain that they and other priests might offer His own body and blood: let him be anathema.

Mt 16:16; Jn 21:15 ff - Vatican I, July 18, 1870 "The Institution of Apostlic Primacy in Blessed Peter," chapter 1

[Against heretics and schismatics]. So we teach and declare that according to the testimonies of the Gospel and the primacy of jurisdiction over the entire Church of God was promised and was conferred immediately and directly upon the blessed Apostle Peter by Christ the Lord. For the one Simon, to whom He had before said: "Thou shalt be called Cephas [John 1:42]," after he had given forth his confession with those words: "Thou art Christ, Son of the living God [Matthew 16:16], the Lord spoke with these solemn words: "Blessed art thou, Simon bar Jonah; because flesh and blood hath not revealed it to thee, but my Father who is in heaven. And I say to thee: That thou art Peter, and upon this rock I will build my church, and the gates of hell shall not prevail against it: and I shall give to thee the keys of the kingdom of heaven. And whatsoever thou shalt bind upon earth, it shall be bound also in heaven: and whatsoever thou shalt loose upon earth, it shall be loosed also in heaven [Matthew 16:17ff]." [Against Richerieus etc.] And upon Simon Peter alone Jesus after His resurrection conferred the jurisdicition of the highest pastor and rector over his entire fold, saying: "Feed my lambs," Feed my sheep [John 21:15ff]." To this teaching of Sacred Scriptures, so manifest as it has been always understood by the Catholic Church, are opposed openly the vicious opinions of those who perversely deny that the form of government in His Church was established by Christ the Lord; that to Peter alone, before the other apostles, whether individually or all together; was confided the true and proper primacy of jurisdiction by Christ; or, of those who affirm that the same primacy was not immediately and directly bestowed upon the blessed Peter himself, but upon the Church, and through this Church upon him as the minister of the Church herself.

The Canon of Scripture

*"Ignorance of Scripture is
ignorance of Christ"*
- St. Jerome

*"Knowledge of Church history is
the death of Protestantism"*
- John Henry Newman

Whether atheist or agnostic, Hindu, Moslem, Protestant, evangelical or fundamentalist, surety of truth is the most difficult thing for someone outside the Catholic Church to know. The central issue is authority. None of the people outside of the Church necessarily recognize a legitimate authority outside of themselves. An individual may insist that s/he recognizes the authority of Jesus Christ, and is led by the Holy Spirit, but, given the 23,000 Christian denominations extant today, the Holy Spirit appears to be agreeable to a number of different, and antagonistic, interpretations of Scripture. It is understandably difficult to distinguish being led by the Holy Spirit from being led by personal tastes. We cannot conclude that someone reading Scripture is not led by the Holy Spirit. It is simply the case that, apart from internal conviction (which may well be inspired by the Holy Spirit), those who do not recognize the authority of the Church have no established authority with whom to test the spirit and verify the correctness of his/her interpretation.

The Evidence of Ancient Texts

The information in this section summarizes the introduction to the Acts of the Apostle volume of the Navarre Bible:

All the books of the New Testament were written in Greek, with the sole exception of the Gospel of Matthew and the first two chapters of Luke, which were probably originally written in Aramaic (or possibly Hebrew). Unfortunately, none of the original texts survived. The oldest version of any surviving New Testament book is a papyrus fragment of St. John's Gospel (18:31-33, 37-38) which dates from roughly 125 A.D. According to a 1976 survey, there are over 5,000 surviving texts:

- 88 papyrus fragments
- 274 manuscripts written in capitals (that is, each letter is separate and their are no accent marks)
- 2795 manuscripts written in lower case letters (that is, the letters in each word are linked)
- 2209 lectionaries for public liturgical use

New copies are continually being discovered. A 1963 catalogue (K. Aland) lists 4689, while a 1976 count was 5366. Over 4000 ancient (100-400 A.D.) translations exist, composed variously in Latin (from 2nd century onward, many prior to St. Jerome's translation), Syriac (2nd to 3rd century), Coptic (3rd century), Armenian (4th century), Ethiopian, Slav, Gothic (4th century), and Arabic. Furthermore, many ancient writers (e.g. Eusebius) quoted Scripture liberally - it is possible to reconstruct virtually the entire New Testament on the basis of these quotations, and the ancient texts from which these quotes come are generally older than the manuscript versions of the Scripture books which have come down to us. Nearly 100 New Testament papyri have survived, all of them Egyptian. Their time of writing was approximately between 100 to 200 AD. In addition, the writings of early Christians quote the New Testament so extensively that virtually the entire New Testament, apart from seven or eight verses, could be reconstructed simply from the works of those same Christians. Keep in mind, however, that the early Christians did not quote chapter and verse, since there were no chapter/verse subdivisions until the Middle Ages (see below).

In comparison, we have only two extant copies of accounts that Hannibal crossed the Alps with elephants, and only one line in all of ancient writing which indicates that Alexander reached India during his conquests, yet both of these events are undisputed by historians.

Proving the Bible and the Church Trustworthy

Some claim that using the Scripture to witness to the authority of the Church, and using the Church to witness to the authority of Scripture, is a circular argument. It is not. It is a spiral. To begin with, assume neither is trustworthy.

- It is the case that an historical person named Jesus existed. No contemporary writers deny his existence, many affirm it.

- We know what he taught from the evidence of witnesses. Some of this evidence is in a book called Scripture, but some is not part of that book.
- Jesus apparently claimed he would be raised from the dead. His followers claim he was raised from the dead. This doesn't mean he was.
- His followers were so adamant he had been raised from the dead they willingly suffered torture and death rather than recant.
- The form of death everyone agrees he underwent was extremely public, and Jesus was known to be a widely recognized person. It is highly unlikely that his enemies would have allowed the wrong man to be killed. The form of death (crucifixion) was such that it is extremely unlikely that he could have faked it. The Romans tended to be quite good at killing their man. Thus, Jesus almost certainly did die on the cross.
- Did He rise from the dead? It is extremely unusual for literally hundreds of people to stick to a story that is false, especially when they are not only threatened with death, but know death is a definite fact awaiting them because of the story they are telling. We have a very high probability that Jesus was crucified, and a very high probability that the witnesses saw what they said they saw. The Resurrection probably happened - that is, what he claimed would happen came true.
- This Jesus person claimed to establish a church. We have historical evidence of a church. Tacitus, Josephus, Seutonius, and Pliny the Younger all vouch for the existence of Christ and his Church. The last, writing at the beginning of the second century, even mentioned that the Christians thought the bread and wine becomes the body and blood of God. We can show a line of unbroken succession of leaders of this church and people in this church. We have a high probability that these events happened - the only evidence against is incredulity.
- The Church witnesses which ancient books are the most trustworthy (i.e., Scripture). Christ said the church was a good witness.

Scripture Translations

The information in this section summarizes Why Do Catholics Do That?, *pp. 24-25.*

The Bible was the first document written in many modern languages. The Church's evanglization needs forced the invention of written Slavonic, Gaelic and German. The oldest surviving German document is a translation of Scripture done by a monk named Ulfilas (381 A.D.). Between the time of Ulfilas and Martin Luther, over a millenium of manuscripts were written; nearly two-dozen mechanically printed German editions of Scripture existed when Luther made his translation. Luther was not the first to translate Scripture into German, much less the first to translate it into the language of the people.

Why didn't more people have Bibles prior to Luther's time? Because they were extremely expensive. In medieval times, a new Bible cost a community about as much as a new church building, it required the slaughter of 400 animals for the vellum which made the pages, years of work by hundreds of scribes who lettered, gilded, and illuminated the text by hand, and it generally merited an ornate, sometimes gold- or jewel-encrusted binding. Given the material and workmanship necessary for the construction of any book, much less the word of God, one Bible was easily worth an entire manor. Most people were illiterate precisely because the text materials required for teaching literacy was so expensive. "A Bible in every house" was economically and culturally impossible. However, despite the high price of the book, churches often kept the Bible on public display in the building, secured only by a chain, so that all who could read might have access to the Scriptures. Gutenburg, a Catholic, printed copies of Scripture as his first job.

Because books were so expensive, the vast majority of people could not read until the invention of the printing press. Martin Luther happened to undertake his translation of Scripture at a time when the price of books had begun to fall drastically, and thus literacy had begun to become affordable. In short, Luther's *sola scriptura* theology was the creation of man-made technology. *Sola scriptura* was literally impossible (pardon the pun) prior to the invention of the printing press. If the Church had taught what Luther advocated, she would have condemned all but the very rich to ignorance of Christ prior to the invention of moveable type. More than 95% of the pre-print technology population was illiterate. Even today, world literacy runs no higher than about 50%. Given that Christ came to save the lowly, the meek and the poor, it seems highly unlikely that He would have made literacy and books, both marks of wealth, prerequisites for entering the Kingdom of Heaven.

As a side-point, chapter and verse divisions were added to Scripture well after Scripture was written. Chapter divisions were introduced around the year 1206 A.D., by Stephen Langton (d. 1228), a professor at the University of Paris and subsequently Archbishop of Canterbury and a cardinal, into the Parisian Bible in that year. The chapter divisions were subsequently added to all editions of the Bible. Chapters were split into verses in the sixteenth century, with Robert Etienne (Stephenus) providing the final form in 1551. The verse divisions are not always consistent (minor variations exist between translations), and in some instances the chapter divisions arbitrarily chop a contiguous story or theme up into artificially separate pieces (*Guide to the Bible*, Robert and Tricot, Paris: Desclee, 1960, I:5), as with chapters 2, 3, and 4 of John's Gospel.

How the Canon was Established

Jn 7:35 The Jews said to one another, "Where does this man intend to go that we shall not find him? Does he intend to go to the Dispersion among the Greeks and teach the Greeks?"

*As a matter of fact, He did intend it.
And therein lies the story...*

Because of the Babylonian Exile and the resulting Diaspora, Hebrew had become an essentially dead language, read only by rabbis, several centuries before Christ was born. Jews outside of Palestine spoke "koine" (common) Greek, those in Palestine spoke primarily Aramaic. In the post-Exile period, targums, Aramaic paraphrase commentaries of sacred Hebrew books, were written within Palestine. Outside of Palestine, the Diaspora Jews relied on Greek translations of Scripture commonly called the "Septuagint," which means "the 70." It was named for the 70 scholars of legend who supposedly translated the sacred Hebrew books into Greek in Alexandria - earning these collections the present-day nickname of "the Alexandrian canon" while the Hebrew text is called the "Palestinian" or "Jamnian" canon. Because scrolls were expensive, scarce, and treasured, it was a rare bookshelf indeed which had a complete collection of either the Hebrew or the Greek versions of Scripture.

By Christ's birth, the canon of Hebrew Scripture had only been partially defined. The Hebrew Scriptures had a tri-partite structure: the Law, the Prophets, and the Writings. While the list of books belonging to the Law and the Prophets was clearly fixed and ordered by 130 B.C., it was not clear what books belonged to the Writings. The Septuagint, on the other hand, arranged books by style; narrative, poetical, and prophetic. Since most post-Exile Jews wrote in Greek and Aramaic, not Hebrew, the Greek collections soon added historical books which the Hebrew version never saw. Because the Septuagint didn't have a standard ordering or a completely standard list of books, the list of books included in the Greek varied according to collection, with no distinction made between earlier and later works. By the time of Christ's Incarnation, the Septuagint had acquired several more books than the Hebrew Scripture had: Tobit, Judith, the Wisdom of Solomon, Sirach, Baruch (including the Letter of Jeremiah), 1-3 Maccabees, the Prayer of Manasseh, Psalm 151, the Book of Jubilees, 1 Esdras, additions to Esther and Daniel, and very rarely, 4 Maccabees, since this last was not widely used and was never considered inspired by Jews or Christians. Since none of these books contained law or prophecy, they all properly belonged to the Writings.

This situation was not considered a serious problem, however, since Jewish teaching relied on oral tradition. Even the Torah was read according to oral tradition. Prior to about the ninth century A.D., the Torah was written as one long word, a string of consonants without spaces, punctuation, or vowels - it was literally the word of God. Students learned how to read the text by listening to their elders read it over and over again. Although targums (translations into the common tongue) existed, the rabbis disliked them - these encouraged private interpretation of Scripture and undermined the Divinely authorized oral teaching authority of the Levitical priests (cf. Mt 23:2-3. Christ commands the people to respect their teaching authority, but not their lived example). What we today call the Talmud had not yet been committed to writing. The Talmud (which means "learnt by heart"), the rabbis' oral tradition of civil and religious law, is made up of two parts, the Mishna (the text of the oral law itself) and the Gemara (commentary). The Mishna was not written down until about the end of the second century A.D., while the Gemara was only written down during the 3rd to the 6th centuries A.D. Oral interpretive tradition was the rule of faith for the Jews.

How did Jesus handle this situation? He acted like the Jewish teacher He was. Nothing indicates Christ authorized either His Apostles or disciples to write anything down. He only authorized them to preach orally, in the ancient Judaic teaching tradition. Of approximately 350 references made to Old Testament Scripture by the inspired writers of the New Testament, over 300 (85%) refer to the Septuagint, not the Hebrew version of Scripture. Jesus, for instance, when discussing "human traditions" (Mark 7:6-8), quotes a version of a passage in Isaiah found only in the Septuagint.

By 70 A.D., when the temple in Jerusalem was razed by the Romans and the Levitical priesthood was wiped out, the Jewish faith was hemorrhaging followers to the rapidly spreading belief that Jewish prophecy had been fulfilled in the person of Jesus. These new "Christians" were as likely to be Gentile as they were Jew, and if they were Jewish, they were quite a bit more likely to be Hellenistic Jews than Palestinian Jews. That is, these Jewish and Gentile "Christians" didn't read or speak Hebrew, they spoke "koine" Greek. Because the Jews of the Diaspora and the Gentiles of eastern Mediterrenean were the first converts, the Greek Septuagint was not only in wide use among Jews, but it was virtually the only text used by Christians. This was part of God's plan.

Jewish Christian oral teaching competed successfully against Jewish oral teaching, and it used Jewish Scripture to do it. This sparked two movements within non-Christian Judaism. First, Jewish scholars began debating whether or not the Christians' "Greek Scripture" was really Scripture. Second, around the year 200, the rabbis began writing down Jewish religious and civil law and their commentaries on it, creating what would eventually become the Talmud six centuries later. Non-Christian Jews ultimately refused the deuterocanonical Old Testament books, probably because of theology (e.g., 1 and 2 Maccabees teaches resurrection of the dead, while Wisdom chapters 1-5 contains an unsettlingly prophetic description of Christ's Passion and Death) and because they were written in Greek, not Hebrew.

Meanwhile the Christians had their own problems. Not only were Jewish brethren arguing that some of the Septuagint wasn't really Scripture, Gentile and Jewish Christians were writing numerous works about the life of Christ and Christian practice/belief, and no one was certain which of those writings should be considered sacred. During the first two centuries of the Church's existence, Christians simply couldn't be sure of the sacredness of many of the books in either their Jewish or their new "Christian" tradition. Even Jude, verse 9, alludes to the Assumption of Moses, a book which was not in the Hebrew canon or the Septuagint and is not now considered part of Sacred Scripture. The arguments led early Christians to distinguish between the *homologoumenoi* (the "accepted" books) and the *antilegomenoi* (the "contested" books), sometimes also called the *amphiballomenoi* (the "contradicted" books).

As God's plan continued to unfold, the language of the western Church switched from Greek to Latin in the first and second centuries and Latin Scripture translations were made. These were always made from the Greek Septuagint, since few Gentile or Jewish Christians knew Hebrew. Over time, 3 and 4 Maccabees, the Prayer of Manasseh, Psalm 151, Enoch, and 1 Esdras, were all dropped from the Latin translation, while the Greek-speaking eastern Church, who didn't need to translate the books, retained everything but 4 Maccabees. The Coptic and Ethiopian churches followed the eastern Church, but also kept the Book of Enoch, a book which was never translated into Latin, and therefore never had common usage in the western Church. Enoch was soon also dropped by the eastern Church due to heretical misuse, though it was widely used and considered inspired by the Church Fathers up to the fourth century - in fact, Jude 14 refers to it. By the time Pope Damasus commissioned Jerome to write a new Latin translation of the Gospels and the Psalms, the Old Latin version already had long usage in the western Church. This laid the groundwork for the four major variations in the canon of the Old Testament we have today: Roman Catholic, Eastern Orthodox, Coptic, and Judaic/Protestant/Evangelical.

While the Old Testament arguments revolved around Jewish acceptance of the books as sacred, New Testament difficulties related mostly to authorship. If the book was not clearly apostolic in origin, the Church tended to dispute or reject it. For instance, the western church was not convinced Hebrews was written by the apostle Paul, while the eastern church was. Meanwhile, the eastern church doubted the Apostle John wrote the Apocalypse, while the western church knew he had.

Several dozen books claimed apostolic origin, and their theological quality varied widely. Some works ultimately deemed apocryphal were and are recognized as essentially good to excellent theological works, e.g., the Didache, the Shepherd of Hermas, but uncertain authorship prevented their acceptance as inspired. Other apocryphal books were not only of uncertain or flagrantly false authorship, but also had serious error mixed in with otherwise acceptable theology, e.g., the Gospel of Thomas, the Acts of Pontius Pilate, and the Gospel of Mary. Many learned orthodox Christians fought to include theologically sound works like the Didache in the canon of the New Testament, arguing for their apostolic origin. However, the typical early Christian was illiterate. He could make no judgements himself about matters of canonicity, inspiration, or the fine points of theology in a written work.

Even the literate Christians faced raging disputes. Marcion (ca. 85-160 A.D.), for instance, denied the inspiration of all but ten Pauline epistles and a version of the Gospel of Luke which lacked the infancy narrative, and asserted the God of the Old Testament was radically different than the God of the New. He consciously copied the organization and rites of the Catholic church, and seriously threatened common Christian belief. No one could tell the canonical books without a scorecard and nobody had one.

The Scorecard:
Councils and papal decrees which defined or re-iterated the list of Sacred books

- 382 - Pope Damasus convoked a synod which produced the Roman Code. The Roman Code identified a list of holy Scripture identical to the Council of Trent's formally defined canon.
- 397 - First Council of Carthage
- 405 - Innocent I wrote a letter to the Gallican bishop Exsuperius of Toulouse which listed the books of Scripture.
- 419 - Second Council of Carthage

In a span of forty years, the Church essentially solved the problem. The "disputed" Old Testament books - Tobias, Judith, Wisdom, Ecclesiasticus, Baruch, 1 and 2 Maccabees, parts of Esther (chapters 11-16, or A-F), and parts of Daniel (3:24-90 and 13, 14) - and the "disputed" New Testament books - Hebrews, James, Jude, 2 Peter, 2 and 3 John, Revelation, parts of Mark (16:9-20), parts of Luke (22:43-44) and parts of John (5:4 and 8:1-11) - were recognized as inspired. Each of the decrees and councils above provided the same list of Scripture. No council or papal decree gave a different list. Prior to these decisions, both Athanasius and Jerome knew of, and to some extent agreed with, the Jewish unwillingness to accept these books, but both bowed to the authority of the Church, accepting the canonical status of all the disputed Old Testament and New Testament books. By 450 A.D., today's list of inspired books was almost universally accepted in the western Church.

Thus, the Christian canon was settled as the non-Christian Jews were still in the process of committing the Talmud to writing. By the early Middle Ages, the Jewish transition from oral to written tradition was made complete with the production of the "Masoretic" text of Hebrew Scripture. As noted above, the Hebrew Scripture was difficult to read without intensive oral instruction, being literally one long word. Between 800 and 925 A.D., the Jewish family Masorete added punctuation, vowels, and spacing to the Hebrew Scripture. The Masoretic version functionally replaced the original Hebrew text. Indeed, until the discovery of the Dead Sea Scrolls in the 1940's, the oldest surviving copy of the Hebrew Palestinian canon into modern times was the Masoretic text known as the Leningrad codex, dated to 1009 A.D. This meant the Septuagint version of the Old Testament available during the Middle Ages was actually older and had undergone less extensive revision than the available Hebrew text. The Septuagint would continue to be the oldest and most reliable version of Holy Writ available into this century, despite Luther's claim to be "going back to the original" when he reverted to the Hebrew canon.

By the 16th century, the Latin words "protocanonical" (meaning "first canon") and "deuterocanonical" (meaning "second canon") had replaced the Greek terms for "accepted" and "contested." The Septuagint books rejected by the Church and all non-Septuagint ancient texts are called "Apocrypha," which means "hidden," a shorthand for "these books are to be hidden from all but the wise," since they tended to be misunderstood by those not well-formed in the mysteries of faith. Around this time, the canonical status of the Christian Old Testament was called into question by Elias Levita, a Jewish contemporary of Luther. He theorized that Ezra presided over "the men of the Great Synagogue" and closed the canon in the 5th century B.C. His "proof" was Nehemiah 8 and 9, the great assembly of the people for the oral reading of the Law after they returned from Exile. Though no historical evidence of a "Great Synagogue" exists, Luther popularized this idea since it supported his bid to discard the Old Testament deuterocanonical books and thereby strengthened his dubious theology. Shortly after the Reformation began, Protestants began jeering the deuterocanonical books as "apocrypha" in order to disparage the inspired quality of that part of Scripture. The Rationalists of the 17th and 18th centuries would also support Levita's theory, since it undermined the authority of the Church.

Today, *sola scriptura* Christians present several arguments against the history and nature of the books. They argue that no ecumenical council defined the canon prior to Trent, and assert Trent arbitrarily added the Old Testament deuterocanonical books to

Scripture. However, this ignores the Second Council of Niceae's (787 AD) formal ratification of the African Code, which contained the canon, and the Council of Florence's (1441 AD) defined list of inspired books. While Trent was the first to use the words "canon" or "canonical," the list of the Council of Florence was identical with all previous lists of Scripture. Thus, the Council of Trent's Sacrosancta decree of April 8, 1546 AD, while the first formal canonical definition of Old and New Testament Scripture to the Church Universal, was the third formal affirmation of their inspiration in ecumenical council, and at least the seventh affirmation overall. Vatican I (1869) and Vatican II (1963) also confirmed Trent's list.

In fact, since 419 A.D., only one documented instance of a council or pope denying the canonicity of an Old Testament deuterocanonical book exists. Pope St. Gregory the Great, writing in his *Morals on the Book of Job* around the year 600 A.D., said of 1 Maccabees "...we are not acting irregularly, if from the books, though not canonical, yet brought out for the edification of the Church, we bring forward testimony. Thus, Eleazar, in the battle smote and brought down the elephant, but fell under the very beast that he killed (1 Macc 6:46)" (*A Library of the Fathers of the Holy Catholic Church*, Oxford, J. Parker, 1848, Morals on the Book of Job, Vol II, parts III & IV, Book XIX.34, p. 424). However, he was not making a formal universal teaching to the faithful, rather, he was writing a commentary on the book of Job as a private theologian. In other words, this book was not a Magisterial teaching.

Unlike Zwingli, Luther did not entirely discard the deuterocanonical books from his translation of Scripture, rather, he relegated them to an appendix situated between the Old Testament and the New Testament. However, Luther wasn't happy with the deuterocanonical New Testament books either; he disliked the Apocalypse, Hebrews, and Jude, and seriously considered "throwing Jimmy [the epistle of James] into the fire" because it contradicted his faith-alone theology. Standing in judgement of Scripture, he called James "an epistle full of straw," while regarding all four books as quasi-canonical. However, the Old Testament deuterocanonical books stayed in the appendix of many Protestant translations for 300 years because they were recognized as useful for moral instruction. Indeed, the Protestant kings of England imposed the death penalty on anyone who omitted the deuterocanonical appendix. The books were only completely discarded in 1827, at the impetus of the British and Foreign Bible Society.

This history creates several problems for *sola scriptura* Christians. To begin with, the version of Scripture they use is not only incomplete by Catholic standards, it is incomplete when compared to three hundred years of common Protestant usage. Today's *sola scriptura* Christians are using a collection of Scripture which has only been in common existence for roughly 150 years.

Furthermore, if Trent's Sacrosancta decree incorrectly added Old Testament deuterocanonical books, how do we know the New Testament is correct? After all, the arguments against the New Testament deuterocanonical books and passages are as valid as those against the Old, i.e., Jewish scholars rejected New Testament writings and Trent erroneously added them to Scripture. Luther's willingness to question the books in both canons of Scripture shows he accepted this line of reasoning.

Some argue that Jewish scholars would know nothing about the New Testament because they did not recognize Christ, while they know the Old Testament because they lived it. However, this introduces a false division between the two Testaments of Scripture. Since the New Testament lies hidden in the Old, while the Old is fulfilled in the New, the Old Testament is just as permeated with Christ as the New. Simply put, Jewish scholars who rejected Christ would be unable to properly recognize Old Testament Scripture, since they would not have the guidance of the Holy Spirit.

Luther supposedly accepted the Hebrew canon only because the Jews would know better than anyone what books were in Scripture. Yet Luther's sermons showed little respect for Jewish theological opinion in other areas or for Jews in general. He put no stock in Old Testament Midrash commentaries or targums. He rejected Purgatory, claiming his newly-defined canon had no prayers for the dead, despite the well-known Jewish tradition prefiguring Purgatory, the praying of Q'addish, the prayer for the purification of the recently deceased. Q'addish is prayed for eleven months following the death of a relative, since it is an insult to think the dead so unclean s/he would need a full year of purification. He ignored the fact that all the first-century Jews who were Christian accepted the Septuagint. He ignored the fact that the non-Christian Jews upon whose opinion he relied for canonicity rejected not only the deuterocanonical Old Testament books, but the entirety of the New Testament. If he accepted Jewish authority to define the canon of the Old Testament, upon what authority did he define the canon of the New? All Christians deny Luther's infallibility. Therefore, we may reasonably ask upon what authority *sola scriptura* Christians base their definition of either canon of Scripture. Remember, Trent was the first formal definition in all Christendom of *either* canon, New or Old, of Scripture.

These are the historical arguments. But what of the arguments against the books themselves? Most of these arguments are addressed in the section below, "Excerpts from the Old Testament Deuterocanonical books." However, it will be noted here that the New Testament "failure" to quote the relevant books is not quite what it seems. Esther, Nehemiah, Song of Songs, Ecclesiastes, and Ruth: none of these are quoted in the New Testament, while the extra-canonical books of Enoch and the Assumption of Moses *are* referred to in the epistle of Jude. To be consistent, *sola scriptura* Christians should discard the former books and add the latter two to the canon of the Old Testament. The earliest Christians would probably have been amazed at this judgement: While the catacombs have frescoes depicting scenes from the deuterocanonical books, such as Tobias and Raphael, Judas Maccabeus, the mother of Maccabees with her seven martyred sons, Daniel in the lion's den, Judith holding the head of Holofernes, and the three boys in the fiery furnace, there are no such frescoes from the apocryphal books.

1100 years after the Second Council of Carthage, Martin Luther would pretend to rely on the authority of Jewish Scripture scholars, the same Jews upon whom he poured verbal vitriol from the pulpit, in order to subvert the authority of the Body of Christ; claiming the former knew what parts of the Old Testament were Holy Scripture while the Church did not. He would adopt the Palestinian canon, today's Protestant canon, in contravention to over a millenia of Septuagint use by all Christians. 23,000 individual "Bible-only" Christian denominations have resulted from his refusal to accept authority.

.Early Christians' comments on the Old Testament Canon

New Testament Deuterocanonical Passages

Many Christians do not realize that some of their favorite passages in the New Testament Gospels are deuterocanonical - their inspiration was in doubt and contested for significant periods of Church history:

Mk 16:9-20 Now when he rose early on the first day of the week, he appeared first to Mary Magdalene, from whom he had cast out seven demons. [10] She went and told those who had been with him, as they mourned and wept. [11] But when they heard that he was alive and had been seen by her, they would not believe it.

[12] After this he appeared in another form to two of them, as they were walking into the country. [13] And they went back and told the rest, but they did not believe them.

[14] Afterward he appeared to the eleven themselves as they sat at table; and he upbraided them for their unbelief and hardness of heart, because they had not believed those who saw him after he had risen. [15] And he said to them, "Go into all the world and preach the gospel to the whole creation. [16] He who believes and is baptized will be saved; but he who does not believe will be condemned. [17] And these signs will accompany those who believe: in my name they will cast out demons; they will speak in new tongues; [18] they will pick up serpents, and if they drink any deadly thing, it will not hurt them; they will lay their hands on the sick, and they will recover."

[19] So then the Lord Jesus, after he had spoken to them, was taken up into heaven, and sat down at the right hand of God. [20] And they went forth and preached everywhere, while the Lord worked with them and confirmed the message by the signs that attended it. Amen.

Lk 22:43-44 43 (And to strengthen him an angel from heaven appeared to him. 44 He was in such agony and he prayed so fervently that his sweat became like drops of blood falling on the ground.)

Jn 5:4 For from time to time an angel of the Lord used to come down into the pool, and the water was stirred up, so that the first one to get in (after the stirring of the water) was healed of whatever disease afflicted him.

Jn 8:1-11 but Jesus went to the Mount of Olives. [2] Early in the morning he came again to the temple; all the people came to him, and he sat down and taught them. ³ The scribes and the Pharisees brought a woman who had been caught in adultery, and placing her in the midst ⁴ they said to him, "Teacher, this woman has been caught in the act of adultery. ⁵ Now in the law Moses commanded us to stone such. What do you say about her?" ⁶ This they said to test him, that they might have some charge to bring against him. Jesus bent down and wrote with his finger on the ground. ⁷ And as they continued to ask him, he stood up and said to them, "Let him who is without sin among you be the first to throw a stone at her." ⁸ And once more he bent down and wrote with his finger on the ground. ⁹ But when they heard it, they went away, one by one, beginning with the eldest, and Jesus was left alone with the woman standing before him. ¹⁰ Jesus looked up and said to her, "Woman, where are they? Has no one condemned you?" ¹¹ She said, "No one, Lord." And Jesus said, "Neither do I condemn you; go, and do not sin again."

How many people are willing to throw out the story of the adulterous woman, the story that Jesus' sweat was like blood during the Agony in the Garden, the story of the angel stirring the pool, or Christ's appearance to Mary Magdelene? Yet, why would one accept deuterocanonical New Testament passages and accounts while rejecting deuterocanonical Old Testament passages and accounts? If the Popes and the Church Councils incorrectly defined the Old Testament, why would they correctly define the New Testament? If bishops who could trace their consecration back to Peter and the Apostles were not infallible in their definitions, why should today's Christians be so certain that THEY have the true canon of Scripture? One could argue that Christians couldn't be wrong on something so basic, and yet, historically speaking, if sola scriptura *Christians are correct, the whole of Christendom MUST have been wrong for some period of time prior to Trent, for the whole Church admitted the deuterocanonical Old Testament books; everyone used them in liturgical worship during the several centuries leading up to Trent. How do we know we aren't still all wrong today, just as they were all wrong in that era? Without an infallible teaching authority, there is simply no way to tell.*

Excerpts from the Old Testament Deuterocanonical books

Sola scriptura *Christians often say that the deutero-canonical books contain flaws which prevent them from being considered canonical. The books of Judith and Tobit are asserted to show that lying pays off, and both books are known to contain geographical and historical errors (see below). Further, the deuterocanonical books are claimed not to have a sufficiently inspired or prophetic nature. Read through these excerpts from the first five chapters of Wisdom, particularly chapters two and five, and decide for yourself how closely it seems to prophesy the events of the New Testament.*

The Wisdom of Solomon
Chapter 1

¹ Love righteousness, you rulers of the earth,
think of the Lord with uprightness,
and seek him with sincerity of heart... ⁷ Because the Spirit of the Lord has filled the world,
and that which holds all things together knows what is said; ⁸ therefore no one who utters unrighteous things will escape notice,
and justice, when it punishes, will not pass him by... ¹² Do not invite death by the error of your life, nor bring on destruction by the works of your hands; ¹³ because God did not make death,
and he does not delight in the death of the living... ¹⁶ But ungodly men by their words and deeds summoned death; considering him a friend, they pined away,
and they made a covenant with him, because they are fit to belong to his party.

Chapter 2

For they reasoned unsoundly, saying to themselves,
"Short and sorrowful is our life,
and there is no remedy when a man comes to his end,
and no one has been known to return from Hades. ² Because we were born by mere chance, and hereafter we shall be as though we had never been;
because the breath in our nostrils is smoke,
and reason is a spark kindled by the beating of our hearts. ³ When it is extinguished, the body will turn to ashes,
and the spirit will dissolve like empty air. ⁴ Our name will be forgotten in time and no one will remember our works;
our life will pass away like the traces of a cloud,
and be scattered like mist that is chased by the rays of the sun

and overcome by its heat. ⁵ For our allotted time is the passing of a shadow,
and there is no return from our death,
because it is sealed up and no one turns back. ⁶ "Come, therefore, let us enjoy the good things that exist,
and make use of the creation to the full as in youth. ⁷ Let us take our fill of costly wine and perfumes,
and let no flower of spring pass by us. ⁸ Let us crown ourselves with rosebuds before they wither. ⁹ Let none of us fail to share in our revelry,
everywhere let us leave signs of enjoyment,
because this is our portion, and this our lot. ¹⁰ Let us oppress the righteous poor man; let us not spare the widow
nor regard the gray hairs of the aged. ¹¹ But let our might be our law of right,
for what is weak proves itself to be useless. ¹² "Let us lie in wait for the righteous man, because he is inconvenient to us and opposes our actions;
he reproaches us for sins against the law,
and accuses us of sins against our training. ¹³ He professes to have knowledge of God, and calls himself a child of the Lord. ¹⁴ He became to us a reproof of our thoughts; ¹⁵ the very sight of him is a burden to us,
because his manner of life is unlike that of others,
and his ways are strange. ¹⁶ We are considered by him as something base,
and he avoids our ways as unclean;
he calls the last end of the righteous happy,
and boasts that God is his father. ¹⁷ Let us see if his words are true,
and let us test what will happen at the end of his life; ¹⁸ for if the righteous man is God's son, he will help him,
and will deliver him from the hand of his adversaries. ¹⁹ Let us test him with insult and torture, that we may find out how gentle he is,
and make trial of his forbearance. ²⁰ Let us condemn him to a shameful death,
for, according to what he says, he will be protected." ²¹ Thus they reasoned, but they were led astray,
for their wickedness blinded them, ²² and they did not know the secret purposes of God, nor hope for the wages of holiness,
nor discern the prize for blameless souls; ²³ for God created man for incorruption, and made him in the image of his own eternity, ²⁴ but through the devil's envy death entered the world,
and those who belong to his party experience it.

Chapter 3

But the souls of the righteous are in the hand of God,
and no torment will ever touch them. ² In the eyes of the foolish they seemed to have died,
and their departure was thought to be an affliction, ³ and their going from us to be their destruction;
but they are at peace. ⁴ For though in the sight of men they were punished,
their hope is full of immortality. ⁵ Having been disciplined a little, they will receive great good,
because God tested them and found them worthy of himself; ⁶ like gold in the furnace he tried them,
and like a sacrificial burnt offering he accepted them. ⁷ In the time of their visitation they will shine forth,
and will run like sparks through the stubble. ⁸ They will govern nations and rule over peoples,
and the Lord will reign over them for ever. ⁹ Those who trust in him will understand truth, and the faithful will abide with him in love,
because grace and mercy are upon his elect,
and he watches over his holy ones. ¹⁰ But the ungodly will be punished as their reasoning deserves,
who disregarded the righteous man and rebelled against the Lord; ¹¹ for whoever despises wisdom and instruction is miserable.
Their hope is vain, their labors are unprofitable,
and their works are useless... ¹⁵ For the fruit of good labors is renowned, and the root of understanding does not fail...

Chapter 5

Then the righteous man will stand with great confidence
in the presence of those who have afflicted him,
and those who make light of his labors. ² When they see him, they will be shaken with dreadful fear, and they will be amazed at his unexpected salvation. ³ They will speak to one another in repentance,
and in anguish of spirit they will groan, and say, ⁴ "This is the man whom we once held in derision and made a byword of reproach—we fools!
We thought that his life was madness
and that his end was without honor. ⁵ Why has he been numbered among the sons of God? And why is his lot among the saints? ⁶ So it was we who strayed from the way of truth,
and the light of righteousness did not shine on us,
and the sun did not rise upon us. ⁷ We took our fill of the paths of lawlessness and destruction,
and we journeyed through trackless deserts,
but the way of the Lord we have not known. ⁸ What has our arrogance profited us? And what good has our boasted wealth brought us? ⁹ "All those things have vanished like a shadow,

and like a rumor that passes by; ¹⁰ like a ship that sails through the billowy water, and when it has passed no trace can be found,
nor track of its keel in the waves; ¹¹ or as, when a bird flies through the air,
no evidence of its passage is found;
the light air, lashed by the beat of its pinions
and pierced by the force of its rushing flight,
is traversed by the movement of its wings,
and afterward no sign of its coming is found there; ¹² or as, when an arrow is shot at a target, the air, thus divided, comes together at once,
so that no one knows its pathway. ¹³ So we also, as soon as we were born, ceased to be, and we had no sign of virtue to show,
but were consumed in our wickedness." ¹⁴ Because the hope of the ungodly man is like chaff carried by the wind, and like a light hoarfrost driven away by a storm; it is dispersed like smoke before the wind,
and it passes like the remembrance of a guest who stays but a day. ¹⁵ But the righteous live for ever, and their reward is with the Lord;
the Most High takes care of them. ¹⁶ Therefore they will receive a glorious crown and a beautiful diadem from the hand of the Lord,
because with his right hand he will cover them,
and with his arm he will shield them. ¹⁷ The Lord will take his zeal as his whole armor, and will arm all creation to repel his enemies; ¹⁸ he will put on righteousness as a breastplate, and wear impartial justice as a helmet; ¹⁹ he will take holiness as an invincible shield, ²⁰ and sharpen stern wrath for a sword, and creation will join with him to fight against the madmen. ²¹ Shafts of lightning will fly with true aim,
and will leap to the target as from a well-drawn bow of clouds, ²² and hailstones full of wrath will be hurled as from a catapult;
the water of the sea will rage against them,
and rivers will relentlessly overwhelm them; ²³ a mighty wind will rise against them, and like a tempest it will winnow them away.
Lawlessness will lay waste the whole earth,
and evil-doing will overturn the thrones of rulers.

There are definite similarities between certain passages in the epistles and in the Old Testament deuterocanonical books:

Mt 22:25-26 Now there were seven brothers among us; the first married, and died, and having no children left his wife to his brother. ²⁶ So too the second and third, down to the seventh.

Mk 12:20-22 There were seven brothers; the first took a wife, and when he died left no children; ²¹ and the second took her, and died, leaving no children; and the third likewise; ²² and the seven left no children.

Lk 20:29-31 Now there were seven brothers; the first took a wife, and died without children; ³⁰ and the second ³¹ and the third took her, and likewise all seven left no children and died.

Tob 7:11 "I have given my daughter to seven husbands, and when each came to her he died in the night. But for the present be merry." And Tobias said, "I will eat nothing here until you make a binding agreement with me."

Christ accepted the reference to Tobit as Scripture for:

Mt 22:29,31-33 But Jesus answered them, "You are wrong, because you know neither the scriptures nor the power of God... ³¹ And as for the resurrection of the dead, have you not read what was said to you by God, ³² 'I am the God of Abraham, and the God of Isaac, and the God of Jacob'? He is not God of the dead, but of the living." ³³ And when the crowd heard it, they were astonished at his teaching.

Mk 12:24, 26-27 Jesus said to them, "Is not this why you are wrong, that you know neither the scriptures nor the power of God?... ²⁶ And as for the dead being raised, have you not read in the book of Moses, in the passage about the bush, how God said to him, 'I am the God of Abraham, and the God of Isaac, and the God of Jacob'? ²⁷ He is not God of the dead, but of the living; you are quite wrong."

Lk 20:34,37 And Jesus said to them...³⁷ "But that the dead are raised, even Moses showed, in the passage about the bush, where he calls the Lord the God of Abraham and the God of Isaac and the God of Jacob."

Indeed, Jesus not only affirms that their reference is to Scripture, He tells them that they do not understand Scripture; all three synoptic accounts show Him explaining His opponents' Scripture reference to Tobit by interpreting it in light of His own Scripture reference to Exodus. He does not draw a distinction between the book of Tobit and the book of Exodus. Further, Jesus is aquainted with the book of Sirach:

Mt 5:23-24, 43-48 So if you are offering your gift at the altar, and there remember that your brother has something against you, [24] leave your gift there before the altar and go; first be reconciled to your brother, and then come and offer your gift... "You have heard that it was said, 'You shall love your neighbor and hate your enemy.' [44] But I say to you, Love your enemies and pray for those who persecute you, [45] so that you may be sons of your Father who is in heaven; for he makes his sun rise on the evil and on the good, and sends rain on the just and on the unjust. [46] For if you love those who love you, what reward have you? Do not even the tax collectors do the same? [47] And if you salute only your brethren, what more are you doing than others? Do not even the Gentiles do the same? [48] You, therefore, must be perfect, as your heavenly Father is perfect.

Sir 28:2-6 Forgive your neighbor the wrong he has done,
and then your sins will be pardoned when you pray. [3] Does a man harbor anger against another,
and yet seek for healing from the Lord? [4] Does he have no mercy toward a man like himself,
and yet pray for his own sins? [5] If he himself, being flesh, maintains wrath,
who will make expiation for his sins? [6] Remember the end of your life, and cease from enmity,
remember destruction and death, and be true to the commandments.

God used not just the book of Exodus, but also the book of Wisdom in order to inform the Gospel of John:

Wis 16:10-12 but thy sons were not conquered even by the teeth of venomous serpents,
for thy mercy came to their help and healed them. [11] To remind them of thy oracles they were bitten,
and then were quickly delivered,
lest they should fall into deep forgetfulness
and become unresponsive to thy kindness. [12] For neither herb nor poultice cured them,
but it was thy word, O Lord, which heals all men.

Jn 1:1 In the beginning was the Word, and the Word was with God, and the Word was God.

Jn 3:14-15 And as Moses lifted up the serpent in the wilderness, so must the Son of man be lifted up, [15] that whoever believes in him may have eternal life."

Other Apostles knew of the deuterocanonical books:

1 Pet 1:6-7 In this you rejoice, though now for a little while you may have to suffer various trials, [7] so that the genuineness of your faith, more precious than gold which though perishable is tested by fire, may redound to praise and glory and honor at the revelation of Jesus Christ.

Wis 3:5-6 Having been disciplined a little, they will receive great good,
because God tested them and found them worthy of himself; [6] like gold in the furnace he tried them,
and like a sacrificial burnt offering he accepted them.

Both Peter, above, and Paul, below, seem to have echoed passages from the book of Wisdom.

Heb 1:3 He reflects the glory of God and bears the very stamp of his nature, upholding the universe by his word of power. When he had made purification for sins, he sat down at the right hand of the Majesty on high...

Wis 7:26-27 For she is a reflection of eternal light,
a spotless mirror of the working of God,
and an image of his goodness. [27] Though she is but one, she can do all things,
and while remaining in herself, she renews all things;
in every generation she passes into holy souls
and makes them friends of God, and prophets...

Eph 6:14-17 Stand therefore, having girded your loins with truth, and having put on the breastplate of righteousness, [15] and having shod your feet with the equipment of the gospel of peace; [16] besides all these, taking the shield of faith, with which you can quench all the flaming darts of the evil one. [17] And take the helmet of salvation, and the sword of the Spirit, which is the word of God.

1 Thess 5:8 But, since we belong to the day, let us be sober, and put on the breastplate of faith and love, and for a helmet the hope of salvation

Wis 5:17-20 The Lord will take his zeal as his whole armor, and will arm all creation to repel his enemies; [18] he will put on righteousness as a breastplate, and wear impartial justice as a helmet; [19] he will take holiness as an invincible shield, [20] and sharpen stern wrath for a sword, and creation will join with him to fight against the madmen.

While the synoptic Gospels show the prophecy of the book of Wisdom being fulfilled...

Wis 2:12-20 "Let us lie in wait for the righteous man, because he is inconvenient to us and opposes our actions; he reproaches us for sins against the law, and accuses us of sins against our training. [13] He professes to have knowledge of God, and calls himself a child of the Lord. [14] He became to us a reproof of our thoughts; [15] the very sight of him is a burden to us, because his manner of life is unlike that of others, and his ways are strange. [16] We are considered by him as something base, and he avoids our ways as unclean; he calls the last end of the righteous happy, and boasts that God is his father. [17] Let us see if his words are true, and let us test what will happen at the end of his life; [18] for if the righteous man is God's son, he will help him, and will deliver him from the hand of his adversaries. [19] Let us test him with insult and torture, that we may find out how gentle he is, and make trial of his forbearance. [20] Let us condemn him to a shameful death, for, according to what he says, he will be protected."

Mt 27:39-43 And those who passed by derided him, wagging their heads [40] and saying, "You who would destroy the temple and build it in three days, save yourself! If you are the Son of God, come down from the cross." [41] So also the chief priests, with the scribes and elders, mocked him, saying, [42] "He saved others; he cannot save himself. He is the King of Israel; let him come down now from the cross, and we will believe in him. [43] He trusts in God; let God deliver him now, if he desires him; for he said, 'I am the Son of God.'"

Mk 15:27-32 And with him they crucified two robbers, one on his right and one on his left. [29] And those who passed by derided him, wagging their heads, and saying, "Aha! You who would destroy the temple and build it in three days, [30] save yourself, and come down from the cross!" [31] So also the chief priests mocked him to one another with the scribes, saying, "He saved others; he cannot save himself. [32] Let the Christ, the King of Israel, come down now from the cross, that we may see and believe."

Lk 23:33 And the people stood by, watching; but the rulers scoffed at him, saying, "He saved others; let him save himself, if he is the Christ of God, his Chosen One!"

Paul and Judith teach the same lessons on being an example of faithfulness, even unto martyrdom...

1 Cor 10:9-10 We must not put the Lord to the test, as some of them did and were destroyed by serpents; [10] nor grumble, as some of them did and were destroyed by the Destroyer.

Jud 8:24-25 "Now therefore, brethren, let us set an example to our brethren, for their lives depend upon us, and the sanctuary and the temple and the altar rest upon us. [25] In spite of everything let us give thanks to the Lord our God, who is putting us to the test as he did our forefathers.

Heb 11 and 2 Mac 6 and 7 both recount the valorous deaths of martyrs.

2 Mac 7:13 When he too had died, they maltreated and tortured the fourth in the same way.

Heb 11:35 Women received their dead by resurrection. Some were tortured, refusing to accept release, that they might rise again to a better life.

What about Baruch? Baruch 6 is an extended commentary on the uselessness of idols - a theme rather common to Scripture. An excerpt is presented here:

Bar 6:35-40,44 Likewise they are not able to give either wealth or money; if one makes a vow to them and does not keep it, they will not require it. [36] They cannot save a man from death or rescue the weak from the strong. [37] They cannot restore sight to a blind man; they cannot rescue a man who is in distress. [38] They cannot take pity on a widow or do good to an orphan. [39] These things that are made of wood and overlaid with gold and silver are like stones from the mountain, and those who serve them will be put to shame. [40] Why then must any one think that they are gods, or call them gods?:... Whatever is done for them is false. Why then must any one think that they are gods, or call them gods?

The book of Tobit is failed on three counts: the first is that the hero, Tobit, seems to undertake ritual magic, in direct contravention to Scripture.

When reading Tobit, as when reading any book of Scripture, it is important to remember that the Old Testament contains typology which prophesies or foreshadows what will happen in the New Testament. "The New Testament lies hidden in the Old Testament, while the Old Testament is revealed in the New," as Augustine said. One of the most ancient symbols for Christ is a fish. Note what the fish in this story does, and how it is used:

Tob 6:2-8, 16-17, 8:2-3, 11:8 Then the young man went down to wash himself. A fish leaped up from the river and would have swallowed the young man; ³ and the angel said to him, "Catch the fish." So the young man seized the fish and threw it up on the land. ⁴ Then the angel said to him, "Cut open the fish and take the heart and liver and gall and put them away safely." ⁵ So the young man did as the angel told him; and they roasted and ate the fish. And they both continued on their way until they came near to Ecbatana. ⁶ Then the young man said to the angel, "Brother Azarias, of what use is the liver and heart and gall of the fish?" ⁷ He replied, "As for the heart and liver, if a demon or evil spirit gives trouble to any one, you make a smoke from these before the man or woman, and that person will never be troubled again. ⁸ And as for the gall, anoint with it a man who has white films in his eyes, and he will be cured."... When you enter the bridal chamber, you shall take live ashes of incense and lay upon them some of the heart and liver of the fish so as to make a smoke. ¹⁷ Then the demon will smell it and flee away, and will never again return. And when you approach her, rise up, both of you, and cry out to the merciful God, and he will save you and have mercy on you.... As he went he remembered the words of Raphael, and he took the live ashes of incense and put the heart and liver of the fish upon them and made a smoke. ³ And when the demon smelled the odor he fled to the remotest parts of Egypt, and the angel bound him.... You therefore must anoint his eyes with the gall; and when they smart he will rub them, and will cause the white films to fall away, and he will see you."

The fish tries to swallow Tobit; it is a fisher of men. Tobit cuts out the heart, liver, and gall and salts the fish (see the exegesis on holy water for an explanation of the Scriptural use of salt as a representation of suffering). The heart and liver are the organs of life in a living creature. So, the book of Tobit portrays a Christ-symbol sown with suffering and roasted, as Christ roasted on the cross in the sun, as an immolation to God. This oblation caused the complete defeat of the demon, who had caused the death of many men in the story. In this defeat, a virginal maiden was rescued in order to be married to the bridegroom who had offered the sacrifice, and who had the legal right to marry her - the Bridegroom marrying the Bride without spot or blemish. Following the marriage, the gall from the fish made the cataracts fall from Tobiah's eyes, healing his blindness, prefiguring Christ's healing of the blind man (Jn 9) and the scales which would fall from Saul's eyes. (Acts 10:18)

Second, some claim Tobit contains inaccuracies, something the Word of God could not possibly have. However, apparent inaccuracies occur in other books as well. For instance, the book of Daniel asserts that the Medes were a world power in the eras between the neo-Babylonians and the Persians (cf Dan 2:31-45, 7:1-7), something completely unknown to ancient history. Belshazzar was never titled a king, despite Daniel's assertions, and he was the son of Nabonidus (556-539 B.C), not of Nebuchadnezzar (605-562 B.C.) (cf. Dan 5:1-30, 7:1-7, 17, 8:1-27). Only Daniel records a Darius the Mede. Darius I was king of Persia (522-486 B.C). Does this mean the Book of Daniel is not Scriptural? No - it means that some "Biblical literalist" Christians don't fully understand the way in which God speaks through the literary forms of Scripture.

Third, it is claimed for both Judith and Tobit that the heroes of the book lied (Jud 9:10,13, Tob 5:5,13), which presents a poor example the word of God would never provide. Yet the Hebrew midwives lie to Pharoah (Ex 1:19), and Judges, in addition to presenting a situation similar to Judith (Judg 4:17-22), also shows a man who offers his own daughter as a holocaust (Judg 11:29-40), and another who gives his wife to a crowd to be raped to death in place of himself and cuts her body into pieces in order to provoke a war (Judg 19:22-30), while Genesis shows Jacob stealing Esau's birthright (Gen 25 and 27) and profiting greatly from this deception. Thus, if we were to say that the name "Yahweh helps" is a lie (the meaning of the name Raphael gives, and certainly a true name given the story), we must discard several other Old Testament books along with Tobit and Judith.

Finally, it is sometimes claimed that Sirach and 2 Maccabees both deny that they are inspired Scripture, since both open with a preface in which the respective authors apologize for any possible errors. However, 1 Cor 1:15 shows Paul forgetting whom he baptized, while 1 Cor 7:12 and 1 Cor 7:40 both are explicitly asserted to be Paul's personal opinion, not God's word. Does this mean 1 Corinthians, or at least the relevant passages named, are not canonical Scripture?

Mt 12:6, 41,42 I tell you, something greater than the temple is here...The men of Nineveh will arise at the judgment with this generation and condemn it; for they repented at the preaching of Jonah, and behold, something greater than Jonah is here. The queen of the South will arise at the judgment with this generation and condemn it; for she came from the ends of the earth to hear the wisdom of Solomon, and behold, something greater than Solomon is here.

Christ is greater than the Law (temple), the Prophets (Jonah) and the Writings (Solomon). But notice the example Christ uses for the Writings: "The Wisdom of Solomon." It is, coincidentally, the traditional title of the deuterocanonical book which describes both His killers and His death.

Private Interpretation of Scripture

Is 53:6 All we like sheep have gone astray; we have turned every one to his own way; and the LORD has laid on him the iniquity of us all.

No truth of Scripture can be obtained with assurance unless it be studied within the light of Sacred Tradition and the teaching authority, that is, the Magisterium, of the Church, who alone has the divine authority, wisdom, and guidance to interpret the gift She received from the Bridegroom.

Current misunderstandings: Many, many people accept sola scriptura, *the idea that Scripture is the sole authority and/or that Scripture can interpret itself in such a way that all one needs to know for salvation is available from the word of Scripture. Yet these same people cannot agree on a simple thing like the regenerative nature of baptism and it's necessity for salvation. Christianity has split into over 23,000 separate sects, each teaching a Scripture so clear on its face that the requirements for salvation are obvious, thus resulting in 23,000 different ideas of how it is obvious.*

Is 28:8-9 For all tables are full of vomit, no place is without filthiness. [9] "Whom will he teach knowledge, and to whom will he explain the message? Those who are weaned from the milk, those taken from the breast?

Isaiah emphasizes that sinful human persons are not qualified to receive the message of God. What person could be qualified?

1 Jn 2:27 but the anointing which you received from him abides in you, and you have no need that any one should teach you; as his anointing teaches you about everything, and is true, and is no lie, just as it has taught you, abide in him.

It is the anointing, i.e., the joining into the Body of Christ, which imparts wisdom. It is through the sacraments and the teaching authority of the Church, the Bride of Christ, that we learn knowledge of God.

Mt 13:10-11 Then the disciples came and said to him, "Why do you speak to them in parables?" [11] And he answered them, "To you it has been given to know the secrets of the kingdom of heaven, but to them it has not been given."

Though the passage says "disciples," Christ is talking to the Apostles - this is clear in Matthew 13:36, when Christ dismisses the crowds and enters the house. The "disciples" follow and ask for further explanation of the parables - a house would not be large enough to house all of his disciples. Only the Apostles are given the ability to fully comprehend Scripture.

Lk 24:45 Then he opened their minds to understand the scriptures...

Luke confirms this - it describes what the risen Christ did for the Apostles in the upper room. Note that Christ explains all of Scripture to two disciples on the road to Emmaus (Luke 24:13-35) yet - although their hearts burned within them - they fail to understand or recognize Christ until the breaking of the <u>bread</u>. However, here in Luke 24:44, the Apostles' minds are opened to the understanding which the simple, non-Apostolic disciples in the previous passage were unable to grasp.

Jude 8 Yet in like manner these men in their dreamings defile the flesh, reject authority, and revile the glorious ones.

The rejection of authority is a sin against God. This applies also to the rejection of the authoritative interpretation of Scripture.

Prov 3:5-6 Trust in the LORD with all your heart, and do not rely on your own insight. ⁶ In all your ways acknowledge him, and he will make straight your paths.

2 Pet 1:20-21 First of all you must understand this, that no prophecy of scripture is a matter of one's own interpretation, ²¹ because no prophecy ever came by the impulse of man, but men moved by the Holy Spirit spoke from God.

We can't rely on our own insight. We need a teacher.

2 Pet 3:15-16 And count the forbearance of our Lord as salvation. So also our beloved brother Paul wrote to you according to the wisdom given him, ¹⁶ speaking of this as he does in all his letters. There are some things in them hard to understand, which the ignorant and unstable twist to their own destruction, as they do the other scriptures.

Scripture itself testifies that Scripture is hard to understand.

2 Cor 1:13 For we write you nothing but what you can read and understand; I hope you will understand fully...

Heb 5:11-12 About this we have much to say which is hard to explain, since you have become dull of hearing. ¹² For though by this time you ought to be teachers, you need some one to teach you again the first principles of God's word.

1 Cor 1:10 I appeal to you, brethren, by the name of our Lord Jesus Christ, that all of you agree and that there be no dissensions among you, but that you be united in the same mind and the same judgment.

At one point, Martin Luther wrote "The epistle of James gives us much trouble. If they will not admit my interpretations, I will make rubble also of it. I almost feel like throwing Jimmy into the stove" (Luther, Vol 4., p. 317). He was also unsure about 2 Peter, Hebrews and Revelation. Yet even Luther began to realize how divisive his own sola scriptura theology was. In his Letter against Zwingli, Luther wrote "If the world lasts long it will be again necessary on account of the different interpretations of Scripture which now exist that to preserve the unity of faith we should receive the councils and decrees and fly to them for refuge."

The following five passages list the gifts of the Holy Spirit:

Is 11:1-3 There shall come forth a shoot from the stump of Jesse, and a branch shall grow out of his roots. ² And the Spirit of the LORD shall rest upon him, the spirit of wisdom and understanding, the spirit of counsel and might, the spirit of knowledge and the fear of the LORD. ³ And his delight shall be in the fear of the LORD.

Note that "his delight" is not knowledge, wisdom, or understanding, but fear of the Lord.

Rom 12:3-8 For by the grace given to me I bid every one among you not to think of himself more highly than he ought to think, but to think with sober judgment, each according to the measure of faith which God has assigned him. ⁴ For as in one body we have many members, and all the members do not have the same function, ⁵ so we, though many, are one body in Christ, and individually members of one another. ⁶ Having gifts that differ according to the grace given to us, let us use them: if prophecy, in proportion to our faith; ⁷ if service, in our serving; he who teaches, in his teaching; ⁸ he who exhorts, in his exhortation; he who contributes, in liberality; he who gives aid, with zeal; he who does acts of mercy, with cheerfulness.

If gifts of grace differ, why should we think that everyone has an equal gift at Scripture interpretation? Is salvation denied to those who cannot read? Or to those who do not have the gift of interpreting Scripture correctly?

1 Cor 12:4-11 Now there are varieties of gifts, but the same Spirit; ⁵ and there are varieties of service, but the same Lord; ⁶ and there are varieties of working, but it is the same God who inspires them all in every one. ⁷ To each is given the manifestation of the Spirit for the common good. ⁸ To one is given through the Spirit the utterance of wisdom, and to another the utterance of knowledge according to the same Spirit, ⁹ to another faith by the same Spirit, to another gifts of healing by the one Spirit, ¹⁰ to another the working of miracles, to another prophecy, to another the ability to distinguish between spirits, to another various kinds of tongues, to another the interpretation of tongues. ¹¹ All these are inspired by one and the same Spirit, who apportions to each one individually as he wills.

1 Cor 12:28-30 And God has appointed in the church first apostles, second prophets, third teachers, then workers of miracles, then healers, helpers, administrators, speakers in various kinds of tongues. ²⁹ Are all apostles? Are all prophets? Are all teachers? Do all work miracles? ³⁰ Do all possess gifts of healing? Do all speak with tongues? Do all interpret?

Eph 4:8-12 Therefore it is said,
"When he ascended on high he led a host of captives, and he gave gifts to men." ⁹ (In saying, "He ascended," what does it mean but that he had also descended into the lower parts of the earth? ¹⁰ He who descended is he who also ascended far above all the heavens, that he might fill all things.) ¹¹ And his gifts were that some should be apostles, some prophets, some evangelists, some pastors and teachers, ¹² to equip the saints for the work of ministry, for building up the body of Christ, ¹³ until we all attain to the unity of the faith and of the knowledge of the Son of God, to mature manhood, to the measure of the stature of the fulness of Christ;

Not one of these passages asserts that the interpretation of Scripture or the ability to discern the correct canon of Scripture is a gift of the Spirit. On the contrary, the fact that three out of four New Testament passages mention teaching as a gift of the Spirit implies most will not be able to interpret Scripture well on their own - they will need an infallibly led teacher.

Jn 14:26 But the Counselor, the Holy Spirit, whom the Father will send in my name, he will teach you all things, and bring to your remembrance all that I have said to you.

Jn 16:13 When the Spirit of truth comes, he will guide you into all the truth; for he will not speak on his own authority, but whatever he hears he will speak, and he will declare to you the things that are to come.

Remember, Jesus' words in the Gospel of John were spoken to the Apostles alone, while they were all gathered at the Last Supper. Only the Apostles were promised the gift of the infallible leadership of the Spirit. The gift was that they would always be reminded of what Christ TOLD them - in other words, the oral transmission of knowledge is safeguarded. According to Scripture, both Christ and the Holy Spirit speak - they do not write. Scripture does not promise the written deposit will be safeguarded, it promises only that the oral deposit will be safeguarded. The Church took it upon herself, in her authority as the Bride of Christ, under the direction of the Holy Spirit, to write down and safeguard the deposit of Scripture, the gift of God.

Lk 24:42-49 They gave him a piece of broiled fish, ⁴³ and he took it and ate before them. ⁴⁴ Then he said to them, "These are my words which I spoke to you, while I was still with you, that everything written about me in the law of Moses and the prophets and the psalms must be fulfilled." ⁴⁵ Then he opened their minds to understand the scriptures, ⁴⁶ and said to them, "Thus it is written, that the Christ should suffer and on the third day rise from the dead, ⁴⁷ and that repentance and forgiveness of sins should be preached in his name to all nations, beginning from Jerusalem. ⁴⁸ You are witnesses of these things. And behold, I send the promise of my Father upon you; but stay in the city, until you are clothed with power from on high."

The gifts of Scriptural interpretation, i.e., the promise of the Father to be led into all truth, is not listed as a separate gift of the Spirit because it is already bound up within a gift of the Spirit, specifically, the gift of <u>apostleship.</u> It was the Apostles, or disciples under the close direction of the Apostles, who wrote out the *knowledge of God which those same Apostles preached every day, the written knowledge we now call Holy Scripture. Not all Christians have the gift of interpreting Scripture - that gift will not come to all Christians "until we all attain to the unity of faith and knowledge of the Son of God, to mature manhood, to the extent of the full stature of Christ." (Ephesians 4:13)*

Early Christians' comments on Private Revelation

Sola Scriptura

Much of the Scripture and exegesis in this section comes from Pat Madrid's tape series "What Still Divides Us?"

Holy Scripture is materially sufficient for knowledge of salvation, that is, implicitly or explicitly, it describes everything necessary for salvation. However, Scripture is not formally sufficient, that is, it does not teach the truths of salvation so clearly that anyone who picks up a Bible can discover those truths for himself. Scripture needs a teacher who bears and embodies the infallible teaching authority of the Holy Spirit if it is to be understood as God intends, for only the Holy Spirit knows the mind of God.

Current misunderstandings: Sola scriptura *Christians claim a) Scripture is the sole and final authority and b) it is formally sufficient for knowledge of salvation, i.e., it expresses itself clearly enough on matters involving salvation that no interpretation is necessary. Yet, while Scripture claims to be inspired in 2 Timothy 3:16, the Qur'an, the Book of Mormon, and the Hindu Vedas all claim to be inspired as well. How do we know ours is and theirs isn't? "Burning in the heart" a la Mormonism doesn't count. How do we know that Scripture is the sole authority? Unfortunately, Scripture itself denies the idea that it is either the sole or the final authority. We know of Scripture's authority because of two good witnesses - the Church and Tradition.*

1 Jn 2:26-27 I write this to you about those who would deceive you; [27] but the anointing which you received from him abides in you, and you have no need that any one should teach you; as his anointing teaches you about everything, and is true, and is no lie, just as it has taught you, abide in him.

This text is used to demonstrate that an infallible teacher for Scripture is not necessary - the anointing received from Christ is sufficient. But if that were the meaning John intended, then why is John writing it at all? The epistle is an instruction in which John gives a new command (1 John 2:8) - why give a new command, or explain the meaning of Christ's message, to people who don't need instruction? John TELLS them that they don't need to be TOLD anything because of their anointing, so John would seem to be saying his own epistle is useless. In fact, John's reference to the "anointing [which] teaches you about everything" is a reference to the catechizing prior to baptism and confirmation, sacraments which poured out the Isaiahan gifts of the Spirit, perfecting understanding. If John really meant that no further catechization were necessary after anointing, then the Spirit's gift of teaching and the Word of Scripture itself would be useless.

1 Thess 5:21 but test everything; hold fast what is good...

The same Christians often assert that a doctrinal practice is licit only if Scripture explicitly affirms or describes the practice. However, Scripture does not explicitly affirm or describe such a test anywhere, thus the rule itself fails its own test. Worse, Scripture did not command any of the Apostles to write down what is in Scripture, nor does Christ command anyone to write anything down (apart from John's Apocalypse). Thus, if this rule were followed, the New Testament and large chunks of the Old must be thrown out; writing down Scripture was itself not licit because Scripture does not affirm the Apostles were authorized by God to write it down. The disciples who were not Apostles (e.g., Mark and Luke) had even less authority to write.

1 Jn 4:1 Beloved, do not believe every spirit, but test the spirits to see whether they are of God; for many false prophets have gone out into the world.

1 Thess 5:19-21 Do not quench the Spirit, [20] do not despise prophesying, [21] but test everything; hold fast what is good

Many claim to be led by the Holy Spirit in their interpretation of Scripture. Yet do they follow the command of Scripture? They should test each spirit, to make sure the spirit of interpretation is from God. How can one test a spirit, except against one's own conscience? The interpretation of one Scripture passage cannot be used to test the interpretation of another Scripture passage, since the same spirit may very well be influencing both interpretations. In order to test the spirit which is giving them their interpretation, their only measure is their own conscience. Yet is not the conscience and soul of every man stained with sin? So we test the spirit and its teaching with a dim eye using a darkened measure. We must instead test with a clear eye using a clear measure.

1 Cor 2:10-11 For the Spirit searches everything, even the depths of God. [11] For what person knows a man's thoughts except the spirit of the man which is in him? So also no one comprehends the thoughts of God except the Spirit of God.

There is only one who is both without sin and who knows the measure of God, and He is Jesus Christ, within whom the Spirit of God rests. It is only the authoritative voice of the Body of Christ, animated by the Holy Spirit, which can properly test the Spirit and render just judgement upon the meaning of Scripture (cf. Apostolic Succession). Scripture confirms this.

Mt 18:16-17 But if he does not listen, take one or two others along with you, that every word may be confirmed by the evidence of two or three witnesses. [17] If he refuses to listen to them, tell it to the church; and if he refuses to listen even to the church, let him be to you as a Gentile and a tax collector.

In the Matthean passage, Scripture witnesses that the Church is the final authority. Her authority must be infallible, for if She were to err, then Christ would be commanding disciples to treat a fellow believer as an unbeliever on the basis of an erroneous judgement. If you cannot trust your church to be a final authority (and who can trust any authority except an infallible authority?), then you are not in the church of Christ described by Scripture. Scripture states that the Church is to be listened to. It states no exceptions. It does not hint at fallible teachings.

Mt 4 *Another argument points to the temptation of Christ. Christ referred only to Scripture and He parried the Devil's quoting of Scripture by again referring to Scripture. He did not refer to His own Divinity, to tradition or Tradition, to the authority of the Church, or to any authority besides Scripture. What those who hold this argument forget is that Jesus Christ is always infallibly led by the Holy Spirit for the right interpretation of Scripture, for He is indissolubly united with the Holy Spirit in the Godhead. Thus, this passage merely affirms what the Church teaches - that only the Body of Christ can interpret Scripture rightly, and only His Body, with Him as the head, can correct those who use it incorrectly.*

Sola scriptura supporters sometimes use Deuteronomy as support for their contention.

Deut 31:9,12 And Moses wrote this law, and gave it to the priests the sons of Levi,...[he said] Assemble the people, men, women, and little ones, and the sojourner within your towns, that they may hear and learn to fear the LORD your God, and be careful to do all the words of this law...

Deut 32:46-47 he said to them, "Lay to heart all the words which I enjoin upon you this day, that you may command them to your children, that they may be careful to do all the words of this law. 47 For it is no trifle for you, but it is your life, and thereby you shall live long in the land which you are going over the Jordan to possess."

These Deuteronomy passages certainly establish Scripture as an authority, but they do not indicate Scripture is the sole authority.

Psalm 119 *is also often used to support* sola scriptura. *It is an extended meditation on knowing and keeping the law. Nowhere does it state that the law (Scripture) is the sole, final, or formally sufficient authority.. Indeed, those who use arguments from the Old Testament to support* sola scriptura *defeat their own purpose, for the Old Testament references to the law are references to the Mosaic law, the law which Paul specifically says was made obsolete (Hebrews 8:13).*

Acts 15:1-2 But some men came down from Judea and were teaching the brethren, "Unless you are circumcised according to the custom of Moses, you cannot be saved." 2 And when Paul and Barnabas had no small dissension and debate with them, Paul and Barnabas and some of the others were appointed to go up to Jerusalem to the apostles and the elders about this question

Notice that Paul and Barnabas did not appeal to Scripture to settle this dispute. Rather, they were deputized to go to Jerusalem and get a definitive ruling from "the apostles and the elders." Further, in Acts 15 and 16, the Council did not appeal to Scripture alone in order to settle the difficulty, rather, they appealed directly to the Holy Spirit and to their own authority, which they put on a co-equal basis with that of God.

Acts 15:28 For it has seemed good to the Holy Spirit and to us to lay upon you no greater burden than these necessary things...

The need for apostolic authority is clear:

Acts 17:1-7 Now when they had passed through Amphipolis and Apollonia, they came to Thessalonica, where there was a synagogue of the Jews. 2 And Paul went in, as was his custom, and for three weeks he argued with them from the scriptures, 3 explaining and proving that it was necessary for the Christ to suffer and to rise from the dead, and saying, "This Jesus, whom I proclaim to you, is the Christ." 4 And some of them were persuaded, and joined Paul and Silas; as did a great many of the devout Greeks and not a few of the leading women. 5 But the Jews were jealous, and taking some wicked fellows of the rabble, they gathered a crowd, set the city in an uproar, and attacked the house of Jason, seeking to bring them out to the people. 6 And when they could not find them, they dragged Jason and some of the brethren before the city authorities, crying, "These men who have turned the world upside down have come here also, 7 and Jason has received them; and they are all acting against the decrees of Caesar, saying that there is another king, Jesus."

According to the analysis presented by Steve Ray in "Why the Bereans Rejected Sola Scriptura," This Rock, March 1997, pp. 22-25, it appears that the Thessalonians were sola scriptura adherents. After all, Paul reasoned with them from the Scriptures for three weeks, but they were not convinced. Christ did not visibly fulfill any of the recognized messianic texts (e.g. Psalms 45, 89; 2 Sam 7:11-16; Mic 5:2-4; Amos 9:11; Mal 3:1-4;4:5; I 9:2-7; 11:1-16; 49:8-13; 52:1-12) nor was he a martyr like the Maccabees who died in defense of the Torah. His life and death challenged the status of Torah (Scripture) as the absolute norm for life. In his manner of living he was a sinner (2 Cor 5:21) and in his death, cursed by God (see The Sign of the Cross*). According to the Jewish followers of* sola scriptura, *Jesus was not blessed by God, but accursed by God and they could prove it from Scripture by the very mode of his death.*

The Thessalonians did not accept oral teaching or the authority of Paul, which was mere human authority by their standards. They accepted only what they privately interpreted from Scripture. Paul's words obviously contradicted the Torah, in their estimate. As a result, Paul was nearly run out of town on a rail.

Acts 17:10-12 The brethren immediately sent Paul and Silas away by night to Beroea; and when they arrived they went into the Jewish synagogue. 11 Now these Jews were more noble than those in Thessalonica, for they received the word with all eagerness, examining the scriptures daily to see if these things were so. 12 Many of them therefore believed, with not a few Greek women of high standing as well as men.

Some argue that Paul did not say only the Church could interpret or that only Peter could interpret. They point out that Scripture praises the practice of the Bereans for studying Scripture. This is true. Note, however the Bereans did not study Scripture on their own. They studied Scripture under Paul's direction, in the light of his oral teaching. Paul was an officially deputed member of the Church, and they accepted Paul's oral teaching authority. Scripture actually demonstrates that Scripture alone was not sufficient for the Bereans, since the Bereans had failed to understand the meaning of Christ's crucifixion until the Church explained Scripture to them. There is no instance in Scripture where a community of Jews or Gentiles managed to discover the truth about Jesus Christ through their own study of Scripture without an apostle, an officer of the Body of Christ, to explain the Good News to them, this despite the fact that news of Jesus Christ quickly traveled as far as Rome, as we know from pagan accounts and from Acts itself (cf. Acts 26:26 "This was not done in a corner.").

Gal 1:11-12,15-20 For I would have you know, brethren, that the gospel which was preached by me is not man's gospel. [12] For I did not receive it from man, nor was I taught it, but it came through a revelation of Jesus Christ.... But when he who had set me apart before I was born, and had called me through his grace, [16] was pleased to reveal his Son to me, in order that I might preach him among the Gentiles, I did not confer with flesh and blood, [17] nor did I go up to Jerusalem to those who were apostles before me, but I went away into Arabia; and again I returned to Damascus.
[18] Then after three years I went up to Jerusalem to visit Cephas, and remained with him fifteen days. [19] But I saw none of the other apostles except James the Lord's brother. [20] (In what I am writing to you, before God, I do not lie!)

Paul learns the Gospel through a special private revelation from Christ Himself. Even so, he goes to Jerusalem to talk with Peter.

Gal 2:1-2 The after fourteen years I went up again to Jerusalem with Barnabas... I went up by revelation; and I laid before them (but privately before those who were of repute) the gospel which I preach among the Gentiles, lest somehow I should be running or had run in vain.

Paul checks his preaching with the men of repute on a regular basis. God tells him to.

2 Pet 3:15-16 And count the forbearance of our Lord as salvation. So also our beloved brother Paul wrote to you according to the wisdom given him, [16] speaking of this as he does in all his letters. There are some things in them hard to understand, which the ignorant and unstable twist to their own destruction, as they do the other scriptures.

Scripture itself testifies that Scripture is hard to understand.

2 Cor 1:13 For we write you nothing but what you can read and understand; I hope you will understand fully...

2 Tim 3:14-17 But as for you, continue in what you have learned and have firmly believed, knowing from whom you learned it [15] and how from childhood you have been acquainted with the sacred writings which are able to instruct you for salvation through faith in Christ Jesus. [16] All scripture is inspired by God and profitable for teaching, for reproof, for correction, and for training in righteousness, [17] that the man of God may be complete, equipped for every good work.

2 Tim 3:14-17 is often used to demonstrate that Scripture is sufficient and the final authority. However, the New Testament was not yet written when Timothy was in his "infancy," so this passage really refers to the Old Testament, not the New. Even if it did refer to the New Testament, it would be insufficient. Scripture does not say it is itself the final authority. Insofar as the idea that it shows Scripture's sufficiency, v. 17 uses the words "arteos" and "exartisminos" for "competent" and "equipped." Arteos is only used in Timothy, exartisminos is used only in Acts 21:5, and once in the Septuagint, thus it is impossible to be sure what he meant by those words, since they can mean anything from "suitable" to "perfected." In neither case does it help the sola scriptura *advocate, sine these two words refer to "the man of God," not to Scripture. But even if they did refer to Scripture...*

James 1:4 And let steadfastness have its full effect (teleos), that you may be perfect and complete, lacking in nothing.

"Teleos" means "perfection," and is generally a stronger word than "arteos" or "exartisminos." This would seem to indicate that perseverance is more important than Scripture in order to become a complete man of God.

2 Tim 2:21 If any one purifies himself from what is ignoble, then he will be a vessel for noble use, consecrated and useful to the master of the house, ready for any good work.

The phrase "any good work" is exactly identical to what is used in 3:15. The word "prepared" (Greek heteomazo) can mean everything from ordinary preparation to divine preparation, so one who cleanses himself is a complete man of God.

1 Jn 2:4-6 He who says "I know him" but disobeys his commandments is a liar, and the truth is not in him; [5] but whoever keeps his word, in him truly love for God is perfected. By this we may be sure that we are in him: [6] he who says he abides in him ought to walk in the same way in which he walked.

John says keeping his word, i.e. doing what Christ commands, is what perfects us - not Scripture itself.

2 Tim 2:15 Do your best to present yourself to God as one approved, a workman who has no need to be ashamed, rightly handling the word of truth.

In Timothy, Paul is speaking to a bishop.

Rom 10:8 But what does it say? The word is near you, on your lips and in your heart (that is, the word of faith which we preach [quoting Deut 30:14])...

Deuteronomy shows sufficiency in quality, but says nothing about Scripture being the only source. Paul refers to Scripture as "profitable" using the Greek word "ophedimos," which implies Scripture is not sufficient in and of itself. Paul does not claim that the sole infallible source of truth is Scripture. Instead, he refers to other, non-written teachings.

2 Tim 1:13-14 Follow the pattern of the sound words which you have heard from me, in the faith and love which are in Christ Jesus; [14] guard the truth that has been entrusted to you by the Holy Spirit who dwells within us.

2 Tim 2:2 and what you have heard from me before many witnesses entrust to faithful men who will be able to teach others also.

2 Tim 3:10-11 Now you have observed my teaching, my conduct, my aim in life, my faith, my patience, my love, my steadfastness, [11] my persecutions, my sufferings, what befell me at Antioch, at Iconium, and at Lystra, what persecutions I endured; yet from them all the Lord rescued me.

If 2 Tim 3:16 is sola scriptura, what is Timothy to do with Paul's oral teaching? The passage implies Paul's impending death. What should Timothy do with Scripture, considering that the canon is not complete? Paul did not say to look on his oral teaching with suspicion after his death.

1 Thess 2:13 And we also thank God constantly for this, that when you received the word of God which you heard from us, you accepted it not as the word of men but as what it really is, the word of God, which is at work in you believers.

The word of God can also come from hearing. Since the Word of God is a Living and vibrant word, why would it lose this characteristic simply because it is transmitted orally? We do not have any of the original manuscripts of the New Testament - we have only copies of copies of copies. If the copied message can be transmitted without error because it is the Word of God, could not the spoken Word of God be transmitted without error? It can - this oral transmission is called Sacred Tradition.

2 Thess 2:15 So then, brethren, stand firm and hold to the traditions which you were taught by us, either by word of mouth or by letter.

2 Jn 12 Though I have much to write to you, I would rather not use paper and ink, but I hope to come to see you and talk with you face to face, so that our joy may be complete.

2 Thess 3:9-10 For what thanksgiving can we render to God for you, for all the joy which we feel for your sake before our God, [10] praying earnestly night and day that we may see you face to face and supply what is lacking in your faith?

Phil 4:9 What you have learned and received and heard and seen in me, do; and the God of peace will be with you.

1 Cor 11:2 I commend you because you remember me in everything and maintain the traditions even as I have delivered them to you.

Acts 20:17,27 And from Miletus he sent to Ephesus and called to him the elders of the church...... or I did not shrink from declaring to you the whole counsel of God.

The Ephesian epistle is only 6 chapters long - is that the whole plan of God?

Eph 3:3 how the mystery was made known to me by revelation, as I have written briefly.

This implies a much more thorough oral transmission of knowledge.

1 Cor 11:34 if any one is hungry, let him eat at home—lest you come together to be condemned. About the other things I will give directions when I come.

This implies that not all teaching was through written word.

Mt 18:16 But if he does not listen, take one or two others along with you, that every word may be confirmed by the evidence of two or three witnesses.

The testimony accepted by the Catholic Church is tripartite - Scripture, Tradition, Church, each established by Christ and guided by Holy Spirit. According to Dei Verbum, the magisterium, which is the teaching office of the Church, finds itself a servant of the Word of God, subject to the authority of Scripture. It guards the deposit of Scripture. Though Scripture is the norm which norms all other norms, but which is itself not normed, yet it needs the interpretation of Sacred Tradition to help us understand what it truly says. Statements change meaning depending on vocal emphasis. For instance, repeat the phrase "I never said you stole money" a few times, and emphasize a different word each time you say it - the implied meaning alters radically with each shift in emphasis. Which words of Scripture are emphasized where? Only a good witness could tell. Only an infallibly guided witness who survived 2000 years of hardship to bring us the subtly nuanced meanings could be trusted. The written word is not sufficient - the oral witness must also be present (cf. How the canon was established below). Even in a court of law, a written deposition does not bear the same weight as oral testimony, because a live witness can be examined, probed, tested for sure knowledge of the event. The Word of God is living and active, sharper than a two-edged sword, but that is so precisely because it is transmitted to us by a living, infallible witness - the Body of Christ.

Col 1:24 Now I rejoice in my sufferings for your sake, and in my flesh I complete what is lacking in Christ's afflictions for the sake of his body, that is, the church...

Jn 21:25 But there are also many other things which Jesus did; were every one of them to be written, I suppose that the world itself could not contain the books that would be written.

Christ's sacrifice on the cross was complete, but there is a sense in which it is lacking. It lacks our participation - we must become partakers of the divine nature in order to complete Christ's work, and we can do that only by imitating Him in obedience, in suffering, in directing that suffering towards the perfection of the Church. The Scriptures are complete, but there is a sense in which they, also, are lacking. They lack an authoritative witness, an interpreter who can describe individually all that Christ said and meant, even those things not recorded, who can fill up the world with Christ; a witness who can help us purify ourselves, before whom we can be obedient to the Divine Word, to God.

Tough Questions about Scripture

1 Cor 4:6 I have applied all this to myself and Apollos for your benefit, brethren, that you may learn by us not to go beyond what is written, that none of you may be puffed up in favor of one against another.

Sola scriptura Christians often argue that Scripture requires us not to go beyond what is written, but they themselves do not follow their own advice. While at least some, if not all, of the following points are believed by such Christians, they have no Scriptural basis for their belief, unless they go beyond the literal meaning of the words of Scripture to an unusual degree. The subjects below cannot be verified by a believer in *sola scriptura*, since no verse or combination of verses in Scripture provides the required information:

***Ex nihilo* Creation:** All Christians know that God created the world out of nothing, but the Scriptures recognized by the reformers do not say this anywhere. Some of the Bible commentaries on Genesis 1:1-2 assert that the Hebrew phrase, "the earth was a formless waste and darkness was on the face of the deep," was a Hebrew metaphor for *ex nihilo* creation, but the evidence in support of this assertion is not particularly compelling. Indeed, before the canon of Scripture was established, the earliest Christians had to demonstrate *ex nihilo* creation through reason alone to their heretical opponents. Clement (ca. 150-215 A.D.) appears to have been the first person to state and give a proof from reason for *ex nihilo* creation, while Tertullian (ca. 160-225 A.D.) conceded that creation out of nothing was not explicitly stated anywhere in the Bible, but argued from the silence of Scripture to say this manner of creation had to be the case. Both Christian apologists realized that God and matter could not be co-eternal - God's existence had to precede the existence of matter or His omnipotence could be called into question. It was only with the definitive listing of the books of Scripture, established between 382 and 419 A.D., that any book of Scripture taught the doctrine explicitly: "I beseech you, my child, to look at the heaven and the earth and see everything that is in them, and recognize that God did not make them out of things that existed" (2 Mac 7:28).

The revelation of Jesus Christ ended with the death of the last Apostle: The question is quite simple: is Scripture closed? For example, would God inspire the writing of any more sacred books today? While not all Christian denominations agree, most recognize that no inspiration coming to us after the death of the last apostle could qualify as Scripture. However, this idea of the closing of the canon of Scripture is not found anywhere within Scripture itself. It is an apostolic teaching borne down through the ages in the body of Sacred Tradition guarded by the teaching authority of the Catholic Church, the Magisterium.

Provide the name of the "beloved disciple": Remarkable, but true: we only know the beloved disciple was John, the author of the Gospel, through Sacred Tradition and the Magisterium. It is to be found nowhere in Sacred Scripture.

Demonstrate which weekday is the Sabbath: The word "sabbath" simply means "day of rest" in Hebrew. Scripture does not indicate which day of the week was the day of rest. In fact, Scripture never names any days of the week at all. How do we know Thursday isn't the "day of rest" or the "first day" of the week? It is only through the oral tradition of the Hebrews, an oral tradition maintained and improved upon by the Jews who found the fulfillment of their faith in Jesus Christ, that we know the Sabbath was Saturday and is now Sunday.

Provide the names of the authors of Matthew's Gospel, Mark's Gospel, Luke's Gospel, John's Gospel, or the Acts of the Apostles: Again, Scripture doesn't tell us that the Gospel of Matthew, for instance, was written by Matthew. The titles to the Gospels are known to us only through Sacred Tradition - Scripture doesn't say who wrote any of the works listed above. Likewise, the chapter and verse divisions are traditions of men, chapter divisions being added in 1206 A.D. by Stephen Langton, a professor at the University of Paris and subsequently Archibshop of Canterbury and a cardinal, while the verse numbering was added in the sixteenth century in order to assist in mechanically printing the text. The final form of the verse numbering scheme was set by Robert Etienne, also called Stephanus, in 1551 A.D.

Scripture is the sole authority: While numerous passages of Scripture state that Scripture is an authority, none state that it is the sole authority. The closest verse in support of the statement is 2 Tim 3:16: "Scripture is inspired by God and profitable for teaching, reproof, correction and for training in righteousness, that the man of God may be complete, equipped for every good work." Supposedly, this implies Scripture must be sufficient in and of itself, or the man of God could not be made complete by using it. Unfortunately for the *sola scriptura* thesis, James 1:4 states that "steadfastness" makes a person "perfect and complete, lacking in nothing," while 2 Tim 2:21 asserts that anyone who "purifies himself from what is ignoble... will be a vessel for noble use, consecrated and useful to the master of the house, ready for any good work." So, which is it, Scripture, steadfastness, or self-purification, that completes? It would seem that all are necessary, but none are sufficient by themselves.

We attain salvation through faith alone: While numerous passages of Scripture state that faith is necessary for salvation, none say that faith alone saves. In fact, Scripture specifically denies that faith alone saves in James 2:24, while simultaneously pointing out the necessity of good works for salvation in several other passages, e.g., Eph 2:8-10, Jn 14:15, 1 Jn 5:1-3, Mt 25:31-46, Gal 6:2, etc.

List the Old Testament canonical books or lists the New Testament canonical books: While we know what books are in Scripture, it is not because Scripture tells us, but because the councils and popes of the Church told us. The first three centuries of the Church saw a wide-ranging dispute over the contents of both the Old and the New Testament, with books in both

Testaments being contested as false. For the Old Testament, Tobias, Judith, Wisdom, Ecclesiasticus, Baruch, 1 and 2 Maccabees, parts of Esther (chapters 11-16, or A-F), and parts of Daniel (3:24-90 and 13, 14) were disputed, for the New Testament, Hebrews, James, Jude, 2 Peter, 2 and 3 John, Revelation, parts of Mark (16:9-20), parts of Luke (22:43-44) and parts of John (5:4 and 8:1-11) were all called into question.

The complete canon of Scripture was first recognized by the Roman Synod convoked by Pope Damasus in 382 A. D., which produced the Roman Code. The Code contained the list of Holy Scripture. Pope Damasus confirmed the Synod and Code. The Council of Hippo (393 A.D.) and the First Council of Carthage (397 A.D.) provided identical lists of Scripture. Pope Innocent I confirmed the list again in 405 A.D. when the Gallican bishop Exsuperius of Toulouse asked him what books should be considered Scripture, and the replied by Pope sending him a letter containing a list identical to every definition so far given. The Second Council of Carthage (419 A.D.) confirmed the list yet again. All five definitions were identical to the Council of Trent's. In fact, every council between 393 A.D. and 1965 A.D. (Vatican II) which pronounced on the matter gave an identical list.

Explain the doctrine of the Trinity: Once a Christian has the doctrine of the Trinity, Scripture can be found to support it, but no verse or combination of verses in Scripture tells us that God is one in divine nature having two processions between three Persons in four relations, each Person wholly and entirely God, all co-equal, co-eternal, none sharing the divine nature, but each possessing it totally unto Himself, the Godhead having but one divine intellect and one divine will.

Tells us the Holy Spirit is one of the three Persons of the Trinity: Certainly Scripture can be found which tells us the Holy Spirit is God, e.g., Acts 5:3-4, but nowhere does it say that God consists of more than one Person. Numerous early heresies concerning the Holy Spirit arose both because Scripture was not yet fully defined and because those elements of Scripture which *were* recognized were simply not all that clear on how the Holy Spirit fit into the Godhead.

Tells us Jesus Christ was both fully God and fully man from the moment of conception (e.g. how do we know His Divinity wasn't infused later in His life?) and/or tells us Jesus Christ is One Person with two complete natures, human and Divine and not some other combination of the two natures (i.e., one or both being either absent or less than complete): Again, remarkably, Scripture is essentially silent on the true nature, or rather natures, of Christ. Scripture says Jesus Christ is God, Scripture says Jesus Christ is human, Scripture says Jesus Christ is like us in all things but sin, but nowhere does Scripture say how or when all of this fits together. Was He this way from the moment of conception, or did His divinity descend upon Him at the baptism by John? As the early years of Church readily indicate, agreement was not complete on this issue. The idea that Jesus Christ is both fully God and fully man, having the fullness of the divine nature and a complete human nature, including human body, human will, human intellect, and human soul was only finally settled by the Magisterium at the Councils of Ephesus and Chalcedon. He was known to be God from the moment of conception because Ephesus (431 A.D.) declared Mary to be Mother of God in order to clarify that very point. The doctrine of Jesus' dual nature was laid out at Chalcedon in 451 A.D.

Tell(s) us Jesus Christ is of the same substance of Divinity as God the Father: The Arian heresy, one of the toughest heresies the Church has ever faced, was fought over precisely this point. In trying to defend monotheism, Arius taught Jesus was the highest of all created beings and the first-born of creation, but not God; he had many Scripture passages to support his position. His opponent, Athanasius, had an equally compelling case from Scripture showing Jesus Christ to be truly God. Because Scripture could not settle the argument, Athanasius appealed to apostolic tradition. Emperor Constantine called the first ecumenical council in history, the Council of Nicaea (325 A.D.), in order to settle the argument. The bishops meeting in council agreed the Athanasian formula expressed the true faith handed down to the bishops from the Apostles. They declared Jesus consubstantial with the Father, not just of nature "like unto" the Father as Arius asserted, but actually of the same divine substance as the Father. They drove home this teaching by formulating what we now call the Nicene Creed. It included the first unScriptural word ever used in a creed, "homoousious," which means "of the same substance as."

In order to settle any of these questions, believers need to turn to the authority established by Christ

Mt 18:15-17 "If your brother sins against you, go and tell him his fault, between you and him alone. If he listens to you, you have gained your brother. [16] But if he does not listen, take one or two others along with you, that every word may be confirmed by the evidence of two or three witnesses. ¹⁷ If he refuses to listen to them, tell it to the church; and if he refuses to listen even to the church, let him be to you as a Gentile and a tax collector.

1 Tim 3:15 you may know how one ought to behave in the household of God, which is the church of the living God, the pillar and bulwark of the truth.

THE CHURCH

Deuteronomy 6:4-5
"Hear, O Israel:
The Lord our God is one Lord;
and you shall love the Lord your God
with all your heart, and
with all your soul, and
with all your might.

Matthew 9:34,10:25
But the Pharisees said,
"He casts out demons by the prince of demons."
[then Jesus said to his disciples]
"[I]t is enough
for the disciple to be like his teacher,
and the servant like his master.
If they have called the master of the house
Be-elzebul,
how much more will they malign
those of his household?"

One

God always intended to establish His family on earth, a kingdom of priests mediating His grace and His light to the world. The Church is the Kingdom of God on earth - the visible and invisible reality who dispenses the mysteries of Christ to the world. She is a sacrament, who actually effects the family which she signifies. She carries four marks: she is one, holy, Catholic, and apostolic; it is through her apostles that her oneness, holiness, and universality are maintained. She is heirarchical, given structure and form by the foundation of her Pope and bishops who both hold us up and mediate God to us through the works of God upon the world that are sacraments. Through her is established the communion of saints, in heaven, on earth, and in purgatory. She is both the means to salvation and the goal of salvation, for we participate in the divine nature, in the Beatific Vision, only through our union with the Body of Christ.

Christian disunity is a source of great sadness which must be overcome. Towards that end, the Church engages in ecumenical discussion, attempting to heal the rifts in the Body of Christ, and bring all back to oneness in His Body. However, while all efforts must be made to overcome mutual mis-understanding, such discussions can never be permitted to weaken the teachings or principles of His Body. (CCC 813-822)

Current misunderstandings: Many Christians assert that we should concentrate on commonalities, not argue over differences, since we are all united in Christ. Such an assertion assumes the existence of <u>"the invisible Church,"</u> and also assumes doctrine isn't important to God. Only the sinner's prayer and a personal relationship with Jesus Christ, uniting one to Christ, matters. Of course, such an idea is itself a doctrine...

1 Cor 14:33 For God is not a God of confusion, but of peace.

Gen 2:4 These are the generations of the heavens and the earth when they were created.

The literal translation of this passage is "This is the book of the geneology of the heavens and the earth."

Gen 5:3 When Adam had lived a hundred and thirty years, he became the father of a son in his own likeness, after his image, and named him Seth.

God intended that we all be one covenant family, from the very beginning. Genesis 3:8-16 descibes how the family of God became a broken human family through the first sin of disobedience.

Gen 9:1,6-11 And God blessed Noah and his sons, and said to them, "Be fruitful and multiply, and fill the earth... Whoever sheds the blood of man, by man shall his blood be shed; for God made man in his own image. [7] And you, be fruitful and multiply, bring forth abundantly on the earth and multiply in it." [8] Then God said to Noah and to his sons with him, [9] "Behold, I establish my covenant with you and your descendants after you, [10] and with every living creature that is with you, the birds, the cattle, and every beast of the earth with you, as many as came out of the ark. [11] I establish my covenant with you, that never again shall all flesh be cut off by the waters of a flood, and never again shall there be a flood to destroy the earth."

God gives to Noah the same command He gave to Adam.

Gen 9:21 Noah was the first tiller of the soil. He planted a vineyard; [21] and he drank of the wine, and became drunk, and lay uncovered in his tent.

But Noah also sins.

Gen 10:1 These are the generations of the sons of Noah,

The literal translation is "This is the geneology of the sons of Noah." Noah was, in a certain sense, a "new Adam." Unfortunately, his sin leads to the division of the human family described in Gen 10.

Gen 12:1-3 Now the LORD said to Abram, "Go from your country and your kindred and your father's house to the land that I will show you. [2] And I will make of you a great nation, and I will bless you, and make your name great, so that you will be a blessing. [3] I will bless those who bless you, and him who curses you I will curse; and by you all the families of the earth shall bless themselves."

God makes three Promises to Abram: a nation, fulfilled in Moses, a great name, fulfilled in David, and a world-wide blessing made through him, Abram - a promise which would be fulfilled in Jesus.

Gen 15:5 And he brought him outside and said, "Look toward heaven, and number the stars, if you are able to number them." Then he said to him, "So shall your descendants be."

The blessing made to Abraham and fulfilled in Christ is the blessing of one worldwide family. One family, not 25,000 families. A family has a structure of authority: father, mother, older brothers and sisters, younger children, infants, all working together.

The Catholic Gospel is quite straightforwards: God loves us deeply, but we have strayed from Him through sin. Jesus Christ is the bridge home, the Bridegroom who marries us into the Trinity, who is the Family of God. When we accept Jesus Christ, God adopts us, through baptism, as His own son or daughter. We don't have merely a personal relationship of friendship, we don't have a merely legal relationship, rather God establishes blood ties with us - we are truly blood relatives, participating through Christ in the divine nature, which is the family relationship of love. God foreshadowed this in Scripture: every redeemer in Scripture is a blood relative (e.g., Abraham rescuing Lot (Gen 14), Tobit saving his father from blindness (Tob 11), etc.).

2 Samuel 7:9,11-14 and I have been with you wherever you went, and have cut off all your enemies from before you; and I will make for you a great name, like the name of the great ones of the earth. ... [11] from the time that I appointed judges over my people Israel; and I will give you rest from all your enemies. Moreover the LORD declares to you that the LORD will make you a house. [12] When your days are fulfilled and you lie down with your fathers, I will raise up your offspring after you, who shall come forth from your body, and I will establish his kingdom. [13] He shall build a house for my name, and I will establish the throne of his kingdom for ever. [14] I will be his father, and he shall be my son. When he commits iniquity, I will chasten him with the rod of men, with the stripes of the sons of men;

When verse 11 promises a "house," the word "house" in Hebrew can mean "son," "dynasty," or "structure." In this case, God intends all three. Solomon, David's son, would build a structure for God, the Temple, and through him the dynasty of the House of David would be continued. Unfortunately, Solomon taxed the people heavily, forcing them to pay 666 talents of gold, he used his authority to amass weapons, wealth and women. The result of these sins was as before - a broken family. By 586 B.C., the temporal power and unity of the House of David would be destroyed. But the promise was not destroyed.

Mt 1:23 "Behold, a virgin shall conceive and bear a son,
and his name shall be called Emmanuel" (which means, God with us).

Mt 28:20 teaching them to observe all that I have commanded you; and lo, I am with you always, to the close of the age."

Matthew's Gospel is constructed to emphasize Emmanuel - God with us. It begins and ends by telling us that God will not leave. The family of God is not going to be torn apart this time. God Himself will build up the family of God on and through His own flesh. We are meant to be one family, united in word, thought, and deed.

1 Cor 1:12-13 For just as the body is one and has many members, and all the members of the body, though many, are one body, so it is with Christ. [13] For by one Spirit we were all baptized into one body—Jews or Greeks, slaves or free—and all were made to drink of one Spirit.

The one body of which Paul speaks was foreshadowed in the Old Testament, in the Chosen People.

Num 16:3 "You have gone too far! For all the congregation are holy, every one of them, and the LORD is among them; why then do you exalt yourselves above the assembly of the LORD?"

Deut 23:3 "No Ammonite or Moabite shall enter the assembly of the LORD; even to the tenth generation none belonging to them shall enter the assembly of the LORD for ever"

The "assembly of the Lord" is the Church of God. It is one assembly, one Church. Any division within that assembly is due to sin, not to the Lord's design. He did not intend many separate churches, nor even many loosely confederated churches - He meant one assembly, one Church, one household, one family. He is the Father, He means to have but one family.

Lk 10:25-37 Jesus replied, "A man was going down from Jerusalem to Jericho, and he fell among robbers, who stripped him and beat him, and departed, leaving him half dead. [31] Now by chance a priest was going down that road; and when he saw him he passed by on the other side. ³² So likewise a Levite, when he came to the place and saw him, passed by on the other side. ³³ But a Samaritan, as he journeyed, came to where he was; and when he saw him, he had compassion, ³⁴ and went to him and bound up his wounds, pouring on oil and wine; then he set him on his own beast and brought him to an inn, and took care of him. ³⁵ And the next day he took out two denarii and gave them to the innkeeper, saying, 'Take care of him; and whatever more you spend, I will repay you when I come back.' ³⁶ Which of these three, do you think, proved neighbor to the man who fell among the robbers?" ³⁷ He said, "The one who showed mercy on him." And Jesus said to him, "Go and do likewise."

Man wounded is wounded by sin. The priest who passed by represents the Mosaic Law, the Levite represents the prophets, the Samaritan represents Christ Himself. Jesus, using the oil of gladness and the wine of His Precious Blood, saved the man's life, placed the man on His own beast, the beast which represents His humanity, and took the man to the inn, which is the Church. He gives the innkeeper two silver pieces, representing the Word of Scripture and the Sacraments. With these instruments, we are tended until Christ comes again.

James 5:16 The prayer of a righteous man has great power in its effects

Jn 17:1-26 When Jesus had spoken these words, he lifted up his eyes to heaven and said, "Father, the hour has come; glorify thy Son that the Son may glorify thee, ² since thou hast given him power over all flesh, to give eternal life to all whom thou hast given him. ³ And this is eternal life, that they know thee the only true God, and Jesus Christ whom thou hast sent. ⁴ I glorified thee on earth, having accomplished the work which thou gavest me to do; ⁵ and now, Father, glorify thou me in thy own presence with the glory which I had with thee before the world was made.

⁶ "I have manifested thy name to the men whom thou gavest me out of the world; thine they were, and thou gavest them to me, and they have kept thy word. ⁷ Now they know that everything that thou hast given me is from thee; ⁸ for I have given them the words which thou gavest me, and they have received them and know in truth that I came from thee; and they have believed that thou didst send me. ⁹ I am praying for them; I am not praying for the world but for those whom thou hast given me, for they are thine; ¹⁰ all mine are thine, and thine are mine, and I am glorified in them. ¹¹ And now I am no more in the world, but they are in the world, and I am coming to thee. Holy Father, keep them in thy name, which thou hast given me, that they may be one, even as we are one. ¹² While I was with them, I kept them in thy name, which thou hast given me; I have guarded them, and none of them is lost but the son of perdition, that the scripture might be fulfilled. ¹³ But now I am coming to thee; and these things I speak in the world, that they may have my joy fulfilled in themselves. ¹⁴ I have given them thy word; and the world has hated them because they are not of the world, even as I am not of the world. ¹⁵ I do not pray that thou shouldst take them out of the world, but that thou shouldst keep them from the evil one. ¹⁶ They are not of the world, even as I am not of the world. ¹⁷ Sanctify them in the truth; thy word is truth. ¹⁸ As thou didst send me into the world, so I have sent them into the world. ¹⁹ And for their sake I consecrate myself, that they also may be consecrated in truth.

²⁰ "I do not pray for these only, but also for those who believe in me through their word, ²¹ that they may all be one; even as thou, Father, art in me, and I in thee, that they also may be in us, so that the world may believe that thou hast sent me. ²² The glory which thou hast given me I have given to them, that they may be one even as we are one, ²³ I in them and thou in me, that they may become perfectly one, so that the world may know that thou hast sent me and hast loved them even as thou hast loved me. ²⁴ Father, I desire that they also, whom thou hast given me, may be with me where I am, to behold my glory which thou hast given me in thy love for me before the foundation of the world. ²⁵ O righteous Father, the world has not known thee, but I have known thee; and these know that thou hast sent me. ²⁶ I made known to them thy name, and I will make it known, that the love with which thou hast loved me may be in them, and I in them."

Christ, perfectly righteous, prayed strenuously for unity. Can the Protestant Reformation, which resulted in fracturing and re-fracturing of Christianity, be Christ's Church?

Jn 10:16 And I have other sheep, that are not of this fold; I must bring them also, and they will heed my voice. So there shall be one flock, one shepherd.

The Gentiles were brought in as Christ prophesied, but the flock has fractured. This fracturing has released great evil into the world. For instance, abortion grew out of the sexual revolution. The sexual revolution grew out of widely available <u>contraceptives</u>. Contraceptives became widely available only because

Christians allowed it. For two millenia prior to 1930, all Christians condemned contraception in the strongest terms. After the 1930 Lambeth conference, Anglican bishops permitted the use of contraception by Christians for the first time in history. Within four decades, all Christian denominations allowed artificial contraception. All but one. Only Catholicism still holds to the ancient Christian teaching. Contraception and its step-sisters, promiscuity and abortion, exemplify what our disunity has brought.

1 Jn 1:10 If we say we have not sinned, we make him a liar, and his word is not in us.

This holds good for sins against unity. "So we humbly be pardon of God and of our separated brethren, just as we forgive them that trespass against us.." (Vatican II, Decree on Ecumenism, Chapter II, paragraph 7.)

Jn 14:18 "I will not leave you desolate; I will come to you."

1 Cor 1:10 I appeal to you, brethren, by the name of our Lord Jesus Christ, that all of you agree and that there be no dissensions among you, but that you be united in the same mind and the same judgment.

Phil 2:2 complete my joy by being of the same mind, having the same love, being in full accord and of one mind.

Eph 2:14-16,22 For he is our peace, who has made us both one, and has broken down the dividing wall of hostility, [15] by abolishing in his flesh the law of commandments and ordinances, that he might create in himself one new man in place of the two, so making peace, [16] and might reconcile us both to God in one body through the cross, thereby bringing the hostility to an end... in whom you also are built into it for a dwelling place of God in the Spirit.

Col 2:18 Let no one disqualify you, insisting on self-abasement and worship of angels, taking his stand on visions, puffed up without reason by his sensuous mind, [19] and not holding fast to the Head, from whom the whole body, nourished and knit together through its joints and ligaments, grows with a growth that is from God.

1 Cor 3:3-7 for you are still of the flesh. For while there is jealousy and strife among you, are you not of the flesh, and behaving like ordinary men? [4] For when one says, "I belong to Paul," and another, "I belong to Apollos," are you not merely men? [5] What then is Apollos? What is Paul? Servants through whom you believed, as the Lord assigned to each. [6] I planted, Apollos watered, but God gave the growth. [7] So neither he who plants nor he who waters is anything, but only God who gives the growth.

The Body of Christ excommunicates in order to promote repentance in the sinner who refuses to bow to the divine authority of the Church.

Rom 16:17 I appeal to you, brethren, to take note of those who create dissensions and difficulties, in opposition to the doctrine which you have been taught; avoid them.

Mt 18:15-20 "If your brother sins against you, go and tell him his fault, between you and him alone. If he listens to you, you have gained your brother. [16] But if he does not listen, take one or two others along with you, that every word may be confirmed by the evidence of two or three witnesses. [17] If he refuses to listen to them, tell it to the church; and if he refuses to listen even to the church, let him be to you as a Gentile and a tax collector. [18] Truly, I say to you, whatever you bind on earth shall be bound in heaven, and whatever you loose on earth shall be loosed in heaven. [19] Again I say to you, if two of you agree on earth about anything they ask, it will be done for them by my Father in heaven. [20] For where two or three are gathered in my name, there am I in the midst of them."

1 Cor 5:1-13 It is actually reported that there is immorality among you, and of a kind that is not found even among pagans; for a man is living with his father's wife. [2] And you are arrogant! Ought you not rather to mourn? Let him who has done this be removed from among you.

[3] For though absent in body I am present in spirit, and as if present, I have already pronounced judgment [4] in the name of the Lord Jesus on the man who has done such a thing. When you are assembled, and my spirit is present, with the power of our Lord Jesus, [5] you are to deliver this man to Satan for the destruction of the flesh, that his spirit may be saved in the day of the Lord Jesus.

[6] Your boasting is not good. Do you not know that a little leaven leavens the whole lump? [7] Cleanse out the old leaven that you may be a new lump, as you really are unleavened. For Christ, our paschal lamb, has been sacrificed. [8] Let us, therefore, celebrate the festival, not with the old leaven, the leaven of malice

and evil, but with the unleavened bread of sincerity and truth. ⁹ I wrote to you in my letter not to associate with immoral men; ¹⁰ not at all meaning the immoral of this world, or the greedy and robbers, or idolaters, since then you would need to go out of the world. ¹¹ But rather I wrote to you not to associate with any one who bears the name of brother if he is guilty of immorality or greed, or is an idolater, reviler, drunkard, or robber—not even to eat with such a one. ¹² For what have I to do with judging outsiders? Is it not those inside the church whom you are to judge? ¹³ God judges those outside. "Drive out the wicked person from among you."

The pain brought upon individuals within the Body affects the whole body.

Eph 4:3 eager to maintain the unity of the Spirit in the bond of peace.

Col 3:14 And above all these put on love, which binds everything together in perfect harmony.

The unity of Christ's Body is assured primarily by love but also by the visible communion present in common liturgical worship, profession of the one apostolic faith, and the apostolic succession handed on through Jesus in Holy Orders.

Rom 12:3-6 For by the grace given to me I bid every one among you not to think of himself more highly than he ought to think, but to think with sober judgment, each according to the measure of faith which God has assigned him. ⁴ For as in one body we have many members, and all the members do not have the same function, ⁵ so we, though many, are one body in Christ, and individually members one of another. ⁶ Having gifts that differ according to the grace given to us, let us use them...

This describes parish life. We are One Body. At Christ's Second Coming, He will not come alone, He will come leading all the saints: His whole body will appear. That is why the Book of the Apocalypse refers not just to the descent of Christ, but to the descent of the Heavenly Jerusalem.

2 Cor 2:1-17 For I made up my mind not to make you another painful visit. ² For if I cause you pain, who is there to make me glad but the one whom I have pained? ³ And I wrote as I did, so that when I came I might not suffer pain from those who should have made me rejoice, for I felt sure of all of you, that my joy would be the joy of you all. ⁴ For I wrote you out of much affliction and anguish of heart and with many tears, not to cause you pain but to let you know the abundant love that I have for you.

⁵ But if any one has caused pain, he has caused it not to me, but in some measure—not to put it too severely—to you all. ⁶ For such a one this punishment by the majority is enough; ⁷ so you should rather turn to forgive and comfort him, or he may be overwhelmed by excessive sorrow. ⁸ So I beg you to reaffirm your love for him. ⁹ For this is why I wrote, that I might test you and know whether you are obedient in everything. ¹⁰ Any one whom you forgive, I also forgive. What I have forgiven, if I have forgiven anything, has been for your sake in the presence of Christ, ¹¹ to keep Satan from gaining the advantage over us; for we are not ignorant of his designs.

¹² When I came to Troas to preach the gospel of Christ, a door was opened for me in the Lord; ¹³ but my mind could not rest because I did not find my brother Titus there. So I took leave of them and went on to Macedonia.

¹⁴ But thanks be to God, who in Christ always leads us in triumph, and through us spreads the fragrance of the knowledge of him everywhere. ¹⁵ For we are the aroma of Christ to God among those who are being saved and among those who are perishing, ¹⁶ to one a fragrance from death to death, to the other a fragrance from life to life. Who is sufficient for these things? ¹⁷ For we are not, like so many, peddlers of God's word; but as men of sincerity, as commissioned by God, in the sight of God we speak in Christ.

All who engage in apologetics of any kind would do well to read this passage and to constantly meditate over it.

Holy

God always intended to give Himself to us, He is impelled to do so for His own Name's sake. Through the sacraments, founded in the blood of Jesus Christ, we partake of divinity. Though the inexpressible gulf between our humanity and God's divinity still exists and will continue to exist through all eternity, we truly participate in the divine nature, each of us becoming not just a legal, but a real child of God. We are made to receive grace. Grace is God's life in us, it is His help given to us so that we may participate in the divine nature, it is not just a state. God's grace comes to us in several ways:

- *actual or helping grace, which impels us towards the sacraments,*
- *sanctifying or habitual grace, which grows within us, perfects us, and enables us to act by His love,*
- *the graces of the sacraments, which effect upon us what they signify,*
- *providential grace, which holds us in existence and keeps us alive from moment to moment,*
- *special graces, or charisms, which are for the good of the whole Church and direct us towards sanctifying grace.*

While we can never merit the grace of initial justification, we can, through prayer and participation in the sacraments, merit more grace for ourselves and others (CCC 823-829, 1998-2005).

Current misunderstandings: Our separated brethren deny that we can truly partake of the divine nature or, in the case of Mormons, they go to the other extreme, claiming each of the saved become completely divine in themselves, gods of their own worlds after death.

When explaining divinization, Thomas Aquinas used the example of an iron poker heated in a fire. Though the red-hot poker never itself becomes fire, yet it participates in every characteristic of the fire. It is the same with us. Though we never possess the divine nature, yet we participate in the divine nature through the perfection brought about in purgation and the sacraments. Through these active experiences of the Divine, we are filled to the capacity of our being with divinity. (CCC 221, 260, 398, 460, 1988, 1999, 2012)

Gen 1:27 So God created man in his own image, in the image of God he created him; male and female he created them.

Gen 5:1-3 This is the book of the generations of Adam. When God created man, he made him in the likeness of God. ² Male and female he created them, and he blessed them and named them Man when they were created. ³ When Adam had lived a hundred and thirty years, he became the father of a son in his own likeness, after his image, and named him Seth....

God created everything for man; He gave us the capacity to master the world. God created us male and female. We are made in the image and likeness of God. We image God because we are persons, we are persons called to enter into relationship with the Trinity. We do this freely and we do it more deeply than any material creature. We possess the capacity and the desire to love and know God, we find perfection in seeking and loving the True, the Good, the Beautiful. Our souls can only find their origin and existence in God. Our image may have been marred by original sin, but it can be restored. It is brought to perfection through Jesus Christ in a way that simply was not possible in Adam, for the New Adam supersedes and perfects the old in a way not available to the first Adam, even if he had not fallen.

Wis 2:23 for God created man for incorruption, and made him in the image of his own eternity...

Mt 5:48 You, therefore, must be perfect, as your heavenly Father is perfect.

What God commands is literally possible. We are called to be perfect, we are to become as God. This can only be attained through participation in the divinity of Jesus.

Gen 3:5 -But the serpent said to the woman, "You will not die. ⁵ For God knows that when you eat of it your eyes will be opened, and you will be like God, knowing good and evil."

Divinization is central to God's plan and satan knows it. Original Sin was brought about because the serpent offered a counterfeit sacrament, a lie, something which appeared to accomplish divinization but did not. The original sin is the attempt "to be like God," i.e., the attempt to be divinized, apart from God. Such a thing cannot be done, the very attempt is an offense against the holiness of God. (CCC 398)

Heb 12:23 and to the assembly of the first-born who are enrolled in heaven, and to a judge who is God of all, and to the spirits of just men made perfect...

Heb 10:14 For by a single offering he has perfected for all time those who are sanctified.

2 Pet 1:3-4 His divine power has granted to us all things that pertain to life and godliness, through the knowledge of him who called us to his own glory and excellence, [4] by which he has granted to us his precious and very great promises, that through these you may escape from the corruption that is in the world because of passion, and become partakers of the divine nature.

Scripture attests that we truly participate in the divine nature.

Jn 17:20-23 "I do not pray for these only, but also for those who believe in me through their word, [21] that they may all be one; even as thou, Father, art in me, and I in thee, that they also may be in us, so that the world may believe that thou hast sent me. [22] The glory which thou hast given me I have given to them, that they may be one even as we are one, [23] I in them and thou in me, that they may become perfectly one, so that the world may know that thou hast sent me and hast loved them even as thou hast loved me.

Col 1:26-27 the mystery hidden for ages and generations but now made manifest to his saints. [27] To them God chose to make known how great among the Gentiles are the riches of the glory of this mystery, which is Christ in you, the hope of glory.

This is possible because Christ truly resides in us, and we in Him, through the sacramental life.

1 Jn 3:1 See what love the Father has given us, that we should be called children of God; and so we are.

We are all made into children of God, truly made perfect as God is perfect before God through Christ. We are individually members of Christ's Body.

Gal 4:4-7 But when the time had fully come, God sent forth his Son, born of woman, born under the law, [5] to redeem those who were under the law, so that we might receive adoption as sons. [6] And because you are sons, God has sent the Spirit of his Son into our hearts, crying, "Abba! Father!" [7] So through God you are no longer a slave but a son, and if a son then an heir.

2 Cor 4:11 For while we live we are always being given up to death for Jesus' sake, so that the life of Jesus may be manifested in our mortal flesh.

Eph 2:15 by abolishing in his flesh the law of commandments and ordinances, that he might create in himself one new man in place of the two, so making peace...

God has only one Son. However, we are made one new man in place of the two, part of the Body of the Son, through the sacramental life. Thus, we become heirs with Christ.

Rom 8:14-17 For all who are led by the Spirit of God are sons of God. [15] For you did not receive the spirit of slavery to fall back into fear, but you have received the spirit of sonship. When we cry, "Abba! Father!" [16] it is the Spirit himself bearing witness with our spirit that we are children of God, [17] and if children, then heirs, heirs of God and fellow heirs with Christ, provided we suffer with him in order that we may also be glorified with him.

Eph 2:21-22 in whom the whole structure is joined together and grows into a holy temple in the Lord; [22] in whom you also are built into it for a dwelling place of God in the Spirit.

2 Cor 5:21 For our sake he made him to be sin who knew no sin, so that in him we might become the righteousness of God.

James 1:17 Every good endowment and every perfect gift is from above, coming down from the Father of lights with whom there is no variation or shadow due to change.

We do not simply put on Christ's righteousness, God, who holds all things in existence, whose Word formed the universe from nothing, actually removes the reality of our sin so that our sin no longer exists. Thus are we made perfect.

Rom 8:28-30 We know that in everything God works for good with those who love him, who are called according to his purpose. [29] For those whom he foreknew he also predestined to be conformed to the image of his Son, in order that he might be the first-born among many brethren. [30] And those whom he predestined he also called; and those whom he called he also justified; and those whom he justified he also glorified.

To be "glorified" means to be filled with the glory of God. To be sanctified is to be made "sanctus," that is, to be made holy.

Scriptural Catholicism   **Church**

1 Thess 4:3 For this is the will of God, your sanctification...

Rom 12:2 Do not be conformed to this world but be transformed by the renewal of your mind, that you may prove what is the will of God, what is good and acceptable and perfect.

1 Thess 5:23 May the God of peace himself sanctify you wholly; and may your spirit and soul and body be kept sound and blameless at the coming of our Lord Jesus Christ.

Heb 6:4 For it is impossible to restore again to repentence those who have once been enlightened, who have tasted the heavenly gift, and have become partakers of the Holy Spirit...

Col 2:9-10 For in him the whole fulness of deity dwells bodily, [10] and you have come to fulness of life in him, who is the head of all rule and authority

Eph 3:5-6,19 which was not made known to the sons of men in other generations as it has now been revealed to his holy apostles and prophets by the Spirit; [6] that is, how the Gentiles are fellow heirs, members of the same body, and partakers of the promise in Christ Jesus through the gospel.... and to know the love of Christ which surpasses knowledge, that you may be filled with all the fulness of God.

Jesus is filled with the whole fulness of deity, we are to be filled with all the fulness of God. This is the promise of Christ - He joins us truly to God by making us truly part of the Son, truly participating in the Divine Nature.

Gal 4:19 My little children, with whom I am again in travail until Christ be formed in you!

That is the object of Paul's work: our divinization. That is why Paul says what he does in Ephesians 5:1

Eph 5:1 Therefore be imitators of God, as beloved children.

2 Cor 7:1 Since we have these promises, beloved, let us cleanse ourselves from every defilement of body and spirit, and make holiness perfect in the fear of God.

Col 1:28 Him we proclaim, warning every man and teaching every man in all wisdom, that we may present every man mature in Christ.

Rom 16:7 Greet Andronicus and Junias, my kinsmen and my fellow prisoners; they are men of note among the apostles, and they were in Christ before me.

1 Pet 4:6 For this is why the gospel was preached even to the dead, that though judged in the flesh like men, they might live in the spirit like God.

John 14:23 If a man loves me, he will keep my word, and my Father will love him, and we will come to him and make our home with him.

1 Cor 3:16-17,19-20 Do you not know that you are God's temple and that God's Spirit dwells in you? [17] If any one destroys God's temple, God will destroy him. For God's temple is holy, and that temple you are... Do you not know that your body is a temple of the Holy Spirit within you, which you have from God? You are not your own; [20] you were bought with a price. So glorify God in your body.

2 Cor 6:16 For we are the temple of the living God...

Rom 8:9 But you are not in the flesh, you are in the Spirit, if in fact the Spirit of God dwells in you.

2 Cor 13:5 Do you not realize that Christ is in you?

Gal 2:20 I have been crucified with Christ; it is no longer I who live but Christ who lives in me...

Phil 1:21 For to me to live is Christ, and to die is gain.
God is not Father simply because He made us. He is our Creator, our Master, because He made us. He is Father because He eternally begets the Son. Thus, it is only our portion in the Body of Christ, only when we partake in and participate in the Divine Nature of Jesus Christ, that God truly becomes our Father, and we truly become His sons and daughters. If we want to become children of God, we must be divinized. That is what the sacraments do. They make us truly his children. St. Athanasius stated it most succinctly: "For the Son of God became man so that we might become God." Through the sacramental life, forged in God's covenant with creation and His work on the Cross, we are truly made into the Body of Christ, who is God.

Eph 5:26-27 that he might sanctify her, having cleansed her by the washing of water with the word, [27]

that he might present the church to himself in splendor, without spot or wrinkle or any such thing, that she might be holy and without blemish.

Divinization is the central mission of the Church (CCC #460). All teaching, all ministry, all work is done with the end of bringing all people to the sacraments so that they may be divinized and have a share in the Body of Christ. Our human nature was made in order to be completely immersed in the divine Fire, the consuming, ravishing love of God. We will participate in this whirling dance with Him forever, pouring ourselves out perfectly to Him and Him to us, eternal interpenetration with the Eternal. This cannot be accomplished except in Jesus Christ, in His suffering, His cross, His sacraments.

Catholic

The Body of Christ is Catholic, that is, she is universal, containing the fullness of the means of salvation, Jesus Christ, and sent by Christ, her Head, to the whole human race. Through their communion with the Church of Rome, all individual churches share in and form this catholicity. She is not just the simple sum of all the individual churches, rather, wherever she puts down roots within a particular community, there is the Catholic Church (CCC 830-856).

Current misunderstandings: Some deny the catholicity of the salvation Christ offers, claiming that God predestined some men to be damned from all eternity, while others were created to be saved from all eternity. This is called "double-predestination." In fact, God made all men to be saved, but, once we have been given the grace to be able to choose salvation, we still must freely choose to accept God's gracious gift. Through the graces mediated by the Church, every man, woman, and child has the ability to be saved.

Tob 13:7-8 I exalt my God;
my soul exalts the King of heaven,
and will rejoice in his majesty. [8] Let all men speak,
and give him thanks in Jerusalem.

Wis 12:12-13 Or who will come before thee to plead as an advocate for unrighteous men? [13] For neither is there any god besides thee, whose care is for all men...

Wis 16:10-12 but thy sons were not conquered even by the teeth of venomous serpents,
for thy mercy came to their help and healed them. [11] To remind them of thy oracles they were bitten,
and then were quickly delivered,
lest they should fall into deep forgetfulness
and become unresponsive to thy kindness. [12] For neither herb nor poultice cured them,
but it was thy word, O Lord, which heals all men.

Sir 44:22 The blessing of all men and the covenant
he made to rest upon the head of Jacob;
he acknowledged him with his blessings,
and gave him his inheritance;
he determined his portions,
and distributed them among twelve tribes.

Mt 12:17 This was to fulfil what was spoken by the prophet Isaiah: [18] "Behold, my servant whom I have chosen,
my beloved with whom my soul is well pleased.
I will put my Spirit upon him,
and he shall proclaim justice to the Gentiles. [19] He will not wrangle or cry aloud,
nor will any one hear his voice in the streets; [20] he will not break a bruised reed
or quench a smoldering wick,
till he brings justice to victory; [21] and in his name will the Gentiles hope."

Jn 4:21-22 Jesus said to her, "Woman, believe me, the hour is coming when neither on this mountain nor in Jerusalem will you worship the Father. [22] You worship what you do not know; we worship what we know, for salvation is from the Jews."

Jesus knows the woman worships what she does not know, but He does not condemn her to hell for it. The Church is the visible institution founded by God through whom all men find salvation, but she is invisibly extended into every person who truly seeks to follow God's laws.

Acts 10:34-35 And Peter opened his mouth and said: "Truly I perceive that God shows no partiality, [35] but in every nation any one who fears him and does what is right is acceptable to him."

Acts 17:22-23 So Paul, standing in the middle of the Are-opagus, said: "Men of Athens, I perceive that in every way you are very religious. [23] For as I passed along, and observed the objects of your worship, I found also an altar with this inscription, 'To an unknown god.' What therefore you worship as unknown, this I proclaim to you.

Both Peter and Paul follow Jesus' lead - the God-fearing Gentiles and the Greek worshippers of the "unknown god" are both searching for Him, and this search is pleasing to God.

Jn 3:17 For God sent the Son into the world, not to condemn the world, but that the world might be saved through him.

Jn 12:30-31 Jesus answered, "This voice has come for your sake, not for mine. [31] Now is the judgment of this world, now shall the ruler of this world be cast out; [32] and I, when I am lifted up from the earth, will draw all men to myself."

Acts 2:38-39 And Peter said to them, "Repent, and be baptized every one of you in the name of Jesus Christ for the forgiveness of your sins; and you shall receive the gift of the Holy Spirit. [39] For the promise is to you and to your children and to all that are far off, every one whom the Lord our God calls to him."

Acts 17:30-31 The times of ignorance God overlooked, but now he commands all men everywhere to repent, [31] because he has fixed a day on which he will judge the world in righteousness by a man whom he has appointed, and of this he has given assurance to all men by raising him from the dead."

Acts 22:15-16 'for you will be a witness for him to all men of what you have seen and heard. [16] And now why do you wait? Rise and be baptized, and wash away your sins, calling on his name.'

Rom 5:18 Then as one man's trespass led to condemnation for all men, so one man's act of righteousness leads to acquittal and life for all men.

Rom 11:32 For God has consigned all men to disobedience, that he may have mercy upon all.

1 Cor 9:22-23 I have become all things to all men, that I might by all means save some. [23] I do it all for the sake of the gospel, that I may share in its blessings.

1 Cor 10:33 just as I try to please all men in everything I do, not seeking my own advantage, but that of many, that they may be saved.

2 Cor 3:2 You yourselves are our letter of recommendation, written on your hearts, to be known and read by all men; [3] and you show that you are a letter from Christ delivered by us, written not with ink but with the Spirit of the living God, not on tablets of stone but on tablets of human hearts.

Gal 6:9-10 And let us not grow weary in well-doing, for in due season we shall reap, if we do not lose heart. [10] So then, as we have opportunity, let us do good to all men, and especially to those who are of the household of faith.

Eph 3:8-10 To me, though I am the very least of all the saints, this grace was given, to preach to the

Gentiles the unsearchable riches of Christ, [9] and to make all men see what is the plan of the mystery hidden for ages in God who created all things; [10] that through the church the manifold wisdom of God might now be made known to the principalities and powers in the heavenly places.

1 Tim 2:1-4 First of all, then, I urge that supplications, prayers, intercessions, and thanksgivings be made for all men, [2] for kings and all who are in high positions, that we may lead a quiet and peaceable life, godly and respectful in every way. [3] This is good, and it is acceptable in the sight of God our Savior, [4] who desires all men to be saved and to come to the knowledge of the truth.

1 Tim 4:10 For to this end we toil and strive, because we have our hope set on the living God, who is the Savior of all men, especially of those who believe.

Tit 2:11 For the grace of God has appeared for the salvation of all men...

James 1:5 If any of you lacks wisdom, let him ask God, who gives to all men generously and without reproaching, and it will be given him.

Apostolic

Jesus Christ vested in the Apostles special authority. This special apostolic authority has been passed down in unbroken succession through the bishops of the Church for two millenia, so that the bishops of the Church truly teach with the voice of the Apostles. Apostolic succession is the backbone of the Church. CCC 2,3, 75-77, 815, 830-830, 858-862, 1087. 1724)

Current misunderstandings: Many Christian churches deny Apostolic succession. Either the Apostles had no special authority ("we are all apostles") or the special authority they may have had died with them.

The following exegesis is based on a series of class lectures given by Barbara Morgan, director of catechetics, Franciscan University:

Jn 5:19 Jesus said to them, "Truly, truly, I say to you, the Son can do nothing of his own accord, but only what he sees the Father doing; for whatever he does, that the Son does likewise."

What Christ witnesses...

Lk 24:48 You are witnesses of these things.

The Apostles witness.

Mk 2:10 But that you may know that the Son of man has authority on earth to forgive sins"

Christ has the power to forgive sins...

Jn 20:21 If you forgive the sins of any, they are forgiven; if you retain the sins of any, they are retained."

And the Apostles are given the same power.

Jn 7:16 So Jesus answered them, "My teaching is not mine, but his who sent me...

Jn 5:30 "I can do nothing on my own authority; as I hear, I judge; and my judgment is just, because I seek not my own will but the will of him who sent me."

Jn 8:28-29 "When you have lifted up the Son of man, then you will know that I am he, and that I do nothing on my own authority but speak thus as the Father taught me.

Jn 12:49 For I have not spoken on my own authority; the Father who sent me has himself given me commandment what to say and what to speak.

Christ does not speak on His own authority, but carries the authority of the Father, which He has been given.

Mt 28:18 And Jesus came and said to them, "All authority in heaven and on earth has been given to me..."

Christ teaches a teaching not his own with all authority and power, authority given by the Father's command, derived from His own just judgment because it echoes what the Father wills and teaches...

Jn 16:11 When the Spirit of truth comes, he will guide you into all the truth; for he will not speak on his own authority, but whatever he hears he will speak, and he will declare to you the things that are to come.

Lk 24:49 "And behold, I send the promise of my Father upon you; but stay in the city, until you are clothed with power from on high."

Mt 28:19-20 Go therefore and make disciples of all nations, baptizing them in the name of the Father and of the Son and of the Holy Spirit, 20 teaching them to observe all that I have commanded you...

The Apostles are to teach a teaching not their own with all authority and power, authority given by Christ's command, derived from His own just judgement because it echoes what the Father wills and teaches.

Heb 3:1 Therefore, holy brethren, who share in a heavenly call, consider Jesus, the apostle and high priest of our confession...

Jesus Christ is the Apostle sent by the Father, and...

Jn 20:21 Jesus said to them again, "Peace be with you. As the Father has sent me, even so I send you."

Christ sends the Apostles EXACTLY as He was sent.

The Father commanded Him, Christ commands them, Christ is clothed with power from on high, so will they be. They are to echo the teaching of Christ, who gave them nothing of His own, but only what the Father told Him. They echo it with the authority of Christ, who carries the Father's authority. They will be guided into all truth by the Spirit of truth, who also speaks only on the Father's authority.

Jn 28:29 "And he who sent me is with me; he has not left me alone, for I always do what is pleasing to him."

Just as the Father never leaves Jesus...

Mt 28:20 and lo, I am with you always, to the close of the age."

So Christ will never leave the Apostles.

Lk 6:13 And when it was day, he called his disciples, and chose from them twelve, whom he named apostles...

Mk 3:13 And he appointed twelve, to be with him, and to be sent out to preach 15 and have authority to cast out demons...

Mt 10:1 And he called to him his twelve disciples and gave them authority over unclean spirits, to cast them out, and to heal every disease and every infirmity.

Thus, when Christ chose twelve apostles from among the disciples and gave them special power...

Acts 14:22-23 strengthening the souls of the disciples, exhorting them to continue in the faith, and saying that through many tribulations we must enter the kingdom of God. 23 And when they had appointed elders for them in every church, with prayer and fasting they committed them to the Lord in whom they believed.

1 Tim 4:14 Do not neglect the gift you have, which was given you by prophetic utterance when the council of elders laid their hands upon you.

Tit 2:15 Declare these things; exhort and reprove with all authority. Let no one disregard you

...those Twelve, to whom He has given unique authority, also have not only the authority, but the duty, to imitate Christ and choose successors from among the believers. These successors are to do the will of the Father just as the Apostles did, and just as Christ did before them. These successors carry the authority of the Apostles, who themselves carry the authority of Jesus Christ, the First Apostle.

Acts 14:14 But when the apostles Barnabas and Paul heard of it, they tore their garments and rushed out among the multitude...

Rom 16:6 Greet Andronicus and Junias, my kinsmen and my fellow prisoners; they are men of note among the apostles, and they were in Christ before me.

Acts 15:24 Since we have heard that some persons from us have troubled you with words, unsettling your minds, although we gave them no instructions...

No one should to attempt to teach without apostolic authority.

Acts 2:42 And they devoted themselves to the apostles' teaching and fellowship, to the breaking of bread and the prayers.

We are to devote ourselves to the apostles' teaching.

2 Pet 3:1-2 This is now the second letter that I have written to you, beloved, and in both of them I have aroused your sincere mind by way of reminder; ² that you should remember the predictions of the holy prophets and the commandment of the Lord and Savior through your apostles.

Lk 10:16 "He who hears you hears me, and he who rejects you rejects me, and he who rejects me rejects him who sent me."

Tit 1:9 he must hold firm to the sure word as taught, so that he may be able to give instruction in sound doctrine and also to confute those who contradict it.

Acts 20:27-31 I did not shrink from declaring to you the whole counsel of God. ²⁸ Take heed to yourselves and to all the flock, in which the Holy Spirit has made you overseers, to care for the church of God which he obtained with the blood of his own Son. ²⁹ I know that after my departure fierce wolves will come in among you, not sparing the flock; ³⁰ and from among your own selves will arise men speaking perverse things, to draw away the disciples after them. ³¹ Therefore be alert, remembering that for three years I did not cease night or day to admonish every one with tears.

The apostolic successors have the responsibility to guard the flock and the Christ-given power to do it.

Acts 8:30-31 So Philip ran to him, and heard him reading Isaiah the prophet, and asked, "Do you understand what you are reading?" ³¹ And he said, "How can I, unless some one guides me?" And he invited Philip to come up and sit with him.

1 Cor 12:28 And God has appointed in the church first apostles, second prophets, third teachers, then workers of miracles, then healers, helpers, administrators, speakers in various kinds of tongues.

God's designation, made through the Church, is what makes someone an apostle. It is not an extinct office, it is the first and most important office of the Church.

Lk 22:29-30 and I assign to you, as my Father assigned to me, a kingdom, ³⁰ that you may eat and drink at my table in my kingdom, and sit on thrones judging the twelve tribes of Israel.

That is why Christ could say this to the Apostles. The Apostles rule over a kingdom, the kingdom of God, the Church. The Church is the Bride of Christ, Christ's Body, with Christ at Her head.

1 Thess 2:7,11 But we were gentle among you, like a nurse taking care of her children... for you know how, like a father with his children, we exhorted each one of you and encouraged you and charged you...

1 Thess 5:12-13 But we beseech you, brethren, to respect those who labor among you and are over you in the Lord and admonish you, ¹³ and to esteem them very highly in love because of their work. Be at peace among yourselves.

The following five Scripture passages and their exegesis summarizes "Replacing Judas: A Lot More than Meets the Eye?" Timothy Gray, Lay Witness *magazine, September 1997, p. 4-5.*

1 Chron 24:5 They organized them by lot, all alike, for there were officers of the sanctuary and officers of God among both the sons of Eleazar and the sons of Ithamar.

1 Chron 25:8 And they cast lots for their duties, small and great, teacher and pupil alike.

1 Chron 24:31 These also, the head of each father's house and his younger brother alike, cast lots, just as their brethren the sons of Aaron, in the presence of King David, Zadok, Ahimelech, and the heads of fathers' houses of the priests and of the Levites.

Lk 1:8-9 Now while he was serving as priest before God when his division was on duty, ⁹ according to the custom of the priesthood, it fell to him by lot to enter the temple of the Lord and burn incense.

The priestly office was filled by lot in Judaic tradition.

Acts 1:15,20-26 In those days Peter stood up among the brethren (the company of persons was in all about a hundred and twenty), and said For it is written in the book of Psalms, 'Let his habitation become desolate, and let there be no one to live in it'; and 'His office let another take.' ²¹ So one of the men who have accompanied us during all the time that the Lord Jesus went in and out among us, ²² beginning from the baptism of John until the day when he was taken up from us—one of these men must become with us a witness to his resurrection." ²³ And they put forward two, Joseph called Barsabbas, who was surnamed Justus, and Matthias. ²⁴ And they prayed and said, "Lord, who knowest the hearts of all men, show which one of these two thou hast chosen ²⁵ to take the place in this ministry and apostleship from which Judas turned aside, to go to his own place." ²⁶ And they cast lots for them, and the lot fell on Matthias; and he was enrolled with the eleven apostles.

Peter, first among the Apostles, declared the problem and the solution. He decided what conditions were necessary for the consecration of one who would "take an office" in the church. The decision of whom to choose for the priestly office was established by lot - the followers of the Jew, Jesus Christ, were Jews who knew the traditions for filling priestly office. But Christ had taught them something more - how to establish the successors of the Apostles in their office, once chosen.

Acts 6:6 These they set before the apostles, and they prayed and laid their hands upon them.

Acts 13:3 Then after fasting and praying they laid their hands on them and sent them off.

1 Tim 4:14 Do not neglect the gift you have, which was given you by prophetic utterance when the council of elders laid their hands upon you.

1 Tim 5:22 Do not be hasty in the laying on of hands, nor participate in another man's sins; keep yourself pure.

2 Tim 1:6 Hence I remind you to rekindle the gift of God that is within you through the laying on of my hands

Through the <u>laying on of hands</u> the office is filled.

Acts 9:15-19 But the Lord said to him, "Go, for he is a chosen instrument of mine to carry my name before the Gentiles and kings and the sons of Israel; ¹⁶ for I will show him how much he must suffer for the sake of my name." ¹⁷ So Ananias departed and entered the house. And laying his hands on him he said, "Brother Saul, the Lord Jesus who appeared to you on the road by which you came, has sent me that you may regain your sight and be filled with the Holy Spirit." ¹⁸ And immediately something like scales fell from his eyes and he regained his sight. Then he rose and was baptized, ¹⁹ and took food and was strengthened. For several days he was with the disciples at Damascus.

Even Paul, who was called in a special way by God, only became a minister after the laying on of hands by an officer of the Church. He stayed several days, receiving instruction.

Col 1:24-26 Now I rejoice in my sufferings for your sake, and in my flesh I complete what is lacking in Christ's afflictions for the sake of his body, that is, the church, ²⁵ of which I became a minister according to the divine office which was given to me for you, to make the word of God fully known, ²⁶ the mystery hidden for ages and generations but now made manifest to his saints.

2 Tim 2:2 and what you have heard from me before many witnesses entrust to faithful men who will be able to teach others also.

2 Tim 3:14 But as for you, continue in what you have learned and have firmly believed, knowing from whom you learned it...

Paul asserts that he is not "the" minister, but only "a" minister, one of those given stewardship. Timothy received it from Paul and the council of elders, who had themselves received the authority from the Apostles. Timothy is to pass this stewardship on to others, those who are faithful, in due course. This stewardship comes from the ministry of the Body of Christ, the Church.

Mt 16:16-19 Simon Peter replied, "You are the Christ, the Son of the living God." ¹⁷ And Jesus answered him,

"Blessed are you, Simon Bar-Jona! For flesh and blood has not revealed this to you, but my Father who is in heaven. ¹⁸ And I tell you, you are Peter, and on this rock I will build my church, and the powers of death shall not prevail against it. ¹⁹ I will give you the keys of the kingdom of heaven, and whatever you bind on earth shall be bound in heaven, and whatever you loose on earth shall be loosed in heaven."

The Church, in Peter, is alone given the keys to the kingdom of heaven.

Jude 1:8,11 Yet in like manner these men in their dreamings defile the flesh, reject authority, and revile the glorious ones... Woe to them! For they walk in the way of Cain, and abandon themselves for the sake of gain to Balaam's error, and perish in Korah's rebellion.

Mt 18:17-18 If he refuses to listen to them, tell it to the church; and if he refuses to listen even to the church, let him be to you as a Gentile and a tax collector. ¹⁸ Truly, I say to you, whatever you bind on earth shall be bound in heaven, and whatever you loose on earth shall be loosed in heaven.

The Church, alive in the Christ-given authority of the Apostles, has ultimate authority to judge the truth or falsehood of a situation, because they have the authority Christ has. She alone guards the full deposit of faith, for Christ is One with His Bride, whose ministers have divine authority.

Acts 5:1-4 But a man named Ananias with his wife Sapphira sold a piece of property, ² and with his wife's knowledge he kept back some of the proceeds, and brought only a part and laid it at the apostles' feet. ³ But Peter said, "Ananias, why has Satan filled your heart to lie to the Holy Spirit and to keep back part of the proceeds of the land? ⁴ While it remained unsold, did it not remain your own? And after it was sold, was it not at your disposal? How is it that you have contrived this deed in your heart? You have not lied to men but to God."⁵ When Ananias heard these words, he fell down and died. And great fear came upon all who heard of it.

Ananias and Sapphira lied to the Apostles, yet Peter says they lied to the Holy Spirit, to God Himself. This sin against the apostles was a deadly sin against God.

Jn 14:15-17 "If you love me, you will keep my commandments. ¹⁶ And I will pray the Father, and he will give you another Counselor, to be with you for ever, ¹⁷ even the Spirit of truth, whom the world cannot receive, because it neither sees him nor knows him; you know him, for he dwells with you, and will be in you.

The Church exists because of apostolic authority. If the Eleven had not carried Jesus' message into the world, Christianity would not have survived. Jesus placed all authority in them and gave them the guidance of the Holy Spirit because He depended on them to do the will of the Father and make Him known to all the nations. The Apostles are the foundation.

Rev 21:14 And the wall of the city had twelve foundations, and on them the twelve names of the twelve apostles of the Lamb.

Their office is not finished because their work is not finished. Their work will not be finished until Jesus comes again.

1 Cor 11:2 I commend you because you remember me in everything and maintain the traditions even as I have delivered them to you.

2 Tim 1:13 Follow the pattern of the sound words which you have heard from me, in the faith and love which are in Christ Jesus...

Jn 16:23 In that day you will ask nothing of me. Truly, truly, I say to you, if you ask anything of the Father, he will give it to you in my name.

Early Christians' comments on Apostolic Succession

The Mystical Body

The Church is the Bride of Christ, Bride without spot or wrinkle, joined to the Bridegroom in indissoluble union, so that the two are one Body, with Jesus Christ at the head. She is one, undivided, visible body, composed of individual members, both sinners and holy people organically united, and endowed with the means of sanctification, the sacraments. Christ founded His Body upon His own preaching, suffering, and death; she came forth from his side on the Cross and was made known to the world at Pentecost, when the Holy Spirit revealed Himself as the soul of the Body. She is not a human society, but a communion of God with man, the Eucharist being the seal and sign which effects her unity and communion. (CCC 787-796)

Current misunderstandings: The doctrine of sola scriptura, *the idea that Scripture is the sole authority by which Christ's truth can be judged, very much weakens or completely erases the understanding of Christ's Body among most Christians. In order for sola scriptura to be true, the authority of the Church must be subordinated, reduced, or entirely erased. Many Christians will assert that they are part of an "invisible Church." Christ's Body becomes an invisible Body, a ghost without infallible authority. The connection between the Resurrected Body of Jesus Christ in the Upper Room, and the Body of Christ which is the Church is lost - the phrases become mere symbols, as does the Real Presence of Christ in the Eucharist, since Christ's words at the Last Supper likewise become symbol, not substance. Thus, "Biblical literalists" find themselves taking huge chunks of New Testament Scripture, such as John 6 and 1 Corinthians, as mere metaphor, while Catholics affirm these same passages to be literally true.*

Jn 15:4-5 Abide in me, and I in you. As the branch cannot bear fruit by itself, unless it abides in the vine, neither can you, unless you abide in me. ⁵ I am the vine, you are the branches.

Jesus established communion between Himself and us. Just as the branches of a vine find their sustenance from the root, so do we find our sustenance in Him.

Jn 6:56 He who eats my flesh and drinks my blood abides in me, and I in him.

This communion is not metaphorical. It is real.

1 Pet 3:18-19 For Christ also died for sins once for all, the righteous for the unrighteous, that he might bring us to God, being put to death in the flesh but made alive in the spirit; ¹⁹ in which he went and preached to the spirits in prison...

Spirit has real, concrete interaction with the world:

Lk 24:39-43 See my hands and my feet, that it is I myself; handle me, and see; for a spirit has not flesh and bones as you see that I have." ⁴⁰ And when he had said this, he showed them his hands and his feet. ⁴¹ And while they still disbelieved for joy, and wondered, he said to them, "Have you anything here to eat?" ⁴² They gave him a piece of broiled fish, ⁴³ and he took it and ate before them.

Jn 20:26-28 Eight days later, his disciples were again in the house, and Thomas was with them. The doors were shut, but Jesus came and stood among them, and said, "Peace be with you." ²⁷ Then he said to Thomas, "Put your finger here, and see my hands; and put out your hand, and place it in my side; do not be faithless, but believing." ²⁸ Thomas answered him, "My Lord and my God!" ²⁹ Jesus said to him, "Have you believed because you have seen me? Blessed are those who have not seen and yet believe."

For all those who think "spiritual" interpretations correspond at all to "symbolic" interpretations, Christ was brought to life in the spirit, but Thomas could still feel the nailholes, and Jesus could still eat fish. That which is spiritual is absolutely real in a concrete sense. Grace does not destroy but improves upon nature, spirit does not replace but improves upon matter. The Church is really His Body.

Acts 9:1-5 But Saul, still breathing threats and murder against the disciples of the Lord, went to the high priest ² and asked him for letters to the synagogues at Damascus, so that if he found any belonging to the Way, men or women, he might bring them bound to Jerusalem. ³ Now as he journeyed he approached Damascus, and suddenly a light from heaven flashed about him. ⁴ And he fell to the ground and heard a voice saying to him, "Saul, Saul, why do you persecute me?" ⁵ And he said, "Who are you, Lord?" And he said, "I am Jesus, whom you are persecuting."

Paul persecuted the Church, the Body of Christ. He did not persecute a spirit, he persecuted Jesus, His living Body, served and ruled by the Twelve Apostles.

1 Cor 11:11 (Nevertheless, in the Lord woman is not independent of man nor man of woman; [12] for as woman was made from man, so man is now born of woman. And all things are from God.)

The only occurrence of the word "independent" in all of Scripture is here, and Scripture tells us that we should not be. There is no such thing as an "independent church." We are one family. We are one Body.

1 Cor 14:33 For God is not a God of confusion, but of peace.

Rom 12:1-5 I appeal to you therefore, brethren, by the mercies of God, to present your bodies as a living sacrifice, holy and acceptable to God, which is your spiritual worship. [2] Do not be conformed to this world but be transformed by the renewal of your mind, that you may prove what is the will of God, what is good and acceptable and perfect.
[3] For by the grace given to me I bid every one among you not to think of himself more highly than he ought to think, but to think with sober judgment, each according to the measure of faith which God has assigned him. [4] For as in one body we have many members, and all the members do not have the same function, [5] so we, though many, are one body in Christ, and individually members one of another.

Col 1:18 He is the head of the body, the church; he is the beginning, the first-born from the dead, that in everything he might be pre-eminent.

He is the Head of the Body, supporting her always.

1 Cor 12:12-27 For just as the body is one and has many members, and all the members of the body, though many, are one body, so it is with Christ. [13] For by one Spirit we were all baptized into one body—Jews or Greeks, slaves or free—and all were made to drink of one Spirit.
[14] For the body does not consist of one member but of many. [15] If the foot should say, "Because I am not a hand, I do not belong to the body," that would not make it any less a part of the body. [16] And if the ear should say, "Because I am not an eye, I do not belong to the body," that would not make it any less a part of the body. [17] If the whole body were an eye, where would be the hearing? If the whole body were an ear, where would be the sense of smell? [18] But as it is, God arranged the organs in the body, each one of them, as he chose. [19] If all were a single organ, where would the body be? [20] As it is, there are many parts, yet one body. [21] The eye cannot say to the hand, "I have no need of you," nor again the head to the feet, "I have no need of you." [22] On the contrary, the parts of the body which seem to be weaker are indispensable, [23] and those parts of the body which we think less honorable we invest with the greater honor, and our unpresentable parts are treated with greater modesty, [24] which our more presentable parts do not require. But God has so composed the body, giving the greater honor to the inferior part, [25] that there may be no discord in the body, but that the members may have the same care for one another. [26] If one member suffers, all suffer together; if one member is honored, all rejoice together.
[27] Now you are the body of Christ and individually members of it

Eph 1:22-23 and he has put all things under his feet and has made him the head over all things for the church, [23] which is his body, the fulness of him who fills all in all.

Eph 3:4-6 When you read this you can perceive my insight into the mystery of Christ, [5] which was not made known to the sons of men in other generations as it has now been revealed to his holy apostles and prophets by the Spirit; [6] that is, how the Gentiles are fellow heirs, members of the same body, and partakers of the promise in Christ Jesus through the gospel.

Eph 4:4-5,7-13,16-15,25 There is one body and one Spirit, just as you were called to the one hope that belongs to your call, [5] one Lord, one faith, one baptism... But grace was given to each of us according to the measure of Christ's gift. [8] Therefore it is said, "When he ascended on high he led a host of captives, and he gave gifts to men." [9] (In saying, "He ascended," what does it mean but that he had also descended into the lower parts of the earth? [10] He who descended is he who also ascended far above all the heavens, that he might fill all things.) [11] And his gifts were that some should be apostles, some prophets, some evangelists, some pastors and teachers, [12] to equip the saints for the work of ministry, for building up the body of Christ, [13] until we all attain to the unity of the faith and of the knowledge of the Son of God, to mature manhood, to the measure of the stature of the fulness of Christ... speaking the truth in love, we are to grow up in every way into him who is the head, into Christ, [16] from whom the whole body, joined and knit together by every joint with which it is supplied, when each part is working properly, makes bodily growth and upbuilds itself in love.... Therefore, putting away falsehood, let every one speak the truth with his neighbor, for we are members one of another.

1 Cor 3:23 and you are Christ's; and Christ is God's.

One Body, one faith, one baptism make us members of one another and all members of Christ, each of us still individuals, but all of us part of Him.

Mt 9:11 And when the Pharisees saw this, they said to his disciples, "Why does your teacher eat with tax collectors and sinners?"

Mk 2:16 And the scribes of the Pharisees, when they saw that he was eating with sinners and tax collectors, said to his disciples, "Why does he eat with tax collectors and sinners?"

Lk 15:2 And the Pharisees and the scribes murmured, saying, "This man receives sinners and eats with them."

Christ does not shun the sinner, nor does His Body. Through Baptism and Reconciliation, all are continuously drawn into union with Him, washed in the nuptial bath of water and the Word.

Eph 5:23-32 For the husband is the head of the wife as Christ is the head of the church, his body, and is himself its Savior. ²⁴ As the church is subject to Christ, so let wives also be subject in everything to their husbands. ²⁵ Husbands, love your wives, as Christ loved the church and gave himself up for her, ²⁶ that he might sanctify her, having cleansed her by the washing of water with the word, ²⁷ that he might present the church to himself in splendor, without spot or wrinkle or any such thing, that she might be holy and without blemish. ²⁸ Even so husbands should love their wives as their own bodies. He who loves his wife loves himself. ²⁹ For no man ever hates his own flesh, but nourishes and cherishes it, as Christ does the church, ³⁰ because we are members of his body. ³¹ "For this reason a man shall leave his father and mother and be joined to his wife, and the two shall become one flesh." ³² This mystery is a profound one, and I am saying that it refers to Christ and the church; ³³ however, let each one of you love his wife as himself, and let the wife see that she respects her husband.

Col 1:24 Now I rejoice in my sufferings for your sake, and in my flesh I complete what is lacking in Christ's afflictions for the sake of his body, that is, the church,

One way in which we participate in Christ's Body is by offering our suffering up for the sanctification of others. This is what it means to "make up what is lacking in the afflictions of Christ." We have to participate, we must become little images of Christ. Just as He suffered for us on the Cross, so we must suffer for each other on our own crosses. This may be done at any time, but our suffering is best offered up in union with His Body, in the sacrifice of the Mass.

Heb 10:10 And by that will we have been sanctified through the offering of the body of Jesus Christ once for all.

We have been consecrated through the offering of the body of Christ.

Eph 1:22-23 and he has put all things under his feet and has made him the head over all things for the church, ²³ which is his body, the fulness of him who fills all in all.

Eph 2:15 by abolishing in his flesh the law of commandments and ordinances, that he might create in himself one new man in place of the two, so making peace.

The Church is the Body of Christ. We have been consecrated through the offering of the Church.

Mt 26:26 Now as they were eating, Jesus took bread, and blessed, and broke it, and gave it to the disciples and said, "Take, eat; this is my body."

Lk 5:34-35 And Jesus said to them, "Can you make wedding guests fast while the bridegroom is with them? ³⁵ The days will come, when the bridegroom is taken away from them, and then they will fast in those days."

Only through the grace of God may we become a perfect image of our Saviour, Jesus Christ. Christ established for us a perfect image of His Sacrifice, so that we might truly become One Body with Him.

Acts 2:1-4 When the day of Pentecost had come, they were all together in one place. ² And suddenly a sound came from heaven like the rush of a mighty wind, and it filled all the house where they were sitting. ³ And there appeared to them tongues as of fire, distributed and resting on each one of them. ⁴ And they were all filled with the Holy Spirit and began to speak in other tongues, as the Spirit gave them utterance.

He announced her existence at Pentecost, having already given His Apostles the instructions they would need to care for His Body.

Mt 28:19-20 Go therefore and make disciples of all nations, baptizing them in the name of the Father and of the Son and of the Holy Spirit, ²⁰ teaching them to observe all that I have commanded you; and lo, I am with you always, to the close of the age."

Jn 17:20-23 "I do not pray for these only, but also for those who believe in me through their word, ²¹ that they may all be one; even as thou, Father, art in me, and I in thee, that they also may be in us, so that the world may believe that thou hast sent me. ²² The glory which thou hast given me I have given to them, that they may be one even as we are one, ²³ I in them and thou in me, that they may become perfectly one, so that the world may know that thou hast sent me and hast loved them even as thou hast loved me."

Eph 3:9-11 and to make all men see what is the plan of the mystery hidden for ages in God who created all things; ¹⁰ that through the church the manifold wisdom of God might now be made known to the principalities and powers in the heavenly places. ¹¹ This was according to the eternal purpose which he has realized in Christ Jesus our Lord...

The Church is not invisble. She makes all men see the plan of the mystery of God. Jesus' Incarnation was intended from the beginning. God established the Church in order to continue the incarnational principle Jesus embodies. The Church is the dispenser of the mysteries, according to the eternal purpose realized in Christ Jesus our Lord.

The Communion of Saints

Daniel 7:18 But the saints of the Most High shall receive the kingdom, and possess the kingdom for ever, for ever and ever.

Those who are part of the Bride, the Body of Christ, cannot be separated from His Body through death. We are all One Body. All who are alive in Christ, whether on earth or in heaven, have the joyful duty of praying to God, asking Him to bestow His favors upon those in need. We who are in need must humble ourselves to ask the prayers and petitions of our brothers and sisters, both those here present and those who have gone before us, our elder brothers and sisters who have attained the reward of salvation through Jesus Christ, and stand before His Throne in heaven. The Church Triumphant (those in Heaven) pray for the Church Militant (those on earth), while the Church Militant prays for the Church Suffering (those in Purgatory). (CCC 946-975)

Current misunderstandings: Asking those who have died to pray for us is seen as foolishness at best, necromancy at worst.

Some argue that we are all saints right now, for Paul addressed Christians as "holy ones" and "saints."

Eph 1:1,8-10,2:19 Paul, an apostle of Christ Jesus by the will of God,
To the saints who are also faithful in Christ Jesus:... which he lavished upon us. ⁹ For he has made known to us in all wisdom and insight the mystery of his will, according to his purpose which he set forth in Christ ¹⁰ as a plan for the fulness of time, to unite all things in him, things in heaven and things on earth..... So then you are no longer strangers and sojourners, but you are fellow citizens with the saints and members of the household of God,...

The Ephesians are called holy ones, and said to already be fellow citizens with the holy ones in the household of God.

Eph 4:1,17,26-31,5:10 I therefore, a prisoner for the Lord, beg you to lead a life worthy of the calling to which you have been called,... Now this I affirm and testify in the Lord, that you must no longer live as the Gentiles do, in the futility of their minds;... Be angry but do not sin; do not let the sun go down on your anger, ²⁷ and give no opportunity to the devil. ²⁸ Let the thief no longer steal, but rather let him labor, doing honest work with his hands, so that he may be able to give to those in need. ²⁹ Let no evil talk come out of your mouths, but only such as is good for edifying, as fits the occasion, that it may impart grace to those who hear. ³⁰ And do not grieve the Holy Spirit of God, in whom you were sealed for the day of redemption. ³¹ Let all bitterness and wrath and anger and clamor and slander be put away from you, with all malice,... and try to learn what is pleasing to the Lord.

But oddly, the entire letter to the Ephesians is filled with admonitions and warnings about how to live an upright life, what action to avoid, what action to embrace. Paul tells them to "try to learn what is pleasing to God," which implies they don't know what is pleasing to God, and also implies they might fail to learn what is pleasing to God.

1 Cor 1:1-9 Paul, called by the will of God to be an apostle of Christ Jesus, and our brother Sosthenes,
 ² To the church of God which is at Corinth, to those sanctified in Christ Jesus, called to be saints together with all those who in every place call on the name of our Lord Jesus Christ, both their Lord and ours:
 ³ Grace to you and peace from God our Father and the Lord Jesus Christ. ⁴ I give thanks to God always for you because of the grace of God which was given you in Christ Jesus, ⁵ that in every way you were enriched in him with all speech and all knowledge— ⁶ even as the testimony to Christ was confirmed among you— ⁷ so that you are not lacking in any spiritual gift, as you wait for the revealing of our Lord Jesus Christ; ⁸ who will sustain you to the end, guiltless in the day of our Lord Jesus Christ. ⁹ God is faithful, by whom you were called into the fellowship of his Son, Jesus Christ our Lord.

Note that Paul begins the letter to the Corinthians by calling them "sanctified" - past tense - and by asserting that they have already been given all discourse and all knowledge through Jesus Christ, so that they are not lacking in any spiritual gift. Past (sanctified), present (not lacking) and future (God will keep you firm until the end) are apparently guaranteed. If this passage is read alone, they appear to already be saved, completely spiritual beings. Yet...

1 Cor 2:14-16, 3:1-3 The unspiritual man does not receive the gifts of the Spirit of God, for they are folly to him, and he is not able to understand them because they are spiritually discerned. ¹⁵ The spiritual man judges all things, but is himself to be judged by no one. ¹⁶ "For who has known the mind of the Lord so as to instruct him?" But we have the mind of Christ. ¹ But I, brethren, could not address you as spiritual men, but as men of the flesh, as babes in Christ. ² I fed you with milk, not solid food; for you were not ready for it; and even yet you are not ready, ³ for you are still of the flesh. For while there is jealousy and strife among you, are you not of the flesh, and behaving like ordinary men?

Now Paul says they are NOT spiritual, they are NOT exhibiting every spiritual gift, they could not even take the fullness of teaching that Paul had to offer, much less what Christ has to offer.

1 Cor 15:2 the gospel...by which you are saved, if you hold it fast—unless you believed in vain.

1 Cor 15:20-35 Come to your right mind, and sin no more. For some have no knowledge of God. I say this to your shame.

The "saints" must hold to the faith they have, for if they do not, they will not be saved. In fact, some of them don't even KNOW God. Why the disparity? Because Paul began by envisioning them as God calls them to be - not as they presently are. In both letters, Paul is pointing out to them that they could one day be, but are not yet, saints. It is the same with us.

Necromancy is forbidden by Scripture - it is clearly an abomination before God:

Deut 18:10-12 There shall not be found among you any one who burns his son or his daughter as an offering, any one who practices divination, a soothsayer, or an augur, or a sorcerer, ¹¹ or a charmer, or a medium, or a wizard, or a necromancer. ¹² For whoever does these things is an abomination to the LORD; and because of these abominable practices the LORD your God is driving them out before you.

Saul practices necromancy:

1 Sam 28:7-19 Then Saul said to his servants, "Seek out for me a woman who is a medium, that I may go to her and inquire of her." And his servants said to him, "Behold, there is a medium at Endor."
 ⁸ So Saul disguised himself and put on other garments, and went, he and two men with him; and they came to the woman by night. And he said,

"Divine for me by a spirit, and bring up for me whomever I shall name to you." ⁹ The woman said to him, "Surely you know what Saul has done, how he has cut off the mediums and the wizards from the land. Why then are you laying a snare for my life to bring about my death?" ¹⁰ But Saul swore to her by the LORD, "As the LORD lives, no punishment shall come upon you for this thing." ¹¹ Then the woman said, "Whom shall I bring up for you?" He said, "Bring up Samuel for me." ¹² When the woman saw Samuel, she cried out with a loud voice; and the woman said to Saul, "Why have you deceived me? You are Saul." ¹³ The king said to her, "Have no fear; what do you see?" And the woman said to Saul, "I see a god coming up out of the earth." ¹⁴ He said to her, "What is his appearance?" And she said, "An old man is coming up; and he is wrapped in a robe." And Saul knew that it was Samuel, and he bowed with his face to the ground, and did obeisance.

¹⁵ Then Samuel said to Saul, "Why have you disturbed me by bringing me up?" Saul answered, "I am in great distress; for the Philistines are warring against me, and God has turned away from me and answers me no more, either by prophets or by dreams; therefore I have summoned you to tell me what I shall do." ¹⁶ And Samuel said, "Why then do you ask me, since the LORD has turned from you and become your enemy? ¹⁷ The LORD has done to you as he spoke by me; for the LORD has torn the kingdom out of your hand, and given it to your neighbor, David. ¹⁸ Because you did not obey the voice of the LORD, and did not carry out his fierce wrath against Amalek, therefore the LORD has done this thing to you this day. ¹⁹ Moreover the LORD will give Israel also with you into the hand of the Philistines; and tomorrow you and your sons shall be with me; the LORD will give the army of Israel also into the hand of the Philistines."

Saul and sons will die and "be with [Samuel]." Samuel, presumably, is not in hell as Christians understand it. Yet, Saul is clearly engaging in necromancy. He is asking for information from a medium, who is not even of Israel and definitely not of God.

1 Chron 10:13-14 So Saul died for his unfaithfulness; he was unfaithful to the LORD in that he did not keep the command of the LORD, and also consulted a medium, seeking guidance, ¹⁴ and did not seek guidance from the LORD. Therefore the LORD slew him, and turned the kingdom over to David the son of Jesse.

Verse 14 - this is the key. If Saul had asked God for guidance, there would have been no difficulty. Instead, *he attempts to circumvent God's plans by contacting the dead illicitly. He asks for help from the prophet of God, but does not ask for that help through God, he sends his request through a medium instead. He does not recognize that the prophets are alive in God, he tries by deceitful ways to slip past God's omnipotence. For this abomination, Saul will lose his life.*

Christ is the One Mediator

1 Tim 2:5-6 For there is one God, and there is one mediator between God and men, the man Christ Jesus, ⁶ who gave himself as a ransom for all, the testimony to which was borne at the proper time.

Jesus Christ is the sole mediator. The communion of saints is only possible because of Christ. (CCC 65-67, 101-104, 422-747, 781-796, 988-1019, 1220, 1228, 1257-1261)

Heb 3:14 For we share in Christ, if only we hold our first confidence firm to the end,

1 Cor 3:9 For we are God's fellow workers...

Jn 14:12-14 "Truly, truly, I say to you, he who believes in me will also do the works that I do; and greater works than these will he do, because I go to the Father. ¹³ Whatever you ask in my name, I will do it, that the Father may be glorified in the Son; ¹⁴ if you ask anything in my name, I will do it."

Subordinate mediation is possible, that is, we can image Christ in our lives by mediating for others as He does for us. "Co-worker" or "fellow worker" doesn't mean we are equal to or work parallel to God - it means we work under and with God. "Co" means "with." God's work is the redemption of every human being. We are God's fellow workers. Therefore, each of us also have the work of redeeming every human being. This is humanly impossible, but is divinely possible through the communion of saints working in the Body of Christ through the Holy Spirit.

Ex 17:8-13 Then came Amalek and fought with Israel at Rephidim. ⁹ And Moses said to Joshua, "Choose for us men, and go out, fight with Amalek; tomorrow I will stand on the top of the hill with the rod of God in my hand." ¹⁰ So Joshua did as Moses told him, and fought with Amalek; and Moses, Aaron, and Hur went up to the top of the hill. ¹¹ Whenever Moses held up his hand, Israel prevailed; and whenever he lowered his hand, Amalek prevailed. ¹² But Moses' hands grew weary; so they took a stone and put it under him, and he sat upon it, and Aaron and Hur held up his hands, one on one side, and the other on the other side; so his hands were steady until the going down of the sun. ¹³ And Joshua mowed down Amalek and his people with the edge of the sword.

Moses suffered for his people, so that God might grant them victory against the Amalekites, for God would not grant the Israelites victory unless Moses cooperated with Him by standing on the hill with his arms outstretched as one crucified. God required Moses to suffer for his people, to act as the head so the body might gain victory through the battle they had to undergo.

Jn 4:7,39-42 There came a woman of Samaria to draw water. Jesus said to her, "Give me a drink."... Many Samaritans from that city believed in him because of the woman's testimony, "He told me all that I ever did." ⁴⁰ So when the Samaritans came to him, they asked him to stay with them; and he stayed there two days. ⁴¹ And many more believed because of his word. ⁴² They said to the woman, "It is no longer because of your words that we believe, for we have heard for ourselves, and we know that this is indeed the Savior of the world."

The Samaritans believed God would send but one prophet, the Messiah. They accepted none of the prophets of the Old Testament. A woman mediated Jesus' word into her whole community, bringing many to believe that He was the Prophet who was to come.

Rom 10:14 But how are men to call upon him in whom they have not believed? And how are they to believe in him of whom they have never heard? And how are they to hear without a preacher?

Preaching is acting as a mediator.

Deut 9:20 And the LORD was so angry with Aaron that he was ready to destroy him; and I prayed for Aaron also at the same time.

2 Cor 1:11 You also must help us by prayer, so that many will give thanks on our behalf for the blessing granted us in answer to many prayers.

1 Tim 2:1-3 First of all, then, I urge that supplications, prayers, intercessions, and thanksgivings be made for all men, ² for kings and all who are in high positions, that we may lead a quiet and peaceable life, godly and respectful in every way. ³ This is good, and it is acceptable in the sight of God our Savior, ⁴ who desires all men to be saved and to come to the knowledge of the truth.

Prayers are necessary from all towards all - all Christians should pray for each other and the world. Praying for someone is mediating for them before God. We are mediators for each other before God. This is only possible because we act in Christ. How does it work?

Rom 12:4-5 For as in one body we have many members, and all the members do not have the same function, ⁵ so we, though many, are one body in Christ, and individually members one of another.

1 Cor 12:12-13, 21-27 For just as the body is one and has many members, and all the members of the body, though many, are one body, so it is with Christ. ¹³ For by one Spirit we were all baptized into one body—Jews or Greeks, slaves or free—and all were made to drink of one Spirit.... The eye cannot say to the hand, "I have no need of you," nor again the head to the feet, "I have no need of you." ²² On the contrary, the parts of the body which seem to be weaker are indispensable, ²³ and those parts of the body which we think less honorable we invest with the greater honor, and our unpresentable parts are treated with greater modesty, ²⁴ which our more presentable parts do not require. But God has so composed the body, giving the greater honor to the inferior part, ²⁵ that there may be no discord in the body, but that the members may have the same care for one another. ²⁶ If one member suffers, all suffer together; if one member is honored, all rejoice together. ²⁷ Now you are the body of Christ and individually members of it.

A Christian is a part of the Body of Christ. Scripture does NOT say that Christians are separated from the body of Christ at death, rather, Scripture says death cannot separate us.

Rom 8:35-39 Who shall separate us from the love of Christ? Shall tribulation, or distress, or persecution, or famine, or nakedness, or peril, or sword? ³⁶ As it is written,"For thy sake we are being killed all the day long; we are regarded as sheep to be slaughtered." ³⁷ No, in all these things we are more than conquerors through him who loved us. ³⁸ For I am sure that neither death, nor life, nor angels, nor principalities, nor things present, nor things to come, nor powers, ³⁹ nor height, nor depth, nor anything else in all creation, will be able to separate us from the love of God in Christ Jesus our Lord.

Mt 22:31-32 And as for the resurrection of the dead, have you not read what was said to you by God, [32] 'I am the God of Abraham, and the God of Isaac, and the God of Jacob'? He is not God of the dead, but of the living."

Mk 12:26-27 And as for the dead being raised, have you not read in the book of Moses, in the passage about the bush, how God said to him, 'I am the God of Abraham, and the God of Isaac, and the God of Jacob'? [27] He is not God of the dead, but of the living; you are quite wrong."

Lk 20:34-38 And Jesus said to them, "The sons of this age marry and are given in marriage; [35] but those who are accounted worthy to attain to that age and to the resurrection from the dead neither marry nor are given in marriage, [36] for they cannot die any more, because they are equal to angels and are sons of God, being sons of the resurrection. [37] But that the dead are raised, even Moses showed, in the passage about the bush, where he calls the Lord the God of Abraham and the God of Isaac and the God of Jacob. [38] Now he is not God of the dead, but of the living; for all live to him."

1 Thess 5:9-10 For God has not destined us for wrath, but to obtain salvation through our Lord Jesus Christ, [10] who died for us so that whether we wake or sleep we might live with him.

Wis 11:26 Thou sparest all things, for they are thine, O Lord who lovest the living.

It is sometimes asserted that those in heaven are alive but "asleep." Such readings misunderstand the context. The "sleep" refers to how the body of the deceased appears to us here on earth - it does not refer to the state of the soul, who is vibrantly and superabundantly loved by God in heaven. It would be inconceivably unjust to be alive in heaven, but unable to praise God or experience His burning love because the soul is in an unconscious stupor.

Jn 12:25-26 He who loves his life loses it, and he who hates his life in this world will keep it for eternal life. [26] If any one serves me, he must follow me; and where I am, there shall my servant be also; if any one serves me, the Father will honor him.

The saints serve Christ, and are with Christ, honored by the Father.

Wis 3:1-5 But the souls of the righteous are in the hand of God,
and no torment will ever touch them. [2] In the eyes of the foolish they seemed to have died, and their departure was thought to be an affliction, [3] and their going from us to be their destruction;
but they are at peace. [4] For though in the sight of men they were punished, their hope is full of immortality. [5] Having been disciplined a little, they will receive great good, because God tested them and found them worthy of himself...

Mt 17:3-5 And behold, there appeared to them Moses and Elijah, talking with him. [4] And Peter said to Jesus, "Lord, it is well that we are here; if you wish, I will make three booths here, one for you and one for Moses and one for Elijah." [5] He was still speaking, when lo, a bright cloud overshadowed them, and a voice from the cloud said, "This is my beloved Son, with whom I am well pleased; listen to him."

Lk 9:30-31 And behold, two men talked with him, Moses and Elijah, [31] who appeared in glory and spoke of his departure, which he was to accomplish at Jerusalem.

Moses was dead, (Elijah arguably isn't since he was taken up in a whirlwind - 2 Kings 2:11), but both still conversed with a living man. Death cannot separate us, for Abraham, Isaac, and Jacob are "living" even though they had "fallen asleep" several centuries earlier. If necromancy consists only in speaking with the dead, then Christ is a necromancer, for He speaks with Moses.

Heb 12:1 Therefore, since we are surrounded by so great a cloud of witnesses, let us also lay aside every weight, and sin which clings so closely, and let us run with perseverance the race that is set before us..

Those living with God in heaven witness our acts here on earth. One must be awake to witness.

Heb 12:22-24 But you have come to Mount Zion and to the city of the living God, the heavenly Jerusalem, and to innumerable angels in festal gathering, [23] and to the assembly of the first-born who are enrolled in heaven, and to a judge who is God of all, and to the spirits of just men made perfect, ²⁴ and to Jesus, the mediator of a new covenant, and to the sprinkled blood that speaks more graciously than the blood of Abel.

Eph 3:14-15 For this reason I bow my knees before the Father, ¹⁵ from whom every family in heaven and on earth is named...

The family of heaven has a share in God's glory.

James 5:16 The prayer of a righteous man has great power in its effects.

The spirits of the just are made perfect in order to enter heaven - they are a great cloud of witnesses. Who is more righteous than someone in heaven, kneeling before the throne of God? For...

Rev 21:27 But nothing unclean shall enter it, nor any one who practices abomination or falsehood, but only those who are written in the Lamb's book of life.

2 Mac 12:42-45 and they turned to prayer, beseeching that the sin which had been committed might be wholly blotted out. And the noble Judas exhorted the people to keep themselves free from sin, for they had seen with their own eyes what had happened because of the sin of those who had fallen. ⁴³ He also took up a collection, man by man, to the amount of two thousand drachmas of silver, and sent it to Jerusalem to provide for a sin offering. In doing this he acted very well and honorably, taking account of the resurrection. ⁴⁴ For if he were not expecting that those who had fallen would rise again, it would have been superfluous and foolish to pray for the dead. ⁴⁵ But if he was looking to the splendid reward that is laid up for those who fall asleep in godliness, it was a holy and pious thought. Therefore he made atonement for the dead, that they might be delivered from their sin.

2 Mac 15:12-16 What he saw was this: Onias, who had been high priest, a noble and good man, of modest bearing and gentle manner, one who spoke fittingly and had been trained from childhood in all that belongs to excellence, was praying with outstretched hands for the whole body of the Jews. ¹³ Then likewise a man appeared, distinguished by his gray hair and dignity, and of marvelous majesty and authority. ¹⁴ And Onias spoke, saying, "This is a man who loves the brethren and prays much for the people and the holy city, Jeremiah, the prophet of God." ¹⁵ Jeremiah stretched out his right hand and gave to Judas a golden sword, and as he gave it he addressed him thus: ¹⁶ "Take this holy sword, a gift from God, with which you will strike down your adversaries."

Even if the canonicity of the Maccabees accounts are not accepted, their historicity must be. Orthodox Jews pray for the dead, both then as now. Christ was an Orthodox Jew.

Rev 5:8 And when he had taken the scroll, the four living creatures and the twenty-four elders fell down before the Lamb, each holding a harp, and with golden bowls full of incense, which are the prayers of the saints;

Angels and martyrs pray to God about what happens on earth.

Rev 6:9-11 When he opened the fifth seal, I saw under the altar the souls of those who had been slain for the word of God and for the witness they had borne; ¹⁰ they cried out with a loud voice, "O Sovereign Lord, holy and true, how long before thou wilt judge and avenge our blood on those who dwell upon the earth?" ¹¹ Then they were each given a white robe and told to rest a little longer, until the number of their fellow servants and their brethren should be complete, who were to be killed as they themselves had been.

Rev 8:3-5 And another angel came and stood at the altar with a golden censer; and he was given much incense to mingle with the prayers of all the saints upon the golden altar before the throne; ⁴ and the smoke of the incense rose with the prayers of the saints from the hand of the angel before God. ⁵ Then the angel took the censer and filled it with fire from the altar and threw it on the earth; and there were peals of thunder, voices, flashes of lightning, and an earthquake.

Some argue against the ability of saints to hear thousands of simultaneous prayers of intercession..

1 Cor 2:9 But, as it is written, "What no eye has seen, nor ear heard,
nor the heart of man conceived, what God has prepared for those who love him,"

1 Cor 15:42-43 So is it with the resurrection of the dead. What is sown is perishable, what is raised is imperishable. ⁴³ It is sown in dishonor, it is raised in glory. It is sown in weakness, it is raised in power.

We know Christ grants great powers to those who love him. Jesus Himself says that those in heaven know of each individual repentance...

Lk 15:7-10 Just so, I tell you, there will be more joy in heaven over one sinner who repents than over ninety-nine righteous persons who need no repentance. ⁸ "Or what woman, having ten silver coins, if she loses one coin, does not light a lamp and sweep the house and seek diligently until she finds it? ⁹ And when she has found it, she calls together her friends and neighbors, saying, 'Rejoice with me, for I have found the coin which I had lost.' ¹⁰ Just so, I tell you, there is joy before the angels of God over one sinner who repents."

Gen 18:32-33 ... Then he said, "Oh let not the Lord be angry, and I will speak again but this once. Suppose ten are found there." He answered, "For the sake of ten I will not destroy it." ³³ And the LORD went his way, when he had finished speaking to Abraham; and Abraham returned to his place.

God often grants prayer based on the merits of the person praying. Abraham shows that the faith of a believer can stand in for the faith of non-believers.

Lk 16:19-31 "There was a rich man, who was clothed in purple and fine linen and who feasted sumptuously every day. ²⁰ And at his gate lay a poor man named Lazarus, full of sores, ²¹ who desired to be fed with what fell from the rich man's table; moreover the dogs came and licked his sores. ²² The poor man died and was carried by the angels to Abraham's bosom. The rich man also died and was buried; ²³ and in Hades, being in torment, he lifted up his eyes, and saw Abraham far off and Lazarus in his bosom. ²⁴ And he called out, 'Father Abraham, have mercy upon me, and send Lazarus to dip the end of his finger in water and cool my tongue; for I am in anguish in this flame.' ²⁵ But Abraham said, 'Son, remember that you in your lifetime received your good things, and Lazarus in like manner evil things; but now he is comforted here, and you are in anguish. ²⁶ And besides all this, between us and you a great chasm has been fixed, in order that those who would pass from here to you may not be able, and none may cross from there to us.' ²⁷ And he said, 'Then I beg you, father, to send him to my father's house, ²⁸ for I have five brothers, so that he may warn them, lest they also come into this place of torment.' ²⁹ But Abraham said, 'They have Moses and the prophets; let them hear them.' ³⁰ And he said, 'No, father Abraham; but if some one goes to them from the dead, they will repent.' ³¹ He said to him, 'If they do not hear Moses and the prophets, neither will they be convinced if some one should rise from the dead.'"

The rich man asked Abraham and Lazarus to intercede for those on earth. Abraham and Lazarus are acting as intercessors here. The prayer is not granted, but neither is the rich man rebuked for asking. If the rich man can shout across a great chasm, we can also shout across the great chasm.

Necromancy refers to asking the dead for something outside of Christ's mediation, while the communion of saints merely means we ask those alive in Christ to pray for us to Christ. Our request is only possible, and can only be fulfilled, because all of us are united in Christ. We are the cells in the Body, cells which live and communicate with each other because this Body is the Body of Christ. Intercession is possible only through Jesus Christ. We have a duty to image Christ. We have a duty to allow others to act as Christ, so that they, too, may increase in grace before God. By ignoring Christ's Body and the people living on earth or in heaven who make up that Body, we ignore Christ and the power Christ gave them to be like Him. Such willful blindness towards God's gifts does not honor God.

Early Christians' comments on Praying to the Saints

Relics of Saints

The bodies of the martyrs and saints and the objects that they handled contain within them the healing power of Jesus Christ, who shows honor to those who love Him by permitting them to imitate Him in all things. (CCC 1667-1679)

Current misunderstandings: Most Christians deny that the relics of saints - their bones, the things they handled during their lives - could have any innate power from God.

Psalm 116:15 Precious in the sight of the LORD is the death of his saints.

Ex 13:19 And Moses took the bones of Joseph with him; for Joseph had solemnly sworn the people of

Israel, saying, "God will visit you; then you must carry my bones with you from here."

Moses honors Joseph by taking his bones. The bones and hair of a saint are a first-class relic.

2 Kings 2:13-14 And he took up the mantle of Elijah that had fallen from him, and went back and stood on the bank of the Jordan. [14] Then he took the mantle of Elijah that had fallen from him, and struck the water, saying, "Where is the LORD, the God of Elijah?" And when he had struck the water, the water was parted to the one side and to the other; and Elisha went over.

Elisha uses Elijah's relic, the mantle, in order to work a miracle. Anything handled or used by a saint is a second-class relic.

2 Kings 13:20-21 So Elisha died, and they buried him. Now bands of Moabites used to invade the land in the spring of the year. [21] And as a man was being buried, lo, a marauding band was seen and the man was cast into the grave of Elisha; and as soon as the man touched the bones of Elisha, he revived, and stood on his feet.

The power of Elisha's relics prefigure the power of Christ, the new Elisha, who would display an even greater power over death.

Lk 8:43-48 And a woman who had had a flow of blood for twelve years and could not be healed by any one, and had spent all her living on physicians, [44] came up behind him, and touched the fringe of his garment; and immediately her flow of blood ceased. [45] And Jesus said, "Who was it that touched me?" When all denied it, Peter said, "Master, the multitudes surround you and press upon you!" [46] But Jesus said, "Some one touched me; for I perceive that power has gone forth from me." [47] And when the woman saw that she was not hidden, she came trembling, and falling down before him declared in the presence of all the people why she had touched him, and how she had been immediately healed. [48] And he said to her, "Daughter, your faith has made you well; go in peace."

Mk 6:56 And wherever he came, in villages, cities, or country, they laid the sick in the market places, and besought him that they might touch even the fringe of his garment; and as many as touched it were made well.

Christ's relics - his clothes, in this case - had healing power.

Acts 5:14-16 And more than ever believers were added to the Lord, multitudes both of men and women, [15] so that they even carried out the sick into the streets, and laid them on beds and pallets, that as Peter came by at least his shadow might fall on some of them. [16] The people also gathered from the towns around Jerusalem, bringing the sick and those afflicted with unclean spirits, and they were all healed.

Peter is the first New Testament person who was permitted to imitate Christ in this way.

Acts 19:11-12 And God did extraordinary miracles by the hands of Paul, [12] so that handkerchiefs or aprons were carried away from his body to the sick, and diseases left them and the evil spirits came out of them.

Then Paul was also given that honor. An object touched to a first-class relic is a third-class relic. One might argue that no one told disciples to keep the relics of holy people, but neither did anyone tell them to throw the relics away. If we are supposed to honor the members of the Body of Christ, then throwing away relics as trash would not do well in fulfilling the command, nor is it being good stewards of our resources.

Church Authority and Infallibility

As the Bride of Christ, who is the Body of Christ, the Church enjoys the authority of Him who has headship over Her. Through the guidance of the Holy Spirit, in matters of doctrinal dispute the teaching authority of the Church is both final and infallibly correct, though not necessarily a complete explanation of revelation. (CCC 748-945)

Current misunderstandings: Many Christians deny that the Church has either final or infallible authority, insisting that such authority is arrogated to God alone in Scripture.

To say a teaching is infallible is not solely a statement about its truth value, for all that the Church teaches is true. Infallibility is the clear definition and description of how the authority of the Church, acting in history, came to a deeper understanding in teaching a specific truth. The inerrancy of Scripture fits hand-in-glove with the infallibility of the Church, of the councils, and of the Pope. "Inerrancy" means that Scripture teaches only what is true. "Infallibility" means that the Church, councils, and Pope teach with authority and do not teach what is error. Thus, the Bride of Christ dips into the inexhaustible well of Scripture, bringing forth only that which is pure, never poisoned with distortions or falsehoods.

Mt 5:14 "You are the light of the world. A city set on a hill cannot be hid."

The word ekklesia (church) appears over one hundred times in the NT, not once meaning a "spiritual" or invisible church. The word "spiritual" is often used in ecumenical discussions of Scripture with a meaning which is indistinguishable from "symbolic." Although our separated brethren insist the term has more substance, it is unclear how "spiritual" differs from "symbolic," given the usage it commonly enjoys.

Mt 13:10 The the disciples came and said to him, "Why do you speak to them in parables?" [11] And he answered them, "To you it has been given to know the secrets of the kingdom of heaven, but to them it has not been given."

1 Cor 12:27-29 Now you are the body of Christ and individually members of it. [28] And God has appointed in the church first apostles, second prophets, third teachers, then workers of miracles, then healers, helpers, administrators, speakers in various kinds of tongues. [29] Are all apostles? Are all propherts? Are all teachers? Do all work miracles?

The Magisterium began here - Christ gave the secrets of the kingdom of heaven to the Apostles, to guard and to treasure. This understanding is not imparted to everyone, for not everyone has the same role in the body of Christ.

Luke's writings are specifically structured so as to demonstrate how Jesus passed His authority on to His Church. The Gospel of Luke describes the authority of Jesus, the Acts of the Apostles describes the authority of the Church.

Lk 1:3 it seemed good to me also, having followed all things closely for some time past, to write an orderly account for you, most excellent Theophilus...

Acts 1:1 In the first book, O Theophilus, I have dealth with all that Jesus began to do and teach...

Both books are addressed to the lover of God...

Lk 1:31 And behold, you will conceive in your womb and bear a son, and you shall call his name Jesus.

Acts 1:2 until the day when he was taken up, after he had given commandment through the Holy Spirit to the apostles whom he had chosen.

Jesus coming was prophecied in Luke, the foreshadowing of Apostles guided by the Spirit is likewise described in Acts.

Lk 1:26-27 In the sixth month the angel Gabriel was sent from God to a city of Galilee named Nazareth, [27] to a virgin betrothed to a man whose name was Joseph, of the house of David; and the virgin's name was Mary.

Acts 1:14 All these with one accord devoted themselves to prayer, together with the women and Mary the mother of Jesus, and with his brethren.

Mary's presence is specifically described in both events...

Lk 1:35 And the angel said to her, "The Holy Spirit will come upon you, and the power of the Most High will overshadow you; therefore the child to be born will be called holy, the Son of God..."

Acts 2:1-12 When the day of Pentecost had come, they were all together in one place. ² And suddenly a sound came from heaven like the rush of a mighty wind, and it filled all the house where they were sitting. ³ And there appeared to them tongues as of fire, distributed and resting on each one of them. ⁴ And they were all filled with the Holy Spirit and began to speak in other tongues, as the Spirit gave them utterance.
⁵ Now there were dwelling in Jerusalem Jews, devout men from every nation under heaven. ⁶ And at this sound the multitude came together, and they were bewildered, because each one heard them speaking in his own language. ⁷ And they were amazed and wondered, saying, "Are not all these who are speaking Galileans? ⁸ And how is it that we hear, each of us in his own native language? ⁹ Parthians and Medes and Elamites and residents of Mesopotamia, Judea and Cappadocia, Pontus and Asia, ¹⁰ Phrygia and Pamphylia, Egypt and the parts of Libya belonging to Cyrene, and visitors from Rome, both Jews and proselytes, ¹¹ Cretans and Arabians, we hear them telling in our own tongues the mighty works of God." ¹² And all were amazed and perplexed, saying to one another, "What does this mean?"

...and the coming of the Spirit is specifically described.

Lk 1:9 according to the custom of the priesthood, it fell to him by lot to enter the temple of the Lord and burn incense. ¹⁰ And the whole multitude of people were praying outside at the hour of incense.

Acts 3:1 Now Peter and John were going up to the temple at the hour of prayer, the ninth hour...

Zachary is given a sign at the same time (the ninth hour) and place (The Temple) Peter and John are...

Lk 4:38 And he arose and left the synagogue, and entered Simon's house. Now Simon's mother-in-law was ill with a high fever, and they besought him for her. ³⁹ And he stood over her and rebuked the fever, and it left her; and immediately she rose and served them.

Acts 3:7 And he took him by the right hand and raised him up; and immediately his feet and ankles were made strong.

... and both Jesus and Peter, representing the Church, begin His ministry with a healing.

Lk 4:43 but he said to them, "I must preach the good news of the kingdom of God to the other cities also; for I was sent for this purpose."

Acts 3:12 And when Peter saw it he addressed the people, "Men of Israel, why do you wonder at this, or why do you stare at us, as though by our own power or piety we had made him walk?"

Both Jesus and Peter follow the healing with a preaching of the Good News. Luke constructed the beginning of both books so that the actions mirrored one another: first Jesus, then the Church He instituted, with Peter at its head. Luke continues this parallel structure within Acts itself. Not only does Luke-Acts have a two-part structure, Acts itself has a two-part structure, first following the actions of Peter, head of the college of Apostles, and then describing the actions of a convert to the faith, one Saul of Tarsus, who became Paul. Thus, Luke tells us of Jesus, spiritual head of the Church, then of Peter, His vicar at the head of the Church and the college of Apostles, then of the Church itself, through the actions of Paul.

Matthew's Gospel has a similar two-part structure, in which Jesus' power is described in Matthew 4:23-9:35 - He is preaching, healing, and casting out spirits. Then Jesus explicitly gives the Twelve the same authority and they begin preaching, healing and casting out spirits. Indeed, the Twelve were so accustomed to wielding Jesus' authority that after the Transfiguration they were amazed to encounter a demon they could NOT cast out. Christ is both human and divine, His Body, which is His Church, is made up of human beings, but is divinely guided and protected through the offices of the Twelve which He established.

Amos 9:10-12 "For lo, I will command,
and shake the house of Israel among all the nations
as one shakes with a sieve,
but no pebble shall fall upon the earth. ¹⁰ All the sinners of my people shall die by the sword,
who say, 'Evil shall not overtake or meet us.' ¹¹ "In that day I will raise up
the booth of David that is fallen
and repair its breaches,
and raise up its ruins,
and rebuild it as in the days of old; ¹² that they may possess the remnant of Edom
and all the nations who are called by my name,"
says the LORD who does this.

Acts 15:13-15 "Brethren, listen to me. [14] Simeon has related how God first visited the Gentiles, to take out of them a people for his name. [15] And with this the words of the prophets agree..."

The Church must be a visible structure, for all Gentiles must find it and be joined to it. This is the will of the Father.

Rom 6:17 But thanks be to God, that you who were once slaves of sin have become obedient from the heart to the standard of teaching to which you were committed...

There is a standard of teaching to which Christians must adhere.

Eph 3:2,7-11 assuming that you have heard of the stewardship of God's grace that was given to me for you... Of this gospel I was made a minister according to the gift of God's grace which was given me by the working of his power. [8]To me, though I am the very least of all the saints, this grace was given, to preach to the Gentiles the unsearchable riches of Christ, [9] and to make all men see what is the plan of the mystery hidden for ages in God who created all things; [10] that through the church the manifold wisdom of God might now be made known to the principalities and powers in the heavenly places. [11] This was according to the eternal purpose which he has realized in Christ Jesus our Lord...

Paul points out that he is merely an officer of the Church, that it is only through the Church that the manifold wisdom of God is revealed. Only the Church can reveal the mystery of Divine salvation. This is all in accord with the eternal purpose of God. He intended, from the beginning of eternity, to set up a Church with offices and ministers through which His Divine wisdom would come.

Is 54:9-17 "For this is like the days of Noah to me: as I swore that the waters of Noah should no more go over the earth, so I have sworn that I will not be angry with you and will not rebuke you. [10] For the mountains may depart and the hills be removed, but my steadfast love shall not depart from you, and my covenant of peace shall not be removed, says the LORD, who has compassion on you. [11] "O afflicted one, storm-tossed, and not comforted, behold, I will set your stones in antimony, and lay your foundations with sapphires. [12] I will make your pinnacles of agate, your gates of carbuncles, and all your wall of precious stones. [13] All your sons shall be taught by the LORD, and great shall be the prosperity of your sons. [14] In righteousness you shall be established; you shall be far from oppression, for you shall not fear; and from terror, for it shall not come near you. [15] If any one stirs up strife, it is not from me; whoever stirs up strife with you shall fall because of you. [16] Behold, I have created the smith who blows the fire of coals, and produces a weapon for its purpose. I have also created the ravager to destroy; [17] no weapon that is fashioned against you shall prosper, and you shall confute every tongue that rises against you in judgment. This is the heritage of the servants of the LORD and their vindication from me, says the LORD."

Christ's Church is prophesied in Isaiah.

Mt 16:18-19 And I tell you, you are Peter, and on this rock I will build my church, and the powers of death shall not prevail against it. [19] I will give you the keys of the kingdom of heaven, and whatever you bind on earth shall be bound in heaven, and whatever you loose on earth shall be loosed in heaven."

The prophecy is fulfilled in Matthew. "Peter" means "rock."

1 Cor 3:10-11 According to the grace of God given to me, like a skilled master builder I laid a foundation, and another man is building upon it. Let each man take care how he builds upon it. [11] For no other foundation can any one lay than that which is laid, which is Jesus Christ.

Eph 2:19-20 but you are fellow citizens with the saints and members of the household of God, [20] built upon the foundation of the apostles and prophets, Christ Jesus himself being the cornerstone...

Rev 21:14 And the wall of the city had twelve foundations, and on them the twelve names of the twelve apostles of the Lamb.

Christ and the apostles are individually each referred to as the foundation. Jesus Christ is the cornerstone (the beginning of a foundation).

1 Tim 3:15 you may know how one ought to behave in the household of God, which is the church of the living God, the pillar and bulwark of the truth.

Scriptural Catholicism — Church

Scripture is truth. Scripture itself attests that the Church is the pillar and foundation of the Truth. Without a pillar and foundation, the structure crumbles.

Eph 3:4-5 When you read this you can perceive my insight into the mystery of Christ, [5] which was not made known to the sons of men in other generations as it has now been revealed to his holy apostles and prophets by the Spirit;

Eph 4:11 And his gifts were that some should be apostles, some prophets, some evangelists, some pastors and teachers,

Acts 1:20 For it is written in the book of Psalms, 'Let his habitation become desolate, and let there be no one to live in it'; and 'His office (episkipous) let another take.'

Acts 20:28 Take heed to yourselves and to all the flock, in which the Holy Spirit has made you overseers (episkipous), to care for the church of God which he obtained with the blood of his own Son.

1 Pet 2:24-25 He himself bore our sins in his body on the tree, that we might die to sin and live to righteousness. By his wounds you have been healed. [25] For you were straying like sheep, but have now returned to the Shepherd and Guardian (episkipous) of your souls.

The word used to designate Christ in 1 Peter is the same word used to designate the overseers appointed by the Holy Spirit in Acts 20. Again, we see Scripture treating Christ's authority in some sense as interchangeable with His Apostles'.

1 Tim 3:2 Now a bishop (episkipous) must be above reproach, the husband of one wife, temperate, sensible, dignified, hospitable, an apt teacher,

Titus 1:7 For a bishop (episkipous), as God's steward, must be blameless; he must not be arrogant or quick-tempered or a drunkard or violent or greedy for gain...

And this authority was something the Apostles handed on.

Mt 18:16-18 But if he does not listen, take one or two others along with you, that every word may be confirmed by the evidence of two or three witnesses. [17] If he refuses to listen to them, tell it to the church; and if he refuses to listen even to the church, let him be to you as a Gentile and a tax collector. [18] Truly, I say to you, whatever you bind on earth shall be bound in heaven, and whatever you loose on earth shall be loosed in heaven.

Mt 5:22 But I say to you that every one who is angry with his brother shall be liable to judgment; whoever insults his brother shall be liable to the council...

Gal 1:8-9 But even if we, or an angel from heaven, should preach to you a gospel contrary to that which we preached to you, let him be accursed. [9] As we have said before, so now I say again, If any one is preaching to you a gospel contrary to that which you received, let him be accursed.

The Church's authority is final. She has the ability to pronounce "anathema;" She can, through Her officers, pronounce someone accursed. Christ gives the authority, and Paul, acting as bishop, exercises it.

1 Thess 5:12-13 But we beseech you, brethren, to respect those who labor among you and are over you in the Lord and admonish you, [13] and to esteem them very highly in love because of their work. Be at peace among yourselves.

Heb 13:17 Obey your leaders and submit to them; for they are keeping watch over your souls, as men who will have to give account. Let them do this joyfully, and not sadly, for that would be of no advantage to you

Do you obey leaders or swap churches?

1 Tim 4:11-16 Command and teach these things. [12] Let no one despise your youth, but set the believers an example in speech and conduct, in love, in faith, in purity. [13] Till I come, attend to the public reading of scripture, to preaching, to teaching. [14] Do not neglect the gift you have, which was given you by prophetic utterance when the council of elders laid their hands upon you. [15] Practice these duties, devote yourself to them, so that all may see your progress. [16] Take heed to yourself and to your teaching; hold to that, for by so doing you will save both yourself and your hearers.

Authority is passed on through imposition of hands.

Lk 22:32 "... but I have prayed for you that your faith may not fail; and when you have turned again, strengthen your brethren."

In Luke 22, Christ prays for Kephas. The "you" is singular.

Tit 1:7-11 For a bishop, as God's steward, must be blameless; he must not be arrogant or quick-tempered or a drunkard or violent or greedy for gain, ⁸ but hospitable, a lover of goodness, master of himself, upright, holy, and self-controlled; ⁹ he must hold firm to the sure word as taught, so that he may be able to give instruction in sound doctrine and also to confute those who contradict it. ¹⁰ For there are many insubordinate men, empty talkers and deceivers, especially the circumcision party; ¹¹ they must be silenced, since they are upsetting whole families by teaching for base gain what they have no right to teach.

Tit 2:15 Declare these things; exhort and reprove with all authority. Let no one disregard you.

Does your church have bishops? Do you permit them all authority over you? The bishop is God's steward. A steward guards and distributes with equity and justice the master's belongings to the household. Only bishops are called stewards of God.

Rom 13:1-7 Let every person be subject to the governing authorities. For there is no authority except from God, and those that exist have been instituted by God. ² Therefore he who resists the authorities resists what God has appointed, and those who resist will incur judgment. ³ For rulers are not a terror to good conduct, but to bad. Would you have no fear of him who is in authority? Then do what is good, and you will receive his approval, ⁴ for he is God's servant for your good. But if you do wrong, be afraid, for he does not bear the sword in vain; he is the servant of God to execute his wrath on the wrongdoer. ⁵ Therefore one must be subject, not only to avoid God's wrath but also for the sake of conscience. ⁶ For the same reason you also pay taxes, for the authorities are ministers of God, attending to this very thing. ⁷ Pay all of them their dues, taxes to whom taxes are due, revenue to whom revenue is due, respect to whom respect is due, honor to whom honor is due.

Tit 1:13-14 This testimony is true. Therefore rebuke them sharply, that they may be sound in the faith, ¹⁴ instead of giving heed to Jewish myths or to commands of men who reject the truth.

Tit 3:8-10 The saying is sure. I desire you to insist on these things, so that those who have believed in God may be careful to apply themselves to good deeds; these are excellent and profitable to men. ⁹ But avoid stupid controversies, genealogies, dissensions, and quarrels over the law, for they are unprofitable and futile. ¹⁰ As for a man who is factious, after admonishing him once or twice, have nothing more to do with him...

Heb 13:7 Remember your leaders, those who spoke to you the word of God; consider the outcome of their life, and imitate their faith.

If everyone can interpret Scripture on their own, of what use are leaders, bishops, people who admonish?

Lk 10:16 "He who hears you hears me, and he who rejects you rejects me, and he who rejects me rejects him who sent me."

1 Thess 1:5 for our gospel came to you not only in word, but also in power and in the Holy Spirit and with full conviction. You know what kind of men we proved to be among you for your sake.

1 Tim 6:2-4 Those who have believing masters must not be disrespectful on the ground that they are brethren; rather they must serve all the better since those who benefit by their service are believers and beloved. Teach and urge these duties. ³ If any one teaches otherwise and does not agree with the sound words of our Lord Jesus Christ and the teaching which accords with godliness, ⁴ he is puffed up with conceit, he knows nothing; he has a morbid craving for controversy and for disputes about words, which produce envy, dissension, slander, base suspicions,

Mt 7:24 "Every one then who hears these words of mine and does them will be like a wise man who built his house upon the rock..."

Mt 16:18 And I tell you, you are Peter, and on this rock I will build my church, and the powers of death shall not prevail against it.

Jn 14:16-18, 26 And I will pray the Father, and he will give you another Counselor, to be with you for ever, ¹⁷ even the Spirit of truth, whom the world cannot receive, because it neither sees him nor knows him;

Scriptural Catholicism — Church

you know him, for he dwells with you, and will be in you. [18] "I will not leave you desolate; I will come to you. [1].... But the Counselor, the Holy Spirit, whom the Father will send in my name, he will teach you all things, and bring to your remembrance all that I have said to you.

Again, Christ's word in John are to the Apostles alone - not to all disciples.

Is 35:8 And a highway shall be there, and it shall be called the Holy Way; the unclean shall not pass over it, and fools shall not err therein.

Scripture attests to an infallible Church.

Jn 16:13 When the Spirit of truth comes, he will guide you into all the truth; for he will not speak on his own authority but whatever he hears he will speak, and he will declare to you the things that are to come.

Development of Doctrine

Jn 16:12-15 "I have yet many things to say to you, but you cannot bear them now. [13] When the Spirit of truth comes, he will guide you into all the truth; for he will not speak on his own authority, but whatever he hears he will speak, and he will declare to you the things that are to come. [14] He will glorify me, for he will take what is mine and declare it to you. [15] All that the Father has is mine; therefore I said that he will take what is mine and declare it to you.

There were many things yet to be revealed, but Christ did not reveal them all to the Apostles even at the Last Supper. Instead, He promises that the Spirit would reveal that fullness of truth to the Apostles, for it is only to the Apostles that He addresses these words.

Jn 13:6 He came to Simon Peter; and Peter said to him, "Lord, do you wash my feet?" [7] Jesus answered him, "What I am doing you do not know now, but afterward you will understand."

Mt 13:52 And he said to them, "Therefore every scribe who has been trained for the kingdom of heaven is like a householder who brings out of his treasure what is new and what is old."

Mk 4:20 But those that were sown upon the good soil are the ones who hear the word and accept it and bear fruit, thirtyfold and sixtyfold and a hundredfold."

Jn 15:2-3, 16 Every branch of mine that bears no fruit, he takes away, and every branch that does bear fruit he prunes, that it may bear more fruit. [3] You are already made clean by the word which I have spoken to you. [4] Abide in me, and I in you. As the branch cannot bear fruit by itself, unless it abides in the vine, neither can you, unless you abide in me... You did not choose me, but I chose you and appointed you that you should go and bear fruit and that your fruit should abide; so that whatever you ask the Father in my name, he may give it to you.

This is said to the Apostles at the Last Supper. They are told that they are to "bear fruit," and already know that they who are "scribe(s) trained for the kingdom of heaven" must bear fruit as scribes do - by making explicit the fullness of truth which is revealed through Jesus Christ.

Eph 3:9-10 and to make all men see what is the plan of the mystery hidden for ages in God who created all things; [10] that through the church the manifold wisdom of God might now be made known to the principalities and powers in the heavenly places.

Just as a tree grows from a seed, so does the seeds of truth planted by Christ grow into the ripened fullness revealed by the Church, through whom the plan of salvation is revealed.

Lk 22:29-30 and I assign to you, as my Father assigned to me, a kingdom, [30] that you may eat and drink at my table in my kingdom, and sit on thrones judging the twelve tribes of Israel.

Christ speaks to the Apostles only.

Rev 2:11 He who has an ear, let him hear what the Spirit says to the churches.

Eph 4:11-12 And his gifts were that some should be apostles, some prophets, some evangelists, some pastors and teachers, [12] to equip the saints for the work of ministry, for building up the body of Christ...

Why have pastors and teachers if Scripture interprets itself?

Acts 15:1-2 But some men came down from Judea and were teaching the brethren, "Unless you are circumcised according to the custom of Moses, you cannot be saved." ² And when Paul and Barnabas had no small dissension and debate with them, Paul and Barnabas and some of the others were appointed to go up to Jerusalem to the apostles and the elders about this question

In Acts 15 and 16, the Council did not appeal to Scripture alone in order to settle the difficulty.

1 Pet 2:13-20 Be subject for the Lord's sake to every human institution, whether it be to the emperor as supreme, ¹⁴ or to governors as sent by him to punish those who do wrong and to praise those who do right. ¹⁵ For it is God's will that by doing right you should put to silence the ignorance of foolish men. ¹⁶ Live as free men, yet without using your freedom as a pretext for evil; but live as servants of God. ¹⁷ Honor all men. Love the brotherhood. Fear God. Honor the emperor.
¹⁸ Servants, be submissive to your masters with all respect, not only to the kind and gentle but also to the overbearing. ¹⁹ For one is approved if, mindful of God, he endures pain while suffering unjustly. ²⁰ For what credit is it, if when you do wrong and are beaten for it you take it patiently? But if when you do right and suffer for it you take it patiently, you have God's approval.

The question is not one of whether or not the consecrated successors always act without sin, rather, it is a question of authority. Scripture commands obedience even to human authority. How much more obedience is due to the divinely instituted authority of the bishops, who are the consecrated successors to the Apostles and to the Pope, who is the Vicar of Jesus Christ Himself?

Jude 1:8,10-11 Yet in like manner these men in their dreamings defile the flesh, reject authority, and revile the glorious ones.... But these men revile whatever they do not understand, and by those things that they know by instinct as irrational animals do, they are destroyed. ¹¹ Woe to them! For they walk in the way of Cain, and abandon themselves for the sake of gain to Balaam's error, and perish in Korah's rebellion.

Jude condemns those who follow after the "rebellion of Korah" - Korah and his followers were condemned and punished by God for their rebellion against the priests who had been appointed to preside over the priestly nation of Israel.

Num 16:1-3 Now Korah the son of Izhar, son of Kohath, son of Levi, and Dathan and Abiram the sons of Eliab, and On the son of Peleth, sons of Reuben, ² took men; and they rose up before Moses, with a number of the people of Israel, two hundred and fifty leaders of the congregation, chosen from the assembly, well-known men; ³ and they assembled themselves together against Moses and against Aaron, and said to them, "You have gone too far! For all the congregation are holy, every one of them, and the LORD is among them; why then do you exalt yourselves above the assembly of the LORD?"

Korah's words sound eerily similar to the words Martin Luther used against the Pope.

Num 16: 4-11,28-33 When Moses heard it, he fell on his face; ⁵ and he said to Korah and all his company, "In the morning the LORD will show who is his, and who is holy, and will cause him to come near to him; him whom he will choose he will cause to come near to him. ⁶ Do this: take censers, Korah and all his company; ⁷ put fire in them and put incense upon them before the LORD tomorrow, and the man whom the LORD chooses shall be the holy one. You have gone too far, sons of Levi!" ⁸ And Moses said to Korah, "Hear now, you sons of Levi: ⁹ is it too small a thing for you that the God of Israel has separated you from the congregation of Israel, to bring you near to himself, to do service in the tabernacle of the LORD, and to stand before the congregation to minister to them; ¹⁰ and that he has brought you near him, and all your brethren the sons of Levi with you? And would you seek the priesthood also? ¹¹ Therefore it is against the LORD that you and all your company have gathered together; what is Aaron that you murmur against him?"... And Moses said, "Hereby you shall know that the LORD has sent me to do all these works, and that it has not been of my own accord. ²⁹ If these men die the common death of all men, or if they are visited by the fate of all men, then the LORD has not sent me. ³⁰ But if the LORD creates something new, and the ground opens its mouth, and swallows them up, with all that belongs to them, and they go down alive into Sheol, then you shall know that these men have despised the LORD."
³¹ And as he finished speaking all these words, the ground under them split asunder; ³² and the earth opened its mouth and swallowed them up, with their households and all the men that belonged to Korah and all their goods. ³³ So they and all that belonged to them went down alive into Sheol; and the earth closed over them, and they perished from the midst of the assembly.

The assembly of the Lord has always had a heirarchy.

1 Jn 2:27 but the anointing which you received from him abides in you, and you have no need that any one should teach you; as his anointing teaches you about everything, and is true, and is no lie, just as it has taught you, abide in him.

John writes of the anointing of baptism and confirmation, anointing received through the Body of Christ, the Church. Not just anyone can teach, but only those commanded by Christ, that is, the Apostles and their successors.

Mt 28:20 ... teaching them to observe all that I have commanded you; and lo, I am with you always, to the close of the age."

Rev 2:16 Repent then. If not, I will come to you soon and war against them with the sword of my mouth.

Acts 16:1-5 And he came also to Derbe and to Lystra. A disciple was there, named Timothy, the son of a Jewish woman who was a believer; but his father was a Greek. ² He was well spoken of by the brethren at Lystra and Iconium. ³ Paul wanted Timothy to accompany him; and he took him and circumcised him because of the Jews that were in those places, for they all knew that his father was a Greek. ⁴ As they went on their way through the cities, they delivered to them for observance the decisions which had been reached by the apostles and elders who were at Jerusalem. ⁵ So the churches were strengthened in the faith, and they increased in numbers daily.

Note that Paul and Timothy delivered the decisions reached by the apostles and the presbyters, who were given office by the imposition of hands.

Acts 15:28 For it has seemed good to the Holy Spirit and to us to lay upon you no greater burden than these necessary things:

The apostles then sent Paul and Silas...

Acts 16:4 As they went on their way through the cities, they delivered to them for observance the decisions which had been reached by the apostles and elders who were at Jerusalem.

The teachings were "necessary things," and could not be rejected. Note the phrasing: the Holy Spirit and the officers of the Church made the decisions on these necessities jointly. What they bind is held bound.

1 Thess 2:6-7 nor did we seek glory from men, whether from you or from others, though we might have made demands as apostles of Christ. ⁷ But we were gentle among you, like a nurse taking care of her children.

Phil 1:27-28 Only let your manner of life be worthy of the gospel of Christ, so that whether I come and see you or am absent, I may hear of you that you stand firm in one spirit, with one mind striving side by side for the faith of the gospel, ²⁸ and not frightened in anything by your opponents. This is a clear omen to them of their destruction, but of your salvation, and that from God.

Phil 2:2 complete my joy by being of the same mind, having the same love, being in full accord and of one mind.

Is 59:19-21 So they shall fear the name of the Lord from the west, and his glory from the rising of the sun; for he will come like a rushing stream, which the wind of the Lord drives. ²⁰ "And he will come to Zion as Redeemer, to those in Jacob who turn from transgression, says the Lord. ²¹ "And as for me, this is my covenant with them, says the Lord: my spirit which is upon you, and my words which I have put in your mouth, shall not depart out of your mouth, or out of the mouth of your children, or out of the mouth of your children's children, says the Lord, from this time forth and for evermore.

Papal Authority

The teaching office of the bishop of Rome, founded by Christ through Peter, is imbued with the peculiar and specific dignity and authority granted to Peter by Jesus Christ. Specifically, the man who is consecrated to the office first established by Christ in Peter has the special gift and guidance of the Holy Spirit, so that, no matter what private opinion he may hold, he may never teach to the whole Church from the chair, i.e., with the authority, of Peter on a matter of faith and morals that which is error. God cares for the Body of Christ through the bishop of Rome, who is the temporal head of the Church, Vicar of Christ, guided by the Holy Spirit until such time as Jesus returns to rule. (CCC 2, 440-443, 552-556, 765, 816, 858-860, 881, 981, 1444)

Current misunderstandings: Those who live according to sola scriptura, *along with every other person, believer or no, who has difficulty bowing to concrete authority, refuse to believe the Pope, a self-acknowledged sinner in need of salvation, could possibly carry the authority of Jesus Christ, or be guided infallibly by the Holy Spirit. Yet, the same individual simultaneously tends to believe that he can individually be led by the Holy Spirit and test a teaching against his own apparently infallible conscience, for a* sola scriptura *believer cannot test the spirit which speaks Scriptural doctrine to him against anything but his own conscience.*

Acts 1:15-17,20-22 In those days Peter stood up among the brethren (the company of persons was in all about a hundred and twenty), and said, [16] "Brethren, the scripture had to be fulfilled, which the Holy Spirit spoke beforehand by the mouth of David, concerning Judas who was guide to those who arrested Jesus. [17] For he was numbered among us, and was allotted his share in this ministry.... [20] For it is written in the book of Psalms, 'Let his habitation become desolate, and let there be no one to live in it'; and 'His office let another take.' [21] So one of the men who have accompanied us during all the time that the Lord Jesus went in and out among us, [22] beginning from the baptism of John until the day when he was taken up from us—one of these men must become with us a witness to his resurrection."

All the disciples accepted Peter's comparison without question or dissent. They saw the apostles as holding offices in the kingdom of God, offices distinct from that of the normal disciple. What sort of office did Peter hold?

The Rock

Jn 1:49-51 Nathana-el answered him, "Rabbi, you are the Son of God! You are the King of Israel!" [50] Jesus answered him, "Because I said to you, I saw you under the fig tree, do you believe? You shall see greater things than these." [51] And he said to him, "Truly, truly, I say to you, you will see heaven opened, and the angels of God ascending and descending upon the Son of man."

Mt 16:16-19 Simon Peter replied, "You are the Christ, the Son of the living God." And Jesus answered him, "Blessed are you, Simon Bar-Jona! For flesh and blood has not revealed this to you, but my Father who is in heaven. [18] And I tell you, you are Peter, and on this rock I will build my church, and the powers of death shall not prevail against it. [19] I will give you the keys of the kingdom of heaven, and whatever you bind on earth shall be bound in heaven, and whatever you loose on earth shall be loosed in heaven."

Note that Nathanael has the same revelation Simon does, but Jesus does not call Nathanael's revelation Rock, he doesn't change Nathanael's name, nor does he bless Nathanael for his revelation. However, when Simon speaks the same idea, Christ responds in a radically different way. Simon says to Jesus, "You are the Messiah," and Jesus replies to Simon "You are the Rock." Each names the other. Furthermore, Christ blesses Simon with a three-part blessing in a manner similar to the Old Testament blessings a father might give his son, each blessing followed by a short explanation of the blessing. Simon is called "blessed," he is given a new name "Rock," and he is given the keys to the kingdom of heaven by the King of the House of David. James Akins' recognition of the three-fold blessing can be found in Pat Madrid's Surprised By Truth, *pp. 64-69.*

God alone is the Rock upon which everything is founded. But the word "rock" is also used to refer to God's special presence in the life of a faithful follower. With the exception of Is 54:10-17, this next section is a quick summary of several, though not all, of the Scriptural arguments presented in the book "Jesus, Peter, and the Keys,"

1 Pet 2:5 and like living stones be yourselves built into a spiritual house, to be a holy priesthood, to offer spiritual sacrifices acceptable to God through Jesus Christ.

Is 28:16 therefore thus says the Lord GOD, "Behold, I am laying in Zion for a foundation a stone, a tested stone, a precious cornerstone, of a sure foundation: 'He who believes will not be in haste.'

Is 51:1-2 "Hearken to me, you who pursue deliverance, you who seek the LORD; look to the rock from which you were hewn, and to the quarry from which you were digged. [2] Look to Abraham your father and to Sarah who bore you; for when he was but one I called him, and I blessed him and made him many.

While Scripture calls faithful followers "living stones," only two people in all of Scripture both had their name changed by God and were called "rock" - Abraham and Peter. Abraham is called the rock from which the Old Covenant people of God were hewn. His name was also changed by God (Gen 17:5). Abraham and Peter - upon each was founded a new people, one in God the Father, the second in Jesus Christ, the second people founded within the first, as the Son is begotten eternally by the Father. It is not their humanity which makes them rocks, but the Holy Spirit working within them in a unique way.

Christ's words to Simon, now Peter, recall the Old Testament promise made by God to His people. This promise is echoed to Simon - the Rock who is the Lord would be laid within. God spoke not just of a man, but of a mighty edifice - the Church, whose sons will be taught by God:

Is 54:10-17 For the mountains may depart and the hills be removed, but my steadfast love shall not depart from you, and my covenant of peace shall not be removed, says the LORD, who has compassion on you. [11] "O afflicted one, storm-tossed, and not comforted, behold, I will set your stones in antimony, and lay your foundations with sapphires. [12] I will make your pinnacles of agate, your gates of carbuncles, and all your wall of precious stones. [13] All your sons shall be taught by the LORD, and great shall be the prosperity of your sons. [14] In righteousness you shall be established; you shall be far from oppression, for you shall not fear; and from terror, for it shall not come near you. [15] If any one stirs up strife, it is not from me; whoever stirs up strife with you shall fall because of you. [16] Behold, I have created the smith who blows the fire of coals, and produces a weapon for its purpose. I have also created the ravager to destroy; [17] no weapon that is fashioned against you shall prosper, and you shall confute every tongue that rises against you in judgment. This is the heritage of the servants of the LORD and their vindication from me, says the LORD."

Jn 1:42 He brought him to Jesus. Jesus looked at him, and said, "So you are Simon the son of John? You shall be called Cephas" (which means Peter).

Gal 2:7,9 but on the contrary, when they saw that I had been entrusted with the gospel to the uncircumcised, just as Peter had been entrusted with the gospel to the circumcised... and when they perceived the grace that was given to me, James and Cephas and John, who were reputed to be pillars...

Mt 7:24 "Every one then who hears these words of mine and does them will be like a wise man who built his house upon the rock..."

Jesus says this nine chapters before He founds His Church on he who He names "Rock." "Kephas" is the Aramaic for rock. Christ spoke primarily Aramaic, not Greek. Greek has feminine and masculine nouns, Aramaic does not. The Greek word for "kephas" is the feminine noun "petra." "Petros" is the masculine form of the word. Christ originally said, "You are kephas and upon this kephas I will build my church" while the Greek translation says "You are petros and upon this petra I will build my church"; the Greek word form changes because it is not appropriate to name Peter with a feminine noun. Some say the use of two different words in the Greek demonstrate a difference in Christ's meaning, "petros" meaning "little rock [Peter]" and "petra" meaning "massive rock [Peter's faith]." However, first-century Greek did not distinguish between "petros" and "petra," except in poetry. If Christ wished to refer to Peter as "little rock," the correct translation from the Aramaic to the Greek would be "lithos," not "petros." Yet even had Christ used "lithos" to refer to Peter (He didn't), it still would have meant nothing. Jesus is called "petra" only three times, but is called "lithos" (little rock) 12 times (e.g. Isaiah 28:16 and 1 Peter 2:6, use "lithos" when referring to Christ, the cornerstone, as does Matthew 21:42,44). Further, Peter calls all believers "lithoi" ("stones") in 1 Peter 2:5.

Rom 9:33 as it is written, "Behold, I am laying in Zion a stone that will make men stumble, a rock that will make them fall; and he who believes in him will not be put to shame."

1 Cor 10:4 and all drank the same supernatural drink. For they drank from the supernatural Rock which followed them, and the Rock was Christ.

1 Pet 2:5-8 and like living stones be yourselves built into a spiritual house, to be a holy priesthood, to offer spiritual sacrifices acceptable to God through Jesus Christ. ⁶ For it stands in scripture: "Behold, I am laying in Zion a stone, a cornerstone chosen and precious, and he who believes in him will not be put to shame." ⁷ To you therefore who believe, he is precious, but for those who do not believe, "The very stone which the builders rejected has become the head of the corner," ⁸ and "A stone that will make men stumble, a rock that will make them fall"; for they stumble because they disobey the word, as they were destined to do.

Early Christians' comments on Peter the Rock

The Keys

This explains "rock," but what does it mean to receive the keys to the kingdom? Keys have a two-fold meaning in Jewish culture and Christ intends both meanings.

Is 22:15-24 Thus says the Lord GOD of hosts, "Come, go to this steward, to Shebna, who is over the household, and say to him: ¹⁶ What have you to do here and whom have you here, that you have hewn here a tomb for yourself, you who hew a tomb on the height, and carve a habitation for yourself in the rock? ¹⁷ Behold, the LORD will hurl you away violently, O you strong man. He will seize firm hold on you, ¹⁸ and whirl you round and round, and throw you like a ball into a wide land; there you shall die, and there shall be your splendid chariots, you shame of your master's house. ¹⁹ I will thrust you from your office, and you will be cast down from your station. ²⁰ In that day I will call my servant Eliakim the son of Hilkiah, ²¹ and I will clothe him with your robe, and will bind your girdle on him, and will commit your authority to his hand; and he shall be a father to the inhabitants of Jerusalem and to the house of Judah. ²² And I will place on his shoulder the key of the house of David; he shall open, and none shall shut; and he shall shut, and none shall open. ²³ And I will fasten him like a peg in a sure place, and he will become a throne of honor to his father's house. ²⁴ And they will hang on him the whole weight of his father's house, the offspring and issue, every small vessel, from the cups to all the flagons.

Shebna was master of the palace, but Eliakim will replace him, Eliakim will be given the key to the House of David. Being given the keys makes one a master of the household. Did such an office exist in Hebrew or other ancient kingdoms? Yes.

1 Kings 18:3 And Ahab called Obadiah, who was over the household.

2 Kings 18:18 And when they called for the king, there came out to them Eliakim the son of Hilkiah, who was over the household

2 Kings 15:5 And Jotham the king's son was over the household, governing the people of the land.

How great was their authority?

Gen 41:40-44 "...you shall be over my house, and all my people shall order themselves as you command; only as regards the throne will I be greater than you." ⁴¹ And Pharaoh said to Joseph, "Behold, I have set you over all the land of Egypt." ⁴² Then Pharaoh took his signet ring from his hand and put it on Joseph's hand, and arrayed him in garments of fine linen, and put a gold chain about his neck; ⁴³ and he made him to ride in his second chariot; and they cried before him, "Bow the knee!" Thus he set him over all the land of Egypt. ⁴⁴ Moreover Pharaoh said to Joseph, "I am Pharaoh, and without your consent no man shall lift up hand or foot in all the land of Egypt."

Joseph had the power to bind and loose in Egypt. He commanded the respect commanded by Pharoah. But keys not only signified the master of the palace, a key was also given to a scribe upon his investiture, to show that he had authority to interpret Scripture.

Lk 11:52 Woe to you lawyers! for you have taken away the key of knowledge; you did not enter yourselves, and you hindered those who were entering.

Rev 1:17-18 When I saw him, I fell at his feet as though dead. But he laid his right hand upon me, saying, "Fear not, I am the first and the last, ¹⁸ and the living one; I died, and behold I am alive for evermore, and I have the keys of Death and Hades."

In His Revelation to John, Jesus portrays Himself carrying the keys to Death and Hades, but where are the keys to heaven?

Early Christians' comments on Papal Authority I
Early Christians' comments on Papal Authority II

Thus, the keys themselves have a two-fold meaning and power. What other evidence do we have that Peter was held in special regard?

The Shepherd

Lk 22:31-32 "Simon, Simon, behold, Satan demanded to have you, that he might sift you like wheat, ³² but I have prayed for you that your faith may not fail; and when you have turned again, strengthen your brethren."

Only Peter is given the command to strengthen his brethren. Christ is the good shepherd. He intends one flock, one shepherd. He is the Bridegroom. He intends one family, not multiple families.

Jn 10:11,16 I am the good shepherd. The good shepherd lays down his life for the sheep... And I have other sheep, that are not of this fold; I must bring them also, and they will heed my voice. So there shall be one flock, one shepherd.

Jn 21:15-19 When they had finished breakfast, Jesus said to Simon Peter, "Simon, son of John, do you love me more than these?" He said to him, "Yes, Lord; you know that I love you." He said to him, "Feed my lambs." ¹⁶ A second time he said to him, "Simon, son of John, do you love me?" He said to him, "Yes, Lord; you know that I love you." He said to him, "Tend my sheep." ¹⁷ He said to him the third time, "Simon, son of John, do you love me?" Peter was grieved because he said to him the third time, "Do you love me?" And he said to him, "Lord, you know everything; you know that I love you." Jesus said to him, "Feed my sheep. ¹⁸ Truly, truly, I say to you, when you were young, you girded yourself and walked where you would; but when you are old, you will stretch out your hands, and another will gird you and carry you where you do not wish to go." ¹⁹ (This he said to show by what death he was to glorify God.) And after this he said to him, "Follow me."

Kings were often referred to as "shepherds of the people" by sources ranging from Homer (7th century BC) through Hesychius (5th century AD) and Holy Scripture follows this tradition. It is claimed that here Christ was merely allowing Peter to make up for his three-fold rejection, and Christ was certainly doing that. However, He was also giving Peter a command to spread the Gospel as a shepherd, a command whose emphasis is uniquely directed to Peter.

Num 27:16-17 "Let the Lord, the God of the spirits of all flesh, appoint a man over the congregation, ¹⁷ who shall go out before them and come in before them, who shall lead them out and bring them in; that the congregation of the Lord may not be as sheep which have no shepherd."

2 Sam 5:2 In times past, when Saul was king over us, it was you that led out and brought in Israel; and the Lord said to you, 'You shall be shepherd of my people Israel, and you shall be prince over Israel.'"

Jer 31:10 "Hear the word of the Lord, O nations, and declare it in the coastlands afar off; say, 'He who scattered Israel will gather him, and will keep him as a shepherd keeps his flock.'"

Ezek 34:23-24 And I will set up over them one shepherd, my servant David, and he shall feed them: he shall feed them and be their shepherd. ²⁴ And I, the Lord, will be their God, and my servant David shall be prince among them; I, the Lord, have spoken.

Zech 10:2-3 For the teraphim utter nonsense, and the diviners see lies; the dreamers tell false dreams, and give empty consolation. Therefore the people wander like sheep; they are afflicted for want of a shepherd. ³ "My anger is hot against the shepherds, and I will punish the leaders; for the Lord of hosts cares for his flock, the house of Judah, and will make them like his proud steed in battle.

But the command to shepherd is not all:

Rev 2:26-27 He who conquers and who keeps my works until the end, I will give him power over the nations, ²⁷ and he shall rule them with a rod of iron, as when earthen pots are broken in pieces, even as I myself have received power from my Father...

The word "poimainein" used in John 21:16 is also used here in Revelation 2:27, where it means "rule." Note that of the 11 times "poimanao" is used in the New

Testament, it means "rule" or "rule and feed" in ten of them. This is also true in the Old Testament, where the verb is used 50 times. In every occurrence, it replaces the Hebrew word "raah," which mean "feed, tend, or rule." For instance, the word translated "break" below is often less-well translated as "rule" and is "poimainein" in the original.

Psalm 2:9 You shall break them with a rod of iron, and dash them in pieces like a potter's vessel."

Thus, Christ's use of verbs reinforces the image of a ruling "shepherd." While Peter was not the first to notice Christ on the seashore prior to this scene, he was the first to leap towards Christ, diving into the sea

Mt 10:2-4 The names of the twelve apostles are these: first, Simon, who is called Peter, and Andrew his brother; James the son of Zebedee, and John his brother; [3] Philip and Bartholomew; Thomas and Matthew the tax collector; James the son of Alphaeus, and Thaddaeus; [4] Simon the Cananaean, and Judas Iscariot, who betrayed him.

Acts 5:29 But Peter and the apostles answered, "We must obey God rather than men..."

Gal 2:7 but on the contrary, when they saw that I had been entrusted with the gospel to the uncircumcised, just as Peter had been entrusted with the gospel to the circumcised.

Peter is first in rank among the Apostles.

Early Christians' comments on Petrine Primacy

Gal 1:15-20 But when he who had set me apart before I was born, and had called me through his grace, [16] was pleased to reveal his Son to me, in order that I might preach him among the Gentiles, I did not confer with flesh and blood, [17] nor did I go up to Jerusalem to those who were apostles before me, but I went away into Arabia; and again I returned to Damascus. [18] Then after three years I went up to Jerusalem to visit Cephas, and remained with him fifteen days. [19] But I saw none of the other apostles except James the Lord's brother. [20] (In what I am writing to you, before God, I do not lie!)

Jude 3 contend for the faith which was once for all delivered to the saints.

Peter (no longer Simon, but always Peter) ranks at the head of the Apostles in the list of the saints. But can anyone have the authority claimed for the Pope?

Mt 23:1-3 Then said Jesus to the crowds and to his disciples, [2] "The scribes and the Pharisees sit on Moses' seat; [3] so practice and observe whatever they tell you, but not what they do; for they preach, but do not practice..."

Early Christians' comments on Peter Successors

Even though the scribes and Pharisees are called "fools," "hypocrites," "blind guides," "vipers" and "whitewashed tombs" in Matthew 23, Christ uses the imperative tense to command his disciples to do what they say. They occupy "the seat of Moses," an authoritative position of power whose establishment is not described in Scripture, but is established, known and acknowledged through long Jewish oral tradition. The authority and validity of this position is explicitly supported by Christ. The same person who disputed with the Pharisees and scribes on cleanliness laws, Sabbath laws, and fasting laws told the people to obey those who occupied positions of theological authority.

Acts 5:1-4 But a man named Ananias with his wife Sapphira sold a piece of property, [2] and with his wife's knowledge he kept back some of the proceeds, and brought only a part and laid it at the apostles' feet. [3] But Peter said, "Ananias, why has Satan filled your heart to lie to the Holy Spirit and to keep back part of the proceeds of the land? [4] While it remained unsold, did it not remain your own? And after it was sold, was it not at your disposal? How is it that you have contrived this deed in your heart? You have not lied to men but to God."[5] When Ananias heard these words, he fell down and died. And great fear came upon all who heard of it.

Ananias and Sapphira paid the ultimate penalty upon Peter's authority. Their lie to the Apostles was judged by Peter to be a lie against God, literally a mortal sin.

Acts 2:14-15 ff But Peter, standing with the eleven, lifted up his voice and addressed them, "Men of Judea and all who dwell in Jerusalem, let this be known to you, and give ear to my words. [15] For these men are not drunk, as you suppose, since it is only the third hour of the day.."

Peter preaches the first sermon in Jerusalem.

Acts 3:4-6 And Peter directed his gaze at him, with John, and said, "Look at us." [5] And he fixed his attention upon them, expecting to receive something from them. [6] But Peter said, "I have no silver and gold, but I give you what I have; in the name of Jesus Christ of Nazareth, walk."

Peter performs the first miracle after Christ's resurrection.

Acts 4:8-13 Then Peter, filled with the Holy Spirit, said to them, "Rulers of the people and elders, [9] if we are being examined today concerning a good deed done to a cripple, by what means this man has been healed, [10] be it known to you all, and to all the people of Israel, that by the name of Jesus Christ of Nazareth, whom you crucified, whom God raised from the dead, by him this man is standing before you well. [11] This is the stone which was rejected by you builders, but which has become the head of the corner. [12] And there is salvation in no one else, for there is no other name under heaven given among men by which we must be saved." [13] Now when they saw the boldness of Peter and John, and perceived that they were uneducated, common men, they wondered; and they recognized that they had been with Jesus.

Peter puts the Sanhedrin on trial for crucifying the Lord. He has the power they formerly wielded.

Acts 8:14-17 Now when the apostles at Jerusalem heard that Samaria had received the word of God, they sent to them Peter and John, [15] who came down and prayed for them that they might receive the Holy Spirit; [16] for it had not yet fallen on any of them, but they had only been baptized in the name of the Lord Jesus. [17] Then they laid their hands on them and they received the Holy Spirit.

Peter confirms the Samaritans, half-Jews whose fathers married outside Israel, into the Christian faith.

Acts 10:25-28,34-35 When Peter entered, Cornelius met him and fell down at his feet and worshiped him. [26] But Peter lifted him up, saying, "Stand up; I too am a man." [27] And as he talked with him, he went in and found many persons gathered; [28] and he said to them, "You yourselves know how unlawful it is for a Jew to associate with or to visit any one of another nation; but God has shown me that I should not call any man common or unclean... And Peter opened his mouth and said: "Truly I perceive that God shows no partiality, [35] but in every nation any one who fears him and does what is right is acceptable to him.

Peter admits the Gentiles to the faith. In short, it was through Peter that the first Jews, the first half-Jews, and the first Gentiles entered the Church. In Pope St. Clement's letter to the church at Corinth AD 96 (5:3-7), Clement appeals to the memory of the two martyrs, Peter and Paul, and explicitly states that the Apostles appointed bishops and made provisions for their succession, adding that "our sin is not small if we eject from the episcopate those who have blamelessly and holily offered its sacrifices [i.e. the Eucharist]" (44:4). He then exhorts the Corinthians to re-instate the clergy they had ejected from their ministry since the priesthood, like the Gospel itself, is something established by Christ and handed down from the Apostles. "But if some be disobedient to the words which have been spoken by him [Christ] through us, let them know that they will entangle themselves in transgression and no little danger... So you will afford us great joy and happiness if you are obedient to what we have written through the Holy Spirit" (59:1, 63:2). Eusebius (AD 260-339) "I have evidence that in many churches this epistle [Clement to the Corinthians] was read loud to the assembled worshippers in early days, as it is in our own."

The Apostle John was alive at the time of the writing of this letter. Even though John, a living witness to, and the beloved disciple of, Jesus Christ was available and closer to Corinth than was Clement, Bishop of Rome, yet the Corinthians did not ask the Apostle to settle their dispute, they sent to Rome for Clement's opinion. And they obeyed Clement's ruling.

The following story should give pause to anyone who claims greater authority than the Bride of Christ, the Body of Christ, who is the household of truth, the Church of the Living God:

Num 16:1-3 Now Korah the son of Izhar, son of Kohath, son of Levi, and Dathan and Abiram the sons of Eliab, and On the son of Peleth, sons of Reuben, [2] took men; and they rose up before Moses, with a number of the people of Israel, two hundred and fifty leaders of the congregation, chosen from the assembly, well-known men; [3] and they assembled themselves together against Moses and against Aaron, and said to them, "You have gone too far! For all the congregation are holy, every one of them, and the LORD is among them; why then do you exalt yourselves above the assembly of the LORD?"

Korah pronounces words eerily similar to the words which came forth from Luther's mouth against the Pope. It should be noted how the rebellion against Moses and Aaron ended:

Num 16:19-35 Then Korah assembled all the congregation against them at the entrance of the tent of meeting. And the glory of the LORD appeared to all the congregation.

⁲⁰ And the LORD said to Moses and to Aaron, ²¹ "Separate yourselves from among this congregation, that I may consume them in a moment." ²² And they fell on their faces, and said, "O God, the God of the spirits of all flesh, shall one man sin, and wilt thou be angry with all the congregation?" ²³ And the LORD said to Moses, ²⁴ "Say to the congregation, Get away from about the dwelling of Korah, Dathan, and Abiram."

²⁵ Then Moses rose and went to Dathan and Abiram; and the elders of Israel followed him. ²⁶ And he said to the congregation, "Depart, I pray you, from the tents of these wicked men, and touch nothing of theirs, lest you be swept away with all their sins." ²⁷ So they got away from about the dwelling of Korah, Dathan, and Abiram; and Dathan and Abiram came out and stood at the door of their tents, together with their wives, their sons, and their little ones. ²⁸ And Moses said, "Hereby you shall know that the LORD has sent me to do all these works, and that it has not been of my own accord. ²⁹ If these men die the common death of all men, or if they are visited by the fate of all men, then the LORD has not sent me. ³⁰ But if the LORD creates something new, and the ground opens its mouth, and swallows them up, with all that belongs to them, and they go down alive into Sheol, then you shall know that these men have despised the LORD."

³¹ And as he finished speaking all these words, the ground under them split asunder; ³² and the earth opened its mouth and swallowed them up, with their households and all the men that belonged to Korah and all their goods. ³³ So they and all that belonged to them went down alive into Sheol; and the earth closed over them, and they perished from the midst of the assembly. ³⁴ And all Israel that were round about them fled at their cry; for they said, "Lest the earth swallow us up!" ³⁵ And fire came forth from the LORD, and consumed the two hundred and fifty men offering the incense.

God has given those who wanted a different church their wish - they now have more churches than they can count. Let us pray the punishment is sufficient.

Tradition

God graciously arranged for the salvation of His people so the whole of His truth and salvific works will be transmitted to all generations. This transmission is guaranteed by the Holy Spirit through the agency of Apostles and their successors, the bishops, and popes. It is also contained and carried within the liturgy, ceremonies, blessings, councils, holy families, and the lives of all holy people, through all of whom the Holy Spirit makes Himself known. Sacred Scripture and Sacred Tradition are two rivers which flow from the same source, the source of Truth who is God alone. Both are treasured, preserved, and guarded as One by the Body of Christ, for they are One in God, who is One. (CCC 80, 83, 84, 95-97, 113, 120, 638, 1124)

Current misunderstandings: Those who follow sola scriptura *theology refuse the authority of all other sources. Since these Christians specifically deny the authority of the Church's Sacred Tradition, they see the guardians of Sacred Tradition as modern-day Pharisees and Scribes. Two passages are used to implicitly associate Roman Catholic leaders with the people who opposed Jesus Christ.*

Mt 15:2-9 "Why do your disciples transgress the tradition of the elders? For they do not wash their hands when they eat." ³ He answered them, "And why do you transgress the commandment of God for the sake of your tradition? ⁴ For God commanded, 'Honor your father and your mother,' and, 'He who speaks evil of father or mother, let him surely die.' ⁵ But you say, 'If any one tells his father or his mother, What you would have gained from me is given to God, he need not honor his father.' ⁶ So, for the sake of your tradition, you have made void the word of God. ⁷ You hypocrites! Well did Isaiah prophesy of you, when he said: ⁸ 'This people honors me with their lips, but their heart is far from me; ⁹ in vain do they worship me, teaching as doctrines the precepts of men.'"

Mk 7:4-13 and when they come from the market place, they do not eat unless they purify themselves; and there are many other traditions which they observe, the washing of cups and pots and vessels of bronze.) ⁵ And the Pharisees and the scribes asked him, "Why do your disciples not live according to the tradition of the elders, but eat with hands defiled?" ⁶ And he said to them, "Well did Isaiah prophesy of you hypocrites, as it is written, 'This people honors me with their lips, but their heart is far from me; ⁷ in vain do they worship me, teaching as doctrines the precepts of men.' ⁸ You leave the commandment of God, and hold fast the tradition of men." ⁹ And he said to them, "You have a fine way of rejecting the commandment of God, in order to keep your tradition! ¹⁰ For Moses said, 'Honor your father and your mother'; and, 'He who speaks evil of father or mother, let him surely die'; ¹¹ but you say, 'If a man tells his father or his mother, What you would have gained from me is Corban' (that is, given to God)— ¹² then you no longer permit him to do anything for his father or mother, ¹³ thus making void the word of God through your tradition which you hand on. And many such things you do."

A careful reading of both passages shows Jesus attacking tradition which breaks covenant ties and the family bond. Human tradition uses God as an excuse to dispense with covenantal duties, but the divine tradition of Scripture honors and nourishes covenantal duties, it does not destroy them. An ironical sidenote: in the March/April 1997 edition of Envoy, pp. 44-45, Mark Shea points out that Mark 7:6-8, the verses most often used against Sacred Tradition, show Christ quoting a version of Is 29:13 found only in the Greek, i.e., the Septuagint version of Isaiah - the Hebrew Scripture version of Isaiah used by sola scriptura *Christians does not contain the verse. (See "The Canon of Scripture" below).*

Deut 32:7 Remember the days of old, consider the years of many generations; ask your father, and he will show you; your elders, and they will tell you.

Psalm 44:1 We have heard with our ears, O God, our fathers have told us, what deeds thou didst perform in their days, in the days of old...

Psalm 78:2-3 I will open my mouth in a parable; I will utter dark sayings from of old, ³ things that we have heard and known, that our fathers have told us.

Are you worshipping as the first disciples worshipped? Do you believe what they believed? How do you know? Scripture relates only the first 50 years of discipleship. Have you read the works of the early disciples *of the Church in order to find out what they believed?*

1 Cor 11:2 I commend you because you remember me in everything and maintain the traditions even as I have delivered them to you.

The word Paul uses for "tradition" here is precisely the same word Christ used in Matthew.

1 Cor 4:16 I urge you, then, be imitators of me.

Phil 4:9 What you have learned and received and heard and seen in me, do; and the God of peace will be with you.

Paul hands on binding tradition, oral tradition. Paul tells us to imitate him. He teaches as Christ taught - in the ancient Jewish oral tradition.

Acts 15:22-23,27-28 Then it seemed good to the apostles and the elders, with the whole church, to choose men from among them and send them to Antioch with Paul and Barnabas. They sent Judas, called Barsabbas, and Silas, leading men among the brethren, ²³with the following letter: "...We have therefore sent Judas and Silas, who themselves will tell you the same things by word of mouth. ²⁸ For it has seemed good to the Holy Spirit and to us..."

The words inspired by God and sent by the Church required not only a written, but also an oral, witness.

Is 59:21 "And as for me, this is my covenant with them, says the LORD: my spirit which is upon you, and my words which I have put in your mouth, shall not depart out of your mouth, or out of the mouth of your children, or out of the mouth of your children's children, says the LORD, from this time forth and for evermore."

Rev 3:3 Remember then what you received and heard; keep that, and repent.

While Scripture speaks of what was written, it also constantly refers to Christ fulfilling what was spoken:

Mt 1:22-23 All this took place to fulfil what the Lord had spoken by the prophet: "Behold, a virgin shall conceive and bear a son, and his name shall be called Emmanuel" (which means, God with us).

Mt 2:15,17-18,23 This was to fulfil what the Lord had spoken by the prophet, "Out of Egypt have I called my son...." Then was fulfilled what was spoken by the prophet Jeremiah: "A voice was heard in Ramah, wailing and loud lamentation, Rachel weeping for her children; she refused to be consoled, because they were no more."... And he went and dwelt in a city called Nazareth, that what was spoken by the prophets might be fulfilled, "He shall be called a Nazarene."

Mt 4:14 that what was spoken by the prophet Isaiah might be fulfilled...

Mt 8:17 This was to fulfil what was spoken by the prophet Isaiah, "He took our infirmities and bore our diseases."

Mt 12:17 This was to fulfil what was spoken by the prophet Isaiah:

Mt 13:14,35 With them indeed is fulfilled the prophecy of Isaiah which says:
'You shall indeed hear but never understand, and you shall indeed see but never perceive... This was to fulfil what was spoken by the prophet: "I will open my mouth in parables, I will utter what has been hidden since the foundation of the world."

Mt 21:4-5 This took place to fulfil what was spoken by the prophet, saying, "Tell the daughter of Zion,
Behold, your king is coming to you,
humble, and mounted on an ass,
and on a colt, the foal of an ass."

Mt 27:9-10 Then was fulfilled what had been spoken by the prophet Jeremiah, saying, "And they took the thirty pieces of silver, the price of him on whom a price had been set by some of the sons of Israel,

Rom 10:17 So faith comes from what is heard, and what is heard comes by the preaching of Christ.

2 Thess 2:15 So then, brethren, stand firm and hold to the traditions which you were taught by us, either by word of mouth or by letter.

Heb 4:2 For good news came to us just as to them; but the message which they heard did not benefit them, because it did not meet with faith in the hearers.

Gal 3:2,5 Let me ask you only this: Did you receive the Spirit by works of the law, or by hearing with faith? ⁵ Does he who supplies the Spirit to you and works miracles among you do so by works of the law, or by hearing with faith?

2 Thess 3:6 Now we command you, brethren, in the name of our Lord Jesus Christ, that you keep away from any brother who is living in idleness and not in accord with the tradition that you received from us.

2 Tim 2:2 and what you have heard from me before many witnesses entrust to faithful men who will be able to teach others also.

This oral tradition is to be passed on through faithful men who can themselves pass it on. This tradition was meant to be maintained. It IS maintained.

Jn Chapters 14 and 15 Christ promises the coming of the Spirit and describes how the Church is rooted in Him. The Church will always be led by the Spirit, because she is One with Christ.

Jn 14:26 But the Counselor, the Holy Spirit, whom the Father will send in my name, he will teach you all things, and bring to your remembrance all that I have said to you.

Jn 17:20-21 "I do not pray for these only, but also for those who believe in me through their word, ²¹ that they may all be one; even as thou, Father, art in me, and I in thee, that they also may be in us, so that the world may believe that thou hast sent me."

It is through "their word," the word of the Apostles transmitted both orally and in writing, that we come to believe in Jesus.

2 Jn 12 Though I have much to write to you, I would rather not use paper and ink, but I hope to come to see you and talk with you face to face, so that our joy may be complete.

Jn 16:13 When the Spirit of truth comes, he will guide you into all the truth; for he will not speak on his own authority, but whatever he hears he will speak, and he will declare to you the things that are to come.

Christ's oral teaching is explicitly guaranteed to be guided by the Holy Spirit.

Mt 28:20 teaching them to observe all that I have commanded you; and lo, I am with you always, to the close of the age."

Christ taught only through speech. He wrote nothing (except in sand). He did not command His disciples or

Apostles to write anything, apart from the Book of Revelation. Instead, He commanded his Apostles to teach. Scripture doesn't say the Apostles had the authority to write. Only Sacred Tradition testifies to their authority to write Christ's teachings down. If the Apostles have the authority to take it upon themselves to pass on teachings through writing, do they not also have the authority to pass on teachings orally, especially since oral teaching authority WAS specifically given to them by Christ? What of disciples such as Mark and Luke, who may not even have walked with Christ at all, but rather wrote according to what Peter and Paul told them? From whence comes their authority to write?

Mt 16:18 And I tell you, you are Peter, and on this rock I will build my church, and the powers of death shall not prevail against it.

Lk 10:16 "He who hears you hears me, and he who rejects you rejects me, and he who rejects me rejects him who sent me."

1 Thess 2:13 And we also thank God constantly for this, that when you received the word of God which you heard from us, you accepted it not as the word of men but as what it really is, the word of God, which is at work in you believers.

Col 2:22 Let no one disqualify you, insisting on self-abasement and worship of angels, taking his stand on visions, puffed up without reason by his sensuous mind, [19] and not holding fast to the Head, from whom the whole body, nourished and knit together through its joints and ligaments, grows with a growth that is from God. [20] If with Christ you died to the elemental spirits of the universe, why do you live as if you still belonged to the world? Why do you submit to regulations, [21] "Do not handle, Do not taste, Do not touch" [22] (referring to things which all perish as they are used), according to human precepts and doctrines?

Note that Paul here insists that we hold fast to Christ, who is specifically referred to as the Head of the Body. We must reject the Mosaic works of the Law, which had strict prohibitions on what could be handled (dead bodies), tasted (pork and shellfish), or touched (blood).

Mt 13:51 And he said to them, "Therefore every scribe who has been trained for the kingdom of heaven is like a householder who brings out of his treasure what is new and what is old."

The treasure is the same throughout all the ages, but not all the secrets of the treasure-store have been brought out. Only those in authority know how to bring out the treasures of the storehouse of God.

Scripture references oral tradition (the exegesis of the following seven Scripture passages summarizes an on-line article on oral tradition on the Catholic Answer Web site, Feb 1997):

Mt 2:23 And he went and dwelt in a city called Nazareth, that what was spoken by the prophets might be fulfilled, "He shall be called a Nazarene."

No verse in the Old or New Testament has such a prophecy. This verse is introduced in a way unlike any other prophecy in the New Testament. It is an oral tradition.

Mt 23:2-3 "The scribes and the Pharisees sit on Moses' seat; [3] so practice and observe whatever they tell you, but not what they do; for they preach, but do not practice.

This phrase "Moses' seat" occurs nowhere else in Scripture, yet is clearly accepted by Jesus' audience as a reference they understand.

Acts 15:21 For from early generations Moses has had in every city those who preach him, for he is read every sabbath in the synagogues."

The tradition of teaching authority passed from Moses to the Pharisees and Scribes, who were listened to respectfully in synagogue. Christ commanded that their teaching authority be respected and followed, although their living example was not to be followed when it contradicted what they taught.

1 Cor 10:1-4 I want you to know, brethren, that our fathers were all under the cloud, and all passed through the sea, [2] and all were baptized into Moses in the cloud and in the sea, [3] and all ate the same supernatural food [4] and all drank the same supernatural drink. For they drank from the supernatural Rock which followed them, and the Rock was Christ.

Neither account of this incident, neither Exodus 17:1-7 or Numbers 20:2-13, mentions the rock following the Chosen People through the desert, nor does any other section of Scripture. This is clearly an oral tradition passed on from Paul to his newly-baptized converts.

2 Tim 3:8 As Jannes and Jambres opposed Moses, so these men also oppose the truth, men of corrupt mind and counterfeit faith;

Neither Exodus 7:8ff, nor any other verse in Scripture tells us what the names of the magicians of Pharoah's court were. It is, again, oral tradition.

James 5:17 Elijah was a man of like nature with ourselves and he prayed fervently that it might not rain, and for three years and six months it did not rain on the earth.

The 1 Kings 17 account of Elijah's altercation with King Ahab says nothing of him praying.

Jn 7:16-18 So Jesus answered them, "My teaching is not mine, but his who sent me; [17] if any man's will is to do his will, he shall know whether the teaching is from God or whether I am speaking on my own authority. [18] He who speaks on his own authority seeks his own glory; but he who seeks the glory of him who sent him is true, and in him there is no falsehood.

During Christ's time, oral tradition was the rule of faith for the Jews. Remember, there is no record of Christ authorizing anyone to make a written record. He only authorized them to preach orally. The Talmud, the first written collection of the oral tradition of the rabbis, is made up of two parts, the Mishna and the Gemara. The Mishna was written down at about the end of the 2nd century A.D., while the Gemara was written down during the 3rd to the 6th centuries. Written targums (commentaries) appeared after the Babylonian Exile, but the rabbis didn't approve of them since they encouraged private interpretation of Scripture, undermining the God-given teaching authority of the Levitical priests (cf. How the canon was established *below). The theological system set up by God for the Hebrews was a combination of written Law and oral interpretation of that Law through the priestly teaching office. The Catholic Church continues the Divine tradition into which the Christ incarnated, safeguarded in truth by the Bridegroom of Israel.*

<u>Early Christians' comments on Sacred Tradition</u>

The Mass - Christ's One Sacrifice

Liturgy is the participation of the People of God in the work of God. God intends for us to participate in His life, He has arranged for us to do it on earth through the liturgy. Through its transcendence, we are brought into the heavenly liturgy. It is the source and manifestation of the Church, the act from which flows all love and charity. It is the highest, most essential act the Church performs. In this communal act, the faithful gather with the clergy, together their gestures express the nature of sacred action, the Word of Sacred Scripture is proclaimed in a dialogue and response between God and man. Through liturgy, signs that effect what they signify, that is, sacraments, are divinely handed down to us, and the hours, days, weeks, months and years are kept holy.

Jesus Christ is truly present, Body, Blood, Soul, and Divinity in His Glorified Body in the Eucharist. The sacrifice of the Mass is not a re-sacrifice of Jesus Christ, for such a thing is an impossible blasphemy, nor is it true that the sacrifice of the Cross is in a mysterious way across all time and space, numerically identical to the Mass (cf. Pope Pius XII, Mediator Dei, 1947), but rather, through the separate consecration of bread into His Flesh and wine into His Blood, Jesus Christ presents Himself in His glorified Body to God, in atonement for our sins and the sins of the whole world. The Eucharistic Celebration is thus one single sacrifice with the sacrifice of Christ because it makes present the sacrifice of the Cross, because it is its memorial, and because it applies the fruit of the Cross. Through the Mass, the sufferings of every member of the Body of Christ are united with the sufferings of Christ on the Cross, and all with the glory of every member of the Body of Christ in heaven, made glorious by Christ. The entire heavenly portion of the Body of Christ, angels and saints, is present at every Mass, celebrating the mystery in which God gave each of them a part, and celebrating the God in whose divinity they partake through the sacrifice. (CCC 1077-1112, 1345-1390, 2655)

According to God's divine Plan and in order to ransom mankind, Jesus' Passion, Death, Resurrection, and Ascension were intended for our salvation and accomplished once for all. The "pasch" is the celebration of the Passover Lamb, a "mystery" is something we can understand, just not completely. The Paschal Mystery is the central event of Christianity, one event composed of four events:

- *In the Passion, He pours Himself out in divine invitation,*
- *In Death, He liberates us from the effects of sin,*
- *In Resurrection, He opens the way for new life with us by justification, brings us filial adoption and defines His Divinity once for all,*
- *In the Ascension, He irreversibly brings humanity into heaven, into divine glory.*

At that point, the kingdom is begun. We participate in the Paschal Mystery by the way we teach and live liturgical and sacramental life. Through the liturgy, "the Mass never ends." We carry the Paschal Mystery to the world, it is linked to the Incarnation. Through redemptive suffering, we literally participate in the Paschal Mystery, the work of God.

Current misunderstandings: Most Christians deny the Real Presence of Jesus Christ in the Eucharist. Consequently, they assert that the Mass is either idolatry or an attempt to re-sacrifice Jesus Christ. Since Christ died once and for all, He cannot be re-sacrificed at daily Mass.

1 Chron 28:19 All this he made clear by the writing from the hand of the LORD concerning it, all the work to be done according to the plan.

For the Jews, the Temple was seen as the center of the created universe. It was a micro-cosm of the universe, the universe was a macro-cosm of the Temple. Through the center of the Temple, which was the Holy of Holies with the Ark of the Covenant at its center, heaven and earth intersected.

Ex 26:30 You shall erect the tabernacle according to the plan for it which has been shown you on the mountain.

Moses' tabernacle, was a copy of the heavenly temple...

Wis 9:8 Thou hast given command to build a temple
 on thy holy mountain,
and an alter in the city of thy habitation,
a copy of the holy tent which thou didst prepare
 from the beginning.

...and Solomon's Temple was built according to a heavenly plan. The three parts of the Temple were made to resemble the three parts of the earth, the outer court with its bronze sea corresponding to the ocean surrounding the land, the holy place with its two doors carved with images of trees, flowers, and cherubim, representing the garden of Eden, the Holy of Holies representing the highest heaven, where God dwells. Only the high priest could enter the Holy of Holies, only the high priest could function both on earth and in heaven, and even then he could do it only symbolically.

1 Cor 3:16 Do you not know that you are God's temple and that God's Spirit dwells in you?

The Temple also corresponded to the creation of man, who is a small world, according to Jewish belief. The worship of the Temple imitated the worship of God in heaven. The book of Revelation describes a two-fold liturgy:

Rev 4:8-11 And the four living creatures, each of them with six wings, are full of eyes all round and within, and day and night they never cease to sing,
"Holy, holy, holy, is the Lord God Almighty,
who was and is and is to come!" [9] And whenever the living creatures give glory and honor and thanks to him who is seated on the throne, who lives for ever and ever, [10] the twenty-four elders fall down before him who is seated on the throne and worship him who lives for ever and ever; they cast their crowns before the throne, singing, [11] "Worthy art thou, our Lord and God, to receive glory and honor and power,
for thou didst create all things,
and by thy will they existed and were created."

The liturgy which celebrates God in creation and...

Rev 5:8-14 And when he had taken the scroll, the four living creatures and the twenty-four elders fell down before the Lamb, each holding a harp, and with golden bowls full of incense, which are the prayers of the saints; [9] and they sang a new song, saying,
"Worthy art thou to take the scroll and to open its seals,
for thou wast slain and by thy blood didst ransom men for God
from every tribe and tongue and people and nation, [10] and hast made them a kingdom and priests to our God, and they shall reign on earth." [11] Then I looked, and I heard around the throne and the living creatures and the elders the voice of many angels, numbering myriads of myriads and thousands of thousands, [12] saying with a loud voice, "Worthy is the Lamb who was slain, to receive power and wealth and wisdom

and might and honor and glory and blessing!" ¹³ And I heard every creature in heaven and on earth and under the earth and in the sea, and all therein, saying, "To him who sits upon the throne and to the Lamb be blessing and honor and glory and might for ever and ever!" ¹⁴ And the four living creatures said, "Amen!" and the elders fell down and worshiped.

...the liturgy which celebrates God in redemption. It is the Lamb's sacrifice which makes Him worthy of breaking open the scroll, the Word. He makes a kingdom of priests for God.

Heb 8:1-3 Now the point in what we are saying is this: we have such a high priest, one who is seated at the right hand of the throne of the Majesty in heaven, ² a minister in the sanctuary and the true tent which is set up not by man but by the Lord. ³ For every high priest is appointed to offer gifts and sacrifices; hence it is necessary for this priest also to have something to offer.

Rev 5:3 And between the throne and the four living creatures and among the elders, I saw a Lamb standing, as though it had been slain,

Priests offer sacrifice. Through His sacrifice, and the divine working of baptismal grace, of sacramental grace in our lives, we are united to Him as He, the Lamb who was slain, offers Himself in eternal self-sacrifice.

Tob 7:13 Then he called his daughter Sarah, and taking her by the hand he gave her to Tobias to be his wife, saying, "Here she is; take her according to the law of Moses, and take her with you to your father." And he blessed them. ¹⁴ Next he called his wife Edna, and took a scroll and wrote out the contract; and they set their seals to it. ¹⁵ Then they began to eat.

1 Kings 21:8 So she wrote letters in Ahab's name and sealed them with his seal, and she sent the letters to the elders and the nobles who dwelt with Naboth in his city.

Jer 32:10 I signed the deed, sealed it, got witnesses, and weighed the money on scales.

Sealed scrolls are marriage contracts, royal decrees and deeds of purchase. The Apocolypse describes not just the liturgy, but also the consequences of liturgy - the marriage covenant, made by royal decree, through a deed of purchase. Liturgy is also a hall of judgement.

Lev 26:18 And if in spite of this you will not hearken to me, then I will chastise you again sevenfold for your sins...

Rev 6:1 Now I saw when the Lamb opened one of the seven seals, and I heard one of the four living creatures say, as with a voice of thunder, "Come!"

The sevenfold curse of Leviticus is played out in John's vision. Liturgy is public worship of God by His creatures in union with Him, it is the participation of the People of God in the work of God - that is what we see performed in Revelation. It is a Trinitarian act in which each person of the Most Holy Trinity pours Himself completely out upon the Church. The book of Revelation represents salvation history centered on Christ, it presents the heavenly liturgy, the Mass. Revelation 1:1 to Revelation 3:22 is the Liturgy of the Word, in which Christ, wearing the outfit of the royal high-priest (Rev 1:13) and standing among the menorrah of the Temple altar, speaks out the Divine Word upon the seven churches over which John was bishop. This is followed by the Liturgy of the Eucharist beginning in Revelation 4:1. The Holy, Holy, Holy is sung (Rev 4:8), incense is burned and hymns of praise are sung (Rev 5:8-10), and the power of heaven is unleashed upon the forces of evil. The "Lamb who was slain" or simply "the Lamb" is the most common title for Christ throughout the remainder of the book, which ends in the marriage feast of the Lamb. With each breaking open of the seal, warfare upon the wicked is waged. Participation in the liturgy of the Mass is the waging of spiritual warfare - it releases great power from heaven.

Gen 14:18 And Mel-chizedek king of Salem brought out bread and wine; he was priest of God Most High.

This prefigures the liturgy of the Mass, which is the work of the Body of Christ.

Gen 22:13 And Abraham lifted up his eyes and looked, and behold, behind him was a ram, caught in a thicket by his horns; and Abraham went and took the ram, and offered it up as a burnt offering instead of his son.

Abram's sacrifice of Isaac prefigures Christ's death on the cross, and therefore, the Mass.

Scriptural Catholicism   **Church**

Mal 1:10-11 Oh, that there were one among you who would shut the doors, that you might not kindle fire upon my altar in vain! I have no pleasure in you, says the Lord of hosts, and I will not accept an offering from your hand. [11] For from the rising of the sun to its setting my name is great among the nations, and in every place incense is offered to my name, and a pure offering; for my name is great among the nations, says the Lord of hosts.

The universal sacrifice of the Mass is prefigured and prophesied in the Old Testament, consummated in the New.

Lk 22:19-20 And he took bread, and when he had given thanks he broke it and gave it to them, saying, "This is my body which is given for you. Do this in remembrance of me." [20] And likewise the cup after supper, saying, "This cup which is poured out for you is the new covenant in my blood.

The verb used, anamnesis, does not simply mean "remember," it means "to make present."

1 Cor 10:16-21 The cup of blessing which we bless, is it not a participation in the blood of Christ? The bread which we break, is it not a participation in the body of Christ? [17] Because there is one bread, we who are many are one body, for we all partake of the one bread. [18] Consider the people of Israel; are not those who eat the sacrifices partners in the altar? [19] What do I imply then? That food offered to idols is anything, or that an idol is anything? [20] No, I imply that what pagans sacrifice they offer to demons and not to God. I do not want you to be partners with demons. [21] You cannot drink the cup of the Lord and the cup of demons. You cannot partake of the table of the Lord and the table of demons.

Heb 13:10 We have an altar from which those who serve the tent have no right to eat.

The altar of the Mass is an altar unlike that of the Temple, for those who serve in the Temple have no right to eat at this altar.

Heb 7:27 He has no need, like those high priests, to offer sacrifices daily, first for his own sins and then for those of the people; he did this once for all when he offered up himself.

Heb 9:24-28 For Christ has entered, not into a sanctuary made with hands, a copy of the true one, but into heaven itself, now to appear in the presence of God on our behalf. [25] Nor was it to offer himself repeatedly, as the high priest enters the Holy Place yearly with blood not his own; [26] for then he would have had to suffer repeatedly since the foundation of the world. But as it is, he has appeared once for all at the end of the age to put away sin by the sacrifice of himself. [27] And just as it is appointed for men to die once, and after that comes judgment, [28] so Christ, having been offered once to bear the sins of many, will appear a second time, not to deal with sin but to save those who are eagerly waiting for him.

Heb 10:10 And by that will we have been sanctified through the offering of the body of Jesus Christ once for all.

Christ's sacrifice on the Cross is final and complete. The sacrifice of the Mass is the witness we, the Body of Christ, bear to that one sacrifice, and through which we are joined to His Body, in spirit and in truth. Just as we are all cells in the Body of Christ, so every offering of the Mass is a "cell" in the Sacrifice of Christ. Through Christ's grace, we can become perfect images of Christ. Through God's grace, each Mass IS a perfect and therefore real presentation of Calvary.

Col 1:24-26 Now I rejoice in my sufferings for your sake, and in my flesh I complete what is lacking in Christ's afflictions for the sake of his body, that is, the church, [25] of which I became a minister according to the divine office which was given to me for you, to make the word of God fully known, [26] the mystery hidden for ages and generations...

Though there is One Body, there are many parts. Though there is One Sacrifice, there are many parts, but all One in Christ Jesus.

Acts 2:42,46-47 And they devoted themselves to the apostles' teaching and fellowship, to the breaking of bread and the prayers... And day by day, attending the temple together and breaking bread in their homes, they partook of food with glad and generous hearts, [47] praising God and having favor with all the people. And the Lord added to their number day by day those who were being saved.

Acts 20:7 On the first day of the week, when we were gathered together to break bread, Paul talked with them, intending to depart on the morrow; and he prolonged his speech until midnight.

"Sabbath" is taken from "shabbat," which means "rest." The sacrifice of the Mass takes place on the first day of the week, Sunday, the new Sabbath.

1 Cor 2:14 The unspiritual man does not receive the gifts of the Spirit of God, for they are folly to him, and he is not able to understand them because they are spiritually discerned.

1 Cor 5:7-8 Cleanse out the old leaven that you may be a new lump, as you really are unleavened. For Christ, our paschal lamb, has been sacrificed. ⁸ Let us, therefore, celebrate the festival, not with the old leaven, the leaven of malice and evil, but with the unleavened bread of sincerity and truth.

What festival will be celebrated? The Mass.

1 Cor 11:23-29 For I received from the Lord what I also delivered to you, that the Lord Jesus on the night when he was betrayed took bread, ²⁴ and when he had given thanks, he broke it, and said, "This is my body which is for you. Do this in remembrance of me." ²⁵ In the same way also the cup, after supper, saying, "This cup is the new covenant in my blood. Do this, as often as you drink it, in remembrance of me." ²⁶ For as often as you eat this bread and drink the cup, you proclaim the Lord's death until he comes.
²⁷ Whoever, therefore, eats the bread or drinks the cup of the Lord in an unworthy manner will be guilty of profaning the body and blood of the Lord. ²⁸ Let a man examine himself, and so eat of the bread and drink of the cup. ²⁹ For any one who eats and drinks without discerning the body eats and drinks judgment upon himself.

Why examine yourself if the Eucharist is only a symbol and not really Christ? How can eating a symbol unworthily cause you to need to answer for the sacrifice of the Cross, "the body and blood of the Lord"? Because it isn't just a symbol - through the Mass God makes the body and blood of the Lord present.

The following isn't Scripture, but it is useful to know:

Ignatius of Antioch to the church at Smyrna 7:1 (AD 110): "They [the heretics] even absent themselves from the Eucharist and the public prayers [cf. Acts 2:42], because they will not admit that the Eucharist is the flesh of our Savior Jesus Christ which suffered for our sins and which the Father in his goodness afterwards raised up again." Antioch is the city where Jesus' followers were first called Christians (Acts 11:26). Ignatius was taught by the Apostle John, who wrote the Gospel of John (cf. John 6:48-58).

Ignatius said to the church at Ephesus "obey [the] bishop and clergy with undivided minds and to share in the one common breaking of the bread - the medicine of immortality and the sovereign remedy by which we escape death and live in Jesus Christ for evermore." (20:3) "the sole Eucharist you should consider valid is one that is celebrated by the bishop himself or by some person authorized by him. where the bishop is to be seen, there let all his people be, just as wherever Jesus Christ is present, there is the Catholic Church." Ignatius' Epistle to the church at Smyrna 8:1-2 Didache (A.D. 60-140)

Is 6:3 "Holy, holy, holy is the LORD of hosts!" they cried one to the other. "All the earth is filled with his glory!"

Rev 4:8 The four living creatures, each of them with six wings, were covered with eyes inside and out. Day and night they do not stop exclaiming: "Holy, holy, holy is the Lord God almighty, who was, and who is, and who is to come."

Rev 19:9 Then the angel said to me, "Write this: Blessed are those who have been called to the wedding feast of the Lamb." And he said to me, "These words are true; they come from God."

<u>Early Christians' comments on the Sacrifice of the Mass</u>

Lk 24:27-32 And beginning with Moses and all the prophets, he interpreted to them in all the scriptures the things concerning himself.
²⁸ So they drew near to the village to which they were going. He appeared to be going further, ²⁹ but they constrained him, saying, "Stay with us, for it is toward evening and the day is now far spent." So he went in to stay with them. ³⁰ When he was at table with them, he took the bread and blessed, and broke it, and gave it to them. ³¹ And their eyes were opened and they recognized him; and he vanished out of their sight. ³² They said to each other, "Did not our hearts burn within us while he talked to us on the road, while he opened to us the scriptures?"

Acts 10:39-41 And we are witnesses to all that he did both in the country of the Jews and in Jerusalem. They put him to death by hanging him on a tree; [40] but God raised him on the third day and made him manifest; [41] not to all the people but to us who were chosen by God as witnesses, who ate and drank with him after he rose from the dead.

Christ is encountered through the liturgy. The liturgy is the living, active word in which we meet the Word. It teaches us about God, so that we may recognize Him when we meet Him. The only people who physically meet Jesus after His resurrection are those who eat and drink with Him. That continues to be true today.

The following is loosely modelled on the much superior analysis presented by Rev. Peter M. J. Stravinskas in The Catholic Church and the Bible, *pp. 83-106. While my commentary below covers only the bare bones of the Mass, Stravinskas sets aside one section of his book to go through essentially all the possible variations in the liturgy, showing the Scriptural components of each variation, and including cross-references to the Catechism. In addition, his book provides an excellent analysis of the relation between Scripture and the Church.*

The Order of Mass

The Mass makes present the entirety of salvation history to the faithful, recalling all that God has done.

Introductory Rites

Priest: In the name of the Father and of the Son and of the Holy Spirit (1 Jn 4:13-14 By this we know that we abide in him and he in us, because he has given us of his own Spirit. [14] And we have seen and testify that the Father has sent his Son as the Savior of the world.)

People: Amen (Neh 5:13 And all the assembly said "Amen")

Priest: The grace of our Lord Jesus Christ and the love of God and the fellowship of the Holy Spirit be with you all.

People: And also with you (2 Cor 13:14 The grace of the Lord Jesus Christ and the love of God and the fellowship of the Holy Spirit be with you all.)

We enter into Mass glorying in nothing but the Sign of the Cross, by which Christ was crucified to us, and we to the world. The grace, love and fellowship of the Trinity is distributed upon us. It is a reminder of Creation - the original work of the Trinity which brought us into existence.

Penitential Rite

All: I confess to Almighty God, and to you my brothers and sisters, that I have sinned through my own fault (James 5:16 Therefore confess your sins to one another, and pray for one another, that you may be healed.) in my thoughts (Mk 7:15 there is nothing outside a man which by going into him can defile him; but the things which come out of a man are what defile him.) and in my words, (James 3:6 The tongue is an unrighteous world among our members, staining the whole body, setting on fire the cycle of nature, and set on fire by hell) in what I have done and what I have failed to do (James 4:17 Whoever knows what is right to do and fails to do it, for him it is sin.) and I ask Blessed Mary Ever-Virgin, all the angels and saints, and you, my brothers and sisters, to pray for me to the Lord Our God. (2 Thess 3:1 Finally, brethren, pray for us.)

Priest: May Almighty God have mercy on us, forgive us our sins, and bring us to everlasting life. (1 Jn 1:9 If we confess our sins, he is faithful and just, and will forgive our sins and cleanse us from all unrighteousness.)

All: Lord have mercy, (Mt 20:31 "Lord have mercy on us, Son of David!") Christ have mercy (Jude 21 wait for the mercy of our Lord Jesus Christ unto eternal life.)

Since the sacrifice of the Mass is one with the Cross, it is for the forgiveness of our sins, so we must call to mind what we have done, and ask the forgiveness of God and the Body of Christ. The Fall of Adam, the prophets calling for repentance, culminating in the baptism of John, a baptism of repentance, are all brought to mind.

Gloria

All: Glory to God in the highest, and peace to his people on earth (Lk 2:14 "Glory to God in the highest, and on earth peace among men with whom he is pleased!"), Lord God, Heavenly King, Almighty God and Father (Rom 15:6 that together you may with one voice glorify the God and Father of our Lord Jesus Christ.) we worship you (Rev 19:10 Worship God..) we give you thanks (Eph 5:20 always and for everything giving thanks in the name of our Lord Jesus Christ to God the Father..) we praise you for your glory (Phil 1:11 filled with the fruits of righteousness which come through Jesus Christ, to the glory and praise of God.) Lord Jesus Christ, only Son of the Father (1 Jn 4:9 In this the love of God was made manifest among us, that God sent his only Son into the world, so that we might live through him.), Lord God, Lamb of God, you take away the sins of the world, have mercy on us (Jn 1:29 Behold, the Lamb of God, who takes away the sin of the world), you are seated at the right hand of the Father, receive our prayer, (Rom 8:34 It is Christ (Jesus) who died, rather, was raised, who also is at the right hand of God, who indeed intercedes for us.), for you alone are the Holy One, (Mk 1:24 I know who you are the Holy One of God.") you alone are the Lord (Rev 15:4 Who shall not fear and glorify thy name, O Lord? For thou alone art holy..) , you alone are the Most High, Jesus Christ (Lk 1:32 He will be great and will be called Son of the Most High,), with the Holy Spirit, in the glory of God the Father. (1 Cor 6:19 Do you not know that your body is a temple of the Holy Spirit within you, which you have from God? You are not your own..)

For this sacrifice, we glorify God. The glory of God enters the created world at the Incarnation, and is made manifest to all in a stable.

Liturgy of the Word

- Old Testament reading,
- Responsorial Psalm taken from the Book of Psalms,
- on holy days and Sundays, a second reading from the Epistles,
- Gospel reading.
- Homily

Wherever the Gospel is proclaimed, Jesus is present. The readings are established for each Sunday of the year in a three-year cycle so that essentially the entire Bible is read to the faithful over the course of the cycle. We hear the Word of God as it was originally proclaimed, by the God's prophets. Each reading demands a response on the part of the faithful, the verbal response representing the response of faith we make in our hearts when we hear God's call to us in Scripture. The homily is a meditation on the Word, making clear what lies hidden in the Scripture, things which are often hard to understand (2 Pet 3:15-16). The proclamations of Jesus' coming made by the prophets, the preaching ministry of Jesus, all are recalled and re-presented here.

Profession of Faith (Nicene Creed)

After hearing God's call, we respond by professing our faith in God, recalling all that He has done for us. We believe what the prophets, Zechariah, Nathaniel, and Peter all proclaimed: God is, God saves.

Liturgy of the Eucharist

Priest: Blessed are you Lord God of all creation. Through your goodness we have this bread to offer, which earth has given and human hands have made (Gen 3:16 In the sweat of your face you shall eat bread till you return to the ground.). It will become for us the bread of life. (Jn 6:35 Jesus said to them, "I am the bread of life...").

People: Blessed be God forever (Psalm 66:20 Blessed be God, because he has not rejected my prayer or removed his steadfast love from me!)

Priest: Blessed are you, Lord, God of all creation. Through your goodness we have this wine to offer, fruit of the vine and work of human hands, (Gen 14:18 And Melchizedek king of Salem brought out bread and wine; he was priest of God Most High) it will become our spiritual drink. (Jn 15:1 I am the true vine...)

People: Blessed be God forever (Psalm 66:20 Blessed be God, because he has not rejected my prayer or removed his steadfast love from me!)

The twin curses of Genesis were increased labor to bring forth fruit from the earth and increased labor in childbirth: curses of famine and sterility. Jesus will strip those curses away by His Cross. We offer up our labors, ourselves, He unites them to His own, Himself, and makes our labors useful through His sacrifice. Jesus' miraculous healing ministry is about to be made present. The gifts brought forward for the feeding of the 5000 (the only miracle present in all four Gospels) is recalled. A miracle is about to happen.

Priest: Pray, brethren, that our sacrifice may be acceptable to God, the Almighty Father. (Heb 9:24 For Christ has entered, not into a sanctuary made with hands, a copy of the true one, but into heaven itself, now to appear in the presence of God on our behalf.)

People: May the Lord accept the sacrifice at your hands, for the praise and glory of His name, for our good, and the good of all his Church. (Heb 12:28 Therefore let us be grateful for receiving a kingdom that cannot be shaken, and thus let us offer to God acceptable worship, with reverence and awe)

The sacrifice of the Cross is for the whole world.

Eucharistic Prayer

Priest: Lift up your hearts.

People: We lift them up to the Lord (Lam 3:41 Let us reach out our hearts toward God in heaven!)

Priest: Let us give thanks to the Lord our God (Psalm 75:1 We give thanks to thee, O God; we give thanks; we call on thy name and recount thy wondrous deeds.)

People: It is right to give Him thanks and praise (Col 1:3 We always give thanks to God, the Father of our Lord Jesus Christ, when we pray for you,)

We must always be ready, waiting on the Lord. We follow Mary's example, who maintained faith in her Son even as He was led to death, our souls magnify the Lord, and our spirits rejoice in God our Saviour.

Preface Acclamation

All: Holy, holy, holy Lord, God of power and might, heaven and earth are full of your glory. Hosanna in the highest. (Is 6:3 "Holy, holy, holy is the LORD of hosts!" they cried one to the other. "All the earth is filled with his glory!") Blessed is He who comes in the name of the Lord. Hosanna in the highest. (Mt 21:9 Hosanna to the Son of David! Blessed is he who comes in the name of the Lord! Hosanna in the highest!")

The praise of the angelic hosts in Isaiah and Revelation and the praise made by the crowds on Jesus' triumphant entry into Jerusalem are both brought together here. Salvation history is being re-presented to us. The fruits of the Tree of Life, the Cross of Jesus will be made available to us, and the glory of God will be made manifest.

Eucharistic Prayer II

(Of the four Eucharistic prayers, this is the oldest and the shortest. The other three are similarly Scriptural.)

Priest: Lord, you are holy indeed, the fountain of all holiness. (Jn 4:11 whoever drinks of the water that I shall give him will never thirst; the water that I shall give him will become in him a spring of water welling up to eternal life.") Let your Spirit come upon these gifts to make them holy, so that they may become for us the Body and Blood of our Lord Jesus Christ. (Lk 1:35 The Holy Spirit will come upon you, and the power of the Most High will overshadow you; therefore the child to be born will be called holy, the Son of God.) Before He was given up to death (Phil 2:8 he humbled himself and became obedient unto death, even death on a cross.), a death He freely accepted (Jn 10:17-18 For this reason the Father loves me, because I lay down my life, that I may take it again. [18] No one takes it from me, but I lay it down of my own accord. I have power to lay it down, and I have power to take it again), He took bread and gave you thanks. He broke the bread, and gave it to his disciples and said: Take this all of you and eat of it: this is my Body, which will be given up for you. When supper was ended, He took the cup. Again He gave you thanks and praise, gave the cup to His disciples and said: Take this all of you and drink from it: this is the cup of my Blood, the blood of the new and everlasting covenant. It will be shed for you and for all men so that sins may be forgiven. Do this in memory of me. (Mt 26:26-28 Now as they were eating, Jesus took bread, and blessed, and broke it, and gave it to the disciples and said, "Take, eat; this is my body." [27] And he took a cup, and when he had given thanks he gave it to them, saying, "Drink of it, all of you; [28] for this is my blood of the covenant, which is poured out for many for the forgiveness of sins.)

Let us proclaim the mystery of faith. (Eph 1:9-10 For he has made known to us in all wisdom and insight the mystery of his will, according to his purpose which he set forth in Christ [10] as a plan for the fulness of time, to unite all things in him, things in heaven and things on earth.)

The sacrifice is again present. We have walked from the moment of Creation, through the Fall, repentance, the Incarnation, Jesus proclamation of the Gospel, our response in faith, culminating in His sacrifice for us. But the Cross is not the end. Salvation history is not over. There is more to come.

All: Dying you destroyed our death, rising you restored our life, Lord Jesus come in glory. (Heb 2:14-15 Since therefore the children share in flesh and blood, he himself likewise partook of the same nature, that through death he might destroy him who has the power of death, that is, the devil, ⁵ and deliver all those who through fear of death were subject to lifelong bondage.)

Priest: In memory of His death and resurrection, we offer you, Father, this life-giving bread, this saving cup (Jn 6:51,54 I am the living bread which came down from heaven; if any one eats of this bread, he will live for ever; and the bread which I shall give for the life of the world is my flesh... he who eats my flesh and drinks my blood has eternal life, and I will raise him up at the last day."). We thank you for counting us worthy to stand in your Presence and serve you. May all of us who share the Body and Blood of Christ be brought together in unity by the Holy Spirit. (1 Cor 10:17 Because there is one bread, we who are many are one body, for we all partake of the one bread..). Lord, remember your Church throughout the world; make us grow in love, together with N. our Pope, N., our bishop, and all the clergy. (Heb 13:17 Obey your leaders and submit to them; for they are keeping watch over your souls, as men who will have to give account. Let them do this joyfully...) Remember our brothers and sisters who have gone to their rest in the hope of rising again. Bring them and all the departed into the light of your presence. (2 Mac 12:45 But if he was looking to the splendid reward that is laid up for those who fall asleep in godliness, it was a holy and pious thought. Therefore he made atonement for the dead, that they might be delivered from their sin..) Have mercy on us all; make us worthy to share eternal life, together with Mary, the virgin mother of God, with the apostles, and with all the saints, who have done your will throughout the ages. May we praise you in union with them and give you glory through your Son, Jesus Christ. (2 Thess 1:4-5 Therefore we ourselves boast of you in the churches of God for your steadfastness and faith in all your persecutions and in the afflictions which you are enduring. ⁵ This is evidence of the righteous judgment of God, that you may be made worthy of the kingdom of God, for which you are suffering.)

God rose from the dead, rescuing us all from death.

Doxology

Priest: Through Him, with Him, in Him, in the unity of the Holy Spirit, all glory and honor is yours Almighty Father, forever and ever.

People: Amen. (Rom 11:36 For from him and through him and to him are all things. To him be glory for ever. Amen.)

The depth of the riches and wisdom and knowledge of God, unsearchable in his judgements, inscrutable in His ways, is now known.

Communion Rite

Lord's Prayer (Mt 6:9-13 Our Father who art in heaven, Hallowed be thy name. ¹⁰ Thy kingdom come. Thy will be done, On earth as it is in heaven. ¹¹ Give us this day our daily bread; ¹² And forgive us our debts, As we also have forgiven our debtors; ¹³ And lead us not into temptation, But deliver us from evil..)

Priest: Deliver us Lord from every evil, and grant us peace in our day. In your mercy keep us free from sin and protect us from all anxiety, as we wait in joyful hope for the coming of our Saviour, Jesus Christ. (Jn 17:15 I do not pray that thou shouldst take them out of the world, but that thou shouldst keep them from the evil one.)

People: For the kingdom, the power, and the glory are yours, now and forever (Didache - teaching of the Apostles, first century and 1 Chron 29:11 Thine, O LORD, is the greatness, and the power, and the glory, and the victory, and the majesty;)

Priest: Lord Jesus Christ, you said to your disciples: I leave you peace, my peace I give you. Look not on our sins, but on the faith of your Church, and grant us the peace and unity of your kingdom, where you live forever and ever. (Jn 14:27 Peace I leave with you; my peace I give to you; not as the world gives do I give to you. Let not your hearts be troubled, neither let them be afraid.)

Priest: The peace of the Lord be with you always. (Jn 20:19 Jesus came and stood among them and said to them, "Peace be with you.")

It is His resurrection, His glorified body, which is made present to us in the Eucharist. As He came to them in a locked room and unrecognized on the road to Emmaus, so He comes to us, unrecognized by many, so that we may feed on His flesh, which is for the life of the world.

Breaking of the Bread

People: Lamb of God, you take away the sins of the world: have mercy on us. Lamb of God, you take away the sins of the world: have mercy on us. Lamb of God you take away the sins of the world: grant us peace. (Jn 1:29 "Behold, the Lamb of God, who takes away the sin of the world!")

His body is our salvation, His flesh cleanses our sins.

Communion

Priest: This is the Lamb of God, who takes away the sins of the world. Happy are those who are called to His Supper. (Rev 19:9 "Write this: Blessed are those who are invited to the marriage supper of the Lamb." And he said to me, "These are true words of God.")

All: Lord, I am not worthy to receive you, but only say the word and I shall be healed. (Lk 7:6-7 "Lord, do not trouble yourself, for I am not worthy to have you come under my roof; [7] ...But say the word, and let my servant be healed).

The vision of Revelation is fulfilled. The Spirit and the Bride say "Come!" Though we are not worthy to be invited to the wedding feast of the Lamb, yet God invites us from the highways and byways of our lives to join Him in the feast. Our marriage to Him is consummated by our taking Him into ourselves. The faithful members of the Bride approach the font of grace, Jesus Christ, and receive the Bridegroom.

Dismissal

Priest: Go in peace, to love and serve the Lord (Rom 10:15 And how can men preach unless they are sent? As it is written, "How beautiful are the feet of those who preach good news!" Mt 28:19 Go therefore and make disciples of all nations...)

People: Thanks be to God. (2 Cor 9:15 Thanks be to God for his inexpressible gift!)

Strengthened with the power of the sacraments, we go into the world to proclaim what He has done for us, and what He will do for all who ask.

SACRAMENTS

Galatians 6:15-16
For neither circumcision counts for
anything, nor uncircumcision,
but a new creation.
Peace and mercy be upon all who walk by this rule,
upon the Israel of God.

Isaiah 55:10-13
"For as the rain and the snow come down from heaven,
and return not thither but water the earth,
making it bring forth and sprout,
giving seed to the sower and bread to the eater,
so shall my word be that goes forth from my mouth;
it shall not return to me empty,
but it shall accomplish that which I purpose,
and prosper in the thing for which I sent it.

"For you shall go out in joy, and be led forth in peace;
the mountains and the hills before you shall break forth into singing,
and all the trees of the field shall clap their hands.
Instead of the thorn shall come up the cypress;
instead of the brier shall come up the myrtle;
and it shall be to the Lord for a memorial,
for an everlasting sign
which shall not be cut off."

The Love of Christ

Phil 2:17 Even if I am to be poured as a libation upon the sacrificial offering of your faith, I am glad and rejoice with you all.

To understand what it means to be a Christian, we must understand what we are being called into. 2 Peter 1:3-4 says we are called to "participate (or share) in the Divine Nature." To know what this participation involves, we must have some idea of what the Divine Nature is. Peter immediately follows his description of what Christians are called to be part of by describing what our goal is: our goal is to become perfect in love (verse 7). John, in his first epistle, describes the key aspect of the Divine Nature: "God is love." We must become perfect in love so we can share in God's life of love. But exactly what *is* God's life of love?

Before the beginning was God. God is He who exists outside of time, outside of space. He is spirit. That means He has no parts which compose Him and no parts into which He could decompose. This is what it means to be perfectly simple, and God is perfectly simple. God has but one mind, one intellect, one will. What God does is love. In fact, God loves so fully, so completely, so well, that it is correct to say that God is love. But how can God love unless there is someone to love? There is someone to love, and there always has been. While God is not composed of parts, He contains within Himself three Persons., God the Father, God the Son, and God the Holy Spirit. The three Persons of the Trinity do not together make up God, rather, each Person is Himself totally and completely distinct, totally and completely God. However, each Person is so fully united to the other two that there is only one God, not three. How then are the three Persons of the Trinity related to each other?

God the Father is the source of all, the source even of the other two Persons of the Trinity. Though every Person of the Trinity is co-eternal, none of them coming into existence before or after the others, still it is the case that the Father is the source of all.

The knowledge of God the Father is perfect, which means that God knows Himself perfectly. In order for something to be perfect, it must have existence, and the self-knowledge of God's own personal existence has His own existence. His personal self-knowledge is Himself a Person, the Second Person of the Trinity. The Second Person of the Trinity, called God the Son, is the perfect image of the Father. Because He who is the perfect self-knowledge of God has His source in God from all eternity, God the Son is eternally begotten by the Father.

God the Father pours Himself out in the self-knowledge who is God the Son. The word we use to describe how He pours Himself out completely into God the Son is *love*. Another word for this complete self-outpouring is *kenosis* - nothing is held back. God the Father loves God the Son completely, pouring Himself out completely to the Son, so completely that the Father is fully within the Son. Since the Son is the perfect image of the Father, the Son also pours Himself out completely to the Father, and is therefore fully in the Father. In fact, the love of self-outpouring between the two Divine Persons is so complete, so perfect, that He, too, has His own existence. The mutual self-outpouring of love between God the Father and God the Son *is* God the Holy Spirit. Of course, since God the Holy Spirit is Himself the complete outpouring of love between the Father and the Son, He is fully within the Father and He is fully within the Son. Similarly, the Father is fully within Him, and the Son is fully within Him. This is the essence of Trinitarian love - each Person pouring Himself out completely into the other two Persons, each Person having the completeness of the other two Persons within Himself.

The three Persons of the Trinity do not share the divine nature, each possesses the divine nature entirely. Each totally, completely possesses the one mind, the one intellect, the one will of God. This is our finite, limited understanding of who God is, of what God's innermost life is about. Before time began, before creation came into existence, this perfect and complete family of Persons existed, Father, Son, and Holy Spirit, each pouring Himself out completely in each of the other two. This is the Divine Passion - three Persons living the one kenosis of pure love. God does not need anyone or anything else, and nothing else exists in this "time" before time, before creation. Because God is the Original Essence, the Original Being, all that comes into existence owes its existence to Him.

When God created, He did not create out of need, but out of superabundant love, out of a free desire to love us into existence. This is the nature of love; that it be free. He intended to create creatures who would share His life of love. All of creation is ordered to man, and man is ordered towards the love of God. Man and woman were created in the image and likeness of God. They were made to be flesh of one flesh and bone of one bone, willed by God to become one flesh. From this union, new created life springs forth, also in the image and likeness of God. The

Eternal Family thus brought about the created image of Himself in the human family, in the love which flows between man and woman with such strength and passion that new creation springs forth, made to share in God's life, completing the created image of God.

Sadly, the first man and woman, having perfect freedom and loved perfectly by God, chose not to love God as they were themselves loved. Though this was a terrible offense against God, yet God still loved them. It is God's nature to love, so He acts the same towards all He creates. He continues to love us, to think of us, every moment, no matter how often we refuse to love or think of Him. If He did not think of us, we would fall out of existence, we would stop being. Yet this never happens. Our existence is a measure of the depth of His love, but it is not the only measure.

At the very moment that the man and the woman chose against His love, He promised to give them a second chance to live in love as He does. He promised to send a Saviour. Further, He allowed the man and the woman to keep much of what He had given them. They continued in their free will, though it was now disordered and incapable of the perfect control it had when they were created. They continued to have the use of their reason, though it was now clouded by their refusal to turn completely towards Him who is the source of all. God even allowed the man and the woman to continue to act in His image, to bring forth new life. Although they had rejected God's love, and thus made both the bringing forth of this new life and the sustenance of life itself very difficult, yet God still allowed them to share in His creative power and in His work of creation. Though they did not choose to live in kenosis, they could still dimly image it.

In order to accomplish the salvation He had promised, God chose for Himself a man from the land of Ur, a man named Abram. Abram was given the choice to follow God. Abram chose to do so. Though Abram and his children continued in the same mistakes their parents had made, God always gave them help to return to Him. This man's children and their children's children became the Chosen People, God's family on earth. The image and likeness of God was writ large, but it was still writ dimly, for the children of that first couple continued to live in sin. Centuries of preparation went by, and God shepherded His created family towards His salvation.

From within His Chosen People, His family on earth, He chose a woman from Galilee, from the town of Nazareth. Just as He had with the first man and woman, God prepared this woman from the first moment of her existence for a very special role. When the time had reached its fullness, again the question was put forward as it had been put forward to the first man, to the first woman. But this question was also dramatically different. God again asked: would she do as God desired? Would she love as God loved? Yet the question was different because God intended something which had never before happened. God intended to enter creation itself, and open the doors for all mankind to participate in His inner life. He was prepared to pour Himself out completely not just into the Divine Persons, but into a human person, Mary. For this reason, He had made this woman capable of pouring herself out to Him to the uttermost limits of her created being. He had made her sinless. All that remained was the question and the answer. Would she freely give her freely loved consent as no other had?

What would her answer be?

"Yes."

In that moment, the Holy Spirit, in the kenosis of divine love, poured Himself out upon her, overshadowing her with the living life of love that accomplishes what God wills. God the Son, wholly present within the Father, wholly present within the Holy Spirit, now poured Himself out into the very creation which had taken form through Him, humbling Himself to take on human form, becoming wholly present within Mary, the young woman from Nazareth. She received what no human being had ever before received, what no human being will ever again receive with the same power and presence. She received the presence of the living God in her own womb. The life which He brought to her womb was not just the image of God, He was God Himself. God's kenosis, the Divine Nature, had entered creation as it had never entered creation before. God's Passion entered into her life, and swept into the world. By her assent to God's love, she was made the Bride into which the Holy Spirit poured Himself, bringing about the Incarnation of the Son.

The Son she carried grew in wisdom and age and favor within her womb, from egg to embryo, from embryo to birth. In His Divine Nature, He possesses the entire intellect, mind, and will of God, for that is who He is. In His human nature, He possesses a human mind, human intellect, human will, human soul, all united with a human body. Thus, He is fully human, fully Divine, one Divine Person, Second Person of the Trinity become Incarnate. In His humanity, He grew within and before her and before all who knew Him in wisdom and grace, while in His Divinity, He who is God had full knowledge of what He planned to accomplish and how it would be accomplished. To that end, He foreshadowed what was to come by being placed in the eating trough which is the manger, in a poor hovel like unto the creation He had deigned to enter.

The Plan is very simple: God extends to all mankind a divine Invitation to enter into and participate in the Divine Nature. In order to accomplish this invitation, He pours Himself out completely, for this is how God invites persons into participation with He Who Is. He called men to Himself, His disciples, and chose twelve as men to be sent, Apostles. But many, very many, refused the invitation to love.

Jesus' outpouring became an outpouring of love into the teeth of love refused, yet His divine, His human, kenosis continued unabated. The Passion of His love became a passion of pain, of torture, and of death, but no matter the rejection, the love of God would not cease, for one human being, Mary, had chosen to love as He loved, and her Bridegroom, God, would never yield. Thus, no matter how many reviled His love, the Passion of the Bridegroom for His Bride burned. He and His love had the will to win. He drew the circle which brought us in. At the end, His thirst for us could be abated only in the final libation.

God did the impossible.
God died.
The silence of the grave saw love conquered.
Conquered.

For a night
    and a day
        and another night,

Silence.

But in the silence of that last pre-dawn light, the whole earth trembled.

The grave opened.
God/man stepped forth.
He had raised Himself from the dead.
He could not stop for death, nor could death stop Him. Even death could not abate His love.

He came again to those whom He had chosen. This time, they did not refuse. They saw the invitation for what it was, finally. They turned, knelt, and worshipped. In the forty days remaining, He taught the Apostles and disciples. He drove home the points they had not understood before, the whole mystery of God who is love. He appeared only to those with whom He ate and drank, sharing His Body with His Body. Then, He ascended into heaven, carrying with Him His body, the body which had won the victory, the humanity for which He had died. He retains His full humanity even now, for His humanity has borne the burden, it has won the honor. In the divine procession of Trinitarian love, human nature now participates, for Jesus is fully human, and He participates fully in the Divine Nature. He sent the Spirit for those waiting on earth. This time, the Spirit did not need to ask, for all in the upper room had answered "Yes." He poured Himself out in that upper room upon Mary and the disciples, kenosis yet again, the Third person of the Trinity dwelling fully within the Bride, the Church. He forms the mystical body of Christ just as He had poured Himself out thirty-three years earlier to form the physical body of Christ. The kenosis of God's love again reverberated through creation, but now, because of the door which opened through Mary's womb, the roar of this wind does not cease.

God's work of creation is not done; it springs anew with every fertile union of man and woman. God's work of new creation is not done; it pours itself out through the Church in the waters of baptism and washes through the whole of creation in the sacramental life. The sacraments are the gift of kenosis to us who live still on earth. We are here to learn how to live out this gift, to learn its uses and its ways. When we live in God, He is our cleansing, our strengthening, our food, our healing, our teacher, our spouse, our last vision. He continues to be personally present in creation through the cleansing kenosis which is baptism, the strengthening kenosis which is confirmation, the healing kenosis which is confession, the teaching kenosis which is Holy Orders, the kenosis of marriage which is Holy Matrimony, the kenosis of sustenance which is the Eucharist, and the last worldly experience which is the Anointing of the Sick. He is present as He has been present since that young Jewish woman brought Him to us. God's kenosis has no end.

At the end of her life, Mary, who was the first human being to experience the fullness of participation in the Divine nature on earth, attained the promise of Scripture, and was brought body and soul into heaven, there to participate in the Divine Nature as the first of the elect in heaven. At the Final Judgment, all will regain their bodies and be able to participate in the kenosis which she experiences now, the fullness which Jesus prepared for us all.

Against that day, God allows us who are baptized to participate in a foretaste of that kenosis. Through the Eucharist, the sacrament for which all other sacraments prepare us, God makes Himself present within the poor hovels of our bodies as He made Himself present in the poor hovel, the manger into which He was born. He is not just spiritually present, but physically present. He pours Himself out to each one of us, Body, Blood, Soul and Divinity, teaching us by example to pour ourselves out to one another, completely, totally, in perfect love. He becomes our food so that we might learn to live as He lives. His love will not be denied. This is the story of our lives - learning how to pour ourselves out as He did, so that we can live as we are called to live, participating in the Divine Nature. The saints are examples of people who have learned how to do it. They who are filled with all the fullness of God teach and guide us in this path, so that we, too, may fulfill Scripture and be filled with all the fullness of God.

This is the purpose of our existence: kenosis. The life within the Trinity, the life first imaged in Adam and Eve, the life poured out on and through Mary, lived by Jesus, poured out on the Cross, poured out in the upper room, poured out in the sacraments, created humanity united with Eternal Family, Bride and Bridegroom, Mary and the Holy Spirit, each baptized person and Jesus, the whole Church and Christ, each person at the Wedding Feast of the Lamb which is the Eucharistic celebration, the feast of the Lamb who was Slain. Kenosis, becoming the Body of Christ, living wholly in Him and He living wholly in us, flesh of one flesh, bone of one bone, the two become one flesh.

This is the Catholic faith.

Sacramental Principles

The Body of Christ acts and moves in the world today as Christ Himself acted in the world two millenia ago - He heals, sanctifies, divinizes us through the things of the created world, in an economy of salvation created and instituted in His Incarnation, Life, Passion, Death, and Resurrection. These special actions of the Body of Christ in the created world are endowed by God with salvific grace, and heal the recipient, for it is Christ who heals through the sacraments (CCC 1114-1130).

Most of Christ's healing miracles involved actual physical contact with the sick person in some way. Similarly, His miracles at Cana, at sea, and with the loaves involved the physical manipulation of the created world. A sacrament is a physical sign which carries with it real, healing, sanctifying grace, grace which accomplishes what the sign signifies. Sacraments divinize us (CCC 1131-1134, 1988)

Mt 8:2 and behold, a leper came to him and knelt before him, saying, "Lord, if you will, you can make me clean." [3] And he stretched out his hand and touched him, saying, "I will; be clean." And immediately his leprosy was cleansed.

Mk 1:40-41 And a leper came to him beseeching him, and kneeling said to him, "If you will, you can make me clean." [41] Moved with pity, he stretched out his hand and touched him, and said to him, "I will; be clean."

Lk 5:13 And he stretched out his hand, and touched him, saying, "I will; be clean." And immediately the leprosy left him.

Mt 8:14-15 And when Jesus entered Peter's house, he saw his mother-in-law lying sick with a fever; [15] he touched her hand, and the fever left her, and she rose and served him.

Mk 1:30-31 Now Simon's mother-in-law lay sick with a fever, and immediately they told him of her. [31] And he came and took her by the hand and lifted her up, and the fever left her; and she served them.

Mt 9:24-25 he said, "Depart; for the girl is not dead but sleeping." And they laughed at him. [25] But when the crowd had been put outside, he went in and took her by the hand, and the girl arose.

Mk 5:40-42 And they laughed at him. But he put them all outside, and took the child's father and mother and those who were with him, and went in where the child was. ⁴¹ Taking her by the hand he said to her, "Talitha cumi"; which means, "Little girl, I say to you, arise." ⁴² And immediately the girl got up and walked (she was twelve years of age), and they were immediately overcome with amazement.

Lk 8:53-55 And they laughed at him, knowing that she was dead. ⁵⁴ But taking her by the hand he called, saying, "Child, arise." ⁵⁵ And her spirit returned, and she got up at once; and he directed that something should be given her to eat.

Lk 7:13-15 And when the Lord saw her, he had compassion on her and said to her, "Do not weep." ¹⁴ And he came and touched the bier, and the bearers stood still. And he said, "Young man, I say to you, arise." ¹⁵ And the dead man sat up, and began to speak. And he gave him to his mother.

Mk 9:26-27 And after crying out and convulsing him terribly, it came out, and the boy was like a corpse; so that most of them said, "He is dead." ²⁷ But Jesus took him by the hand and lifted him up, and he arose.

Lk 13:12-13 And when Jesus saw her, he called her and said to her, "Woman, you are freed from your infirmity." ¹³ And he laid his hands upon her, and immediately she was made straight, and she praised God.

Lk 14:2-4 And behold, there was a man before him who had dropsy. ³ And Jesus spoke to the lawyers and Pharisees, saying, "Is it lawful to heal on the sabbath, or not?" ⁴ But they were silent. Then he took him and healed him, and let him go.

Mt 9:28-30 When he entered the house, the blind men came to him; and Jesus said to them, "Do you believe that I am able to do this?" They said to him, "Yes, Lord." ²⁹ Then he touched their eyes, saying, "According to your faith be it done to you." ³⁰ And their eyes were opened. And Jesus sternly charged them, "See that no one knows it."

Mk 8:22-25 And they came to Beth-saida. And some people brought to him a blind man, and begged him to touch him. ²³ And he took the blind man by the hand, and led him out of the village; and when he had spit on his eyes and laid his hands upon him, he asked him, "Do you see anything?" ²⁴ And he looked up and said, "I see men; but they look like trees, walking." ²⁵ Then again he laid his hands upon his eyes; and he looked intently and was restored, and saw everything clearly.

Mk 7:33-35 And taking him aside from the multitude privately, he put his fingers into his ears, and he spat and touched his tongue; ³⁴ and looking up to heaven, he sighed, and said to him, "Ephphatha," that is, "Be opened." ³⁵ And his ears were opened, his tongue was released, and he spoke plainly.

Jn 9:6-7 As he said this, he spat on the ground and made clay of the spittle and anointed the man's eyes with the clay, ⁷ saying to him, "Go, wash in the pool of Siloam" (which means Sent). So he went and washed and came back seeing.

Christ could have chosen never to touch or feed a single person. Without even a spoken word in the created world, He could have willed hunger and thirst to miraculously abate, the sick to heal. He had no need to put his fingers into the deaf man's ears or rub mud made of clay and spittle onto a blind man's eyes, or even to vocally command demons begone. Yet He did these things. He did not do them just a few times: every miracle involved at least a spoken command, the vast majority of His healing miracles specifically record Him touching the recipients. Indeed, the very word "rebuke" may imply a touch, for Luke records only that Christ rebuked the fever in Peter's mother-in-law, while the other two synoptic Gospels tell us that He touched her and her fever left. Why? Why does Christ put such emphasis on His created body, on the desire to speak with, to touch His people in order to heal them? Why did Christ wash the Apostle's <u>feet</u>? Why does He retain His human nature and human body to this very moment, and intend to retain it for all eternity? Why would God choose to be, now and forever, a finite man?

Mt 17:27 "However, not to give offense to them, go to the sea and cast a hook, and take the first fish that comes up, and when you open its mouth you will find a shekel; take that and give it to them for me and for yourself."

Even the temple priests are satisfied through a miracle of creation. Note Christ pays the temple tax not only for himself, but also for <u>Peter.</u>

Lev 15:25-26 "If a woman has a discharge of blood for many days... all the days of the discharge she shall continue in uncleanness; as in the days of her impurity, she shall be unclean. ²⁶ Every bed on which she lies, all the days of her discharge, shall be to her as the bed of her impurity; and everything on which she sits shall be unclean, as in the uncleanness of her impurity. ²⁷ And whoever touches these things shall be unclean, and shall wash his clothes, and bathe himself in water, and be unclean until the evening.

Lev 17:14 ...the life of every creature is its blood

Mt 9:20-22 And behold, a woman who had suffered from a hemorrhage for twelve years came up behind him and touched the fringe of his garment; ²¹ for she said to herself, "If I only touch his garment, I shall be made well." ²² Jesus turned, and seeing her he said, "Take heart, daughter; your faith has made you well." And instantly the woman was made well.

Mk 5:27-34 She had heard the reports about Jesus, and came up behind him in the crowd and touched his garment. ²⁸ For she said, "If I touch even his garments, I shall be made well." ²⁹ And immediately the hemorrhage ceased; and she felt in her body that she was healed of her disease. ³⁰ And Jesus, perceiving in himself that power had gone forth from him, immediately turned about in the crowd, and said, "Who touched my garments?" ³¹ And his disciples said to him, "You see the crowd pressing around you, and yet you say, 'Who touched me?'" ³² And he looked around to see who had done it. ³³ But the woman, knowing what had been done to her, came in fear and trembling and fell down before him, and told him the whole truth. ³⁴ And he said to her, "Daughter, your faith has made you well; go in peace, and be healed of your disease."

Lk 8:43-48 And a woman who had had a flow of blood for twelve years and could not be healed by any one, and had spent all her living on physicians, ⁴⁴ came up behind him, and touched the fringe of his garment; and immediately her flow of blood ceased. ⁴⁵ And Jesus said, "Who was it that touched me?" When all denied it, Peter said, "Master, the multitudes surround you and press upon you!" ⁴⁶ But Jesus said, "Some one touched me; for I perceive that power has gone forth from me." ⁴⁷ And when the woman saw that she was not hidden, she came trembling, and falling down before him declared in the presence of all the people why she had touched him, and how she had been immediately healed. ⁴⁸ And he said to her, "Daughter, your faith has made you well; go in peace."

Luke provides the archetype for sacrament. Blood is the source of life - the woman's life was draining away in uncleanness. She (we) come to the Body of Christ in search of healing - we must reach out and touch Him as a sign of our faith, and so that our faith may increase. He is not defiled by our touch, rather, He makes us clean and heals us by His intimate presence, our response to His call. We must respond, we must touch Him, but only He can heal and cleanse us. He heals us now as He healed us then, through the things of the created world, in which He took on created form. Jesus Christ is the only Sacrament, the source from which the seven sacraments flow. This is the Resurrection - Christ moving among us in the created world. He is with us always, until the end of the world.

Lk 4:40 Now when the sun was setting, all those who had any that were sick with various diseases brought them to him; and he laid his hands on every one of them and healed them.

Mk 6:56 And wherever he came, in villages, cities, or country, they laid the sick in the market places, and besought him that they might touch even the fringe of his garment; and as many as touched it were made well.

God the Father intended this from the beginning. He intends us to have to come to Jesus, touch Him, be joined to Him, in order to be saved. The Passion, Death, Resurrection and Ascension of His Son made the Plan effective, wins the graces and gives the Plan the power it requires. The Holy Spirit, sent by the Father and the Son, gives us the ability to utilize the fruits of grace won for us. These fruits of grace are made available to us only through Jesus' Body, energized by His Spirit, that is, we obtain the graces of salvation only through the Church (CCC 1077, 1084, 1091, 1116-1117).

Eph 3:9-10 and to make all men see what is the plan of the mystery hidden for ages in God who created all things; ¹⁰ that through the church the manifold wisdom of God might now be made known to the principalities and powers in the heavenly places.

God created the world through Jesus. Through the Church, Jesus' Body, He brings the New Creation of the sacraments. This is the mystery of God's salvation.

Holy Matrimony

Is 62:4-5 You shall no more be termed Forsaken,
and your land shall no more be termed Desolate;
but you shall be called My delight is in her,
and your land Married;
for the LORD delights in you,
and your land shall be married.
For as a young man marries a virgin,
so shall your sons marry you,
and as the bridegroom rejoices over the bride,
so shall your God rejoice over you.

Marriage is the type by which God's plan of salvation is made known to all, the created image of the way God saves us. We can only understand the sacraments and the sacramental life by first understanding marriage. It is the first sacrament in temporal terms. The natural bond uniting Adam and Eve into flesh of one flesh and bone of one bone is found constantly in the Old Testament as the living example God uses to express His covenant with His Chosen People. In the New Testament, Jesus Christ, the Bridegroom, elevates marriage, making it the means by which He unites Himself with all who will be saved through the New Covenant, making believers in Him, through baptism, flesh of His flesh, and bone of His bone, one Body with His Bride, the Church. He works in the dust, pours out upon us the waters of the New Creation, and forms His Bride. (CCC 1601-1666)

Current misunderstandings: Many Christian denominations do not fully understand the covanental nature of marriage, or the outpouring of the Spirit which occurs in marriage. They consequently permit the offenses of contraception and divorce to be undertaken against this covenantal act.

Gen 1:26-28,31 Then God said, "Let us make man in our image, after our likeness; and let them have dominion over the fish of the sea, and over the birds of the air, and over the cattle, and over all the earth, and over every creeping thing that creeps upon the earth." [27] So God created man in his own image, in the image of God he created him; male and female he created them. [28] And God blessed them, and God said to them, "Be fruitful and multiply, and fill the earth and subdue it; and have dominion over the fish of the sea and over the birds of the air and over every living thing that moves upon the earth."...And God saw everything that he had made, and behold, it was very good. And there was evening and there was morning, a sixth day.

Gen 2:18-25 Then the LORD God said, "It is not good that the man should be alone; I will make him a helper fit for him." [19] So out of the ground the LORD God formed every beast of the field and every bird of the air, and brought them to the man to see what he would call them; and whatever the man called every living creature, that was its name. [20] The man gave names to all cattle, and to the birds of the air, and to every beast of the field; but for the man there was not found a helper fit for him. [21] So the LORD God caused a deep sleep to fall upon the man, and while he slept took one of his ribs and closed up its place with flesh; [22] and the rib which the LORD God had taken from the man he made into a woman and brought her to the man. [23] Then the man said,
"This at last is bone of my bones
and flesh of my flesh;
she shall be called Woman,
because she was taken out of Man." [24] Therefore a man leaves his father and his mother and cleaves to his wife, and they become one flesh. [25] And the man and his wife were both naked, and were not ashamed.

The Hebrew word "holy" means "set apart." It is also the word for "marriage." Note that the use of sexuality was ordained prior to the Fall - the first couple were told to "be fruitful and multiply." As Paul is at pains to point out, marriage is not a sin. It is, in fact, the first sacrament in the temporal order, elevated by Christ to the level of sacrament, and is the created model for the Trinity.

Eph 5:2,21-33 And walk in love, as Christ loved us and gave himself up for us, a fragrant offering and sacrifice to God... Be subject to one another out of reverence for Christ. [22] Wives, be subject to your husbands, as to the Lord. [23] For the husband is the head of the wife as Christ is the head of the church, his body, and is himself its Savior. [24] As the church is subject to Christ, so let wives also be subject in everything to their husbands. [25] Husbands, love your wives, as Christ loved the church and gave himself up for her, [26] that he might sanctify her, having cleansed her by the washing of water with the word, [27] that he might present the church to himself in splendor, without spot or wrinkle or any such thing, that she might be holy and without blemish. [28] Even so husbands should love their wives as their own bodies. He who loves his wife loves himself. [29] For no man ever hates his own flesh, but nourishes and cherishes it, as Christ does the church, [30] because we are members of his body. [31] "For this reason a man shall leave his father and mother and be joined to his wife, and the two shall become one flesh." ³² This mystery is a profound one, and I am saying that it refers to Christ and the church; ³³ however, let each one of you love his wife as himself, and let the wife see that she respects her husband.

Note that marriage is the only one of the seven sacraments to be referred to by Scripture as a "mystery." Yet the Greek word for "sacrament" is "mysterium," that is, mystery. In matrimony, the spouses are united by the very same bond that unites Christ to the Church. Thus, all sacraments are a sharing in the central mystery, the mystery of the Bridegroom and the Bride.

Gen 24:48-51,58-67 Then I bowed my head and worshiped the LORD, and blessed the LORD, the God of my master Abraham, who had led me by the right way to take the daughter of my master's kinsman for his son. ⁴⁹ Now then, if you will deal loyally and truly with my master, tell me; and if not, tell me; that I may turn to the right hand or to the left."
⁵⁰ Then Laban and Bethuel answered, "The thing comes from the LORD; we cannot speak to you bad or good. ⁵¹ Behold, Rebekah is before you, take her and go, and let her be the wife of your master's son, as the LORD has spoken."... And they called Rebekah, and said to her, "Will you go with this man?" She said, "I will go." ⁵⁹ So they sent away Rebekah their sister and her nurse, and Abraham's servant and his men. ⁶⁰ And they blessed Rebekah, and said to her, "Our sister, be the mother of thousands of ten thousands; and may your descendants possess the gate of those who hate them!" ⁶¹ Then Rebekah and her maids arose, and rode upon the camels and followed the man; thus the servant took Rebekah, and went his way.
⁶² Now Isaac had come from Beer-lahai-roi, and was dwelling in the Negeb. ⁶³ And Isaac went out to meditate in the field in the evening; and he lifted up his eyes and looked, and behold, there were camels coming. ⁶⁴ And Rebekah lifted up her eyes, and when she saw Isaac, she alighted from the camel, ⁶⁵ and said to the servant, "Who is the man yonder, walking in the field to meet us?" The servant said, "It is my master." So she took her veil and covered herself. ⁶⁶ And the servant told Isaac all the things that he had done. ⁶⁷ Then Isaac brought her into the tent, and took Rebekah, and she became his wife; and he loved her. So Isaac was comforted after his mother's death.

Tob 7:9-14 So he communicated the proposal to Raguel. And Raguel said to Tobias, "Eat, drink, and be merry; ¹⁰ for it is your right to take my child. But let me explain the true situation to you. ¹¹ I have given my daughter to seven husbands, and when each came to her he died in the night. But for the present be merry." And Tobias said, "I will eat nothing here until you make a binding agreement with me." ¹² So Raguel said, "Take her right now, in accordance with the law. You are her relative, and she is yours. The merciful God will guide you both for the best." ¹³ Then he called his daughter Sarah, and taking her by the hand he gave her to Tobias to be his wife, saying, "Here she is; take her according to the law of Moses, and take her with you to your father." And he blessed them. ¹⁴ Next he called his wife Edna, and took a scroll and wrote out the contract; and they set their seals to it.

Tob 8:4-9 When the door was shut and the two were alone, Tobias got up from the bed and said, "Sister, get up, and let us pray that the Lord may have mercy upon us." ⁵ And Tobias began to pray,
"Blessed art thou, O God of our fathers,
and blessed be thy holy and glorious name for ever.
Let the heavens and all thy creatures bless thee. ⁶ Thou madest Adam and gavest him Eve his wife
as a helper and support.
From them the race of mankind has sprung.
Thou didst say, 'It is not good that the man should be alone;
let us make a helper for him like himself.' ⁷ And now, O Lord, I am not taking this sister of mine because of lust, but with sincerity. Grant that I may find mercy and may grow old together with her." ⁸ And she said with him, "Amen." ⁹ Then they both went to sleep for the night.

Song 2:8-10,14,16;8:6-7 The voice of my beloved!
Behold, he comes,
leaping upon the mountains,
bounding over the hills. ⁹ My beloved is like a gazelle, or a young stag.
Behold, there he stands
behind our wall,
gazing in at the windows,
looking through the lattice. ¹⁰ My beloved speaks and says to me:
"Arise, my love, my fair one,
and come away;... O my dove, in the clefts of the rock, in the covert of the cliff,
let me see your face,
let me hear your voice,
for your voice is sweet,
and your face is comely. My beloved is mine and I am his,
he pastures his flock among the lilies. ...

Set me as a seal upon your heart,
as a seal upon your arm;
for love is strong as death,
jealousy is cruel as the grave.
Its flashes are flashes of fire,
a most vehement flame. ⁷ Many waters cannot quench love,
neither can floods drown it.
If a man offered for love
all the wealth of his house,
it would be utterly scorned.

Sir 26:1-4, 13-18 Happy is the husband of a good wife;
the number of his days will be doubled. ² A loyal wife rejoices her husband,
and he will complete his years in peace. ³ A good wife is a great blessing;
she will be granted among the blessings of the man who fears the Lord. ⁴ Whether rich or poor, his heart is glad,
and at all times his face is cheerful.. A wife's charm delights her husband,
and her skill puts fat on his bones. ¹⁴ A silent wife is a gift of the Lord,
and there is nothing so precious as a disciplined soul. ¹⁵ A modest wife adds charm to charm,
and no balance can weigh the value of a chaste soul. ¹⁶ Like the sun rising in the heights of the Lord,
so is the beauty of a good wife in her well-ordered home. ¹⁷ Like the shining lamp on the holy lampstand,
so is a beautiful face on a stately figure. ¹⁸ Like pillars of gold on a base of silver, so are beautiful feet with a steadfast heart.

Jer 31:31-34 "Behold, the days are coming, says the Lord, when I will make a new covenant with the house of Israel and the house of Judah, ³² not like the covenant which I made with their fathers when I took them by the hand to bring them out of the land of Egypt, my covenant which they broke, though I was their husband, says the Lord. ³³ But this is the covenant which I will make with the house of Israel after those days, says the Lord: I will put my law within them, and I will write it upon their hearts; and I will be their God, and they shall be my people. ³⁴ And no longer shall each man teach his neighbor and each his brother, saying, 'Know the Lord,' for they shall all know me, from the least of them to the greatest, says the Lord; for I will forgive their iniquity, and I will remember their sin no more."

Rom 8:31-35,37-39 What then shall we say to this? If God is for us, who is against us? ³² He who did not spare his own Son but gave him up for us all, will he not also give us all things with him? ³³ Who shall bring any charge against God's elect? It is God who justifies; ³⁴ who is to condemn? Is it Christ Jesus, who died, yes, who was raised from the dead, who is at the right hand of God, who indeed intercedes for us? ³⁵ Who shall separate us from the love of Christ? Shall tribulation, or distress, or persecution, or famine, or nakedness, or peril, or sword?... No, in all these things we are more than conquerors through him who loved us. ³⁸ For I am sure that neither death, nor life, nor angels, nor principalities, nor things present, nor things to come, nor powers, ³⁹ nor height, nor depth, nor anything else in all creation, will be able to separate us from the love of God in Christ Jesus our Lord.

Rom 12:1-2,9-13 I appeal to you therefore, brethren, by the mercies of God, to present your bodies as a living sacrifice, holy and acceptable to God, which is your spiritual worship. ² Do not be conformed to this world but be transformed by the renewal of your mind, that you may prove what is the will of God, what is good and acceptable and perfect..... Let love be genuine; hate what is evil, hold fast to what is good; ¹⁰ love one another with brotherly affection; outdo one another in showing honor. ¹¹ Never flag in zeal, be aglow with the Spirit, serve the Lord. ¹² Rejoice in your hope, be patient in tribulation, be constant in prayer. ¹³ Contribute to the needs of the saints, practice hospitality.

1 Cor 6:13-20 "Food is meant for the stomach and the stomach for food"—and God will destroy both one and the other. The body is not meant for immorality, but for the Lord, and the Lord for the body. ¹⁴ And God raised the Lord and will also raise us up by his power. ¹⁵ Do you not know that your bodies are members of Christ? Shall I therefore take the members of Christ and make them members of a prostitute? Never! ¹⁶ Do you not know that he who joins himself to a prostitute becomes one body with her? For, as it is written, "The two shall become one flesh." ¹⁷ But he who is united to the Lord becomes one spirit with him. ¹⁸ Shun immorality. Every other sin which a man commits is outside the body; but the immoral man sins against his own body. ¹⁹ Do you not know that your body is a temple of the Holy Spirit within you, which you have from God? You are not your own; ²⁰ you were bought with a price. So glorify God in your body.

1 Cor 12:31-13:8 But earnestly desire the higher gifts. And I will show you a still more excellent way. ¹ If I speak in the tongues of men and of angels, but have not love, I am a noisy gong or a clanging cymbal. ² And if I have prophetic powers, and understand all mysteries and all knowledge, and if I have all faith, so as to remove mountains, but have not love, I am nothing. ³ If I give away all I have, and if I deliver my body to be burned, but have not love, I gain nothing.

⁴ Love is patient and kind; love is not jealous or boastful; ⁵ it is not arrogant or rude. Love does not insist on its own way; it is not irritable or resentful; ⁶ it does not rejoice at wrong, but rejoices in the right. ⁷ Love bears all things, believes all things, hopes all things, endures all things.

⁸ Love never ends; as for prophecies, they will pass away; as for tongues, they will cease; as for knowledge, it will pass away.

1 Pet 3:1-9 Likewise you wives, be submissive to your husbands, so that some, though they do not obey the word, may be won without a word by the behavior of their wives, ² when they see your reverent and chaste behavior. ³ Let not yours be the outward adorning with braiding of hair, decoration of gold, and wearing of fine clothing, ⁴ but let it be the hidden person of the heart with the imperishable jewel of a gentle and quiet spirit, which in God's sight is very precious. ⁵ So once the holy women who hoped in God used to adorn themselves and were submissive to their husbands, ⁶ as Sarah obeyed Abraham, calling him lord. And you are now her children if you do right and let nothing terrify you.

⁷ Likewise you husbands, live considerately with your wives, bestowing honor on the woman as the weaker sex, since you are joint heirs of the grace of life, in order that your prayers may not be hindered.

⁸ Finally, all of you, have unity of spirit, sympathy, love of the brethren, a tender heart and a humble mind. ⁹ Do not return evil for evil or reviling for reviling; but on the contrary bless, for to this you have been called, that you may obtain a blessing.

1 Jn 3:18-24 Little children, let us not love in word or speech but in deed and in truth.

¹⁹ By this we shall know that we are of the truth, and reassure our hearts before him ²⁰ whenever our hearts condemn us; for God is greater than our hearts, and he knows everything. ²¹ Beloved, if our hearts do not condemn us, we have confidence before God; ²² and we receive from him whatever we ask, because we keep his commandments and do what pleases him. ²³ And this is his commandment, that we should believe in the name of his Son Jesus Christ and love one another, just as he has commanded us. ²⁴ All who keep his commandments abide in him, and he in them. And by this we know that he abides in us, by the Spirit which he has given us.

1 Jn 4:7-12 Beloved, let us love one another; for love is of God, and he who loves is born of God and knows God. ⁸ He who does not love does not know God; for God is love. ⁹ In this the love of God was made manifest among us, that God sent his only Son into the world, so that we might live through him. ¹⁰ In this is love, not that we loved God but that he loved us and sent his Son to be the expiation for our sins. ¹¹ Beloved, if God so loved us, we also ought to love one another. ¹² No man has ever seen God; if we love one another, God abides in us and his love is perfected in us.

1 Tim 2:15 Yet woman will be saved through bearing children, if she continues in faith and love and holiness, with modesty.

1 Thess 4:4 that each one of you know how to control his own body in holiness and honor,...

Hosea *Through his unfaithful wife and broken marriage, he was a prophetic picture of apostate Israel. This entire book is the clearest image of Israel's condition and it was given to us by God through the image of a broken marriage. Marriage is a constant image of his covenant relationship with us. Many prophets refer to apostasy of covenant as "adultery."*

Mt 19:1-9 Now when Jesus had finished these sayings, he went away from Galilee and entered the region of Judea beyond the Jordan; ² and large crowds followed him, and he healed them there.

³ And Pharisees came up to him and tested him by asking, "Is it lawful to divorce one's wife for any cause?" ⁴ He answered, "Have you not read that he who made them from the beginning made them male and female, ⁵ and said, 'For this reason a man shall leave his father and mother and be joined to his wife, and the two shall become one flesh'? ⁶ So they are no longer two but one flesh. What therefore God has joined together, let not man put asunder." ⁷ They said to him, "Why then did Moses command one to give a certificate of divorce, and to put her away?" ⁸ He said to them, "For your hardness of heart Moses allowed you to divorce your wives, but from the beginning it was not so. ⁹ And I say to you: whoever divorces his wife, except for unchastity, and marries another,

commits adultery; and he who marries a divorced woman, commits adultery."

God treated Israel as the Israelites treated each other - they insisted on bills of divorce for themselves, so God showed them what bills of divorce meant.

Is 50:1-2 Thus says the LORD: "Where is your mother's bill of divorce, with which I put her away? Or which of my creditors is it to whom I have sold you? Behold, for your iniquities you were sold, and for your transgressions your mother was put away. ² Why, when I came, was there no man? When I called, was there no one to answer? Is my hand shortened, that it cannot redeem? Or have I no power to deliver? Behold, by my rebuke I dry up the sea, I make the rivers a desert; their fish stink for lack of water, and die of thirst.

Jer 3:8 She saw that for all the adulteries of that faithless one, Israel, I had sent her away with a decree of divorce; yet her false sister Judah did not fear, but she too went and played the harlot.

But Christ's covenant does not permit such ill-use of one another...

Mt 19:4-5 He answered, "Have you not read that he who made them from the beginning made them male and female, ⁵ and said, 'For this reason a man shall leave his father and mother and be joined to his wife, and the two shall become one flesh'?

Mk 10:7-9 'For this reason a man shall leave his father and mother and be joined to his wife, ⁸ and the two shall become one flesh.' So they are no longer two but one flesh. ⁹ What therefore God has joined together, let not man put asunder."

Heb 13:4 Let marriage be held in honor among all, and let the marriage bed be undefiled; for God will judge the immoral and adulterous.

Mt 22:35-40 And one of them, a lawyer, asked him a question, to test him. ³⁶ "Teacher, which is the great commandment in the law?" ³⁷ And he said to him, "You shall love the Lord your God with all your heart, and with all your soul, and with all your mind. ³⁸ This is the great and first commandment. ³⁹ And a second is like it, You shall love your neighbor as yourself. ⁴⁰ On these two commandments depend all the law and the prophets."

Jn 15:9-16 As the Father has loved me, so have I loved you; abide in my love. ¹⁰ If you keep my commandments, you will abide in my love, just as I have kept my Father's commandments and abide in his love. ¹¹ These things I have spoken to you, that my joy may be in you, and that your joy may be full.
¹² "This is my commandment, that you love one another as I have loved you. Greater love has no man than this, that a man lay down his life for his friends. ¹⁴ You are my friends if you do what I command you. ¹⁵ No longer do I call you servants, for the servant does not know what his master is doing; but I have called you friends, for all that I have heard from my Father I have made known to you. ¹⁶ You did not choose me, but I chose you and appointed you that you should go and bear fruit and that your fruit should abide; so that whatever you ask the Father in my name, he may give it to you.

Jn 17:20-26 "I do not pray for these only, but also for those who believe in me through their word, ²¹ that they may all be one; even as thou, Father, art in me, and I in thee, that they also may be in us, so that the world may believe that thou hast sent me. ²² The glory which thou hast given me I have given to them, that they may be one even as we are one, ²³ I in them and thou in me, that they may become perfectly one, so that the world may know that thou hast sent me and hast loved them even as thou hast loved me. ²⁴ Father, I desire that they also, whom thou hast given me, may be with me where I am, to behold my glory which thou hast given me in thy love for me before the foundation of the world. ²⁵ O righteous Father, the world has not known thee, but I have known thee; and these know that thou hast sent me. ²⁶ I made known to them thy name, and I will make it known, that the love with which thou hast loved me may be in them, and I in them."

Jn 2:1-11 On the third day there was a marriage at Cana in Galilee, and the mother of Jesus was there; ² Jesus also was invited to the marriage, with his disciples. ³ When the wine failed, the mother of Jesus said to him, "They have no wine." ⁴ And Jesus said to her, "O woman, what have you to do with me? My hour has not yet come." ⁵ His mother said to the servants, "Do whatever he tells you." ⁶ Now six stone jars were standing there, for the Jewish rites of purification, each holding twenty or thirty gallons. ⁷ Jesus said to them, "Fill the jars with water." And they filled them up to the brim. ⁸ He said to them, "Now draw some out, and take it to the steward of the feast." So they took it. ⁹ When the steward of the feast tasted the water now become wine, and did not know where it came from (though the servants who had drawn the water knew), the steward of the feast called the bridegroom [10] and said to him, "Every man serves the good wine first; and when men have drunk freely, then the poor wine; but you have kept the good wine until now." [11] This, the first of his signs, Jesus did at Cana in Galilee, and manifested his glory; and his disciples believed in him.

The first miracle of the Incarnate Word was accomplished at a wedding feast. At a wedding, it was the bridegroom's obligation to supply the wine. This account tells us the name of both the Bridegroom and the Bride. It was here at the Wedding Feast, where the marriage between God and man is begun, that his disciples first began to believe. This union will not be broken. Even the Apostles will attest to it.

Acts 15:28 For it has seemed good to the Holy Spirit and to us....

The Bride works in union with the Bridegroom.
The Wedding Feast is the icon for the whole public ministry of Christ, surveying the whole purpose of the Incarnation. The Bride and Bridegroom at the Wedding Feast is Christ's favorite description for the Kingdom of Heaven.

Jn 3:29 He who has the bride is the bridegroom; the friend of the bridegroom, who stands and hears him, rejoices greatly at the bridegroom's voice; therefore this joy of mine is now full.

Mt 9:15 And Jesus said to them, "Can the wedding guests mourn as long as the bridegroom is with them? The days will come, when the bridegroom is taken away from them, and then they will fast.

Mt 25:1,10 "Then the kingdom of heaven shall be compared to ten maidens who took their lamps and went to meet the bridegroom... And while they went to buy, the bridegroom came, and those who were ready went in with him to the marriage feast; and the door was shut.

Mk 2:19-20 "Can the wedding guests fast while the bridegroom is with them? As long as they have the bridegroom with them, they cannot fast. [20] The days will come, when the bridegroom is taken away from them, and then they will fast in that day.

Lk 5:34-35 And Jesus said to them, "Can you make wedding guests fast while the bridegroom is with them? [35] The days will come, when the bridegroom is taken away from them, and then they will fast in those days."

Lk 12:35-36 "Let your loins be girded and your lamps burning, [36] and be like men who are waiting for their master to come home from the marriage feast, so that they may open to him at once when he comes and knocks.

Lk 14:6 Now he told a parable to those who were invited, when he marked how they chose the places of honor, saying to them, [8] "When you are invited by any one to a marriage feast, do not sit down in a place of honor, lest a more eminent man than you be invited by him; [9] and he who invited you both will come and say to you, 'Give place to this man,' and then you will begin with shame to take the lowest place.

Mt 22:1-9 And again Jesus spoke to them in parables, saying, [2] "The kingdom of heaven may be compared to a king who gave a marriage feast for his son, [3] and sent his servants to call those who were invited to the marriage feast; but they would not come. [4] Again he sent other servants, saying, 'Tell those who are invited, Behold, I have made ready my dinner, my oxen and my fat calves are killed, and everything is ready; come to the marriage feast.' [5] But they made light of it and went off, one to his farm, another to his business, [6] while the rest seized his servants, treated them shamefully, and killed them. [7] The king was angry, and he sent his troops and destroyed those murderers and burned their city. [8] Then he said to his servants, 'The wedding is ready, but those invited were not worthy. [9] Go therefore to the thoroughfares, and invite to the marriage feast as many as you find.' [10] And those servants went out into the streets and gathered all whom they found, both bad and good; so the wedding hall was filled with guests.
[11] "But when the king came in to look at the guests, he saw there a man who had no wedding garment; [12] and he said to him, 'Friend, how did you get in here without a wedding garment?' And he was speechless. [13] Then the king said to the attendants, 'Bind him hand and foot, and cast him into the outer darkness; there men will weep and gnash their teeth.' [14] For many are called, but few are chosen."

Note that guests who treat marriage and the marriage feast lightly receive total destruction and death by fire from the king.

Rev 18:23 and the light of a lamp
shall shine in thee no more;
and the voice of bridegroom and bride
shall be heard in thee no more;

The loss of the wedding couple is the last and greatest sign signaling the loss of salvation for Babylon.

2 Cor 11:2 I feel a divine jealousy for you, for I betrothed you to Christ to present you as a pure bride to her one husband.

Rev 21:2-4 And I saw the holy city, new Jerusalem, coming down out of heaven from God, prepared as a bride adorned for her husband; ³ and I heard a loud voice from the throne saying, "Behold, the dwelling of God is with men. He will dwell with them, and they shall be his people, and God himself will be with them; ⁴ he will wipe away every tear from their eyes, and death shall be no more, neither shall there be mourning nor crying nor pain any more, for the former things have passed away...." Then came one of the seven angels who had the seven bowls full of the seven last plagues, and spoke to me, saying, "Come, I will show you the Bride, the wife of the Lamb." ¹⁰ And in the Spirit he carried me away to a great, high mountain, and showed me the holy city Jerusalem coming down out of heaven from God,

Rev 22:17 The Spirit and the Bride say, "Come."

Rev 19:1,5-9 After this I heard what seemed to be the loud voice of a great multitude in heaven, crying, "Hallelujah! Salvation and glory and power belong to our God... 5 And from the throne came a voice crying, "Praise our God, all you his servants,
you who fear him, small and great." ⁶ Then I heard what seemed to be the voice of a great multitude, like the sound of many waters and like the sound of mighty thunderpeals, crying,
"Hallelujah! For the Lord our God the Almighty reigns. ⁷ Let us rejoice and exult and give him the glory,
for the marriage of the Lamb has come,
and his Bride has made herself ready; ⁸ it was granted her to be clothed with fine linen, bright and pure"—
for the fine linen is the righteous deeds of the saints.

⁹ And the angel said to me, "Write this: Blessed are those who are invited to the marriage supper of the Lamb." And he said to me, "These are true words of God."

The Wedding Feast is the reward for those who persevere to the end.

Divorce

Divorce is impossible - what God has joined, no man may break asunder. In order for a valid marriage to have occurred, both parties must make full, free, and knowledgeable assent to entrance into the sacrament. A serious defect of understanding, freedom, or intent may erect such an impediment to the graces proper to marriage that the bond of marriage is never actually established to begin with, despite the appearance of such. If, after proper investigation of the circumstances surrounding the event, such impediments are shown to have been present, the Church may declare that a valid sacramental marriage was not, in fact, undertaken. This formal declaration is called an "annulment" - it is the formal recognition that one or both parties were operating under such impediments that the graces proper to the establishment of the bond of marriage were not conferred, and no marriage was ever established.

Current misunderstandings: Many Christian denominations permit divorce.

Mt 5:31-32 "It was also said, 'Whoever divorces his wife, let him give her a certificate of divorce.' ³² But I say to you that every one who divorces his wife, except on the ground of unchastity, makes her an adulteress; and whoever marries a divorced woman commits adultery.

Mt 19:3-9 And Pharisees came up to him and tested him by asking, "Is it lawful to divorce one's wife for any cause?" ⁴ He answered, "Have you not read that he who made them from the beginning made them male and female, ⁵ and said, 'For this reason a man shall leave his father and mother and be joined to his wife, and the two shall become one flesh'? ⁶ So they are no longer two but one flesh. What therefore God has joined together, let not man put asunder." ⁷ They said to him, "Why then did Moses command one to give a certificate of divorce, and to put her away?" ⁸ He said to them, "For your hardness of heart Moses allowed you to divorce your wives, but from the beginning it was not so. ⁹ And I say to you: whoever divorces his wife, except for unchastity, and marries another, commits adultery."

Porneia, the word translated here as "unchastity" means "sexual unlawfulness." It probably refers to a couple living together without being formally engaged or married, or to an attempt to marry someone who is too close in consanguinity, that is, too close of a blood relative, to validly do so.

Mal 2:15-16 Has not the one God made and sustained for us the spirit of life? And what does he desire? Godly offspring. So take heed to yourselves, and let none be faithless to the wife of his youth. ¹⁶ "For I hate divorce, says the LORD the God of Israel, and covering one's garment with violence, says the LORD of hosts. So take heed to yourselves and do not be faithless.

Some attempt to say Christian divorce is acceptable in cases of infidelity or adultery. This cannot be true. Not only does it offend Scripture, it offends reason. By this reasoning, all a married man need do in order to divorce his first wife and marry the second is to have relations with the woman he intends to marry, and the first covenant would be broken. Marriage is the key to our relationship with Christ. If we violate our marriage to our spouse, we violate our marriage to Christ.

Mk 10:2-9 And Pharisees came up and in order to test him asked, "Is it lawful for a man to divorce his wife?" ³ He answered them, "What did Moses command you?" ⁴ They said, "Moses allowed a man to write a certificate of divorce, and to put her away." ⁵ But Jesus said to them, "For your hardness of heart he wrote you this commandment. ⁶ But from the beginning of creation, 'God made them male and female.' ⁷ 'For this reason a man shall leave his father and mother and be joined to his wife, ⁸ and the two shall become one flesh.' So they are no longer two but one flesh. ⁹ What therefore God has joined together, let not man put asunder."

1 Cor 7:10-15 To the married I give charge, not I but the Lord, that the wife should not separate from her husband ¹¹ (but if she does, let her remain single or else be reconciled to her husband)—and that the husband should not divorce his wife.

¹² To the rest I say, not the Lord, that if any brother has a wife who is an unbeliever, and she consents to live with him, he should not divorce her. ¹³ If any woman has a husband who is an unbeliever, and he consents to live with her, she should not divorce him. ¹⁴ For the unbelieving husband is consecrated through his wife, and the unbelieving wife is consecrated through her husband. Otherwise, your children would be unclean, but as it is they are holy. ¹⁵ But if the unbelieving partner desires to separate, let it be so; in such a case the brother or sister is not bound. For God has called us to peace.

This passage is the basis for the "Pauline privilege." Marriage is a sacrament. A sacrament may only be validly conferred onto a baptized person (except for baptism itself, which is the sacrament of entry into the Body of Christ, and the gateway to all other sacraments). Both partners must be baptized in order for a sacramental marriage to have occurred. If two unbaptized people marry, a natural, non-sacramental marriage occurs. If one member of a natural marriage is subsequently baptized, the natural marriage may, under certain circumstances, be dissolved in order to protect the faith of the baptized member.

Early Christians' comments on Divorce and Remarriage

Birth Control

Most of the Scripture and commentary concerning Judah and Onan summarizes Brian W. Harrison "Onan's Real Sin," This Rock, April 1997, pp. 40-42.

The use of artificial birth control is an intrinsic evil, being an act which destroys not only the procreative but the unitive aspects of the sexual act. The use of artificial fertilization is also wrong, and made more heinous by the use of active elements, sperm or ovum, which derive from a third party, not least because it breaks the essential unitive aspect of the marital act. However, the use of medical treatment which permits the completion of the marital act between husband and wife, or which enhances the fertility of this act, is acceptable.

Current misunderstandings: From the foundation of Christianity, for the course of nearly two millenia, all Christian denominations without exception condemned the use of artificial birth control as an intrinsic evil. Within the last two hundred years, new concepts of social engineering and eugenics have run riot through European and American society. These concepts, which reached an apex in Europe in the early part of this century, influenced a 1930 conference of Anglican bishops held in Lambeth, England to such an extent that eugenicists actually took part in the conference. The Anglicans, after study and in light of social pressures, concluded that artificial birth control could be used by married couples only, and only under certain extreme circumstances. With this ruling, the Anglican Church broke ranks with all other Christian denominations and the constant teaching of all Christianity. The floodgates opened. Within twenty years, every major Christian denomination but one had fallen away from a teaching two millenia old. Every major Christian denomination but one.

Gen 1:28 And God blessed them, and God said to them, "Be fruitful and multiply, and fill the earth and subdue it; and have dominion over the fish of the sea and over the birds of the air and over every living thing that moves upon the earth."

Consider the case of Judah and his son Onan. In the Old Testament, family lines had to be preserved. If a man died before his wife bore him offspring, it was the duty of the man's brother or father to bring forth offspring for his dead brother's/son's line by having relations with the dead brother's wife until she conceived.

Gen 38:6-10 And Judah took a wife for Er his first-born, and her name was Tamar. ⁷ But Er, Judah's first-born, was wicked in the sight of the Lord; and the Lord slew him. ⁸ Then Judah said to Onan, "Go in to your brother's wife, and perform the duty of a brother-in-law to her, and raise up offspring for your brother." ⁹ But Onan knew that the offspring would not be his; so when he went in to his brother's wife he spilled the semen on the ground, lest he should give offspring to his brother. ¹⁰ And what he did was displeasing in the sight of the Lord, and he slew him also.

Some argue that Onan was killed for his failure to do his duty, not because of his practice of birth control. However, this simply misreads the text. Onan was slain for what he DID in the sight of the Lord, not for what he failed to do in the sight of the Lord. Even if verse 10 weren't part of Scripture, the "family duty" argument is Scripturally incoherent. After Onan's death, it was Judah's duty to bring forth children for his dead son's line. But Judah did not do his duty either, nor did he fulfill his promises.

Gen 38:11-18 Then Judah said to Tamar his daughter-in-law, "Remain a widow in your father's house, till Shelah my son grows up"—for he feared that he would die, like his brothers. So Tamar went and dwelt in her father's house.

¹² In course of time the wife of Judah, Shua's daughter, died; and when Judah was comforted, he went up to Timnah to his sheepshearers, he and his friend Hirah the Adullamite ¹³ And when Tamar was told, "Your father-in-law is going up to Timnah to shear his sheep," ¹⁴ she put off her widow's garments, and put on a veil, wrapping herself up, and sat at the entrance to Enaim, which is on the road to Timnah; for she saw that Shelah was grown up, and she had not been given to him in marriage. ¹⁵ When Judah saw her, he thought her to be a harlot, for she had covered her face. ¹⁶ He went over to her at the road side, and said, "Come, let me come in to you," for he did not know that she was his daughter-in-law. She said, "What will you give me, that you may come in to me?" ¹⁷ He answered, "I will send you a kid from the flock." And she said, "Will you give me a pledge, till you send it?" ¹⁸ He said, "What pledge shall I give you?" She replied, "Your signet and your cord, and your staff that is in your hand." So he gave them to her, and went in to her, and she conceived by him.

Gen 38:25-26 As she was being brought out, she sent word to her father-in-law, "By the man to whom these belong, I am with child." And she said, "Mark, I pray you, whose these are, the signet and the cord and the staff." ²⁶ Then Judah acknowledged them and said, "She is more righteous than I, inasmuch as I did not give her to my son Shelah." And he did not lie with her again.

Though Judah did not do his familial duty, nor did he allow his son to carry out that duty, neither Judah nor his son Shelah were killed. Onan's death, therefore, did not result from his failure to do his familial duty, but resulted from some other aspect of his behaviour. Onan willingly undertook the act which would normally bring about new life, but he actively tried to close off the possibility that such a life would be engendered. Onan engaged in a form of birth control, Judah did not.

There is a further consideration. What are the penalties Scripture prescribes for failing to marry the wife of one's dead brother, as opposed to the wasting of seed?

Deut 25:7-10 And if the man does not wish to take his brother's wife, then his brother's wife shall go up to the gate to the elders, and say, 'My husband's brother refuses to perpetuate his brother's name in Israel; he will not perform the duty of a husband's brother to me.' ⁸ Then the elders of his city shall call him, and speak to him: and if he persists, saying, 'I do not wish to take her,' ⁹ then his brother's wife shall go up to him in the presence of the elders, and pull his sandal off his foot, and spit in his face; and she shall answer and say, 'So shall it be done to the man who does not build up his brother's house.' ¹⁰ And the name of his house shall be called in Israel, The house of him that had his sandal pulled off.

If the man refuses to keep up the lineage, the man is simply struck with his own shoe and spat upon. He is not killed. The act which wastes seed is dealt with much more harshly:

Lev 18:22-23, 20:13 You shall not lie with a male as with a woman; it is an abomination. ²³ And you shall not lie with any beast and defile yourself with it, neither shall any woman give herself to a beast to lie with it: it is perversion.... If a man lies with a male as with a woman, both of them have committed an abomination; they shall be put to death, their blood is upon them.

THIS is the act which warrants the death penalty. We are supposed to take the same joy in the generative act that God took in the act of Creation. Wasting or destroying the materials with which one creates is not joyful, it tears down creation just as the serpent attempted to tear down Creation.

Scripture always refers to acceptable acts of intercourse in general terms, i.e., "going into" his wife or "knowing" her. When the description is more explicit, e.g., "lying with" someone or "uncovering ... nakedness," the reference is always to shameful or sinful acts. The description of Onan's act was very explicit.

Rom 1:25-27 because they exchanged the truth about God for a lie and worshiped and served the creature rather than the Creator, who is blessed for ever! Amen.
²⁶ For this reason God gave them up to dishonorable passions. Their women exchanged natural relations for unnatural, ²⁷ and the men likewise gave up natural relations with women and were consumed with passion for one another, men committing shameless acts with men and receiving in their own persons the due penalty for their error.

Sexuality which is closed off to the possibility of procreation is sinful.

Jer 1:5 "Before I formed you in the womb I knew you, and before you were born I consecrated you...

God's greatest gifts are children.

Psalm 127:3-5 Lo, sons are a heritage from the LORD,
 the fruit of the womb a reward.
 ⁴ Like arrows in the hand of a warrior are the sons of one's youth.
 ⁵ Happy is the man who has his quiver full of them!
He shall not be put to shame
 when he speaks with his enemies in the gate.

Psalm 128:3,5-6 Your wife will be like a fruitful vine within your house;
your children will be like olive shoots
around your table. ⁴ Lo, thus shall the man be blessed who fears the LORD. ⁵ The LORD bless you from Zion!
 May you see the prosperity of Jerusalem all the days of your life!
⁶ May you see your children's children! Peace be upon Israel!

Gen 3:16-17 To the woman he said, "I will greatly multiply you pain in childbearing; in pain you shall bring forth children, yet your desire shall be for your husband, and he shall rule over you. ¹⁷ and to Adam he said, "Because you have listened to the voice of your wife, and have eaten of the tree of whichI caommanded you, 'You shall not eat of it,' cursed is the ground because of you; in toil you shall eat of it all the days of your life..'

The twin curses of original sin were problems with fertility and childbirth and worry about famine.

Gen 3:12 The man said, "The woman whom thou gavest to be with me, she gave me fruit of the tree, and I ate."

Adam repudiated his wife before God ("this woman whom YOU gave me"). Abraham, Isaac, and Jacob will do exactly as Adam did; each will repudiate his wife...

Gen 12:10-13 Now there was a famine in the land. So Abram went down to Egypt to sojourn there, for the famine was severe in the land. ¹¹ When he was about to enter Egypt, he said to Sarai his wife, "I know that you are a woman beautiful to behold; ¹² and when the

Egyptians see you, they will say, 'This is his wife'; then they will kill me, but they will let you live. [13] Say you are my sister, that it may go well with me because of you, and that my life may be spared on your account."

Gen 26:6-7 So Isaac dwelt in Gerar. [7] When the men of the place asked him about his wife, he said, "She is my sister"; for he feared to say, "My wife," thinking, "lest the men of the place should kill me for the sake of Rebekah"; because she was fair to look upon.

Gen 29:25 And in the morning, behold, it was Leah; and Jacob said to Laban, "What is this you have done to me? Did I not serve with you for Rachel? Why then have you deceived me?"

each will be struck by infertility and famine...

Gen 12:10 Now there was a famine in the land. So Abram went down to Egypt to sojourn there, for the famine was severe in the land.

Gen 16:1 Now Sarai, Abram's wife, bore him no children.

Gen 25:21 And Isaac prayed to the LORD for his wife, because she was barren; and the LORD granted his prayer, and Rebekah his wife conceived..

Gen 26:1 Now there was a famine in the land, besides the former famine that was in the days of Abraham. And Isaac went to Gerar, to Abimelech king of the Philistines.

Gen 29:31-32 When the LORD saw that Leah was hated, he opened her womb; but Rachel was barren. [32] And Leah conceived and bore a son, and she called his name Reuben; for she said, "Because the LORD has looked upon my affliction; surely now my husband will love me."

Gen 30:1-2 When Rachel saw that she bore Jacob no children, she envied her sister; and she said to Jacob, "Give me children, or I shall die!" [2] Jacob's anger was kindled against Rachel, and he said, "Am I in the place of God, who has withheld from you the fruit of the womb?"

Gen 30:9 When Leah saw that she had ceased bearing children, she took her maid Zilpah and gave her to Jacob as a wife.

Gen 41:54 Moreover, all the earth came to Egypt to Joseph to buy grain, because the famine was severe over all the earth.

It is no coincidence that the first three patriarchs, Abraham, Isaac, and Jacob, all suffered from the curses of infertility and famine. The curses meted out to Adam as a result of his infidelity towards God reverberated through the subsequent covenant between God and man. Mankind learns that it is only the Lord who gives life, and that life is a gift from God.

Mt 1:19-20 and her husband Joseph, being a just man and unwilling to put her to shame, resolved to divorce her quietly. [20] But as he considered this, behold, an angel of the Lord appeared to him in a dream, saying, "Joseph, son of David, do not fear to take Mary your wife, for that which is conceived in her is of the Holy Spirit; [21] she will bear a son, and you shall call his name Jesus, for he will save his people from their sins."

Significantly, Joseph was about to repudiate Mary, and was prevented from doing so only through the warning of an angel. The time of famine and sterility was coming to a radical end...

Jn 3:29 He who has the bride is the bridegroom; the friend of the bridegroom, who stands and hears him, rejoices greatly at the bridegroom's voice; therefore this joy of mine is now full.

Rev 19:9 And the angel said to me, "Write this: Blessed are those who are invited to the marriage supper of the Lamb." And he said to me, "These are true words of God."

Jesus Christ, the Bridegroom, smashes the twin curses of Genesis. His Body, hanging on the Cross, is the fruit of the Tree of Life. When we who are the Bride receive the Bridegroom into ourselves at the wedding feast, we are fed with the everlasting food of His Body, and we are made fruitful thereby. Contraception does not just violate the marriage bond, it also violates the sacrament marriage images: the Eucharist.

2 Pet 1:3-4 His divine power has granted to us all things that pertain to life and godliness, through the knowledge of him who called us to his own glory and excellence, [4] by which he has granted to us his precious and very great promises, that through these you may escape from the corruption that is in the world because of passion, and become partakers of the divine nature.

It is a violation against the very nature we are called to participate in - divinity.

Is 45:9-11 "Woe to him who strives with his Maker, an earthen vessel with the potter! Does the clay say to him who fashions it, 'What are you making'? or 'Your work has no handles'? [10] Woe to him who says to a father, 'What are you begetting?' or to a woman, 'With what are you in travail?'" [11] Thus says the LORD, the Holy One of Israel, and his Maker: "Will you question me about my children, or command me concerning the work of my hands?

Jn 15:1-17 "I am the true vine, and my Father is the vinedresser. [2] Every branch of mine that bears no fruit, he takes away, and every branch that does bear fruit he prunes, that it may bear more fruit. [3] You are already made clean by the word which I have spoken to you. [4] Abide in me, and I in you. As the branch cannot bear fruit by itself, unless it abides in the vine, neither can you, unless you abide in me. [5] I am the vine, you are the branches. He who abides in me, and I in him, he it is that bears much fruit, for apart from me you can do nothing. [6] If a man does not abide in me, he is cast forth as a branch and withers; and the branches are gathered, thrown into the fire and burned. [7] If you abide in me, and my words abide in you, ask whatever you will, and it shall be done for you. [8] By this my Father is glorified, that you bear much fruit, and so prove to be my disciples. [9] As the Father has loved me, so have I loved you; abide in my love. [10] If you keep my commandments, you will abide in my love, just as I have kept my Father's commandments and abide in his love. [11] These things I have spoken to you, that my joy may be in you, and that your joy may be full.
[12] "This is my commandment, that you love one another as I have loved you. [13] Greater love has no man than this, that a man lay down his life for his friends. [14] You are my friends if you do what I command you. [15] No longer do I call you servants, for the servant does not know what his master is doing; but I have called you friends, for all that I have heard from my Father I have made known to you. [16] You did not choose me, but I chose you and appointed you that you should go and bear fruit and that your fruit should abide; so that whatever you ask the Father in my name, he may give it to you. [17] This I command you, to love one another.

Contraception expresses hatred for one's own flesh, a wish for sterility instead of the fecundity which is the natural order of a healthy body.

Phil 3:2 Look out for the dogs, look out for the evil-workers, look out for those who mutilate the flesh.

While Paul was talking here about the Jewish converts who insisted on circumcising Gentiles, the warning seems to be an uncomfortably accurate description of surgical sterilization.

Eph 5:29-32 For no man ever hates his own flesh, but nourishes and cherishes it, as Christ does the church, [30] because we are members of his body. [31] "For this reason a man shall leave his father and mother and be joined to his wife, and the two shall become one flesh." [32] This mystery is a profound one, and I mean in reference to Christ and the church...

Fyodor Dostoevsky, in The Brothers Karamazov, *put it best when he had the defense attorney at the trial of a man accused of parricide say: "The conventional answer (to the question "Who is my father?") is: 'He begot you, and you are his flesh and blood, and therefore you are bound to love him.' The youth involuntarily reflects: 'But did he love me when he begot me?' he asks, wondering more and more, 'Was it for my sake he begot me? He did not know me, not even my sex, at that moment, at the moment of passion, perhaps, inflamed by wine..."*

"Did he love me when he begot me?" When we actively put up chemical or physical walls between ourselves, our lover, and the child which, perhaps, might be begotten, will we truly have loved that child into existence, as God loved us into existence? Are we acting in the image of the living God?

Early Christians' comments on Birth Control

Abortion

The Scripture quotes in this section, and the references to the Talmud, come from Brian Clowes', The Facts of Life, *pp. 199-200, 219.*

Abortion is an intrinsic evil. Anyone who procures an abortion, or anyone who assists in the procurement of an abortion is guilty by that very act of a terrible abomination before God. Yet, it is also true that every sin can be forgiven. We need only turn again to God and ask His forgiveness, and it will flow like a river. As far as east is from west, so far will He cast away the sins of those who ask forgiveness, and He will remember their transgressions no more. (CCC 2270-2275)

Current misunderstandings: Some Christians assert that abortion is a morally acceptable choice.

Gen 9:6 Whoever sheds the blood of man in a man, his blood will be shed...

The Talmud defines "man in a man" as a preborn baby in his mother's womb. In the Mishneh Torah, *Maimonedes states "A descendant of Noah who kills any human being, even an infant in his mother's womb, is to be put to death."*

Some argue that the book of Exodus permits abortion:

Ex 21:22-25 "When men strive together, and hurt a woman with child, so that there is a miscarriage, and yet no harm follows, the one who hurt her shall be fined, according as the woman's husband shall lay upon him; and he shall pay as the judges determine. [23] If any harm follows, then you shall give life for life, [24] eye for eye, tooth for tooth, hand for hand, foot for foot, [25] burn for burn, wound for wound, stripe for stripe.

The Hebrew term used here for miscarried baby is y'ladeha which means "child," not u'bar or v'lad, meaning "embryo" or "fetus." The payment prescribed here does not mean that the child is deemed less than fully human, for the passage clearly describes an unintentionally caused miscarriage. A man could accidentally cause the death of another and not be condemned to death.

Num 35:22-34 "But if he stabbed him suddenly without enmity, or hurled anything on him without lying in wait, [23] or used a stone, by which a man may die, and without seeing him cast it upon him, so that he died, though he was not his enemy, and did not seek his harm; [24] then the congregation shall judge between the manslayer and the avenger of blood, in accordance with these ordinances; [25] and the congregation shall rescue the manslayer from the hand of the avenger of blood, and the congregation shall restore him to his city of refuge, to which he had fled, and he shall live in it until the death of the high priest who was anointed with the holy oil.

While it is true that the man who causes miscarriage does not flee to a city of refuge as does one who kills an adult, yet this does not mean that Jewish law saw the preborn child as less than human.

Ex 21:20-21 "When a man strikes his slave, male or female, with a rod and the slave dies under his hand, he shall be punished. [21] But if the slave survives a day or two, he is not to be punished; for the slave is his money."

The Law for harming a slave involved penalties different from either of the previous, but the Law clearly understood both free man and slave as fully human, for the Law had provisions for the freeing of the same slave on the year of Jubilee. The question in these cases does not concern a question about the humanity or worth of the victim, but of authority. Deliberate killing was an attack on the gift of life from God, while unintended killing was not.

Life begins at conception:

Gen 16:11 And the angel of the LORD said to her, "Behold, you are with child, and shall bear a son; you shall call his name Ishmael; because the LORD has given heed to your affliction."

Gen 25:21-26 And Isaac prayed to the LORD for his wife, because she was barren; and the LORD granted his prayer, and Rebekah his wife conceived. [22] The children struggled together within her...

Rom 9:10-13 And not only so, but also when Rebecca had conceived children by one man, our forefather Isaac, [11] though they were not yet born and had done nothing either good or bad, in order that God's purpose of election might continue, not because of works but because of his call, [12] she was told, "The elder will serve the younger." [13] As it is written, "Jacob I loved, but Esau I hated."

Hos 12:2-3 The LORD has an indictment against Judah, and will punish Jacob according to his ways, and requite him according to his deeds. [3] In the womb he took his brother by the heel, and in his manhood he strove with God.

Psalm 51:5 Behold, I was brought forth in iniquity, and in sin did my mother conceive me.

Lk 1:35 And the angel said to her, "The Holy Spirit will come upon you, and the power of the Most High will overshadow you; therefore the child to be born will be called holy, the Son of God."

Jer 1:5 "Before I formed you in the womb I knew you, and before you were born I consecrated you; I appointed you a prophet to the nations."

Is 44:2,24 Thus says the Lord who made you, who formed you from the womb and will help you: Fear not, O Jacob my servant, Jeshurun whom I have chosen... Thus says the Lord, your Redeemer, who formed you from the womb...

Is 46:3 "Hearken to me, O house of Jacob, all the remnant of the house of Israel, who have been borne by me from your birth, carried from the womb..."

Is 49:1,2 Listen to me, O coastlands, and hearken, you peoples from afar. The Lord called me from the womb, from the body of my mother he named my name. ² He made my mouth like a sharp sword, in the shadow of his hand he hid me; he made me a polished arrow, in his quiver he hid me away.

Is 49:15-16 "Can a woman forget her sucking child, that she should have no compassion on the son of her womb? Even these may forget, yet I will not forget you. ¹⁶ Behold, I have graven you on the palms of my hands

Job 10:8-12 Thy hands fashioned and made me;
and now thou dost turn about and destroy me.
⁹ Remember that thou hast made me of clay;
and wilt thou turn me to dust again?
¹⁰ Didst thou not pour me out like milk
and curdle me like cheese?
¹¹ Thou didst clothe me with skin and flesh,
and knit me together with bones and sinews.
¹² Thou hast granted me life and steadfast love;
and thy care has preserved my spirit.

Job 31:15 Did not he who made me in the womb make him? And did not one fashion us in the womb?

Eccles 11:5 As you do not know how the spirit comes to the bones in the womb of a woman with child, so you do not know the work of God who makes everything.

Lk 1:41-44 And when Elizabeth heard the greeting of Mary, the babe leaped in her womb; and Elizabeth was filled with the Holy Spirit ⁴² and she exclaimed with a loud cry, "Blessed are you among women, and blessed is the fruit of your womb! ⁴³ And why is this granted me, that the mother of my Lord should come to me? ⁴⁴ For behold, when the voice of your greeting came to my ears, the babe in my womb leaped for joy.

God knew us from the very beginning:

Eph 1:4 even as he chose us in him before the foundation of the world, that we should be holy and blameless before him.

Mt 25:34 Then the King will say to those at his right hand, 'Come, O blessed of my Father, inherit the kingdom prepared for you from the foundation of the world...

Psalm 139:13-14 For thou didst form my inward parts,
thou didst knit me together in my mother's womb.
¹⁴ I praise thee, for thou art fearful and wonderful.
Wonderful are thy works!
Thou knowest me right well;

Job 10:8-12 Thy hands fashioned and made me;
and now thou dost turn about and destroy me.
⁹ Remember that thou hast made me of clay;
and wilt thou turn me to dust again?
¹⁰ Didst thou not pour me out like milk
and curdle me like cheese?
¹¹ Thou didst clothe me with skin and flesh,
and knit me together with bones and sinews.
¹² Thou hast granted me life and steadfast love;
and thy care has preserved my spirit.

2 Mac 7:22 "I do not know how you came into being in my womb. It was not I who gave you life and breath, nor I who set in order the elements within each of you... "

Gen 4:1 Now Adam knew Eve his wife, and she conceived and bore Cain, saying, "I have gotten a man with the help of the Lord."

Children are created not just through the work of man, but with the help and joy of the Lord. That is why a child with a physical defect is no less a gift from God:

Jn 9:1-3 As he passed by, he saw a man blind from his birth. ² And his disciples asked him, "Rabbi, who sinned, this man or his parents, that he was born blind?" ³ Jesus answered, "It was not that this man sinned, or his parents, but that the works of God might be made manifest in him."

Acts 17:27-29 that they should seek God, in the hope that they might feel after him and find him. Yet he is not far from each one of us, ²⁸ for 'In him we live and move and have our being'; as even some of your poets have said,
'For we are indeed his offspring.' ²⁹ Being then God's offspring, we ought not to think that the Deity is like gold, or silver, or stone, a representation by the art and imagination of man.

Psalm 94:9 He who planted the ear, does he not hear? He who formed the eye, does he not see?

Lev 19:14 You shall not curse the deaf or put a stumbling block before the blind, but you shall fear your God: I am the LORD.

Is 45:9-12 "Woe to him who strives with his Maker, an earthen vessel with the potter! Does the clay say to him who fashions it, 'What are you making'? or 'Your work has no handles'? ¹⁰ Woe to him who says to a father, 'What are you begetting?' or to a woman, 'With what are you in travail?'" ¹¹ Thus says the LORD, the Holy One of Israel, and his Maker: "Will you question me about my children, or command me concerning the work of my hands? ¹² I made the earth, and created man upon it; it was my hands that stretched out the heavens, and I commanded all their host.

Children must not be sacrificed for any reason:

Ezek 16:20-21 And you took your sons and your daughters, whom you had borne to me, and these you sacrificed to them to be devoured. Were your harlotries so small a matter ²¹ that you slaughtered my children and delivered them up as an offering by fire to them?

Jer 32:35 They built the high places of Baal in the valley of the son of Hinnom, to offer up their sons and daughters to Molech, though I did not command them, nor did it enter into my mind, that they should do this abomination, to cause Judah to sin.

Ex 1:15-17 Then the king of Egypt said to the Hebrew midwives, one of whom was named Shiphrah and the other Puah, ¹⁶ "When you serve as midwife to the Hebrew women, and see them upon the birthstool, if it is a son, you shall kill him; but if it is a daughter, she shall live." ¹⁷ But the midwives feared God, and did not do as the king of Egypt commanded them, but let the male children live.

Psalm 106:37-42 They sacrificed their sons and their daughters to the demons;
³⁸ they poured out innocent blood,
   the blood of their sons and daughters,
whom they sacrificed to the idols of Canaan;
   and the land was polluted with blood.
³⁹ Thus they became unclean by their acts,
   and played the harlot in their doings.
⁴⁰ Then the anger of the LORD was kindled against his people,
   and he abhorred his heritage;
⁴¹ he gave them into the hand of the nations,
   so that those who hated them ruled over them.
⁴² Their enemies oppressed them,
and they were brought into subjection under their power.

2 Kings 16:3 but he walked in the way of the kings of Israel. He even burned his son as an offering, according to the abominable practices of the nations whom the LORD drove out before the people of Israel.

2 Kings 17:17 And they burned their sons and their daughters as offerings, and used divination and sorcery, and sold themselves to do evil in the sight of the LORD, provoking him to anger.

2 Kings 21:6 And he burned his son as an offering, and practiced soothsaying and augury, and dealt with mediums and with wizards. He did much evil in the sight of the LORD, provoking him to anger.

Deut 12:31 You shall not do so to the LORD your God; for every abominable thing which the LORD hates they have done for their gods; for they even burn their sons and their daughters in the fire to their gods.

Deut 18:10 There shall not be found among you any one who burns his son or his daughter as an offering, any one who practices divination, a soothsayer, or an augur, or a sorcerer...

Lev 18:21,30 You shall not give any of your children to devote them by fire to Molech, and so profane the name of your God: I am the LORD.... So keep my charge never to practice any of these abominable customs which were practiced before you, and never to defile yourselves by them: I am the LORD your God."

Mt 2:16 Then Herod, when he saw that he had been tricked by the wise men, was in a furious rage, and he sent and killed all the male children in Bethlehem and in all that region who were two years old or under, according to the time which he had ascertained from the wise men.

These children were sacrificed in order to attain material, temporal goods. To what gods of material, temporal good are today's children sacrificed? We have a duty to protect women and children, especially women and children abandoned or left without husband or father:

James 1:27 Religion that is pure and undefiled before God and the Father is this: to visit orphans and widows in their affliction, and to keep oneself unstained from the world.

Zech 7:9-10 "Thus says the LORD of hosts, Render true judgments, show kindness and mercy each to his brother, ¹⁰ do not oppress the widow, the fatherless, the sojourner, or the poor; and let none of you devise evil against his brother in your heart."

Is 1:23 Your princes are rebels and companions of thieves. Every one loves a bribe and runs after gifts. They do not defend the fatherless, and the widow's cause does not come to them.

Is 10:1-2 Woe to those who decree iniquitous decrees, and the writers who keep writing oppression, ² to turn aside the needy from justice and to rob the poor of my people of their right, that widows may be their spoil, and that they may make the fatherless their prey!

Prov 24:11-12 Rescue those who are being taken away to death; hold back those who are stumbling to the slaughter. ¹² If you say, "Behold, we did not know this," does not he who weighs the heart perceive it? Does not he who keeps watch over your soul know it, and will he not requite man according to his work?

Is 1:15-17 When you spread forth your hands, I will hide my eyes from you; even though you make many prayers, I will not listen; your hands are full of blood. ¹⁶ Wash yourselves; make yourselves clean; remove the evil of your doings from before my eyes; cease to do evil, ¹⁷ learn to do good; seek justice, correct oppression; defend the fatherless, plead for the widow.

Jer 7:5-6 "For if you truly amend your ways and your doings, if you truly execute justice one with another, ⁶ if you do not oppress the alien, the fatherless or the widow, or shed innocent blood in this place, and if you do not go after other gods to your own hurt, ⁷ then I will let you dwell in this place, in the land that I gave of old to your fathers for ever.

Gal 6:9-10 And let us not grow weary in well-doing, for in due season we shall reap, if we do not lose heart. ¹⁰ So then, as we have opportunity, let us do good to all men, and especially to those who are of the household of faith.

We sin by commissioning abortion, performing abortion, or assisting in the procuring of abortion. We also sin by refusing to provide the financial, emotional, or spiritual support we have available to a mother who is being tempted into the lure of this deeply evil act. All who strengthen abortion's appeal suffer from a heart hardened to the benificence of God, and the opportunities He gives us to give of ourselves and become like unto Him. Yet those who ask forgiveness of even these sins will be forgiven, if they are truly repentant.

Psalm 103:11-12 For as the heavens are high above the earth, so great is his steadfast love toward those who fear him; ¹² as far as the east is from the west, so far does he remove our transgressions from us.

Jer 31:33-34 But this is the covenant which I will make with the house of Israel after those days, says the LORD: I will put my law within them, and I will write it upon their hearts; and I will be their God, and they shall be my people. ³⁴ And no longer shall each man teach his neighbor and each his brother, saying, 'Know the LORD,' for they shall all know me, from the least of them to the greatest, says the LORD; for I will forgive their iniquity, and I will remember their sin no more."

The real horror of abortion lies not in the destruction of a child's innocent life, heinous though it is, for the child does not go to eternal punishment. Rather, the horror lies in the depth of sin into which it plunges complicit souls. The broken bodies of the children are but crumbs which fall from the gibbering mouth of satan. He delights in the souls of those who participate in the whirlwind of killing, either by commission or omission. We can obtain forgiveness for ourselves and for those who participate by asking God to forgive our hardness of heart, to replace our hearts of stone with real hearts. We will be judged on this.

<u>Early Christians' comments on Abortion</u>

Baptism

Baptism is the marriage vow which the Bridegroom makes to us, through which He adopts us, cleanses us in nuptial bath and allows us to vow fidelity to Him. Through this unmerited free gift of grace, justification, sanctification and divinization, we are united to His Body and become Child of God and Bride of Christ. For these reasons, it is necessary for salvation.

Baptism has three forms: baptism of faith, baptism of blood, and baptism of water. Baptism of faith applies to those unable to be baptized with water, but who desire baptism, or to those who would desire water baptism if only they knew of its necessity. Baptism of blood applies to those who have not been baptized with water, but who die for their witness of the truth of the natural law written in their hearts by God, thereby witnessing Jesus Christ, through whom the natural world was created. Baptism by water is alone the fullness of the sacrament. It applies to those baptized in the name of the Father and of the Son and of the Holy Spirit, by one who intends to do what the Church does (although he who baptizes need not himself be baptized). Water baptism may use immersion or pouring. Water baptism alone indelibly marks us as Christ's and washes us clean of all sin. It alone allows, after proper instruction, the baptized person to partake of all Christ's sacraments. Water baptism may be undertaken regardless of the age or mental capacities of the recipient, for the faith of the guardian of such a person stands in for the faith of the recipient. No sacrament depends on our faith for efficacy, rather, each pours out God's Spirit upon us through the things of the created world. (CCC 398, 213-1284, 2670)

What happens to unbaptized children who die before they attain the age of reason? We do not know, but we trust in the infinite mercy of God, who may lead them to salvation in a mysterious way known only to Him. Salvation is available to all through the merits of Jesus Christ. The concept of Limbo has not been formally defined by the Body of Christ, it is not part of doctrine or dogma - it is only theological opinion. (CCC 1261)

Current misunderstandings: All misunderstandings arise from some combination of the following ideas:
- *baptism is not necessary for salvation,*
- *baptism is necessary for salvation but must be undertaken by immersion to be valid,*
- *baptism is necessary for the salvation of those who have reached the age of reason, but cannot be validly conferred upon children under the age of reason or the mentally infirm who are incapable of understanding the assent of faith.*
- *baptism is a necessary seal, but it does not wash away sin*

Types for Baptism

Is 55:10-11 "For as the rain and the snow come down from heaven, and return not thither but water the earth, making it bring forth and sprout, giving seed to the sower and bread to the eater, [11] so shall my word be that goes forth from my mouth; it shall not return to me empty, but it shall accomplish that which I purpose, and prosper in the thing for which I sent it.

The waters of baptism rain down upon the earth, making it fertile and fruitful, giving the seed of the Gospel to him who sows, and the Bread of Life to him who eats, through the Word that goes forth from His mouth.

Gen 1:1-2 In the beginning God created the heavens and the earth. [2] The earth was without form and void, and darkness was upon the face of the deep; and the Spirit of God was moving over the face of the waters

Creation was baptized into existence; the wind of the Spirit moved over the waters, and the waters brought forth living creatures, as do the waters of Baptism. We are each little fishes in the image of the Big Fish, Jesus Christ.

Gen 7:4 "For in seven days I will send rain upon the earth forty days and forty nights; and every living thing that I have made I will blot out from the face of the ground."

Not only was the Ark the baptism and salvation of Noah and his family, it marked the start of a new creation, for they were given the same command given to Adam and Eve: "Be fruitful and multiply, and fill the earth" (Gen 9:1-4).

Ex 2:1-10 Now a man from the house of Levi went and took to wife a daughter of Levi. [2] The woman conceived and bore a son; and when she saw that he was a goodly child, she hid him three months. [3] And when she could hide him no longer she took for him a basket made of bulrushes, and daubed it with bitumen and pitch; and she put the child in it and placed it among the reeds at the river's brink. [4] And his sister stood at a distance, to know what would be done to him. ⁵ Now the daughter of Pharaoh came down to bathe at the river, and her maidens walked beside the river; she saw the basket among the reeds and sent her maid to fetch it. ⁶ When she opened it she saw the child; and lo, the babe was crying. She took pity on him and said, "This is one of the Hebrews' children." ⁷ Then his sister said to Pharaoh's daughter, "Shall I go and call you a nurse from the Hebrew women to nurse the child for you?" ⁸ And Pharaoh's daughter said to her, "Go." So the girl went and called the child's mother. ⁹ And Pharaoh's daughter said to her, "Take this child away, and nurse him for me, and I will give you your wages." So the woman took the child and nursed him. ¹⁰ And the child grew, and she brought him to Pharaoh's daughter, and he became her son; and she named him Moses, for she said, "Because I drew him out of the water."

The three-month old infant Moses was saved through water. Through the salvation of this infant, the whole nation was saved.

Ex 14:21 Then Moses stretched out his hand over the sea; and the Lord drove the sea back by a strong east wind all night, and made the sea dry land, and the waters were divided.

God divided the waters and the land in Genesis and again here, as He saves the nation of Israel.

Ex 15:19 For when the horses of Pharaoh with his chariots and his horsemen went into the sea, the LORD brought back the waters of the sea upon them; but the people of Israel walked on dry ground in the midst of the sea.

Just as the Egyptians were wiped out in the miraculous parting of the waters, so are our sins wiped out in the miraculous waters of baptism. We are a new creation.

1 Cor 10:1 I want you to know, brethren, that our fathers were all under the cloud, and all passed through the sea, ² and all were baptized into Moses in the cloud and in the sea,

The people of Israel underwent a baptism at the Red Sea - they who faced death did not die.

Ex 15:23-25 When they came to Marah, they could not drink the water of Marah because it was bitter; therefore it was named Marah. ²⁴ And the people murmured against Moses, saying, "What shall we drink?" ²⁵ And he cried to the Lord; and the Lord showed him a tree, and he threw it into the water, and the water was made sweet.

The people were saved from death by thirst through the immersion of the tree, representing the Cross, into the bitter waters, thereby making the waters sweet. The murmuring of the people is quieted by the burying of the Cross in the waters. Again, they who faced death did not die.

Josh 3:15-16 and when those who bore the ark had come to the Jordan, and the feet of the priests bearing the ark were dipped in the brink of the water (the Jordan overflows all its banks throughout the time of harvest), ¹⁶ the waters coming down from above stood and rose up in a heap far off, at Adam, the city that is beside Zarethan, and those flowing down toward the sea of the Arabah, the Salt Sea, were wholly cut off; and the people passed over opposite Jericho.

Instead, the next generation entered the Promised Land, baptized through the waters of the Jordan, into new life, a land flowing with milk and honey.

1 Kings 18:30-39 Then Elijah said to all the people, "Come near to me"; and all the people came near to him. And he repaired the altar of the LORD that had been thrown down; ³¹ Elijah took twelve stones, according to the number of the tribes of the sons of Jacob, to whom the word of the LORD came, saying, "Israel shall be your name"; ³² and with the stones he built an altar in the name of the LORD. And he made a trench about the altar, as great as would contain two measures of seed. ³³ And he put the wood in order, and cut the bull in pieces and laid it on the wood. And he said, "Fill four jars with water, and pour it on the burnt offering, and on the wood." ³⁴ And he said, "Do it a second time"; and they did it a second time. And he said, "Do it a third time"; and they did it a third time. ³⁵ And the water ran round about the altar, and filled the trench also with water. ³⁶ And at the time of the offering of the oblation, Elijah the prophet came near and said, "O LORD, God of Abraham, Isaac, and Israel, let it be known this day that thou art God in Israel, and that I am thy servant, and that I have done all these things at thy word. ³⁷ Answer me, O LORD, answer me, that this people may know that thou, O LORD, art God, and that thou hast turned their hearts back." ³⁸ Then the fire of the LORD fell, and consumed the burnt offering, and the wood, and the stones, and the dust, and licked up the water that was in the trench. ³⁹ And when all the people saw it, they fell on their faces; and they said, "The LORD, he is God; the LORD, he is God."

Elijah builds the altar on a foundation of twelve stones, the foundation of the twelve tribes of Israel and the twelve Apostles. He baptizes the sacrificial offering in a three-fold washing with water...

Heb 12:29 Our God is a consuming fire.

When Elijah calls down the Holy Spirit, the sacrifice is totally consumed in a kenosis of fire.

2 Kings 5:11-14 But Naaman was angry, and went away, saying, "Behold, I thought that he would surely come out to me, and stand, and call on the name of the LORD his God, and wave his hand over the place, and cure the leper. ¹² Are not Abana and Pharpar, the rivers of Damascus, better than all the waters of Israel? Could I not wash in them, and be clean?" So he turned and went away in a rage. ¹³ But his servants came near and said to him, "My father, if the prophet had commanded you to do some great thing, would you not have done it? How much rather, then, when he says to you, 'Wash, and be clean'?" ¹⁴ So he went down and dipped himself seven times in the Jordan, according to the word of the man of God; and his flesh was restored like the flesh of a little child, and he was clean.

Naaman did not believe that the waters of the Jordan had any special power, but he failed to realize that God is the one who gives the power to cleanse men through the created things and the work of creation. Leprosy, an ancient sign of sinfulness, was removed by the seven-fold washing in the waters blessed by the man of God. Namaan was returned to a pure state.

The exegesis on 2 Kings 2:7-11 is taken from Danielou's Bible and the Liturgy, *pp. 99-114.*

Elijah prefigures baptism by crossing the Jordan before being taken up to heaven.

2 Kings 2:7-11 Fifty men of the sons of the prophets also went, and stood at some distance from them, as they both were standing by the Jordan. ⁸ Then Elijah took his mantle, and rolled it up, and struck the water, and the water was parted to the one side and to the other, till the two of them could go over on dry ground. ⁹ When they had crossed, Elijah said to Elisha, "Ask what I shall do for you, before I am taken from you." And Elisha said, "I pray you, let me inherit a double share of your spirit." ¹⁰ And he said, "You have asked a hard thing; yet, if you see me as I am being taken from you, it shall be so for you; but if you do not see me, it shall not be so." ¹¹ And as they still went on and talked, behold, a chariot of fire and horses of fire separated the two of them. And Elijah went up by a whirlwind into heaven.

John's baptism is a type for the baptism which Christ will institute.

Mk 1:4 John the baptizer appeared in the wilderness, preaching a baptism of repentance for the forgiveness of sins.

Lk 3:3 and he went into all the region about the Jordan, preaching a baptism of repentance for the forgiveness of sins

Jn 1:29 The next day he saw Jesus coming toward him, and said, "Behold, the Lamb of God, who takes away the sin of the world!

Jn 1:33 I myself did not know him; but he who sent me to baptize with water said to me, 'He on whom you see the Spirit descend and remain, this is he who baptizes with the Holy Spirit.'

Significantly, John himself did not recognize Salvation until the descent of the Spirit. This descent of the Spirit was effected through baptism with water.

Establishment of Baptism

Jn 2:1-11 On the third day there was a marriage at Cana in Galilee, and the mother of Jesus was there; ² Jesus also was invited to the marriage, with his disciples. ³ When the wine failed, the mother of Jesus said to him, "They have no wine." ⁴ And Jesus said to her, "O woman, what have you to do with me? My hour has not yet come." ⁵ His mother said to the servants, "Do whatever he tells you." ⁶ Now six stone jars were standing there, for the Jewish rites of purification, each holding twenty or thirty gallons. ⁷ Jesus said to them, "Fill the jars with water." And they filled them up to the brim. ⁸ He said to them, "Now draw some out, and take it to the steward of the feast." So they took it. ⁹ When the steward of the feast tasted the water now become wine, and did not know where it came from (though the servants who had drawn the water knew), the steward of the feast called the bridegroom ¹⁰ and said to him, "Every man serves the good wine first; and when men have drunk freely, then the poor wine; but you have kept the good wine until now." ¹¹ This, the first of his signs, Jesus did at Cana in Galilee, and manifested his glory; and his disciples believed in him.

The purifying water held in the jars used for Jewish purification was called "baptismoi." The power of Christ is first revealed in the transformation He worked through this water.

Gen 49:11 Binding his foal to the vine
and his ass's colt to the choice vine,
he washes his garments in wine
and his vesture in the blood of grapes...

Deut 32:14 Curds from the herd, and milk from the flock,
with fat of lambs and rams,
herds of Bashan and goats,
with the finest of the wheat—
and of the blood of the grape you drank wine.

Cleansing water is transformed by Jesus Christ into the "blood of the grape" at a wedding feast. In His first miracle, and in one incredibly compact act, the Bridegroom tells us that we are <u>cleansed and married into His Body</u> through water transformed by <u>His Blood</u>, itself the sign, seal, and covenant made present in the <u>Wedding Feast</u>. The next two chapters of John explain how this happens.

With the exception of the exegesis of John 3:23, 25-30, the following exegesis of John's Gospel is a summary of information presented in Scott Hahn's tape set "The Gospel of John."

Jn 2:23-25 Now when he was in Jerusalem at the Passover feast, many believed in his name when they saw the signs which he did; ²⁴ but Jesus did not trust himself to them, ²⁵ because he knew all men and needed no one to bear witness of man; for he himself knew what was in man.

Faith in Him is a start, but it is not completion. Nicodemus, a man of the class described in John 2:23, who believes in His name, visits Jesus to tell Him of his belief.

Jn 3:1-3 Now there was a man of the Pharisees, named Nicodemus, a ruler of the Jews. ² This man came to Jesus by night and said to him, "Rabbi, we know that you are a teacher come from God; for no one can do these signs that you do, unless God is with him." ³ Jesus answered him, "Truly, truly, I say to you, unless one is born anew, he cannot see the kingdom of God."

The name Nicodemus means "people-crusher." Jesus intentionally uses a word for "anew" which has two meanings. It can mean "above" or it can mean "again." The context makes it impossible to tell which is meant.

Jn 3:4-6 Nicodemus said to him, "How can a man be born when he is old? Can he enter a second time into his mother's womb and be born?" ⁵ Jesus answered, "Truly, truly, I say to you, unless one is born of water and the Spirit, he cannot enter the kingdom of God. ⁶ That which is born of the flesh is flesh, and that which is born of the Spirit is spirit.

Nicodemus misunderstands Christ to mean a birth after the manner of all flesh. Jesus corrects Him - he must be born of water and the spirit. In verse 6, Christ merely re-emphasizes that "water and spirit" do not refer to birth from the womb, but to a spiritual re-birth. Being brought to life in the Spirit is a very concrete thing, as Peter tells us...

1 Pet 3:18-19 For Christ also died for sins once for all, the righteous for the unrighteous, that he might bring us to God, being put to death in the flesh but made alive in the spirit; ¹⁹ in which he went and preached to the spirits in prison...

Remember Thomas, who put his hands into Christ's pierced flesh, the flesh of the risen Christ, who was brought to life in the Spirit? Who will say that being born of the Spirit by the washing with water is not a concrete thing?

1 Cor 15:45-49 Thus it is written, "The first man Adam became a living being"; the last Adam became a life-giving spirit. ⁴⁶ But it is not the spiritual which is first but the physical, and then the spiritual. ⁴⁷ The first man was from the earth, a man of dust; the second man is from heaven. ⁴⁸ As was the man of dust, so are those who are of the dust; and as is the man of heaven, so are those who are of heaven.

The spiritual does not destroy the physical, rather, the spiritual perfects the physical. Grace perfects nature. Our first, natural birth was of water in the womb. Our second, heavenly birth is of water and the Spirit. Christ images all creation in us through the order of creation He has established.

1 Jn 5:6-9 This is he who came by water and blood, Jesus Christ, not with the water only but with the water and the blood. ⁷ And the Spirit is the witness, because the Spirit is the truth. ⁸ There are three witnesses, the Spirit, the water, and the blood; and these three agree. ⁹ If we receive the testimony of men, the testimony of God is greater; for this is the testimony of God that he has borne witness to his Son.

God's testimony is the testimony of the waters of baptism, made efficacious through the blood of Jesus Christ.

Early Christian comments on Baptismal Rebirth

Jn 3:7-8 Do not marvel that I said to you, 'You must be born anew.' ⁸ The wind blows where it wills, and you hear the sound of it, but you do not know whence it comes or whither it goes; so it is with every one who is born of the Spirit.

Again, Jesus uses a word for "wind" which can mean either "wind" or "Spirit" and the context makes it impossible to tell which is meant. Jesus is deliberately using confusing terminology in order to rock this Pharisee back on his heels, and force him out of his material thoughts towards a deeper spiritual reality - the reality of regenerative baptism. Now He makes Nicodemus fully realize just how little he knows about the way heaven works.

Jn 3:9-15 Nicodemus said to him, "How can this be?" ¹⁰ Jesus answered him, "Are you a teacher of Israel, and yet you do not understand this? ¹¹ Truly, truly, I say to you, we speak of what we know, and bear witness to what we have seen; but you do not receive our testimony. ¹² If I have told you earthly things and you do not believe, how can you believe if I tell you heavenly things? ¹³ No one has ascended into heaven but he who descended from heaven, the Son of man. ¹⁴ And as Moses lifted up the serpent in the wilderness, so must the Son of man be lifted up, ¹⁵ that whoever believes in him may have eternal life."

Christ explicitly connects His crucifixion with baptism. Just as the serpent Moses lifted up healed the people of the poison, so Christ lifted up on the cross will heal the people of the poison of sin. Baptism accomplishes this cleansing - it is a heavenly act accomplished through an earthly thing, just as Christ is a heavenly Person made present to Nicodemus as a true earthly man.

Jn 3:16-17 For God so loved the world that he gave his only Son, that whoever believes in him should not perish but have eternal life. ¹⁷ For God sent the Son into the world, not to condemn the world, but that the world might be saved through him.

Note that John 3:16 is not restrictive. "Everyone who believes in him... [might] have eternal life," yet this passage does not set up pre-conditions for belief, or explain what constitutes belief in him. That explanation is given elsewhere (see "Salvation through Faith and Works"). How will the baptism of water have efficacy? Through the crucifixion of God's only Son, who will be lifted up just as the serpent was lifted up. It is the water flowing from the side of the Body of Christ, water flowing alongside His Precious Blood, which makes water cleansing to the soul through the action of the Holy Spirit. It is, in fact, the water flowing from the Body of Christ which fills the baptismal fonts of the Body of Christ, the Church.

Christ will baptize, but He is obviously not yet crucified, so how can His baptism be effective? Because it comes from God, and God's grace is timeless. The One Sacrifice will be made - guaranteed - so the Spirit can cleanse and seal through His baptism even before the crucifixion.

Early Christians' comments on Baptismal Grace

Jn 3:18 He who believes in him is not condemned; he who does not believe is condemned already, because he has not believed in the name of the only Son of God.

The people of John 2:23 believed - so did Nicodemus. But Christ is talking about a belief made living through baptism. As soon as Jesus finishes explaining the importance of baptism to Nicodemus, He heads out to baptize.

Jn 3:22 After this Jesus and his disciples went into the land of Judea; there he remained with them and baptized.

Marriage to the Bridegroom

Jn 3:23,25-30 John also was baptizing at Aenon near Salim, because there was much water there; and people came and were baptized.... Now a discussion arose between John's disciples and a Jew over purifying. ²⁶ And they came to John, and said to him, "Rabbi, he who was with you beyond the Jordan, to whom you bore witness, here he is, baptizing, and all are going to him." ²⁷ John answered, "No one can receive anything except what is given him from heaven. ²⁸ You yourselves bear me witness, that I said, I am not the Christ, but I have been sent before him. ²⁹ He who has the bride is the bridegroom; the friend of the bridegroom, who stands and hears him, rejoices greatly at the bridegroom's voice; therefore this joy of mine is now full. ³⁰ He must increase, but I must decrease."

Several things are attested to here:
- *Everyone is coming to Christ,*
- *What Christ dispenses in baptism comes from heaven, it is a work of God, not man,*
- *John specifically links Christ's baptism with marriage, calling Christ the Bridegroom, and saying the Bride belongs to Him, Remember, this is at the beginning of Christ's ministry, well before Paul uses the phrase,*
- *John the Baptist recognizes that the Body of Christ increases through the use of baptism. Through it, we are married to, joined to, the Body of Christ.*

Jn 4:1-2 Now when the Lord knew that the Pharisees had heard that Jesus was making and baptizing more disciples than John ² (although Jesus himself did not baptize, but only his disciples)...

Jesus did not baptize Himself. Why not? Let us examine another person who did not baptize:

1 Cor 1:16 (I did baptize also the household of Stephanas. Beyond that, I do not know whether I baptized any one else.)

Paul also denied that he baptized...

1 Cor 3:4-6 For when one says, "I belong to Paul," and another, "I belong to Apollos," are you not merely men? ⁵ What then is Apollos? What is Paul? Servants through whom you believed, as the Lord assigned to each. ⁶ I planted, Apollos watered, but God gave the growth.

Because "Apollos watered" - it was Apollos, the local presbyter, who baptized after Paul preached, but it is God who regenerates through baptism and causes the growth. Christ didn't baptize for the same reason Paul refrained from baptizing - it was important to establish the Apostles in their role as bishops, teaching them through practice how baptism was to be done. Even at this point, Christ is preparing His bishops for His Death, Resurrection, and Ascension. This is not surprising. His whole mission on earth will eventually depend on these twelve men doing all and exactly what He taught them, doing it with no written instructions, no one to help them but the Paraclete. As it is, one, Judas, will fail.

Jn 4:10,13-14 Jesus answered her, "If you knew the gift of God, and who it is that is saying to you, 'Give me a drink,' you would have asked him, and he would have given you living water... Every one who drinks of this water will thirst again, ¹⁴ but whoever drinks of the water that I shall give him will never thirst; the water that I shall give him will become in him a spring of water welling up to eternal life."

John caps the long discussion of water and baptism with the woman at the well. Christ asserts again that He is the source of living water, that the water He gives out is a wellspring of eternal life. This revelation is followed by yet another discussion of marriage.

Jn 4:16-18 Jesus said to her, "Go, call your husband, and come here." ¹⁷ The woman answered him, "I have no husband." Jesus said to her, "You are right in saying, 'I have no husband'; ¹⁸ for you have had five husbands, and he whom you now have is not your husband; this you said truly."

Christ uses the word "ba'al" for "husband." This word, which a concubine uses for her master, also means "god." Christ refers to the Samaritans' worship of false idols. That is why the woman replies as she does:

Jn 4:19-26 The woman said to him, "Sir, I perceive that you are a prophet. ²⁰ Our fathers worshiped on this mountain; and you say that in Jerusalem is the place where men ought to worship." ²¹ Jesus said to her, "Woman, believe me, the hour is coming when neither on this mountain nor in Jerusalem will you worship the Father. ²² You worship what you do not know; we worship what we know, for salvation is from the Jews. ²³ But the hour is coming, and now is, when the true worshipers will worship the Father in spirit and truth, for such the Father seeks to worship him. ²⁴ God is spirit, and those who worship him must worship in spirit and truth." ²⁵ The woman said to him, "I know that Messiah is coming (he who is called Christ); when he comes, he will show us all things." ²⁶ Jesus said to her, "I who speak to you am he."

The Samaritans recognized only the Pentateuch, rejecting all Old Testament prophetic books as uninspired. They looked only for one prophet, foretold by Moses, the prophet not yet come into the world, the Messiah. Christ, the promised Messiah, has told this Samaritan how to attain eternal life - through acceptance of living water.

Zech 12:10, 13:1 "And I will pour out on the house of David and the inhabitants of Jerusalem a spirit of compassion and supplication, so that, when they look on him whom they have pierced, they shall mourn for him, as one mourns for an only child, and weep bitterly over him, as one weeps over a first-born... On that day there shall be a fountain opened for the house of David and the inhabitants of Jerusalem to cleanse them from sin and uncleanness.

Jn 19:33-35 but when they came to Jesus and saw that he was already dead, they did not break his legs. [34] But one of the soldiers pierced his side with a spear, and at once there came out blood and water. [35] He who saw it has borne witness—his testimony is true, and he knows that he tells the truth—that you also may believe.

Baptism is a marriage bond to God. Christ, the source from whom Living Water flows, marries us into His Body, making us clean, purifying us, so that we have within us a wellspring of eternal life. It is no coincidence that the attestation of the witness appears at precisely this point. An officer of the Body of Christ attests to the source of the water that same Body applies in baptism.

Jn 8:34-36 Jesus answered them, "Truly, truly, I say to you, every one who commits sin is a slave to sin. [35] The slave does not continue in the house for ever; the son continues for ever. [36] So if the Son makes you free, you will be free indeed.

Christ's sacrifice is open to the whole world.

Regenerative Baptism

Jn 10-11 *Prior to the raising of Lazarus, Jesus was west of the Jordan. He waited two days, then crossed the Jordan and raised Lazarus from the dead, thus fulfilling Joshua 1:11 "In three days you will pass over the Jordan" and after this crossing God will accomplish wonders (Joshua 3:5) - Thomas confirms the baptismal significance of Christ's Jordan crossing* by saying "Let us also go and die with Him" (Jn 11:6). *Baptism is new life.*

We are buried with Him in baptism and rise from death as we rise from our washing, clean, divinized.

Rom 4:23-25 But the words, "it was reckoned to him," were written not for his sake alone, [24] but for ours also. It will be reckoned to us who believe in him that raised from the dead Jesus our Lord, [25] who was put to death for our trespasses and raised for our justification.

Rom 6:1-6 What shall we say then? Are we to continue in sin that grace may abound? [2] By no means! How can we who died to sin still live in it? [3] Do you not know that all of us who have been baptized into Christ Jesus were baptized into his death? [4] We were buried therefore with him by baptism into death, so that as Christ was raised from the dead by the glory of the Father, we too might walk in newness of life. [5] For if we have been united with him in a death like his, we shall certainly be united with him in a resurrection like his. [6] We know that our old self was crucified with him so that the sinful body might be destroyed, and we might no longer be enslaved to sin.

Col 2:12-14 and you were buried with him in baptism, in which you were also raised with him through faith in the working of God, who raised him from the dead. [13] And you, who were dead in trespasses and the uncircumcision of your flesh, God made alive together with him, having forgiven us all our trespasses, [14] having canceled the bond which stood against us with its legal demands; this he set aside, nailing it to the cross.

Gal 3:27 For as many of you as were baptized into Christ have put on Christ.

We are raised from the waters of baptism justified, cleansed, made perfect through the Holy Spirit. Baptism is what incorporates us into the Body of Christ - not the sinner's prayer.

Acts 22:16 And now why do you wait? Rise and be baptized, and wash away your sins, calling on his name.'

1 Cor 6:11 And such were some of you. But you were washed, you were sanctified, you were justified in the name of the Lord Jesus Christ and in the Spirit of our God.

Heb 10:22 let us draw near with a true heart in full assurance of faith, with our hearts sprinkled clean from an evil conscience and our bodies washed with pure water.

Eph 5:26 that he might sanctify her, having cleansed her by the washing of water with the word,

Tit 3:5 he saved us, not because of deeds done by us in righteousness, but in virtue of his own mercy, by the washing of regeneration and renewal in the Holy Spirit...

Rev 7:14 "And he said to me, 'These are they who have come out of the great tribulation; they have washed their robes and made them white in the blood of the Lamb.'"

Without the regenerative cleansing of baptism, we will not be One Body with God.

Rev 19:13-14 He is clad in a robe dipped in blood, and the name by which he is called is The Word of God. [14] And the armies of heaven, arrayed in fine linen, white and pure, followed him on white horses.

Those who are baptized in His blood and wrapped in righteous deeds are part of the armies of heaven.

Necessary for Salvation

Mk 16:16 He who believes and is baptized will be saved; but he who does not believe will be condemned.

Jn 3:5 "Truly, truly, I say to you, unless one is born of water and the Spirit, he cannot enter the kingdom of God."

While disbelief may condemn, salvation requires both belief and baptism.

Mt 28:19 Go therefore and make disciples of all nations, baptizing them in the name of the Father and of the Son and of the Holy Spirit..

Baptism creates disciples. Jesus thought baptism so important that two out of the four Gospels end with Him reminding the Apostles about it one last time before He ascends to the Father.

1 Pet 3:20-21 who formerly did not obey, when God's patience waited in the days of Noah, during the building of the ark, in which a few, that is, eight persons, were saved through water. [21] Baptism, which corresponds to this, now saves you, not as a removal of dirt from the body but as an appeal to God for a clear conscience, through the resurrection of Jesus Christ,

Baptism saves you now. It is salvation.

Acts 16:15 And when she was baptized, with her household, she besought us, saying, "If you have judged me to be faithful to the Lord, come to my house and stay." And she prevailed upon us.

Acts 16:27-34 When the jailer woke and saw that the prison doors were open, he drew his sword and was about to kill himself, supposing that the prisoners had escaped. [28] But Paul cried with a loud voice, "Do not harm yourself, for we are all here." [29] And he called for lights and rushed in, and trembling with fear he fell down before Paul and Silas, [30] and brought them out and said, "Men, what must I do to be saved?" [31] And they said, "Believe in the Lord Jesus, and you will be saved, you and your household." [32] And they spoke the word of the Lord to him and to all that were in his house. [33] And he took them the same hour of the night, and washed their wounds, and he was baptized at once, with all his family. [34] Then he brought them up into his house, and set food before them; and he rejoiced with all his household that he had believed in God.

Note that he rejoices in having come to faith in God only after he and his family were baptised in their home.

Mk 10:38 But Jesus said to them, "You do not know what you are asking. Are you able to drink the cup that I drink, or to be baptized with the baptism with which I am baptized?"

Lk 12:50 I have a baptism to be baptized with; and how I am constrained until it is accomplished!

Eph 4:5 one Lord, one faith, one baptism,

Paul equates the one baptism with the One God and the One Faith. Faith and baptism are necessary.

Rev 22:14 Blessed are those who wash their robes, that they may have the right to the tree of life and that they may enter the city by the gates..

It is only through baptism, the washing in His passion, death, resurrection, and ascension, that we are raised up to heaven.

Acts 19:1-5 While Apollos was at Corinth, Paul passed through the upper country and came to Ephesus. There he found some disciples. ² And he said to them, "Did you receive the Holy Spirit when you believed?" And they said, "No, we have never even heard that there is a Holy Spirit." ³ And he said, "Into what then were you baptized?" They said, "Into John's baptism." ⁴ And Paul said, "John baptized with the baptism of repentance, telling the people to believe in the one who was to come after him, that is, Jesus." ⁵ On hearing this, they were baptized in the name of the Lord Jesus.

1 Cor 1:13 Is Christ divided? Was Paul crucified for you? Or were you baptized in the name of Paul?

There is but one baptism, the baptism of Jesus. Because baptism is a work of God, a person validly baptized, that is, baptized with a three-fold washing in the name of the Father, of the Son, and of the Holy Spirit, cannot be "re-baptized."

Lk 7:29-30 (When they heard this all the people and the tax collectors justified God, having been baptized with the baptism of John; ³⁰ but the Pharisees and the lawyers rejected the purpose of God for themselves, not having been baptized by him.)

If John's baptism was necessary for the Pharisees and the lawyers, how much more seroiusly should we take the baptism of the Messiah, to whom John always pointed?

Heb 6:4-6 For it is impossible to restore again to repentance those who have once been enlightened, who have tasted the heavenly gift, and have become partakers of the Holy Spirit, ⁵ and have tasted the goodness of the word of God and the powers of the age to come, ⁶ if they then commit apostasy, since they crucify the Son of God on their own account and hold him up to contempt.

Heb 10:26 For if we sin deliberately after receiving the knowledge of the truth, there no longer remains a sacrifice for sins,

Yet, as Hebrews points out, we can lose our salvation after baptism. How can we be <u>washed clean again</u>?

<u>Early Christians on Trinitarian Baptism</u>
<u>Early Christians on the Necessity of Baptism</u>

Immersion

The disciples of Pentecost know that baptism is a marriage to the Bridegroom that regenerates the soul, and the head Apostle explains it to those who would be new converts:

Acts 2:38-41 And Peter said to them, "Repent, and be baptized every one of you in the name of Jesus Christ for the forgiveness of your sins; and you shall receive the gift of the Holy Spirit. ³⁹ For the promise is to you and to your children and to all that are far off, every one whom the Lord our God calls to him." ⁴⁰ And he testified with many other words and exhorted them, saying, "Save yourselves from this crooked generation." ⁴¹ So those who received his word were baptized, and there were added that day about three thousand souls.

Many claim that "baptism," which means "to immerse," is only valid if the person to be baptized is fully immersed in water. There is insufficient water in that area of the country to have baptized three thousand persons by immersion.

According to Liddell and Scott's Greek-English Lexicon, 7th Edition, "baptismo" means "a dipping in water, ablution." This does not necessarily mean full immersion, as Jewish purification ritual shows:

Num 19:9-19 And a man who is clean shall gather up the ashes of the heifer, and deposit them outside the camp in a clean place; and they shall be kept for the congregation of the people of Israel for the water for impurity, for the removal of sin. ¹⁰ And he who gathers the ashes of the heifer shall wash his clothes, and be unclean until evening. And this shall be to the people of Israel, and to the stranger who sojourns among them, a perpetual statute.
¹¹ "He who touches the dead body of any person shall be unclean seven days; ¹² he shall cleanse himself with the water on the third day and on the seventh day, and so be clean; but if he does not cleanse himself on the third day and on the seventh day, he will not become clean. ¹³ Whoever touches a dead person, the

body of any man who has died, and does not cleanse himself, defiles the tabernacle of the LORD, and that person shall be cut off from Israel; because the water for impurity was not thrown upon him, he shall be unclean; his uncleanness is still on him.

¹⁴ "This is the law when a man dies in a tent: every one who comes into the tent, and every one who is in the tent, shall be unclean seven days. ¹⁵ And every open vessel, which has no cover fastened upon it, is unclean. ¹⁶ Whoever in the open field touches one who is slain with a sword, or a dead body, or a bone of a man, or a grave, shall be unclean seven days. ¹⁷ For the unclean they shall take some ashes of the burnt sin offering, and running water shall be added in a vessel; ¹⁸ then a clean person shall take hyssop, and dip it in the water, and sprinkle it upon the tent, and upon all the furnishings, and upon the persons who were there, and upon him who touched the bone, or the slain, or the dead, or the grave; ¹⁹ and the clean person shall sprinkle upon the unclean on the third day and on the seventh day; thus on the seventh day he shall cleanse him, and he shall wash his clothes and bathe himself in water, and at evening he shall be clean.

Remember, the purification water was referred to as "baptismoi," yet full immersion was not a requirement.

Acts 9:17-19 So Ananias departed and entered the house. And laying his hands on him he said, "Brother Saul, the Lord Jesus who appeared to you on the road by which you came, has sent me that you may regain your sight and be filled with the Holy Spirit." ¹⁸ And immediately something like scales fell from his eyes and he regained his sight. Then he rose and was baptized, ¹⁹ and took food and was strengthened.

First century houses did not have bathtubs. Paul could not have been immersive.

Ezek 36:25 I will sprinkle clean water upon you, and you shall be clean from all your uncleannesses, and from all your idols I will cleanse you.

God promised the cleansing of sin by the sprinkling of clean water.

Acts 8:12-16 But when they believed Philip as he preached good news about the kingdom of God and the name of Jesus Christ, they were baptized, both men and women. ¹³ Even Simon himself believed, and after being baptized he continued with Philip. And seeing signs and great miracles performed, he was amazed.

¹⁴ Now when the apostles at Jerusalem heard that Samaria had received the word of God, they sent to them Peter and John, ¹⁵ who came down and prayed for them that they might receive the Holy Spirit; ¹⁶ for it had not yet fallen on any of them, but they had only been baptized in the name of the Lord Jesus.

This passage, which provides evidence of the sacrament of <u>confirmation,</u> also testifies that believers were baptized.

Acts 8:17-24 Then they laid their hands on them and they received the Holy Spirit. ¹⁸ Now when Simon saw that the Spirit was given through the laying on of the apostles' hands, he offered them money, ¹⁹ saying, "Give me also this power, that any one on whom I lay my hands may receive the Holy Spirit." ²⁰ But Peter said to him, "Your silver perish with you, because you thought you could obtain the gift of God with money! ²¹ You have neither part nor lot in this matter, for your heart is not right before God. ²² Repent therefore of this wickedness of yours, and pray to the Lord that, if possible, the intent of your heart may be forgiven you. ²³ For I see that you are in the gall of bitterness and in the bond of iniquity." ²⁴ And Simon answered, "Pray for me to the Lord, that nothing of what you have said may come upon me."

Baptism and confirmation are gifts from God, not works of men. Note also that Simon also received an early form of the sacrament of confession, by confessing his sins and asking pardon of the officers of the Church.

Acts 8:25-38 Now when they had testified and spoken the word of the Lord, they returned to Jerusalem, preaching the gospel to many villages of the Samaritans. ²⁶ But an angel of the Lord said to Philip, "Rise and go toward the south to the road that goes down from Jerusalem to Gaza." This is a desert road. ²⁷ And he rose and went. And behold, an Ethiopian, a eunuch, a minister of the Candace, queen of the Ethiopians, in charge of all her treasure, had come to Jerusalem to worship ²⁸ and was returning; seated in his chariot, he was reading the prophet Isaiah. ²⁹ And the Spirit said to Philip, "Go up and join this chariot." ³⁰ So Philip ran to him, and heard him reading Isaiah the prophet, and asked, "Do you understand what you are reading?" ³¹ And he said, "How can I, unless some one guides me?" And he invited Philip to come up and sit with him. ³² Now the passage of the scripture which he was reading was this:

"As a sheep led to the slaughter
or a lamb before its shearer is dumb,
so he opens not his mouth. [33] In his humiliation justice was denied him.
Who can describe his generation?
For his life is taken up from the earth." [34] And the eunuch said to Philip, "About whom, pray, does the prophet say this, about himself or about some one else?" [35] Then Philip opened his mouth, and beginning with this scripture he told him the good news of Jesus. [36] And as they went along the road they came to some water, and the eunuch said, "See, here is water! What is to prevent my being baptized?" [38] And he commanded the chariot to stop, and they both went down into the water, Philip and the eunuch, and he baptized him.

Acts 10:44-48 While Peter was still saying this, the Holy Spirit fell on all who heard the word. [45] And the believers from among the circumcised who came with Peter were amazed, because the gift of the Holy Spirit had been poured out even on the Gentiles. [46] For they heard them speaking in tongues and extolling God. Then Peter declared, [47] "Can any one forbid water for baptizing these people who have received the Holy Spirit just as we have?" [48] And he commanded them to be baptized in the name of Jesus Christ. Then they asked him to remain for some days.

The passage above demonstrates that baptism of faith and desire, precedes the baptism of water, which washes away sin.

Infant Baptism

Since baptism is necessary for salvation, infants must be baptized.

Mt 18:10 "See that you do not despise one of these little ones; for I tell you that in heaven their angels always behold the face of my Father who is in heaven."

Mt 18:14 So it is not the will of my Father who is in heaven that one of these little ones should perish

Mt 19:13-15 Then children were brought to him that he might lay his hands on them and pray. The disciples rebuked the people; [14] but Jesus said, "Let the children come to me, and do not hinder them; for to such belongs the kingdom of heaven." [15] And he laid his hands on them and went away.

Circumcision is a necessary covenant sign in the Old Testament

Gen 17:12-14 He that is eight days old among you shall be circumcised; every male throughout your generations, whether born in your house, or bought with your money from any foreigner who is not of your offspring, [13] both he that is born in your house and he that is bought with your money, shall be circumcised. So shall my covenant be in your flesh an everlasting covenant. [14] Any uncircumcised male who is not circumcised in the flesh of his foreskin shall be cut off from his people; he has broken my covenant."

Circumcision had to take place on the eighth day - the day which would become the day of new creation in Jesus Christ, Resurrection Day. Baptism replaces circumcision as a sign of membership and entrance into the New Covenant, it is the perfection of the old sign.

Col 2:11-12 In him also you were circumcised with a circumcision made without hands, by putting off the body of flesh in the circumcision of Christ; [12] and you were buried with him in baptism, in which you were also raised with him through faith in the working of God, who raised him from the dead.

If circumcision was acceptable for infants, then baptism is also acceptable for infants. After all, why would the perfection of Jewish faith cut off Jewish children who were originally not only permitted, but required, to enter into covenant with God? Christ came not to restrict, but to expand and perfect the saving plan of God.

Lk 18:15-17 Now they were bringing even infants to him that he might touch them; and when the disciples saw it, they rebuked them. [16] But Jesus called them to him, saying, "Let the children come to me, and do not hinder them; for to such belongs the kingdom of God. [17] Truly, I say to you, whoever does not receive the kingdom of God like a child shall not enter it."

Acts 2:38-39 And Peter said to them, "Repent, and be baptized every one of you in the name of Jesus Christ for the forgiveness of your sins; and you shall receive the gift of the Holy Spirit. [39] For the promise is to you and to your children and to all that are far off, every one whom the Lord our God calls to him."

Even the children are called.

1 Cor 7:12-14 To the rest I say, not the Lord, that if any brother has a wife who is an unbeliever, and she consents to live with him, he should not divorce her. [13] If any woman has a husband who is an unbeliever, and he consents to live with her, she should not divorce him. [14] For the unbelieving husband is consecrated through his wife, and the unbelieving wife is consecrated through her husband. Otherwise, your children would be unclean, but as it is they are holy.

Every Christian prays for unbelievers, that they might come to believe. It is the faith of the believer which saves the unbeliever, for God grants the unbeliever the grace of faith on account of our faith and prayers, the faith of we who believe. In the same way, but in superior fashion, does the faith of the parents stand in for the faith of the child at baptism, for baptism is not just prayer or supplication, it is a Divine act, performed by God on the human person.

Mk 2:1-6 And when he returned to Caperna-um after some days, it was reported that he was at home. [2] And many were gathered together, so that there was no longer room for them, not even about the door; and he was preaching the word to them. [3] And they came, bringing to him a paralytic carried by four men. [4] And when they could not get near him because of the crowd, they removed the roof above him; and when they had made an opening, they let down the pallet on which the paralytic lay. [5] And when Jesus saw their faith, he said to the paralytic, "My son, your sins are forgiven."

Note what Christ does here - he looks on the faith of the four friends who broke open the roof. It is on the basis of the friends' faith that the paralytic is forgiven his sins. The faith of the believer can bring about the healing of an unbeliever.

Mt 8:5-8,10,13 As he entered Caperna-um, a centurion came forward to him, beseeching him [6] and saying, "Lord, my servant is lying paralyzed at home, in terrible distress." [7] And he said to him, "I will come and heal him." [8] But the centurion answered him, "Lord, I am not worthy to have you come under my roof; but only say the word, and my servant will be healed..." [10] When Jesus heard him, he marveled, and said to those who followed him, "Truly, I say to you, not even in Israel have I found such faith... [13] And to the centurion Jesus said, "Go; be it done for you as you have believed." And the servant was healed at that very moment.

1 Jn 4:19 We love because he first loved us.

Each of us, adult or infant, is called to God through baptism not because of our assent, but because He first loved us.

Origen (185-253 AD): The Church received from the Apostles the tradition of giving baptism even to infants" (Commentaries on Romans 5:9). The Council of Carthage (A.D. 252) condemns those who postpone baptism until the eighth day after birth. Baptism perfects Jewish circumcision. St. Cyprian of Carthage wrote to Fidius, "As to what pertains to the case of infants: you said that they ought not to be baptized within the second or third day after their birth,... In our council it seemed to us far otherwise. No one agreed to the course which you thought should be taken. Rather, we all judged that the mercy and grace of God ought to be denied to no man born."

<u>Early Christians' comments on Baptizing Babies</u>

Confirmation

In Confirmation, the wedding vows taken in Baptism are strengthened against all trials. Note the "laying on of hands" has two distinctly different effects in Scripture - it results in Confirmation and Holy Orders. Confirmation is called "the completion of baptism," because it finishes the work of God's grace begun in baptism. It is the fullness of the gift of the Holy Spirit (CCC 1285-1321). The Scripture verses below are provided primarily for completeness, to demonstrate that this sacrament has Scriptural foundations.

Current misunderstandings: Some view Confirmation as a rite of passage which the recipient personally chooses to accept in order to signify their acceptance of the Faith. In fact, confirmation matures the gifts of the Spirit received in baptism; once baptism has been received, confirmation must necessarily follow as day follows dawn. The choice is made in baptism.

Acts 8:14-17 Now when the apostles at Jerusalem heard that Samaria had received the word of God, they sent to them Peter and John, ¹⁵ who came down and prayed for them that they might receive the Holy Spirit; ¹⁶ for it had not yet fallen on any of them, but they had only been baptized in the name of the Lord Jesus. ¹⁷ Then they laid their hands on them and they received the Holy Spirit.

Acts 19:1-6 While Apollos was at Corinth, Paul passed through the upper country and came to Ephesus. There he found some disciples. ² And he said to them, "Did you receive the Holy Spirit when you believed?" And they said, "No, we have never even heard that there is a Holy Spirit." ³ And he said, "Into what then were you baptized?" They said, "Into John's baptism." ⁴ And Paul said, "John baptized with the baptism of repentance, telling the people to believe in the one who was to come after him, that is, Jesus." ⁵ On hearing this, they were baptized in the name of the Lord Jesus. ⁶ And when Paul had laid his hands upon them, the Holy Spirit came on them; and they spoke with tongues and prophesied.

Heb 6:1-2 Therefore let us leave the elementary doctrine of Christ and go on to maturity, not laying again a foundation of repentance from dead works and of faith toward God, ² with instruction about ablutions, the laying on of hands, the resurrection of the dead, and eternal judgment.

Wis 9:17 Who has learned thy counsel, unless thou hast given wisdom and sent thy holy Spirit from on high?

2 Cor 1:21 But it is God who establishes us with you in Christ, and has commissioned us...

Note the importance of the above passage. Christ alone baptizes, Christ alone consecrates, Christ alone anoints each of us. Those who lay on hands are acting in the image of Christ, and may only act in that way through the special charism granted them through the Body of Christ.

Eph 1:13 In him you also, who have heard the word of truth, the gospel of your salvation, and have believed in him, were sealed with the promised Holy Spirit...

Early Christians' comments on Confirmation

Holy Orders

In this sacrament, Christ prepares for the Wedding Feast of the Lamb by appointing servants who will oversee its preparation and offer the Sacred Banquet. The bishop is the duly consecrated successor to the apostles, following them in an unbroken line from the Twelve, and holding the fullness of the sacrament of Holy Orders. The priests are consecrated assistants to the successors of the Apostles, sharing in the apostolic authority of their bishops. The deacons are consecrated assistants to the priests, and have a share in the authority of the bishop as well. Each is divinized and divinizes. (CCC 1533-1600)

Current misunderstandings: Many Christians tend not to accept the idea of apostolic succession, the idea that the apostles consecrated successors to themselves who carried the authority of the apostles, nor the idea of an established heirarchy within the Body of Christ. Yet Scripture clearly attests to both.

Lk 22:19 And he took bread, and when he had given thanks he broke it and gave it to them, saying, "This is my body which is given for you. Do this in remembrance of me. [20] And likewise the cup after supper, saying, "This cup which is poured out for you is the new covenant in my blood."

1 Cor 11:24 and when he had given thanks, he broke it, and said, "This is my body which is for you. Do this in remembrance of me."

Jn 20:22 And when he had said this, he breathed on them, and said to them, "Receive the Holy Spirit...."

God only breathes on man twice in Scripture, in Genesis, when He makes man in the image and likeness of God, and here. A priest performing sacramental duties is acting in the image of Jesus Christ - thus, it is only Christ who baptizes, Christ who consecrates, Christ who forgives sins, and no one else. This gift is passed on from Christ to the Apostles and to those consecrated to act as Christ acted through the Apostles. Every Catholic bishop can show his line of spiritual descent, i.e., who consecrated him, who consecrated his consecrator, and so on, all the way back to the Apostles. Apart from the Eastern Orthodox Churches, no other Christian denomination can make this claim.

Acts 20:28 Take heed to yourselves and to all the flock, in which the Holy Spirit has made you overseers (episkipous), to care for the church of God which he obtained with the blood of his own Son

1 Pet 2:24-25 He himself bore our sins in his body on the tree, that we might die to sin and live to righteousness. By his wounds you have been healed. [25] For you were straying like sheep, but have now returned to the Shepherd and Guardian (episkipous) of your souls.

The word used to designate Christ in 1 Peter, episkipous, is the same word used to designate the overseers, i.e., the priests, in Acts 20:28.

Acts 1:20-21 For it is written in the book of Psalms,
'Let his habitation become desolate,
and let there be no one to live in it'; and
'His office let another take.' [21] So one of the men who have accompanied us during all the time that the Lord Jesus went in and out among us,

Peter referred to the position Judas held as an office, and no one disputed him. The key attribute to a holder of the office is that he be a "witness to the resurrection." The Resurrection is witnessed in the daily sacrifice of the Mass. Certain of the believers are set apart in a special way, through the imposition of hands. These are the consecrated successors to the apostles.

Acts 6:6 These they set before the apostles, and they prayed and laid their hands upon them.

Acts 13:3 Then after fasting and praying they laid their hands on them and sent them off.

Acts 14:22-23 strengthening the souls of the disciples, exhorting them to continue in the faith, and saying that through many tribulations we must enter the kingdom of God. [23] And when they had appointed elders for them in every church, with prayer and fasting they committed them to the Lord in whom they believed.

1 Tim 4:14 Do not neglect the gift you have, which was given you by prophetic utterance when the council of elders laid their hands upon you.

2 Tim 1:6 Hence I remind you to rekindle the gift of God that is within you through the laying on of my hands;

Notice that the imposition of hands is used in two different ways in Scripture - one for the presbyters, and

one for the bringing down of the <u>Holy Spirit</u>, in a completion of baptism.

Ex 19:6 and you shall be to me a kingdom of priests and a holy nation. These are the words which you shall speak to the children of Israel."

Is 61:6 but you shall be called the priests of the LORD, men shall speak of you as the ministers of our God; you shall eat the wealth of the nations, and in their riches you shall glory.

Some argue that this makes us all priests, and this is true. We are a nation of priests by our baptism. Yet the nation of priests which was the Chosen People had a special tribe of priests set apart...

Lev 8:23-24 And Moses killed it, and took some of its blood and put it on the tip of Aaron's right ear and on the thumb of his right hand and on the great toe of his right foot. ^{24} And Aaron's sons were brought, and Moses put some of the blood on the tips of their right ears and on the thumbs of their right hands and on the great toes of their right feet; and Moses threw the blood upon the altar round about.

Only the Aaronic priesthood had the right to offer sacrifice for the nation of Israel.

1 Tim 5:22 Do not be hasty in the laying on of hands, nor participate in another man's sins; keep yourself pure.

Tit 1:5 This is why I left you in Crete, that you might amend what was defective, and appoint elders in every town as I directed you

Lk 10:16 "He who hears you hears me, and he who rejects you rejects me, and he who rejects me rejects him who sent me."

1 Pet 2:9 But you are a chosen race, a royal priesthood, a holy nation, God's own people, that you may declare the wonderful deeds of him who called you out of darkness into his marvelous light.

We are all made priests by our baptism. However, there is a special group of men set apart to minister for the whole Body of Christ.

<u>Early Christians' comments on Bishops, Priests, Deacons (Holy Orders)</u>

Women's Ordination

No woman can be consecrated into the sacrament of Holy Orders.

Current misunderstandings: Some hold that women are capable of being ordained. While Scripture shows women were prophets, sources of wisdom, and sources of salvation for both the Israelites and all of mankind, no passage in Scripture shows women offering sacrifice. A priest's primary duty is to offer sacrifice.

Gen 1:27 So God created man in his own image, in the image of God he created him; male and female he created them.

Gal 3:28 There is neither Jew nor Greek, there is neither slave nor free, there is neither male nor female; for you are all one in Christ Jesus.

These two verses are sometimes taken in combination to support the idea that Christ did not intend a male-only priesthood. Since there is no male or female in Christ, and both mand and woman are created in the image and likeness of God, women must be capable of being ordained. Unfortunately for this line of reasoning, Galatians is not here speaking of holy orders, but of baptismal salvation, as parallel passages make clear:

1 Cor 12:13 For by one Spirit we were all baptized into one body—Jews or Greeks, slaves or free—and all were made to drink of one Spirit.

Rom 10:12-13 For there is no distinction between Jew and Greek; the same Lord is Lord of all and bestows his riches upon all who call upon him. ^{13} For, "every one who calls upon the name of the Lord will be saved."

Col 3:11 Here there cannot be Greek and Jew, circumcised and uncircumcised, barbarian, Scythian, slave, free man, but Christ is all, and in all.

The Romans, the Galatians, the Corinthians and the Colossians were each denying that certain members of their community could be saved. Paul intended to remind each audience that Christ's salvation was open to all - no one could lose the right to salvation simply because of social status. Since one's salvation is not dependent on being ordained a priest, Galatians does not apply to the problem of Holy Orders.

Rom 16:1-2 I commend to you our sister Phoebe, a deaconess of the church at Cenchre-ae, ² that you may receive her in the Lord as befits the saints, and help her in whatever she may require from you, for she has been a helper of many and of myself as well.

This verse says quite a bit less than it appears to. The earliest Christians agree that women who served the Church in various capacities were given the name "deacons" (the translation here is actually faulty - the word "deaconess" doesn't appear until the second century). However, the earliest Christians also agree that female deacons never had the same functions, duties, or sacramental charism as even a male deacon, much less a priest.

Ex 33:7 Now Moses used to take the tent and pitch it outside the camp, far off from the camp; and he called it the tent of meeting. And every one who sought the LORD would go out to the tent of meeting, which was outside the camp.

1 Sam 2:22 Now Eli was very old, and he heard all that his sons were doing to all Israel, and how they lay with the women who served at the entrance to the tent of meeting.

Although it is difficult to be certain, the Old Testament makes some allusions to a group of women who appeared to have some sort of guard duty at the doors. This guard duty was certainly present in the early Church, for the earliest Christians would permit none but the baptized to enter the building in which the liturgy of the Mass was being celebrated. Thus, one of the primary functions of the diaconesses was doorkeeping; they were charged with making sure that none but those baptized into the family of God could enter. They also performed the chrism anointing of women being baptised or being anointed in illness, since these anointings were done over and upon the whole body of the nude believer, and it was (reasonably) believed that a celibate male should not be put in a position of temptation.

Even the strongest proponents of women's ordination agree that no orthodox Christian knew of anyone except heretics who attempted to ordain women. In fact, only three heretical sects ever attempted it: the Montanists, the Marcionites, and the Collyridians. The first two Gnostic sects ordained women because both taught that women had to "become like men" in order to be saved (the Gnostic Gospel of Thomas *and* Gospel of Mary Magdalene *both agreed on this point). The third sect worshipped the Blessed Virgin Mary as a goddess - they ordained women because they understood that the priest (or, in this case, priestess) should be in the image and likeness of God. Thus, though they heretically considered Mary to be God, they were at least self-consistent in attempting to ordain women.*

Early Christians' comments on Women Priests

Call No Man "Father"

The use of titles for those who have been properly installed in the offices of the Body of Christ is an appropriate way to honor the authority of Christ which these persons carry. This includes the titles used to reference our spiritual fathers, the priests.

Current misunderstandings: Since Jesus forbad the title "Father" to anyone but God, Catholic use of this title in reference to men is a violation of Scripture.

Mt 23:6-9 and they love the place of honor at feasts and the best seats in the synagogues, ⁷ and salutations in the market places, and being called rabbi by men. ⁸ But you are not to be called rabbi, for you have one teacher, and you are all brethren. ⁹ And call no man your father on earth, for you have one Father, who is in heaven.

Jesus tells us not to use the title "Father"...

Lk 16:24 And he called out, 'Father Abraham, have mercy upon me, and send Lazarus to dip the end of his finger in water and cool my tongue; for I am in anguish in this flame.'

Yet He Himself uses the word in parables...

Jn 7:22 Moses gave you circumcision (not that it is from Moses, but from the fathers)...

He calls other human beings "father"...

Mk 11:9-10 And those who went before and those who followed cried out, "Hosanna! Blessed is he who comes in the name of the Lord! ¹⁰ Blessed is the kingdom of our father David that is coming! Hosanna in the highest!"

And He allows others to use it as well without rebuke.

Acts 7:1-2 And the high priest said, "Is this so?" ² And Stephen said: "Brethren and fathers, hear me. The God of glory appeared to our father Abraham, when he was in Mesopotamia, before he lived in Haran...

Stephen, the first martyr, uses the title right before he sees a vision of Jesus beckoning him to heaven...

Rom 4:1 What then shall we say about Abraham, our forefather according to the flesh?

Rom 4:16-18 That is why it depends on faith, in order that the promise may rest on grace and be guaranteed to all his descendants—not only to the adherents of the law but also to those who share the faith of Abraham, for he is the father of us all, ¹⁷ as it is written, "I have made you the father of many nations"—in the presence of the God in whom he believed, who gives life to the dead and calls into existence the things that do not exist. ¹⁸ In hope he believed against hope, that he should become the father of many nations; as he had been told, "So shall your descendants be."

And Paul uses the term extensively. Some say the prohibition is not on naming biological fathers such as Abraham and David, but on naming anyone a spiritual father...

1 Cor 4:14-16 I do not write this to make you ashamed, but to admonish you as my beloved children. ¹⁵ For though you have countless guides in Christ, you do not have many fathers. For I became your father in Christ Jesus through the gospel. ¹⁶ I urge you, then, be imitators of me.

Yet Paul calls himself a spiritual "father," and urges us to imitate him...

1 Thess 2:11 for you know how, like a father with his children, we exhorted each one of you and encouraged you and charged you...

In fact, he refers to all the elders of the Church as "father"...

1 Jn 2:13-14 I am writing to you, fathers, because you know him who is from the beginning. I am writing to you, young men, because you have overcome the evil one. I write to you, children, because you know the Father. ¹⁴ I write to you, fathers, because you know him who is from the beginning. I write to you, young men, because you are strong, and the word of God abides in you, and you have overcome the evil one.

And Paul acknowledges they are fathers because of their knowledge of God. In fact, it is from God that the designation "father" derives.

Eph 3:14-15 For this reason I bow my knees before the Father, ¹⁵ from whom every family in heaven and on earth is named...

The spiritual fatherhood of the priest is derived from the same place biological fatherhood draws its power - both are a participation and a sharing in the Fatherhood of God.

Celibacy

Fasting teaches control of bodily appetites and demonstrates love for God. The fast which is celibacy is a good and wholesome thing. All who dedicate their lives to God through the special ministering offices of the Body of Christ imitate Christ and must therefore seek out the special gifts of grace which this fast brings, so as to best accomplish Christ's work. The fast of celibacy is a discipline which enhances the ministerial office and allows more complete concentration on God's will. This discipline is imposed through the authority of the Church, and will remain in effect as long as the fruits of the discipline are visible within Christ's ministry to the world.

Current misunderstandings: Many Christians say the celibacy of Catholic religious is an offense against God, arguing that Scripture demonstrates married bishops, so the Church does not have the right to impose celibacy on its clergy.

Celibacy was prefigured in the priesthood of the Old Testament.

1 Sam 21:5 And the priest answered David, "I have no common bread at hand, but there is holy bread; if only the young men have kept themselves from women." ⁵ And David answered the priest, "Of a truth women have been kept from us as always when I go on an expedition; the vessels of the young men are holy, even when it is a common journey; how much more today will their vessels be holy?"

Is 52:11 Depart, depart, go out thence, touch no unclean thing; go out from the midst of her, purify yourselves, you who bear the vessels of the LORD.

Lev 21:6-7 They shall be holy to their God, and not profane the name of their God; for they offer the offerings by fire to the LORD, the bread of their God; therefore they shall be holy. ⁷ They shall not marry a harlot or a woman who has been defiled; neither shall they marry a woman divorced from her husband; for the priest is holy to his God.

Jerusalem was the "virgin," the Lord's bride:

Lam 1:7,15 Jerusalem remembers
    in the days of her affliction and bitterness
    all the precious things
that were hers from days of old....
    "The LORD flouted all my mighty men
        in the midst of me;
    he summoned an assembly against me
        to crush my young men;
    the Lord has trodden as in a wine press
the virgin daughter of Judah.

Is 23:12 And he said: "You will no more exult, O oppressed virgin daughter of Sidon; arise, pass over to Cyprus, even there you will have no rest."

Wis 3:14 Blessed also is the eunuch whose hands have done no lawless deed,
and who has not devised wicked things against the Lord;
for special favor will be shown him for his faithfulness, and a place of great delight in the temple of the Lord.

Some say the following passages shows priests should be married:

1 Cor 9:4 This is my defense to those who would examine me. ⁴ Do we not have the right to our food and drink? ⁵ Do we not have the right to be accompanied by a wife, as the other apostles and the brothers of the Lord and Cephas?

1 Tim 3:2-4 Now a bishop must be above reproach, the husband of one wife, temperate, sensible, dignified, hospitable, an apt teacher, ³ no drunkard, not violent but gentle, not quarrelsome, and no lover of money. ⁴ He must manage his own household well, keeping his children submissive and respectful in every way; ⁵ for if a man does not know how to manage his own household, how can he care for God's church?

However, they forget that both Paul and Christ Himself recommended otherwise.

Mt 19:10 The disciples said to him, "If such is the case of a man with his wife, it is not expedient to marry."

Mt 19:11-12 But he said to them, "Not all men can receive this saying, but only those to whom it is given. ¹² For there are eunuchs who have been so from birth, and there are eunuchs who have been made eunuchs by men, and there are eunuchs who have made themselves eunuchs for the sake of the kingdom of heaven. He who is able to receive this, let him receive it."

1 Cor 7:1-7 Now concerning the matters about which you wrote. It is well for a man not to touch a woman. ² But because of the temptation to immorality, each man should have his own wife and each woman her own husband. ³ The husband should give to his wife her conjugal rights, and likewise the wife to her husband. ⁴ For the wife does not rule over her own body, but the husband does; likewise the husband does not rule over his own body, but the wife does. ⁵ Do not refuse one another except perhaps by agreement for a season, that you may devote yourselves to prayer; but then come together again, lest Satan tempt you through lack of self-control. ⁶ I say this by way of concession, not of command. ⁷ I wish that all were as I myself am. But each has his own special gift from God, one of one kind and one of another.

1 Cor 7:32-38 I want you to be free from anxieties. The unmarried man is anxious about the affairs of the Lord, how to please the Lord; ³³ but the married man is anxious about worldly affairs, how to please his wife, ³⁴ and his interests are divided. And the unmarried woman or girl is anxious about the affairs of the Lord, how to be holy in body and spirit; but the married woman is anxious about worldly affairs, how to please her husband. ³⁵ I say this for your own benefit, not to lay any restraint upon you, but to promote good order and to secure your undivided devotion to the Lord. ³⁶ If any one thinks that he is not behaving properly toward his betrothed, if his passions are strong, and it has to be, let him do as he wishes: let them marry—it is no sin. ³⁷ But whoever is firmly established in his heart, being under no necessity but having his desire under control, and has determined this in his heart, to keep her as his betrothed, he will do well. ³⁸ So that he who marries his betrothed does well; and he who refrains from marriage will do better.

Note that here Paul has to take care to warn that marriage is not a sin. His emphasis on the importance and virtue of celibacy is so strong that he is afraid his readers will think marriage a mistake.

Mt 22:30 For in the resurrection they neither marry nor are given in marriage, but are like angels in heaven.

Celibacy is a sign of the Kingdom of Heaven. St. John the Baptist, Joseph, Mary, St. John the Apostle, St. Paul - all were celibate.

Rev 14:1-5 And I heard a voice from heaven like the sound of many waters and like the sound of loud thunder; the voice I heard was like the sound of harpers playing on their harps, ³ and they sing a new song before the throne and before the four living creatures and before the elders. No one could learn that song except the hundred and forty-four thousand who had been redeemed from the earth. ⁴ It is these who have not defiled themselves with women, for they are chaste; it is these who follow the Lamb wherever he goes; these have been redeemed from mankind as first fruits for God and the Lamb, ⁵ and in their mouth no lie was found, for they are spotless.

Only the virgins can sing the song of the Lamb.

Mt 19:29-30 And every one who has left houses or brothers or sisters or father or mother or children or lands, for my name's sake, will receive a hundredfold, and inherit eternal life. ³⁰ But many that are first will be last, and the last first.

Mk 10:29-31 Jesus said, "Truly, I say to you, there is no one who has left house or brothers or sisters or mother or father or children or lands, for my sake and for the gospel, ³⁰ who will not receive a hundredfold now in this time, houses and brothers and sisters and mothers and children and lands, with persecutions, and in the age to come eternal life. ³¹ But many that are first will be last, and the last first."

Lk 18:29-30 And he said to them, "Truly, I say to you, there is no man who has left house or wife or brothers or parents or children, for the sake of the kingdom of God, ³⁰ who will not receive manifold more in this time, and in the age to come eternal life."

Those who will enter into ministry know the preconditions established. If they cannot accept the conditions which the Body of Christ asks of them, they may serve the Lord in many other ways besides religious life. The Church imposes the discipline for the benefit of the ministers of the Lord.

The Eucharist

Is 45:15 Truly, thou art a God who hidest thyself, O God of Israel, the Savior.

Lk 2:34 34 and Simeon blessed them and said to Mary his mother, "Behold, this child is set for the fall and rising of many in Israel, and for a sign that is spoken against..."

The Eucharist is the consummation of the wedding vow made in Baptism and strengthened in Confirmation. The marriage is consummated at the Mass, which is the Wedding Feast of the Lamb, when the Bridegroom enters into we who are the Bride, and each member of the Bride is made fruitful thereby. In the extension of the Cross which is the Mass, at the words of consecration, through the power of the Holy Spirit, the Body, Blood, Soul, and Divinity of the glorified Christ is made present to all, so that we may consume His flesh and His blood as Christ commanded in His Scriptures, and so that we may worship and adore Him in spirit and in truth. Jesus Christ is fully present in both the consecrated host and in the consecrated cup, so that, though one be called His Flesh, and the other His Blood, and though both be separately consecrated, yet they each contain the fullness of Body, Blood, Soul, and Divinity who is Jesus Christ. (CCC 1322-1344, 1391-1419, 1524-1525)

Current misunderstandings: Most Christians deny the Real Presence of Jesus Christ in the Eucharist. At best, Christ is seen as being truly present, but His presence does not completely replace the substance of the bread. At worst, the process is seen as strictly a symbolic memorial. Only the Eastern Orthodox and the Catholic Churches adhere to the ancient belief, only the Catholic Church explicitly understands Him to completely replace the substance of the bread and wine. Interestingly, these are also the only two faiths which teach an infallible Church, and maintain the seven sacraments. The more attenuated the idea of Christ's presence in the Eucharist, the more attenuated the idea of the Church as the Body of Christ, or the sacraments as conduits of God's grace. Therefore, baptism becomes only a seal, and not regenerative, because there is no sacramental life to be baptized into.

God dwelt among His people in the Old Testament in the Ark of the Covenant:

Psalm 68:7-8 O God, when thou didst go forth before thy people, when thou didst march through the wilderness, [Selah] ⁸ the earth quaked, the heavens poured down rain, at the presence of God; yon Sinai quaked at the presence of God, the God of Israel.

God dwelt among His people when Jesus walked the earth:

Jn 1:14 And the Word became flesh and dwelt among us, full of grace and truth; we have beheld his glory, glory as of the only Son from the Father..

God dwells among His people in the ages since the crucifixion in the Resurrected Body of Christ present in the Eucharist:

Mt 28:20 and lo, I am with you always, to the close of the age."

Types for the Eucharist

Gen 3:22 Then the LORD God said, "Behold, the man has become like one of us, knowing good and evil; and now, lest he put forth his hand and take also of the tree of life, and eat, and live for ever"

Acts 13:29 And when they had fulfilled all that was written of him, they took him down from the tree, and laid him in a tomb.

Rev 22:14 Blessed are those who wash their robes, that they may have the right to the tree of life and that they may enter the city by the gates..

Christ was hung on a tree. He is the source of life. Jesus Christ is the fruit of the tree of life.

Gen 22:9-13 When they came to the place of which God had told him, Abraham built an altar there, and laid the wood in order, and bound Isaac his son, and laid him on the altar, upon the wood. ¹⁰ Then Abraham put forth his hand, and took the knife to slay his son. ¹¹ But the angel of the LORD called to him from heaven, and said, "Abraham, Abraham!" And he said, "Here am I." ¹² He said, "Do not lay your hand on the lad or do anything to him; for now I know that you fear God, seeing you have not withheld your son, your only son, from me." ¹³ And Abraham lifted up his eyes and looked, and behold, behind him was a ram, caught in a thicket by his horns; and Abraham went and took the ram, and offered it up as a burnt offering instead of his son.

Abraham offered up his only son on the altar he built on Mount Moriah, the future site of Jerusalem. God saved his first-born son, as He would later save all the first-born sons of Israel in the land of Egypt, providing Abraham a substitution sacrifice - a ram, caught by its crown in thorns nearby. The ram was offered instead of Abraham's first-born. The flesh of sacrificial animals was eaten by the worshipper.

Ex 12:1-10 The LORD said to Moses and Aaron in the land of Egypt, ² "This month shall be for you the beginning of months; it shall be the first month of the year for you. ³ Tell all the congregation of Israel that on the tenth day of this month they shall take every man a lamb according to their fathers' houses, a lamb for a household; ⁴ and if the household is too small for a lamb, then a man and his neighbor next to his house shall take according to the number of persons; according to what each can eat you shall make your count for the lamb. ⁵ Your lamb shall be without blemish, a male a year old; you shall take it from the sheep or from the goats; ⁶ and you shall keep it until the fourteenth day of this month, when the whole assembly of the congregation of Israel shall kill their lambs in the evening. ⁷ Then they shall take some of the blood, and put it on the two doorposts and the lintel of the houses in which they eat them. ⁸ They shall eat the flesh that night, roasted; with unleavened bread and bitter herbs they shall eat it. ⁹ Do not eat any of it raw or boiled with water, but roasted, its head with its legs and its inner parts. ¹⁰ And you shall let none of it remain until the morning, anything that remains until the morning you shall burn.

The Passover lamb had to be eaten - it was a divine commandment.

Ex 12:11-15 In this manner you shall eat it: your loins girded, your sandals on your feet, and your staff in your hand; and you shall eat it in haste. It is the LORD's passover. ¹² For I will pass through the land of Egypt that night, and I will smite all the first-born in the land of Egypt, both man and beast; and on all the gods of Egypt I will execute judgments: I am the LORD. ¹³ The blood shall be a sign for you, upon the houses where you are; and when I see the blood, I will pass over you, and no plague shall fall upon you to destroy you, when I smite the land of Egypt.
¹⁴ "This day shall be for you a memorial day, and you shall keep it as a feast to the LORD; throughout your generations you shall observe it as an ordinance for ever. ¹⁵ Seven days you shall eat unleavened bread; on the first day you shall put away leaven out of your houses, for if any one eats what is leavened, from the first day until the seventh day, that person shall be cut off from Israel.

The Passover sacrifice is a perpetual ordinance. The Hebrew people are to keep this sacrifice for the entire life of the people. They must sacrifice the Paschal Lamb and consume its flesh.

Lev 17:11-12 For the life of the flesh is in the blood; and I have given it for you upon the altar to make atonement for your souls; for it is the blood that makes atonement, by reason of the life. ¹² Therefore I have said to the people of Israel, No person among you shall eat blood, neither shall any stranger who sojourns among you eat blood.

As the Israelites would later write in their legal code, blood was the source of all life. By marking their houses with blood, they were proclaiming themselves to be the seat of life for all peoples, thus the angel of death would pass over them. Those with no blood on their lintels were people dead to God. But God put a strong stricture on the Hebrews - they could not consume blood. They were not yet ready to incorporate the source of life into their lives. The Mosaic law would be an external source of life, as the blood on the door signified, but it was not an internal wellspring of life. That internal wellspring of God's life within them had not yet come into the world.

Ex 22:21 "You shall not wrong a stranger or oppress him, for you were strangers in the land of Egypt.

Ex 23:43-49 And the LORD said to Moses and Aaron, "This is the ordinance of the passover: no foreigner shall eat of it; ⁴⁴ but every slave that is bought for money may eat of it after you have circumcised him. ⁴⁵ No sojourner or hired servant may eat of it. ⁴⁶ In one house shall it be eaten; you shall not carry forth any of the flesh outside the house; and you shall not break a bone of it. ⁴⁷ All the congregation of Israel shall keep it. ⁴⁸ And when a stranger shall sojourn with you and would keep the passover to the LORD, let all his males be circumcised, then he may come near and keep it; he shall be as a native of the land. But no uncircumcised person shall eat of it. ⁴⁹ There shall be one law for the native and for the stranger who sojourns among you."

While the foreigner and sojourner had to be respected and well-treated, they could not partake of the Passover. Only those who belonged to God could do so. Also, of all the Old Testament sacrifices, only the Passover was "an ordinance forever." While all sacrifice prefigured Christ's one sacrifice, the Passover, being a perpetual ordinance, prefigured Christ in an entirely unique and superlative way.

Lev 7:7 The guilt offering is like the sin offering, there is one law for them; the priest who makes atonement with it shall have it.

Sacrifical offerings had to be eaten.

Lev 7:15-20 And the flesh of the sacrifice of his peace offerings for thanksgiving shall be eaten on the day of his offering; he shall not leave any of it until the morning. [16] But if the sacrifice of his offering is a votive offering or a freewill offering, it shall be eaten on the day that he offers his sacrifice, and on the morrow what remains of it shall be eaten, [17] but what remains of the flesh of the sacrifice on the third day shall be burned with fire. [18] If any of the flesh of the sacrifice of his peace offering is eaten on the third day, he who offers it shall not be accepted, neither shall it be credited to him; it shall be an abomination, and he who eats of it shall bear his iniquity.
[19] "Flesh that touches any unclean thing shall not be eaten; it shall be burned with fire. All who are clean may eat flesh, [20] but the person who eats of the flesh of the sacrifice of the LORD's peace offerings while an uncleanness is on him, that person shall be cut off from his people.

The "thanksgiving sacrifice" ("eucharasis" in the Greek) can also be translated "fulfillment sacrifice." It was offered up at the fulfillment of a vow or promise, not as reparation. Its characteristic feature was the sacred banquet at which the offerer and his guests ate of the meat of the sacrificed animal on the same day it was offered. Interestingly, the meat could not be eaten on the third day, and the people who partook of it had to be utterly clean.

Lev 7:35-36 This is the portion of Aaron and of his sons from the offerings made by fire to the LORD, consecrated to them on the day they were presented to serve as priests of the LORD; [36] the LORD commanded this to be given them by the people of Israel, on the day that they were anointed; it is a perpetual due throughout their generations."

Lev 10:16-20 Now Moses diligently inquired about the goat of the sin offering, and behold, it was burned! And he was angry with Eleazar and Ithamar, the sons of Aaron who were left, saying, [17] "Why have you not eaten the sin offering in the place of the sanctuary, since it is a thing most holy and has been given to you that you may bear the iniquity of the congregation, to make atonement for them before the LORD? [18] Behold, its blood was not brought into the inner part of the sanctuary. You certainly ought to have eaten it in the sanctuary, as I commanded." [19] And Aaron said to Moses, "Behold, today they have offered their sin offering and their burnt offering before the LORD; and yet such things as these have befallen me! If I had eaten the sin offering today, would it have been acceptable in the sight of the LORD?" [20] And when Moses heard that, he was content.

For each of the sacrifices offered by the Aaronic priesthood, the sacrifical meat absolutely had to be eaten, and it had to be eaten in a state of cleanness. Aaron was rightly concerned that his sons didn't fulfill the prerequisites.

Lev 24:5-9 "And you shall take fine flour, and bake twelve cakes of it; two tenths of an ephah shall be in each cake. [6] And you shall set them in two rows, six in a row, upon the table of pure gold. [7] And you shall put pure frankincense with each row, that it may go with the bread as a memorial portion to be offered by fire to the LORD. [8] Every sabbath day Aaron shall set it in order before the LORD continually on behalf of the people of Israel as a covenant for ever. [9] And it shall be for Aaron and his sons, and they shall eat it in a holy place, since it is for him a most holy portion out of the offerings by fire to the LORD, a perpetual due."

Twelve loaves for the twelve tribes and the twelve apostles who would come, six loaves on each side because the seventh, the bread in which we rest, had not yet come. The Scriptures had not yet been fulfilled. The true showbread of the Lord will be instituted by God Himself.

Ex 16:16-30 This is what the LORD has commanded: 'Gather of it, every man of you, as much as he can eat; you shall take an omer apiece, according to the number of the persons whom each of you has in his tent.'" [17] And the people of Israel did so; they gathered, some more, some less. [18] But when they measured it with an omer, he that gathered much had nothing over, and he that gathered little had no lack; each gathered according to what he could eat. [19] And Moses said to

them, "Let no man leave any of it till the morning." [20] But they did not listen to Moses; some left part of it till the morning, and it bred worms and became foul; and Moses was angry with them. [21] Morning by morning they gathered it, each as much as he could eat; but when the sun grew hot, it melted.
[22] On the sixth day they gathered twice as much bread, two omers apiece; and when all the leaders of the congregation came and told Moses, [23] he said to them, "This is what the LORD has commanded: 'Tomorrow is a day of solemn rest, a holy sabbath to the LORD; bake what you will bake and boil what you will boil, and all that is left over lay by to be kept till the morning.'" [24] So they laid it by till the morning, as Moses bade them; and it did not become foul, and there were no worms in it. [25] Moses said, "Eat it today, for today is a sabbath to the LORD; today you will not find it in the field. [26] Six days you shall gather it; but on the seventh day, which is a sabbath, there will be none." [27] On the seventh day some of the people went out to gather, and they found none. [28] And the LORD said to Moses, "How long do you refuse to keep my commandments and my laws? [29] See! The LORD has given you the sabbath, therefore on the sixth day he gives you bread for two days; remain every man of you in his place, let no man go out of his place on the seventh day." [30] So the people rested on the seventh day.

Again, we see that the manna could be kept for two days under special conditions, but never for three. The bread which fell from heaven for the physical sustenance of the Chosen People, and the flesh sacrifices in which man fulfilled his portion of the covenant promise did not avail by the third day - they were things of this world, and they passed away into corruption, useless in the sight of God and of man.

1 Cor 10:3-4 and all ate the same supernatural food [4] and all drank the same supernatural drink. For they drank from the supernatural Rock which followed them, and the Rock was Christ.

Paul recognized that the water from the rock, the manna, were both prefigurements of something far greater.

Ex 24:9-11 Then Moses and Aaron, Nadab, and Abihu, and seventy of the elders of Israel went up, [10] and they saw the God of Israel; and there was under his feet as it were a pavement of sapphire stone, like the very heaven for clearness. [11] And he did not lay his hand on the chief men of the people of Israel; they beheld God, and ate and drank.

The Mosaic covenant was consummated with a covenant meal in the presence of God.

1 Sam 16:1 The LORD said to Samuel, "How long will you grieve over Saul, seeing I have rejected him from being king over Israel? Fill your horn with oil, and go; I will send you to Jesse the Bethlehemite, for I have provided for myself a king among his sons."

The name "Bethlehem" means "house of bread." Remember this. Samuel is going to the House of Bread to find the King who is to be consecrated. From this king's line will come the Messiah.

1 Sam 16:5 And he said, "Peaceably; I have come to sacrifice to the LORD; consecrate yourselves, and come with me to the sacrifice." And he consecrated Jesse and his sons, and invited them to the sacrifice.

Note the kind of sacrificial banquet Samuel offers - this is the fulfillment banquet spoken of in Leviticus, the eucharasis.

1 Sam 16:6-7 When they came, he looked on Eliab and thought, "Surely the LORD'S anointed is before him." [7] But the LORD said to Samuel, "Do not look on his appearance or on the height of his stature, because I have rejected him; for the LORD sees not as man sees; man looks on the outward appearance, but the LORD looks on the heart."

The very first person Samuel sees seems good to him. Samuel is ready to consecrate the king. But God stops him. We are not to judge by appearance when searching out the son of Jesse, the anointed King who resides in the House of Bread, Bethlehem. We find the King only when we see as God sees, because man sees only the appearance, but God knows the heart of everything. Remember this.

1 Sam 16:10-12 And Jesse made seven of his sons pass before Samuel. And Samuel said to Jesse, "The LORD has not chosen these." And Samuel said to Jesse, "Are all your sons here?" and he said, "There remains yet the youngest, but behold, he is keeping the sheep." And Samuel said to Jesse, "Send and fetch him; for we will not sit down till he comes here." And he sent, and brought him in. Now he was ruddy, and had beautiful eyes, and was handsome. And the LORD said, "Arise, anoint him; for this is he."

Seven sons passed by, it was the eighth who was anointed king. Christ will rise after three days in the tomb, but He will not arise on the seventh day, the Sabbath. He rises on the eighth day, the day of New Creation.

1 Kings 19:4-8 But he himself went a day's journey into the wilderness, and came and sat down under a broom tree; and he asked that he might die, saying, "It is enough; now, O Lord, take away my life; for I am no better than my fathers." ⁵ And he lay down and slept under a broom tree; and behold, an angel touched him, and said to him, "Arise and eat." ⁶ And he looked, and behold, there was at his head a cake baked on hot stones and a jar of water. And he ate and drank, and lay down again. ⁷ And the angel of the Lord came again a second time, and touched him, and said, "Arise and eat, else the journey will be too great for you." ⁸ And he arose, and ate and drank, and went in the strength of that food forty days and forty nights to Horeb the mount of God.

Elijah was strengthened for his journey to the holy mountain by the eating of the bread provided by God.

1 Kings 19:12-13 And after the earthquake a fire, but the Lord was not in the fire; and after the fire a still small voice. ¹³ And when Elijah heard it, he wrapped his face in his mantled and went out and stood at the entrance of the cave.

And it was this journey which brought him to perceive the "still small voice" and presence of God.

2 Kings 4:42-44 A man came from Baal-shalishah, bringing the man of God bread of the first fruits, twenty loaves of barley, and fresh ears of grain in his sack. And Elisha said, "Give to the men, that they may eat." ⁴³ But his servant said, "How am I to set this before a hundred men?" So he repeated, "Give them to the men, that they may eat, for thus says the Lord, 'They shall eat and have some left.'" ⁴⁴ So he set it before them. And they ate, and had some left, according to the word of the Lord.

Elisha miraculously multiplied the loaves - he has a double portion of Elijah's spirit. Christ will do a greater thing than this.

1 Kings 18:30-39 Then Elijah said to all the people, "Come near to me"; and all the people came near to him. And he repaired the altar of the Lord that had been thrown down; ³¹ Elijah took twelve stones, according to the number of the tribes of the sons of Jacob, to whom the word of the Lord came, saying, "Israel shall be your name"; ³² and with the stones he built an altar in the name of the Lord. And he made a trench about the altar, as great as would contain two measures of seed. ³³ And he put the wood in order, and cut the bull in pieces and laid it on the wood. And he said, "Fill four jars with water, and pour it on the burnt offering, and on the wood." ³⁴ And he said, "Do it a second time"; and they did it a second time. And he said, "Do it a third time"; and they did it a third time. ³⁵ And the water ran round about the altar, and filled the trench also with water. ³⁶ And at the time of the offering of the oblation, Elijah the prophet came near and said, "O Lord, God of Abraham, Isaac, and Israel, let it be known this day that thou art God in Israel, and that I am thy servant, and that I have done all these things at thy word. ³⁷ Answer me, O Lord, answer me, that this people may know that thou, O Lord, art God, and that thou hast turned their hearts back." ³⁸ Then the fire of the Lord fell, and consumed the burnt offering, and the wood, and the stones, and the dust, and licked up the water that was in the trench. ³⁹ And when all the people saw it, they fell on their faces; and they said, "The Lord, he is God; the Lord, he is God."

Elijah builds the altar on a foundation of twelve stones, the foundation of the twelve tribes of Israel and the twelve Apostles. The offering is a bull cut in pieces and laid upon the wood, it is buried in a three-fold washing with water...

Heb 12:29 Our God is a consuming fire.

and the Holy Spirit completely consumes the substance of the sacrifice - there remained in its place only fire. In this sacrifice, the people recognize the presence of God.

Is 6:5-7 And I said: "Woe is me! For I am lost; for I am a man of unclean lips, and I dwell in the midst of a people of unclean lips; for my eyes have seen the King, the Lord of hosts!"
⁶ Then flew one of the seraphim to me, having in his hand a burning coal which he had taken with tongs from the altar. ⁷ And he touched my mouth, and said: "Behold, this has touched your lips; your guilt is taken away, and your sin forgiven."

When the burning coal of God's Eucharistic presence was touched to Isaiah's mouth, he was healed of his uncleanness.

Prov 9:1-5 Wisdom has built her house, she has set up her seven pillars. ² She has slaughtered her beasts, she has mixed her wine, she has also set her table. ³ She has sent out her maids to call from the highest places in the town, ⁴ "Whoever is simple, let him turn in here!" To him who is without sense she says, ⁵ "Come, eat of my bread and drink of the wine I have mixed.

Psalm 116:13 I will lift up the cup of salvation and call on the name of the LORD,

Psalm 31:20 O how abundant is thy goodness,
which thou hast laid up for those who fear thee,
and wrought for those who take refuge in thee,
in the sight of the sons of men!

Ex 29:44-46 I will consecrate the tent of meeting and the altar; Aaron also and his sons I will consecrate, to serve me as priests. ⁴⁵ And I will dwell among the people of Israel, and will be their God. ⁴⁶ And they shall know that I am the LORD their God, who brought them forth out of the land of Egypt that I might dwell among them; I am the LORD their God.

Mal 1:1,10-11 The oracle of the word of the LORD to Israel by Malachi..... Oh, that there were one among you who would shut the doors, that you might not kindle fire upon my altar in vain! I have no pleasure in you, says the LORD of hosts, and I will not accept an offering from your hand. ¹¹ For from the rising of the sun to its setting my name is great among the nations, and in every place incense is offered to my name, and a pure offering; for my name is great among the nations, says the LORD of hosts.

We know this to be a true oracle, for it is canonical Scripture. The temple gates have been shut for two millenia. Yet, who but Christ can offer "a pure offering?" How could this sacrifice be brought "everywhere"?

The Establishment of the Eucharist

Lk 2:6-7 And while they were there, the time came for her to be delivered. ⁷ And she gave birth to her first-born son and wrapped him in swaddling cloths, and laid him in a manger, because there was no place for them in the inn.

A manger is an eating trough. See also "Sacraments Produce Grace."

Jn 1:35 The next day again John was standing with two of his disciples; ³⁶ and he looked at Jesus as he walked, and said, "Behold, the Lamb of God!"

John's comment specifically refers to the one perpetual sacrifice, the one ordinance of God which the whole Hebrew people had to keep, the Passover. The ram offered by Abraham on Mount Moriah, the future site of Jerusalem, the Passover lamb, the Levitical sacrifices, the manna, the manger - the whole covenantal theme of God's salvation plan is coming to fruition. Its theme is our need for sustenance. The Passover lamb had to be eaten.

How does Christ use food metaphors?

Mt 16:5-12 When the disciples reached the other side, they had forgotten to bring any bread. ⁶ Jesus said to them, "Take heed and beware of the leaven of the Pharisees and Sadducees." ⁷ And they discussed it among themselves, saying, "We brought no bread." ⁸ But Jesus, aware of this, said, "O men of little faith, why do you discuss among yourselves the fact that you have no bread? ⁹ Do you not yet perceive? Do you not remember the five loaves of the five thousand, and how many baskets you gathered? ¹⁰ Or the seven loaves of the four thousand, and how many baskets you gathered? ¹¹ How is it that you fail to perceive that I did not speak about bread? Beware of the leaven of the Pharisees and Sadducees." ¹² Then they understood that he did not tell them to beware of the leaven of bread, but of the teaching of the Pharisees and Sadducees.

Jn 4:7-8, 31-38 There came a woman of Samaria to draw water. Jesus said to her, "Give me a drink." ⁸ For his disciples had gone away into the city to buy food.... Meanwhile the disciples besought him, saying, "Rabbi, eat." ³² But he said to them, "I have food to eat of which you do not know." ³³ So the disciples said to one another, "Has any one brought him food?" ³⁴ Jesus said to them, "My food is to do the will of him who sent me, and to accomplish his work. ³⁵ Do you not say, 'There are yet four months, then comes the harvest'? I tell you, lift up your eyes, and see how the fields are already white for harvest. ³⁶ He who reaps receives wages, and gathers fruit for eternal life, so that sower and reaper may rejoice together. ³⁷ For here the saying holds true, 'One sows and another reaps.' ³⁸ I sent you to reap that for which you did not labor; others have labored, and you have entered into their labor."

When using such metaphors, Christ explains exactly how the food imagery is a metaphor, He corrects the disciples when they mistake His food metaphors for literal truth. Compare the two passages above to the passage in which Christ does not intend His food reference to be taken as a metaphor at all. Christ will combine every thread of Old Testament foreshadowing in order to teach His disciples the living reality.

Jn 6:4 Now the Passover, the feast of the Jews, was at hand...

The Aaronic sacrifices were performed every day, through all the wanderings in the desert, during the conquering of the Promised Land, and after each rebuilding of the Temple, offered for a thousand years until the final destruction of the Temple in 70 A.D. By Christ's time, the sacrifices had been established for generations. Thus, when Christ speaks the words of John 6 in the synagogue at Capernaum, He speaks to an audience which knows full well what the priests were required to do with the sacrifices offered in the temple every day, an audience which was itself preparing for the greatest sacrifice of all, the Passover, even as the Lamb of God spoke.

Jn 6:10-14 Jesus said, "Make the people sit down." Now there was much grass in the place; so the men sat down, in number about five thousand. 11 Jesus then took the loaves, and when he had given thanks, he distributed them to those who were seated; so also the fish, as much as they wanted. 12 And when they had eaten their fill, he told his disciples, "Gather up the fragments left over, that nothing may be lost." 13 So they gathered them up and filled twelve baskets with fragments from the five barley loaves, left by those who had eaten. 14 When the people saw the sign which he had done, they said, "This is indeed the prophet who is to come into the world!"

Slaves stood when they ate. Only free people ate while reclining. Christ's multiplication of the loaves not only reminds us of the plenitude of the Messianic era, it also reminds us of the manna with which God fed the Chosen People after their release from bondage in Egypt.

Jn 6:19-20 When they had rowed about three or four miles, they saw Jesus walking on the sea and drawing near to the boat. They were frightened, 20 but he said to them, "It is I; do not be afraid."

Moses parted the Red Sea. Christ supercedes that - He does not even need dry ground. He walks on the water. He has complete mastery over the physical world. Remember this.

Jn 6:22-31 On the next day the people who remained on the other side of the sea saw that there had been only one boat there, and that Jesus had not entered the boat with his disciples, but that his disciples had gone away alone. 23 However, boats from Tiberi-as came near the place where they ate the bread after the Lord had given thanks. 24 So when the people saw that Jesus was not there, nor his disciples, they themselves got into the boats and went to Caperna-um, seeking Jesus. 25 When they found him on the other side of the sea, they said to him, "Rabbi, when did you come here?" 26 Jesus answered them, "Truly, truly, I say to you, you seek me, not because you saw signs, but because you ate your fill of the loaves. 27 Do not labor for the food which perishes, but for the food which endures to eternal life, which the Son of man will give to you; for on him has God the Father set his seal." 28 Then they said to him, "What must we do, to be doing the works of God?" 29 Jesus answered them, "This is the work of God, that you believe in him whom he has sent." 30 So they said to him, "Then what sign do you do, that we may see, and believe you? What work do you perform? 31 Our fathers ate the manna in the wilderness; as it is written, 'He gave them bread from heaven to eat.'"

The word Christ uses for "endures" in the phrase "work for food which endures" is a primitive verb. It means "to stay, remain." There is no shadow of movement or transition in this verb. Common meals, manna, even the sacrificial offerings, all of this food becomes corrupt and perishes. But He is about to tell them of a food that does not perish, as the food of the table and of the Aaronic sacrifices do. Indeed, later in John's Gospel, the crowd will affirm that the presence of God is a gift which God gives and does not take back:

Jn 12:34 The crowd answered him, "We have heard from the law that the Christ remains for ever.

Jn 6:32-33 Jesus then said to them, "Truly, truly, I say to you, it was not Moses who gave you the bread from heaven; my Father gives you the true bread from heaven. 33 For the bread of God is that which comes down from heaven, and gives life to the world."

The crowd is looking for food, but Christ rejects the idea that simple physical bread, even that created by supernatural means (manna), is worth discussing. He says they need the only true bread there is, the true bread of God.

Wis 16:20 Instead of these things thou didst give thy people food of angels, and without their toil thou didst supply them from heaven with bread ready to eat, providing every pleasure and suited to every taste.

Jn 6:34-40 They said to him, "Lord, give us this bread always."
^{35} Jesus said to them, "I am the bread of life; he who comes to me shall not hunger, and he who believes in me shall never thirst. ^{36} But I said to you that you have seen me and yet do not believe. ^{37} All that the Father gives me will come to me; and him who comes to me I will not cast out. ^{38} For I have come down from heaven, not to do my own will, but the will of him who sent me; ^{39} and this is the will of him who sent me, that I should lose nothing of all that he has given me, but raise it up at the last day. ^{40} For this is the will of my Father, that every one who sees the Son and believes in him should have eternal life; and I will raise him up at the last day."

They still think He is talking about manna or a loaf of normal bread, and they ask for it. He corrects them a second time. They are to look for Him. He is the bread of life. They look straight at the bread of life and fail to see it (Him) because they look with the eyes of man instead of with the eyes of faith. He commands them again to have faith, and see as God does, see as Samuel did, see the truth.

Jn 6:41-42 The Jews then murmured at him, because he said, "I am the bread which came down from heaven." ^{42} They said, "Is not this Jesus, the son of Joseph, whose father and mother we know? How does he now say, 'I have come down from heaven'?"

The crowd is confused by His correction. So far, He has commanded them to come to Him, and they are His disciples. Have they not already done this? He must be speaking in a metaphorical sense. He clearly did not descend from heaven. They know His father. Yet how can one metaphorically "come down from heaven"? They are asking the wrong question. Christ will re-focus their attention on the REAL mystery.

Jn 6:43-51 Jesus answered them, "Do not murmur among yourselves. ^{44} No one can come to me unless the Father who sent me draws him; and I will raise him up at the last day. ^{45} It is written in the prophets, 'And they shall all be taught by God.' Every one who has heard and learned from the Father comes to me. ^{46} Not that any one has seen the Father except him who is from God; he has seen the Father. ^{47} Truly, truly, I say to you, he who believes has eternal life. ^{48} I am the bread of life. ^{49} Your fathers ate the manna in the wilderness, and they died. ^{50} This is the bread which comes down from heaven, that a man may eat of it and not die. ^{51} I am the living bread which came down from heaven; if any one eats of this bread, he will live for ever; and the bread which I shall give for the life of the world is my flesh."

Christ insists that they stop murmuring - the reason the Israelites got only manna after they were freed from slavery in Egypt and walked through the Red Sea parted by Moses was due to their murmuring. Christ has fed the free man and walked on water. The Old Testament is being played out again. But the bread that comes this time will be different - it will be His own flesh. Seeing may be believing, but believing is not enough. They must eat this bread. This is the first of six repeated commands to do so.

Jn 6:52 The Jews then disputed among themselves, saying, "How can this man give us his flesh to eat?"

His Jewish disciples suddenly realize that He is not speaking metaphorically. They still don't see the supernatural reality, but even their limited understanding of what He is saying has just been radically altered. He does not correct them when they ask how He can give them His flesh to eat. Now that they understand His real point, He goes on to say something far more shocking:

Jn 6:53 So Jesus said to them, "Truly, truly, I say to you, unless you eat the flesh of the Son of man and drink his blood, you have no life in you...

His Jewish disciples know their Scripture:

Is 49:26 I will make your oppressors eat their own flesh, and they shall be drunk with their own blood as with wine. Then all flesh shall know that I am the LORD your Savior, and your Redeemer, the Mighty One of Jacob."

2 Sam 23:17 and said, "Far be it from me, O LORD, that I should do this. Shall I drink the blood of the men who went at the risk of their lives?"

Job 39:30 His young ones suck up blood; and where the slain are, there is he."

Ezek 39:17-20 "As for you, son of man, thus says the Lord GOD: Speak to the birds of every sort and to all beasts of the field, 'Assemble and come, gather from all sides to the sacrificial feast which I am preparing for you, a great sacrificial feast upon the mountains of Israel, and you shall eat flesh and drink blood. [18] You shall eat the flesh of the mighty, and drink the blood of the princes of the earth - of rams, of lambs, and of goats, of bulls, all of them fatlings of Bashan. [19] And you shall eat fat till you are filled, and drink blood till you are drunk, at the sacrificial feast which I am preparing for you. [20] And you shall be filled at my table with horses and riders, with mighty men and all kinds of warriors,' says the Lord GOD.

Num 23:24 "Behold, a people! As a lioness it rises up and as a lion it lifts itself;
it does not lie down till it devours the prey, and drinks the blood of the slain."

Deut 32:42 'I will make my arrows drunk with blood, and my sword shall devour flesh—
with the blood of the slain and the captives, from the long-haired heads of the enemy.'

Jer 46:10 That day is the day of the Lord GOD of hosts,
a day of vengeance,
to avenge himself on his foes.
The sword shall devour and be sated,
and drink its fill of their blood.
For the Lord GOD of hosts holds a sacrifice
in the north country by the river Euphrates.

1 Chron 11:19 "Far be it from me before my God that I should do this. Shall I drink the lifeblood of these men? For at the risk of their lives they brought it."

Interestingly, the 1 Chronicles and 2 Sam excerpts quote King David as he refuses to drink water captured for him from the cistern at Bethlehem, by a trinity of troops who obtained it at the risk of their lives.

The Semite idiom "eat the flesh and drink the blood" means to do someone serious injury, especially by slander; it is an idiom used by the writers of the New Testament...

Rev 16:6 "For men have shed the blood of saints and prophets, and thou hast given them blood to drink. It is their due!"

...and still used by Arabs today. If Jesus were speaking metaphorically, He would be exhorting His disciples to slander Him, to cheat Him, to kill Him in order to gain eternal life. The disciples realize that He cannot be speaking metaphorically. He is literally serious - they must really eat His flesh and drink His blood at some future time. They no longer dispute His claim that He came down from heaven. He has successfully refocused their attention. It seems Jesus is demanding cannibalism, for the word He uses for "eat" (phago) is very blunt. It is used in reference to the eating of meat. The noun (phagos) derived from this verb means "glutton." But Christ, ever the teacher, wants to make sure they have gotten the point:

Jn 6:54-59 ...he who eats (phago) my flesh and drinks my blood has eternal life, and I will raise him up at the last day. [55] For my flesh is food indeed, and my blood is drink indeed. [56] He who eats (trogos) my flesh and drinks my blood abides in me, and I in him. [57] As the living Father sent me, and I live because of the Father, so he who eats (trogos) me will live because of me. [58] This is the bread which came down from heaven, not such as the fathers ate (phago) and died; he who eats (phago) this bread will live for ever." [59] This he said in the synagogue, as he taught at Caperna-um.

After the mention of drinking His Blood, He starts using a different verb. While "phago" means "to eat meat," "trogos" means "to gnaw or crunch." Once the disciples get the idea, however preposterous, that they need to eat His flesh, He follows up by emphasizing and re-emphasizing how serious He is about their doing exactly that. They will not eat as their ancestors did, they will gnaw and crunch on His flesh, the true bread. Remember, this is being said in synagogue to Jews who know the Aaronic sacrifices, and it is being said on the eve of Passover, as the lambs are being gathered for slaughter in Jerusalem.

Furthermore, He doesn't stop with just the eating of His flesh. They must drink His blood. This means He considers Himself the source of life, the well-spring of life, and He is asserting that they can internalize the well-spring of life. Instead of being externally righteous, as were the Hebrews led out of Egypt, they will be internally pure, cleansed, holy. But to be that, they must drink His blood. It is this passage which explains why Paul says the Mosaic works of the law are no longer of any use. Christ perfects those laws in a radical way.

Christ has stated twelve times that He is the bread of life, the food that endures. He has stated six times that His flesh and blood are to be eaten. No other teaching in Scripture gets the emphasis this teaching gets.

Jn 6:60-63 Many of his disciples, when they heard it, said, "This is a hard saying; who can listen to it?" [61] But Jesus, knowing in himself that his disciples murmured at it, said to them, "Do you take offense at this? [62] Then what if you were to see the Son of man ascending where he was before? [63] It is the spirit that gives life, the flesh is of no avail; the words that I have spoken to you are spirit and life.

Note that He does NOT mean to indicate that His flesh is of no avail. He says "the flesh." Paul explains what that phrase means:

1 Cor 2:14-3:3 The unspiritual man does not receive the gifts of the Spirit of God, for they are folly to him, and he is not able to understand them because they are spiritually discerned. [15] The spiritual man judges all things, but is himself to be judged by no one. [16] "For who has known the mind of the Lord so as to instruct him?" But we have the mind of Christ.... [1] But I, brethren, could not address you as spiritual men, but as men of the flesh, as babes in Christ. [2] I fed you with milk, not solid food; for you were not ready for it; and even yet you are not ready, [3] for you are still of the flesh. For while there is jealousy and strife among you, are you not of the flesh, and behaving like ordinary men?

Christ means that acting in an ordinary way is of no avail; we have to see the supernatural reality which He has given us, and which He will give them through the power of the Cross - His own flesh and blood made present in His glorified Body for our food.

Jn 6:64-66 But there are some of you that do not believe." For Jesus knew from the first who those were that did not believe, and who it was that would betray him. [65] And he said, "This is why I told you that no one can come to me unless it is granted him by the Father." [66] After this many of his disciples drew back and no longer went about with him.

This is the only instance in Scripture in which disciples leave Jesus. These people have been His disciples, they have seen Him perform incredible miracles, they have stood with Him despite the attacks of the Pharisees, Sadducees, the scribes and the Sanhedrin, but this teaching is too much. They cannot make the leap of faith.

Jn 6:67-71 Jesus said to the twelve, "Do you also wish to go away?" [68] Simon Peter answered him, "Lord, to whom shall we go? You have the words of eternal life; [69] and we have believed, and have come to know, that you are the Holy One of God." [70] Jesus answered them, "Did I not choose you, the twelve, and one of you is a devil?" [71] He spoke of Judas the son of Simon Iscariot, for he, one of the twelve, was to betray him.

Even Peter, speaking for the Twelve, can barely restrain his incredulity. His words imply that they WOULD go somewhere else, but there is nowhere to go. Incidentally, the phrase "the words I have spoken are spirit" do not mean "the words I have spoken are symbolic." "Spirit" is never used that way anywhere in Scripture, for example..

1 Pet 3:18 For Christ also died for sins once for all, the righteous for the unrighteous, that he might bring us to God, being put to death in the flesh but made alive in the spirit...

Remember Thomas? Thomas could put his hands into Christ's side, and watch him eat a piece of fish. In Scripture, the spiritual has a fuller reality than the merely physical. Christ did not mean something symbolic. Through His use of verbs, evocation, subject, emphasis, and timing, He brought out a teaching so scandalous that His own disciples could not accept it. The scandal of the Cross is fully revealed in the Eucharist. The spiritual does not destroy the physical, nor is it something separate from the physical, rather, the spiritual perfects the physical, grace perfects nature.

Mk 4:35-41 On that day, when evening had come, he said to them, "Let us go across to the other side." [36] And leaving the crowd, they took him with them in the boat, just as he was. And other boats were with him. [37] And a great storm of wind arose, and the waves beat into the boat, so that the boat was already filling. [38] But he was in the stern, asleep on the cushion; and they woke him and said to him, "Teacher, do you not care if we perish?" [39] And he awoke and rebuked the wind, and said to the sea, "Peace! Be still!" And the wind ceased, and there was a great calm. [40] He said to them, "Why are you afraid? Have you no faith?" [41] And they were filled with awe, and said to one another, "Who then is this, that even wind and sea obey him?"

Mt 21:18-19 In the morning, as he was returning to the city, he was hungry. ¹⁹ And seeing a fig tree by the wayside he went to it, and found nothing on it but leaves only. And he said to it, "May no fruit ever come from you again!" And the fig tree withered at once.

Jesus has total control over the created world - it does what He commands it to do. When He commands the bread to be His Body, the reality occurs. He commands His Apostles to do as He has done and gives them the power to do it.

Mt 26:26-30 Now as they were eating, Jesus took bread, and blessed, and broke it, and gave it to the disciples and said, "Take, eat; this is my body." ²⁷ And he took a cup, and when he had given thanks he gave it to them, saying, "Drink of it, all of you; ²⁸ for this is my blood of the covenant, which is poured out for many for the forgiveness of sins. ²⁹ I tell you I shall not drink again of this fruit of the vine until that day when I drink it new with you in my Father's kingdom."
³⁰ And when they had sung a hymn, they went out to the Mount of Olives.

Mk 14:22-26 And as they were eating, he took bread, and blessed, and broke it, and gave it to them, and said, "Take; this is my body." ²³ And he took a cup, and when he had given thanks he gave it to them, and they all drank of it. ²⁴ And he said to them, "This is my blood of the covenant, which is poured out for many. ²⁵ Truly, I say to you, I shall not drink again of the fruit of the vine until that day when I drink it new in the kingdom of God."
²⁶ And when they had sung a hymn, they went out to the Mount of Olives.

Lk 22:14-20 And when the hour came, he sat at table, and the apostles with him. ¹⁵ And he said to them, "I have earnestly desired to eat this passover with you before I suffer; ¹⁶ for I tell you I shall not eat it until it is fulfilled in the kingdom of God." ¹⁷ And he took a cup, and when he had given thanks he said, "Take this, and divide it among yourselves; ¹⁸ for I tell you that from now on I shall not drink of the fruit of the vine until the kingdom of God comes." ¹⁹ And he took bread, and when he had given thanks he broke it and gave it to them, saying, "This is my body which is given for you. Do this in remembrance of me." ²⁰ And likewise the cup after supper, saying, "This cup which is poured out for you is the new covenant in my blood.

The commentary involving the Passover meal and the implications of the fourth cup summarizes Dr. Scott Hahn's tape presentation "The Fourth Cup."

The Passover meal is shared "in remembrance." The word used for "remembrance" is "anamnesis," which means "to make present." For a first-century Jew, the Passover, through faith, unites every present participant to the participants in the original Passover; they become one Chosen People through this sacrifice. Christ commands remembrance in a Passover context, as God commanded it of all Jews at the first Passover. Note that the Last Supper is the only time Christ uses the word "covenant" in all four Gospels.

The Seder (Passover) meal consists of four parts, each part is completed by the mixing and drinking of a cup of wine. The Khaddish, a Judaic prayer of festival blessing, is spoken over the first cup. The bitter herbs are then served. This was probably the dish in which Jesus and Judas dipped bread together.

The second course is served, and then Psalm 113, which is called the Little Hallel (little song of praise), is sung. The second cup is mixed and shared.

The third course is served, and the Passover lamb and unleavened bread is eaten, after which the third cup is drunk. This third cup is called the cup of blessing.

1 Cor 10:16 The cup of blessing which we bless, is it not a participation in the blood of Christ? The bread which we break, is it not a participation in the body of Christ?

After this, the meal reaches its climax with the singing of Psalms 114-118, which is called the Great Hallel (great praise). Then the fourth cup is mixed and drunk to complete the ritual. It is called the "cup of consummation." It is clear that the cup which is shared among the apostles is the cup of blessing, both from the description, "while they were eating," and Paul's own testimony which will be discussed shortly.

Christ starts the Passover meal, but He doesn't complete it. He offers the unleavened bread ("This is my body") and the third cup ("This is my blood") while they were still eating the Passover lamb. He proclaims the bread to be His body, and the cup to be His blood, and these are consumed "while they were eating." He states that He will not taste of the fruit of the vine again until the coming His Father's Kingdom. The Great Hallel is sung, but Christ and the apostles leave the upper room without drinking the fourth cup. The Passover is not complete - the cup of consummation has not been consumed.

Lk 22:42 "Father, if thou art willing, remove this cup from me; nevertheless not my will, but thine, be done."

Mt 26:39 And going a little farther he fell on his face and prayed, "My Father, if it be possible, let this cup pass from me; nevertheless, not as I will, but as thou wilt."

Mk 14:36 And he said, "Abba, Father, all things are possible to thee; remove this cup from me; yet not what I will, but what thou wilt."

Jesus has not drunk the fourth cup of the Passover, but He has a cup to drink which the Apostles do not yet know.

Jn 19:13-14 When Pilate heard these words, he brought Jesus out and sat down on the judgment seat at a place called The Pavement, and in Hebrew, Gabbatha. [14] Now it was the day of Preparation of the Passover; it was about the sixth hour.

The sixth hour is important because it was at that hour the Passover lambs were slaughtered for the evening sacrifice. How can this be? Didn't Christ already celebrate the Passover? He did - according to the Pharisaic calendar. But the Sadducees followed a slightly different calendar. The Pharisees celebrated Passover on Tuesday, while the Sadducees celebrated Passover on Friday. God's plan allowed Christ to both offer His own flesh and blood under the forms of bread and wine with His Apostles at the Last Supper, and still truly be offered up as the Paschal Lamb on Passover at His Crucifixion. He is both high priest and victim. Standing before the crowd on the cold stone pavement, He had not yet completed the Passover sacrifice He had begun with His Apostles.

Lk 23:36 The soldiers also mocked him, coming up and offering him vinegar,

Mk 15:22 And they brought him to the place called Golgotha (which means the place of a skull). [23] And they offered him wine mingled with myrrh; but he did not take it.

Mt 27:33 And when they came to a place called Golgotha (which means the place of a skull), [34] they offered him wine to drink, mingled with gall; but when he tasted it, he would not drink it.

They offer Him wine at the beginning of the crucifixion. He refuses to drink.

Mk 15:36-37 And one ran and, filling a sponge full of vinegar, put it on a reed and gave it to him to drink, saying, "Wait, let us see whether Elijah will come to take him down." [37] And Jesus uttered a loud cry, and breathed his last.

Mt 27:48-50 And one of them at once ran and took a sponge, filled it with vinegar, and put it on a reed, and gave it to him to drink. [49] But the others said, "Wait, let us see whether Elijah will come to save him." [50] And Jesus cried again with a loud voice and yielded up his spirit.

Jn 19:29-30 A bowl full of vinegar stood there; so they put a sponge full of the vinegar on hyssop and held it to his mouth. [30] When Jesus had received the vinegar, he said, "It is finished"; and he bowed his head and gave up his spirit.

Seconds before His death, Jesus drinks the wine and says "It is consummated" or "It is finished." Was He speaking of the work of redemption?

Rom 4:25 who was put to death for our trespasses and raised for our justification.

Unlikely. The work of justification would not be completed until the Resurrection. So, what was finished? The Passover. The fourth cup had been drunk on the cross. Christ was High Priest of the Sacrifice even as He hung on the Cross, His skin flayed off His back as one might skin a lamb, His flesh roasted in the sun as He carried the Cross. The fruit of the tree of life, the Paschal Lamb, is prepared. What must be done with the Lamb?

The Eucharist in the Early Church

Lk 24:13-35 That very day two of them were going to a village named Emmaus, about seven miles from Jerusalem, [14] and talking with each other about all these things that had happened. [15] While they were talking and discussing together, Jesus himself drew near and went with them. ¹⁶ But their eyes were kept from recognizing him. ¹⁷ And he said to them, "What is this conversation which you are holding with each other as you walk?" And they stood still, looking sad. ¹⁸ Then one of them, named Cleopas, answered him, "Are you the only visitor to Jerusalem who does not know the things that have happened there in these days?" ¹⁹ And he said to them, "What things?" And they said to him, "Concerning Jesus of Nazareth, who was a prophet mighty in deed and word before God and all the people, ²⁰ and how our chief priests and rulers delivered him up to be condemned to death, and crucified him. ²¹ But we had hoped that he was the one to redeem Israel. Yes, and besides all this, it is now the third day since this happened. ²² Moreover, some women of our company amazed us. They were at the tomb early in the morning ²³ and did not find his body; and they came back saying that they had even seen a vision of angels, who said that he was alive. ²⁴ Some of those who were with us went to the tomb, and found it just as the women had said; but him they did not see." ²⁵ And he said to them, "O foolish men, and slow of heart to believe all that the prophets have spoken! ²⁶ Was it not necessary that the Christ should suffer these things and enter into his glory?" ²⁷ And beginning with Moses and all the prophets, he interpreted to them in all the scriptures the things concerning himself.

²⁸ So they drew near to the village to which they were going. He appeared to be going further, ²⁹ but they constrained him, saying, "Stay with us, for it is toward evening and the day is now far spent." So he went in to stay with them. ³⁰ When he was at table with them, he took the bread and blessed, and broke it, and gave it to them. ³¹ And their eyes were opened and they recognized him; and he vanished out of their sight. ³² They said to each other, "Did not our hearts burn within us while he talked to us on the road, while he opened to us the scriptures?" ³³ And they rose that same hour and returned to Jerusalem; and they found the eleven gathered together and those who were with them, ³⁴ who said, "The Lord has risen indeed, and has appeared to Simon!" ³⁵ Then they told what had happened on the road, and how he was known to them in the breaking of the bread..

Note that the two disciples had all of Scripture explained to them by the best teacher the world has ever seen, yet they still failed to recognize Jesus. It was only in the breaking of the bread that Christ was recognized. Their eyes were opened, not by Scripture alone, but by word and act. What of the others?

Mk 16:9-13 Now when he rose early on the first day of the week, he appeared first to Mary Magdalene, from whom he had cast out seven demons. ¹⁰ She went and told those who had been with him, as they mourned and wept. ¹¹ But when they heard that he was alive and had been seen by her, they would not believe it. After this he appeared in another form to two of them, as they were walking into the country. ¹³ And they went back and told the rest, but they did not believe them.

Mark summarizes the Emmaus story much more succinctly than Luke. The witnesses witness, but even the Apostles themselves do not believe. Witness and word alone were not enough to kindle faith. Christ had to act so that they would understand the truth.

Jn 20:19-28 On the evening of that day, the first day of the week, the doors being shut where the disciples were, for fear of the Jews, Jesus came and stood among them and said to them, "Peace be with you." ²⁰ When he had said this, he showed them his hands and his side. Then the disciples were glad when they saw the Lord. ²¹ Jesus said to them again, "Peace be with you. As the Father has sent me, even so I send you." ²² And when he had said this, he breathed on them, and said to them, "Receive the Holy Spirit. ²³ If you forgive the sins of any, they are forgiven; if you retain the sins of any, they are retained."

²⁴ Now Thomas, one of the twelve, called the Twin, was not with them when Jesus came. ²⁵ So the other disciples told him, "We have seen the Lord." But he said to them, "Unless I see in his hands the print of the nails, and place my finger in the mark of the nails, and place my hand in his side, I will not believe."

²⁶ Eight days later, his disciples were again in the house, and Thomas was with them. The doors were shut, but Jesus came and stood among them, and said, "Peace be with you." ²⁷ Then he said to Thomas, "Put your finger here, and see my hands; and put out your hand, and place it in my side; do not be faithless, but believing." ²⁸ Thomas answered him, "My Lord and my God!" ²⁹ Jesus said to him, "Have you believed because you have seen me? Blessed are those who have not seen and yet believe."

Lk 24:37-43 But they were startled and frightened, and supposed that they saw a spirit. ³⁸ And he said to them, "Why are you troubled, and why do questionings rise in your hearts? ³⁹ See my hands and my feet, that it is I myself; handle me, and see; for a spirit has not flesh and bones as you see that I have." ⁴⁰ And when he had said this, he showed them his hands and his feet. ⁴¹ And while they still disbelieved for joy, and wondered, he said to them, "Have you anything here to eat?" [42] They gave him a piece of broiled fish, [43] and he took it and ate before them.

Christ was not just a spiritual presence - a ghost. He was physical being glorified in the spirit. Thus, He displaced the air in the locked room as readily as He displaces the substance of bread with His own Body while maintaining the appearance of bread. The King born in the House of Bread and laid in an eating trough is real and present. His Real Presence is what the Resurrection is all about.

Mt 28:20 and lo, I am with you always, to the close of the age."

How did the Apostles understand it?

Acts 2:42-47 And they devoted themselves to the apostles' teaching and fellowship, to the breaking of bread and the prayers. [43] And fear came upon every soul; and many wonders and signs were done through the apostles. [44] And all who believed were together and had all things in common; [45] and they sold their possessions and goods and distributed them to all, as any had need. [46] And day by day, attending the temple together and breaking bread in their homes, they partook of food with glad and generous hearts, [47] praising God and having favor with all the people. And the Lord added to their number day by day those who were being saved.

Acts 27:34-35 Therefore I urge you to take some food; it will give you strength, since not a hair is to perish from the head of any of you." [35] And when he had said this, he took bread, and giving thanks to God in the presence of all he broke it and began to eat.

Acts 2:24,31 But God raised him up, having loosed the pangs of death, because it was not possible for him to be held by it.... he was not abandoned to Hades, nor did his flesh see corruption.

Over half of Peter's first speech to unbelievers taught exactly one thing: the death and resurrection of Jesus Christ. In fact, in Acts, Peter will make five speeches with this theme, and Paul will make a sixth (see Acts 3:12-26, 4:8-12, 5:29-32, 10:34-43, and 13:16-41). This list doesn't count passing references to such speeches as:

Acts 17:32 Now when they heard of the resurrection of the dead, some mocked; but others said, "We will hear you again about this."

Acts 23:6 But when Paul perceived that one part were Sadducees and the other Pharisees, he cried out in the council, "Brethren, I am a Pharisee, a son of Pharisees; with respect to the hope and the resurrection of the dead I am on trial."

The Greeks at the Areopagus willingly listened to everything but the Resurrection. At Paul's trial, his mention of the Resurrection nearly caused a riot. The disciples at Capernaum didn't believe, the disciples on the road to Emmaus didn't believe, the Apostles themselves didn't believe. At two millenia distance, it is difficult to appreciate exactly how outrageous the Resurrection was and is. The Resurrection was the single largest stumbling block in the spreading of the faith. The Docetist heresy, already raging by 100 A.D., claimed Christ had not really died. It was put down only because eyewitnesses of the crucifixion still lived and categorically condemned Docetist teaching as a lie. Christ died. He rose. Witnesses knew.

The daily Eucharistic meal was and is a central proof for those who see with eyes even greater than Samuel's as he searched Bethlehem for a king, who see with the eyes of faith. It is the central scandal of Christianity.

1 Cor 10:14-22 Therefore, my beloved, shun the worship of idols. [15] I speak as to sensible men; judge for yourselves what I say. [16] The cup of blessing which we bless, is it not a participation in the blood of Christ? The bread which we break, is it not a participation in the body of Christ? [17] Because there is one bread, we who are many are one body, for we all partake of the one bread. [18] Consider the people of Israel; are not those who eat the sacrifices partners in the altar? [19] What do I imply then? That food offered to idols is anything, or that an idol is anything? [20] No, I imply that what pagans sacrifice they offer to demons and not to God. I do not want you to be partners with demons. [21] You cannot drink the cup of the Lord and the cup of demons. You cannot partake of the table of the Lord and the table of demons. [22] Shall we provoke the Lord to jealousy? Are we stronger than he?

Paul uses precisely the same word for "bread" that Christ used in John 6. He asks us to consider "Israel according to the flesh" - as the disciples at Capernaum had considered Christ's words according to the flesh. He acknowledges that meat sacrificed to idols is *nothing - it has no supernatural reality. Implicitly, he contrasts it with the Eucharistic meal, where the sacrifice *IS* something, and God *IS* someone.*

1 Cor 11:23-34 For I received from the Lord what I also delivered to you, that the Lord Jesus on the night when he was betrayed took bread, [24] and when he had given thanks, he broke it, and said, "This is my body which is for you. Do this in remembrance of me." [25] In the same way also the cup, after supper, saying, "This cup is the new covenant in my blood. Do this, as often as you drink it, in remembrance of me." [26] For as often as you eat this bread and drink the cup, you proclaim the Lord's death until he comes.
[27] Whoever, therefore, eats the bread or drinks the cup of the Lord in an unworthy manner will be guilty of profaning the body and blood of the Lord. [28] Let a man examine himself, and so eat of the bread and drink of the cup. [29] For any one who eats and drinks without discerning the body eats and drinks judgment upon himself. [30] That is why many of you are weak and ill, and some have died. [31] But if we judged ourselves truly, we should not be judged. [32] But when we are judged by the Lord, we are chastened so that we may not be condemned along with the world.
[33] So then, my brethren, when you come together to eat, wait for one another— [34] if any one is hungry, let him eat at home—lest you come together to be condemned. About the other things I will give directions when I come.

Paul does not refer to either "wine" or to "blood," but to "the cup of the Lord." Can one be required to answer for the body and blood of the Lord if he eats merely natural bread, and drinks from a cup containing merely wine?

Jn 13:26,30 So when he had dipped the morsel, he gave it to Judas, the son of Simon Iscariot... So, after receiving the morsel, he immediately went out; and it was night.

Judas ate of the morsel and immediately entered the darkness. Recall that it was Judas who did not believe Jesus' teaching in John 6. The phrase "answer for the Body and Blood" is a phrase which was used against those accused of murder. Where is Christ's Body or Blood, that one must answer for it? This matter was so important that Paul wrote immediately - he dare not wait until he had free time to come and correct the error in person.

Even though he speaks in words extraordinarily reminiscent of Leviticus 7:20, he doesn't say the person eating unworthily has to answer for the bread and wine offered to the Lord. Rather, such a person answers for the Body and Blood of Jesus Christ. Yet we know from Leviticus that cereal sacrifices were common. How is it that Paul does not call this a cereal sacrifice, but an offense against Christ's Body and Blood? He is both the most orthodox of Jews and a devout follower of Christ. He would not profane Christ's name by confusing a cereal offering with Christ's Resurrected Body and Blood.

Heb 9:13-14 For if the sprinkling of defiled persons with the blood of goats and bulls and with the ashes of a heifer sanctifies for the purification of the flesh, [14] how much more shall the blood of Christ, who through the eternal Spirit offered himself without blemish to God, purify your conscience from dead works to serve the living God.

The Levitical thanksgiving sacrifice (called "eucharasis" in Greek) could not "touch any unclean thing," for if it did, it could not be consumed. We know that Christ called Himself "the food that stays" - His body does not perish as does ordinary substances of this world. The real substance of Christ's Body and Blood in the Eucharist completely replaces that of the bread and wine, there can be no mingling of the two substances. Neither could His Presence depart after the consecration, for then it would not be "the food that endures."

Acts 10:40-41 but God raised him on the third day and made him manifest; [41] not to all the people but to us who were chosen by God as witnesses, who ate and drank with him after he rose from the dead.

Christ appears only to those who ate and drank with Him.

Mt 8:10-11 When Jesus heard him, he marveled, and said to those who followed him, "Truly, I say to you, not even in Israel have I found such faith. [11] I tell you, many will come from east and west and sit at table with Abraham, Isaac, and Jacob in the kingdom of heaven,...

Rev 3:20 Behold, I stand at the door and knock; if any one hears my voice and opens the door, I will come in to him and eat with him, and he with me...

Rev 5:6,9-10 And between the throne and the four living creatures and among the elders, I saw a Lamb standing, as though it had been slain, with seven horns and with seven eyes, which are the seven spirits of God sent out into all the earth;... and they sang a new song, saying,
"Worthy art thou to take the scroll and to open its seals,
for thou wast slain and by thy blood didst ransom men for God
from every tribe and tongue and people and nation, [10] and hast made them a kingdom and priests to our God, and they shall reign on earth."

Rev 7:17 For the Lamb in the midst of the throne will be their shepherd, and he will guide them to springs of living water;
and God will wipe away every tear from their eyes."

Rev 19:9 And the angel said to me, "Write this: Blessed are those who are invited to the marriage supper of the Lamb." And he said to me, "These are true words of God."

Rev 21:22 And I saw no temple in the city, for its temple is the Lord God the Almighty and the Lamb.

Rev 21:2 And I saw the holy city, new Jerusalem, coming down out of heaven from God, prepared as a bride adorned for her husband...

The wedding feast is the consummation of the marriage between the Bride and the Bridegroom, in which the Bride receives the Bridegroom into Herself, as a Bride does on her wedding night, being made fruitful thereby. Because He gives her His Body and Blood, He is one Body with Her.

Lk 14:15 When one of those who sat at table with him heard this, he said to him, "Blessed is he who shall eat bread in the kingdom of God!"

We are called to be perfect images of Christ. Christ established for us a perfect image of His Sacrifice, an image so perfect that He Himself is fully and actually present at the sacrifice we, the Church, offer. Through this sacrifice, the sacrifice of the <u>Mass,</u> His One Sacrifice becomes present to His Body which is the <u>Church.</u> The reality of Christ's Resurrected Body in the Eucharist brings together several strands of Old and New Testament prophecy - the tree of life, the gifts of Melchisedek, the Passover, the gift of manna, the Aaronic sacrifices, the search for the king, the place of Christ's birth, the wedding feast of the Lamb. The Eucharist is the source and goal of our faith. The whole of Scripture points to it, prepares for it, teaches us how to live so that we may receive it. Through it, we are truly made part of the Body of Christ, and truly become sons of the living God.

Early Christians' comments on the Real Presence

The mystery of the Eucharist is the central mystery of the Church. Do not expect to understand it after one reading or one explanation. The best analogy I can give is as follows. You have seen a silk rose. If you touch such a rose, are you touching a rose? No, you are touching silk. Assume that the silk has been genetically engineered to give off a pleasing rose-like odor. Is it a rose? No, it is still silk. No matter how you engineer the silk, the rose which results is only a rose to the senses. It is really silk to the touch. At the consecration and forever after, until it is consumed and loses the appearance of bread and/or wine, the host and/or the cup is no longer bread and/or wine. It is Jesus Christ. Your senses may smell, see, taste, touch bread, but you really smell, see, taste, touch the flesh of Jesus Christ.

Reconciliation:
Reunion with the Church

The Sacrament of Reconciliation renews our wedding vow to the Bridegroom after we have fallen away in sin. God shepherds us toward this sacrament with His grace, and through this sacrament, He forgives us and takes us back as His own true Bride. As the Body of Christ, the Church has the power to re-unite to herself those who have fallen away from Christ through sin. This authority is granted by Jesus Christ through His Suffering, Death, and Resurrection, to the Apostles and to their consecrated successors. The sacrament of reconciliation "is a drawing near to the holiness of God, a rediscovery of one's true identity... a regaining of lost joy, the joy of being saved" (Reconciliation and Penance, Reconciliato et Paenitentia, #31 III). Since every sin affects all of society (1 Cor 12), the ecclesial community of the Church formally welcome the penitent back into the Body of Christ, putting on the penitent the robe and rings of grace. Within this sacrament, Christ Himself both forgives the sinner and again permits him to share in the sufferings of the Cross. (CCC 1420-1470, 1485-1498)

Current misunderstandings: Most Christians insist no one need go to a priest to confess sins, rather one should only approach Jesus Christ in his heart, for only Christ can forgive sins. Oddly enough, while they deny that human mediation is necessary for the cleansing of sin, all denominations require a human mediator for baptism; i.e., no Christian denomination allows a believer to baptize himself. This is true even for those denominations which assert baptism does not cleanse from sin, but is only a seal.

Acts 8:13,18-24 Even Simon himself believed, and after being baptized he continued with Philip. And seeing signs and great miracles performed, he was amazed.... Now when Simon saw that the Spirit was given through the laying on of the apostles' hands, he offered them money, [19] saying, "Give me also this power, that any one on whom I lay my hands may receive the Holy Spirit." [20] But Peter said to him, "Your silver perish with you, because you thought you could obtain the gift of God with money! [21] You have neither part nor lot in this matter, for your heart is not right before God. [22] Repent therefore of this wickedness of yours, and pray to the Lord that, if possible, the intent of your heart may be forgiven you. [23] For I see that you are in the gall of bitterness and in the bond of iniquity." [24] And Simon answered, "Pray for me to the Lord, that nothing of what you have said may come upon me."

Simon asks the Apostles to mediate his forgiveness. The Apostles hold a priestly office.

Num 5:6-7 "Say to the people of Israel, When a man or woman commits any of the sins that men commit by breaking faith with the LORD, and that person is guilty, [7] he shall confess his sin which he has committed; and he shall make full restitution for his wrong, adding a fifth to it, and giving it to him to whom he did the wrong.

The sacrament of Confession was prefigured in the Old Testament...

Lev 26:39-40 And those of you that are left shall pine away in your enemies' lands because of their iniquity; and also because of the iniquities of their fathers they shall pine away like them.
[40] "But if they confess their iniquity and the iniquity of their fathers in their treachery which they committed against me, and also in walking contrary to me...

2 Sam 12:13 David said to Nathan, "I have sinned against the LORD." And Nathan said to David, "The LORD also has put away your sin; you shall not die.

Psalm 32:5 I acknowledged my sin to thee, and I did not hide my iniquity;
   I said, "I will confess my transgressions to the LORD";
then thou didst forgive the guilt of my sin.

Prov 28:13 He who conceals his transgressions will not prosper,
but he who confesses and forsakes them will obtain mercy.

...and in the baptism of John in preparation for the coming of the Messiah.

Mt 3:5-6 Then went out to him Jerusalem and all Judea and all the region about the Jordan, [6] and they were baptized by him in the river Jordan, confessing their sins.

Mk 1:5 And there went out to him all the country of Judea, and all the people of Jerusalem; and they were baptized by him in the river Jordan, confessing their sins

The section from Isaiah to 2 Cor 2:10 below is a very quick summary of Tim Staple's "I Confess," Envoy, Nov. 97-Feb. 98, pp. 42-44.

Is 43:25 "I, I am He who blots out your transgressions for my own sake, and I will not remember your sins."

Only God forgives sins...

Lev 19:20-22 "If a man lies carnally with a woman who is a slave, betrothed to another man and not yet ransomed or given her freedom, an inquiry shall be held. They shall not be put to death, because she was not free; 21 but he shall bring a guilt offering for himself to the LORD, to the door of the tent of meeting, a ram for a guilt offering. 22 And the priest shall make atonement for him with the ram of the guilt offering before the LORD for his sin which he has committed; and the sin which he has committed shall be forgiven him.

but the priest intercedes and mediates for sinners.

Heb 3:1 Therefore, holy brethren, who share in a heavenly call, consider Jesus, the apostle and high priest of our confession

Christ is the only High Priest...

1 Pet 2:9 But you are a chosen race, a royal priesthood, a holy nation, God's own people, that you may declare the wonderful deeds of him who called you out of darkness into his marvelous light.

But everyone is a member of the holy priesthood of believers, through their portion in Christ's body. In this passage Peter refers to the Old Testament, Exodus 19:6, and Isaiah 61:6. Israel, a nation of holy priests, had the Aaronic and Levitical priesthoods as mediators. Thus, Peter expressly links the Israelite manner of priesthood with the New Covenant's manner of priesthood. Christ, who alone can forgive sins, explicitly gives the power to forgive sins to the Apostles, making them the new mediating priesthood for the Body of new believers God would build up as His own.

Jn 13:5-15 Then he poured water into a basin, and began to wash the disciples' feet, and to wipe them with the towel with which he was girded. 6 He came to Simon Peter; and Peter said to him, "Lord, do you wash my feet?" 7 Jesus answered him, "What I am doing you do not know now, but afterward you will understand." 8 Peter said to him, "You shall never wash my feet." Jesus answered him, "If I do not wash you, you have no part in me." 9 Simon Peter said to him, "Lord, not my feet only but also my hands and my head!" 10 Jesus said to him, "He who has bathed does not need to wash, except for his feet, but he is clean all over; and you are clean, but not every one of you." 11 For he knew who was to betray him; that was why he said, "You are not all clean."

12 When he had washed their feet, and taken his garments, and resumed his place, he said to them, "Do you know what I have done to you? 13 You call me Teacher and Lord; and you are right, for so I am. 14 If I then, your Lord and Teacher, have washed your feet, you also ought to wash one another's feet. 15 For I have given you an example, that you also should do as I have done to you.

<u>Baptism</u> washes one clean of sins, but Christ washes the Apostles' feet. He expressly says that the Apostles will not understand what He is doing until "afterward" - a reference to His death. Christ is not just demonstrating humility, for Christ has already said that the Apostles won't fully understand His action now, yet Peter understands that Jesus is humbling Himself before him. Christ gives them a hint by stating that whoever has bathed has no need of washing again, except for his feet. The feet are the only part of the body which is in habitual contact with the ground, with the world. The Hebrew euphemism for relieving oneself is "to cover one's feet" (cf. 1 Sam 24:3, where Saul enters the cave to "ease nature."), when Christ washes feet, He washes away more than dust. If this action were not a type for confession, then why has no Christian denominations instituted the "seal" of the washing of feet, in order to fulfill the command of John 13:14-15? The Last Supper begins with the washing of feet. Thus, even though baptism cleanses, more cleansing is required throughout life. Without that cleansing, we risk having no part in Christ. When do the Apostles finally understand what Christ did?

Jn 20:21-23 Jesus said to them again, "Peace be with you. As the Father has sent me, even so I send you." 22 And when he had said this, he breathed on them, and said to them, "Receive the Holy Spirit. 23 If you forgive the sins of any, they are forgiven; if you retain the sins of any, they are retained."

Jesus Christ sends the Apostles in the SAME way He was sent from the Father: with the Divine authority to reconcile and reunite the world to God through the forgiveness of sins. God breathes on man only twice in

all of Scripture - once in Genesis when He breathes the breath of life into Adam, through whom we were all given life, and again here, at the completion of the New Creation, when He breathes on the Apostles, through whom we all attain new life in Christ. The risen Christ, who alone won our redemption, gave the Apostles the power to raise people from spiritual death, which is sin. In this way, the Body of Christ is continually drawing all men to Jesus.

Lk 22:29-30 and I assign to you, as my Father assigned to me, a kingdom, [30] that you may eat and drink at my table in my kingdom, and sit on thrones judging the twelve tribes of Israel.

2 Cor 2:10 Any one whom you forgive, I also forgive. What I have forgiven, if I have forgiven anything, has been for your sake in the presence of Christ,...

Mind-reading is not part of the sacramental gift. Sins must be stated to be forgiven. Just as no one can baptize themselves, but must instead go to another to be cleansed in baptism, so we must go to another to be cleansed in confession.

2 Cor 5:18-20 All this is from God, who through Christ reconciled us to himself and gave us the ministry of reconciliation; [19] that is, in Christ God was reconciling the world to himself, not counting their trespasses against them, and entrusting to us the message of reconciliation. [20] So we are ambassadors for Christ, God making his appeal through us. We beseech you on behalf of Christ, be reconciled to God.

James 5:15 Is any one among you suffering? Let him pray. Is any cheerful? Let him sing praise. [14] Is any among you sick? Let him call for the elders of the church, and let them pray over him, anointing him with oil in the name of the Lord; [15] and the prayer of faith will save the sick man, and the Lord will raise him up; and if he has committed sins, he will be forgiven. [16] Therefore confess your sins to one another, and pray for one another, that you may be healed.

A specific action of the elders is needed in order for sins to be forgiven and the penitant accepted back into the community.

1 Jn 1:9 If we confess our sins, he is faithful and just, and will forgive our sins and cleanse us from all unrighteousness.

We are forgiven the minute we ask forgiveness - that's what makes repentance possible in confession. Confession to a priest is necessary for the same reason the confession of marriage vows is necessary - it affirms or reaffirms our covenant with the Body of Christ. Following both marriage and confession, the Bride and Bridegroom are united into one Body.

Acts 19:18 Many also of those who were now believers came, confessing and divulging their practices.

James 5:16 Therefore confess your sins to one another, and pray for one another, that you may be healed. The prayer of a righteous man has great power in its effects.

Eph 4:15-16 Rather, speaking the truth in love, we are to grow up in every way into him who is the head, into Christ, [16] from whom the whole body, joined and knit together by every joint with which it is supplied, when each part is working properly, makes bodily growth and upbuilds itself in love.

Eph 5:29 For no man ever hates his own flesh, but nourishes and cherishes it, as Christ does the church...

1 Cor 12:22-25 On the contrary, the parts of the body which seem to be weaker are indispensable, [23] and those parts of the body which we think less honorable we invest with the greater honor, and our unpresentable parts are treated with greater modesty, [24] which our more presentable parts do not require. But God has so composed the body, giving the greater honor to the inferior part, [25] that there may be no discord in the body, but that the members may have the same care for one another.

The commentary on leprosy comes from apologetics lectures given by Pat Madrid on the sacrament of confession.

Just as lepers needed to be re-integrated into the community after they were cured from leprosy, so do sinners need to be re-integrated into the Body of Christ.

Lk 17:11-14 On the way to Jerusalem he was passing along between Samaria and Galilee. [12] And as he entered a village, he was met by ten lepers, who stood at a distance [13] and lifted up their voices and said, "Jesus, Master, have mercy on us." [14] When he saw them he said to them, "Go and show yourselves to the priests." And as they went they were cleansed.

Lk 5:13-14 And he stretched out his hand, and touched him, saying, "I will; be clean." And immediately the leprosy left him. ¹⁴ And he charged him to tell no one; but "go and show yourself to the priest, and make an offering for your cleansing, as Moses commanded, for a proof to the people."

Mt 8:2-4 and behold, a leper came to him and knelt before him, saying, "Lord, if you will, you can make me clean." ³ And he stretched out his hand and touched him, saying, "I will; be clean." And immediately his leprosy was cleansed. ⁴ And Jesus said to him, "See that you say nothing to any one; but go, show yourself to the priest, and offer the gift that Moses commanded, for a proof to the people."

Mk 1:40-45 And a leper came to him beseeching him, and kneeling said to him, "If you will, you can make me clean." ⁴¹ Moved with pity, he stretched out his hand and touched him, and said to him, "I will; be clean." ⁴² And immediately the leprosy left him, and he was made clean. ⁴³ And he sternly charged him, and sent him away at once, ⁴⁴ and said to him, "See that you say nothing to any one; but go, show yourself to the priest, and offer for your cleansing what Moses commanded, for a proof to the people." ⁴⁵ But he went out and began to talk freely about it, and to spread the news, so that Jesus could no longer openly enter a town, but was out in the country; and people came to him from every quarter.

The need for re-integration into the Body of Christ after sin is part of human existence. We need to be healed. We can do that only by removing and renouncing that which brought us harm and death.

1 Jn 1:8-9 If we say we have no sin, we deceive ourselves, and the truth is not in us. ⁹ If we confess our sins, he is faithful and just, and will forgive our sins and cleanse us from all unrighteousness.

Lk 15:18-19 I will arise and go to my father, and I will say to him, "Father, I have sinned against heaven and before you; ¹⁹ I am no longer worthy to be called your son; treat me as one of your hired servants.'"

1 Jn 2:15-17 Do not love the world or the things in the world. If any one loves the world, love for the Father is not in him. ¹⁶ For all that is in the world, the lust of the flesh and the lust of the eyes and the pride of life, is not of the Father but is of the world. ¹⁷ And the world passes away, and the lust of it; but he who does the will of God abides for ever.

It is through the sacrament of Reconciliation that we publicly accuse ourselves of sinfulness and renounce our attachment to sin in sorrow. In this sacrament, we pass through the mystery of the Cross in order to reach union with God and sanctification. The Holy Spirit brings the penitent sinner a real participation in the grieving the crucified Christ experienced for our particular sin. Accepting penance is accepting the burden of Christ, it is an immersion in Christ's Passion.

Early Christians' comments on Confession

Anointing of the Sick

In this sacrament, Jesus heals His Bride's physical illness or, if the fullness of time has been reached, welcomes each one of us into His Father's House after our honeymoon on earth. The anointing with oil by the elders of the church is for the healing of the body and the forgiveness of sins. (CCC 1499-1532)

Current misunderstandings: While most of our separated brethren do not take much issue with this sacrament (apart from asking for the Scriptural justification every once in a great while), it is also the case that essentially no Church except the Catholic and Eastern Orthodox Churches ever DOES what Scripture commands in this regard.

James 5:14-15 Is any among you sick? Let him call for the elders of the church, and let them pray over him, anointing him with oil in the name of the Lord; [15] and the prayer of faith will save the sick man, and the Lord will raise him up; and if he has committed sins, he will be forgiven.

Mk 6:12-13 So they went out and preached that men should repent. [13] And they cast out many demons, and anointed with oil many that were sick and healed them.

Does your Christian denomination do this? If not, why did they stop? This is what God commands. Is your church doing everything God commands?

Divinization

Through the sacraments, founded in the blood of Jesus Christ, we partake of divinity. Though the inexpressible gulf between our humanity and God's divinity still exists and will exist through all eternity, we truly participate in the divine nature, each of us becoming not just a legal, but a real child of God.

When explaining divinization, Thomas Aquinas used the example of an iron poker heated in a fire. Though the red-hot poker never itself becomes fire, yet it participates in every characteristic of the fire. So do we participate in the divine nature through the perfection brought about in purgation and the sacraments. Through these active experiences of the Divine, we are filled to the capacity of our being with divinity.

Current Misunderstandings: Our separated brethren deny that we can truly partake of the divine nature or, in the case of Mormons, they go to the other extreme and claim that each of the saved become completely divine, gods of their own worlds after death.

Gen 1:27 So God created man in his own image, in the image of God he created him; male and female he created them.

Gen 5:1-3 This is the book of the generations of Adam. When God created man, he made him in the likeness of God. 2 Male and female he created them, and he blessed them and named them Man when they were created. 3 When Adam had lived a hundred and thirty years, he became the father of a son in his own likeness, after his image, and named him Seth....

We are made in the image and likeness of God. That image may have been marred by original sin, but it can be restored. It is brought to perfection through Jesus Christ in a way that simply was not possible in Adam, for the New Adam supersedes and perfects the old in a way not available to the first Adam, even if he had not fallen.

Mt 5:48 You, therefore, must be perfect, as your heavenly Father is perfect.

God commanded it, so it is literally possible. It can only be attained through participation in the divinity of Jesus.

Heb 12:23 and to the assembly of the first-born who are enrolled in heaven, and to a judge who is God of all, and to the spirits of just men made perfect...

Heb 10:14 For by a single offering he has perfected for all time those who are sanctified.

2 Pet 1:3-4 His divine power has granted to us all things that pertain to life and godliness, through the knowledge of him who called us to his own glory and excellence, 4 by which he has granted to us his precious and very great promises, that through these you may escape from the corruption that is in the world because of passion, and become partakers of the divine nature.

Scripture attests that we truly participate in the divine nature.

Jn 17:20-23 "I do not pray for these only, but also for those who believe in me through their word, 21 that they may all be one; even as thou, Father, art in me, and I in thee, that they also may be in us, so that the world may believe that thou hast sent me. 22 The glory which thou hast given me I have given to them, that they may be one even as we are one, 23 I in them and thou in me, that they may become perfectly one, so that the world may know that thou hast sent me and hast loved them even as thou hast loved me.

Col 2:9-10 For in him the whole fulness of deity dwells bodily, 10 and you have come to fulness of life in him, who is the head of all rule and authority

Col 1:26-27 the mystery hidden for ages and generations but now made manifest to his saints. 27 To them God chose to make known how great among the Gentiles are the riches of the glory of this mystery, which is Christ in you, the hope of glory.

This is possible because Christ truly resides in us, and we in Him, through the sacramental life.

1 Jn 3:1 See what love the Father has given us, that we should be called children of God; and so we are.

We are all made into firstborn children of God, truly made perfect as God is perfect before God through Christ. We are individually members of Christ's Body.

Gal 4:4-7 But when the time had fully come, God sent forth his Son, born of woman, born under the law, 5 to redeem those who were under the law, so that we might receive adoption as sons. 6 And because you are sons, God has sent the Spirit of his Son into our hearts, crying, "Abba! Father!" 7 So through God you are no longer a slave but a son, and if a son then an heir.

2 Cor 4:11 For while we live we are always being given up to death for Jesus' sake, so that the life of Jesus may be manifested in our mortal flesh.

Eph 2:15 by abolishing in his flesh the law of commandments and ordinances, that he might create in himself one new man in place of the two, so making peace...

God has only one Son. However, we are made one new man in place of the two, part of the Body of the Son, through the sacramental life. Thus, we become heirs with Christ.

Rom 8:14-17 For all who are led by the Spirit of God are sons of God. 15 For you did not receive the spirit of slavery to fall back into fear, but you have received the spirit of sonship. When we cry, "Abba! Father!" 16 it is the Spirit himself bearing witness with our spirit that we are children of God, 17 and if children, then heirs, heirs of God and fellow heirs with Christ, provided we suffer with him in order that we may also be glorified with him.

Eph 2:21-22 in whom the whole structure is joined together and grows into a holy temple in the Lord; 22 in whom you also are built into it for a dwelling place of God in the Spirit.

James 1:17 Every good endowment and every perfect gift is from above, coming down from the Father of lights with whom there is no variation or shadow due to change.

We do not simply put on Christ's righteousness, God, who holds all things in existence, whose Word formed the universe from nothing, actually removes the reality of our sin so that our sin no longer exists. Thus are we made perfect.

Rom 12:2 Do not be conformed to this world but be transformed by the renewal of your mind, that you may prove what is the will of God, what is good and acceptable and perfect.

Heb 6:4 For it is impossible to restore again to repentence those who have once been enlightened, who have tasted the heavenly gift, and have become partakers of the Holy Spirit...

Eph 3:5-6,19 which was not made known to the sons of men in other generations as it has now been revealed to his holy apostles and prophets by the Spirit; 6 that is, how the Gentiles are fellow heirs, members of the same body, and partakers of the promise in Christ Jesus through the gospel.... and to know the love of Christ which surpasses knowledge, that you may be filled with all the fulness of God.

The promise of Christ is to be filled with all the fullness of God (cf. Col 2:9 on the previous page) - being truly part of the Son, truly participating in the Divine Nature. That is why Paul says what he does in Ephesians 5:1

Eph 5:1 Therefore be imitators of God, as beloved children.

2 Cor 7:1 Since we have these promises, beloved, let us cleanse ourselves from every defilement of body and spirit, and make holiness perfect in the fear of God.

Col 1:28 Him we proclaim, warning every man and teaching every man in all wisdom, that we may present every man mature in Christ.

Rom 16:7 Greet Andronicus and Junias, my kinsmen and my fellow prisoners; they are men of note among the apostles, and they were in Christ before me.

1 Pet 4:6 For this is why the gospel was preached even to the dead, that though judged in the flesh like men, they might live in the spirit like God.

John 14:23 If a man loves me, he will keep my word, and my Father will love him, and we will come to him and make our home with him.

1 Cor 3:16-17,19-20 Do you not know that you are God's temple and that God's Spirit dwells in you? 17 If any one destroys God's temple, God will destroy him. For God's temple is holy, and that temple you are... Do you not know that your body is a temple of the Holy Spirit within you, which you have from God? You are not your own; 20 you were bought with a price. So glorify God in your body.

2 Cor 6:16 For we are the temple of the living God...

Rom 8:9 But you are not in the flesh, you are in the Spirit, if in fact the Spirit of God dwells in you.

2 Cor 13:5 Do you not realize that Christ is in you?

Gal 2:20 I have been crucified with Christ; it is no longer I who live but Christ who lives in me...

Phil 1:21 For to me to live is Christ, and to die is gain.

God is not Father because He made us. He is our Creator, our Master, because He made us. He is

Father because He eternally begets the Son. Thus, it is only our portion in the Body of Christ, only when we partake in and participate in the Divine Nature of Jesus Christ, that God truly becomes our Father, and we truly become His sons and daughters. If we want to become children of God, we must be divinized. That is what the sacraments do. They make us truly his children. St. Athanasius stated it most succinctly: "For the Son of God became man so that we might become God." Through the sacramental life, forged in God's covenant with creation and His work on the Cross, we are truly made into the Body of Christ, who is God.

Divinization is the central mission of the Church (Catechism of the Catholic Church, #460, 1988, 1999). All teaching, all ministry, all work is done with the end of bringing all people to the sacraments so that they may be divinized and have a share in the Body of Christ. Our human nature was made in order to be completely immersed in the divine Fire, the consuming, ravishing love of God, in a whirling dance with Him forever, pouring ourselves out perfectly to Him and Him to us, eternal interpenetration with the Eternal. This cannot be accomplished except in Jesus Christ, in His suffering, His cross, His sacraments.

SACRAMENTALS

1 Tim 4:4-5
For everything created by God is good,
and nothing is to be rejected
if it is received with thanksgiving;
for then it is consecrated
by the word of God and prayer.

"Sacramentals... are sacred signs which bear a resemblance to the sacraments.... By them men are disposed to receive the chief effect of the sacraments, and various occasions of life are rendered holy."
Catechism of the Catholic Church, #1667

In order to dispense the actual graces which flow from the Paschal Mystery into every situation of our lives, the Church provides the children of God with sacramentals. These sacred signs signify the effects of her prayers and intercessions. Through the power of Holy Orders, the ministers of Christ shower the blessings of Christ unto His children. In like manner, objects are set apart and made holy unto the Lord, their use ordained towards Him. Through these blessings and holy things given by the Bride to her children, the people of God are given the helping graces necessary to confidently approach the throne of grace, the sacraments, in which we find participation in the divine life of God, are gathered up in His arms, and are joined to His Body.

Blessings

Gen 12:2 And I will make of you a great nation, and I will bless you, and make your name great, so that you will be a blessing.

Gen 49:22-27 Joseph is a fruitful bough,
a fruitful bough by a spring;
his branches run over the wall. [23] The archers fiercely attacked him,
shot at him, and harassed him sorely; [24] yet his bow remained unmoved,
his arms were made agile
by the hands of the Mighty One of Jacob
(by the name of the Shepherd, the Rock of Israel), [25] by the God of your father who will help you,
by God Almighty who will bless you
with blessings of heaven above,
blessings of the deep that couches beneath,
blessings of the breasts and of the womb. [26] The blessings of your father
are mighty beyond the blessings of the eternal mountains,
the bounties of the everlasting hills;
may they be on the head of Joseph,
and on the brow of him who was separate from his brothers.

Num 6:22-26 The LORD said to Moses, [23] "Say to Aaron and his sons, Thus you shall bless the people of Israel: you shall say to them, [24] The LORD bless you and keep you: [25] The LORD make his face to shine upon you, and be gracious to you: [26] The LORD lift up his countenance upon you, and give you peace.

These verses from Numbers are part of the liturgy which ends the sacrifice of the Mass.

1 Chron 23:13 The sons of Amram: Aaron and Moses. Aaron was set apart to consecrate the most holy things, that he and his sons for ever should burn incense before the LORD, and minister to him and pronounce blessings in his name for ever.

Psalm 72:15 May prayer be made for him continually, and blessings invoked for him all the day!

Prov 10:6 Blessings are on the head of the righteous, but the mouth of the wicked conceals violence.

Heb 11:20-21 By faith Isaac invoked future blessings on Jacob and Esau. [21] By faith Jacob, when dying, blessed each of the sons of Joseph, bowing in worship over the head of his staff.

Eph 1:3 Blessed be the God and Father of our Lord Jesus Christ, who has blessed us in Christ with every spiritual blessing in the heavenly places.

Lk 6:28 bless those who curse you, pray for those who abuse you.

Exorcisms likewise fall under sacramental power.

Mk 1:25-26 But Jesus rebuked him, saying, "Be silent, and come out of him!" [26] And the unclean spirit, convulsing him and crying with a loud voice, came out of him.

Images

Honor given to the Body of Christ is honor given to Christ Himself. Thus, the use of icons, statues, medals, scapulars, photographs or other images which remind us of those living in the Body of Christ are appropriate ways to focus our attention on His Glorified Mystical Body and become aware of the cloud of witnesses who surround us. Such images are never to be used as charms or amulets, but only as reminders of loved ones who are not with us in body, though they are with us in spirit through the Body of Christ. (CCC 1159-1162)

Current misunderstandings: Most Christians find the veneration of the saints to be an abomination, because it detracts from the honor due to God. Therefore, the use of statues or other images is seen as a veiled form of idolatry, and a violation of the Ten Commandments.

Ex 20:4-5 "You shall not make for yourself a graven image, or any likeness of anything that is in heaven above, or that is in the earth beneath, or that is in the water under the earth; ⁵ you shall not bow down to them or serve them; for I the LORD your God am a jealous God, visiting the iniquity of the fathers upon the children to the third and the fourth generation..."

Ex 25:18-21 And you shall make two cherubim of gold; of hammered work shall you make them, on the two ends of the mercy seat. ¹⁹ Make one cherub on the one end, and one cherub on the other end; of one piece with the mercy seat shall you make the cherubim on its two ends. ²⁰ The cherubim shall spread out their wings above, overshadowing the mercy seat with their wings, their faces one to another; toward the mercy seat shall the faces of the cherubim be. ²¹ And you shall put the mercy seat on the top of the ark; and in the ark you shall put the testimony that I shall give you.

Immediately after telling the Israelites not to carve graven images, He commands them to do so. God cannot command that which is against His nature. God does not violate His own laws. A thing is not good because God says it is good, a thing is good because it reflects the nature of who God is. If statues and images were instrinsically evil and an offense against God, He would not have had the ark of His Presence engraved with them. Some argue that God merely forbad men to make such images, that the God may make images for Himself, if He chooses. This is a difficult argument to maintain, given how the Israelites used these images:

Josh 3:14-16 So, when the people set out from their tents, to pass over the Jordan with the priests bearing the ark of the covenant before the people, ¹⁵ and when those who bore the ark had come to the Jordan, and the feet of the priests bearing the ark were dipped in the brink of the water (the Jordan overflows all its banks throughout the time of harvest), ¹⁶ the waters coming down from above stood and rose up in a heap far off, at Adam, the city that is beside Zarethan, and those flowing down toward the sea of the Arabah, the Salt Sea, were wholly cut off; and the people passed over opposite Jericho

The Israelites used the ark, covered in graven images, to win battles and part the Jordan. God does not need an image to win a battle or part a river. God commanded MEN to make images for MEN to use.

Josh 7:6-7 Then Joshua rent his clothes, and fell to the earth upon his face before the ark of the LORD until the evening, he and the elders of Israel; and they put dust upon their heads. ⁷ And Joshua said, "Alas, O Lord GOD, why hast thou brought this people over the Jordan at all, to give us into the hands of the Amorites, to destroy us? Would that we had been content to dwell beyond the Jordan!

Joshua directly violates the command against the use of graven images by bowing before them. Joshua is not forbidden entry into the Promised Land for his idolatry, instead God permits it. Indeed, because of the actions of Joshua and the elders, God tells them how to win military victory. Though all the people of Moses' and Joshua's generation were forbidden to enter the Promised Land because of their idolatry of the Golden Calf, Joshua is permitted to enter and in fact does enter. Yet didn't he here commit idolatry? God apparently doesn't think so. Why not? Because the graven images of the ark are being used properly. While the casual observer might think Joshua is bowing down to graven images (for God reveals Himself to those whom He will, and a casual observer would not necessarily know of the presence of God upon the Ark), yet Joshua is merely using the images on the ark and the ark itself as a means of focusing his worship on the God who is beyond all created things.

Judg 20:27 And the people of Israel inquired of the LORD (for the ark of the covenant of God was there in those days)...

The Israelites consulted God through the use of an object covered in graven images. He responds by giving them military victory.

2 Sam 6:13-16 and when those who bore the ark of the LORD had gone six paces, he sacrificed an ox and a fatling. [14] And David danced before the LORD with all his might; and David was girded with a linen ephod. [15] So David and all the house of Israel brought up the ark of the LORD with shouting, and with the sound of the horn. [16] As the ark of the LORD came into the city of David, Michal the daughter of Saul looked out of the window, and saw King David leaping and dancing before the LORD; and she despised him in her heart.

David sacrifices before the graven images - when Michal, Saul's daughter saw him whirling and dancing before the graven images she disapproved and was struck sterile by God for the rest of her life.

1 Kings 3:15 And Solomon awoke, and behold, it was a dream. Then he came to Jerusalem, and stood before the ark of the covenant of the LORD, and offered up burnt offerings and peace offerings, and made a feast for all his servants.

Solomon offers sacrifice in front of graven images in thanksgiving for the gift of wisdom. The case of the two mothers disputing over the infant boy immediately follows. Solomon's successful solution demonstrates that God has indeed given him this gift.

1 Kings 8:5 And King Solomon and all the congregation of Israel, who had assembled before him, were with him before the ark, sacrificing so many sheep and oxen that they could not be counted or numbered.

After Solomon makes "countless" sacrifices in front of the graven images, the glory of the Lord filled the Temple so fully that the ministering priests couldn't see to minister.

Were David and Solomon offering sacrifice to the graven images? The casual observer might think so. Yet each was actually using the images to focus his worship on the Lord.

1 Chron 13:6 And David and all Israel went up to Baalah, that is, to Kiriath-jearim which belongs to Judah, to bring up from there the ark of God, which is called by the name of the LORD who sits enthroned above the cherubim.

1 Chron 16:4 Moreover he appointed certain of the Levites as ministers before the ark of the LORD, to invoke, to thank, and to praise the LORD, the God of Israel

Why before the ark? Isn't God everywhere present? People are appointed to minister in front of the graven images, yet no harm comes to them.

Psalm 132:8 Arise, O LORD, and go to thy resting place, thou and the ark of thy might.

The ark is even called mighty - how can images approach the might of God?

Deut 6:4-5 Hear, O Israel: the Lord our God is one Lord; [5] and you shall love the Lord your God with all your heart, and with all your soul, and with all your might.

Col 1:15 He is the image of the invisible God, the first-born of all creation...

Christ is the icon, the image, of God.

Gen 1:27 So God created man in his own image, in the image of God he created him; male and female he created them.

Gen 5:1-3 When God created man, he made him in the likeness of God. [2] Male and female he created them, and he blessed them and named them Man when they were created. [3] When Adam had lived a hundred and thirty years, he became the father of a son in his own likeness, after his image...

Lev 19:18 You shall not take vengeance or bear any grudge against the sons of your own people, but you shall love your neighbor as yourself: I am the Lord.

And we are images of God as well, through Jesus Christ. Even though we are images of God, the love we bear for each other is not idolatry. Our existence depends on God. When we keep that in mind as we love one another, we honor the Persons from whom our existence derives: God. We are living reminders to each other of God's love borne through each of us. Images recall not only the great gifts of His creation but every one of the living reminders of love He has sent us throughout history, the great saints through which He exercises His power.

Num 21:8-9 And the Lord said to Moses, "Make a fiery serpent, and set it on a pole; and every one who is bitten, when he sees it, shall live." ⁹ So Moses made a bronze serpent, and set it on a pole; and if a serpent bit any man, he would look at the bronze serpent and live.

Now, it is true that God commanded Moses to use this image. But why a SERPENT? One might reply that the serpent symbolizes Christ raised up on the cross, and so it does. But the very problem modern Christians have with statues is their symbolism. God used the very image of Satan found in Genesis to symbolize Jesus Christ, so that by looking upon a serpent, the people might be healed. If the serpent can symbolize the living God, Jesus Christ, on the cross, isn't it possible for a statue of Mary to symbolize the incarnation of Christ on earth? Couldn't a statue of Joseph symbolize the loving protection with which Christ guards His people, just as Joseph guarded the Holy Family? Doesn't the whole family of saints both symbolize and actualize, i.e, make up a part of, the Living Body of Jesus Christ?

Jn 3:14-15 And as Moses lifted up the serpent in the wilderness, so must the Son of man be lifted up, ¹⁵ that whoever believes in him may have eternal life."

Jesus certainly approved of the use of images.

1 Kings 6:23-35 In the inner sanctuary he made two cherubim of olivewood, each ten cubits high. ²⁴ Five cubits was the length of one wing of the cherub, and five cubits the length of the other wing of the cherub; it was ten cubits from the tip of one wing to the tip of the other. ²⁵ The other cherub also measured ten cubits; both cherubim had the same measure and the same form. ²⁶ The height of one cherub was ten cubits, and so was that of the other cherub. ²⁷ He put the cherubim in the innermost part of the house; and the wings of the cherubim were spread out so that a wing of one touched the one wall, and a wing of the other cherub touched the other wall; their other wings touched each other in the middle of the house. ²⁸ And he overlaid the cherubim with gold.
²⁹ He carved all the walls of the house round about with carved figures of cherubim and palm trees and open flowers, in the inner and outer rooms. ³⁰ The floor of the house he overlaid with gold in the inner and outer rooms.
³¹ For the entrance to the inner sanctuary he made doors of olivewood; the lintel and the doorposts formed a pentagon. ³² He covered the two doors of olivewood with carvings of cherubim, palm trees, and open flowers; he overlaid them with gold, and spread gold upon the cherubim and upon the palm trees.
³³ So also he made for the entrance to the nave doorposts of olivewood, in the form of a square, ³⁴ and two doors of cypress wood; the two leaves of the one door were folding, and the two leaves of the other door were folding. ³⁵ On them he carved cherubim and palm trees and open flowers; and he overlaid them with gold evenly applied upon the carved work.

Think on this. Throughout salvation history, every place God chooses to dwell is either itself an image, i.e., human beings, an icon, i.e., Jesus, or covered with graven images, i.e., the Ark of the Covenant and the Temple. Clearly, the prohibition on graven images is not total - it depends on how one uses them. Nearly all Christian denominations use them. For instance, it is the rare Christian church which does not have a cross in or near the church. Yet none of those crosses are the True Cross upon which Jesus gave His life for us. If it is not the tree upon which Jesus hung, then it is a statue of the tree, an icon of that Cross. Just as no Christian prays to the Cross, but rather uses the image of the Cross to focus worship on God, and as a constant reminder of what God has done for us, so the holy men and women of God are likewise gifts of God, signs of what God has done for us, for He raised them up in our midst.

If we use images for idolatry, i.e., we think the statue contains a spirit, or we think the statue is itself a god, we have committed a mortal sin. However, if the image is used to focus attention on the gifts, the honors, the glories bestowed by God to His faithful, it is a proper and fitting way to honor the glory of God in His creation. God made us. We are material creatures. He knows how we think, and what we need. He permits us to use material things which remind us of His presence in our lives, whether it be a reminder of the presence of God over the ark, the presence of Christ in Galilee, or the presence of God in the lives of the saints who make up the Body of Christ. If Catholics truly worshipped any statue or image as God, we would say so - after all, we readily admit that we worship as God what appears to be unleavened bread and grape wine. Catholics do not worship statues.

Holy Water

Holy water, that is, water mixed with salt and blessed by a priest, washes away venial sin by the renewal of our baptismal vows.

Current misunderstandings: Many Christians see the use of holy water as a superstition.

Num 5:17 and the priest shall take holy water in an earthen vessel, and take some of the dust that is on the floor of the tabernacle and put it into the water.

Num 8:7 And thus you shall do to them, to cleanse them: sprinkle the water of expiation upon them, and let them go with a razor over all their body, and wash their clothes and cleanse themselves.

Num 19:17 For the unclean they shall take some ashes of the burnt sin offering, and running water shall be added in a vessel...

Psalm 51:2 Wash me thoroughly from my iniquity, and cleanse me from my sin!

So, why is holy water important? Because it foreshadows the Passion of Jesus Christ, containing within it references to the themes of suffering, covenant and sacrifice which repeat constantly throughout Scripture.

Salt, a component of holy water, is first mentioned in connection with two important events - the rescue of Lot from captivity by Abram, and the gifts of bread and wine offered by Melchizedek.

Gen 14:3,8-18 And all these joined forces in the Valley of Siddim (that is, the Salt Sea)... Then the king of Sodom, the king of Gomorrah, the king of Admah, the king of Zeboiim, and the king of Bela (that is, Zoar) went out, and they joined battle in the Valley of Siddim [9] with Ched-or-laomer king of Elam, Tidal king of Goiim, Amraphel king of Shinar, and Arioch king of Ellasar, four kings against five. [10] Now the Valley of Siddim was full of bitumen pits; and as the kings of Sodom and Gomorrah fled, some fell into them, and the rest fled to the mountain. [11] So the enemy took all the goods of Sodom and Gomorrah, and all their provisions, and went their way; [12] they also took Lot, the son of Abram's brother, who dwelt in Sodom, and his goods, and departed. [13] Then one who had escaped came, and told Abram the Hebrew, who was living by the oaks of Mamre the Amorite, brother of Eshcol and of Aner; these were allies of Abram. [14] When Abram heard that his kinsman had been taken captive, he led forth his trained men, born in his house, three hundred and eighteen of them, and went in pursuit as far as Dan. [15] And he divided his forces against them by night, he and his servants, and routed them and pursued them to Hobah, north of Damascus. [16] Then he brought back all the goods, and also brought back his kinsman Lot with his goods, and the women and the people.
[17] After his return from the defeat of Ched-or-laomer and the kings who were with him, the king of Sodom went out to meet him at the Valley of Shaveh (that is, the King's Valley). [18] And Mel-chizedek king of Salem brought out bread and wine; he was priest of God Most High.

The kings of this world, of Sodom and Gomorrah, could not prevail in the valley of salt. Lot was captured by the victors. Abram rescued Lot from their grasp, releasing his cousin from captivity and conquering the kings of this world. Melchizedek offers up <u>bread and wine</u> on Abram's behalf in thanksgiving for the victory and the rescue.

Gen 19:26 But Lot's wife behind him looked back, and she became a pillar of salt.

When Lot's wife turns away from God and back towards the sins of this world, she is turned into a pillar of salt. The next occurence of the word adds liturgical themes to the foreshadowing of the Eucharist.

Ex 30:35 and make an incense blended as by the perfumer, seasoned with salt, pure and holy;

Tobit exorcised a demon (Tob 6:17-18, 8:2-3) using a fish, the ancient Christ symbol, strewn with salt (Tob 6:6). Sacrifice required salt:

Ezra 6:9 And whatever is needed—young bulls, rams, or sheep for burnt offerings to the God of heaven, wheat, salt, wine, or oil, as the priests at Jerusalem require—let that be given to them day by day without fail...

Ezra 7:21-22 21 I, Artaxerxes the king, issue this decree to all the treasurers of West-of-Euphrates: Whatever Ezra the priest, scribe of the law of the God of heaven, requests of you, dispense to him accurately, 22 within these limits: silver, one hundred talents;

wheat, one hundred kors; wine, one hundred baths; oil, one hundred baths; salt, without limit.

Being added to the holocaust offering AFTER purification:

Ezek 43:23-24 "And I, Ar-ta-xerxes the king, make a decree to all the treasurers in the province Beyond the River: Whatever Ezra the priest, the scribe of the law of the God of heaven, requires of you, be it done with all diligence, ²² up to a hundred talents of silver, a hundred cors of wheat, a hundred baths of wine, a hundred baths of oil, and salt without prescribing how much.

Salt is an image of wasteland, desolation. It is hard to bear:

Sir 22:15 Sand, salt, and a piece of iron are easier to bear than a stupid man.

An image of God's wrath:

Sir 39:23 The nations will incur his wrath, just as he turns fresh water into salt.

An insipid thing cannot be eaten without it:

Job 6:6 Can that which is tasteless be eaten without salt,

It signifies a burned out waste, a desert:

Wis 10:7 Evidence of their wickedness still remains: a continually smoking wasteland, plants bearing fruit that does not ripen, and a pillar of salt standing as a monument to an unbelieving soul.

Deut 29:22-23 when they see the afflictions of that land and the sicknesses with which the Lord has made it sick— ²³ the whole land brimstone and salt, and a burnt-out waste, unsown, and growing nothing, where no grass can sprout, an overthrow like that of Sodom and Gomorrah, Admah and Zeboiim, which the Lord overthrew in his anger and wrath—

Zeph 2:9 Therefore, as I live," says the Lord of hosts, the God of Israel,
"Moab shall become like Sodom,
and the Ammonites like Gomorrah,
a land possessed by nettles and salt pits,
and a waste for ever.

A sign of one who trusts in himself, not God:

Jer 17:5-6 Thus says the Lord: "Cursed is the man who trusts in man
and makes flesh his arm, whose heart turns away from the Lord. ⁶ He is like a shrub in the desert, and shall not see any good come. He shall dwell in the parched places of the wilderness, in an uninhabited salt land.

Being under a salt tax signified dominion, being freed of the salt tax showed relative freedom:

1 Mac 10:29 "And now I free you and exempt all the Jews from payment of tribute and salt tax and crown levies,"

1 Mac 11:35 And the other payments henceforth due to us of the tithes, and the taxes due to us, and the salt pits and the crown taxes due to us— from all these we shall grant them release.

In the exercise of their free will, the people become like a wild ass, living in salt flats:

Job 39:5-8 "Who has let the wild ass go free? Who has loosed the bonds of the swift ass, ⁶ to whom I have given the steppe for his home, and the salt land for his dwelling place? ⁷ He scorns the tumult of the city; he hears not the shouts of the driver. ⁸ He ranges the mountains as his pasture, and he searches after every green thing.

The only people ever recorded as being slain in the Salt Valley were the descendants of Esau, a wild ass of a man (cf. Ishmael, Gen 16:11), who sold his inheritance for a mess of pottage (Gen 25:30-34) - the satisfaction of the sensual delights of this world. His descendants were called the Edomites and they inhabited the land of Seir. They were slain in the Salt Valley by David, King of Israel, and his generals. Psalm 60, which begins with a scene of desolation, was written after David's battle in the Valley of Salt.

2 Sam 8:13 And David won a name for himself. When he returned, he slew eighteen thousand Edomites in the Valley of Salt

2 Kings 14:7 He killed ten thousand Edomites in the Valley of Salt and took Sela by storm, and called it Jokthe-el, which is its name to this day.

1 Chron 18:12 And Abishai, the son of Zeruiah, slew eighteen thousand Edomites in the Valley of Salt.

2 Chron 25:11 But Amaziah took courage, and led out his people, and went to the Valley of Salt and smote ten thousand men of Seir.

Judg 9:45 And Abimelech fought against the city all that day; he took the city, and killed the people that were in it; and he razed the city and sowed it with salt.

But salt is necessary for our existence...

Sir 39:26-27 Basic to all the needs of man's life are water and fire and iron and salt and wheat flour and milk and honey, the blood of the grape, and oil and clothing. ²⁷ All these are for good to the godly, just as they turn into evils for sinners.

The only time salt definitely purified, instead of being added after purification was complete, was here:

2 Kings 2:20-22 He said, "Bring me a new bowl, and put salt in it." So they brought it to him. ²¹ Then he went to the spring of water and threw salt in it, and said, "Thus says the LORD, I have made this water wholesome; henceforth neither death nor miscarriage shall come from it." ²² So the water has been wholesome to this day, according to the word which Elisha spoke.

It purifies Living Water, a clear Christological reference. Just as the seraph lifted in the desert healed the people of the poison (Num 21:9), and prefigured the crucified Christ, so the salt strewn in the poisonous waters healed the waters of their poison and prefigured the suffering Christ.

Ezek 16:4 And as for your birth, on the day you were born your navel string was not cut, nor were you washed with water to cleanse you, nor rubbed with salt, nor swathed with bands.

Holy water is inextricably linked to the Living Waters of baptism (baptismal water is NEVER salted) in part because baptismal water washes away the salt of suffering which covers the newborn. Christ, the Living Water, takes on our salt, our suffering..

Ezek 47:8-11 And he said to me, "This water flows toward the eastern region and goes down into the Arabah; and when it enters the stagnant waters of the sea, the water will become fresh. ⁹ And wherever the river goes every living creature which swarms will live, and there will be very many fish; for this water goes there, that the waters of the sea may become fresh; so everything will live where the river goes. ¹⁰ Fishermen will stand beside the sea; from En-gedi to En-eglaim it will be a place for the spreading of nets; its fish will be of very many kinds, like the fish of the Great Sea. ¹¹ But its swamps and marshes will not become fresh; they are to be left for salt.

Living water (i.e. flowing water, such as a river), is not made desolate by meeting the salt water, rather the salt water is made fresh. The marshes and swamps, which are neither water or land, but stand between, are like the people who are neither hot nor cold (Rev 3:15-16) - they will be left for salt.

The boundaries of Israel began and ended in the Salt Sea:

Num 34:3,12 your south side shall be from the wilderness of Zin along the side of Edom, and your southern boundary shall be from the end of the Salt Sea on the east;. and the boundary shall go down to the Jordan, and its end shall be at the Salt Sea. This shall be your land with its boundaries all round."

Deut 3:15-17 To Machir I gave Gilead, ¹⁶ and to the Reubenites and the Gadites I gave the territory from Gilead as far as the valley of the Arnon, with the middle of the valley as a boundary, as far over as the river Jabbok, the boundary of the Ammonites ¹⁷ the Arabah also, with the Jordan as the boundary, from Chinnereth as far as the sea of the Arabah, the Salt Sea, under the slopes of Pisgah on the east.

The borders of the tribe of Judah and Benjamin, the only two tribes who stayed even partially true to God, were partially defined by the Salt Sea:

Josh 15:1-5 The lot for the tribe of the people of Judah according to their families reached southward to the boundary of Edom, to the wilderness of Zin at the farthest south. ² And their south boundary ran from the end of the Salt Sea, from the bay that faces southward; ³ it goes out southward of the ascent of Akrabbim, passes along to Zin, and goes up south of Kadesh-barnea, along by Hezron, up to Addar, turns about to Karka, ⁴ passes along to Azmon, goes out by the Brook of Egypt, and comes to its end at the sea. This shall be your south boundary. ⁵ And the east boundary is the Salt Sea, to the mouth of the Jordan.

Josh 18:11,19 he lot of the tribe of Benjamin according to its families came up, and the territory allotted to it fell between the tribe of Judah and the tribe of Joseph..... then the boundary passes on to the north of the shoulder of Beth-hoglah; and the boundary ends at the northern bay of the Salt Sea, at the south end of the Jordan: this is the southern border.

When Israel entered into the land flowing with milk and honey, the Jordan waters flowing to the Salt Sea disappeared entirely, allowing them to cross.

Josh 3:16-17 the waters coming down from above stood and rose up in a heap far off, at Adam, the city that is beside Zarethan, and those flowing down toward the sea of the Arabah, the Salt Sea, were wholly cut off; and the people passed over opposite Jericho. ¹⁷ And while all Israel were passing over on dry ground, the priests who bore the ark of the covenant of the LORD stood on dry ground in the midst of the Jordan, until all the nation finished passing over the Jordan.

Salt therefore becomes a sign of covenant:

2 Chron 13:4-5 Then Abijah stood up on Mount Zemaraim which is in the hill country of Ephraim, and said, "Hear me, O Jeroboam and all Israel! ⁵ Ought you not to know that the LORD God of Israel gave the kingship over Israel for ever to David and his sons by a covenant of salt?

Ezra 4:14 Now because we eat the salt of the palace and it is not fitting for us to witness the king's dishonor, therefore we send and inform the king...

It is in the cereal offering that the full typology is revealed:

Lev 2:11-13 No cereal offering which you bring to the LORD shall be made with leaven; for you shall burn no leaven nor any honey as an offering by fire to the LORD. ¹² As an offering of first fruits you may bring them to the LORD, but they shall not be offered on the altar for a pleasing odor. ¹³ You shall season all your cereal offerings with salt; you shall not let the salt of the covenant with your God be lacking from your cereal offering; with all your offerings you shall offer salt.

The Leviticus passage is interesting because it is the only sacrifice with a three-fold command to be salted. This cereal offering foreshadows the Eucharist, just as Melchizedek's offering had, and the Levitical cereal offering was itself referenced by Christ.

Mt 5:13 "You are the salt of the earth; but if salt has lost its taste, how shall its saltness be restored? It is no longer good for anything except to be thrown out and trodden under foot by men.

Mk 9:50 Salt is good; but if the salt has lost its saltness, how will you season it? Have salt in yourselves, and be at peace with one another."

Lk 14:34-35 "Salt is good; but if salt has lost its taste, how shall its saltness be restored? ³⁵ It is fit neither for the land nor for the dunghill; men throw it away. He who has ears to hear, let him hear."

Col 4:6 Let your speech always be gracious, seasoned with salt, so that you may know how you ought to answer every one.

James 3:12 Can a fig tree, my brethren, yield olives, or a grapevine figs? No more can salt water yield fresh.

We who are in the Body of Christ must season ourselves with suffering, and direct that suffering in offering towards God. Replace the word "salt" in the passages above with "suffering," and the passages are transformed. Water mixed with salt and blessed, i.e., holy water, is a type for the Living Water and His Passion, and a constant reminder of our baptism.

Ashes and Incense

The Scripture for this subject comes from Scripture by Topic, *pp. 360-361. The exegesis is my own.*

The use of ashes and incense in the liturgy corresponds to the divine plan for our redemption. It not only reminds us of our final end, but through faith, brings us into conformance with God's will for us.

Current misunderstandings: The use of ashes and incense is seen as empty ritual by most Christians, bordering on idolatry.

Mt 11:21 "Woe to you, Chorazin! woe to you, Beth-saida! for if the mighty works done in you had been done in Tyre and Sidon, they would have repented long ago in sackcloth and ashes.

Gen 3:19 In the sweat of your face you shall eat bread till you return to the ground, for out of it you were taken; you are dust, and to dust you shall return."

Gen 18:27 Abraham answered, "Behold, I have taken upon myself to speak to the Lord, I who am but dust and ashes.

Esther 4:1 When Mordecai learned all that had been done, Mordecai rent his clothes and put on sackcloth and ashes, and went out into the midst of the city, wailing with a loud and bitter cry...

Job 42:6 therefore I despise myself, and repent in dust and ashes."

Lam 3:16 He has made my teeth grind on gravel, and made me cower in ashes...

Incense, too, is a blessing and a reminder of God's constant presence, and our duties towards Him.

Lk 1:10 And the whole multitude of the people were praying outside at the hour of incense

Psalm 141:2 Let my prayer be counted as incense before thee,
and the lifting up of my hands as an evening sacrifice!

Ex 30:8 and when Aaron sets up the lamps in the evening, he shall burn it, a perpetual incense before the Lord throughout your generations.

It is offered even in heaven:

Rev 5:8 And when he had taken the scroll, the four living creatures and the twenty-four elders fell down before the Lamb, each holding a harp, and with golden bowls full of incense, which are the prayers of the saints...

Rev 8:3-4 And another angel came and stood at the altar with a golden censer; and he was given much incense to mingle with the prayers of all the saints upon the golden altar before the throne [4]and the smoke of the incense rose with the prayers of the saints from the hand of the angel before God.

SALVATION

"Conversion means accepting,
by a personal decision,
the saving sovereignty of Christ
and becoming his disciple."
- *Mission of the Redeemer,* Pope John Paul II

1 Peter 2:1-3
So put away all malice and all guile
and insincerity and envy and all slander.
Like newborn babes, long for the pure spiritual milk,
that by it you may grow up to salvation;
for you have tasted the kindness of the Lord.

John 4:22
... salvation is from the Jews.

Salvation Through Faith and Works

1 Cor 13:2 and if I have all faith, so as to remove mountains, but have not love, I am nothing.

We are saved by grace alone. No one can merit the initial grace of forgiveness and justification, which is the adoption into God's Body as His true child through baptism. All our merit and all that we merit ultimately derives from God's gracious condescension in adopting us as His own. Through this baptism, which cleanses us, adopts us, makes us a true child of God, we are enabled to become partakers by grace in the divine nature. As His true children, we obtain, as every child does, a right to a share in the life of our Father. Moved by the Holy Spirit, we, His children, image the First-Born, winning additional merit for ourselves and for others through our response in faith and action. Faith and action are similar responses with different outward forms. Thus, the sacraments are actual outpourings of the divine Life, grace, in which we must participate with faith in order to attain salvation, not that our faith makes the sacraments operative, rather, our submission to the Divinely instituted sacraments in both faith and action constitute the formal cooperation with grace in which we freely submit our will to that of Jesus Christ and thereby become One with His Body. (CCC 144-184, 161, 1996)

Current misunderstandings: Sole fide *theology teaches that we are saved by grace alone, but that the only proper response to grace is faith - one need do nothing but believe in order to be saved.* Sole fide *theology does not merely reject the idea that human work can, by itself, lead to salvation, an idea which all Christians, Catholics included, reject. Rather, it teaches that one need not respond to grace through definitive action at all - a response of faith is sufficient. In this theology, action has no effect on salvation whatsoever. Walking in the ways of God does not save, since good acts come after salvation has been attained through faith, and failing to walk in His ways does not condemn, since we are saved by the cloak of Christ's righteousness, which no wrongful action can remove from us. Some followers of* sole fide *acknowledge the fact that sinfulness can condemn us, but continue to refuse the idea that following God's ways can do anything to save us.*

Acts 15:11 "But we believe that we shall be saved through the grace of the Lord Jesus, just as they will."

Eph 2:8-10 For by grace you have been saved through faith; and this is not your own doing, it is the gift of God— [9] not because of works, lest any man should boast. [10] For we are his workmanship, created in Christ Jesus for good works, which God prepared beforehand, that we should walk in them.

All denominations agree on one thing: grace alone saves. Grace comes to us as an unmerited gift from God. It is God's life within us. It is power. We must respond to that grace, utilize that power, in order to be saved. But what are the fruits of grace? The first fruit of grace is that we are created for good works. Works are not the fruit of faith, they are the direct fruit of grace, just as faith is.

Heb 11:6 And without faith it is impossible to please him. For whoever would draw near to God must believe that he exists and that he rewards those who seek him.

This passage from Hebrews describes the minimum response necessary for salvation - we must believe that God exists and that He rewards those who seek Him. Faith in God is one of the fruits of grace. How can we come to know Him?

Jn 1:1-3 In the beginning was the Word, and the Word was with God, and the Word was God. [2] He was in the beginning with God; [3] all things were made through him, and without him was not anything made that was made.

We come to know Him through Jesus Christ, for, whether the evidence be the material world created through Him or the person of Jesus Christ Himself, it is only through the Person of Christ that all evidence of God comes to us:

Wis 13:1-9 For all men who were ignorant of God were foolish by nature; and they were unable from the good things that arc seen to know him who exists,
nor did they recognize the craftsman while paying heed to his works; [2] but they supposed that either fire or wind or swift air,
or the circle of the stars, or turbulent water,
or the luminaries of heaven were the gods that rule the world. [3] If through delight in the beauty of these things men assumed them to be gods, let them know how much better than these is their Lord,

for the author of beauty created them. ⁴ And if men were amazed at their power and working, let them perceive from them
how much more powerful is he who formed them. ⁵ For from the greatness and beauty of created things
comes a corresponding perception of their Creator. ⁶ Yet these men are little to be blamed, for perhaps they go astray
while seeking God and desiring to find him. ⁷ For as they live among his works they keep searching,
and they trust in what they see, because the things that are seen are beautiful. ⁸ Yet again, not even they are to be excused; ⁹ for if they had the power to know so much that they could investigate the world,
how did they fail to find sooner the Lord of these things?

Psalm 19:1-5 The heavens are telling the glory of God;
and the firmament proclaims his handiwork. ² Day to day pours forth speech,
and night to night declares knowledge. ³ There is no speech, nor are there words;
their voice is not heard;
⁴ yet their voice goes out through all the earth,
and their words to the end of the world.
In them he has set a tent for the sun,
⁵ which comes forth like a bridegroom leaving his chamber,
and like a strong man runs its course with joy.

Rom 1:19-20 For what can be known about God is plain to them, because God has shown it to them. ²⁰ Ever since the creation of the world his invisible nature, namely, his eternal power and deity, has been clearly perceived in the things that have been made. So they are without excuse...

Acts 14:15-17 "Men, why are you doing this? We also are men, of like nature with you, and bring you good news, that you should turn from these vain things to a living God who made the heaven and the earth and the sea and all that is in them. ¹⁶ In past generations he allowed all the nations to walk in their own ways; ¹⁷ yet he did not leave himself without witness, for he did good and gave you from heaven rains and fruitful seasons, satisfying your hearts with food and gladness."

Acts 17:22-27 So Paul, standing in the middle of the Are-opagus, said: "Men of Athens, I perceive that in every way you are very religious. ²³ For as I passed along, and observed the objects of your worship, I found also an altar with this inscription, 'To an unknown god.' What therefore you worship as unknown, this I proclaim to you. ²⁴ The God who made the world and everything in it, being Lord of heaven and earth, does not live in shrines made by man, ²⁵ nor is he served by human hands, as though he needed anything, since he himself gives to all men life and breath and everything. ²⁶ And he made from one every nation of men to live on all the face of the earth, having determined allotted periods and the boundaries of their habitation, ²⁷ that they should seek God, in the hope that they might feel after him and find him. Yet he is not far from each one of us...

Rom 2:13-16 For it is not the hearers of the law who are righteous before God, but the doers of the law who will be justified. ¹⁴ When Gentiles who have not the law do by nature what the law requires, they are a law to themselves, even though they do not have the law. ¹⁵ They show that what the law requires is written on their hearts, while their conscience also bears witness and their conflicting thoughts accuse or perhaps excuse them ¹⁶ on that day when, according to my gospel, God judges the secrets of men by Christ Jesus.

Acts 10:34-35 And Peter opened his mouth and said: "Truly I perceive that God shows no partiality, ³⁵ but in every nation any one who fears him and does what is right is acceptable to him."

Early Christians' comments on Salvation Outside the Church.

Scripture is truth. Truth cannot contradict truth. While there are many passages which emphasize the importance of faith, often without mentioning the importance of works at all, the passages below emphasize the importance of works, often without mentioning faith at all. Just as Ephesians 2:8-10 says it is faith that saves, not works, so Scripture also says:

James 2:24 You see that a man is justified by works and not by faith alone.

Zech 1:3 Therefore say to them, Thus says the Lord of hosts: Return to me, says the Lord of hosts, and I will return to you, says the Lord of hosts.

The idea that work alone leads to salvation is as wrong as the idea that faith alone leads to salvation. Grace alone brings salvation. Grace is power which we initially receive as an unmerited gift. Once we have received that unmerited gift, we can grow in justification through good works..

Rom 6:3-4 Do you not know that all of us who have been baptized into Christ Jesus were baptized into his death? ⁴ We were buried therefore with him by baptism into death, so that as Christ was raised from the dead by the glory of the Father, we too might walk in newness of life.

Grace produces two co-equal fruits in us - faith and works. We must respond to grace, we must utilize the power God gives us. Just as God made man by indissolubly joining an immortal soul to a material body, so salvation is attained through the indissoluble union of faith (the response of the spirit) and works (the response of the body) to grace, the inner life of the Trinity, very God dwelling within us. Just as we are not really complete after the separation of soul from body which occurs at death until we are rejoined with our bodies at the Final Judgement, so faith and works cannot be torn apart. We respond with our whole being to the grace of God, and that response requires a response of both body and soul. Grace requires different kinds of responses depending on individual circumstances. Each writer of Holy Scripture was trying to emphasize the importance of a different aspect of grace working in our lives to an audience which didn't understand that aspect. Neither faith nor work precedes the other, but both act together, reinforcing each other.

Jn 5:33-36 You sent to John, and he has borne witness to the truth. ³⁴ Not that the testimony which I receive is from man; but I say this that you may be saved. ³⁵ He was a burning and shining lamp, and you were willing to rejoice for a while in his light. ³⁶ But the testimony which I have is greater than that of John; for the works which the Father has granted me to accomplish, these very works which I am doing, bear me witness that the Father has sent me.

We are supposed to act in the image of Christ. Christ specifically states that He does not accept human testimony. However, He also specifically states that His works, the works He is currently performing prior to the Passion, Death, and Resurrection, are greater testimony than anything John says. If we image Christ, then our good works are not ours, but God's works through us. Therefore, to deny the usefulness of good works is to deny the testimony of God.

Jn 10:37-38 If I am not doing the works of my Father, then do not believe me; ³⁸ but if I do them, even though you do not believe me, believe the works, that you may know and understand that the Father is in me and I am in the Father."

Mt 6:1-4 1 "Beware of practicing your piety before men in order to be seen by them; for then you will have no reward from your Father who is in heaven.
² "Thus, when you give alms, sound no trumpet before you, as the hypocrites do in the synagogues and in the streets, that they may be praised by men. Truly, I say to you, they have received their reward. ³ But when you give alms, do not let your left hand know what your right hand is doing, ⁴ so that your alms may be in secret; and your Father who sees in secret will reward you.

Mt 7:12 So whatever you wish that men would do to you, do so to them; for this is the law and the prophets.

Mt 7:19-23 Every tree that does not bear good fruit is cut down and thrown into the fire. ²⁰ Thus you will know them by their fruits.
"Not every one who says to me, 'Lord, Lord,' shall enter the kingdom of heaven, but he who does the will of my Father who is in heaven. ²² On that day many will say to me, 'Lord, Lord, did we not prophesy in your name, and cast out demons in your name, and do many mighty works in your name?' ²³ And then will I declare to them, 'I never knew you; depart from me, you evildoers.'

Mt 19:16-21 And behold, one came up to him, saying, "Teacher, what good deed must I do, to have eternal life?" ¹⁷ And he said to him, "Why do you ask me about what is good? One there is who is good. If you would enter life, keep the commandments." ¹⁸ He said to him, "Which?" And Jesus said, "You shall not kill, You shall not commit adultery, You shall not steal, You shall not bear false witness, ¹⁹ Honor your father and mother, and, You shall love your neighbor as yourself." ²⁰ The young man said to him, "All these I have observed; what do I still lack?" ²¹ Jesus said to him, "If you would be perfect, go, sell what you possess and give to the poor, and you will have treasure in heaven; and come, follow me."

Mt 25:31-46 "When the Son of man comes in his glory, and all the angels with him, then he will sit on his glorious throne. ³² Before him will be gathered all the nations, and he will separate them one from another as a shepherd separates the sheep from the goats, ³³ and he will place the sheep at his right hand, but the goats at the left. ³⁴ Then the King will say to those at his right hand, 'Come, O blessed of my Father, inherit the kingdom prepared for you from the foundation of the world; ³⁵ for I was hungry and you gave me food, I was thirsty and you gave me drink, I was a stranger and you welcomed me, ³⁶ I was naked and you clothed me, I was sick and you visited me, I was in prison and you came to me.' ³⁷ Then the righteous will answer him, 'Lord, when did we see thee hungry and feed thee, or thirsty and give thee drink? ³⁸ And when did we see thee a stranger and welcome thee, or naked and clothe thee? ³⁹ And when did we see thee sick or in prison and visit thee?' ⁴⁰ And the King will answer them, 'Truly, I say to you, as you did it to one of the least of these my brethren, you did it to me.' ⁴¹ Then he will say to those at his left hand, 'Depart from me, you cursed, into the eternal fire prepared for the devil and his angels; ⁴² for I was hungry and you gave me no food, I was thirsty and you gave me no drink, ⁴³ I was a stranger and you did not welcome me, naked and you did not clothe me, sick and in prison and you did not visit me.' ⁴⁴ Then they also will answer, 'Lord, when did we see thee hungry or thirsty or a stranger or naked or sick or in prison, and did not minister to thee?' ⁴⁵ Then he will answer them, 'Truly, I say to you, as you did it not to one of the least of these, you did it not to me.' ⁴⁶ And they will go away into eternal punishment, but the righteous into eternal life."

Note that in the passage above, the saved did not even recognize Christ. They simply acted as they knew God wanted them to act, yet still they were saved, while those who knew Christ but did not act were condemned. Participation is necessary for salvation.

Jn 14:15,21 "If you love me, you will keep my commandments... He who has my commandments and keeps them, he it is who loves me; and he who loves me will be loved by my Father, and I will love him and manifest myself to him."

Here, Christ says that it is action, not faith alone, which saves. In fact, Christ does not even refer to faith as a necessary condition here, even though other passages attest to the need for it.

2 Cor 5:10 For we must all appear before the judgment seat of Christ, so that each one may receive good or evil, according to what he has done in the body.

Jn 5:29 and come forth, those who have done good, to the resurrection of life, and those who have done evil, to the resurrection of judgment

Jn 9:3-4 It was not that this man sinned, or his parents, but that the works of God might be made manifest in him. ⁴ We must work the works of him who sent me, while it is day; night comes, when no one can work.

Jesus' work is our work. We work together.

1 Jn 5:1-31 Every one who believes that Jesus is the Christ is a child of God, and every one who loves the parent loves the child. ² By this we know that we love the children of God, when we love God and obey his commandments. ³ For this is the love of God, that we keep his commandments. And his commandments are not burdensome.

Lk 6:35-38 But love your enemies, and do good, and lend, expecting nothing in return; and your reward will be great, and you will be sons of the Most High; for he is kind to the ungrateful and the selfish. ³⁶ Be merciful, even as your Father is merciful.
³⁷ "Judge not, and you will not be judged; condemn not, and you will not be condemned; forgive, and you will be forgiven; ³⁸ give, and it will be given to you; good measure, pressed down, shaken together, running over, will be put into your lap. For the measure you give will be the measure you get back."

Sir 15:15 If you will, you can keep the commandments,
and to act faithfully is a matter of your own choice

Dan 4:27 Therefore, O king, let my counsel be acceptable to you; break off your sins by practicing righteousness, and your iniquities by showing mercy to the oppressed, that there may perhaps be a lengthening of your tranquillity."

Tob 4:7-11 Give alms from your possessions to all who live uprightly, and do not let your eye begrudge the gift when you make it. Do not turn your face away from any poor man, and the face of God will not be turned away from you. ⁸ If you have many possessions, make your gift from them in proportion; if few, do not be afraid to give according to the little you have. ⁹ So you will be laying up a good treasure for yourself against the day of necessity. ¹⁰ For charity delivers from death and keeps you from entering the darkness; ¹¹ and for all who practice it charity is an excellent offering in the presence of the Most High.

Scriptural Catholicism — Salvation

Tob 12:8 Prayer is good when accompanied by fasting, almsgiving, and righteousness. A little with righteousness is better than much with wrongdoing. It is better to give alms than to treasure up gold.

Sir 3:30 Water extinguishes a blazing fire: so almsgiving atones for sin...

1 Cor 3:8 He who plants and he who waters are equal, and each shall receive his wages according to his labor.

Rom 8:17 and if children, then heirs, heirs of God and fellow heirs with Christ, provided we suffer with him in order that we may also be glorified with him.

Rev 20:12 And I saw the dead, great and small, standing before the throne, and books were opened. Also another book was opened, which is the book of life. And the dead were judged by what was written in the books, by what they had done.

Works of the Law

Rom 2:5-10,13 But by your hard and impenitent heart you are storing up wrath for yourself on the day of wrath when God's righteous judgment will be revealed. ⁶ For he will render to every man according to his works: ⁷ to those who by patience in well-doing seek for glory and honor and immortality, he will give eternal life; ⁸ but for those who are factious and do not obey the truth, but obey wickedness, there will be wrath and fury. ⁹ There will be tribulation and distress for every human being who does evil, the Jew first and also the Greek, ¹⁰ but glory and honor and peace for every one who does good, the Jew first and also the Greek... For it is not the hearers of the law who are righteous before God, but the doers of the law who will be justified.

In Romans 2:6 the word for "work" is "ergon," that is, it is same as the word used in Ephesians 2:8. But how can this be? Paul attacks works:

Rom 3:20 For no human being will be justified in his sight by works of the law, since through the law comes knowledge of sin.

Gal 2:16 ...a man is not justified by works of the law but through faith in Jesus Christ, even we have believed in Christ Jesus, in order to be justified by faith in Christ, and not by works of the law, because by works of the law shall no one be justified.

Gal 3:2-10 Let me ask you only this: Did you receive the Spirit by works of the law, or by hearing with faith? ³ Are you so foolish? Having begun with the Spirit, are you now ending with the flesh? ⁴ Did you experience so many things in vain? —if it really is in vain. ⁵ Does he who supplies the Spirit to you and works miracles among you do so by works of the law, or by hearing with faith?
⁶ Thus Abraham "believed God, and it was reckoned to him as righteousness." ⁷ So you see that it is men of faith who are the sons of Abraham. ⁸ And the scripture, foreseeing that God would justify the Gentiles by faith, preached the gospel beforehand to Abraham, saying, "In you shall all the nations be blessed." ⁹ So then, those who are men of faith are blessed with Abraham who had faith.
¹⁰ For all who rely on works of the law are under a curse; for it is written, "Cursed be every one who does not abide by all things written in the book of the law, and do them."

Is not this proof positive that works has no power? It is. But the works Paul speaks of with such derision are not the same works James speaks of with such approval. Paul is combatting a very specific problem - the Judaizers, who insist that the works of circumcision and animal sacrifices must be done in order to be a good Christian.

Acts 13:38-39 Let it be known to you therefore, brethren that through this man forgiveness of sins is proclaimed to you, ³⁹ and by him every one that believes is freed from everything from which you could not be freed by the law of Moses.

We are freed from the "works of the law" of Moses.

Gal 3:16-17 Now the promises were made to Abraham and to his offspring. It does not say, "And to offsprings," referring to many; but, referring to one, "And to your offspring," which is Christ. ¹⁷ This is what I mean: the law, which came four hundred and thirty years afterward, does not annul a covenant previously ratified by God, so as to make the promise void.

Paul's attack on the law is an attack on the law instituted by God and Moses upon the Chosen People, four hundred and thirty years after God made covenant with Abraham. That is why Paul was not schizophrenic when he attacked the law in one chapter of Galatians and said just a few paragraphs later:

Gal 6:2 Bear one another's burdens, and so fulfil the law of Christ.

We are under a law, but it is not the old law.

Rom 3:28-30 For we hold that a man is justified by faith apart from works of law. ²⁹ Or is God the God of Jews only? Is he not the God of Gentiles also? Yes, of Gentiles also, ³⁰ since God is one; and he will justify the circumcised on the ground of their faith and the uncircumcised through their faith.

The Romans passage could be translated "For we consider that a person is justified by faith apart from the Torah" (Surprised By Truth, p. 63). Simply acting righteously is not enough. What is inside has to match what is outside - the work Christ requires has to be performed with a pure heart, pure intentions, and pure love. The Chosen People were saved from temporal death by the external sprinkling of blood on their doors. The Body of Christ is saved from eternal condemnation by having, cooperating with, and shining forth the pure Blood of Christ in their hearts.

2 Cor 3:7-11 Now if the dispensation of death, carved in letters on stone, came with such splendor that the Israelites could not look at Moses' face because of its brightness, fading as this was ⁸ will not the dispensation of the Spirit be attended with greater splendor? ⁹ For if there was splendor in the dispensation of condemnation, the dispensation of righteousness must far exceed it in splendor. ¹⁰ Indeed, in this case, what once had splendor has come to have no splendor at all, because of the splendor that surpasses it. ¹¹ For if what faded away came with splendor, what is permanent must have much more splendor.

Neither the works of circumcision or the Mosaic law justified. If they had, Abraham would have been justified by circumcision. That is not what happened. Abraham responds in faith to God's call in Genesis 12:

Gen 12:1 Now the LORD said to Abram, "Go from your country and your kindred and your father's house to the land that I will show you. ² And I will make of you a great nation, and I will bless you, and make your name great, so that you will be a blessing. ³ I will bless those who bless you, and him who curses you I will curse; and by you all the families of the earth shall bless themselves." So Abram went, as the Lord had told him; and Lot went with him. Abram was seventy-five years old when he departed from Har-an.

Heb 11:8 By faith Abraham obeyed when he was called to go out to a place which he was to receive as an inheritance; and he went out, not knowing where he was to go.

He was seventy-five years old when he makes his faith response to God and commits himself to the Lord...

Gen 15:6 And he believed the LORD; and he reckoned it to him as righteousness.

But it isn't until Genesis 15 that Abraham is made righteous. Yet Abraham travelled in faith through Canaan, down into Egypt to avoid famine, got embroiled with Pharoah, travelled back into the Negeb, and lived through a war, rescuing his cousin Lot, before God finally blessed him with righteousness.

Gen 17:9-11 And God said to Abraham, "As for you, you shall keep my covenant, you and your descendants after you throughout their generations. ¹⁰ This is my covenant, which you shall keep, between me and you and your descendants after you: Every male among you shall be circumcised. ¹¹ You shall be circumcised in the flesh of your foreskins, and it shall be a sign of the covenant between me and you.

Rom 4:9-12 Is this blessing pronounced only upon the circumcised, or also upon the uncircumcised? We say that faith was reckoned to Abraham as righteousness. ¹⁰ How then was it reckoned to him? Was it before or after he had been circumcised? It was not after, but before he was circumcised. ¹¹ He received circumcision as a sign or seal of the righteousness which he had by faith while he was still uncircumcised. The purpose was to make him the father of all who believe without being circumcised and who thus have righteousness reckoned to them, ¹² and likewise the father of the circumcised who are not merely circumcised but also follow the example of the faith which our father Abraham had before he was circumcised.

Abraham was righteous BEFORE circumcision. However, he wasn't righteous simply because he had faith in God. He had a long walk first, in which faith and works responding to grace reinforced and built each other up.

Rom 4:9 We say that faith was reckoned to Abraham as righteousness.

And so it was. But that was not enough.

James 2:21 Was not Abraham our father justified by works, when he offered his son Isaac upon the altar?

Faith was his righteousness, works his justification. Thus...

1 Cor 9:20-21 To the Jews I became as a Jew, in order to win Jews; to those under the law I became as one under the law—though not being myself under the law—that I might win those under the law. [21] To those outside the law I became as one outside the law—not being without law toward God but under the law of Christ—that I might win those outside the law.

Rom 3:21-22 But now the righteousness of God has been manifested apart from law, although the law and the prophets bear witness to it, [22] the righteousness of God through faith in Jesus Christ for all who believe.

Truth does not contradict truth. We are not under the Old Law, we are under the law of Christ. Faith is the beginning of righteousness, but there is much more which must be done in order to achieve justification.

Col 1:24-26 Now I rejoice in my sufferings for your sake, and in my flesh I complete what is lacking in Christ's afflictions for the sake of his body, that is, the church, [25] of which I became a minister according to the divine office which was given to me for you, to make the word of God fully known, [26] the mystery hidden for ages and generations but now made manifest to his saints.

When we suffer in union with Christ, we make up what is lacking in the sufferings of Christ.

Gal 5:4-6 You are severed from Christ, you who would be justified by the law; you have fallen away from grace. [5] For through the Spirit, by faith, we wait for the hope of righteousness. [6] For in Christ Jesus neither circumcision nor uncircumcision is of any avail, but faith working through love.

Galatians 5:6 truly summarizes the position of the Catholic Church.

Mk 2:1-5 And when he returned to Caperna-um after some days, it was reported that he was at home. [2] And many were gathered together, so that there was no longer room for them, not even about the door; and he was preaching the word to them. [3] And they came, bringing to him a paralytic carried by four men. [4] And when they could not get near him because of the crowd, they removed the roof above him; and when they had made an opening, they let down the pallet on which the paralytic lay. [5] And when Jesus saw their faith, he said to the paralytic, "My son, your sins are forgiven."

Mark's account is a beautiful example of the principle. Christ sees the faith and works of the four friends who lowered the paralytic through the roof, and on the basis of their faith and works, He forgives the paralytic's sins. The four friends understand the law of Christ. Faith alone is not enough. Each must...

Gal 6:2 Bear one another's burdens, and so fulfil the law of Christ.

Gal 6:6-10 Let him who is taught the word share all good things with him who teaches. [7] Do not be deceived; God is not mocked, for whatever a man sows, that he will also reap. [8] For he who sows to his own flesh will from the flesh reap corruption; but he who sows to the Spirit will from the Spirit reap eternal life. [9] And let us not grow weary in well-doing, for in due season we shall reap, if we do not lose heart. [10] So then, as we have opportunity, let us do good to all men, and especially to those who are of the household of faith.

Mk 9:41 For truly, I say to you, whoever gives you a cup of water to drink because you bear the name of Christ, will by no means lose his reward.

Phil 2:12-13 Therefore, my beloved, as you have always obeyed, so now, not only as in my presence but much more in my absence, work out your own salvation with fear and trembling; [13] for God is at work in you, both to will and to work for his good pleasure.

James 1:22-27 But be doers of the word, and not hearers only, deceiving yourselves. [23] For if any one is a hearer of the word and not a doer, he is like a man who observes his natural face in a mirror; [24] for he observes himself and goes away and at once forgets what he was like. [25] But he who looks into the perfect law, the law of liberty, and perseveres, being no hearer that forgets but a doer that acts, he shall be blessed in his doing.

²⁶ If any one thinks he is religious, and does not bridle his tongue but deceives his heart, this man's religion is vain. ²⁷ Religion that is pure and undefiled before God and the Father is this: to visit orphans and widows in their affliction, and to keep oneself unstained from the world.

James 2:6-26 But you have dishonored the poor man. Is it not the rich who oppress you, is it not they who drag you into court? ⁷ Is it not they who blaspheme that honorable name which was invoked over you?

⁸ If you really fulfil the royal law, according to the scripture, "You shall love your neighbor as yourself," you do well. ⁹ But if you show partiality, you commit sin, and are convicted by the law as transgressors. ¹⁰ For whoever keeps the whole law but fails in one point has become guilty of all of it. ¹¹ For he who said, "Do not commit adultery," said also, "Do not kill." If you do not commit adultery but do kill, you have become a transgressor of the law. ¹² So speak and so act as those who are to be judged under the law of liberty. ¹³ For judgment is without mercy to one who has shown no mercy; yet mercy triumphs over judgment.

¹⁴ What does it profit, my brethren, if a man says he has faith but has not works? Can his faith save him? ¹⁵ If a brother or sister is ill-clad and in lack of daily food, ¹⁶ and one of you says to them, "Go in peace, be warmed and filled," without giving them the things needed for the body, what does it profit? ¹⁷ So faith by itself, if it has no works, is dead. ¹⁸ But some one will say, "You have faith and I have works." Show me your faith apart from your works, and I by my works will show you my faith. ¹⁹ You believe that God is one; you do well. Even the demons believe—and shudder. ²⁰ Do you want to be shown, you shallow man, that faith apart from works is barren? ²¹ Was not Abraham our father justified by works, when he offered his son Isaac upon the altar? ²² You see that faith was active along with his works, and faith was completed by works, ²³ and the scripture was fulfilled which says, "Abraham believed God, and it was reckoned to him as righteousness"; and he was called the friend of God. ²⁴ You see that a man is justified by works and not by faith alone. ²⁵ And in the same way was not also Rahab the harlot justified by works when she received the messengers and sent them out another way? ²⁶ For as the body apart from the spirit is dead, so faith apart from works is dead.

The only time the word "alone" appears with the word "faith" in the Greek text is in James 2:24 we are "not saved by faith alone." Luther added the word "alone" to the phrase "you are saved by faith" in both Galatians and Romans 3:28 in order to shore up his flawed theology. When he was accused of altering the word of God, he responded: "You tell me what a great fuss the Papists are making because the word 'alone' is not in the text of Paul. If your Papist makes such an unnecessary row about the word 'alone,' say right out to him: 'Dr. Martin Luther will have it so,' and say:'Papists and asses are one and the same thing.' I will have it so, and I order it to be so, and my will is reason enough. I know very well that the word 'alone' is not in the Latin or the Greek text, and it was not necessary for the Papists to teach me that. It is true those letters are not in it, which letters the jackasses look at, as a cow stares at a new gate... It shall remain in my New Testament, and if all the Popish donkeys were to get mad and beside themselves, they will not get it out." (<u>Rebuilding a Lost Faith</u>*, John Stoddard, p. 136-137)*

Note also James' argument in v. 19 - even demons believe that Christ is Lord, believe that He is risen from the dead. They proclaimed Him the Anointed One of God when He threatened to cast them out. Yet their belief and proclamation will not save them. Faith alone does not save.

1 Jn 3:18 Little children, let us not love in word or speech but in deed and in truth.

James 4:17 Whoever knows what is right to do and fails to do it, for him it is sin.

1 Jn 2:3 And by this we may be sure that we know him, if we keep his commandments.

1 Jn 4:17-21 In this is love perfected with us, that we may have confidence for the day of judgment, because as he is so are we in this world. ¹⁸ There is no fear in love, but perfect love casts out fear. For fear has to do with punishment, and he who fears is not perfected in love. ¹⁹ We love, because he first loved us. ²⁰ If any one says, "I love God," and hates his brother, he is a liar; for he who does not love his brother whom he has seen, cannot love God whom he has not seen. ²¹ And this commandment we have from him, that he who loves God should love his brother also..

1 Jn 5:2-4 By this we know that we love the children of God, when we love God and obey his commandments. ³ For this is the love of God, that we keep his commandments. And his commandments are not burdensome. ⁴ For whatever is born of God overcomes the world; and this is the victory that overcomes the world, our faith. ⁵ Who is it that overcomes the world but he who believes that Jesus is the Son of God?

2 Tim 2:11-12 The saying is sure: If we have died with him, we shall also live with him; ¹² if we endure, we shall also reign with him; if we deny him, he also will deny us...

1 Cor 6:20 you were bought with a price. So glorify God in your body.

1 Jn 4:11-12 Beloved, if God so loved us, we also ought to love one another. ¹² No man has ever seen God; if we love one another, God abides in us and his love is perfected in us.

Heb 6:7-10 For land which has drunk the rain that often falls upon it, and brings forth vegetation useful to those for whose sake it is cultivated, receives a blessing from God. ⁸ But if it bears thorns and thistles, it is worthless and near to being cursed; its end is to be burned.
⁹ Though we speak thus, yet in your case, beloved, we feel sure of better things that belong to salvation. ¹⁰ For God is not so unjust as to overlook your work and the love which you showed for his sake in serving the saints, as you still do.

Just as verse 7 above testifies to the fact that our response in works to grace wins us additional grace, so verse 10 demonstrates that our works are part of our love. Faith alone is insufficient.

Jn 2:23-25 Now when he was in Jerusalem at the Passover feast, many believed in his name when they saw the signs which he did; ²⁴ but Jesus did not trust himself to them, ²⁵ because he knew all men and needed no one to bear witness of man; for he himself knew what was in man.

Jn 8:29-31,37-38 And he who sent me is with me; he has not left me alone, for I always do what is pleasing to him." ³⁰ As he spoke thus, many believed in him.
³¹ Jesus then said to the Jews who had believed in him, "If you continue in my word, you are truly my disciples... I know that you are descendants of Abraham; yet you seek to kill me, because my word finds no place in you. ³⁸ I speak of what I have seen with my Father, and you do what you have heard from your father."

These two passages attest to the insufficiency of faith alone, for both groups of Jews believed in Christ, but neither was accepted by Him - one group was even accused of trying to kill Him. Further, the second passage attests strongly to the need for works. They must ACT in addition to believe, they must "continue in His word," anything less is seeking to kill Christ.

Imputed Righteousness

Many Christians will often insist that Christ's righteousness is imputed to each of those who are saved, but is external to them. For the sinners who accept Christ as their personal saviour, Christ's righteousness does not wash away their sins, rather, it covers their sinfulness like snow covers a dunghill. Christ had something to say about being cloaked in righteousness without being truly cleansed.

Rev 19:7-8 Let us rejoice and exult and give him the glory,
for the marriage of the Lamb has come,
and his Bride has made herself ready;
⁸ it was granted her to be clothed with fine linen, bright and pure" - for the fine linen is the righteous deeds of the saints.

It would seem the only cloak wrapped around the Church is that of righteous deeds.

Rev 19:13-14 He is clad in a robe dipped in blood, and the name by which he is called is The Word of God. ¹⁴ And the armies of heaven, arrayed in fine linen, white and pure, followed him on white horses.

Those who are baptized in His blood and wrapped in righteous deeds are part of the armies of heaven.

Mt 23:27-28 "Woe to you, scribes and Pharisees, hypocrites! for you are like whitewashed tombs, which outwardly appear beautiful, but within they are full of dead men's bones and all uncleanness. ²⁸ So you also outwardly appear righteous to men, but within you are full of hypocrisy and iniquity."

Acts 23:2-3 And the high priest Ananias commanded those who stood by him to strike him on the mouth. ³ Then Paul said to him, "God shall strike you, you whitewashed wall! Are you sitting to judge me according to the law, and yet contrary to the law you order me to be struck?"

Ezek 13:10-16 Because, yea, because they have misled my people, saying, 'Peace,' when there is no peace; and because, when the people build a wall, these prophets daub it with whitewash; [11] say to those who daub it with whitewash that it shall fall! There will be a deluge of rain, great hailstones will fall, and a stormy wind break out; [12] and when the wall falls, will it not be said to you, 'Where is the daubing with which you daubed it?' [13] Therefore thus says the Lord GOD: I will make a stormy wind break out in my wrath; and there shall be a deluge of rain in my anger, and great hailstones in wrath to destroy it. [14] And I will break down the wall that you have daubed with whitewash, and bring it down to the ground, so that its foundation will be laid bare; when it falls, you shall perish in the midst of it; and you shall know that I am the LORD. [15] Thus will I spend my wrath upon the wall, and upon those who have daubed it with whitewash; and I will say to you, The wall is no more, nor those who daubed it, [16] the prophets of Israel who prophesied concerning Jerusalem and saw visions of peace for her, when there was no peace, says the Lord GOD.

God has no love for the appearance of righteousness without the underlying reality of righteousness. If He pronounces this curse on such whitewashed walls, why would He allow those who believe in Him to become like this?

Mt 23:25-26 "Woe to you, scribes and Pharisees, hypocrites! for you cleanse the outside of the cup and of the plate, but inside they are full of extortion and rapacity. [26] You blind Pharisee! first cleanse the inside of the cup and of the plate, that the outside also may be clean.

Lk 11:38-41 The Pharisee was astonished to see that he did not first wash before dinner. [39] And the Lord said to him, "Now you Pharisees cleanse the outside of the cup and of the dish, but inside you are full of extortion and wickedness. [40] You fools! Did not he who made the outside make the inside also? [41] But give for alms those things which are within; and behold, everything is clean for you.

Rom 5:19 For as by one man's disobedience many were made sinners, so by one man's obedience many will be made righteous.

The sin of Adam MADE men sinners, the obedience of Christ MADE men righteous. Just as we really have Adam's sin, so we really are cleansed and obtain Christ's righteousness. It is not just a legal statement, it is a reality formed by the Word of God, whose Word forms reality.

Psalm 51:1-2, 7, 9-10 Have mercy on me, O God, ... blot out my transgressions. Wash me thoroughly from my iniquity, and cleanse me from my sin! Purge me with hyssop, and I shall be clean; wash me, and I shall be whiter than snow... Hide thy face from my sins, and blot out all my iniquities. Create in me a clean heart, O God, and put a new and right spirit within me.

Christ certainly gives us legal righteousness, but righteousness doesn't stop just with legalities. God deals in reality. God's Word is effective, His Word forms reality. Therefore, His Word actually removes our sin. He says we are to be holy as He is holy, and He gives us the means to accomplish this: the blood of Jesus Christ.

Rev 22:11 "Let the evildoer still do evil, and the filthy still be filthy, and the righteous still do right and the holy still be holy."

In fact, imputed righteousness assumes the filthy are still really filthy - Scripture clearly describes a place for those who are really still filthy, while it describes a different place for the righteous who DO right and the holy who ARE really holy. We can really be made holy. God says so.

Psalm 103:11-12 For as the heavens are high above the earth,
> so great is his steadfast love toward those who
>> fear him;
[12] as far as the east is from the west,
so far does he remove our transgressions from us.

2 Cor 5:17 Therefore if anyone is in Christ, he is a new creation; the old has passed away, behold, the new has come.

Once Saved, Always Saved

Every person can and must maintain the hope of salvation in Jesus Christ. However, free will is inherent and freedom to act present as a gift from God in every person at every moment. Any person might freely choose to reject God's saving grace through deliberate thought or action against, or deliberate failure to act in accordance with, God's wishes, thereby stripping from themselves the ability to enter into the Beatific Vision. Thus, we cannot presume to know our own salvation anymore than we can know the salvation of any other person; rather, we must work out our salvation by a constant, positive response to grace, in fear and trembling, with our face turned always towards the hope who is Jesus Christ. (CCC 141-184).

Current misunderstandings: Since Christ died once for all, and since Christ's blood is effective, many Christian denominations believe that saying the unScriptural sinner's prayer and accepting Jesus Christ as your personal Lord and Saviour assures salvation. Martin Luther himself taught that one might commit adultery 100 times and still be saved, for God will forgive those who accept His Son, and put Him on as a cloak of righteousness. Some agree with Luther, others argue that the elect can be known by their works, i.e., "By their fruits, ye shall know them," implying that a true disciple of Christ would never commit adultery or other heinous sin. That could be true, but how does one KNOW whether or not s/he will commit heinous sin sometime in the future? If I don't know the future, I can't know I am saved now, for I may give the lie to my "guaranteed" salvation by committing that sin next week which I abhor today.

1 Jn 5:13 I write this to you who believe in the name of the Son of God, that you may know that you have eternal life.

Eph 2:8 For by grace you have been saved...

Salvation is, in a sense, a completed action in the life of all who have been baptized. (cf. Matthew 16:16, Romans 6:3, Galatians 3:27) However...

1 Cor 1:18 For the word of the cross is folly to those who are perishing, but to us who are being saved it is the power of God.

Mt 10:22 But he who endures to the end will be saved

Justification is spoken of in the past, present and future tenses.

1 Cor 4:4-5 I am not aware of anything against myself, but I am not thereby acquitted. It is the Lord who judges me. ⁵ Therefore do not pronounce judgment before the time, before the Lord comes, who will bring to light the things now hidden in darkness and will disclose the purposes of the heart. Then every man will receive his commendation from God.

Paul acknowledges that he himself cannot make a judgment on whether or not he will be saved.

Phil 3:11-12 that if possible I may attain the resurrection from the dead.
¹² Not that I have already obtained this or am already perfect; but I press on to make it my own, because Christ Jesus has made me his own.

Even though Paul is a possession of Christ, still he does not have the resurrection of the dead as a sure prize.

1 Cor 9:25-27 Every athlete exercises self-control in all things. They do it to receive a perishable wreath, but we an imperishable. ²⁶ Well, I do not run aimlessly, I do not box as one beating the air; ²⁷ but I pommel my body and subdue it, lest after preaching to others I myself should be disqualified.

Indeed, he fears losing this prize.

Phil 2:12 Therefore, my beloved, as you have always obeyed, so now, not only as in my presence but much more in my absence, work out your own salvation with fear and trembling...

Are you a better Christian than Paul?

Jn 10:27-29 My sheep hear my voice, and I know them, and they follow me; ²⁸ and I give them eternal life, and they shall never perish, and no one shall snatch them out of my hand. ²⁹ My Father, who has given them to me, is greater than all, and no one is able to snatch them out of the Father's hand.

Ex 32:33 But the LORD said to Moses, "Whoever has sinned against me, him will I blot out of my book."

No external agent, no person on earth, can snatch us out of God's hand, but each of us can choose to abandon Him, each of us can leave, if we so choose. If we choose to leave and reject what He has given us, He will honor our choice.

Lk 15:11-14 And he said, "There was a man who had two sons; [12] and the younger of them said to his father, 'Father, give me the share of property that falls to me.' And he divided his living between them. [13] Not many days later, the younger son gathered all he had and took his journey into a far country, and there he squandered his property in loose living. [14] And when he had spent everything, a great famine arose in that country, and he began to be in want.

If we repent, the Father will welcome us back. But we must respond to the grace He gives us and desire to return. If we do not, He will let us stay where we choose, with the swine...

Acts 8:13,18-24 Even Simon himself believed, and after being baptized he continued with Philip. And seeing signs and great miracles performed, he was amazed.... Now when Simon saw that the Spirit was given through the laying on of the apostles' hands, he offered them money, [19] saying, "Give me also this power, that any one on whom I lay my hands may receive the Holy Spirit." [20] But Peter said to him, "Your silver perish with you, because you thought you could obtain the gift of God with money! [21] You have neither part nor lot in this matter, for your heart is not right before God. [22] Repent therefore of this wickedness of yours, and pray to the Lord that, if possible, the intent of your heart may be forgiven you. [23] For I see that you are in the gall of bitterness and in the bond of iniquity." [24] And Simon answered, "Pray for me to the Lord, that nothing of what you have said may come upon me."

Simon Magus believed, was baptized, travelled with Phillip, but still nearly lost his salvation.

Rom 11:22-23 Note then the kindness and the severity of God: severity toward those who have fallen, but God's kindness to you, provided you continue in his kindness; otherwise you too will be cut off. [23] And even the others, if they do not persist in their unbelief, will be grafted in, for God has the power to graft them in again.

Repentance is always possible, but is not guaranteed. Salvation can be lost if kindness is lost, if belief is lost. And both can be lost.

Col 1:21-23 And you, who once were estranged and hostile in mind, doing evil deeds, [22] he has now reconciled in his body of flesh by his death, in order to present you holy and blameless and irreproachable before him, [23] provided that you continue in the faith, stable and steadfast, not shifting from the hope of the gospel which you heard, which has been preached to every creature under heaven, and of which I, Paul, became a minister.

Why persevere if we are saved no matter what we do?

Heb 6:4-6 For it is impossible to restore again to repentance those who have once been enlightened, who have tasted the heavenly gift, and have become partakers of the Holy Spirit, [5] and have tasted the goodness of the word of God and the powers of the age to come, [6] if they then commit apostasy, since they crucify the Son of God on their own account and hold him up to contempt.

Heb 10:26-29 For if we sin deliberately after receiving the knowledge of the truth, there no longer remains a sacrifice for sins, [27] but a fearful prospect of judgment, and a fury of fire which will consume the adversaries. [28] A man who has violated the law of Moses dies without mercy at the testimony of two or three witnesses. [29] How much worse punishment do you think will be deserved by the man who has spurned the Son of God, and profaned the blood of the covenant by which he was sanctified, and outraged the Spirit of grace?

Both of the above passages indicate not only that we can be lost, but that, once we turn out backs on Christ after having accepted Him, our guilt and punishment is much, much worse. Peter agrees.

2 Pet 2:20-21 For if, after they have escaped the defilements of the world through the knowledge of our Lord and Savior Jesus Christ, they are again entangled in them and overpowered, the last state has become worse for them than the first. [21] For it would have been better for them never to have known the way of righteousness than after knowing it to turn back from the holy commandment delivered to them.

Heb 3:12-14 Take care, brethren, lest there be in any of you an evil, unbelieving heart, leading you to fall away from the living God. ¹³ But exhort one another every day, as long as it is called "today," that none of you may be hardened by the deceitfulness of sin. ¹⁴ For we share in Christ, if only we hold our first confidence firm to the end...

1 Cor 15:1-2 Now I would remind you, brethren, in what terms I preached to you the gospel, which you received, in which you stand, ² by which you are saved, if you hold it fast—unless you believed in vain.

Salvation can be lost. You will only be saved if you hold fast and do not let go.

Mt 5:19-30 Whoever then relaxes one of the least of these commandments and teaches men so, shall be called least in the kingdom of heaven; but he who does them and teaches them shall be called great in the kingdom of heaven. ²⁰ For I tell you, unless your righteousness exceeds that of the scribes and Pharisees, you will never enter the kingdom of heaven.
²¹ "You have heard that it was said to the men of old, 'You shall not kill; and whoever kills shall be liable to judgment.' ²² But I say to you that every one who is angry with his brother shall be liable to judgment; whoever insults his brother shall be liable to the council, and whoever says, 'You fool!' shall be liable to the hell of fire. ²³ So if you are offering your gift at the altar, and there remember that your brother has something against you, ²⁴ leave your gift there before the altar and go; first be reconciled to your brother, and then come and offer your gift. ²⁵ Make friends quickly with your accuser, while you are going with him to court, lest your accuser hand you over to the judge, and the judge to the guard, and you be put in prison; ²⁶ truly, I say to you, you will never get out till you have paid the last penny.
²⁷ "You have heard that it was said, 'You shall not commit adultery.' ²⁸ But I say to you that every one who looks at a woman lustfully has already committed adultery with her in his heart. ²⁹ If your right eye causes you to sin, pluck it out and throw it away; it is better that you lose one of your members than that your whole body be thrown into hell. ³⁰ And if your right hand causes you to sin, cut it off and throw it away; it is better that you lose one of your members than that your whole body go into hell.

Gal 5:19-21 Now the works of the flesh are plain: fornication, impurity, licentiousness, ²⁰ idolatry, sorcery, enmity, strife, jealousy, anger, selfishness, dissension, party spirit, ²¹ envy, drunkenness, carousing, and the like. I warn you, as I warned you before, that those who do such things shall not inherit the kingdom of God.

Eph 5:5-7 Be sure of this, that no fornicator or impure man, or one who is covetous (that is, an idolater), has any inheritance in the kingdom of Christ and of God. ⁶ Let no one deceive you with empty words, for it is because of these things that the wrath of God comes upon the sons of disobedience. ⁷ Therefore do not associate with them...

1 Cor 6:9-10 Do you not know that the unrighteous will not inherit the kingdom of God? Do not be deceived; neither the immoral, nor idolaters, nor adulterers, nor sexual perverts, ¹⁰ nor thieves, nor the greedy, nor drunkards, nor revilers, nor robbers will inherit the kingdom of God. ¹¹ And such were some of you. But you were washed, you were sanctified, you were justified in the name of the Lord Jesus Christ and in the Spirit of our God.

Notice that Paul does not except those who have already "accepted Jesus Christ as their personal Lord and Saviour." Anyone, believer or not, who does the things he lists will not inherit the kingdom. Period.

Sir 5:1-7 Do not set your heart on your wealth, nor say, "I have enough." ² Do not follow your inclination and strength,
walking according to the desires of your heart. ³ Do not say, "Who will have power over me?"
for the Lord will surely punish you. ⁴ Do not say, "I sinned, and what happened to me?"
for the Lord is slow to anger. ⁵ Do not be so confident of atonement
that you add sin to sin. ⁶ Do not say, "His mercy is great,
he will forgive the multitude of my sins,"
for both mercy and wrath are with him,
and his anger rests on sinners. ⁷ Do not delay to turn to the Lord,
nor postpone it from day to day;
for suddenly the wrath of the Lord will go forth,
and at the time of punishment you will perish.

Perserverance is emphasized and re-emphasized as very important - but how could perserverance be important if praying the sinner's prayer is enough to assure ourselves of salvation?

1 Tim 2:3-4 This is good, and it is acceptable in the sight of God our Savior, ⁴ who desires all men to be saved and to come to the knowledge of the truth.

God wants us in heaven, but we have free will. We can choose hell.

1 Tim 4:16 Take heed to yourself and to your teaching; hold to that, for by so doing you will save both yourself and your hearers.

2 Tim 2:11-13 The saying is sure:
If we have died with him, we shall also live with him;
¹² if we endure, we shall also reign with him;
if we deny him, he also will deny us; ¹³ if we are faithless, he remains faithful— for he cannot deny himself.

James 1:12 Blessed is the man who endures trial, for when he has stood the test he will receive the crown of life which God has promised to those who love him.

Mt 10:22 and you will be hated by all for my name's sake. But he who endures to the end will be saved.

Jn 15:6 If a man does not abide in me, he is cast forth as a branch and withers; and the branches are gathered, thrown into the fire and burned.

Rev 2:10-11 Do not fear what you are about to suffer. Behold, the devil is about to throw some of you into prison, that you may be tested, and for ten days you will have tribulation. Be faithful unto death, and I will give you the crown of life. ¹¹ He who has an ear, let him hear what the Spirit says to the churches. He who conquers shall not be hurt by the second death.'

Rev 3:5 He who conquers shall be clad thus in white garments, and I will not blot his name out of the book of life; I will confess his name before my Father and before his angels.

Revelation shows that Christ will not erase some names, but implies that He will erase others.

Mt 10:33 but whoever denies me before men, I also will deny before my Father who is in heaven.

Lk 12:9 but he who denies me before men will be denied before the angels of God

Mk 13:13 and you will be hated by all for my name's sake. But he who endures to the end will be saved.

Mt 24:13 But he who endures to the end will be saved.

Mortal and Venial Sin

There is sin which destroys our life in Christ. This sin is called mortal sin, for by it we are cut off from the source of grace, and are dead to Christ, having rejected His salvific grace in us. We are only brought back to life in Christ, and brought back in the ability to share in the sacramental life of grace, through the sacrament of Confession, in which Christ revives the life of grace within us through a gift of grace, cleansing our soul of sin. There is also sin which does not destroy our life in Christ, but wounds it, and leads to a partial separation from His Body. This sin is called venial sin. We can continue to partake of the life of Christ poured out in the sacraments when we are in this state, but are urged to avail ourselves of the cleansing grace of Confession at our earliest opportunity. (CCC 1852-1864)

Current misunderstandings: Many Christians claim that all sins are equally heinous before God - stealing a penny is as bad as slaughtering an entire household.

Num 15:30 But the person who does anything with a high hand, whether he is native or a sojourner, reviles the LORD, and that person shall be cut off from among his people.

Lev 18:26-30 But you shall keep my statutes and my ordinances and do none of these abominations, either the native or the stranger who sojourns among you [27] (for all of these abominations the men of the land did, who were before you, so that the land became defiled); [28] lest the land vomit you out, when you defile it, as it vomited out the nation that was before you. [29] For whoever shall do any of these abominations, the persons that do them shall be cut off from among their people. [30] So keep my charge never to practice any of these abominable customs which were practiced before you, and never to defile yourselves by them: I am the LORD your God."

Lev 20:1-7 The LORD said to Moses, [2] "Say to the people of Israel, Any man of the people of Israel, or of the strangers that sojourn in Israel, who gives any of his children to Molech shall be put to death; the people of the land shall stone him with stones. [3] I myself will set my face against that man, and will cut him off from among his people, because he has given one of his children to Molech, defiling my sanctuary and profaning my holy name. [4] And if the people of the land do at all hide their eyes from that man, when he gives one of his children to Molech, and do not put him to death, [5] then I will set my face against that man and against his family, and will cut them off from among their people, him and all who follow him in playing the harlot after Molech.
[6] "If a person turns to mediums and wizards, playing the harlot after them, I will set my face against that person, and will cut him off from among his people. [7] Consecrate yourselves therefore, and be holy; for I am the LORD your God.

Ex 21:17 "Whoever curses his father or his mother shall be put to death."

Sins are said to be mortal when they kill the life of grace within your soul. In the Old Testament, "these things happened to them as a warning" (1 Cor 10:11).

Sir 3:30 Water extinguishes a blazing fire:
so almsgiving atones for sin...

Many of the sins done against the Lord can be expiated through sacrifice and almsgiving, as Numbers 15, the first several chapters of Leviticus, and Sirach demonstrate.

Mt 5:17 "Think not that I have come to abolish the law and the prophets; I have come not to abolish them but to fulfil them.

Mortal sin and venial sin existed in the Old Covenant. It also exists in the New Covenant.

Acts 5:1-4 But a man named Ananias with his wife Sapphira sold a piece of property, [2] and with his wife's knowledge he kept back some of the proceeds, and brought only a part and laid it at the apostles' feet. [3] But Peter said, "Ananias, why has Satan filled your heart to lie to the Holy Spirit and to keep back part of the proceeds of the land? [4] While it remained unsold, did it not remain your own? And after it was sold, was it not at your disposal? How is it that you have contrived this deed in your heart? You have not lied to men but to God."[5] When Ananias heard these words, he fell down and died. And great fear came upon all who heard of it.

Ananias and Sapphira paid the ultimate penalty upon Peter's authority. Their lie to the Apostles was judged by Peter to be a lie against God, literally a mortal sin.

1 Jn 5:16-17 If any one sees his brother committing what is not a mortal sin, he will ask, and God will give him life for those whose sin is not mortal. There is sin which is mortal; I do not say that one is to pray for that. ¹⁷ All wrongdoing is sin, but there is sin which is not mortal.

1 John 5:16 is often the easiest way to make a sola scriptura *enthusiast sit up and take notice. For some reason, even people who have read Scripture cover to cover twelve times simply don't remember seeing this verse until it is pointed out to them.*

Mt 5:28 But I say to you that every one who looks at a woman lustfully has already committed adultery with her in his heart.

Mt 6:23 but if your eye is not sound, your whole body will be full of darkness. If then the light in you is darkness, how great is the darkness!

Mt 12:31 Therefore I tell you, every sin and blasphemy will be forgiven men, but the blasphemy against the Spirit will not be forgiven. ³² And whoever says a word against the Son of man will be forgiven; but whoever speaks against the Holy Spirit will not be forgiven, either in this age or in the age to come.

Mk 3:28-30 Truly, I say to you, all sins will be forgiven the sons of men, and whatever blasphemies they utter; ²⁹ but whoever blasphemes against the Holy Spirit never has forgiveness, but is guilty of an eternal sin"— ³⁰ for they had said, "He has an unclean spirit."

The sin of refusing to ask for forgiveness is a sin against the Holy Spirit - God can forgive anyone for any sin, but He does not forgive those who do not ask forgiveness (CCC 1864).

Mt 15:19 For out of the heart come evil thoughts, murder, adultery, fornication, theft, false witness, slander.

James 4:1-4 What causes wars, and what causes fightings among you? Is it not your passions that are at war in your members? ² You desire and do not have; so you kill. And you covet and cannot obtain; so you fight and wage war. You do not have, because you do not ask. ³ You ask and do not receive, because you ask wrongly, to spend it on your passions. ⁴ Unfaithful creatures! Do you not know that friendship with the world is enmity with God? Therefore whoever wishes to be a friend of the world makes himself an enemy of God.

Rom 1:29-31, They were filled with all manner of wickedness, evil, covetousness, malice. Full of envy, murder, strife, deceit, malignity, they are gossips, ³⁰ slanderers, haters of God, insolent, haughty, boastful, inventors of evil, disobedient to parents, ³¹ foolish, faithless, heartless, ruthless. ³² Though they know God's decree that those who do such things deserve to die, they not only do them but approve those who practice them.

Rom 13:13-14 let us conduct ourselves becomingly as in the day, not in reveling and drunkenness, not in debauchery and licentiousness, not in quarreling and jealousy. ¹⁴ But put on the Lord Jesus Christ, and make no provision for the flesh, to gratify its desires.

Mk 10:19 You know the commandments: 'Do not kill, Do not commit adultery, Do not steal, Do not bear false witness, Do not defraud, Honor your father and mother.'"

Lk 18:20 You know the commandments: 'Do not commit adultery, Do not kill, Do not steal, Do not bear false witness, Honor your father and mother.'"

A violation of the Ten Commandments is serious sin.

2 Cor 5:10 For we must all appear before the judgment seat of Christ, so that each one may receive good or evil, according to what he has done in the body.

Gal 5:19-21 Now the works of the flesh are plain: fornication, impurity, licentiousness, ²⁰ idolatry, sorcery, enmity, strife, jealousy, anger, selfishness, dissension, party spirit,

Eph 5:5 Be sure of this, that no fornicator or impure man, or one who is covetous (that is, an idolater), has any inheritance in the kingdom of Christ and of God.

1 Cor 6:9-10 Do you not know that the unrighteous will not inherit the kingdom of God? Do not be deceived; neither the immoral, nor idolaters, nor adulterers, nor sexual perverts, ¹⁰ nor thieves, nor the greedy, nor drunkards, nor revilers, nor robbers will inherit the kingdom of God.

There are sins which can lose us our salvation. Paul tells us which sins those are. They are mortal sin. Not all sins are mortal, nor are all sins venial, else Paul would not bother to distinguish them.

Rev 21:8 But as for the cowardly, the faithless, the polluted, as for murderers, fornicators, sorcerers, idolaters, and all liars, their lot shall be in the lake that burns with fire and sulphur, which is the second death."

Rev 21:27 But nothing unclean shall enter it, nor any one who practices abomination or falsehood, but only those who are written in the Lamb's book of life.

Abomination and falsehood prevent entry to heaven.

Rev 22:14-15 Blessed are those who wash their robes, that they may have the right to the tree of life and that they may enter the city by the gates. [15] Outside are the dogs and sorcerers and fornicators and murderers and idolaters, and every one who loves and practices falsehood.

<u>Early Christians' comments on Mortal Sin</u>

Redemptive Suffering

Several Scripture passages in the sections Redemptive Suffering *and* Temporal Consequences of Sin *came from* Scripture by Topic. *The exegesis is my own.*

We image Christ through suffering; our individual suffering can and should be offered up to God not only for our salvation, but for the salvation of others and for the whole world. This offering of our suffering may be done at any time, but is best done in the holy sacrifice of the Mass, in which we unite our suffering with that of Christ on the cross, and thereby become images of Christ, living as part of the Body of Christ, which suffering alone redeemed the whole world. (CCC 307, 618, 793, 1004, 1368, 1506-1508, 1521, 2846-2848)

Current misunderstandings: Almost none of our separated brethren understand the role of suffering in the world. They see it as something to be undergone in obedient silence, but they do not understand that bearing pain is meritorious not only for self, but for others.

Col 1:24 Now I rejoice in my sufferings for your sake, and in my flesh I complete what is lacking in Christ's afflictions for the sake of his body, that is, the church...

Paul states something here which passes almost unnoticed by many sola scriptura *Christians - that there is a sense in which Christ's afflictions are lacking. While Christ's Passion superabundantly completed the salvation of all mankind, yet mankind must formally co-operate with the grace poured out on the Cross. Paul indicates this can be accomplished not through the sinner's prayer, but through suffering.*

1 Cor 3:9 For we are God's fellow workers...

Eph 3:2 assuming that you have heard of the stewardship of God's grace that was given to me for you...

Paul was a steward of God's grace. Stewards dispense that over which they have stewardship. Thus, Paul was a co-redeemer and co-mediator of grace with Christ by his own admission - a true co-worker.

Jn 9:3-4 It was not that this man sinned, or his parents, but that the works of God might be made manifest in him. ⁴ We must work the works of him who sent me, while it is day; night comes, when no one can work.

We must work the works of God, who sent Jesus. Jesus sees us as His co-workers, His partners. Whatever work God does in the created world, we are supposed to be doing as well. Without God, we could do none of it. With Him, we can do all of it. He doesn't need our help, He chooses that we help Him.

Rom 8:17 and if children, then heirs, heirs of God and fellow heirs with Christ, provided we suffer with him in order that we may also be glorified with him.

We must suffer with Him - He suffered for all of us, so we must suffer with Him for all. If we do not, we will not be glorified with Him.

Phil 2:13 Even if I am to be poured as a libation upon the sacrificial offering of your faith, I am glad and rejoice with you all.

Eph 3:7-8, 10-11, 13 Of this gospel I was made a minister according to the gift of God's grace which was given me by the working of his power. ⁸ To me, though I am the very least of all the saints, this grace was given, to preach to the Gentiles the unsearchable riches of Christ... that through the church the manifold wisdom of God might now be made known to the principalities and powers in the heavenly places. ¹¹ This was according to the eternal purpose which he has realized in Christ Jesus our Lord, ... So I ask you not to lose heart over what I am suffering for you, which is your glory.

Paul's suffering is for the glory of the eternal purpose of Christ, our glory.

2 Thess 1:4-5 Therefore we ourselves boast of you in the churches of God for your steadfastness and faith in all your persecutions and in the afflictions which you are enduring. ⁵ This is evidence of the righteous judgment of God, that you may be made worthy of the kingdom of God, for which you are suffering...

Like Paul, we also suffer for all the kingdom of God, in imitation of Christ...

1 Thess 1:6-7 And you became imitators of us and of the Lord, for you received the word in much affliction, with joy inspired by the Holy Spirit; ⁷ so that you became an example to all the believers in Macedonia and in Achaia.

1 Pet 4:1-2 Since therefore Christ suffered in the flesh, arm yourselves with the same thought, for whoever has suffered in the flesh has ceased from sin, ² so as to live for the rest of the time in the flesh no longer by human passions but by the will of God.

Heb 3:14 For we share in Christ, if only we hold our first confidence firm to the end...

1 Thess 2:13-14 And we also thank God constantly for this, that when you received the word of God which you heard from us, you accepted it not as the word of men but as what it really is, the word of God which is at work in you believers. ¹⁴ For you, brethren, became imitators of the churches of God in Christ Jesus which are in Judea; for you suffered the same things from your own countrymen as they did from the Jews...

In fact, our redemptive suffering proves that we have really received the word of God.

Phil 1:7, 12-14,23-24,29-30 It is right for me to feel thus about you all, because I hold you in my heart, for you are all partakers with me of grace, both in my imprisonment and in the defense and confirmation of the gospel.... I want you to know, brethren, that what has happened to me has really served to advance the gospel, ¹³ so that it has become known throughout the whole praetorian guard and to all the rest that my imprisonment is for Christ; ¹⁴ and most of the brethren have been made confident in the Lord because of my imprisonment, and are much more bold to speak the word of God without fear.... I am hard pressed between the two. My desire is to depart and be with Christ, for that is far better. ²⁴ But to remain in the flesh is more necessary on your account.... For it has been granted to you that for the sake of Christ you should not only believe in him but also suffer for his sake,³⁰ engaged in the same conflict which you saw and now hear to be mine.

Furthermore, Paul's suffering, our suffering, is shared by all who are in the Church, and can be applied not just to his personal redemption, but to the <u>whole Church</u>. He (and we) join(s) his suffering to the Cross, and so completes the sacrifice by helping Christ distribute the graces Christ alone won for us.

Phil 3:10-11 that I may know him and the power of his resurrection, and may share his sufferings, becoming like him in his death, ¹¹ that if possible I may attain the resurrection from the dead.

Jesus' work is the salvation of every human being who ever lived, so our work is also the salvation of every human being that every lived. That is why all of our suffering must be offered up to God, in union with the sacrifice of the cross, so that we become the partners and co-workers that God intends us to be.

1 Jn 3:16 By this we know love, that he laid down his life for us; and we ought to lay down our lives for the brethren.

Lk 23:28 But Jesus turning to them said, "Daughters of Jerusalem, do not weep for me, but weep for yourselves and for your children."

Gal 6:2 Bear one another's burdens, and so fulfil the law of Christ.

Mt 27:32 As they went out, they came upon a man of Cyrene, Simon by name; this man they compelled to carry his cross.

Mk 15:21 And they compelled a passer-by, Simon of Cyrene, who was coming in from the country, the father of Alexander and Rufus, to carry his cross.

Lk 23:26 And as they led him away, they seized one Simon of Cyrene, who was coming in from the country, and laid on him the cross, to carry it behind Jesus.

Lk 9:23 And he said to all, "If any man would come after me, let him deny himself and take up his cross daily and follow me."

Mt 10:38 and he who does not take his cross and follow me is not worthy of me.

1 Pet 2:19,21 For one is approved if, mindful of God, he endures pain while suffering unjustly... For to this you have been called, because Christ also suffered for you, leaving you an example, that you should follow in his steps

Jesus uses Simon of Cyrene to teach us how to act. We are to participate in His Passion.

Phil 2:17, 25, 30 Even if I am to be poured as a libation upon the sacrificial offering of your faith, I am glad and rejoice with you all.... I have thought it necessary to send to you Epaphroditus my brother and fellow worker and fellow soldier, and your messenger and minister to my need... for he nearly died for the work of Christ, risking his life to complete your service to me.

Heb 11:40 And all these, though well attested by their faith, did not receive what was promised, ⁴⁰ since God had foreseen something better for us, that apart from us they should not be made perfect.

Our suffering and work in Christ Jesus brought even the Old Testament heroes to perfection.

2 Cor 1:6,11 If we are afflicted, it is for your comfort and salvation; and if we are comforted, it is for your comfort, which you experience when you patiently endure the same sufferings that we suffer....You also must help us by prayer, so that many will give thanks on our behalf for the blessing granted us in answer to many prayers.

2 Tim 1:8 Do not be ashamed then of testifying to our Lord, nor of me his prisoner, but share in suffering for the gospel in the power of God...

2 Tim 2:3 Share in suffering as a good soldier of Christ Jesus.

2 Tim 4:5 As for you, always be steady, endure suffering, do the work of an evangelist, fulfil your ministry.

Suffering is part of the ministry of the evangelist.

1 Pet 5:9 Resist him, firm in your faith, knowing that the same experience of suffering is required of your brotherhood throughout the world.

2 Cor 2:5 But if any one has caused pain, he has caused it not to me, but in some measure—not to put it too severely—to you all.

1 Cor 12:24 If one member suffers, all suffer together; if one member is honored, all rejoice together.

Gal 6:14 But far be it from me to glory except in the cross of our Lord Jesus Christ, by which the world has been crucified to me, and I to the world.

1 Pet 4:16 yet if one suffers as a Christian, let him not be ashamed, but under that name let him glorify God.

Lk 14:27 Whoever does not bear his own cross and come after me, cannot be my disciple.

It is in our suffering that we take on the priestly role proper to every follower of Christ. We offer up our own sacrifice of ourselves, to cleanse not only our own souls, but the souls of others, to save not just ourselves, but every man from the fires of hell. We are a royal nation of priests. This is NOT an empty title. The role of every priest is to offer sacrifice to God for the expiation of sin and in glory of His name. As cells in the Body of Christ, members of His Body, we are under obligation to carry out our duties. All the Persons of the Trinity participated in accomplishing our salvation. All the persons of the Body participate in accomplishing each person's salvation.

Temporal Consequences of Sin

Christ's Passion, Death and Resurrection atones for the guilt of our sin, our co-operation with Satan, but the consequences of that cooperation, the consequences which bring evil into the world, can only be removed through our positive, active response to and cooperation with the grace of forgiveness brought to us through the Cross. God forgives us, but requires us to mortify ourselves in imitation of His Son in acknowledgement. Through our self-mortification the consequences of sin are removed (CCC 1865-1869).

Current misunderstandings: Many Christians deny sin's dual effect. They insist that Christ's death not only removes our guilt, but also removes the temporal consequences of sin, consequences which flow through creation, bringing evil.

2 Sam 12:13 David said to Nathan, "I have sinned against the Lord." And Nathan said to David, "The Lord also has put away your sin; you shall not die.

2 Sam 24:10-13 But David's heart smote him after he had numbered the people. And David said to the Lord, "I have sinned greatly in what I have done. But now, O Lord, I pray thee, take away the iniquity of thy servant; for I have done very foolishly." [11] And when David arose in the morning, the word of the Lord came to the prophet Gad, David's seer, saying, [12] "Go and say to David, 'Thus says the Lord, Three things I offer you; choose one of them, that I may do it to you." [13] So Gad came to David and told him, and said to him, "Shall three years of famine come to you in your land? Or will you flee three months before your foes while they pursue you? Or shall there be three days' pestilence in your land? Now consider, and decide what answer I shall return to him who sent me."...

David sinned by taking a census of the people when the Lord did not command him to do so. A census is only useful for two things: counting the people for war or for levying taxes. David intended to inflict one or both on the people, but repented of it. The Lord forgives his sin, but requires restitution. After the plague sweeps the land, David repents even more greatly, and acts to stop the temporal consequence of the king's sin, which is calamity among his people.

2 Sam 24:22-25 Then Araunah said to David, "Let my lord the king take and offer up what seems good to him; here are the oxen for the burnt offering, and the threshing sledges and the yokes of the oxen for the wood. ²³ All this, O king, Araunah gives to the king." And Araunah said to the king, "The LORD your God accept you." ²⁴ But the king said to Araunah, "No, but I will buy it of you for a price; I will not offer burnt offerings to the LORD my God which cost me nothing." So David bought the threshing floor and the oxen for fifty shekels of silver. ²⁵ And David built there an altar to the LORD, and offered burnt offerings and peace offerings. So the LORD heeded supplications for the land, and the plague was averted from Israel.

Deut 32:51-52 because you broke faith with me in the midst of the people of Israel at the waters of Meri-bath-kadesh, in the wilderness of Zin; because you did not revere me as holy in the midst of the people of Israel. ⁵² For you shall see the land before you; but you shall not go there, into the land which I give to the people of Israel."

1 Cor 5:3-5 For though absent in body I am present in spirit, and as if present, I have already pronounced judgment ⁴ in the name of the Lord Jesus on the man who has done such a thing. When you are assembled, and my spirit is present, with the power of our Lord Jesus, ⁵ you are to deliver this man to Satan for the destruction of the flesh, that his spirit may be saved in the day of the Lord Jesus.

Dan 4:27 Therefore, O king, let my counsel be acceptable to you; break off your sins by practicing righteousness, and your iniquities by showing mercy to the oppressed, that there may perhaps be a lengthening of your tranquillity."

We atone for our evil through our own fasting, prayer, alms-giving and suffering.

Purgatory

The smallest drop of Christ's blood is sufficient to obtain salvation for all the sins of all the people who ever have, do, or will live. However, sin entails for us a double consequence - not only does it deprive us from communion with God, but it also exhibits an unhealthy attachment to created things (this is called the "temporal punishment" of sin). Christ forgives our sins and, through His blood, restores our communion with God, but we must still be purified of our attachment to creatures. This purification can only be accomplished through a purging, either in this world or the next, from such attachments. This purging can be accomplished in this world, through a spirit of fervent charity, or in the next, through bathing in God's consuming fire of love. (CCC 1030-1032).

Current misunderstandings: Sola fide *theology implies no one is really ever cleansed of sin, rather, every person puts on the cloak of Christ's righteousness, and thus enters heaven. Since Christ's blood does not cleanse us, but merely covers us, it follows that no one need suffer or be purged from sin, since Christ simply covers all our sin by the work of the Cross.*

Ex 3:6 And he said, "I am the God of your father, the God of Abraham, the God of Isaac, and the God of Jacob." And Moses hid his face, for he was afraid to look at God.

Ex 33:11 Thus the LORD used to speak to Moses face to face, as a man speaks to his friend.

Ex 34:33-35 And when Moses had finished speaking with them, he put a veil on his face; ³⁴ but whenever Moses went in before the LORD to speak with him, he took the veil off, until he came out; and when he came out, and told the people of Israel what he was commanded, ³⁵ the people of Israel saw the face of Moses, that the skin of Moses' face shone; and Moses would put the veil upon his face again, until he went in to speak with him.

Moses did not begin by talking to God face-to-face. God made Himself present through the angel in the burning bush because Moses was not yet ready to see God face to face. Through his trials, Moses grew in closeness to God until he had to veil himself when he emerged from the Tent of Meeting because the rest of Israel couldn't stand to look at him. Purgation, on earth or after death, prepares us to meet God.

Heb 9:27 And just as it is appointed for men to die once, and after that comes judgment...

Mt 12:32 And whoever says a word against the Son of man will be forgiven; but whoever speaks against the Holy Spirit will not be forgiven, either in this age or in the age to come.

Not forgiven in this age or the age to come - what could be forgiven in heaven? or hell? Yet Jesus implies some sort of post-death forgiveness can occur for some sins, because He takes care to point out it won't happen for the sin of speaking against the Holy Spirit.

Rev 21:27 But nothing unclean shall enter it, nor any one who practices abomination or falsehood, but only those who are written in the Lamb's book of life.

Perfection is needed in order to enter heaven.

Phil 3:11-12 That if possible I may attain the resurrection from the dead. [12] Not that I have already obtained this or am already perfect; but I press on to make it my own, because Christ Jesus has made me his own.

1 Cor 4:4 I am not aware of anything against myself, but I am not thereby acquitted. It is the Lord who judges me.

Even Saint Paul had not attained perfection.

Mt 5:25-26 Make friends quickly with your accuser, while you are going with him to court, lest your accuser hand you over to the judge, and the judge to the guard, and you be put in prison; [26] truly, I say to you, you will never get out till you have paid the last penny.

Lk 12:58-59 As you go with your accuser before the magistrate, make an effort to settle with him on the way, lest he drag you to the judge, and the judge hand you over to the officer, and the officer put you in prison. [59] I tell you, you will never get out till you have paid the very last copper."

Mt 18:23-35 "Therefore the kingdom of heaven may be compared to a king who wished to settle accounts with his servants. [24] When he began the reckoning, one was brought to him who owed him ten thousand talents; [25] and as he could not pay, his lord ordered him to be sold, with his wife and children and all that he had, and payment to be made. [26] So the servant fell on his knees, imploring him, 'Lord, have patience with me, and I will pay you everything.' [27] And out of pity for him the lord of that servant released him and forgave him the debt. [28] But that same servant, as he went out, came upon one of his fellow servants who owed him a hundred denarii; and seizing him by the throat he said, 'Pay what you owe.' [29] So his fellow servant fell down and besought him, 'Have patience with me, and I will pay you.' [30] He refused and went and put him in prison till he should pay the debt. [31] When his fellow servants saw what had taken place, they were greatly distressed, and they went and reported to their lord all that had taken place. [32] Then his lord summoned him and said to him, 'You wicked servant! I forgave you all that debt because you besought me; [33] and should not you have had mercy on your fellow servant, as I had mercy on you?' [34] And in anger his lord delivered him to the jailers, till he should pay all his debt. [35] So also my heavenly Father will do to every one of you, if you do not forgive your brother from your heart."

Jesus warns us of a prison, a place where we will not be released until we have paid for all of our failures to follow the law of love. Note that a man in debtors' prison could enlist the help of friends and family out in the world to help him pay off his debt.

Lk 16:19-31 "There was a rich man, who was clothed in purple and fine linen and who feasted sumptuously every day. [20] And at his gate lay a poor man named Lazarus, full of sores, [21] who desired to be fed with what fell from the rich man's table; moreover the dogs came and licked his sores. [22] The poor man died and was carried by the angels to Abraham's bosom. The rich man also died and was buried; [23] and in Hades, being in torment, he lifted up his eyes, and saw Abraham far off and Lazarus in his bosom. [24] And he called out, 'Father Abraham, have mercy upon me, and send Lazarus to dip the end of his finger in water and cool my tongue; for I am in anguish in this flame.' [25] But Abraham said, 'Son, remember that you in your lifetime received your good things, and Lazarus in like manner evil things; but now he is comforted here, and you are in anguish. [26] And besides all this, between us and you a great chasm has been fixed, in order that those who would pass from here to you may not be able, and none may cross from there to us.' [27] And he said, 'Then I beg you, father, to send him to my father's house, [28] for I have five brothers, so that he may warn them, lest they also come into this place of torment.' [29] But Abraham said, 'They have Moses and the prophets; let them hear them.' ³⁰ And he said, 'No, father Abraham; but if some one goes to them from the dead, they will repent.' ³¹ He said to him, 'If they do not hear Moses and the prophets, neither will they be convinced if some one should rise from the dead.'"

God is love. Hell is being completely cut off from God. Hell is being completely cut off from love. In Hell, one can feel no love for anyone, not even one's self - it is total exclusion from love, from God. The rich man is clearly not in heaven, but he just as clearly feels compassion for his brothers and is concerned about their well-being, so he is clearly not in hell. Where is he? Incidentally, this is the only parable in which Christ gives one of the persons in the story a name - Lazarus. Many Christian commentators think this is not a parable, but a description of an historical event known to Christ.

Is 6:6-7 Then flew one of the seraphim to me, having in his hand a burning coal which he had taken with tongs from the altar. ⁷ And he touched my mouth, and said: "Behold, this has touched your lips; your guilt is taken away, and your sin forgiven."

The word "seraphim" means "the burning ones" and these are traditionally said to be the angels closest to God. God's presence is often described as fire (the burning bush, tongues of fire, pillar of fire, etc.). Think on what this means. Heaven is the burning fire of God's love. Hell is a burning fire. Purgatory is also a fire which burns away that which is unclean. The presence of God pervades the universe - how we respond to God's love determines where we will end. Total acceptance means we are ravished by it, total rejection means we are forever burned by it, limited, hesitant acceptance means we must be burnished by it, to burn off that which does not accept and leave only that which does. Isaiah's lips are cleansed by the holy fire, but not without pain, suffering, purgation.

Psalm 139:7-12 Whither shall I go from thy Spirit?
　Or whither shall I flee from thy presence?
　⁸ If I ascend to heaven, thou art there!
　If I make my bed in Sheol, thou art there!
　⁹ If I take the wings of the morning
　　and dwell in the uttermost parts of the sea,
　¹⁰ even there thy hand shall lead me,
　　and thy right hand shall hold me.
　¹¹ If I say, "Let only darkness cover me,
　　and the light about me be night,"
　¹² even the darkness is not dark to thee,
　the night is bright as the day;
for darkness is as light with thee.

Heb 12:29 For our God is a consuming fire.

1 Jn 4:8 ...God is love.

Since we are part of the Body of Christ, we can pray for those being purified in Christ.

1 Cor 12:26 If one member suffers, all suffer together; if one member is honored, all rejoice together.

Sir 7:32-33 Stretch forth your hand to the poor, so that your blessing may be complete. ³³ Give graciously to all the living, and withhold not kindness from the dead.

Gal 6:2 Bear one another's burdens, and so fulfil the law of Christ.

1 Tim 2:1 First of all, then, I urge that supplications, prayers, intercessions, and thanksgivings be made for all men...

Job 1:5 And when the days of the feast had run their course, Job would send and sanctify them, and he would rise early in the morning and offer burnt offerings according to the number of them all; for Job said, "It may be that my sons have sinned, and cursed God in their hearts." Thus Job did continually.

Mt 22:32 He is not God of the dead, but of the living.

Job offered oblations for the possible sins of his living sons, that they might be purified.

2 Tim 1:16-18 May the Lord grant mercy to the household of Onesiphorus, for he often refreshed me; he was not ashamed of my chains, ¹⁷ but when he arrived in Rome he searched for me eagerly and found me— ¹⁸ may the Lord grant him to find mercy from the Lord on that Day—and you well know all the service he rendered at Ephesus.

Onesiphorus is almost certainly dead, else why would Paul ask the Lord to grant mercy to his family apart from him? Yet Paul also asks the Lord to grant Onesiphorus mercy. If there is no Purgatory, why does Paul ask this? Those in hell cannot be helped by prayers and those in heaven have no need of prayers.

1 Jn 5:16 If any one sees his brother committing what is not a mortal sin, he will ask, and God will give him life for those whose sin is not mortal. There is sin which is mortal; I do not say one is to pray for that.

Purgatory cleanses one from venial sin.

2 Mac 12:41-46 So they all blessed the ways of the Lord, the righteous Judge, who reveals the things that are hidden; ⁴² and they turned to prayer, beseeching that the sin which had been committed might be wholly blotted out. And the noble Judas exhorted the people to keep themselves free from sin, for they had seen with their own eyes what had happened because of the sin of those who had fallen. ⁴³ He also took up a collection, man by man, to the amount of two thousand drachmas of silver, and sent it to Jerusalem to provide for a sin offering. In doing this he acted very well and honorably, taking account of the resurrection. ⁴⁴ For if he were not expecting that those who had fallen would rise again, it would have been superfluous and foolish to pray for the dead. ⁴⁵ But if he was looking to the splendid reward that is laid up for those who fall asleep in godliness, it was a holy and pious thought. Therefore he made atonement for the dead, that they might be delivered from their sin.

We can pray and offer up our personal sacrifices for one another, even for those in purgatory.

Rev 20:12 And I saw the dead, great and small, standing before the throne, and books were opened. Also another book was opened, which is the book of life. And the dead were judged by what was written in the books, by what they had done.

1 Cor 3:10-15 According to the grace of God given to me, like a skilled master builder I laid a foundation, and another man is building upon it. Let each man take care how he builds upon it. ¹¹ For no other foundation can any one lay than that which is laid, which is Jesus Christ. ¹² Now if any one builds on the foundation with gold, silver, precious stones, wood, hay, straw— ¹³ each man's work will become manifest; for the Day will disclose it, because it will be revealed with fire, and the fire will test what sort of work each one has done. ¹⁴ If the work which any man has built on the foundation survives, he will receive a reward. ¹⁵ If any man's work is burned up, he will suffer loss, though he himself will be saved, but only as through fire.

1 Pet 1:6-7 In this you rejoice, though now for a little while you may have to suffer various trials, ⁷ so that the genuineness of your faith, more precious than gold which though perishable is tested by fire, may redound to praise and glory and honor at the revelation of Jesus Christ.

Wis 3:1-8 But the souls of the righteous are in the hand of God,
and no torment will ever touch them. ² In the eyes of the foolish they seemed to have died,
and their departure was thought to be an affliction, ³ and their going from us to be their destruction;
but they are at peace. ⁴ For though in the sight of men they were punished,
their hope is full of immortality. ⁵ Having been disciplined a little, they will receive great good,
because God tested them and found them worthy of himself; ⁶ like gold in the furnace he tried them,
and like a sacrificial burnt offering he accepted them. ⁷ In the time of their visitation they will shine forth,
and will run like sparks through the stubble. ⁸ They will govern nations and rule over peoples,
and the Lord will reign over them for eve

1 Pet 3:18-19 For Christ also died for sins once for all, the righteous for the unrighteous, that he might bring us to God, being put to death in the flesh but made alive in the spirit; ¹⁹ in which he went and preached to the spirits in prison,

1 Pet 4:6 For this is why the gospel was preached even to the dead, that though judged in the flesh like men, they might live in the spirit like God.

At the end of time, Purgatory (called Hades in the Greek, Sheol in Hebrew) will have completed its cleansing work, will be emptied and will pass away.

Rev 20:13-14 And the sea gave up the dead in it, Death and Hades gave up the dead in them, and all were judged by what they had done. ¹⁴ Then Death and Hades were thrown into the lake of fire. This is the second death, the lake of fire...

<u>Early Christians' comments on Purgatory</u>

Indulgences

The temporal punishments of sin which remain after the forgiveness of the guilt of sin can be removed. This remission is not itself a forgiveness of sins, nor is it a sacrament, but it requires and presupposes that the sin has been forgiven, that the sinner has shown true contrition and undertaken confession. It is granted to the living by way of absolution and to <u>the dead</u> by way of <u>intercession</u>. For an indulgenced act to be effective, the cleansed sinner must not only accomplish the act, but must also have the proper attitude and intention, i.e., disattachment from all sin. Without such an orientation, the indulgenced act is worthless. (CCC 1471-1484,1494)

Current misunderstandings: This subject is difficult largely because it requires a deep understanding of how sin sends its roots through our lives. While all Christians affirm the need for the forgiveness of sin, many do not formally acknowledge the temporal consequences of sin, nor the need for those temporal consequences to be repaired. When we sin, we build up our own will in opposition to Christ's will for us. When we are <u>forgiven</u> for sin, the sin is wiped from our soul, but the habit of opposition we have built up in our will remains. In order to successfully avoid sin in the future, we must re-learn the submission of our wills to Christ; we must break down our own wills so that we can again submit to Him in docility. This self-created impediment to Him is one way to think about the temporal punishments of sin. Only Christ can give us the grace to accomplish the necessary submission of our will. While the temporal consequences of sin are sometimes tacitly acknowledged in Christian theology, only Catholics formally discuss or acknowledge how these are dealt with.

Lk 12:33-34 Sell your possessions, and give alms; provide yourselves with purses that do not grow old, with a treasure in the heavens that does not fail, where no thief approaches and no moth destroys. ³⁴ For where your treasure is, there will your heart be also.

The smallest drop of Christ's blood was sufficient to wipe away the stain of sin from the souls of all who ever have or ever will live. Yet Christ poured Himself out completely for us, and He allowed His martyrs to imitate Him by pouring out their own blood as well.

Col 1:24 Now I rejoice in my sufferings for your sake, and in my flesh I complete what is lacking in Christ's afflictions for the sake of his body, that is, the church...

This infinite treasury of merit is an inexhaustible treasure in heaven, built up pre-eminently by the sufferings of Christ and secondarily by His martyrs, who imitate Him, for the use of all the faithful.

Mt 16:19 I will give you the keys of the kingdom of heaven, and whatever you bind on earth shall be bound in heaven, and whatever you loose on earth shall be loosed in heaven."

Mt 18:18 Truly, I say to you, whatever you bind on earth shall be bound in heaven, and whatever you loose on earth shall be loosed in heaven.

Christ gave the power to bind and loose to Peter, the first <u>Pope</u>, and the Apostles. What they bind or loose in heaven is bound or loosed on earth. This binding and loosing includes the binding and loosing of the treasury of merit created by Christ's suffering and death.

Heb 5:7-8 In the days of his flesh, Jesus offered up prayers and supplications, with loud cries and tears, to him who was able to save him from death, and he was heard for his godly fear. ⁸ Although he was a Son, he learned obedience through what he suffered...

Obedience was the only thing Scripture affirms Christ had to learn. He had to learn it so that His Body would learn it. He learned it through suffering. The treasury of merit in heaven is the complete merit of docility and obedience, built up by the suffering of Christ and His martyrs.

In the parable of the unjust judge who ruled for the widow (Luke 18:2-8 - see "Repetitious Prayer"), Christ compared God to an unjust judge, and us sinners to the righteous widow, turning the real situation on its head in order to drive home the reality of God's perfect justice. In this parable, a similar style is used:

Lk 16:1-12 He also said to the disciples, "There was a rich man who had a steward, and charges were brought to him that this man was wasting his goods. ² And he called him and said to him, 'What is this that I hear about you? Turn in the account of your stewardship, for you can no longer be steward.' ³ And the steward said to himself, 'What shall I do, since my master is taking the stewardship away from me? I am not strong enough to dig, and I am ashamed to beg. ⁴ I have decided what to do, so that people may receive me into their houses when I am put out of the stewardship.' ⁵ So, summoning his master's debtors one by one, he said to the first, 'How much do you owe my master?' ⁶ He said, 'A hundred measures of oil.' And he said to him, 'Take your bill, and sit down quickly and write fifty.' ⁷ Then he said to another, 'And how much do you owe?' He said, 'A hundred measures of wheat.' He said to him, 'Take your bill, and write eighty.' ⁸ The master commended the dishonest steward for his shrewdness; for the sons of this world are more shrewd in dealing with their own generation than the sons of light. ⁹ And I tell you, make friends for yourselves by means of unrighteous mammon, so that when it fails they may receive you into the eternal habitations.

¹⁰ "He who is faithful in a very little is faithful also in much; and he who is dishonest in a very little is dishonest also in much. ¹¹ If then you have not been faithful in the unrighteous mammon, who will entrust to you the true riches? ¹² And if you have not been faithful in that which is another's, who will give you that which is your own?

In this topsy-turvy parable, heaven is not the master's house, as one would normally expect, but is the homes in which the debtors dwell ("eternal dwellings"). The master's house is, instead, the created world; his storehouse, represents all the things of the created world. The debtors themselves are those who see heaven as their home. The steward, representing the Church, is rewarded for making wise use of the resources of the created world in order bring all who owe allegiance to the king into heaven. In reality, the treasury of merit is not a resource of the created world, rather it is true wealth which belongs to the whole Church. This true wealth, unlike the wealth of this world, is guarded by the most faithful of stewards, the Bride of Christ, who dispenses the merits of the treasure to all the faithful who are in debt. Through clear acts of submission and obedience, we may draw upon the treasury of meritorious obedience which Christ earned for us. We become obedient to our Mother, the Church, as Christ was obedient to His parents.

Lk 2:51-52 And he went down with them and came to Nazareth, and was obedient to them; and his mother kept all these things in her heart. ⁵² And Jesus increased in wisdom and in stature, and in favor with God and man.

Col 1:22 he has now reconciled in his body of flesh by his death, in order to present you holy and blameless and irreproachable before him,

1 Jn 2:2 and he is the expiation for our sins, and not for ours only but also for the sins of the whole world.

This storehouse was established for the purification of the whole world.

2 Cor 2:5-10 But if any one has caused pain, he has caused it not to me, but in some measure—not to put it too severely—to you all. ⁶ For such a one this punishment by the majority is enough; ⁷ so you should rather turn to forgive and comfort him, or he may be overwhelmed by excessive sorrow. ⁸ So I beg you to reaffirm your love for him. ⁹ For this is why I wrote, that I might test you and know whether you are obedient in everything. ¹⁰ Any one whom you forgive, I also forgive. What I have forgiven, if I have forgiven anything, has been for your sake in the presence of Christ...

What harms one part of the Body harms the whole Body. What heals one part of the Body heals the whole Body. When one part of the Body learns obedience, then all are able to learn it. This total submission of ourselves to Christ is a necessary part of our purification, so that we may enter heaven. We are helped into heaven by Christ and by those whom He allows to image Him - He helps us through them, so that they may be true images of Him.

More on Indulgences

Hell

The Scripture in the section comes largely from Scripture By Topic.

Hell exists. It is a mercy reserved for those who deny God, or choose not to live in Him. The Scripture given below is only a partial sampling. (CCC 633, 1033-1037, 1861)

Current misunderstandings: Some Christians deny the existence of hell.

Wis 11:24 for thou lovest all things that exist, and hast loathing for none of the things which thou hast made, for thou wouldst not have made anything if thou hadst hated it.

God created us because He loves us. He never stops loving us. He would never annihilate us, or blot us out of existence, because He has too much love for each one of us to do such a thing. He does not desire us in hell. He always loves us, even when we choose to reject Him completely, even when we choose to reject His love completely.

Psalm 139:7-12 Whither shall I go from thy Spirit?
Or whither shall I flee from thy presence?
⁸ If I ascend to heaven, thou art there!
If I make my bed in Sheol, thou art there!
⁹ If I take the wings of the morning
and dwell in the uttermost parts of the sea,
¹⁰ even there thy hand shall lead me,
and thy right hand shall hold me.
¹¹ If I say, "Let only darkness cover me,
and the light about me be night,"
¹² even the darkness is not dark to thee,
the night is bright as the day;
for darkness is as light with thee.

We can't escape the presence of the God who is love. Ever.

Prov 25:20-22 He who sings songs to a heavy heart is like one who takes off a garment on a cold day, and like vinegar on a wound. ²¹ If your enemy is hungry, give him bread to eat; and if he is thirsty, give him water to drink; ²² for you will heap coals of fire on his head...

In fact, His pure love for us despite and in the teeth of our total rejection of that love IS the experience we call hell.

Psalm 9:17 The wicked shall depart to Sheol, all the nations that forget God.

Dan 12:2 And many of those who sleep in the dust of the earth shall awake, some to everlasting life, and some to shame and everlasting contempt.

Ezek 31:16-17 I will make the nations quake at the sound of its fall, when I cast it down to Sheol with those who go down to the Pit; and all the trees of Eden, the choice and best of Lebanon, all that drink water, will be comforted in the nether world. ¹⁷ They also shall go down to Sheol with it, to those who are slain by the sword; yea, those who dwelt under its shadow among the nations shall perish.

Prov 7:27 Her house is the way to Sheol,
going down to the chambers of death.

Psalm 55:15 Let death come upon them;
let them go down to Sheol alive;
let them go away in terror into their graves.

Psalm 21:10 You will make them as a blazing oven when you appear.
The LORD will swallow them up in his wrath; and
fire will consume them.

What appears to be wrath from our point of view is actually the consuming fire of God's love.

Is 5:14 Therefore Sheol has enlarged its appetite and opened its mouth beyond measure, and the nobility of Jerusalem and her multitude go down, her throng and he who exults in her.

Is 66:24 "And they shall go forth and look on the dead bodies of the men that have rebelled against me; for their worm shall not die, their fire shall not be quenched, and they shall be an abhorrence to all flesh."

Sir 21:9-10 An assembly of the wicked is like tow gathered together,
and their end is a flame of fire. ¹⁰ The way of sinners is smoothly paved with stones, but at its end is the pit of Hades.

Mk 9:43-48 And if your hand causes you to sin, cut it off; it is better for you to enter life maimed than with two hands to go to hell, to the unquenchable fire. ⁴⁵ And if your foot causes you to sin, cut it off; it is better for you to enter life lame than with two feet to be thrown into hell. ⁴⁷ And if your eye causes you to sin, pluck it out; it is better for you to enter the kingdom of God with one eye than with two eyes to be thrown into hell, ⁴⁸ where their worm does not die, and the fire is not quenched.

Mt 10:28 And do not fear those who kill the body but cannot kill the soul; rather fear him who can destroy both soul and body in hell.

2 Pet 2:4 For if God did not spare the angels when they sinned, but cast them into hell and committed them to pits of nether gloom to be kept until the judgment...

2 Pet 2:9 then the Lord knows how to rescue the godly from trial, and to keep the unrighteous under punishment until the day of judgment,

Rev 20:10,15 and the devil who had deceived them was thrown into the lake of fire and sulphur where the beast and the false prophet were, and they will be tormented day and night for ever and ever....and if any one's name was not found written in the book of life, he was thrown into the lake of fire.

Rev 21:8 But as for the cowardly, the faithless, the polluted, as for murderers, fornicators, sorcerers, idolaters, and all liars, their lot shall be in the lake that burns with fire and sulphur, which is the second death."

Mt 18:8-9 And if your hand or your foot causes you to sin, cut it off and throw it away; it is better for you to enter life maimed or lame than with two hands or two feet to be thrown into the eternal fire. ⁹ And if your eye causes you to sin, pluck it out and throw it away; it is better for you to enter life with one eye than with two eyes to be thrown into the hell of fire.

Mt 25:41 Then he will say to those at his left hand, 'Depart from me, you cursed, into the eternal fire prepared for the devil and his angels;

2 Thess 1:9 They shall suffer the punishment of eternal destruction and exclusion from the presence of the Lord and from the glory of his might,

Mt 3:12 His winnowing fork is in his hand, and he will clear his threshing floor and gather his wheat into the granary, but the chaff he will burn with unquenchable fire."

Mt 25:46 "And they will go away into eternal punishment, but the righteous into eternal life."

God called each one of us immediately into existence at our conception. He loved us into existence even more thoroughly than our parents did. He loved us into existence despite the fact that He knew we would be born into a state of original sin, an unwillingness to love Him completely in return. He called us into existence because He had promised to heal us of this lack of love. He provided the means to heal us, we have only to cooperate with the healing. He never stops loving us. He will let us choose to refuse to love Him for all eternity, if we so desire, but He won't snuff out our existence simply because we refuse to love Him. Since God creates nothing except good things, existence is a good thing, and God will not wipe good out of existence. Hell is the eternity of knowing and feeling God's love surround us, and rejecting that love totally, firm in our conviction that we do not want to love Him, that we do not want any part of His love. Hell is not God torturing us, it is us torturing ourselves in the pure undimmed light of God, with all illusions removed.

Our existence is radically contingent on God; our physical death doesn't alter our existence, it merely changes how we experience our existence - it puts us face-to-face with the ultimate reality. We don't control the fact that we exist: God does. God won't let us fall out of existence. The fact of our own existence, the fact of God's love for us, is not within our free will - it is within God's free will. He chose for us to exist and He chose to love us, and His will does not change.

Heaven

What is heaven? It is participating in the life of the Trinity. The Father, the Son and the Holy Spirit each pour themselves out completely on one another, holding nothing back. The Father pours Himself out completely on the Son and the Spirit, "taking care" of them, not worrying about Himself because the Son and the Spirit pour themselves out completely on the Father and "take care" of the Father. The Son and Spirit do the same for each other. Each pours Himself out completely on the other two persons of the Trinity. (CCC 325-326, 1023-1029)

2 Pet 1:3-4 His divine power has granted to us all things that pertain to life and godliness, through the knowledge of him who called us to his own glory and excellence, ⁴ by which he has granted to us his precious and very great promises, that through these you may escape from the corruption that is in the world because of passion, and become partakers of the divine nature.

From the beginning of time, this is what we were created to do. We are created to participate in this life. The closest analogy Jesus' could find was also His favorite: He described heaven as a wedding feast.

Mt 25:1,10 "Then the kingdom of heaven shall be compared to ten maidens who took their lamps and went to meet the bridegroom... And while they went to buy, the bridegroom came, and those who were ready went in with him to the marriage feast; and the door was shut."

Mt 22:1-9 And again Jesus spoke to them in parables, saying, ² "The kingdom of heaven may be compared to a king who gave a marriage feast for his son, ³ and sent his servants to call those who were invited to the marriage feast; but they would not come. ⁴ Again he sent other servants, saying, 'Tell those who are invited, Behold, I have made ready my dinner, my oxen and my fat calves are killed, and everything is ready; come to the marriage feast.' ⁵ But they made light of it and went off, one to his farm, another to his business, ⁶ while the rest seized his servants, treated them shamefully, and killed them. ⁷ The king was angry, and he sent his troops and destroyed those murderers and burned their city. ⁸ Then he said to his servants, 'The wedding is ready, but those invited were not worthy. ⁹ Go therefore to the thoroughfares, and invite to the marriage feast as many as you find.' ¹⁰ And those servants went out into the streets and gathered all whom they found, both bad and good; so the wedding hall was filled with guests.
¹¹ "But when the king came in to look at the guests, he saw there a man who had no wedding garment; ¹² and he said to him, 'Friend, how did you get in here without a wedding garment?' And he was speechless. ¹³ Then the king said to the attendants, 'Bind him hand and foot, and cast him into the outer darkness; there men will weep and gnash their teeth.' ¹⁴ For many are called, but few are chosen."

The Wedding Feast is the foreshadowing for what will come, a time of celebration, pure bliss for each participant. However, only those who choose to participate in the exchange of total love with the God who is love will be given the ability to do so.

Mt 8:11-12 I tell you, many will come from east and west and sit at table with Abraham, Isaac, and Jacob in the kingdom of heaven, ¹² while the sons of the kingdom will be thrown into the outer darkness; there men will weep and gnash their teeth."

Mt 13:41-43 The Son of man will send his angels, and they will gather out of his kingdom all causes of sin and all evildoers, ⁴² and throw them into the furnace of fire; there men will weep and gnash their teeth. ⁴³ Then the righteous will shine like the sun in the kingdom of their Father.

God made us to shine like the sun, but He wants us to desire our own glorification as well...

Deut 30:19 I call heaven and earth to witness against you this day, that I have set before you life and death, blessing and curse; therefore choose life, that you and your descendants may live...

If we choose life...

1 Cor 2:9 "...no eye has seen, nor ear heard, nor the heart of man conceived, what God has prepared for those who love him..."

What, exactly, will it be like? We don't know for certain. The one thing we do know is that it won't be boring. We won't simply be singing "Hosanna," throwing down our crowns, picking them up, and throwing them down again. Every person desires, every person craves, love. In heaven, each of us will not only be loved to the tips of our toes and the tops of our heads, we will know that love to the core of our being in a way that no human mind, no human love, can fathom or reach. That love will empower us, enliven us, enrich us, enkindle in us knowledge and a response of love beyond anything we presently understand. Heaven is participation in infinity, not in an endless dull-gray infinity, but in a richly sumptuous, wonderfully woven height and depth and breadth, more stars than the starriest night, more beauty than the loveliest vista, more energy and more peace combined in one person, in each person, than we have ever known.

Rev 19:1,5-9 After this I heard what seemed to be the loud voice of a great multitude in heaven, crying, "Hallelujah! Salvation and glory and power belong to our God... 5 And from the throne came a voice crying, "Praise our God, all you his servants,
you who fear him, small and great." ⁶ Then I heard what seemed to be the voice of a great multitude, like the sound of many waters and like the sound of mighty thunderpeals, crying,
"Hallelujah! For the Lord our God the Almighty reigns. ⁷ Let us rejoice and exult and give him the glory,
for the marriage of the Lamb has come,
and his Bride has made herself ready; ⁸ it was granted her to be clothed with fine linen, bright and pure"—
for the fine linen is the righteous deeds of the saints.
⁹ And the angel said to me, "Write this: Blessed are those who are invited to the marriage supper of the Lamb." And he said to me, "These are true words of God."

It is greater than anything we know because it is not something we could ever come to know through our own ability. In Heaven, God gives us a power infinitely beyond the greatest of our own powers. He gives us participation in Him, what He is, what He does.

Acts 1:9-11 And when he had said this, as they were looking on, he was lifted up, and a cloud took him out of their sight. ¹⁰ And while they were gazing into heaven as he went, behold, two men stood by them in white robes, ¹¹ and said, "Men of Galilee, why do you stand looking into heaven? This Jesus, who was taken up from you into heaven, will come in the same way as you saw him go into heaven."

We participate with everything we are. The resurrection of the dead is not just bonus points at the end of time. We will have our bodies, for Heaven is a place for men, and man is body and soul together. God created us to be united body and soul, indissolubly.

The breaking of the bond between the two is the evil of death, but the Resurrection bursts the ramparts of death asunder. While those in heaven now are happy, they will be even happier after the resurrection, when soul and body are again reunited, and we live as God intended us to live from the beginning. Heaven is a sensory experience as well as a spiritual completion. We will need every cell of our created being, body and soul, to fully experience and appreciate Heaven. Jesus brought His body into heaven, He keeps His humanity even now, and will continue to keep it for all eternity. This is how much He loves man. He is willing to stay within the limits of a human body for all eternity, so that each of us may have the opportunity to touch Him, to embrace Him, to hear His voice and gaze into His eyes. We will see God face to face, and know Him, His love.

Rev 21:2-4 And I saw the holy city, new Jerusalem, coming down out of heaven from God, prepared as a bride adorned for her husband; ³ and I heard a loud voice from the throne saying, "Behold, the dwelling of God is with men. He will dwell with them, and they shall be his people, and God himself will be with them; ⁴ he will wipe away every tear from their eyes, and death shall be no more, neither shall there be mourning nor crying nor pain any more, for the former things have passed away...." Then came one of the seven angels who had the seven bowls full of the seven last plagues, and spoke to me, saying, "Come, I will show you the Bride, the wife of the Lamb." ¹⁰ And in the Spirit he carried me away to a great, high mountain, and showed me the holy city Jerusalem coming down out of heaven from God...

The Wedding Feast is the divine reward for those who persevere to the end. God gives Himself completely, just as He always has. But this time, we will be able to appreciate Him completely, with every fiber of our being.

Rev 22:17 The Spirit and the Bride say, "Come."

MARY

Luke 1:38
"Behold,
I am the handmaid of the Lord;
let it be done to me
according to your word."

John 2:5
"Do whatever he tells you."

From all eternity God intended to enlist the free cooperation of a human being to accomplish his plan. He enlisted the aid of a daughter of Israel, Mary. She is the first bride of God, through whom He brought forth the Son. She is, without doubt, the most complex and nuanced subject of Scriptural exegesis. For this reason, the Scripture under this heading has more commentary than any other subject treated in this work. Mary is the archetype for the Bride, the Church. Unless you have spent time studying the interplay of the sacraments, sin, salvation, grace, and authority, you may have a difficult time understanding Marian teaching. On the other hand, if you understand Marian doctrine, you understand all the Church is, for she is the Bride of Christ. (CCC 487-511, 721, 963-975)

Four dogmas and one doctrine concern Mary.
The four dogmas:
(1) She is the Mother of God, defined at the Council of Ephesus, 431 A.D. (CCC 495),
(2) She is perpetually virginal, defined by the First Lateran Council, 649 A.D., under Pope Martin I, and confirmed by the ecumenical Second Council of Constantinople (CCC 496-511),
(3) She is Immaculately Conceived, that is, she was conceived without sin, and lived her whole life without sinning, defined by Pope Pius IX, Dec. 8, 1854, in Ineffebilus Deus *(CCC 411, 490-493),*
(4) She was assumed bodily into heaven through the power of God, defined by Pope Pius XII, Nov. 1, 1950, in Munificentissimus Deus *(CCC 966, 974).*

The doctrine: Mary is the mother of the Church and our spiritual mother in the order of grace (CCC 495, 963, 968-970). For this reason, we may properly call her:
(1) our maternal mediator with God, being the Advocate for all the peoples of the world before the throne of Christ (CCC 970),
(2) the Mediatrix of all graces, for all grace came into the world through her womb, and the timeless work of the Holy Spirit continues to pour through her now in the same way He worked through her in the Annunciation, (CCC 618, 964, 968-970)
(3) the Co-Redemptrix, who worked as the squire of God in subordination to Christ, actively participating with and under Him, in His redemption of the world. (CCC 618, 964, 968-970)

Gen 3:15 I will put enmity between you and the woman, and between your seed and her seed;
he shall bruise your head,
and you shall bruise his heel."

This is the Proto-evangelium - the first declaration of the coming of a Saviour. It is one of the foundational Scripture passages for all Marian doctrine and dogma. The pivotal aspects are the reference to enmity, seed, and Saviour.

The word "enmity" had connotations to the Hebrew mind which simply do not obtain today. Enmity for them did not just mean distaste, it meant total opposition, polar separation, a complete antipathy of interest and inclination. If you had enmity for someone, you shared no common ground with that person at all. The enmity spoken of here is a future enmity, an enmity which "will" be placed between the woman and the serpent. It cannot refer to Eve, for Eve already has common ground with the serpent - she has done what the serpent asked. It refers to a future woman. That woman will never share common ground with the serpent, she will never do what the serpent asks.

Note also the phrase "her seed." This phrase occurs nowhere else in Scripture. Strictly speaking, it should be a nonsensical expression, since seed (and lineage) was understood to come from the man, not from the woman. The fact that the words were used as they were indicates that a woman will play a unique role in the lineage which will result in the destruction of the power of Satan. This relationship between offspring and woman is not only unique to her as parent, but unique to her, period.

Finally, note the parallelism of the passage. Serpent vs. woman, serpent's offspring vs. woman's offspring. Woman and offspring share the same enmity towards serpent and offspring. She will stand in perfect harmony with her offspring, both will stand in total opposition to the serpent. The serpent's head will be crushed while the serpent will merely "lie in wait," paralyzed and unable to move.

Who does the crushing of the serpent's head? According to Franciscan University's Dr. Mark Miravelle and his class lectures on the subject, the oldest extant manuscripts in the Greek show a neuter pronoun, the oldest Hebrew texts use a pronoun which meant variously "he" or "she" depending on the time period. It is unknown exactly when Genesis was written. Jerome, using texts no longer available to us and conversing with Jewish scholars now long dead, translated the text into Latin as "she will crush your head," while the 1985 New Vulgate uses the neuter.

Rom 16:20 then the God of peace will soon crush Satan under your feet.

Why is the gender ambivalent? Because the crushing of the head is done by the Church, the Church is represented by Mary, and both are given the power to do this by their Son, the Bridegroom and the Head of the Body, Jesus Christ.

Early Christians' comments on Mary, Mother of God

Jer 31:22 For the LORD has created a new thing on the earth: a woman protects a man."

Why is this a new thing? Because the woman in question will bring forth a saviour.

Mary, the Sinless New Eve

"The infusion of Mary's soul was effected without original sin...From the first moment she began to live she was free from all sin." - Martin Luther, Sermon: "On the Day of the Conception of the Mother of God." Luther believed in the Immaculate Conception right up until his death.

Gen 2:21-24 So the LORD God caused a deep sleep to fall upon the man, and while he slept took one of his ribs and closed up its place with flesh; [22] and the rib which the LORD God had taken from the man he made into a woman and brought her to the man. [23] Then the man said,
"This at last is bone of my bones
and flesh of my flesh;
she shall be called Woman,
because she was taken out of Man." [24] Therefore a man leaves his father and his mother and cleaves to his wife, and they become one flesh.

Gen 3:6 So when the woman saw that the tree was good for food, and that it was a delight to the eyes, and that the tree was to be desired to make one wise, she took of its fruit and ate; and she also gave some to her husband, and he ate.

Adam and Eve were created sinless. Eve commits one sin - she eats of the fruit of the tree. Adam commits two sins. He eats of the fruit himself, and he fails to preserve Eve from sinning - he fails in his role of headship. For these failures, both were banished from the garden and death entered the world. The sin in the Garden was a corporate sin - the couple sinned together. Just as a transgression of your parents against your grandfather might cause your parents to lose their inheritance, resulting in a loss which will affect their own children, i.e., you, so the disorder Adam and Eve introduced affected everyone that came from them, and everything they had rule over. In them, we all lost our inheritance and our rights to the grace of God's presence and preternatural existence. This privation of privilege and grace is original sin. In order to regain our inheritance, we must be brought into a new family relationship with God.

Rom 5:14 Yet death reigned from Adam to Moses, even over those whose sins were not like the transgression of Adam, who was a type of the one who was to come.

1 Cor 15:45-49 Thus it is written, "The first man Adam became a living being"; the last Adam became a life-giving spirit. [46] But it is not the spiritual which is first but the physical, and then the spiritual. [47] The first man was from the earth, a man of dust; the second man is from heaven. [48] As was the man of dust, so are those who are of the dust; and as is the man of heaven, so are those who are of heaven. [49] Just as we have borne the image of the man of dust, we shall also bear the image of the man of heaven.

Christ is the new Adam. Scripture is clear on that. Who, then, is the new Eve?

Eph 1:3-10 Blessed be the God and Father of our Lord Jesus Christ, who has blessed us in Christ with every spiritual blessing in the heavenly places, [4] even as he chose us in him before the foundation of the world, that we should be holy and blameless before him. [5] He destined us in love to be his sons through Jesus Christ, according to the purpose of his will, [6] to the praise of his glorious grace which he freely bestowed on us in the Beloved. [7] In him we have redemption through his blood, the forgiveness of our trespasses, according to the riches of his grace [8] which he lavished upon us. [9] For he has made known to us in all wisdom and insight the mystery of his will, according to his purpose which he set forth in Christ [10] as a plan for the fulness of time, to unite all things in him, things in heaven and things on earth.

The New Eve is the woman chosen before the foundation of the world to be holy and blameless before him, according to the purpose of His will.

Lk 1:28 And he came to her and said, "Hail, full of grace, the Lord is with you!"

Two words in this greeting need to be studied: "chairoo" (Hail) and "kekaritomene" (full of grace). "Hail" which is "chairoo" in the Greek, is a greeting reserved for royalty, and it is generally followed by the title of the royal person greeted. It is used only six times in Scripture.

Mt 26:48-49 Now the betrayer had given them a sign, saying, "The one I shall kiss is the man; seize him." 49 And he came up to Jesus at once and said, "Hail, Master!" And he kissed him.

By using "chairoo" in front of the Roman guard, Judas implies Jesus seeks political kingship.

Mk 15:18 And they began to salute him, "Hail, King of the Jews!"

Jn 19:3 they came up to him, saying, "Hail, King of the Jews!" and struck him with their hands

Mt 27:29 and plaiting a crown of thorns they put it on his head, and put a reed in his right hand. And kneeling before him they mocked him, saying, "Hail, King of the Jews!"

The soldiers mock those political aspirations.

Mt 28:8-9 So they departed quickly from the tomb with fear and great joy, and ran to tell his disciples. 9 And behold, Jesus met them and said, "Hail!" And they came up and took hold of his feet and worshiped him.

Jesus acknowledges the royal priesthood of believers.

Lk 1:28 And he came to her and said, "Hail, O favored one, the Lord is with you!"

In Mary's case, the angel, speaking with the voice and message of God, greets a fifteen year old Jewish girl with the royal title "kekaritomene," a perfect passive participle which is more accurately translated "you who are fully transfigured by grace." Before Jesus hails us, made a kingdom of royal priests through His Passion, Death and Resurrection, Jesus first gave the gifts which flow from His Cross to the woman who will be His mother. He gives her those gifts before she even hears the question, for the angel recognized his queen. So should we, and for a very simple reason. Names signify something about essence in Scripture: "Sarai" means "princess" while "Sarah" means "princess of the multitudes," "Abram-Abraham" likewise is a change from "father" to "father of the multitudes," Jacob means "heel-catcher" and YHWH means "I Am Who Am." Nearly every name in Scripture carries a meaning which is important, sometimes crucially important, to the story being told.

Gal 2:21 I do not nullify the grace of God; for if justification were through the law, then Christ died to no purpose.

The word "kekaritomene," derived from the verb which means "to endow, to grace," bespeaks an action completed in the past, but still relevant to the present. A slightly better translation might be "Hail, you who have been transformed in grace" or "Hail, you who have been fully graced." Mary, living under the Old Law, had already been transformed in grace by the time the angel greets her, transformed before Jesus dies on the Cross thirty-three years in the future, transformed even before He took flesh within her womb. How did this happen?

Jn 19:33-34 But when they came to Jesus and saw that he was already dead, they did not break his legs, 34 but one soldier thrust his lance into his side, and immediately blood and water flowed out.

The first Eve was formed from the first Adam's side as he slept on the ground. She was made sinless, as was he. The second Eve was formed from the second Adam's side as He slept on the cross. From His side flowed the blood and water which preserved her from the sin she would otherwise have certainly fallen into. Thus, she was made sinless in her humanity, just as He was in His. Christ acquired His humanity as all men do, from His parents. In the generative order, He had one human parent. His humanity was given to Him by His mother - it was given sinless, because she was sinless. She was sinless because Her Son and Saviour died to preserve her so. Adam failed in his role of headship. He failed to preserve Eve from sin. Jesus does not fail in HIS role of headship. He successfully preserves the New Eve from sin.

But Scripture says:

Rom 3:10-12 as it is written:
"None is righteous, no, not one; 11 no one understands, no one seeks for God. 12 All have turned aside, together they have gone wrong;

no one does good, not even one." (Psalm 10:7)

Rom 3:23 since all have sinned and fall short of the glory of God...

Are infants guilty of personal sin? What of the mentally incompetent? What of Paul himself?

Phil 3:6 as to zeal a persecutor of the church, as to righteousness under the law blameless.

Paul claims to be blameless, free from personal sin under the Old Law, a law which does not cleanse. How can he make such a claim?

Mk 1:5 And there went out to him all the country of Judea, and all the people of Jerusalem; and they were baptized by him in the river Jordan, confessing their sins.

Did John the Baptist actually baptize EVERY PERSON who lived in Jerusalem and the whole country of Judea? A single man baptizing several millions, is certainly a remarkable event. However...

Lk 7:29-30 (When they heard this all the people and the tax collectors justified God, having been baptized with the baptism of John; ³⁰ but the Pharisees and the lawyers rejected the purpose of God for themselves, not having been baptized by him.)

Were the Pharisees and lawyers NOT inhabitants of Jerusalem or Judea?

Mt 15:1 Then Pharisees and scribes came to Jesus from Jerusalem and said...

No, they came from Jerusalem. Scripture sometimes deals in hyperbole in order to make a point. However, Mary made a sin offering. Was this not sign of personal sin?

Lk 2:24 and to offer a sacrifice according to what is said in the law of the Lord, "a pair of turtledoves, or two young pigeons."

Mary did make a sin offering, but all women had to do so after childbirth and menstruation. They had come into contact with blood, which made one ritually unclean. Menstruation is not a sin, neither is childbirth, especially giving birth to the Saviour. Mary's sin offering was an obedient response to an external purity ritual, it has no bearing on her personal sinfulness.

Heb 4:15 For we have not a high priest who is unable to sympathize with our weaknesses, but one who in every respect has been tempted as we are, yet without sin.

Just as Jesus was tested, so was Mary. But Christ intervened every time the serpent spoke, so that she would not even be inclined towards the serpent.

Rom 9:21 Has the potter no right over the clay, to make out of the same lump one vessel for beauty and another for menial use?

Lk 1:42 and she exclaimed with a loud cry, "Blessed are you among women, and blessed is the fruit of your womb!

The blessing of God which rests upon Mary is made parallel with the blessing of God which rests upon Christ's humanity. This repeat of the Genesis parallelism suggests that Mary, like Christ, was free from sin from her conception.

There are additional reasons to believe Mary was created sinless by virtue of Christ's salvific work on the Cross. In addition to the parallelism with the New Genesis (Adam and Eve formed sinless, the new Adam and the new Eve also formed sinless), we must consider the nature of the love flowing within the Trinity, the nature of sacramental marriage, the work Mary had to accomplish, and the effects of pride.

The nature of the Trinity is pure love. God so loves His Son, and the Son so loves the Father, that the Holy Spirit, the Third Person of the Trinity, proceeds from that love. Would God have created a mother for His Son, whom He loved so much, who was anything less than perfect? Would Jesus permit Satan to lay the smallest finger upon His own mother?

Further, consider her role as mother. A mother is the living example for her child. Though Jesus would never sin no matter what example He was given, in order to fulfill all righteousness His mother was a perfect example for Him, walking perfectly in the ways of grace.

Related to that, we must consider the nature of marriage. Marriage requires totally free consent.

There can be no compulsion in a marriage, or it is not a true marriage. Mary bore the son of God; she was, in a very real way, the spouse of the Holy Spirit, who engendered Jesus Christ in her womb. In order for her to freely consent to this sacramental marriage, she needed true and total freedom, with no shadow of sin darkening her intellect, will or spirit. God granted her that grace for His own name's sake.

Ezek 20:9 But I acted for the sake of my name, that it should not be profaned in the sight of the nations among whom they dwelt, in whose sight I made myself known to them in bringing them out of the land of Egypt

Consider the role of John the Baptist:

Lk 1:15,41,44 for he will be great before the Lord, and he shall drink no wine nor strong drink, and he will be filled with the Holy Spirit, even from his mother's womb.... And when Elizabeth heard the greeting of Mary, the babe leaped in her womb; and Elizabeth was filled with the Holy Spirit... "For behold, when the voice of your greeting came to my ears, the babe in my womb leaped for joy."

John the Baptist had only two works: to proclaim the coming of the Lord and to provide a baptism of repentance. After those works were accomplished and Jesus's ministry began, Jesus increased while John decreased. For this work, John was sanctified in the womb. Mary's work is much greater than John's - for her work, she was sanctified from the moment of conception. In fact, it was through her greeting that John the Baptist would be sanctified in the womb and leap with the joy of receiving the Holy Spirit.

Finally, we must consider God's reaction to pride. Pride is the first sin, committed by Satan, and it lies at the root of all sin. Pride says, "Not Thy will, but MY will be done." God shows Himself in those who are humble and low-born.

Num 12:3 Now the man Moses was very meek, more than all men that were on the face of the earth.

Ex 33:11 Thus the LORD used to speak to Moses face to face, as a man speaks to his friend.

He shows Himself most fully in those who have the least pride. Jesus Christ is the completed fullness of God's revelation, so He must have come in the midst of absolute humility, with no trace of pride, either internally or externally. For this reason, Mary must have been absolutely devoid of the sin of pride. Where there is no pride, there can be no other sin. She did not accomplish this on her own, but God accomplished it in her.

Lk 1:46-49 And Mary said,
"My soul magnifies the Lord, [47] and my spirit rejoices in God my Savior, [48] for he has regarded the low estate of his handmaiden.
For behold, henceforth all generations will call me blessed; [49] for he who is mighty has done great things for me, and holy is his name.

Indeed, Mary herself proclaims that God is her saviour. If a person loses his balance on the edge of a pit and falls in, the one who pulls him out has saved him from the pit. Likewise, the person who loses his balance on the edge of a pit, but does not fall in because that same rescuer reaches out and grabs him, is also saved by that rescuer. Christ preserved Mary from the pit, and is rightly her Saviour. Aquinas rightly denied the proposition that Mary did not need a Saviour. He did not deny the Immaculate Conception, he denied all explanations of it which said she had no need of a Saviour.

Rom 5:19 For as by one man's disobedience many were made sinners, so by one man's obedience many will be made righteous.

Here is the relationship between Adam and Christ: Christ's obedience brings righteousness to us all. However, it also describes the relationship between Eve and Mary - Eve's disobedience made us all sinners, Mary's obedience brought Righteousness into the world.

Rom 1:5 through whom we have received grace and apostleship to bring about the obedience of faith for the sake of his name among all the nations,

Rom 16:26 but is now disclosed and through the prophetic writings is made known to all nations, according to the command of the eternal God, to bring about the obedience of faith...

Paul's letter to the Romans opens and closes by equating obedience and faith. Mary perfected both in her "Fiat - let it be done to me according to Thy word." The greatest apostle is the apostle who most perfectly proclaims the Good News. No one in all of history has ever or will ever proclaim the Good News as perfectly as the Blessed Virgin Mary. Her perfect obedience allowed her to make the perfect proclamation of the Good News, with perfect faith. She made the proclamation in a stable, for there was no room in the inn, yet at that proclamation the very heavens shouted for joy.

Prov 31:10-12 A good wife who can find?
She is far more precious than jewels. [11] The heart of her husband trusts in her,
and he will have no lack of gain. [12] She does him good, and not harm,
all the days of her life.

From the earliest times, every Christian writer who spoke of Mary referred to her as the New Eve. The Trinity is the foundational doctrine of Christianity. The word "Trinity," however, is not to be found in Scripture. It is first used in 181 A.D., by Theophilus of Antioch. By 181 A.D., the earliest Christians have already referred to Mary as "the New Eve" at least three times in their writings (the Epistle of Mathatais the Diognetes refers to Mary as both "sinless" and the "New Eve," ca. 100 A.D., St. Justin Martyr calls her "the New Eve" in his "Dialogue with Trypho," 150 A.D., as does St. Ireneaus in "Against Heresies," book 3, 180 A.D.). She who is the ark of the New Covenant was made holy before God came to dwell in her.

Ex 30:26 And you shall anoint with it the tent of meeting and the ark of the testimony...

Ex 40:9 take the anointing oil, and anoint the tabernacle and all that is in it, and consecrate it and all its furniture; and it shall become holy.

<u>Early Christians discuss Mary: Full of Grace</u>

Mary, Ark of the Covenant

This section comes largely from Pat Madrid's tape "Do Whatever He Tells You"

2 Sam 6:9 And David was afraid of the LORD that day; and he said, "How can the ark of the LORD come to me?"

Lk 1:41-43 ... And when Elizabeth heard the greeting of Mary, the babe leaped in her womb; and Elizabeth was filled with the Holy Spirit [42] and she exclaimed with a loud cry, "Blessed are you among women, and blessed is the fruit of your womb! [43] And why is this granted me, that the mother of my Lord should come to me?

Elizabeth's words are identical to David's upon seeing the Ark of the Covenant.

2 Sam 6:12-14 And it was told King David, "The LORD has blessed the household of Obed-edom and all that belongs to him, because of the ark of God." So David went and brought up the ark of God from the house of Obed-edom to the city of David with rejoicing; [13] and when those who bore the ark of the LORD had gone six paces, he sacrificed an ox and a fatling. [14] And David danced before the LORD with all his might; and David was girded with a linen ephod.

Lk 1:41 And when Elizabeth heard the greeting of Mary, the babe leaped in her womb; and Elizabeth was filled with the Holy Spirit...

John the Baptist danced for joy in Elizabeth's womb, just as David danced before the ark.

Ex 40:34-35 Then the cloud covered the tent of meeting, and the glory of the LORD filled the tabernacle. [35] And Moses was not able to enter the tent of meeting, because the cloud abode upon it, and the glory of the LORD filled the tabernacle.

Lk 1:35 And the angel said to her,
"The Holy Spirit will come upon you,
and the power of the Most High will overshadow you;
therefore the child to be born will be called holy,
the Son of God.

The verb "overshadow" used in Luke is the same verb used in Exodus to describe how the Lord "filled" the tabernacle.

Heb 9:3-4 Behind the second curtain stood a tent called the Holy of Holies, [4]having the golden altar of incense and the ark of the covenant covered on all sides with gold, which contained a golden urn holding the manna, and Aaron's rod that budded, and the tables of the covenant

The ark carried the Ten Commandments (the Word), the rod of Aaron (power), and manna (food). Mary carries the Word of God, the Power of God, and the True Bread which is come down from heaven. She is the Ark of the New Covenant. That is why Jeremiah could prophesy:

Jer 3:15-19 "'And I will give you shepherds after my own heart, who will feed you with knowledge and understanding. ¹⁶ And when you have multiplied and increased in the land, in those days, says the LORD, they shall no more say, "The ark of the covenant of the LORD." It shall not come to mind, or be remembered, or missed; it shall not be made again. ¹⁷ At that time Jerusalem shall be called the throne of the LORD, and all nations shall gather to it, to the presence of the LORD in Jerusalem, and they shall no more stubbornly follow their own evil heart. ¹⁸ In those days the house of Judah shall join the house of Israel, and together they shall come from the land of the north to the land that I gave your fathers for a heritage.

That time is now. The original ark will not be remade, nor missed. God has given us new shepherds after His own heart, the houses of Judah and Israel are joined. Through Mary's "Yes," the promise has been fulfilled.

Mary, Perpetual Virgin

Is 7:14 Therefore the Lord himself will give you a sign. Behold, a young woman shall conceive and bear a son, and shall call his name Immanu-el.

Some argue that the phrase "young woman" does not imply "virgin." There are two versions of the Old Testament, one called the Septuagint, the other referred to as the Jamnian canon. The Jamnian canon has the word "young woman," while the Septuagint has the word "virgin." Please see the discussion on the <u>canon</u> for more details. The Septuagint is the canonical version accepted by the Catholic Church and used by Christ and the Apostles. Keep in mind also that the sign value of a young woman bearing a child is not nearly so great as that of a virgin bearing a child. Why King Ahaz (the person to whom the prophecy was made) would regard the former as fulfillment of prophecy is not at all clear, while his (and our) motivation to consider the latter to be fulfillment is, to say the least, somewhat easier to understand.

Is 66:6-8 "Hark, an uproar from the city! A voice from the temple! The voice of the LORD, rendering recompense to his enemies! ⁷ "Before she was in labor she gave birth; before her pain came upon her she was delivered of a son. ⁸ Who has heard such a thing? Who has seen such things? Shall a land be born in one day? Shall a nation be brought forth in one moment? For as soon as Zion was in labor she brought forth her sons.

She will give birth to the Saviour without experiencing pain. Thus, in a certain sense, the virgin birth prefigured the Resurrection. Just as Christ miraculously leaves His mother's womb, so will He miraculously leave the tomb. As Father Frederick Miller pointed out in lecture at Franciscan University, the Father's glory is magnified by His eternal begetting of the Son. Mary's absence of pain is a created image of the Father's magnified glory.

Mic 5:1-2 Now you are walled about with a wall;
siege is laid against us;
with a rod they strike upon the cheek
the ruler of Israel. ² But you, O Bethlehem Ephrathah,
who are little to be among the clans of Judah,
from you shall come forth for me
one who is to be ruler in Israel,
whose origin is from of old,
from ancient days.

The birth will take place in Bethlehem.

Joel 2:29 Even upon the menservants and maidservants in those days, I will pour out my spirit.

Again, Father Miller points out that Mary's virginity mirrors the virginal love of Father. God the Father was, in fact, called "the Virgin of Virgins" by the early Cistercians. Jerusalem was the virgin bride, the New Jerusalem is adorned as a wife for her husband. "Virginity" means to hold oneself back in order to give oneself completely away. God gives Himself completely to the Son and completely to the finite creature, Mary, in the Son. Mary, finite creature that she is, gives herself completely to the Father. St. Louis de Montfort said God the Father communicated to Mary His fruitfulness insofar as a creature was able to contain it, in order to give birth to the uncreated Son and the created saints. Mary brings forth a Divine Person - the creature in the image and likeness of the Creator. This is only possible in sinlessness - in it she brings forth all the members of the mystical body, through the preaching of the Word and the sacraments.

Lk 1:34-35,38 And Mary said to the angel, "How shall this be, since I have no husband?" ³⁵ And the angel said to her,
"The Holy Spirit will come upon you,
and the power of the Most High will overshadow you;
therefore the child to be born will be called holy,

the Son of God.... And Mary said, "Behold, I am the handmaid of the Lord; let it be to me according to your word." And the angel departed from her.

Again, the translation of these verses is not good. The correct translation is actually "How shall this be done?" not "How can this be done? Mary was not expressing disbelief that God could do it, she was asking how God planned on accomplishing it.

Further, in the original Greek, the angel says "With God, every word (rama) shall not be impossible." Greek used the double negative for emphasis. However, the angel's declaration was simply incredible to the Hebrew reader because the Hebrews understood God's word to be actual - it is reality, not possibility. God's word creates reality. Why then did the angel say that every word of God was possible? Because every word of God in Scripture, every prediction, every prophecy and promise, was contingent on the response of a fifteen year old girl.

Mary replied "Behold the handmaid of the Lord, let it be done to me according to thy word (rama)." With that assent, the Word of God became flesh and dwelt among us. The Eternal Word becomes audible to creation in Mary's womb.

Mary's birth of the Son in time is the temporal icon for eternal begetting of the Son by the Father. The point of the analogy is not the generative act but the result. Mary is the masterwork of the mission of the Son and the Spirit: both are sent to manifest the Father (CCC 721). Jesus has two births: the Eternal birth from the Father, and the temporal from Mary, His mother. The Church celebrates three Masses on this day: Christmas midnight Mass symbolizes the eternal birth from the Father, the dawn Mass symbolizes the nativity in Bethlehem, and the Mass at noon signifies the birth of Christ in our soul; all three are ONE birth. Our souls need to be virginal, i.e., cleansed by sanctifying grace.

Song 4:12 A garden locked is my sister, my bride, a garden locked, a fountain sealed

The Song of Songs has long been held to be not only a description of Christ's love for the Church, but of God's love for Mary, who is the Bride of the Holy Spirit, for God does not rape nor does He fornicate, but He marries.

Ezek 44:2-3 And he said to me, "This gate shall remain shut; it shall not be opened, and no one shall enter by it; for the Lord, the God of Israel, has entered by it; therefore it shall remain shut. ³ Only the prince may sit in it to eat bread before the Lord; he shall enter by way of the vestibule of the gate, and shall go out by the same way."

Ezekial's poetic vision of the Temple of the New Jerusalem confirms the reference made in Isaiah. The mother of the Lord will be a virgin.

Mt 1:24-25 When Joseph woke from sleep, he did as the angel of the Lord commanded him; he took his wife, ²⁵ but knew her not until she had borne a son; and he called his name Jesus.

This does NOT mean he had <u>marital relations</u> with her afterward (see "Brothers of Christ").

Mt 27:59-60 And Joseph took the body, and wrapped it in a clean linen shroud, ⁶⁰ and laid it in his own new tomb, which he had hewn in the rock;

Lk 23:53 Then he took it down and wrapped it in a linen shroud, and laid him in a rock-hewn tomb, where no one had ever yet been laid.

Jn 19:41 Now in the place where he was crucified there was a garden, and in the garden a new tomb where no one had ever been laid.

Jerome, arguably the greatest Biblical scholar in the history of the Western Church, asserted Mary's perpetual virginity complemented Christ's burial in the "virginal" sepulchre - no one would be buried in Christ's tomb, and no child would be born of Mary's womb, after Him.

<u>Early Christians' comments on Mary Ever-Virgin</u>

Brothers of Christ

"Christ...was the only Son of Mary, and the Virgin Mother bore no more children besides Him...'brothers' really means 'cousins' here, and Holy Writ and the Jews have always called cousins brothers" - Martin Luther, Sermons on John, Chap. 1-4

Jesus was the only son of Mary. Mary did not have marital relations with Joseph, rather she remained a virgin throughout her whole life, her virginity remaining intact even during and after the birth of the Lord, as a sign of her undefiled devotion to God, an unmerited gift from God to Mary. (CCC 411, 490-493)

Current misunderstandings: Because the people of the Near East were a tribal people, the languages they use do not make the same familial distinctions made in non-tribal languages, such as Greek and English. Neither Hebrew nor Aramaic has a word which distinguishes "brother" from "cousin" - the same word is used for both relations, since a tribe considers all who are descended from the same patriarch brothers. However, Greek does have a separate word for each state. The Greek translation of the Hebrew Scriptures (i.e., the Septuagint translation) recognizes the translation difficulty and solves it by using the word "brother" (adelphos) exclusively - it doesn't use "cousin" at all. Likewise, every occurrence of the word "brother" in the New Testament is also adelphos. Consequently, if two people in Scripture are called "brothers," the reader can only determine the blood relationship between the two people by the context - neither the Greek nor the Hebrew distinguishes. For various reasons relating to Church authority and the archetype which Mary represents in Scripture, it is theologically useful for many Christians to impugn various Catholic teachings about Mary. In this case, her eternal virginity is attacked through inadvertent or deliberate misunderstandings of context involving the words "brother," "until" (Matthew 1:24-25), and "first-born," the argument being that "until" implicitly means "things were one way until the event, another way after the event," and that "first-born" implies other children.

Not all uses of the word "brother" indicate two men with the same mother:

Deut 23:8 "You shall not abhor an Edomite, for he is your brother; you shall not abhor an Egyptian, because you were a sojourner in his land.

Neh 5:7 I took counsel with myself, and I brought charges against the nobles and the officials. I said to them, "You are exacting interest, each from his brother." And I held a great assembly against them...

2 Kings 10:13-14 ... Jehu met the kinsmen of Ahaziah king of Judah, and he said, "Who are you?" And they answered, "We are the kinsmen of Ahaziah, and we came down to visit the royal princes and the sons of the queen mother." [14] He said, "Take them alive." And they took them alive, and slew them at the pit of Beth-eked, forty-two persons, and he spared none of them.

The word translated here as "kinsmen" is the same word which is translated "brother" elsewhere.

Jer 34:9 that every one should set free his Hebrew slaves, male and female, so that no one should enslave a Jew, his brother.

2 Sam 1:26 I am distressed for you, my brother Jonathan; very pleasant have you been to me; your love to me was wonderful...

1 Kings 9:11-13 and Hiram king of Tyre had supplied Solomon with cedar and cypress timber and gold, as much as he desired, King Solomon gave to Hiram twenty cities in the land of Galilee. [12] But when Hiram came from Tyre to see the cities which Solomon had given him, they did not please him. [13] Therefore he said, "What kind of cities are these which you have given me, my brother?" So they are called the land of Cabul to this day.

1 Kings 20:32 So they girded sackcloth on their loins, and put ropes on their heads, and went to the king of Israel and said, "Your servant Ben-hadad says, 'Pray, let me live.'" And he said, "Does he still live? He is my brother."

Amos 1:9 Thus says the LORD:
"For three transgressions of Tyre,
and for four, I will not revoke the punishment;
because they delivered up a whole people to Edom,
and did not remember the covenant of brotherhood.

Was this practice of calling non-blood relations "brother" altered in the New Testament Greek?

Mt 12:46-50 While he was still speaking to the people, behold, his mother and his brothers stood outside, asking to speak to him. [48] But he replied to the man who told him, "Who is my mother, and who are my brothers?" [49] And stretching out his hand toward his disciples, he said, "Here are my mother and my brothers! [50] For whoever does the will of my Father in heaven is my brother, and sister, and mother."

Mk 3:31-33 And his mother and his brothers came; and standing outside they sent to him and called him. [32] And a crowd was sitting about him; and they said to him, "Your mother and your brothers are outside, asking for you." [33] And he replied, "Who are my mother and my brothers?" [34] And looking around on those who sat about him, he said, "Here are my mother and my brothers! ³⁵ Whoever does the will of God is my brother, and sister, and mother."

Some would say these passages show Jesus had blood brothers. Yet...

Mt 5:22-24 But I say to you that every one who is angry with his brother shall be liable to judgment; whoever insults his brother shall be liable to the council, and whoever says, 'You fool!' shall be liable to the hell of fire. ²³ So if you are offering your gift at the altar, and there remember that your brother has something against you, ²⁴ leave your gift there before the altar and go; first be reconciled to your brother, and then come and offer your gift.

Mt 18:15, 21,35 "If your brother sins against you, go and tell him his fault, between you and him alone. If he listens to you, you have gained your brother....Then Peter came up and said to him, "Lord, how often shall my brother sin against me, and I forgive him? As many as seven times?" ²² Jesus said to him, "I do not say to you seven times, but seventy times seven. [The parable of the ungrateful servant follows] So also my heavenly Father will do to every one of you, if you do not forgive your brother from your heart."

...if we think the Greek word "adelphos" was meant to indicate only sons of one mother, then Jesus only forbids us to be angry with our own mother's sons. Anger with daughters would presumably be acceptable. People who insist on "blood brothers" in Mk 3 and Mt 12 never insist on it for Mt 5 and Mt 18, even though the word is identical in all four passages.

Mk 6:3 Is not this the carpenter, the son of Mary and brother of James and Joses and Judas and Simon, and are not his sisters here with us?"

Mt 13:55 Is not this the carpenter's son? Is not his mother called Mary? And are not his brothers James and Joseph and Simon and Judas?

Note that Christ isn't called "a son of Mary," but "the son of Mary," nor is he called "a carpenter's son" but "the carpenter's son."

Mk 3:21 And when his family heard it, they went out to seize him, for people were saying, "He is beside himself."

The word "brothers" above is translated "family" by the RSV. In first-century Jewish society, a younger brother would NEVER presume to tell his older brother (especially his first-born older brother) or his father what to do. It was a violation of honor, respect, and conduct.

Additional evidence - the geneologies:

Mk 15:40 There were also women looking on from afar, among whom were Mary Magdalene, and Mary the mother of James the younger and of Joses, and Salome,

Lk 6:15-16 and Matthew, and Thomas, and James the son of Alphaeus, and Simon who was called the Zealot, ¹⁶ and Judas the son of James, and Judas Iscariot, who became a traitor.

Mt 10:2-3 James the son of Zebedee, and John his brother; ³ Philip and Bartholomew; Thomas and Matthew the tax collector; James the son of Alphaeus, and Thaddaeus;

Mt 27:56 among whom were Mary Magdalene, and Mary the mother of James and Joseph, and the mother of the sons of Zebedee.

Jn 19:25-27 So the soldiers did this. But standing by the cross of Jesus were his mother, and his mother's sister, Mary the wife of Clopas, and Mary Magdalene. ²⁶ When Jesus saw his mother, and the disciple whom he loved standing near, he said to his mother, "Woman, behold, your son!" ²⁷ Then he said to the disciple, "Behold, your mother!" And from that hour the disciple took her to his own home.

Mary Magdalen's offspring: none apparent.

Mary, wife of Clopas' (or Cleophas) offspring: James the younger, Joseph, and sons of Zebedee (Matthew 27:56, Mark 15:40, John 19:25). James is called son of Alphaeus in Matthew 10:3, but Alphaeus and Clopas could be the same person, or the mother of James could have re-married. According to Hegesippus, Cleophas was the brother of Joseph, Mary's husband, which would make James a first-cousin.

The Blessed Virgin Mary's offspring: Jesus.

Also, note that Mary is given into the care of "the beloved disciple," who is clearly not Mary's son. This is not proper for a man whose mother has other sons - she would have been given into the care of a family member, not an unrelated person.

Scriptural Catholicism — Mary

The "until" argument:

Mt 1:24-25 When Joseph woke from sleep, he did as the angel of the Lord commanded him; he took his wife, 25 but knew her not until she had borne a son; and he called his name Jesus.

Many argue the use of the word "until," or heos *in the Greek, indicates Joseph had marital relations with Mary after the birth of Jesus. In fact, Scripture frequently uses the word "until" to indicate an important event in an on-going process. It does not necessarily indicate that the process changed or stopped after the important event occurred.*

Mt 22:43-44 He said to them, "How is it then that David, inspired by the Spirit, calls him Lord, saying, 44 'The Lord said to my Lord,
Sit at my right hand,
till I put thy enemies under thy feet'?

The word "till" here is also heos. *If it HAD to mean a termination of a previous state, then the Lord would stop sitting at the Father's right hand once His enemies are put under His feet.*

Mt 18:21 Then Peter came up and said to him, "Lord, how often shall my brother sin against me, and I forgive him? As many as seven times?" 22 Jesus said to him, "I do not say to you seven times, but seventy times seven.

Although the translation doesn't show it, the word heos *actually appears twice in this passage, both in "till seven times?" and in "until seventy times seven." Again, this would mean there is some point at which we can stop forgiving our brother.*

2 Pet 1:9 And we have the prophetic word made more sure. You will do well to pay attention to this as to a lamp shining in a dark place, until the day dawns and the morning star rises in your hearts.

Does this mean we don't have to pay attention to the prophetic word once we accept Jesus into our heart?

Gen 8:5 And the waters continued to abate until the tenth month; in the tenth month, on the first day of the month, the tops of the mountains were seen.

The waters diminished "until" the tenth month, but they kept diminishing even after that (or we would all be living on one square foot of land). In fact, the sacred author could have used at least two other forms of the word "until," akhree *or* mekhree, *to indicate the termination of a previous process. He didn't. He chose instead* heos, *the word which indicates a continuous process. The use of the word "until" in Mt 1:24-25 does not imply Joseph began having relations with Mary after Jesus' birth.*

The first-born argument:

Ex 34:20 All the first-born of your sons you shall redeem. And none shall appear before me empty.

Does this mean the first-born son wouldn't be redeemed until the second son was born? "First-born" means no more than it says. This son was born, and he was the first. It doesn't imply a second.

Mary, Queen of Heaven

2 Tim 4:8 Henceforth there is laid up for me the crown of righteousness, which the Lord, the righteous judge, will award to me on that Day, and not only to me but also to all who have loved his appearing.

This section comes largely from Dr. Scott Hahn's tape "Immaculately Conceived."

The title "Queen of Heaven" is very difficult for some sola scriptura *Christians, and for a very good reason:*

Jer 7:18 The children gather wood, the fathers kindle fire, and the women knead dough, to make cakes for the queen of heaven; and they pour out drink offerings to other gods, to provoke me to anger.

Jer 44:7-8,11,15-17,24-27 And now thus says the LORD God of hosts, the God of Israel: Why do you commit this great evil against yourselves, to cut off from you man and woman, infant and child, from the midst of Judah, leaving you no remnant? 8 Why do you provoke me to anger with the works of your hands, burning incense to other gods in the land of Egypt where you have come to live, that you may be cut off and become a curse and a taunt among all the nations of the earth.. 11 "Therefore thus says the LORD of hosts, the God of Israel: Behold, I will set my face against you for evil, to cut off all Judah...

¹⁵ Then all the men who knew that their wives had offered incense to other gods, and all the women who stood by, a great assembly, all the people who dwelt in Pathros in the land of Egypt, answered Jeremiah: ¹⁶ "As for the word which you have spoken to us in the name of the LORD, we will not listen to you. ¹⁷ But we will do everything that we have vowed, burn incense to the queen of heaven and pour out libations to her, as we did, both we and our fathers, our kings and our princes, in the cities of Judah and in the streets of Jerusalem; for then we had plenty of food, and prospered, and saw no evil...
²⁴ Jeremiah said to all the people and all the women, "Hear the word of the LORD, all you of Judah who are in the land of Egypt, ²⁵ Thus says the LORD of hosts, the God of Israel: You and your wives have declared with your mouths, and have fulfilled it with your hands, saying, 'We will surely perform our vows that we have made, to burn incense to the queen of heaven and to pour out libations to her.' Then confirm your vows and perform your vows! ²⁶ Therefore hear the word of the LORD, all you of Judah who dwell in the land of Egypt: Behold, I have sworn by my great name, says the LORD, that my name shall no more be invoked by the mouth of any man of Judah in all the land of Egypt, saying, 'As the Lord GOD lives.' ²⁷ Behold, I am watching over them for evil and not for good; all the men of Judah who are in the land of Egypt shall be consumed by the sword and by famine, until there is an end of them.

It is important to know the context of these remarks in ancient Jewish society, and the practices of pagan cults. The title "Queen of Heaven" was first attached to the Assyro-Babylonian fertility goddess Ishtar, daughter of the moon-god, whose worship was introduced under King Manessah and was revived after King Josiah's death. The baking of bread cakes in the shape of stars and the burning of incense were the way in which sacrifice was made to this goddess, who was associated with the planet Venus. This is the pagan cult which Jeremiah rightly condemns.

Rev 12:1 And a great portent appeared in heaven, a woman clothed with the sun, with the moon under her feet, and on her head a crown of twelve stars...

The Church was and is fully aware of this pagan cult, for Mary is Christ's triumph over this cult. As is so often the case, these pagans had a dim, twisted idea of reality and how God works. Just as the demi-gods of Greek and Roman legend, half-human, half-divine, are dim, twisted images of the fully-human, fully-divine Christ, the "fertility goddess" figure is a very dim, twisted, mistaken view of Mary, the simple Jewish woman through whose womb the living God, the Creator of all that exists, entered the world. She crushes the moon-god and his children under her feet. Ishtar, who pretended to be queen of heaven, is overthrown by Jesus, who crowns the true Queen of Heaven, His Mother.

The first century heresy of Collyridianism, which arose out of Arabia, attempted to replace Ishtar with Mary. Collyridianism held Mary to be divine and offered her sacrifice, through the baking of bread cakes and the burning of incense. The heresy was immediately put down by the Church, and has never revived. While Mary must be treated with the same honor with which God treats her, it is blasphemy to offer sacrifice to a human being. Only God is due sacrifice.

So, how does Jesus Christ honor His mother? For centuries before Christ's birth, the queen of a Near Eastern kingdom was not the wife of the king, but the king's mother. She assisted the king in ruling over the land, was his counselor, led the people in song worship, and was a major advocate for the people before him. Scripture confirms the existence of the institution of Queen Mother in Israel and her role:

Ex 15:20-21 Then Miriam, the prophetess, the sister of Aaron, took a timbrel in her hand; and all the women went out after her with timbrels and dancing. ²¹ And Miriam sang to them:
"Sing to the LORD, for he has triumphed gloriously; the horse and his rider he has thrown into the sea."

Jer 13:18,20 Say to the king and the queen mother:
"Take a lowly seat,
for your beautiful crown
has come down from your head."... "Lift up your eyes and see
those who come from the north.
Where is the flock that was given you,
your beautiful flock?

Prov 31:1-2,8-9 - (*written by a Queen Mother*) The words of Lemuel, king of Massa, which his mother taught him:² What, my son? What, son of my womb?What, son of my vows?... Open your mouth for the dumb,
for the rights of all who are left desolate. ⁹ Open your mouth, judge righteously, maintain the rights of the poor and needy.

2 Chron 22:2-4 Ahaziah was forty-two years old when he began to reign, and he reigned one year in Jerusalem. His mother's name was Athaliah, the granddaughter of Omri. ³ He also walked in the ways of the house of Ahab, for his mother was his counselor in doing wickedly. ⁴ He did what was evil in the sight of the LORD, as the house of Ahab had done; for after the death of his father they were his counselors, to his undoing.

2 Kings 11:1-3 Now when Athaliah the mother of Ahaziah saw that her son was dead, she arose and destroyed all the royal family. ² But Jehosheba, the daughter of King Joram, sister of Ahaziah, took Joash the son of Ahaziah, and stole him away from among the king's sons who were about to be slain, and she put him and his nurse in a bedchamber. Thus she hid him from Athaliah, so that he was not slain; ³ and he remained with her six years, hid in the house of the LORD, while Athaliah reigned over the land.

1 Kings 15:9-13 In the twentieth year of Jeroboam king of Israel Asa began to reign over Judah, ¹⁰ and he reigned forty-one years in Jerusalem. His mother's name was Maacah the daughter of Abishalom. ¹¹ And Asa did what was right in the eyes of the LORD, as David his father had done. ¹² He put away the male cult prostitutes out of the land, and removed all the idols that his fathers had made. ¹³ He also removed Maacah his mother from being queen mother because she had an abominable image made for Asherah; and Asa cut down her image and burned it at the brook Kidron.

2 Kings 10:13-14 Jehu met the kinsmen of Ahaziah king of Judah, and he said, "Who are you?" And they answered, "We are the kinsmen of Ahaziah, and we came down to visit the royal princes and the sons of the queen mother." ¹⁴ He said, "Take them alive." And they took them alive, and slew them at the pit of Beth-eked, forty-two persons, and he spared none of them.

Jezebel was the only Queen Mother the Northern Kingdom had. Her death without replacement signalled the political instability and eventual fall of the Northern Kingdom. When the Davidic line goes underground during the Babylonian captivity, so does the position of Queen Mother. It re-emerges with the Davidic line demonstrated in Mark 1. Christ is king in the line of Solomon and David, therefore His mother must occupy the position of Queen Mother.

Psalm 45:1-9 My heart overflows with a goodly theme;
I address my verses to the king;
my tongue is like the pen of a ready scribe.
² You are the fairest of the sons of men;
 grace is poured upon your lips;
therefore God has blessed you for ever.
³ Gird your sword upon your thigh, O mighty one,
in your glory and majesty!
⁴ In your majesty ride forth victoriously
for the cause of truth and to defend the right;
 let your right hand teach you dread deeds!
⁵ Your arrows are sharp
 in the heart of the king's enemies;
the peoples fall under you.
⁶ Your divine throne endures for ever and ever.
Your royal scepter is a scepter of equity;
⁷ you love righteousness and hate wickedness.
Therefore God, your God, has anointed you
 with the oil of gladness above your fellows;
⁸ your robes are all fragrant with myrrh and aloes
 and cassia.
From ivory palaces stringed instruments make
 you glad;
⁹ daughters of kings are among your ladies of
 honor;
at your right hand stands the queen in gold of Ophir.

Phil 2:6-11 who, though he was in the form of God, did not count equality with God a thing to be grasped, ⁷ but emptied himself, taking the form of a servant, being born in the likeness of men. ⁸ And being found in human form he humbled himself and became obedient unto death, even death on a cross. ⁹ Therefore God has highly exalted him and bestowed on him the name which is above every name, ¹⁰ that at the name of Jesus every knee should bow, in heaven and on earth and under the earth, ¹¹ and every tongue confess that Jesus Christ is Lord, to the glory of God the Father.

The word used for "servant" in Phillippians is "doulos" - the word for "handmaid" in Luke, below, is the feminine form of "doulous."

Lk 1:38,46-55 And Mary said, "Behold, I am the handmaid of the Lord; let it be to me according to your word." And the angel departed from her....And Mary said,
"My soul magnifies the Lord, ⁴⁷ and my spirit rejoices in God my Savior, ⁴⁸ for he has regarded the low estate of his handmaiden.

For behold, henceforth all generations will call me blessed; [49] for he who is mighty has done great things for me,
and holy is his name. [50] And his mercy is on those who fear him
from generation to generation. [51] He has shown strength with his arm,
he has scattered the proud in the imagination of their hearts, [52] he has put down the mighty from their thrones,
and exalted those of low degree; [53] he has filled the hungry with good things,
and the rich he has sent empty away. [54] He has helped his servant Israel,
in remembrance of his mercy, [55] as he spoke to our fathers,
to Abraham and to his posterity for ever."

1 Pet 5:4-5 And when the chief Shepherd is manifested you will obtain the unfading crown of glory. [5] Likewise you that are younger be subject to the elders. Clothe yourselves, all of you, with humility toward one another, for "God opposes the proud, but gives grace to the humble."

Peter, Paul, and Luke stress humbleness and obedience, and both assert that exaltation results from those virtues: Christ is above every other name, his mother is uniquely blessed, and uniquely crowned. What honor is due to a queen mother?

1 Kings 2:19 So Bathsheba went to King Solomon, to speak to him on behalf of Adonijah. And the king rose to meet her, and bowed down to her; then he sat on his throne, and had a seat brought for the king's mother; and she sat on his right.

King Solomon pays filial honor to his mother, honoring God's commandments. God commands that we must honor our mother. If we are truly brothers of Jesus Christ, then Mary is truly our mother, and our queen, for Christ is truly the King of kings and Lord of lords.

1 Cor 9:25 Every athlete exercises self-control in all things. They do it to receive a perishable wreath, but we an imperishable.

2 Tim 4:8 Henceforth there is laid up for me the crown of righteousness, which the Lord, the righteous judge, will award to me on that Day, and not only to me but also to all who have loved his appearing.

Who loved His appearing more than the one who gave Him birth?

James 1:12 Blessed is the man who endures trial, for when he has stood the test he will receive the crown of life which God has promised to those who love him.

Keep this verse in mind when you read of Mary's heart being pierced by a sword, or when you think on her standing at the foot of the cross, watching her only Son's blood running in rivulets down the wood.

Wis 5:16 Therefore they will receive a glorious crown and a beautiful diadem from the hand of the Lord, because with his right hand he will cover them, and with his arm he will shield them.

1 Pet 5:4 And when the chief Shepherd is manifested you will obtain the unfading crown of glory.

Rev 2:10 Be faithful unto death, and I will give you the crown of life.

Song 6:10 Who is she that comes forth as the morning rising, fair as the moon, bright as the sun, terrible as an army set in battle array?

One of the most ancient Marian prayers known, the Sub Tuum Praesidium, written no later than 250 A.D., acknowledges her role: "We fly to your patronage, O Holy Mother of God, despise not our petitions in our necessities, but deliver us from all dangers, O glorious and blessed Virgin!" It is a direct prayer to Mary, Queen Mother and Theotokos (God-bearer) at least 200 years before the formal definition at Ephesus, composed amidst the countless martyrdoms flowing from Roman persecution.

Mary, Our Mother

"Mary is the Mother of Jesus and the Mother of us all...There where He is, we ought also to be; and all that He has ought to be ours, and His Mother is also our mother." - Martin Luther, Sermon, Christmas, 1529

Lk 1:45 "And blessed is she who believed that there would be fulfilledment of what was spoken to her from the Lord."

As Elizabeth observes, Mary heard the word of God and kept it in her heart and in her womb.

Lk 11:27-28 As he said this, a woman in the crowd raised her voice and said to him, "Blessed is the womb that bore you, and the breasts that you sucked!" 28 But he said, "Blessed rather are those who hear the word of God and keep it!"

Again, the translation is poor. The Greek is better translated "Yes, but blessed are those who hear the word of God and keep it!" Jesus does not deny Mary's blessedness, He confirms that she is even more blessed because of her obedience than because of her motherhood.

Mt 12:49-50 And stretching out his hand toward his disciples, he said, "Here are my mother and my brothers! 50 For whoever does the will of my Father in heaven is my brother, and sister, and mother."

Mk 3:34-35 And looking around on those who sat about him, he said, "Here are my mother and my brothers! 35 Whoever does the will of God is my brother, and sister, and mother."

Lk 8:21 But he said to them, "My mother and my brothers are those who hear the word of God and do it."

However, Christ insists we understand: Mary is our spiritual mother. She is not to be called blessed simply because she physically gave Him birth, but because she hears the word of God and keeps it always.

Lk 1:31-35,38 And behold, you will conceive in your womb and bear a son, and you shall call his name Jesus. 32 He will be great, and will be called the Son of the Most High;
and the Lord God will give to him the throne of his father David, 33 and he will reign over the house of Jacob for ever;
and of his kingdom there will be no end." 34 And Mary said to the angel, "How shall this be, since I have no husband?" 35 And the angel said to her,
"The Holy Spirit will come upon you,
and the power of the Most High will overshadow you; therefore the child to be born will be called holy, the Son of God.... And Mary said, "Behold, I am the handmaid of the Lord; let it be to me according to your word." And the angel departed from her.

Gal 4:4-7 But when the time had fully come, God sent forth his Son, born of woman, born under the law, 5 to redeem those who were under the law, so that we might receive adoption as sons. 6 And because you are sons, God has sent the Spirit of his Son into our hearts, crying, "Abba! Father!" 7 So through God you are no longer a slave but a son, and if a son then an heir.

Mary is the mother of the man who is our brother. We are sons of God, she is the mother of God, and of us.

Heb 2:11-12 For he who sanctifies and those who are sanctified have all one origin. That is why he is not ashamed to call them brethren, 12 saying,
"I will proclaim thy name to my brethren,
in the midst of the congregation I will praise thee."

The Second Person of the Trinity has His divine origin in God the Father, Jesus has His temporal origin in Mary. Through our baptism, we are joined to Him, participating in the divine nature and sharing His temporal origin.

Psalm 87:5 "One and all were born in her;
and he who has established her
is the Most High Lord." (NAB translation)

Psalm 86:16 Turn to me and take pity on me; give thy strength to thy servant, and save the son of thy handmaid.

David calls himself the child of God's handmaid. It is interesting to note that the word "handmaid" appears only once in the New Testament, but almost two dozen times in the Old Testament. In each case, the woman who is called or calls herself a "handmaid" prefigures some aspect of Mary's role.

Judg 9:18 and you have risen up against my father's house this day, and have slain his sons, seventy men on one stone, and have made Abimelech, the son of his maidservant, king over the citizens of Shechem, because he is your kinsman

Abimelech's claim to the throne lies in the fact that he is the son of the old king's handmaid.

Ex 2:5 Now the daughter of Pharaoh came down to bathe at the river, and her maidens walked beside the river; she saw the basket among the reeds and sent her maid to fetch it

Moses, the prophet who prefigures Christ, is rescued by a handmaid. All Israel is rescued through Moses.

1 Sam 1:11 And [Hannah] vowed a vow and said, "O LORD of hosts, if thou wilt indeed look on the affliction of thy maidservant, and remember me, and not forget thy maidservant, but wilt give to thy maidservant a son, then I will give him to the LORD all the days of his life, and no razor shall touch his head."

Hannah bore Samuel, the prophet who would anoint both Saul and David king over Israel.

1 Sam 25:24-25,32-35 She fell at his feet and said, "Upon me alone, my lord, be the guilt; pray let your handmaid speak in your ears, and hear the words of your handmaid. ²⁵ Let not my lord regard this ill-natured fellow, Nabal; for as his name is, so is he; Nabal is his name, and folly is with him; but I your handmaid did not see the young men of my lord, whom you sent.... And David said to Abigail, "Blessed be the LORD, the God of Israel, who sent you this day to meet me! ³³ Blessed be your discretion, and blessed be you, who have kept me this day from bloodguilt and from avenging myself with my own hand! ³⁴ For as surely as the LORD the God of Israel lives, who has restrained me from hurting you, unless you had made haste and come to meet me, truly by morning there had not been left to Nabal so much as one male." ³⁵ Then David received from her hand what she had brought him; and he said to her, "Go up in peace to your house; see, I have hearkened to your voice, and I have granted your petition."

Abigail successfully intercedes for her guilty husband Nabal, sparing him from the wrath of King David. David is so impressed by how eloquently she intercedes for her husband that he later marries her after her husband is struck down by the Lord.

2 Sam 14:15 Now I have come to say this to my lord the king because the people have made me afraid; and your handmaid thought, 'I will speak to the king; it may be that the king will perform the request of his servant. ¹⁶ For the king will hear, and deliver his servant from the hand of the man who would destroy me and my son together from the heritage of God.' ¹⁷ And your handmaid thought, 'The word of my lord the king will set me at rest'; for my lord the king is like the angel of God to discern good and evil. The LORD your God be with you!"

Joab did not himself intercede before the king, but sent a maidservant to do so.

1 Kings 1:13 Go in at once to King David, and say to him, 'Did you not, my lord the king, swear to your maidservant, saying, "Solomon your son shall reign after me, and he shall sit upon my throne"? Why then is Adonijah king?'

Bathsheba, wife of the king and mother of Solomon, successfully intercedes with the king for her child. She is Solomon's Queen Mother.

1 Kings 3:20 And she arose at midnight, and took my son from beside me, while your maidservant slept, and laid it in her bosom, and laid her dead son in my bosom.

The sinless woman successfully fights for her child's life before the king.

Jud 11:5,12:4 Judith replied to him, "Accept the words of your servant, and let your maidservant speak in your presence, and I will tell nothing false to my lord this night... 12:4 Judith replied, "As your soul lives, my lord, your servant will not use up the things I have with me before the Lord carries out by my hand what he has determined to do."

Judith saves all Israel from invasion by Holofernes and the Assyrian army he leads. She accomplishes this by entering Holofernes camp, cutting off Holofernes head, and displaying it from the walls of the fortified city Holofernes had under siege. The entire army flees in terror as the Israelites attack. The sacred author portrays Judith as the pure defender of Israel.

Wis 9:5 For I am thy slave and the son of thy maidservant,
a man who is weak and short-lived,
with little understanding of judgment and laws;

Solomon, king of Israel, again affirms that the Queen Mother is the handmaid of the Lord, and he, the King of Israel, is her son.

Lk 7:12-15 As he drew near to the gate of the city, behold, a man who had died was being carried out, the only son of his mother, and she was a widow; and a large crowd from the city was with her. ¹³ And when the Lord saw her, he had compassion on her and said to her, "Do not weep." ¹⁴ And he came and touched the bier, and the bearers stood still. And he said, "Young man, I say to you, arise." ¹⁵ And the dead man sat up, and began to speak. And he gave him to his mother.

This passage is the closest parallel in all Scripture to His relationship to His mother in His Passion, Death, and Resurrection. The parallels between what happens here and what happens at the foot of the Cross cannot be ignored.

Lk 23:27-28 And there followed him a great multitude of the people, and of women who bewailed and lamented him. ²⁸ But Jesus turning to them said, "Daughters of Jerusalem, do not weep for me, but weep for yourselves and for your children..."

The word Jesus habitually uses to address Mary is "gune," which means "woman," but has the specific meaning "wife." The word is derived from "ginomai" which means, among other things, "to be married." Mary is the spouse of the Holy Spirit - if God is our Father, then Mary is our mother.

Jn 19:26-27 When Jesus saw his mother, and the disciple whom he loved standing near, he said to his mother, "Woman, behold, your son!" ²⁷ Then he said to the disciple, "Behold, your mother!" And from that hour the disciple took her to his own home.

Verse 27 is incorrectly translated on at least two counts. First, the word "home" was added by the English translator - it does not exist in the Greek. Second, the Greek does not say "his own" but "their own." Thus, the correct translation would be "And from that hour, the disciple took her to their own." Mary is a gift from God to each of us who is His beloved disciple. We are to take her into our own. After He brings us back to life, He gives each of us to His mother, and gives each of us His mother.

Rev 12:17 Then the dragon was angry with the woman, and went off to make war on the rest of her offspring, on those who keep the commandments of God and bear testimony to Jesus.

The dragon wages war against HER offspring, those who keep God's commandments and bear witness to Jesus. Do you do these things? Then you are her children in the order of grace. "All Mary wants to do is give the heavenly Father children." (Fr. Frederick Miller)

Maternal Mediation

Mary's motherhood, however, does give her an extraordinary role. She stands at the apex of the communion of saints, as Queen Mother, Advocate, Mediatrix of All Graces, and the squire of God, the Co-Redemptrix. (CCC 618, 968)

Gal 4:4 But when the time had fully come, God sent forth his Son, born of woman, born under the law,...

Heb 10:10 And by that will we have been sanctified through the offering of the body of Jesus Christ once for all.

It is the body of Christ which sanctifies us. Mary, the squire of God, gave Christ the instrument which He used to accomplish our sanctification in the battle against Satan. The prophets and patriarchs of old were instruments of God's will and purpose, mediators between the Trinity and mankind, but none of these human instruments reached the heights which Mary reached, perfectly transmitting God's will and intention, indeed, His very life, into the world.

Heb 4:11-13 Let us therefore strive to enter that rest, that no one fall by the same sort of disobedience. ¹² For the word of God is living and active, sharper than any two-edged sword, piercing to the division of soul and spirit, of joints and marrow, and discerning the thoughts and intentions of the heart. ¹³ And before him no creature is hidden, but all are open and laid bare to the eyes of him with whom we have to do.

The passage is preceded by a discussion of the Sabbath rest established by God in Genesis 2. Paul is specifically linking Jesus Christ, the Word of God, to the New Creation, the perfect rest promised to us by God, a rest prophesied but never delivered in the Old Testament. The Word of God, sharp enough to pierce the division between soul and spirit, and able to lay bare everyone to His eyes, is delivered into creation by the squire He appoints.

Lk 2:32-34 "...a light for revelation to the Gentiles, and for glory to they people Israel." ³³ And his father and his mother marveled at what was said about him; ³⁴ and Simeon blessed them and said to Mary his mother,
   "Behold, this child is set for the fall and rising of many in Israel, and for a sign that is spoken against
   ³⁵ (and a sword will pierce through your own soul also),
   that thoughts out of many hearts may be revealed."

The Word of God pierces Mary's soul in an absolutely unique way. The two-edged sword of God is carried by His mother. Through her assent to His will, He takes up His humanity from her hands, welds it to His Divinity, and wields Himself, laying bare the hearts of many. She has a unique share in this work.

Eph 3:2 assuming that you have heard of the stewardship of God's grace that was given to me for you...

Paul was a self-proclaimed steward of God's grace. A steward guards and distributes his master's belongings with equity and justice to the members of the master's household. Here, Paul claimed to be designated by God to distribute grace to everyone for God by the fact that he preached the Gospel. If Paul can claim to be a steward of God's grace through preaching the Word, then consider Mary, who preached the Word more completely, more effectively, than any Apostle or disciple who ever lived. She preached His Word in complete silence, in a stable. Through the stewardship given to her by the Holy Spirit, the grace of God came into the world for the salvation of men; wrapped in swaddling clothes, laid in a manger.

1 Cor 9:22 I have become all things to all men, that I might by all means save some.

1 Tim 4:16 Take heed to yourself and to your teaching: hold to that, for by so doing you will save both yourself and your hearers.

If Paul could claim to be a saviour, and could instruct Timothy in how to be a saviour, then Mary has a claim at least as strong as either to the same title and honor. Paul and Timothy can only claim to have preached the Word while Mary's submission to God's will actually allows us to meet Him in the flesh.

Lk 1:15,41-45 for he will be great before the Lord, and he shall drink no wine nor strong drink, and he will be filled with the Holy Spirit, even from his mother's womb. ...And when Elizabeth heard the greeting of Mary, the babe leaped in her womb; and Elizabeth was filled with the Holy Spirit [42] and she exclaimed with a loud cry, "Blessed are you among women, and blessed is the fruit of your womb! [43] And why is this granted me, that the mother of my Lord should come to me? [44] For behold, when the voice of your greeting came to my ears, the babe in my womb leaped for joy. [45] And blessed is she who believed that there would be a fulfilment of what was spoken to her from the Lord."

In this remarkable story, Elizabeth receives an outpouring of inspiration through the Holy Spirit, and John the Baptist is sanctified in the womb just as the angel prophesied, due simply to Mary's presence and greeting. Mary was the instrument which brought about Elizabeth's inspired recognition and John's sanctification. How does Elizabeth respond? By blessing Mary first, then Jesus. She does not do this because Mary is more important than Jesus, rather she does this because she understands the ways of God. If you would honor God, you must first honor the finest work of His hands, His mother.

Jn 2:1-5 On the third day there was a marriage at Cana in Galilee, and the mother of Jesus was there; [2] Jesus also was invited to the marriage, with his disciples. [3] When the wine failed, the mother of Jesus said to him, "They have no wine." [4] And Jesus said to her, "O woman, what have you to do with me? My hour has not yet come." [5] His mother said to the servants, "Do whatever he tells you."

John 2:2 may imply that Jesus was invited to the wedding only because Mary was. His first public miracle was made at His mother's request. It was made because she was interceeding for someone in need. Christ asks, "What is the relationship between you and I?" Mary is not asking Jesus to do something He does not desire to do - she desires only what God desires. God simply requires of her what He requires of us all - we are to participate in the work.

Jn 2:11 This, the first of his signs, Jesus did at Cana in Galilee, and manifested his glory; and his disciples believed in him.

Mary's assent was necessary before Jesus would condescend to enter into the world, her prayer was necessary before He would condescend to begin His work in the world. He performed this first miracle even though His "time had not yet come," simply because she asked. The last words Scripture records from her mouth are also found here. They sum up her mission - she commands us always and constantly to "Do whatever He tells you." She leads us to Her Son better than anyone, for she loves Her Son better than any of us. She loves Him as only a mother can.

Is 53:3,11 He was despised and rejected by men; a man of sorrows, and acquainted with grief; and as one from whom men hide their faces he was despised, and we esteemed him not.... he shall see the fruit of the travail of his soul and be satisfied; by his knowledge shall the righteous one, my servant, make many to be accounted righteous; and he shall bear their iniquities.

The same prophet who foretold the virginal birth foretells the Suffering Servant. The mother of such a servant would suffer for and with her son.

Lk 2:34 and Simeon blessed them and said to Mary his mother,
"Behold, this child is set for the fall and rising of many in Israel,
and for a sign that is spoken against [35] (and a sword will pierce through your own soul also), that thoughts out of many hearts may be revealed."

Jn 19:25-27 So the soldiers did this. But standing by the cross of Jesus were his mother, and his mother's sister, Mary the wife of Clopas, and Mary Magdalene. [26] When Jesus saw his mother, and the disciple whom he loved standing near, he said to his mother, "Woman, behold, your son!"[27] Then he said to the disciple, "Behold, your mother!" And from that hour the disciple took her to his own home.

Mary's suffering at seeing her innocent and perfect Son cruelly tortured to death was immense, but she offered Him to the Father. She alone could look on the cross and say "There is flesh of my flesh and bone of my bone." Remember this. She alone, of all the people on earth, bore an echo of Christ's face in her own. Half of His DNA was hers. When you look upon Christ, you see the echo of Mary's face. When you look upon Mary, you see the echo of Christ. His face, twisted in an agony of pain on the Cross, was mirrored in her face, twisted in an agony of sorrow at His feet. He gave her to His beloved disciple, that is, to each of us, and each of us are to take her into our home. This is not an invitation. It is a command.

Rev 12:1-2 And a great portent appeared in heaven, a woman clothed with the sun, with the moon under her feet, and on her head a crown of twelve stars; [2] she was with child and she cried out in her pangs of birth, in anguish for delivery.

While giving birth to Christ was a joy without pain, giving birth to the Church was the searing pain of the Cross, a pain she shared spiritually with her Son as no one else could.

Acts 1:14 All these with one accord devoted themselves to prayer, together with the women and Mary the mother of Jesus, and with his brothers.

Mary prayed for the coming of her spouse, the Holy Spirit, so that the Body of Christ, the Church, might be formed on earth in the same way the Body of Christ was formed in her womb thirty-three years before. The formation of the Church required immense sacrifice from Mary, not in the sense that God required her sacrifice in order to redeem men - only Christ's sacrifice was required for our redemption - but in the sense that the pain brought to her mother's heart was prophesied to be part of what would reveal the thoughts of many. God permitted her to share in the sacrificial redemptive act of His Son.

Mal 3:1 "Behold, I send my messenger to prepare the way before me, and the Lord whom you seek will suddenly come to his temple...

Where God dwells, that is His Temple. He dwelt in the womb of Mary. She is the throne of grace in which He sat.

Heb 4:16 Let us then with confidence draw near to the throne of grace, that we may receive mercy and find grace to help in time of need.

Mary stands at our side as we approach Christ, encouraging us towards Him, guiding us as a mother guides her smallest child. She comforts us as Christ the Healer administers the medicine needed to bring us to health. She helps us open our hearts in trust to Him who is our Saviour and hers.

The Assumption of Mary

The Assumption is the rainbow in the heavens, God's sign to all Christians of the joy which awaits them. Mary, first among Christians, is lifted up to heaven body and soul by the power of God, there to enjoy heaven in its fullness. For we who are made to be the union of soul and body, the fullness of the experience of heaven is only possible when our souls are reunited with our bodies at resurrection of the dead.

Gen 5:23 Thus all the days of Enoch were three hundred and sixty-five years. [24] Enoch walked with God; and he was not, for God took him.

2 Kings 2:11 And as they still went on and talked, behold, a chariot of fire and horses of fire separated the two of them. And Elijah went up by a whirlwind into heaven.

Mt 27:52-53 the tombs also were opened, and many bodies of the saints who had fallen asleep were raised, ⁵³ and coming out of the tombs after his resurrection they went into the holy city and appeared to many.

Jude 9 But when the archangel Michael, contending with the devil, disputed about the body of Moses, he did not presume to pronounce a reviling judgment upon him, but said, "The Lord rebuke you."

Enoch and Elijah were both taken into heaven, Matthew reports a resurrection before the end of the world, and Jude reminds us that all Israel believed Moses' body had been assumed into heaven.

Psalm 132:8 Arise, O LORD, and go to thy resting place, thou and the ark of thy might.

Mary is the Ark of the New Covenant. But David was not the only one to see the vision. Mary's position in heaven was recorded by John, the beloved disciple who cared for Mary in their old age.

Rev 11:19-12:17 Then God's temple in heaven was opened, and the ark of his covenant was seen within his temple; and there were flashes of lightning, voices, peals of thunder, an earthquake, and heavy hail. ¹And a great portent appeared in heaven, a woman clothed with the sun, with the moon under her feet, and on her head a crown of twelve stars; ² she was with child and she cried out in her pangs of birth, in anguish for delivery. ³ And another portent appeared in heaven; behold, a great red dragon, with seven heads and ten horns, and seven diadems upon his heads. ⁴ His tail swept down a third of the stars of heaven, and cast them to the earth. And the dragon stood before the woman who was about to bear a child, that he might devour her child when she brought it forth; ⁵ she brought forth a male child, one who is to rule all the nations with a rod of iron, but her child was caught up to God and to his throne, ⁶ and the woman fled into the wilderness, where she has a place prepared by God, in which to be nourished for one thousand two hundred and sixty days. ⁷ Now war arose in heaven, Michael and his angels fighting against the dragon; and the dragon and his angels fought, ⁸ but they were defeated and there was no longer any place for them in heaven. ⁹ And the great dragon was thrown down, that ancient serpent, who is called the Devil and Satan, the deceiver of the whole world—he was thrown down to the earth, and his angels were thrown down with him. ¹⁰ And I heard a loud voice in heaven, saying, "Now the salvation and the power and the kingdom of our God and the authority of his Christ have come, for the accuser of our brethren has been thrown down, who accuses them day and night before our God. ¹¹ And they have conquered him by the blood of the Lamb and by the word of their testimony, for they loved not their lives even unto death. ¹² Rejoice then, O heaven and you that dwell therein! But woe to you, O earth and sea, for the devil has come down to you in great wrath, because he knows that his time is short!"

¹³ And when the dragon saw that he had been thrown down to the earth, he pursued the woman who had borne the male child. ¹⁴ But the woman was given the two wings of the great eagle that she might fly from the serpent into the wilderness, to the place where she is to be nourished for a time, and times, and half a time. ¹⁵ The serpent poured water like a river out of his mouth after the woman, to sweep her away with the flood. ¹⁶ But the earth came to the help of the woman, and the earth opened its mouth and swallowed the river which the dragon had poured from his mouth. ¹⁷ Then the dragon was angry with the woman, and went off to make war on the rest of her offspring, on those who keep the commandments of God and bear testimony to Jesus. And he stood on the sand of the sea.

Jn 12:26 If any one serves me, he must follow me; and where I am, there shall my servant be also; if any one serves me, the Father will honor him.

Who served Christ more faithfully than the woman who assented to be His Mother?

The Virtues of Mary

The Blessed Virgin's exemplary holiness encourages the faithful to "raise their eyes to Mary who shines forth before the whole community of the elect as a model of the virtues." It is a question of solid, evangelical virtues:

Faith and the docile acceptance of the Word of God, her generous obedience, her worship of God manifested in alacrity in the fulfillment of religious duties:

Lk 1:26-38 In the sixth month the angel Gabriel was sent from God to a city of Galilee named Nazareth, [27] to a virgin betrothed to a man whose name was Joseph, of the house of David; and the virgin's name was Mary. [28] And he came to her and said, "Hail, O favored one, the Lord is with you!" [29] But she was greatly troubled at the saying, and considered in her mind what sort of greeting this might be. [30] And the angel said to her, "Do not be afraid, Mary, for you have found favor with God. [31] And behold, you will conceive in your womb and bear a son, and you shall call his name Jesus. [32] He will be great, and will be called the Son of the Most High;
and the Lord God will give to him the throne of his father David, [33] and he will reign over the house of Jacob for ever;
and of his kingdom there will be no end." [34] And Mary said to the angel, "How shall this be, since I have no husband?" [35] And the angel said to her,
"The Holy Spirit will come upon you,
and the power of the Most High will overshadow you;
therefore the child to be born will be called holy,
the Son of God.
[36] And behold, your kinswoman Elizabeth in her old age has also conceived a son; and this is the sixth month with her who was called barren. [37] For with God nothing will be impossible." [38] And Mary said, "Behold, I am the handmaid of the Lord; let it be to me according to your word." And the angel departed from her.

Lk 1:45 And blessed is she who believed that there would be a fulfilment of what was spoken to her from the Lord."

Lk 11:27-28 As he said this, a woman in the crowd raised her voice and said to him, "Blessed is the womb that bore you, and the breasts that you sucked!" [28] But he said, "Blessed rather are those who hear the word of God and keep it!"

Jn 2:5 His mother said to the servants, "Do whatever he tells you."

her solicitous charity and genuine humility, her gratitude for gifts received:

Lk 1:39-56 In those days Mary arose and went with haste into the hill country, to a city of Judah, [40] and she entered the house of Zechariah and greeted Elizabeth. [41] And when Elizabeth heard the greeting of Mary, the babe leaped in her womb; and Elizabeth was filled with the Holy Spirit [42] and she exclaimed with a loud cry, "Blessed are you among women, and blessed is the fruit of your womb! [43] And why is this granted me, that the mother of my Lord should come to me? [44] For behold, when the voice of your greeting came to my ears, the babe in my womb leaped for joy. [45] And blessed is she who believed that there would be a fulfilment of what was spoken to her from the Lord." [46] And Mary said,
"My soul magnifies the Lord, [47] and my spirit rejoices in God my Savior, [48] for he has regarded the low estate of his handmaiden.
For behold, henceforth all generations will call me blessed; [49] for he who is mighty has done great things for me,
and holy is his name. [50] And his mercy is on those who fear him
from generation to generation. [51] He has shown strength with his arm,
he has scattered the proud in the imagination of their hearts, [52] he has put down the mighty from their thrones,
and exalted those of low degree; [53] he has filled the hungry with good things,
and the rich he has sent empty away. [54] He has helped his servant Israel,
in remembrance of his mercy, [55] as he spoke to our fathers,
to Abraham and to his posterity for ever." [56] And Mary remained with her about three months, and returned to her home.

profound wisdom (cf. Lk. 1:29,34 above):

Lk 2:19 But Mary kept all these things, pondering them in her heart.

in her offering in the Temple:

Lk 2:22-24 And when the time came for their purification according to the law of Moses, they brought him up to Jerusalem to present him to the Lord [23] (as it is written in the law of the Lord, "Every male that opens the womb shall be called holy to the Lord") [24] and to offer a sacrifice according to what is said in the law of the Lord, "a pair of turtledoves, or two young pigeons."

and in her prayer in the midst of the apostolic community:

Acts 1:12-14 Then they returned to Jerusalem from the mount called Olivet, which is near Jerusalem, a sabbath day's journey away; [13] and when they had entered, they went up to the upper room, where they were staying, Peter and John and James and Andrew, Philip and Thomas, Bartholomew and Matthew, James the son of Alphaeus and Simon the Zealot and Judas the son of James. [14] All these with one accord devoted themselves to prayer, together with the women and Mary the mother of Jesus, and with his brothers.

her fortitude in exile:

Mt 2:13-20 Now when they had departed, behold, an angel of the Lord appeared to Joseph in a dream and said, "Rise, take the child and his mother, and flee to Egypt, and remain there till I tell you; for Herod is about to search for the child, to destroy him." [14] And he rose and took the child and his mother by night, and departed to Egypt, [15] and remained there until the death of Herod. This was to fulfil what the Lord had spoken by the prophet, "Out of Egypt have I called my son."

[16] Then Herod, when he saw that he had been tricked by the wise men, was in a furious rage, and he sent and killed all the male children in Bethlehem and in all that region who were two years old or under, according to the time which he had ascertained from the wise men. [17] Then was fulfilled what was spoken by the prophet Jeremiah: [18] "A voice was heard in Ramah, wailing and loud lamentation,
Rachel weeping for her children;
she refused to be consoled,
because they were no more."

[19] But when Herod died, behold, an angel of the Lord appeared in a dream to Joseph in Egypt, saying, [20] "Rise, take the child and his mother, and go to the land of Israel, for those who sought the child's life are dead."

and in suffering (cf. Lk. 2:34-35, 49):

Jn 19:25 So the soldiers did this. But standing by the cross of Jesus were his mother, and his mother's sister, Mary the wife of Clopas, and Mary Magdalene.

her poverty reflecting dignity and trust in God (cf. Lk. 1:48, 2:24);

her attentive care for her Son, from His humble birth to the ignominy of the cross (cf. Lk. 2:1-7; Jn. 19:25-27);

her delicate forethought:

Jn 2:1-5ff On the third day there was a marriage at Cana in Galilee, and the mother of Jesus was there; [2] Jesus also was invited to the marriage, with his disciples. [3] When the wine failed, the mother of Jesus said to him, "They have no wine." [4] And Jesus said to her, "O woman, what have you to do with me? My hour has not yet come." [5] His mother said to the servants, "Do whatever he tells you."

her virginal purity (cf. Lk. 1:26-38):

Mt 1:20-25 But as he considered this, behold, an angel of the Lord appeared to him in a dream, saying, "Joseph, son of David, do not fear to take Mary your wife, for that which is conceived in her is of the Holy Spirit; [21] she will bear a son, and you shall call his name Jesus, for he will save his people from their sins." [22] All this took place to fulfil what the Lord had spoken by the prophet: [23] "Behold, a virgin shall conceive and bear a son,
and his name shall be called Emmanuel" (which means, God with us). [24] When Joseph woke from sleep, he did as the angel of the Lord commanded him; he took his wife, [25] but knew her not until she had borne a son; and he called his name Jesus.

and her strong and chaste married love. These virtues of the Mother will also adorn her children who steadfastly study her example in order to reflect it in their own lives. And this progress in virtue will appear as the consequence and the already mature fruit of that pastoral zeal which springs from devotion to the Blessed Virgin.

Martin Luther on Mary and Marian Veneration

"Christ...was the only Son of Mary, and the Virgin Mother bore no more children besides Him...'brothers' really means 'cousins' here , and Holy Writ and the Jews have always called cousins brothers" (Sermons on John, Chap. 1-4)

"God says...Mary's Son is My only Son.' Thus Mary is the Mother of God."

"The veneration of Mary is inscribed in the very depths of the human heart." (Sermon; Sept. 1, 1522)

"The infusion of Mary's soul was effected without original sin...From the first moment she began to live she was free from all sin." - Martin Luther, Sermon: "On the Day of the Conception of the Mother of God."

Luther believed in the Immaculate Conception right up until his death.

"We can never honor her enough. Still, honor and praise must be given to her in such a way as to injure neither Christ nor the Scriptures." (Sermon: Christimas, 1531) And Catholics do honor her but not in a way injurious to Christ nor the Scriptures.

"Whoever possesses a good faith says the Hail Mary without danger." (Sermon: March 11, 1523).

PRAYER

James 5:16
The prayer
of a righteous man has
great power
in its effects.

The Sign of the Cross

Most of the Scripture in this section was taken from Danielou's Bible and the Liturgy *pp. 54-70.*

All things are to be done in the name of Christ, using the sign by which He conquered sin and death. While Christ carried our curse, becoming, in a certain sense, a curse for our sakes, He was not Himself cursed, for God does not curse Himself, nor undertake blasphemies against His own name. Rather, Jesus was beloved of the Father for having done the Father's will perfectly. On the Cross, the love of the Father poured out on His Son in acknowledgement of the love the Son bore the Father through the pouring out of His own life for the sake of His Father's will. (CCC 2598-2754, particularly 2663-2672))

Current misunderstandings: Many Christians either do not understand or actively argue against the use of the prayer of the Sign of the Cross, saying that it ties the supplicant to the curse of the Cross, instead of the Redemption of Christ.

Deut 21:22-23 "And if a man has committed a crime punishable by death and he is put to death, and you hang him on a tree, 23 his body shall not remain all night upon the tree, but you shall bury him the same day, for a hanged man is accursed by God; you shall not defile your land which the LORD your God gives you for an inheritance.

Gal 3:13 Christ redeemed us from the curse of the law, having become a curse for us—for it is written, "Cursed be every one who hangs on a tree"

The argument is that Christ bears the curse of Deuteronomy, and the cross is therefore a cursed sign. In this understanding, Christ is the target for the divine wrath, which was poured out in a fury upon Him. This mistaken reading overlooks the fact that Christ was doing the will of His Father, for He finally carried out the covenant duties for all mankind, which included accepting the punishment due us for our transgressions. Thus, Jesus Christ lived a life of perfect obedience to the Father. Hanging obediently on the Cross, Jesus is not the target of wrath, but is bathed in the great and perfect love of the Father.

Gal 6:14 But far be it from me to glory except in the cross of our Lord Jesus Christ, by which the world has been crucified to me, and I to the world.

Mt 28:19 Go therefore and make disciples of all nations, baptizing them in the name of the Father and of the Son and of the Holy Spirit...

The cross is a sign to be gloried in. It is no longer a curse, for no one glories in God's curse. It is the sign of obedience and salvation.

Gen 4:15 Then the LORD said to him, "Not so! If any one slays Cain, vengeance shall be taken on him sevenfold." And the LORD put a mark on Cain, lest any who came upon him should kill him.

God marked Cain with a sign of protection.

Ezek 9:4 And the LORD said to him, "Go through the city, through Jerusalem, and put a mark upon the foreheads of the men who sigh and groan over all the abominations that are committed in it."

Marks of protection were also to be placed on the holy ones.

Gal 6:17 Henceforth let no man trouble me; for I bear on my body the marks of Jesus.

Rev 7:4 And I heard the number of the sealed, a hundred and forty-four thousand sealed, out of every tribe of the sons of Israel,

The sign of the cross, called "the sphragis," was given at baptism, and was considered a seal or brand, showing everyone that the Shepherd owned this sheep. The sign continued to be used on a daily basis by all who glory in Christ's saving work, as a constant reminder to the Christian that he belonged to Christ. "Many [even] tattooed themselves on the hand or the arm with the name of Jesus or the cross" (Procopius of Gaza, 87:2401).

Repetitious Prayer

The praying of the Rosary is a proper way to praise God through honoring the work of His hands, the Blessed Virgin Mary, and meditating on the events of His life and the promises of His salvation. (CCC 2613)

Current misunderstandings: Most sola scriptura Christians do NOT like the Rosary. Honor given to Mary is honor which detracts from Jesus Christ (the idea that one might honor an artist by extolling the beauty of His work is often lost). A single Scripture passage is therefore used to attack the Rosary in the only way possible - it constitutes repetitious prayer. While this charge is sometimes also used in conjunction with litanies and the types of prayer associated with certain indulgences, the last two are generally attacked directly as "unScriptural" without bothering to resort to Matthew's Gospel.

Mt 6:7-8 And in praying do not heap up empty phrases as the Gentiles do; for they think that they will be heard for their many words. [8] Do not be like them, for your Father knows what you need before you ask him.

Have you said the Our Father today? Did you say it yesterday? If so, you are prayng repetitiously. If we are permitted to say the same prayer twice in our lives, what is the Scripturally-approved time limit between the first time one says the prayer and the second time one says it? May we only implore God's help and mercy in our lives once, in order to avoid repetition? Or only once per subject? This seems unlikely. Perhaps we should examine other examples of Christ's prayer advice to us:

Lk 18:10-14 "Two men went up into the temple to pray, one a Pharisee and the other a tax collector. [11] The Pharisee stood and prayed thus with himself, 'God, I thank thee that I am not like other men, extortioners, unjust, adulterers, or even like this tax collector. [12] I fast twice a week, I give tithes of all that I get.' [13] But the tax collector, standing far off, would not even lift up his eyes to heaven, but beat his breast, saying, 'God, be merciful to me a sinner!' [14] I tell you, this man went down to his house justified rather than the other; for every one who exalts himself will be humbled, but he who humbles himself will be exalted."

The tax collector engages in repetitious prayer and is exalted.

Lk 18:2-8 "In a certain city there was a judge who neither feared God nor regarded man; [3] and there was a widow in that city who kept coming to him and saying, 'Vindicate me against my adversary.' [4] For a while he refused; but afterward he said to himself, 'Though I neither fear God nor regard man, [5] yet because this widow bothers me, I will vindicate her, or she will wear me out by her continual coming.'" [6] And the Lord said, "Hear what the unrighteous judge says. [7] And will not God vindicate his elect, who cry to him day and night? Will he delay long over them? [8] I tell you, he will vindicate them speedily. Nevertheless, when the Son of man comes, will he find faith on earth?"

Lk 11:5-9 And he said to them, "Which of you who has a friend will go to him at midnight and say to him, 'Friend, lend me three loaves; [6] for a friend of mine has arrived on a journey, and I have nothing to set before him'; [7] and he will answer from within, 'Do not bother me; the door is now shut, and my children are with me in bed; I cannot get up and give you anything'? [8] I tell you, though he will not get up and give him anything because he is his friend, yet because of his importunity he will rise and give him whatever he needs. [9] And I tell you, Ask, and it will be given you; seek, and you will find; knock, and it will be opened to you..."

Christ recommends repetitious prayer.

Acts 10:1-5 At Caesarea there was a man named Cornelius, a centurion of what was known as the Italian Cohort, [2] a devout man who feared God with all his household, gave alms liberally to the people, and prayed constantly to God. [3] About the ninth hour of the day he saw clearly in a vision an angel of God coming in and saying to him, "Cornelius." [4] And he stared at him in terror, and said, "What is it, Lord?" And he said to him, "Your prayers and your alms have ascended as a memorial before God. [5] And now send men to Joppa, and bring one Simon who is called Peter...

Cornelius prays constantly and is rewarded.

Mt 26:39-44 And going a little farther he fell on his face and prayed, "My Father, if it be possible, let this cup pass from me; nevertheless, not as I will, but as thou wilt." [40] And he came to the disciples and found them sleeping; and he said to Peter, "So, could you not watch with me one hour? [41] Watch and pray that you may not enter into temptation; the spirit indeed is willing, but the flesh is weak." [42] Again, for the second time, he went away and prayed, "My Father, if this cannot pass unless I drink it, thy will be done." [43] And again he came and found them sleeping, for their eyes were heavy. ⁴⁴ So, leaving them again, he went away and prayed for the third time, saying the same words.

Even Christ engages in repetitious prayer.

Litany

When God replies to Job out of the whirlwind, He spends four chapters (38-41) engaged in thematic repetition - a series of rhetorical questions directed towards Job. Dan 3:52-90, Psalm 103, the beginning of Psalm 118, and Psalm 148, all have examples of litany-like repetitious prayer, but Psalms 136 and 150 are the finest examples of litany:

Psalm 136 O give thanks to the LORD, for he is good, for his steadfast love endures for ever. ² O give thanks to the God of gods,
for his steadfast love endures for ever. ³ O give thanks to the Lord of lords,
for his steadfast love endures for ever;
⁴ to him who alone does great wonders,
for his steadfast love endures for ever;
⁵ to him who by understanding made the heavens,
for his steadfast love endures for ever;
⁶ to him who spread out the earth upon the waters,
for his steadfast love endures for ever;
⁷ to him who made the great lights,
for his steadfast love endures for ever;
⁸ the sun to rule over the day,
for his steadfast love endures for ever;
⁹ the moon and stars to rule over the night,
for his steadfast love endures for ever;
¹⁰ to him who smote the first-born of Egypt,
for his steadfast love endures for ever;
¹¹ and brought Israel out from among them,
for his steadfast love endures for ever;
¹² with a strong hand and an outstretched arm,
for his steadfast love endures for ever;
¹³ to him who divided the Red Sea in sunder,
for his steadfast love endures for ever;
¹⁴ and made Israel pass through the midst of it,
for his steadfast love endures for ever;
¹⁵ but overthrew Pharaoh and his host in the Red Sea,
for his steadfast love endures for ever;
¹⁶ to him who led his people through the wilderness,
for his steadfast love endures for ever;
¹⁷ to him who smote great kings,
for his steadfast love endures for ever;
¹⁸ and slew famous kings,
for his steadfast love endures for ever;
¹⁹ Sihon, king of the Amorites,
for his steadfast love endures for ever;
²⁰ and Og, king of Bashan,
for his steadfast love endures for ever;
²¹ and gave their land as a heritage,
for his steadfast love endures for ever;
²² a heritage to Israel his servant,
for his steadfast love endures for ever.
²³ It is he who remembered us in our low estate,
for his steadfast love endures for ever;
²⁴ and rescued us from our foes,
for his steadfast love endures for ever;
²⁵ he who gives food to all flesh,
for his steadfast love endures for ever.
²⁶ O give thanks to the God of heaven,
for his steadfast love endures for ever.

Rom 1:9-10 For God is my witness, whom I serve with my spirit in the gospel of his Son, that without ceasing I mention you always in my prayers, ¹⁰ asking that somehow by God's will I may now at last succeed in coming to you.

2 Tim 1:3 I thank God whom I serve with a clear conscience, as did my fathers, when I remember you constantly in my prayers.

One might argue that the verses above tell us to pray to God <u>directly</u>, and not to Mary, but in that case the discussion is not about repetitious prayer anymore. Scripture clearly shows that repetitious prayer in and of itself is not the problem - rather it is the use of prayer as an incantation which is to be avoided. Pagans think an incantation forces a spirit to appear or forces a spirit to undertake some action. Prayer is never to be used with the intention of forcing something to happen, but in a spirit of begging God for assistance. This unconscious attempt to equate the Rosary with necromancy is no more than that, and fails precisely because prayers to the saints are NOT <u>necromancy.</u>

How many times may you honor God in a day? How often may you tell someone you love them? Who honors the Body of Christ, and His saints who are the cells of His Body, gives honor to God.

The Hail Mary

The prayer:

"Hail Mary, full of grace, the Lord is with thee, blessed art thou amongst women, and blessed is the fruit of thy womb, Jesus. Holy Mary, Mother of God, pray for us sinners, now and at the hour of our death. Amen."

The prayer, Scripturally analyzed:

Lk 1:28 "Hail, full of grace, the Lord is with you." *Hail Mary, full of grace, the Lord is with thee...*

Lk 1:38 "Blessed are you among women, and blessed is the fruit of your womb!" *blessed art thou amongst women, and blessed is the fruit of thy womb, Jesus.*

1 Cor 7:34 "And the unmarried woman or girl is anxious about the affairs of the Lord, how to be holy in body and spirit." *Holy Mary,*

Lk 2:6-7 "And while they were there, the time came for her to be delivered. 7 And she gave birth to her first-born son..." *Mother of God,*

2 Cor 1:11 "You also must help us by prayer, so that many will give thanks on our behalf for the blessing granted us in answer to many prayers." *pray for us sinners now...*

Mt 10:22 "But he who endures to the end will be saved." *and at the hour of our death. Amen.*
(CCC 2676-2677)

The Rosary

The Rosary is an extended meditation on the life of Christ and His salvific mission. A complete Rosary consists of fifteen decades: five Joyful Mysteries, five Sorrowful Mysteries, and five Glorious Mysteries. Each decade of the Rosary consists of an Our Father, followed by ten Hail Marys. While the Doxology (the "Glory Be") is not a strictly necessary part of the Rosary, it is almost always said at the end of every decade. Generally, a set of five decades (i.e., the Joyful, or the Sorrowful, or the Glorious Mysteries) is prayed in one session. (CCC 971,2678,2708)

Joyful
Annunciation *Lk 1:26-38*
Visitation *Lk 1:39-45*
Birth *Mt 1:25, Lk 2:6-7*
Presentation *Lk 2:22-38*
Finding in the Temple *Lk 2:41-52*

Sorrowful
Agony in the Garden *Mt 26:36-46, Mk 14:32-42, Lk 22:39-46*
Scourging at the Pillar *Mt 20:19, 27:26, Mk 15:15, Lk 23:22, Jn 19:1*
Crowning with Thorns *Mt 27:29-30, Mk 15:16-20, Jn 19:2-5*
Carrying of the Cross *Mt 27:31-34, Mk 15:22-23, Lk 23:26-33, Jn 19:16-17*
Dying on the Cross *Mt 27:45-56, Mk 15:33-41, Lk 23:44-49, Jn 19:30-37*

Glorious
Resurrection *Mt 28:1-10, Mk 16:1-11, Lk 24:1-12, Jn 20:1-18*
Ascension *Mk 16:19, Lk 24:50-51*
Descent of the Holy Spirit *Acts 2:1-12*
Mary's Assumption *Psalm 132:8, Rev 12:1-18*
Mary, Crowned Heaven's Queen *1 Cor 9:25, 2 Tim 4:8, Jas 1:12, 1 Pet 5:4, Rev 2:10, Rev 12:1*

Every mystery of the Rosary is a mediation on Christ. Some say the last two mysteries, which meditate on Mary's Bodily Assumption into Heaven and her being crowned Queen of Heaven, is detraction from Christ. However, she is the archetypical Christian - by meditating on the glories given her by God, we come to a deeper understanding of the glories God has in store for us at the Final Judgement. We must always keep in mind these glories are reserved for those who are most obedient, most humble, and most docile to God's will, as Mary was.

A second argument asserts that this is a profane prayer, since each decade has ten Hail Marys as opposed to a single Our Father. However, Scripture indicates that this is as it should be:

1 Cor 3:10-11 According to the grace of God given to me, like a skilled master builder I laid a foundation, and another man is building upon it. Let each man take care how he builds upon it. [11] For no other foundation can any one lay than that which is laid, which is Jesus Christ.

Is 28:16 therefore thus says the Lord GOD, "Behold, I am laying in Zion for a foundation a stone, a tested stone, a precious cornerstone, of a sure foundation: 'He who believes will not be in haste.'

Christ is the cornerstone, the first stone laid in a foundation. Thus, the prayer Christ taught us is the cornerstone prayer, the first prayer prayed in a decade of the Rosary.

1 Pet 2:5 and like living stones be yourselves built into a spiritual house, to be a holy priesthood, to offer spiritual sacrifices acceptable to God through Jesus Christ.

We are to build ourselves up like many living stones. Mary was such a perfect follower of God that God gifted her with allowing the Second Person of the Trinity to enter creation through her womb. The better we imitate Mary, the more fully Jesus the Christ will take form within us. Each Hail Mary is a request for Mary to pray to God for us, that He might give us the grace to become perfect followers of Christ as she was - that each of us become living stones. We are praying that God allows us to become like living stones, built up into a spiritual house. Praying ten Hail Marys symbolizes praying for the completion of that formation of Christ within us, for Scripture counts the gestation of pregnancy according to the lunar cycle - ten months:

Wis 7:1-2 I also am mortal, like all men,
a descendant of the first-formed child of earth;
and in the womb of a mother I was molded into flesh, [2]
within the period of ten months, compacted with blood,
from the seed of a man and the pleasure of marriage.

The Rosary is the prayer for the building up of the Church. It follows the design laid out by Scripture, for the completion of the Body of Christ.

The Sub Tuum Praesidium (ca. 250 A.D.)

The Prayer (composed at or before 250 A.D.): "We fly to your patronage, O Holy Mother of God, despise not our petitions in our necessities, but deliver us from all dangers, O glorious and blessed Virgin!" (CCC 2673-2682, 2617-2619)

The prayer, Scripturally analyzed:

Song 6:10 Who is she who comes forth as the morning rising, fair as the moon, bright as the sun, terrible as an army set in battle array?
We fly to your patronage, O Holy Mother of God...

Esther 5:2,3 She found favor in his sight... and the king said to her, "What is it...? What is your request? It shall be given you, even to the half of my kingdom."
despise not our petitions in our necessities...

Esther 9:22 ...[These are] the days on which the Jews got relief from their enemies, and as the month that had been turned for them from sorrow into gladness and from mourning into a holiday; that they should make them days of feasting and gladness...
but deliver us from all dangers, O glorious and blessed Virgin!

Memorare

The Prayer: "Remember, O most gracious Virgin Mary that never was it known that anyone who fled to thy protection, implored thy help, or sought thy intercession was left unaided. Inspired by this confidence, I fly unto thee, O virgin of virgins, my mother. To thee I come, before thee I stand sinful and sorrowful. O Mother of Mercy, despise not my petitions, but in thy mercy hear and answer me. Amen."

Lk 1:26-27 In the sixth month the angel Gabriel was sent from God to a city of Galilee named Nazareth, 27 to a virgin betrothed to a man whose name was Joseph, of the house of David; and the virgin's name was Mary.
Remember, O most gracious Virgin Mary...

Esther 4:8-9 Mordecai also gave [the messenger] a copy of the written decree issued in Susa for their destruction... to show it to [her] and explain to her and charge her to go to the king to make supplication to him and entreat him for her people. "Beseech the Lord and speak to the king concerning us; and deliver us from death."
that never was it known that anyone who fled to thy protection, implored thy help, or sought thy intercession was left unaided...

Jn 19:26-27 When Jesus saw his mother, and the disciple whom he loved standing near, he said to his mother, "Woman, behold, your son!" 27 Then he said to the disciple, "Behold, your mother!" And from that hour the disciple took her to his own home.
Inspired by this confidence, I fly unto thee, O virgin of virgins, my mother. To thee I come, before thee I stand...

Psalm 51:3 For I know my transgressions, and my sin is ever before me.
sinful and sorrowful...

Lk 1:35, 2:6-7 Therefore the child to be born will be called holy, the Son of God....While they were there, the time came for her to be delivered, and she gave birth to her firstborn son...
Dan 9:9 To the Lord our God belong mercy and forgiveness...
O Mother of Mercy,

1 Kings 2:20 And the king said to her, "Make your request, my mother; for I will not refuse you."
despise not my petitions, but in thy mercy hear and answer me. Amen.

Hail Holy Queen

The Prayer: "Hail holy Queen, Mother of Mercy, our life, our sweetness, and our hope, to thee do we cry poor banished children of Eve, to thee do we send up our sighs, mourning and weeping in this vale of tears.

Turn then, O most gracious Advocate, thine eyes of mercy towards us, and after this our exile, show unto us the blessed fruit of your womb, Jesus. O clement, O loving, O sweet Virgin Mary. Pray for us, O Most Holy Mother of God, that we may be made worthy of the promises of Christ.

Almighty and everlasting God, by the cooperation of the Holy Spirit you prepared the body and soul of Mary, glorious Virgin and Mother, to become the worthy habitation of your Son; grant that by her gracious intercession, in whose commemoration we rejoice, we may be delivered from present evils and from everlasting death. Through the same Christ our Lord. Amen.

May the divine assistance remain always with us. Amen."

Rev 12:1 And a great portent appeared in heaven, a woman clothed with the sun, with the moon under her feet, and on her head a crown of twelve stars.
Hail holy Queen...

Mt 1:25, 2:1 but knew her not until she had borne a son; and he called his name Jesus.... born in Bethlehem of Judea...
Tob 3:2 "Righteous art thou, O Lord; all thy deeds and all thy ways are mercy and truth..."
Mother of Mercy...

Rev 12:2,17 She was with child and she cried out in her pangs of birth, in anguish for delivery... Then the dragon was angry with the woman, and went off to make war on the rest of her offspring, on those who keep the commandments of God and bear testimony to Jesus.
our life, our sweetness, and our hope, to thee do we cry ...

Gen 5:3 When Adam had lived a hundred and thirty years, he became the father of a son in his own likeness, after his image...
poor banished children of Eve,

2 Sam 14:15 "and your handmaid thought, 'I will speak to the king; it may be that the king will perform the request of his servant...' "
to thee do we send up our sighs,

Psalm 6:6 every night I flood my bed with tears; I drench my couch with my weeping.
mourning and weeping in this vale of tears.

Jn 2:3 When the wine failed, the mother of Jesus said to him, "They have no wine."
Turn then, O most gracious Advocate, thine eyes of mercy towards us,

Gen 3:23-24 therefore the Lord God sent him forth from the garden of Eden, to till the ground from which he was taken. ^{24} He drove out the man...
and after this our exile,

Gal 4:4-5 But when the time had fully come, God sent forth his Son, born of woman, born under the law, ^{5} to redeem those who were under the law, so that we might receive adoption as sons.
show unto us the blessed fruit of your womb, Jesus.

Lk 1:38 And Mary said, "Behold, I am the handmaid of the Lord; let it be to me according to your word."

Lk 1:36, 39-40, 56 "And behold, your kinswoman Elizabeth in her old age has also conceived a son; and this is the sixth month with her who was called barren." ...In those days Mary arose and went with haste into the hill country, to a city of Judah, ^{40} and she entered the house of Zechariah and greeted Elizabeth..... And Mary remained with her about three months, and returned to her home.
O clement, O loving, O sweet Virgin Mary.

2 Cor 1:10-11 on him we have set our hope that he will deliver us again. ^{11} You also must help us by prayer
Pray for us, O Most Holy Mother of God,

Heb 6:11-12 And we desire each one of you to show the same earnestness in realizing the full assurance of hope until the end, ^{12} so that you may not be sluggish, but imitators of those who through faith and patience inherit the promises.
that we may be made worthy of the promises of Christ.

Dan 13:42 Then Susanna cried out with a loud voice, and said: "O eternal God, who dost discern what is secret, who art aware of all things before they come to be... "
Almighty and everlasting God,

1 Cor 6:19 Do you not know that your body is a temple of the Holy Spirit within you, which you have from God? You are not your own...
by the cooperation of the Holy Spirit you prepared the body and soul of Mary, glorious Virgin and Mother,

Jn 2:5 His mother said to the servants, "Do whatever he tells you."
to become the worthy habitation of your Son;

1 Kings 2:20 Then she said, "I have one small request to make of you; do not refuse me." And the king said to her, "Make your request, my mother; for I will not refuse you."
grant that by her gracious intercession, in whose commemoration we rejoice,

Esther 4:8-9 Mordecai also gave [the messenger] a copy of the written decree issued in Susa for their destruction... to show it to [her] and explain to her and charge her to go to the king to make supplication to him and entreat him for her people. "Beseech the Lord and speak to the king concerning us; and deliver us from death."
we may be delivered from present evils and from everlasting death.

Rom 2:16 God judges the secrets of men by Christ Jesus.
Through the same Christ our Lord. Amen.

2 Chron 14:10 O Lord, there is none like thee to help, between the mighty and the weak. Help us, O Lord our God, for we rely on thee, and in thy name we have come against this multitude. O Lord, thou art our God; let not man prevail against thee.
May the divine assistance remain always with us. Amen.

Liturgy of the Hours

The work of God done by men, presented in the liturgy of the Mass, is extended throughout the hours, days, weeks, month and year through the liturgical calendar and the prayer of the Church which is called the Liturgy of the Hours. In the extension of the Mass which is the Liturgy of the Hours, the whole Church meditates on the Word of God. Each principle hour of the day, one or more psalms are prayed together with other selections from Scripture and meditations on Scripture written by two millenia of the greatest Christian saints. Through this liturgy, the Church grows in an ever richer understanding of the Word of God. This form of prayer is required of all religious, and warmly commended to the lay faithful.

Josh 1:8 This book of the law shall not depart out of your mouth, but you shall meditate on it day and night, that you may be careful to do according to all that is written in it; for then you shall make your way prosperous, and then you shall have good success.

1 Kings 8:57-60 The Lord our God be with us, as he was with our fathers; may he not leave us or forsake us; ⁵⁸ that he may incline our hearts to him, to walk in all his ways, and to keep his commandments, his statutes, and his ordinances, which he commanded our fathers. ⁵⁹ Let these words of mine, wherewith I have made supplication before the Lord, be near to the Lord our God day and night, and may he maintain the cause of his servant, and the cause of his people Israel, as each day requires; ⁶⁰ that all the peoples of the earth may know that the Lord is God; there is no other.

1 Chron 9:33 Now these are the singers, the heads of fathers' houses of the Levites, dwelling in the chambers of the temple free from other service, for they were on duty day and night.

Lk 1:8-9 Now while he was serving as priest before God when his division was on duty, ⁹ according to the custom of the priesthood, it fell to him by lot to enter the temple of the Lord and burn incense.

Neh 1:3-6 And I said, "O Lord God of heaven, the great and terrible God who keeps covenant and steadfast love with those who love him and keep his commandments; ⁶ let thy ear be attentive, and thy eyes open, to hear the prayer of thy servant which I now pray before thee day and night for the people of Israel thy servants, confessing the sins of the people of Israel, which we have sinned against thee. Yea, I and my father's house have sinned.

Psalm 1:1-3 Blessed is the man
   who walks not in the counsel of the wicked,
       nor stands in the way of sinners,
   nor sits in the seat of scoffers;
 ² but his delight is in the law of the LORD,
   and on his law he meditates day and night.
 ³ He is like a tree
   planted by streams of water,
 that yields its fruit in its season,
   and its leaf does not wither.
In all that he does, he prospers

Lk 18:6-8 And the Lord said, "Hear what the unrighteous judge says. ⁷ And will not God vindicate his elect, who cry to him day and night? Will he delay long over them? ⁸ I tell you, he will vindicate them speedily."

Rev 4:8 And the four living creatures, each of them with six wings, are full of eyes all round and within, and day and night they never cease to sing,
"Holy, holy, holy, is the Lord God Almighty,
who was and is and is to come!"

Jud 11:17 For your servant is religious, and serves the God of heaven day and night...

2 Mac 13:10 But when Judas heard of this, he ordered the people to call upon the Lord day and night, now if ever to help those who were on the point of being deprived of the law and their country and the holy temple...

Sir 39:33 The works of the Lord are all good, and he will supply every need in its hour.

Our Father

This section summarizes Thomas Aquinas' commentary on the Our Father, using his Scripture references. It is interwoven with with a summary of the Scripture and commentary found in CCC 2777-2865.

The Our Father is the summary of the Gospel Jesus taught; it is essential for us. It gives us our attitude about prayer, it tells us about our essential relationship with our Father-Creator, and it orients us to the Christian life.

Lk 11:2-4 And he said to them, "When you pray, say: "Father, hallowed be thy name. Thy kingdom come. ³ Give us each day our daily bread; ⁴ and forgive us our sins, for we ourselves forgive every one who is indebted to us; and lead us not into temptation."

Mt 6:9-13 Pray then like this:
Our Father who art in heaven,
Hallowed be thy name. ¹⁰ Thy kingdom come.
Thy will be done,
On earth as it is in heaven. ¹¹ Give us this day our daily bread; ¹² And forgive us our debts,
As we also have forgiven our debtors; ¹³ And lead us not into temptation,
But deliver us from evil.

Our Father

He is the Holy One of Israel, who appeared before Moses in a burning bush and slowly revealed more and more of Himself, until Moses could speak to Him face to face, as a man might with a friend - when he emerged from the Tent of Meeting, he had to cover his face with a veil, for it shone with a preternatural light.

Mt 11:27 All things have been delivered to me by my Father; and no one knows the Son except the Father, and no one knows the Father except the Son and any one to whom the Son chooses to reveal him.

He it is whom Jesus taught us to dare to call our Father. God is our Father for two reasons:

Deut 32:6 Is not he your father, who created you, who made you and established you?

He created us in His image and likeness, governing us as masters of ourselves, allowing us free will...

Wis 14:2 but it is thy providence, O Father, that steers its course...

Wis 12:18 Thou who art sovereign in strength dost judge with mildness,
and with great forbearance thou dost govern us...

... and He adopted us as sons

Rom 8:15 For you did not receive the spirit of slavery to fall back into fear, but you have received the spirit of sonship. When we cry, "Abba! Father!"

Heb 2:11-12 For he who sanctifies and those who are sanctified have all one origin. That is why he is not ashamed to call them brethren, [12] saying,
"I will proclaim thy name to my brethren,
in the midst of the congregation I will praise thee."

Mt 11:25 At that time Jesus declared, "I thank thee, Father, Lord of heaven and earth, that thou hast hidden these things from the wise and understanding and revealed them to babes..."

We find out who we are through Jesus revelation of the Father. Thus, we owe Him honor:

Mal 1:6 "A son honors his father, and a servant his master. If then I am a father, where is my honor?

1 Cor 6:20 So glorify God in your body.

We owe Him imitation:

Jer 3:19 And I thought you would call me, My Father, and would not turn from following me.

Mt 5:48 You, therefore, must be perfect, as your heavenly Father is perfect.

We owe Him obedience:

Ex 24:7 Then he took the book of the covenant, and read it in the hearing of the people; and they said, "All that the LORD has spoken we will do, and we will be obedient."

Heb 12:9 Shall we not much more be subject to the Father of spirits and live?

We owe Him patience when He corrects us:

Prov 3:11-12 My son, do not despise the LORD's discipline
or be weary of his reproof, [12] for the LORD reproves him whom he loves,
as a father the son in whom he delights.

We likewise owe our neighbor love as our brother and God's child and reverence, because he is God's child:

1 Jn 4:20 If any one says, "I love God," and hates his brother, he is a liar; for he who does not love his brother whom he has seen, cannot love God whom he has not seen.

Mal 2:10 Have we not all one father? Has not one God created us? Why then are we faithless to one another, profaning the covenant of our fathers?

who art in heaven

This directs our thoughts to our final end, not a place, but a way of being...

Mt 6:21 For where your treasure is, there will your heart be also.

1 Cor 15:48-49 As was the man of dust, so are those who are of the dust; and as is the man of heaven, so are those who are of heaven. Just as we have borne the image of the man of dust, we shall also bear the image of the man of heaven.

Eph 2:4-6 But God, who is rich in mercy, out of the great love with which he loved us, [5] even when we were dead through our trespasses, made us alive together with Christ (by grace you have been saved), [6] and raised us up with him, and made us sit with him in the heavenly places in Christ Jesus...

God dwells in the saints...

Jer 14:9 Yet thou, O LORD, art in the midst of us,
and we are called by thy name;

Psalm 19:2 The heavens are telling the glory of God...

...through faith, love, and the keeping of the commandments:

Eph 3:17 and that Christ may dwell in your hearts through faith...

1 Jn 4:16 God is love, and he who abides in love abides in God, and God abides in him.

Jn 14:23 "If a man loves me, he will keep my word, and my Father will love him, and we will come to him and make our home with him."

Col 3:2 Set your minds on things that are above, not on things that are on earth.

Thus, this phrase gives us confidence in prayer, for it reminds us of the power of Him to whom we pray, it brings us into communion with Him through remembering His communion with the saints, and in our petitions we show our confidence in Him. Heavenly desire and heavenly life equip a man for prayer and enable him to pray.

First Petition
Hallowed be thy name

In this first petition, we ask that His Name be manifested and proclaimed to us.

Eph 1:4 that we should be holy and blameless before him.

Mk 16:17-18 And these signs will accompany those who believe: in my name they will cast out demons; they will speak in new tongues; [18] they will pick up serpents, and if they drink any deadly thing, it will not hurt them; they will lay their hands on the sick, and they will recover."

Acts 4:12 And there is salvation in no one else, for there is no other name under heaven given among men by which we must be saved.

Phil 2:10 that at the name of Jesus every knee should bow, in heaven and on earth and under the earth...

His Name works wonders, it saves us, it signifies His perfect love for us, and we rightly acclaim it most holy

Deut 4:24 For the LORD your God is a devouring fire...

Psalm 17:29 Yea, thou dost light my lamp;
the LORD my God lightens my darkness.

1 Cor 6:11 But you were washed, you were sanctified, you were justified in the name of the Lord Jesus Christ and in the Spirit of our God.

for through it we are purified as through fire, and our lives our brought out of darkness and into light.

Rev 1:5-6 To him who loves us and has freed us from our sins by his blood [6] and made us a kingdom, priests to his God and Father, to him be glory and dominion for ever and ever. Amen.

Second Petition
Thy Kingdom come

His kingdom is desired for three reasons: to safeguard the just, to punish the wicked, and to destroy death.

Phil 3:21 who will change our lowly body to be like his glorious body, by the power which enables him even to subject all things to himself.

Psalm 110:1 The LORD says to my lord:
"Sit at my right hand,
till I make your enemies your footstool."

1 Cor 15:26 The last enemy to be destroyed is death.

We need a reverent disposition in order to ask for this.

Tit 2:12 training us to renounce irreligion and worldly passions, and to live sober, upright, and godly lives in this world..

His Kingdom is desirable

Rom 14:17 For the kingdom of God is not food and drink but righteousness and peace and joy in the Holy Spirit

Is 60:21 Your people shall all be righteous...

Rom 8:21 because the creation itself will be set free from its bondage to decay

Is 28:5 In that day the LORD of hosts will be a crown of glory, and a diadem of beauty, to the remnant of his people...

Is 64:4 From of old no one has heard or perceived by the ear, no eye has seen a God besides thee, who works for those who wait for him.

Rom 6:12 Let not sin therefore reign in your mortal bodies, to make you obey their passions.

This petition teaches us to obey God and to be meek.

Mt 5:4 "Blessed are the meek, for they shall inherit the earth."

Third Petition
Thy Will be done on earth as it is in heaven

Jn 13:34 A new commandment I give to you, that you love one another; even as I have loved you, that you also love one another.

1 Tim 2:3-4 This is good, and it is acceptable in the sight of God our Savior, ⁴ who desires all men to be saved and to come to the knowledge of the truth.

This is His will. The Holy Spirit's gift of knowledge teaches us to do His will, not our own.

Prov 3:5 Trust in the LORD with all your heart, and do not rely on your own insight.

Prov 11:2 When pride comes, then comes disgrace; but with the humble is wisdom.

Prov 26:12 Do you see a man who is wise in his own eyes?
There is more hope for a fool than for him.

We should ask nothing of God except that His will be done for us, since our heart will be made right by this.

Jn 6:38,40 For I have come down from heaven, not to do my own will, but the will of him who sent me... ⁴⁰ For this is the will of my Father, that every one who sees the Son and believes in him should have eternal life; and I will raise him up at the last day."

God wills us to have eternal life. Already fulfilled in the angels and the saints in heaven, we will attain it when we follow the Physician's commands....

Mt 19:17 If you would enter life, keep the commandments.

Mt 5:48 You, therefore, must be perfect, as your heavenly Father is perfect.

He wishes man to cooperate with His will...

Zech 1:3 Therefore say to them, Thus says the LORD of hosts: Return to me, says the LORD of hosts, and I will return to you, says the LORD of hosts.

1 Cor 15:10 But by the grace of God I am what I am, and his grace toward me was not in vain.

Finally, He wills that we overcome our rebellion towards Him...

Heb 5:8 Although he was a Son, he learned obedience through what he suffered

1 Thess 4:3 For this is the will of God, your sanctification.

1 Cor 15:43 It is sown in dishonor, it is raised in glory. It is sown in weakness, it is raised in power.

It cannot be fulfilled in this life. We mourn because we have not yet reached the prize, we mourn because the commandments are sweet to the soul, but bitter to the body, we mourn because of our own inability to avoid sin. Thus, this petition directs us to the beatitude...

Mt 5:4 "Blessed are those who mourn, for they shall be comforted."

Fourth Petition
Give us this day our daily bread

The three previous petitions ask for spiritual blessings which are begun here but only perfected in eternal life. This petition begins the request for the gifts necessary to live out this life on earth.

Sir 39:26 Basic to all the needs of man's life are water and ... wheat flour

1 Tim 6:8 but if we have food and clothing, with these we shall be content.

Prov 30:8 give me neither poverty nor riches; feed me with the food that is needful for me...

Prov 23:21 for the drunkard and the glutton will come to poverty...

We should look only for what we need, and feed those who do not have the essentials of food and drink...

1 Chron 29:14 For all things come from thee, and of thy own have we given thee.

Deut 8:3 And he humbled you and let you hunger and fed you with manna, which you did not know, nor did your fathers know; that he might make you know that man does not live by bread alone, but that man lives by everything that proceeds out of the mouth of the LORD.

For God provides all that we have in any case.

Eccl 6:1-2 There is an evil which I have seen under the sun, and it lies heavy upon men: ² a man to whom God gives wealth, possessions, and honor, so that he lacks nothing of all that he desires, yet God does not give him power to enjoy them, but a stranger enjoys them;...

It is safer to be poor than to risk the loss of our soul through riches...

Amos 8:11 "Behold, the days are coming," says the Lord GOD,
"when I will send a famine on the land;
not a famine of bread, nor a thirst for water,
but of hearing the words of the LORD.

Mt 6:31 Therefore do not be anxious, saying, 'What shall we eat?' or 'What shall we drink?' or 'What shall we wear?'

Nor should we be worried about these things. Ask only for what is needed at the present time, and it will be given unto you....

Jn 6:51 I am the living bread which came down from heaven; if any one eats of this bread, he will live for ever; and the bread which I shall give for the life of the world is my flesh."

The word "daily" (epiousios) occurs in the New Testament only in the Lord's Prayer. Our daily, constant need is to eat the living flesh of the Son of Man, present in the Eucharist...

Mt 4:4 "It is written,'Man shall not live by bread alone,but by every word that proceeds from the mouth of God.'"

And to feast on His Word. Thus, this petition points us toward the beatitude....

Mt 5:6 "Blessed are those who hunger and thirst for righteousness, for they shall be satisfied.

Fifth Petition
Forgive us our debts, as we forgive our debtors

The "as" is found in several places in Jesus' teaching.

Mt 5:48 You, therefore, must be perfect, as your heavenly Father is perfect.

Lk 6:36 Be merciful, even as your Father is merciful.

Jn 13:34 A new commandment I give to you, that you love one another; even as I have loved you...

We make petition because none but Christ and the Blessed Virgin have ever lived life here below without committing sin. As sinners, we need counsel.

Dan 4:27 Therefore, O king, let my counsel be acceptable to you; break off your sins by practicing righteousness, and your iniquities by showing mercy to the oppressed, that there may perhaps be a lengthening of your tranquillity."

1 Jn 1:8 If we say we have no sin, we deceive ourselves, and the truth is not in us.

In this petition, each person who prays admits his unrighteousness. Yet we should always have hope, in order to avoid deeper sin.

Eph 4:19 they have become callous and have given themselves up to licentiousness, greedy to practice every kind of uncleanness.

God will forgive us if we ask His favor.

Mt 18:32 I forgave you all that debt because you besought me.

We must have true contrition with firm purpose of amendment.

Psalm 32:4 I acknowledged my sin to thee,
　　and I did not hide my iniquity;
　I said, "I will confess my transgressions to the
　　　LORD";
then thou didst forgive the guilt of my sin.

Why should we confess to a priest?

Jn 20:22 And when he had said this, he breathed on them, and said to them, "Receive the Holy Spirit. [23] If you forgive the sins of any, they are forgiven; if you retain the sins of any, they are retained."

Because priests alone have the power of the keys, and each time we confess the sin, we break its power over us, and as often as we undertake indulgences, we remit the punishment due to our sin, through the merits of Christ's Cross. We are all debtors, but our debt as Christians is unique:

Rom 13:8 Owe no one anything, except to love one another...

In order to obtain forgiveness, we must first forgive our neighbor.

Lk 6:37 forgive, and you will be forgiven

Either by seeking out him who offended you...

Psalm 34:8 seek peace, and pursue it.

Or by forgiving the offender his sin...

Sir 28:2 Forgive your neighbor the wrong he has done, and then your sins will be pardoned when you pray.

This leads us to another beatitude...

Mt 5:7 "Blessed are the merciful, for they shall obtain mercy."

Sixth Petition
And lead us not into temptation

Not only must we confess and repent our sins, we must work hard to avoid sin. It does little good to repent and then not strive to avoid falling into sin again. In the previous petition, we asked to be forgiven, in this, we ask for the strength and disposition to avoid it. The word "lead" here is difficult to translate, meaning both "do not allow us to enter into" and "do not allow us to yield to" temptation.

Is 1:16 Wash yourselves; make yourselves clean; remove the evil of your doings from before my eyes; cease to do evil...

Psalm 34:14 Depart from evil, and do good; seek peace, and pursue it.

God permits us to be tested so that we may know the strength of the virtues He has given us, and be a good example to others. God tempts man towards good deeds.

Deut 13:3 for the LORD your God is testing you, to know whether you love the LORD your God with all your heart and with all your soul.

Temptations toward evil come from our own flesh...

James 1:13-15 Let no one say when he is tempted, "I am tempted by God"; for God cannot be tempted with evil and he himself tempts no one; [14] but each person is tempted when he is lured and enticed by his own desire. [15] Then desire when it has conceived gives birth to sin; and sin when it is full-grown brings forth death.

Wis 9:15 for a perishable body weighs down the soul, and this earthy tent burdens the thoughtful mind.

Rom 7:22-23 For I delight in the law of God, in my inmost self, [23] but I see in my members another law at war with the law of my mind and making me captive to the law of sin which dwells in my members.

Mt 26:41 Watch and pray that you may not enter into temptation; the spirit indeed is willing, but the flesh is weak."

And from the devil...

Eph 6:12 For we are not contending against flesh and blood, but against the principalities, against the powers, against the world rulers of this present darkness, against the spiritual hosts of wickedness in the heavenly places.

1 Pet 5:8 Be sober, be watchful. Your adversary the devil prowls around like a roaring lion, seeking some one to devour.

2 Cor 11:14 And no wonder, for even Satan disguises himself as an angel of light.

Temptations conquered are rewarded, therefore...

James 1:2,12 Count it all joy, my brethren, when you meet various trials... Blessed is the man who endures trial, for when he has stood the test he will receive the crown of life which God has promised to those who love him.

Sir 2:1 My son, if you come forward to serve the Lord, prepare yourself for temptation.

Psalm 71:9 forsake me not when my strength is spent.

To be tempted is human, but to consent is devilish...

1 Cor 10:13 No temptation has overtaken you that is not common to man. God is faithful, and he will not let you be tempted beyond your strength, but with the temptation will also provide the way of escape, that you may be able to endure it.

Even the smallest amount of charity can resist sin...

Song 8:7 Many waters cannot quench love,
neither can floods drown it.

He teaches us what to do, therefore ask for His guidance.

Psalm 13:3-4 Consider and answer me, O Lord my God;
lighten my eyes, lest I sleep the sleep of death; [4] lest my enemy say, "I have prevailed over him"

This petition leads us likewise to beatitude...

Mt 5:8 "Blessed are the pure in heart, for they shall see God."

Seventh Petition
But deliver us from evil

God has taught us how to seek forgiveness of our sins and avoid evil, now He tells us to pray for safety from evil. He may deliver us by preventing their occurrence, though most are not saved in this way, for...

2 Tim 3:12 Indeed all who desire to live a godly life in Christ Jesus will be persecuted...

We may feel utterly crushed by the weight of evil

2 Cor 1:8 For we do not want you to be ignorant, brethren, of the affliction we experienced in Asia; for we were so utterly, unbearably crushed that we despaired of life itself.

and yet, God comforts us

2 Cor 7:6-7 But God, who comforts the downcast, comforted us by the coming of Titus, [7] and not only by his coming but also by the comfort with which he was comforted in you, as he told us of your longing, your mourning, your zeal for me, so that I rejoiced still more.

Jn 17:15 I do not pray that thou shouldst take them out of the world, but that thou shouldst keep them from the evil one.

He makes sure our trials are short...

2 Cor 4:17 For this slight momentary affliction is preparing for us an eternal weight of glory beyond all comparison

Rom 5:3 More than that, we rejoice in our sufferings, knowing that suffering produces endurance, [4] and endurance produces character, and character produces hope, [5] and hope does not disappoint us, because God's love has been poured into our hearts through the Holy Spirit which has been given to us.

Because of all these things, this petition asks for the gift of peace.

Mt 5:9 "Blessed are the peacemakers, for they shall be called sons of God."

Amen.
This is said to ratify all the petitions.
It means, "It is true" or "So be it."

GLOSSARY

Warning: Due to slight variations between Bible translations, chapter, verse and Psalm numbers may not correspond exactly to the version of Scripture which you use.

Pharisees - This strict Hebrew religious community dates from the second century B.C., after the Jews united under the Maccabees. These laymen intended to live out the Mosaic Law as fully and completely as possible; to this end, they separated themselves from the surrounding community, in order to avoid being drawn away from the Law. They intended the Law to permeate every aspect of life, and worked to complete the written and oral Law so that this would be possible. They had a greater sense of charity and were more permissive in their application of the Law than were the Sadducees. They affirmed the existence of angels and the resurrection of the dead. During Christ's time, the group was gaining immense strength. Paul was a Pharisee.

Sadducees - This party also arose during the second century B.C. Their watchwords were intelligence, diplomacy and prudence. They adhered to the letter of the Law, but accomodated themselves to the world on those matters to which the Law made no explicit reference. While the Pharisees added to the written Law, the Sadducees opposed such additions. Indeed, some Sadducees asserted that only the Pentateuch was inspired. Its members denied the existence of angels and the resurrection of the dead. They believed the safest way to avoid war was to learn to live alongside pagans, thus they tended to be statesmen and diplomats. They tended to reject the idea that God would intervene in human affairs, and held to a strict interpretation of the Law. During Christ's time, the group was in decline.

Samaritans - The descendants of the ten tribes who were lost in the Diaspora, these people inter-married with the conquerers, and were therefore no longer of pure Israelite ancestry. The tribe of Judah, which had largely avoided inter-marriage, looked upon the Samaritans as half-breed mongrels. The Samaritans returned the favor by expressly rejecting the canonicity of all of the prophetic books, since all but one of the prophets came from the Southern Kingdom. The Samaritans accepted only the inspiration of the Pentateuch. They asserted that only one prophet would come, the Saviour, the Messiah.

Scribes - A Hebrew term referring to an official of the court or someone of accomplishment, such as a Jewish scholar or lawyer, or a member of the Sanhedrin. Scribes were very often Pharisees.

RESOURCES (5/2/98):

Books:

Butler, Dahlgren, and Hess. *Jesus, Peter and the Keys*, Queenship Publishing Co., Santa Barbara, CA, ISBN 1-882972-54-6

Catechism of the Catholic Church, Libreria Editrice Vaticana, 1994, ISBN 0-932406-23-8

Clowes, Brian. *The Facts of Life*, Human Life International, Front Royal, Virginia, 1997. ISBN 1-55922-043-0

Danielou, Jean S.J., *The Bible and the Liturgy*, University of Notre Dame Press, Notre Dame, Indiana, 1987

Denziger, Heinrich. *Sources of Catholic Dogma*, Herder Books, St. Louis, MO, 1957

Johnson, Kevin Orlin. *Why Do Catholics Do That?* Ballantine Books, 1995, ISBN 0-345-39726-6

Keating, Karl. *Catholicism and Fundamentalism*, Ignatius Press, 1988, ISBN 0-89870-177-5

Madrid, Patrick. *Surprised by Truth*, , Basilica Press, San Diego, 1994, ISBN 0-9642610-8-1

Navarre Bible series, Four Courts Press (a multivolume work, books can be purchased separately)

Ott, Ludwig. *Fundamentals of Catholic Dogma*, Tan Book Publishers, Rockford, IL, 1974

Pelikan, Jaroslav. *Mary Through the Ages*, Yale University Press, New Haven and London, 1996, ISBN 0-300-06951-0

Stravinskas, Peter M.J. *The Catholic Church and the Bible*, Ignatius Press, San Francisco, 1987, ISBN 0-89870-588-6

Vaughan, Rev. Kenelm and Rev. Newton Thompson, S.T.D. *Scripture by Topic*, Roman Catholic Books, Fort Collins, CO, 1943, reprinted 1997, ISBN 0-912141-51-4

Magazines and Magazine Articles:

Envoy Magazine, New Hope Ky, 40052-9989, 1-800-55-ENVOY

Lay Witness, Catholics United for the Faith, 827 N. Fourth, Steubenville, OH 43952, 1-800-MY-FAITH. Their free Faith Fact series is an excellent resource.

This Rock, Catholic Answers, P.O. Box 17490, San Diego, CA 92177, 1-800-291-8000

Gray, Timothy. "Replacing Judas: A Lot More than Meets the Eye?", *Lay Witness*, September 1997, pp. 4-5.

Harrison, Brian W. "Onan's Real Sin," *This Rock,* April 1997, pp. 40-42.

Peters, Joel, S. "Christ's Divinity Proved by the JW Bible," *This Rock,* December 1996, pp. 18-25.

Ray, Steve. "Why the Bereans Rejected Sola Scriptura," *This Rock,* March 1997, pp. 22-25.

Shea, Mark. "Five Myths About Seven Books," *Envoy*, March/April 1997, pp. 44-45.

Staples, Tim. "I Confess," *Envoy*, November, 97-Feb 98, pp. 42-44.

Staples, Tim. "Jesus Christ is not God - the JW argument," *Envoy*, Premier Issue, pp. 21-23.

Scott Hahn tapes:

A Study of the Book of Galatians
A Study of the Book of John
The Fourth Cup
God's Plan of Salvation: Immaculately Conceived

Patrick Madrid tapes:
"Do whatever He tells you" - Mary and Her message for Christians
"What Still Divides Us - A debate on sola scriptura and sole fide"

James Akin tape:
Can you trust the Gospels?

Archbishop Fulton Sheen tape:
The Sacraments and Grace

How To Contact the Author
For information on speaking engagements or
to obtain additional copies of this book,
contact:

Steve Kellmeyer
skellmeyer@bridegroompress.com

Web Sites:
BridegroomPress.com

1 Chron 10:13-14, 79
1 Chron 11:19, 163
1 Chron 13:6, 182
1 Chron 16:4, 182
1 Chron 18:12, 185
1 Chron 23:13, 180
1 Chron 24:31, 71
1 Chron 24:5, 71
1 Chron 25:8, 71
1 Chron 28:19, 104
1 Chron 29:11, 111
1 Chron 29:14, 258
1 Chron 9:33, 253
1 Cor 1:10, 47, 62
1 Cor 1:12-13, 60
1 Cor 1:13, 144
1 Cor 1:15, 45
1 Cor 1:16, 141
1 Cor 1:18, 200
1 Cor 1:1-9, 78
1 Cor 1:2, 12
1 Cor 10:1, 137
1 Cor 10:11, 204
1 Cor 10:1-11, 30
1 Cor 10:13, 260
1 Cor 10:1-4, 102
1 Cor 10:1-4,6, 23
1 Cor 10:14-22, 168
1 Cor 10:16, 165
1 Cor 10:16-21, 106
1 Cor 10:17, 111
1 Cor 10:33, 68
1 Cor 10:3-4, 158
1 Cor 10:4, 95
1 Cor 10:7-11, 23
1 Cor 10:9-10, 44
1 Cor 11:11, 75
1 Cor 11:2, 53, 73, 100
1 Cor 11:23, 31
1 Cor 11:23-29, 107
1 Cor 11:23-34, 169
1 Cor 11:24, 32, 149
1 Cor 11:34, 54
1 Cor 12:12-13, 80
1 Cor 12:12-27, 75
1 Cor 12:13, 150
1 Cor 12:22-25, 173
1 Cor 12:24, 208

1 Cor 12:26, 212
1 Cor 12:27-29, 85
1 Cor 12:28, 71
1 Cor 12:28-30, 48
1 Cor 12:31-13, 123
1 Cor 12:31-13:8, 123
1 Cor 12:4-11, 48
1 Cor 12:4-6, 21
1 Cor 13:2, 190
1 Cor 14:33, 59, 75
1 Cor 15:10, 257
1 Cor 15:1-2, 202
1 Cor 15:2, 78
1 Cor 15:20-35, 78
1 Cor 15:26, 256
1 Cor 15:42-43, 82
1 Cor 15:43, 257
1 Cor 15:45-49, 139, 223
1 Cor 15:48- 49, 255
1 Cor 2:10-11, 50
1 Cor 2:14, 107
1 Cor 2:14-16, 78
1 Cor 2:14-3:3, 164
1 Cor 2:9, 82, 218
1 Cor 3:10-11, 87, 250
1 Cor 3:10-15, 213
1 Cor 3:16, 104
1 Cor 3:16-17, 13
1 Cor 3:16-17,19-20, 66, 177
1 Cor 3:23, 76
1 Cor 3:3-7, 62
1 Cor 3:4-6, 141
1 Cor 3:8, 194
1 Cor 3:9, 15, 79, 206
1 Cor 4:14-16, 152
1 Cor 4:16, 100
1 Cor 4:4, 211
1 Cor 4:4-5, 200
1 Cor 4:6, 54
1 Cor 5:1-13, 62
1 Cor 5:3-5, 210
1 Cor 5:7-8, 107
1 Cor 6:11, 12, 142, 256
1 Cor 6:13-20, 122
1 Cor 6:19, 109, 253
1 Cor 6:20, 198, 255

1 Cor 6:9-10, 202, 205
1 Cor 7:10-15, 127
1 Cor 7:12, 45
1 Cor 7:12-14, 147
1 Cor 7:1-7, 153
1 Cor 7:32-38, 153
1 Cor 7:34, 249
1 Cor 7:40, 45
1 Cor 9:20-21, 196
1 Cor 9:22, 239
1 Cor 9:22-23, 68
1 Cor 9:25, 235
1 Cor 9:25-27, 200
1 Cor 9:4, 153
1 Jn 1:10, 62
1 Jn 1:1-4, 20
1 Jn 1:8, 258
1 Jn 1:8-9, 174
1 Jn 1:9, 108, 173
1 Jn 2:13-14, 152
1 Jn 2:15-17, 174
1 Jn 2:2, 215
1 Jn 2:26-27, 49
1 Jn 2:27, 46, 92
1 Jn 2:3, 197
1 Jn 2:4-6, 53
1 Jn 3:1, 65, 176
1 Jn 3:16, 208
1 Jn 3:18, 197
1 Jn 3:18-24, 123
1 Jn 4:1, 50
1 Jn 4:11-12, 198
1 Jn 4:13-14, 10, 108
1 Jn 4:16, 256
1 Jn 4:17-21, 197
1 Jn 4:19, 147
1 Jn 4:20, 255
1 Jn 4:7-12, 123
1 Jn 4:8, 212
1 Jn 4:9, 109
1 Jn 5:13, 200
1 Jn 5:1-31, 193
1 Jn 5:16, 213
1 Jn 5:16-17, 204
1 Jn 5:20, 18
1 Jn 5:2-4, 197
1 Jn 5:6-9, 13, 140
1 Jn 5:7-8, 18

1 Kings 1:13, 237
1 Kings 15:9-13, 234
1 Kings 18:3, 95
1 Kings 18:30-39, 137, 159
1 Kings 19:12-13, 159
1 Kings 19:4-8, 159
1 Kings 2:19, 235
1 Kings 2:20, 251, 253
1 Kings 20:32, 230
1 Kings 21:8, 105
1 Kings 3:15, 182
1 Kings 3:20, 237
1 Kings 6:23-35, 183
1 Kings 8:5, 182
1 Kings 8:57-60, 253
1 Kings 9:11-13, 230
1 Mac 10:29, 185
1 Mac 11:35, 185
1 Pet 1:3-4, 25
1 Pet 1:6-7, 43, 213
1 Pet 2:1-3, 189
1 Pet 2:13-20, 91
1 Pet 2:19,21, 208
1 Pet 2:24-25, 88, 149
1 Pet 2:5, 94, 250
1 Pet 2:5-8, 95
1 Pet 2:9, 150, 172
1 Pet 3:18, 164
1 Pet 3:18-19, 74, 139, 213
1 Pet 3:18-21, 25
1 Pet 3:1-9, 123
1 Pet 3:20-21, 143
1 Pet 4:1-2, 207
1 Pet 4:16, 209
1 Pet 4:6, 66, 177, 213
1 Pet 5:4, 235
1 Pet 5:4-5, 235
1 Pet 5:8, 259
1 Pet 5:9, 208
1 Sam 1:11, 237
1 Sam 16:1, 158
1 Sam 16:10-12, 158
1 Sam 16:5, 158
1 Sam 16:6-7, 158
1 Sam 2:22, 151
1 Sam 21:5, 152

1 Sam 24:3, 172
1 Sam 25:24-25,32-35, 237
1 Sam 28:7-19, 78
1 Thess 1:5, 89
1 Thess 1:6-7, 207
1 Thess 2:11, 152
1 Thess 2:13, 53, 102
1 Thess 2:13-14, 207
1 Thess 2:6-7, 92
1 Thess 2:7,11, 71
1 Thess 4:3, 66, 257
1 Thess 4:4, 123
1 Thess 5:12-13, 71, 88
1 Thess 5:19-21, 50
1 Thess 5:21, 50
1 Thess 5:23, 66
1 Thess 5:8, 43
1 Thess 5:9-10, 81
1 Tim 2:1, 212
1 Tim 2:1-3, 80
1 Tim 2:1-4, 69
1 Tim 2:15, 123
1 Tim 2:3-4, 203, 257
1 Tim 2:5-6, 15, 16, 79
1 Tim 3:15, 57, 87
1 Tim 3:2, 88
1 Tim 3:2-4, 153
1 Tim 4:10, 69
1 Tim 4:11-16, 88
1 Tim 4:14, 70, 72, 149
1 Tim 4:16, 203, 239
1 Tim 4:4-5, 179
1 Tim 5:22, 72, 150
1 Tim 6:2-4, 89
1 Tim 6:8, 257
2 Chron 14:10, 253
2 Chron 13:4-5, 187
2 Chron 22:2-4, 234
2 Chron 25:11, 186
2 Chron 35:3, 112
2 Cor 1:10-11, 252
2 Cor 1:11, 80, 249
2 Cor 1:13, 47, 52
2 Cor 1:21, 25, 148
2 Cor 1:6,11, 208
2 Cor 1:8, 260
2 Cor 11:14, 259

2 Cor 11:2, 126
2 Cor 13:14, 7, 10, 108, 175, 225
2 Cor 13:5, 66, 177
2 Cor 2:10, 173
2 Cor 2:1-17, 63
2 Cor 2:5, 208
2 Cor 2:5-10, 215
2 Cor 3:2, 68
2 Cor 3:7-11, 195
2 Cor 4:11, 65, 176
2 Cor 4:17, 260
2 Cor 5:10, 193, 205
2 Cor 5:17, 199
2 Cor 5:18-20, 173
2 Cor 5:21, 65
2 Cor 6:16, 66, 177
2 Cor 7:1, 66, 177
2 Cor 7:6-7, 260
2 Cor 9:15, 112
2 Jn 12, 53, 101
2 Kings 10:13-14, 230, 234
2 Kings 11:1-3, 234
2 Kings 13:20-21, 84
2 Kings 14:7, 185
2 Kings 15:5, 95
2 Kings 16:3, 134
2 Kings 17:17, 134
2 Kings 18:18, 95
2 Kings 2:11, 241
2 Kings 2:13-14, 84
2 Kings 2:20-22, 186
2 Kings 2:7-11, 138
2 Kings 21:6, 134
2 Kings 4:42-44, 159
2 Kings 5:11-14, 138
2 Mac 12:41-46, 213
2 Mac 12:42-45, 82
2 Mac 12:45, 111
2 Mac 13:10, 254
2 Mac 15:12-16, 82
2 Mac 7:13, 44
2 Mac 7:22, 133
2 Mac 7:28, 55
2 Pet 1:1, 12
2 Pet 1:20-21, 47, 52
2 Pet 1:21, 13

2 Pet 1:3-4, 25, 65, 176, 218
2 Pet 1:9, 232
2 Pet 2:20-21, 201
2 Pet 2:4, 217
2 Pet 2:6, 30
2 Pet 3:1-2, 71
2 Pet 3:15-16, 47
2 Sam 1:26, 230
2 Sam 12:13, 171, 209
2 Sam 14:15, 237, 252
2 Sam 23:17, 162
2 Sam 24:10-13, 209
2 Sam 5:2, 96
2 Sam 6:12-14, 227
2 Sam 6:13-16, 182
2 Sam 6:9, 227
2 Sam 8:13, 185
2 Samuel 7:9,11-14, 60
2 Thess 1:4-5, 111, 207
2 Thess 1:9, 217
2 Thess 2:15, 53, 101
2 Thess 3:1, 108
2 Thess 3:6, 101
2 Thess 3:9-10, 53
2 Tim 1:13, 73
2 Tim 1:16-18, 212
2 Tim 1:3, 248
2 Tim 1:6, 72, 149
2 Tim 1:8, 208
2 Tim 2:11-12, 198
2 Tim 2:11-13, 203
2 Tim 2:15, 53
2 Tim 2:2, 53, 72, 101
2 Tim 2:21, 53, 55
2 Tim 2:3, 208
2 Tim 3:10-11, 53
2 Tim 3:12, 260
2 Tim 3:14, 72
2 Tim 3:14-17, 52
2 Tim 3:16, 49, 55
2 Tim 3:8, 103
2 Tim 4:5, 208
2 Tim 4:8, 232, 235
Abraham, 18, 22, 24, 81, 83, 94, 105, 121, 123, 130, 151, 152, 169,

188, 197, 198, 211, 212, 235, 242
Acts 1:1, 85
Acts 1:12-14, 242
Acts 1:14, 85, 240
Acts 1:15,20-26, 72
Acts 1:15-17, 93
Acts 1:2, 85
Acts 1:20, 88
Acts 1:20-21, 149
Acts 1:9-11, 219
Acts 10:1-5, 247
Acts 10:18, 45
Acts 10:25-28, 98
Acts 10:34-35, 68, 191
Acts 10:39-41, 108
Acts 10:40-41, 169
Acts 10:44-48, 146
Acts 13:29, 155
Acts 13:3, 72, 149
Acts 13:38-39, 194
Acts 14:14, 71
Acts 14:15-17, 191
Acts 14:22-23, 70, 149
Acts 15:11, 190
Acts 15:1-2, 51, 90
Acts 15:13-15, 87
Acts 15:21, 102
Acts 15:22-23,27-28, 100
Acts 15:24, 71
Acts 15:28, 51, 92
Acts 16:15, 143
Acts 16:1-5, 92
Acts 16:16-18, 20
Acts 16:27-34, 143
Acts 16:4, 92
Acts 17:10-12, 51
Acts 17:1-7, 51
Acts 17:22-23, 68
Acts 17:22-27, 191
Acts 17:27-29, 134
Acts 17:30-31, 68
Acts 17:32, 168
Acts 19:11-12, 84
Acts 19:13-15, 20
Acts 19:1-5, 144
Acts 19:1-6, 144, 148

Acts 19:18, 173
Acts 19:5, 25
Acts 2:1-12, 86
Acts 2:1-4, 76
Acts 2:14-15, 97
Acts 2:24,31, 168
Acts 2:33, 10
Acts 2:37-39, 25
Acts 2:38-39, 68, 146
Acts 2:38-41, 144
Acts 2:42, 71
Acts 2:42,46-47, 106
Acts 2:42-47, 168
Acts 20:17,27, 53
Acts 20:27-31, 71
Acts 20:28, 13, 21, 149
Acts 20:7, 106
Acts 22:15-16, 68
Acts 22:16, 142
Acts 23:2-3, 198
Acts 23:6, 168
Acts 27:34-35, 168
Acts 3:1, 86
Acts 3:12, 86
Acts 3:4-6, 98
Acts 3:7, 86
Acts 4:12, 256
Acts 4:8-13, 98
Acts 5:1-4, 73, 97, 204
Acts 5:14-16, 84
Acts 5:29, 97
Acts 5:3-4, 13
Acts 6:6, 72, 149
Acts 7:1-2, 152
Acts 8:12-16, 145
Acts 8:13,18-24, 171
Acts 8:14-17, 98, 148
Acts 8:17, 25
Acts 8:17-24, 145
Acts 8:25-38, 145
Acts 8:30-31, 71
Acts 9:1-5, 74
Acts 9:15-19, 72
Acts 9:17-19, 145
Amos 1:9, 230
Amos 8:11, 258
Amos 9:10-12, 86
anathema, 31, 32, 88
angel, 10, 15, 16, 17, 19, 20, 39, 40, 45, 82, 88, 107, 126, 130, 145, 156, 159, 170, 188, 219, 227, 228, 229, 234, 236, 239, 242, 243, 247, 251
Anointing of the Sick, 32, 175
Apostolic Succession, 69
Ashes, 40, 45, 144, 145, 169, 184, 188
AUTHORITY, 11, 12, 19, 20, 32, 33, 35, 37, 38, 39, 40, 46, 47, 48, 49, 50, 51, 52, 54, 66, 69, 73, 74, 82, 85, 88, 89, 93, 95, 97, 98, 102, 103, 149, 151, 152, 171, 172, 222, 230, 241
baptism, 23, 25, 31, 46, 50, 72, 75, 92, 93, 120, 127, 136, 137, 138, 140, 141, 142, 143, 144, 145, 146, 147, 148, 150, 155, 171, 172, 173, 190, 246
baptismoi, 24, 139, 145
Bar 6:35-40,44, 44
Bereans, 51, 52
Birth Control, 127
Bridegroom, 11, 24, 45, 46, 74, 76, 96, 103, 121, 125, 138, 139, 140, 141, 144, 170
Celibacy, 152, 154
Church, 12, 13, 17, 21, 26, 31, 32, 33, 34, 36, 37, 38, 39, 40, 46, 48, 49, 50, 52, 53, 54, 57, 59, 61, 62, 69, 70, 71, 72, 73, 74, 75, 76, 77, 78, 85, 87, 88, 89, 90, 92, 93, 94, 98, 100, 101, 102, 103, 106, 107, 108, 110, 111, 120, 121, 126, 128, 131, 136, 145, 147, 149, 151, 152, 153, 154, 155, 170, 171, 173, 175, 181, 196, 206, 207, 214, 215, 222, 225, 228, 229, 230, 233, 240, 250
Col 1:15, 21, 182
Col 1:15-19, 17
Col 1:18, 75
Col 1:21-23, 201
Col 1:22, 215
Col 1:24, 54, 76, 206, 214
Col 1:24-26, 72, 106, 195
Col 1:26-27, 65, 176
Col 1:28, 66, 177
Col 1:3, 110
Col 2:11-12, 146
Col 2:12-14, 142
Col 2:16-17, 30
Col 2:18, 62
Col 2:22, 102
Col 2:9, 18
Col 2:9-10, 66, 176
Col 3:11, 150
Col 3:14, 63
Col 3:2, 256
Col 4:6, 187
Confirmation, 50, 92, 145, 148, 207, 236
Council of Trent, 31, 32
Dan 12:2, 216
Dan 13:42, 252
Dan 2:31-45, 45
Dan 4:27, 193, 210, 258
Dan 5:1-30, 45
Dan 9:9, 251
Deut 12:31, 134
Deut 13:3, 259
Deut 13:7-11, 18
Deut 18:10, 134
Deut 18:10-12, 78
Deut 21:22-23, 246
Deut 23:3, 60
Deut 23:8, 230
Deut 25:7-10, 128
Deut 29:22-23, 185
Deut 3:15-17, 186
Deut 30:19, 218
Deut 31:9,12, 50
Deut 32:14, 24, 139
Deut 32:42, 163
Deut 32:46-47, 51
Deut 32:51-52, 210
Deut 32:7, 100
Deut 4:24, 256
Deut 6:4-5, 8, 58, 182
Deut 8:3, 258
Deut 9:20, 80
Divinization, 64
Dostoevsky, 131
Dt 32:14, 24
Eccl 6:1-2, 258
Eccles 11:5, 133
Elisha, 84, 138, 159, 186
Eph 1:1,8-10, 77
Eph 1:13, 12, 148
Eph 1:22-23, 75, 76
Eph 1:3, 180
Eph 1:3-10, 223
Eph 1:4, 133, 256
Eph 1:9-10, 110
Eph 2:14-16,22, 62
Eph 2:15, 65, 76, 176
Eph 2:18, 10
Eph 2:19-20, 87
Eph 2:21-22, 65, 177
Eph 2:4-6, 255
Eph 2:8, 200
Eph 2:8-10, 190
Eph 3:14-15, 15, 82, 152
Eph 3:14-17, 10
Eph 3:17, 255
Eph 3:2, 87, 206, 239
Eph 3:3, 54
Eph 3:4-5, 88
Eph 3:4-6, 75
Eph 3:5-6,19, 66, 177
Eph 3:7-8, 207
Eph 3:8-10, 68
Eph 3:9-10, 26, 90, 119
Eph 3:9-11, 77
Eph 4:1,17, 77
Eph 4:11, 88
Eph 4:11-12, 90
Eph 4:15-16, 173

Eph 4:19, 258
Eph 4:3, 63
Eph 4:30, 12
Eph 4:4-5, 75
Eph 4:5, 143
Eph 4:8-12, 48
Eph 5:1, 66, 177
Eph 5:2,21-33, 120
Eph 5:20, 109
Eph 5:23-32, 76
Eph 5:26, 143
Eph 5:26-27, 66
Eph 5:29, 173
Eph 5:29-32, 131
Eph 5:5, 205
Eph 5:5-7, 202
Eph 6:12, 259
Eph 6:14-17, 43
Esther 4:1, 188
Esther 4:8-9, 251, 253
Esther 5:2,3, 250
Esther 9:22, 250
Eucharist, 23, 31, 74, 98, 103, 104, 107, 109, 155, 160, 169, 170, 184, 187
Ex 1:15-17, 134
Ex 1:19, 45
Ex 12:1-10, 156
Ex 12:11-15, 156
Ex 13:19, 83
Ex 15:19, 137
Ex 15:20-21, 233
Ex 15:23-25, 137
Ex 17:8-13, 79
Ex 19:6, 150
Ex 2:1-10, 136
Ex 2:5, 236
Ex 20:1-11, 9
Ex 20:3, 18
Ex 20:4-5, 181
Ex 21:17, 204
Ex 21:20-21, 132
Ex 21:22-25, 132
Ex 22:21, 156
Ex 23:43-49, 156
Ex 24:7, 255
Ex 24:9-11, 158

Ex 25:18-21, 181
Ex 26:30, 104
Ex 29:44-46, 160
Ex 3:14, 18
Ex 3:6, 210
Ex 30:26, 227
Ex 30:35, 184
Ex 30:8, 188
Ex 33:11, 210, 226
Ex 33:7, 151
Ex 34:20, 232
Ex 34:33-35, 210
Ex 40:34-35, 227
Ex 40:9, 227
Ezek 11:19-20, 21
Ezek 13:10-16, 199
Ezek 16:20-21, 134
Ezek 16:4, 186
Ezek 20:9, 226
Ezek 3:12,14, 10
Ezek 31:16-17, 216
Ezek 34:23-24, 96
Ezek 36:25, 145
Ezek 36:26, 10
Ezek 39:17-20, 163
Ezek 43:23-24, 185
Ezek 44:2-3, 229
Ezek 47:8-11, 186
Ezek 9:4, 246
Ezra 4:14, 187
Ezra 6:9, 184
Ezra 7:21-22, 184
Gal 1:11-12,15-20, 52
Gal 1:12, 16
Gal 1:15-20, 97
Gal 1:8-9, 88
Gal 2:16, 194
Gal 2:17, 12
Gal 2:20, 66, 177
Gal 2:21, 224
Gal 2:7, 94, 97
Gal 3:13, 246
Gal 3:16, 15
Gal 3:16-17, 194
Gal 3:2,5, 101
Gal 3:2-10, 194
Gal 3:27, 142
Gal 3:28, 150

Gal 4:19, 66
Gal 4:24, 30
Gal 4:4, 15, 238
Gal 4:4-5, 252
Gal 4:4-6, 12
Gal 4:4-7, 65, 176, 236
Gal 4:6-7, 10
Gal 5:19-21, 202, 205
Gal 5:4-6, 196
Gal 6:14, 208, 246
Gal 6:15-16, 23, 113
Gal 6:17, 246
Gal 6:2, 195, 196, 208, 212
Gal 6:6-10, 196
Gal 6:9-10, 68, 135
Gen 1:1, 21
Gen 1:1-2, 22, 136
Gen 1:26, 8
Gen 1:26-28,31, 120
Gen 1:27, 8, 64, 150, 182
Gen 1:28, 128
Gen 10:1, 59
Gen 11:7, 8
Gen 12:1, 195
Gen 12:10-13, 129
Gen 12:1-3, 59
Gen 12:2, 180
Gen 14:18, 105, 109
Gen 14:3,8-18, 184
Gen 15:6, 195
Gen 16:1, 130
Gen 16:11, 132
Gen 17:12-14, 146
Gen 17:9-11, 195
Gen 18:1, 8
Gen 18:13-14, 130
Gen 18:27, 188
Gen 18:32-33, 83
Gen 19:26, 184
Gen 2:18, 8
Gen 2:18-25, 120
Gen 2:19-25, 23
Gen 2:21-24, 223
Gen 2:4, 59
Gen 2:6-7, 22
Gen 22:13, 105

Gen 22:9-13, 155
Gen 24:48-51, 121
Gen 25, 45
Gen 25:21, 130
Gen 25:21-26, 132
Gen 26:1, 130
Gen 26:6-7, 130
Gen 29:25, 130
Gen 3:12, 129
Gen 3:15, 15, 222
Gen 3:16, 109
Gen 3:16-17, 129
Gen 3:19, 188
Gen 3:22, 8, 155
Gen 3:23-24, 252
Gen 3:27, 8
Gen 3:5, 64
Gen 3:6, 223
Gen 30:1-2, 130
Gen 30:9, 130
Gen 38:11-18, 128
Gen 38:25-26, 128
Gen 38:6-10, 128
Gen 4:1, 133
Gen 4:15, 246
Gen 41:40-44, 95
Gen 41:54, 130
Gen 49:11, 139
Gen 49:22-27, 180
Gen 5:1-3, 64, 175, 182
Gen 5:23, 240
Gen 5:3, 59, 252
Gen 7:4, 136
Gen 8:5, 232
Gen 9:1,6-11, 59
Gen 9:21, 59
Gen 9:6, 132
gifts of the Holy Spirit, 47
Gnostic, 151
Gospel of Mary Magdalene, 151
Gospel of Thomas, 36, 151
graven images, 181, 182, 183
Heb 1:1, 13
Heb 1:1-8, 16

Heb 1:3, 43
Heb 1:6, 20
Heb 1:9-13, 17
Heb 10:1, 30
Heb 10:10, 76, 106, 238
Heb 10:14, 65, 176
Heb 10:15-17, 13
Heb 10:22, 143
Heb 10:26, 144
Heb 10:26-29, 201
Heb 11:20-21, 180
Heb 11:35, 44
Heb 11:40, 208
Heb 11:6, 190
Heb 11:8, 195
Heb 12:1, 81
Heb 12:22-24, 81
Heb 12:23, 64, 176
Heb 12:28, 110
Heb 12:29, 138, 159, 212
Heb 12:9, 255
Heb 13:10, 106
Heb 13:17, 88, 111
Heb 13:4, 124
Heb 13:7, 89
Heb 2:11-12, 236, 255
Heb 2:14-15, 110
Heb 2:9, 16
Heb 3:1, 70, 172
Heb 3:12-14, 202
Heb 3:14, 79, 207
Heb 3:4-6, 18
Heb 3:7-11, 13
Heb 4:11-13, 238
Heb 4:15, 225
Heb 4:16, 240
Heb 4:2, 101
Heb 5:11-12, 47
Heb 5:7-8, 214
Heb 5:8, 257
Heb 6:11-12, 252
Heb 6:1-2, 148
Heb 6:4, 66, 177
Heb 6:4-6, 144, 201
Heb 6:7-10, 198
Heb 7:27, 106
Heb 8:1-3, 105

Heb 8:5, 30
Heb 9:13-14, 169
Heb 9:2,9-10, 25
Heb 9:24, 30, 109
Heb 9:24-28, 106
Heb 9:27, 211
Heb 9:3-4, 227
Hell, 31, 32, 79, 108, 202, 203, 211, 212, 216, 217
Holy Matrimony, 120
Holy Orders, 148, 149, 150
Hos 12:2-3, 132
Hos 2:16, 24
Ignatius, 107
Imputed Righteousness, 198
Incense, 45, 72, 82, 91, 99, 106, 160, 184, 188, 232, 233
Indulgences, 214, 215, 247
Inerrancy, 85
Infallibility, 38, 85
Is 1:15-17, 135
Is 1:16, 259
Is 1:23, 135
Is 10:1-2, 135
Is 11:1-3, 47
Is 22:15-24, 95
Is 23:12, 153
Is 28:16, 94, 250
Is 28:5, 256
Is 28:8-9, 46
Is 35:4-6, 17
Is 35:8, 90
Is 43:25, 172
Is 44:2,24, 133
Is 44:24, 21
Is 45:15, 155
Is 45:9-11, 131
Is 45:9-12, 134
Is 46:3, 133
Is 49:1,2, 133
Is 49:15-16, 133
Is 49:26, 162
Is 5:14, 216

Is 50:1-2, 124
Is 51:1-2, 94
Is 52:11, 153
Is 53:3,11, 239
Is 53:6, 46
Is 54:10-17, 94
Is 54:9-17, 87
Is 55:10-11, 136
Is 55:10-13, 113
Is 59:19-21, 92
Is 59:21, 100
Is 6:3, 9, 107, 110
Is 6:5-7, 159
Is 6:6-7, 212
Is 60:21, 256
Is 61:6, 150
Is 62:4-5, 11, 120
Is 64:4, 256
Is 66:24, 216
Is 66:6-8, 228
Is 7:14, 228
Is 9:6, 16
Isaac, 21, 22, 24, 81, 105, 121, 130, 169, 197
James 1:12, 203, 235
James 1:13-15, 259
James 1:17, 65, 177
James 1:2,12, 259
James 1:22-27, 196
James 1:27, 135
James 1:4, 52, 55
James 1:5, 69
James 2:21, 196
James 2:24, 191
James 2:6-26, 197
James 3:12, 187
James 3:6, 108
James 4:1-4, 205
James 4:17, 108, 197
James 5:10, 30
James 5:14, 32
James 5:14-15, 175
James 5:15, 173
James 5:16, 61, 82, 108, 173, 245
James 5:17, 103
Jer 1:5, 129, 133
Jer 13:18,20, 233

Jer 14:9, 255
Jer 17:5-6, 185
Jer 23:5, 17
Jer 3:15-19, 228
Jer 3:19, 255
Jer 3:8, 124
Jer 31:10, 96
Jer 31:22, 223
Jer 31:31-34, 122
Jer 31:33-34, 135
Jer 32:10, 105
Jer 32:35, 134
Jer 33:20-22, 22
Jer 34:9, 230
Jer 44:6:-27, 232
Jer 44:7-8,11,15-17,24-27, 232
Jer 46:10, 163
Jer 7:18, 232
Jer 7:5-6, 135
Jn 1:1, 10, 18, 43
Jn 1:1, 14, 23
Jn 1:1-3, 20, 190
Jn 1:14, 155
Jn 1:18, 16
Jn 1:29, 109, 112
Jn 1:29 29, 138
Jn 1:33, 138
Jn 1:42, 94
Jn 1:49-51, 93
Jn 10:16, 61
Jn 10:17-18, 110
Jn 10:27-29, 200
Jn 10:28-30, 18
Jn 10:30, 11
Jn 10:37-38, 192
Jn 10:6, 29
Jn 11:6, 142
Jn 12:23-24, 24
Jn 12:25-26, 81
Jn 12:26, 241
Jn 12:30-31, 68
Jn 12:34, 161
Jn 12:49, 70
Jn 13:26,30, 169
Jn 13:34, 257, 258
Jn 13:5-15, 172

Jn 13:6, 90
Jn 14:1, 18
Jn 14:12-14, 79
Jn 14:15,21, 193
Jn 14:15-17, 73
Jn 14:16, 26, 12
Jn 14:16,26, 10
Jn 14:16-18, 89
Jn 14:18, 62
Jn 14:23, 256
Jn 14:26, 13, 48, 101
Jn 14:27, 111
Jn 14:28, 16
Jn 15:1, 109
Jn 15:1-17, 131
Jn 15:2-3, 16, 90
Jn 15:26, 13
Jn 15:4-5, 74
Jn 15:6, 203
Jn 15:9-16, 124
Jn 16:11, 70
Jn 16:12-15, 90
Jn 16:13, 48, 90, 101
Jn 16:13-15, 12
Jn 16:14, 14
Jn 16:14-15, 14, 18
Jn 16:23, 73
Jn 16:25, 29
Jn 16:29-30, 29
Jn 17:1-26, 61
Jn 17:15, 111, 260
Jn 17:20-23, 65, 77, 176
Jn 17:20-26, 124
Jn 17:3, 16, 21
Jn 18:4-6, 19
Jn 19:25, 243
Jn 19:25-27, 231, 240
Jn 19:26-27, 238, 251
Jn 19:29-30, 166
Jn 19:3, 224
Jn 19:33-34, 224
Jn 19:33-35, 142
Jn 19:41, 229
Jn 2:11, 239
Jn 2:1-11, 124, 138
Jn 2:1-5, 239, 243
Jn 2:23-25, 139, 198
Jn 2:3, 252

Jn 2:3-6, 24
Jn 2:5, 221, 242, 253
Jn 20:17, 16
Jn 20:19, 111
Jn 20:19-28, 167
Jn 20:21, 69, 70
Jn 20:21-23, 22, 172
Jn 20:22, 14, 31, 149, 259
Jn 20:26-28, 74
Jn 20:28-29, 19
Jn 21:15, 32
Jn 21:15-19, 96
Jn 21:25, 54
Jn 28:29, 70
Jn 3:1-3, 139
Jn 3:14-15, 43, 183
Jn 3:16, 18
Jn 3:16-17, 140
Jn 3:17, 68
Jn 3:18, 140
Jn 3:22, 140
Jn 3:23,25-30, 140
Jn 3:29, 125, 130
Jn 3:4-6, 139
Jn 3:5, 31, 143
Jn 3:7-8, 140
Jn 3:9-15, 140
Jn 4:10,13-14, 141
Jn 4:11, 110
Jn 4:1-2, 141
Jn 4:16-18, 141
Jn 4:19-26, 141
Jn 4:21-22, 68
Jn 4:22, 189
Jn 4:23, 24
Jn 4:7,39-42, 80
Jn 4:7-8, 31-38, 160
Jn 5:18, 18
Jn 5:19, 14, 69
Jn 5:25, 24
Jn 5:29, 193
Jn 5:30, 69
Jn 5:33-36, 192
Jn 5:4, 39
Jn 6:10-14, 161
Jn 6:19-20, 161
Jn 6:22-31, 161

Jn 6:32-33, 161
Jn 6:34-40, 162
Jn 6:35, 109
Jn 6:38,40, 257
Jn 6:4, 161
Jn 6:41-42, 162
Jn 6:43-51, 162
Jn 6:51, 258
Jn 6:51,54, 111
Jn 6:52, 162
Jn 6:53, 162
Jn 6:54-59, 163
Jn 6:56, 74
Jn 6:57, 25
Jn 6:60-63, 164
Jn 6:64-66, 164
Jn 6:67-71, 164
Jn 7:16, 21, 69
Jn 7:16-18, 103
Jn 7:22, 151
Jn 7:35, 35
Jn 8:1-11, 39
Jn 8:28-29, 69
Jn 8:29-31, 198
Jn 8:33, 18
Jn 8:34-36, 142
Jn 8:58-59, 18
Jn 9, 45
Jn 9:1-7, 24
Jn 9:3-4, 193, 206
Jn 9:38, 19
Jn 9:6-7, 22, 118
Job 10:8-12, 133
Job 31:15, 133
Job 39:27, 163
Job 39:5-8, 185
Job 42:6, 188
Job 6:6, 185
Joel 2:28-32, 10
Joel 2:29, 228
John 14:23, 66, 177
Joseph, 95, 183, 229, 243
Josh 1:11, 142
Josh 1:8, 253
Josh 15:1-5, 186
Josh 18:11,19, 186
Josh 3:15-16, 137

Josh 3:16-17, 187
Josh 3:5, 142
Josh 7:6-7, 181
Josh 7:6-8, 181
Jud 11:17, 254
Jud 11:5,12:4, 237
Jud 8:24-25, 44
Jud 9:10, 45
Jude 1:8, 73, 91
Jude 1:9, 19
Jude 14, 36
Jude 20-21, 10
Jude 21, 108
Jude 3, 97
Jude 7, 30
Jude 8, 47
Jude 9, 241
Judg 11:29-40, 45
Judg 19:22-30, 45
Judg 20:27, 181
Judg 4:17-22, 45
Judg 9:18, 236
Judg 9:45, 186
Keys, 32, 73, 87, 93, 95, 96, 214
Korah, 91, 98, 99
Lam 1:7,15, 153
Lam 3:16, 188
Lam 3:41, 110
Lev 10:16-20, 157
Lev 15:25-26, 118
Lev 17:11-12, 156
Lev 17:14, 119
Lev 18:21,30, 134
Lev 18:22-23, 129
Lev 18:26-30, 204
Lev 19:14, 134
Lev 19:18, 182
Lev 19:20-22, 172
Lev 2:11-13, 187
Lev 20:1-7, 204
Lev 21:6-7, 153
Lev 24:5-9, 157
Lev 26:18, 105
Lev 26:39-40, 171
Lev 6:19-22, 157
Lev 7:15-20, 157
Lev 7:35-36, 157

Lev 7:7, 157
Lev 8:23-24, 150
litany, 248
liturgy, 108, 109, 138, 188, 246
Lk 1:10, 188
Lk 1:15,41,44, 226
Lk 1:15,41-45, 239
Lk 1:26-27, 85, 251
Lk 1:26-38, 242
Lk 1:28, 224, 249
Lk 1:3, 85
Lk 1:31, 85
Lk 1:31, 35, 15
Lk 1:31-35,38, 236
Lk 1:32, 109
Lk 1:34-35,38, 228
Lk 1:35, 10, 85, 110, 132, 227
Lk 1:35, 2:6-7, 251
Lk 1:36, 39-40, 56, 252
Lk 1:38, 221, 249, 252
Lk 1:38,46-55, 234
Lk 1:39-56, 242
Lk 1:41, 227
Lk 1:41-43, 227
Lk 1:41-44, 133
Lk 1:42, 225
Lk 1:43, 15
Lk 1:45, 242
Lk 1:46-49, 226
Lk 1:78-79, 30
Lk 1:8-9, 72, 253
Lk 1:9, 86
Lk 10:16, 71, 89, 102, 150
Lk 10:17, 20
Lk 10:22, 11
Lk 10:25-37, 60
Lk 11:2-4, 254
Lk 11:27-28, 236, 242
Lk 11:38-41, 199
Lk 11:52, 95
Lk 11:5-9, 247
Lk 12:33-34, 214
Lk 12:35-36, 125
Lk 12:50, 143
Lk 12:58-59, 211

Lk 12:9, 203
Lk 13:12-13, 118
Lk 13:32, 20
Lk 14:15, 170
Lk 14:2-4, 118
Lk 14:27, 209
Lk 14:34-35, 187
Lk 14:6, 125, 218
Lk 15:11-14, 201
Lk 15:18-19, 174
Lk 15:2, 76
Lk 15:7-10, 83
Lk 16:1-12, 214
Lk 16:19-31, 83, 211
Lk 16:24, 151
Lk 17:11-14, 173
Lk 18:10-14, 247
Lk 18:15-17, 146
Lk 18:20, 205
Lk 18:2-8, 247
Lk 18:29-30, 154
Lk 18:6-8, 254
Lk 2:14, 108
Lk 2:19, 242
Lk 2:22-24, 242
Lk 2:24, 225
Lk 2:32-34, 238
Lk 2:34, 155, 240
Lk 2:51-52, 215
Lk 2:6-7, 160, 249
Lk 20:29-31, 42
Lk 20:34,37, 42
Lk 20:34-38, 81
Lk 22:14-20, 165
Lk 22:19, 31, 32, 149
Lk 22:19-20, 106
Lk 22:29-30, 71, 73, 90, 173
Lk 22:31-32, 96
Lk 22:32, 89
Lk 22:42, 166
Lk 22:43-44 43, 39
Lk 23:26, 208
Lk 23:27-28, 238
Lk 23:28, 208
Lk 23:36, 166
Lk 23:53, 229
Lk 24:13-35, 166

Lk 24:27-32, 107
Lk 24:37-43, 167
Lk 24:39-43, 74
Lk 24:42-49, 48
Lk 24:45, 47
Lk 24:48, 69
Lk 24:49, 70
Lk 3:3, 138
Lk 4:33-36, 20
Lk 4:38, 86
Lk 4:40, 119
Lk 4:40-41, 20
Lk 4:43, 86
Lk 5:13, 117
Lk 5:13-14, 174
Lk 5:20-21, 11
Lk 5:34-35, 76, 125
Lk 6:13, 70
Lk 6:15-16, 231
Lk 6:28, 180
Lk 6:35-38, 193
Lk 6:36, 258
Lk 6:37, 259
Lk 7:12-15, 237
Lk 7:13-15, 118
Lk 7:29-30, 144, 225
Lk 7:6-7, 112
Lk 8:21, 236
Lk 8:43-48, 84, 119
Lk 8:53-55, 118
Lk 9:23, 208
Lk 9:30-31, 81
Lk 9:42, 20
Luther, 34, 37, 38, 39, 47, 91, 99, 197, 200, 223, 229, 235, 243, 244
Mal 1:1,10-11, 160
Mal 1:10-11, 106
Mal 1:6, 255
Mal 2:10, 255
Mal 2:15-16, 127
Mal 3:1, 240
Mary, 15, 19, 24, 36, 39, 40, 108, 111, 151, 155, 167, 183, 221, 222, 223, 225, 226, 227, 228, 229, 230, 233, 234, 235, 236, 238, 239, 240, 241,

242, 243, 244, 247, 248, 249, 250, 251, 252, 253
Mass, 32, 76, 103, 104, 105, 106, 107, 108, 149, 170, 206
Mic 5:1-2, 228
Mk 1:11, 11
Mk 1:24, 109
Mk 1:25-26, 180
Mk 1:25-27, 19
Mk 1:30-31, 117
Mk 1:4, 138
Mk 1:40-41, 117
Mk 1:40-45, 174
Mk 1:5, 171, 225
Mk 10:19, 205
Mk 10:2-9, 127
Mk 10:29-31, 154
Mk 10:38, 143
Mk 10:7-9, 124
Mk 11:9-10, 151
Mk 12:20-22, 42
Mk 12:24, 26-27, 42
Mk 12:26-27, 81
Mk 13:13, 203
Mk 14:22-26, 165
Mk 14:36, 166
Mk 15:18, 224
Mk 15:21, 208
Mk 15:22, 166
Mk 15:27-32, 44
Mk 15:36-37, 166
Mk 15:40, 231
Mk 16:16, 143
Mk 16:17-18, 256
Mk 16:9-13, 167
Mk 16:9-20, 39
Mk 2:10, 69
Mk 2:1-5, 196
Mk 2:16, 76
Mk 2:1-6, 147
Mk 2:19-20, 125
Mk 2:5-7, 11
Mk 3:13, 70
Mk 3:1-6, 11
Mk 3:21, 231
Mk 3:28-30, 205
Mk 3:31-33, 230

Mk 3:34-35, 236
Mk 4:20, 90
Mk 4:35-41, 164
Mk 5:27-34, 119
Mk 5:40-42, 118
Mk 6:12-13, 175
Mk 6:3, 231
Mk 6:56, 84, 119
Mk 7:15, 108
Mk 7:33-35, 118
Mk 7:4-13, 99
Mk 8:22-24, 118
Mk 9:25-27, 20
Mk 9:26-27, 118
Mk 9:41, 196
Mk 9:43-48, 217
Mk 9:50, 187
Mortal and Venial Sin, 204
Moses, 18, 19, 23, 24, 36, 39, 40, 48, 50, 81, 83, 90, 91, 97, 98, 99, 100, 102, 103, 107, 121, 123, 126, 127, 137, 140, 150, 156, 157, 158, 161, 162, 167, 174, 183, 194, 201, 211, 212, 223, 227, 236, 241, 242
Mt 1:19-20, 130
Mt 1:20-25, 243
Mt 1:22-23, 16, 100
Mt 1:23, 60
Mt 1:24-25, 229, 232
Mt 1:25, 2:1, 252
Mt 10:1, 70
Mt 10:19-20, 21
Mt 10:22, 200, 203, 249
Mt 10:2-3, 231
Mt 10:2-4, 97
Mt 10:28, 217
Mt 10:33, 203
Mt 10:38, 208
Mt 11:11, 16
Mt 11:21, 188
Mt 11:25, 255
Mt 11:2-6, 17
Mt 11:27, 11, 254
Mt 12:17, 68, 101

Mt 12:31, 205
Mt 12:46-50, 230
Mt 12:49-50, 236
Mt 12:6, 41,42, 45
Mt 12:8, 11
Mt 13:10, 85
Mt 13:10-11, 46
Mt 13:14,35, 101
Mt 13:34-35, 29
Mt 13:41-43, 218
Mt 13:51, 102
Mt 13:52, 90
Mt 13:55, 231
Mt 15:1, 225
Mt 15:19, 205
Mt 15:2-9, 99
Mt 16:16, 17, 32
Mt 16:16-19, 72, 93
Mt 16:18, 89, 102
Mt 16:18-19, 87
Mt 16:19, 214
Mt 16:5-12, 160
Mt 17:17-18, 19
Mt 17:27, 118
Mt 17:3-5, 81
Mt 18:10, 146
Mt 18:14, 146
Mt 18:15, 21, 231
Mt 18:15-17, 56
Mt 18:15-20, 56, 62
Mt 18:16, 54
Mt 18:16-17, 50
Mt 18:16-18, 88
Mt 18:17-18, 73
Mt 18:18, 214
Mt 18:21, 232
Mt 18:23-35, 211
Mt 18:32, 258
Mt 18:8-9, 217
Mt 19:10, 153
Mt 19:11-12, 153
Mt 19:13-15, 146
Mt 19:16-21, 192
Mt 19:17, 257
Mt 19:1-9, 123
Mt 19:29-30, 154
Mt 19:3-9, 126
Mt 19:4-5, 124

Mt 2:11, 19
Mt 2:13-20, 243
Mt 2:15,17-18,23, 100
Mt 2:16, 134
Mt 2:23, 102
Mt 20:31, 108
Mt 21:18-19, 165
Mt 21:4-5, 101
Mt 21:9, 110
Mt 22:1-9, 125, 218
Mt 22:25-26, 42
Mt 22:29,31-33, 42
Mt 22:30, 154
Mt 22:31-32, 81
Mt 22:32, 212
Mt 22:35-40, 124
Mt 22:43-44, 232
Mt 23:1-3, 97
Mt 23:2-3, 35, 102
Mt 23:27-28, 198
Mt 23:6-9, 151
Mt 24:13, 203
Mt 25:1,10, 125, 218
Mt 25:31, 11
Mt 25:31-46, 192
Mt 25:34, 133
Mt 25:41, 217
Mt 25:46, 217
Mt 26:26, 31, 76
Mt 26:26-28, 110
Mt 26:26-30, 165
Mt 26:39, 166
Mt 26:39-44, 247
Mt 26:41, 259
Mt 26:48-49, 224
Mt 27:29, 224
Mt 27:32, 208
Mt 27:33, 166
Mt 27:39-43, 44
Mt 27:48-50, 166
Mt 27:52-53, 241
Mt 27:59-60, 229
Mt 27:9-10, 101
Mt 28:18, 70
Mt 28:19, 7, 10, 112, 143, 246
Mt 28:19-20, 70, 77

Mt 28:20, 60, 70, 92, 101, 155, 168
Mt 28:8-9, 224
Mt 28:9, 19
Mt 3:12, 217
Mt 3:16, 22
Mt 3:16-17, 10
Mt 3:5-6, 171
Mt 4, 50
Mt 4:14, 30, 101
Mt 4:4, 258
Mt 5:13, 187
Mt 5:14, 85
Mt 5:17, 11, 204
Mt 5:19-30, 202
Mt 5:22-24, 231
Mt 5:23-24, 43-48, 43
Mt 5:25-26, 211
Mt 5:28, 205
Mt 5:31-32, 126
Mt 5:4, 257
Mt 5:48, 64, 176, 255, 257, 258
Mt 5:6, 258
Mt 5:7, 259
Mt 5:8, 260
Mt 5:9, 260
Mt 6:1-4, 192
Mt 6:21, 255
Mt 6:23, 205
Mt 6:31, 258
Mt 6:7-8, 247
Mt 6:9-13, 111, 254
Mt 7:12, 192
Mt 7:19-23, 192
Mt 7:24, 89, 94
Mt 8:10-11, 169
Mt 8:11-12, 218
Mt 8:14-15, 117
Mt 8:17, 101
Mt 8:2, 117
Mt 8:2-4, 174
Mt 9:11, 76
Mt 9:15, 11, 125
Mt 9:20-22, 119
Mt 9:24-25, 117
Mt 9:28-30, 118
Mt 9:34,10:25, 58

necromancy, 77, 78, 79, 81, 83, 248
Neh 1:3-6, 253
Neh 5:13, 108
Neh 5:7, 230
Num 12:3, 226
Num 15:30, 204
Num 16: 4-11, 91
Num 16:1-3, 91, 98
Num 16:19-35, 99
Num 16:3, 60
Num 19:11-12, 24
Num 19:17, 184
Num 19:9-19, 144
Num 21:8-9, 183
Num 23:24, 163
Num 27:16-17, 96
Num 34:3,12, 186
Num 35:22-34, 132
Num 5:17, 184
Num 5:6-7, 171
Num 6:22-26, 180
Num 8:7, 184
Origen, 147
Paul, 12, 13, 16, 17, 20, 31, 44, 45, 47, 51, 52, 53, 66, 72, 77, 78, 84, 87, 91, 92, 100, 102, 103, 106, 120, 131, 141, 143, 144, 145, 148, 150, 152, 153, 154, 158, 163, 168, 169, 200, 202, 205, 206, 211, 212, 225, 239
Peter, 13, 17, 25, 32, 37, 40, 43, 47, 52, 56, 68, 72, 73, 81, 84, 87, 88, 93, 94, 95, 96, 97, 98, 102, 108, 118, 119, 139, 144, 145, 146, 148, 149, 164, 168, 171, 172, 191, 201, 214, 235, 243, 247
Pharisees, 11, 40, 58, 97, 99, 102, 118, 123, 126, 127, 139, 141, 164, 168, 198, 202
Phil 1:11, 109
Phil 1:21, 66, 177
Phil 1:27-28, 92

Phil 1:7, 12-14, 207
Phil 2:10, 256
Phil 2:12, 200
Phil 2:12-13, 196
Phil 2:13, 207
Phil 2:17, 114, 208
Phil 2:2, 62, 92
Phil 2:6, 16
Phil 2:6-11, 234
Phil 3:10-11, 208
Phil 3:11-12, 200, 211
Phil 3:2, 131
Phil 3:21, 256
Phil 3:6, 225
Phil 4:9, 53, 100
Pope John Paul II, 189
Pope Pius XII, 103, 222
Pope St. Clement, 98
Prov 1:5-6, 29
Prov 10:6, 180
Prov 11:2, 257
Prov 23:21, 257
Prov 24:11-12, 135
Prov 25:20-22, 216
Prov 26:12, 257
Prov 28:13, 171
Prov 3:11-12, 255
Prov 3:5, 257
Prov 3:5-6, 47
Prov 30:8, 257
Prov 31:10-12, 227
Prov 31:1-2,8-9, 233
Prov 7:27, 216
Prov 8:22, 9
Prov 9:1-5, 160
Psalm 1:1-3, 254
Psalm 103:11-12, 135, 199
Psalm 106:37-42, 134
Psalm 110:1, 256
Psalm 110:1-3, 17
Psalm 116:13, 160
Psalm 116:15, 83
Psalm 119, 51
Psalm 127:3-5, 129
Psalm 128:3,5-6, 129
Psalm 13:3-4, 260
Psalm 132:8, 182, 241

Psalm 136, 248
Psalm 139:13-14, 133
Psalm 139:7-12, 216
Psalm 141:2, 188
Psalm 17:29, 256
Psalm 19:1-5, 191
Psalm 19:2, 255
Psalm 2:7, 17
Psalm 2:9, 97
Psalm 21:10, 216
Psalm 22:28, 16
Psalm 31:20, 160
Psalm 32:4, 258
Psalm 32:5, 171
Psalm 34:14, 259
Psalm 34:8, 259
Psalm 44:1, 100
Psalm 44:2, 100
Psalm 45:1-9, 234
Psalm 51:1-2, 199
Psalm 51:2, 184
Psalm 51:3, 251
Psalm 51:5, 132
Psalm 55:15, 216
Psalm 6:6, 252
Psalm 66:20, 109
Psalm 68:7-8, 155
Psalm 71:9, 260
Psalm 72:15, 180
Psalm 75:1, 110
Psalm 78:2-3, 100
Psalm 86:16, 236
Psalm 87:5, 236
Psalm 9:17, 216
Psalm 94:9, 134
Purgatory, 38, 77, 210, 212, 213
Real Presence, 31, 74, 104, 155, 168, 170
Reconciliation, 171
Redemptive Suffering, 206
Rev 1:17-18, 95
Rev 1:5-6, 256
Rev 11:19-12:17, 241
Rev 12:1, 233, 252
Rev 12:1-2, 240
Rev 12:17, 238

Rev 12:2,17, 252
Rev 14:1-5, 154
Rev 15:4, 109
Rev 16:6, 163
Rev 17:14, 18
Rev 18:23, 126, 219
Rev 19:1,5-9, 126, 219
Rev 19:10, 109
Rev 19:13-14, 143, 198
Rev 19:7-8, 198
Rev 19:9, 107, 112, 170
Rev 2:10, 235
Rev 2:10-11, 203
Rev 2:11, 90
Rev 2:16, 92
Rev 2:26-27, 96
Rev 20:10,15, 217
Rev 20:12, 194, 213
Rev 20:13-14, 213
Rev 21:14, 73, 87
Rev 21:2, 170
Rev 21:22, 170
Rev 21:2-4, 126, 219
Rev 21:27, 82, 206, 211
Rev 21:5-6, 20
Rev 21:8, 206, 217
Rev 22:13,16, 20
Rev 22:14, 155
Rev 22:14-15, 206
Rev 22:16, 15
Rev 22:17, 126, 219
Rev 3:20, 169
Rev 3:3, 100
Rev 3:5, 203
Rev 4:8, 9, 107, 254
Rev 4:8-11, 104
Rev 4:9-11, 19
Rev 5:3, 105
Rev 5:6,9-10, 170
Rev 5:6-7,12-14, 19
Rev 5:8, 82, 188
Rev 5:8-14, 104
Rev 6:1, 105
Rev 6:9-11, 82
Rev 7:11, 19
Rev 7:14, 143
Rev 7:17, 170
Rev 7:4, 246

Rev 8:3-4, 188
Rev 8:3-5, 82
Rom 1:19-20, 191
Rom 1:25-27, 129
Rom 1:29-31, 205
Rom 1:3-4, 15
Rom 1:5, 226
Rom 1:9, 248
Rom 10:12-13, 150
Rom 10:14, 80
Rom 10:15, 112
Rom 10:17, 101
Rom 10:8, 53
Rom 11:22-23, 201
Rom 11:32, 68
Rom 11:36, 111
Rom 12:1-2, 122
Rom 12:1-5, 75
Rom 12:2, 66, 177
Rom 12:3-6, 63
Rom 12:3-8, 47
Rom 12:4-5, 80
Rom 13:13-14, 205
Rom 13:1-7, 89
Rom 13:8, 259
Rom 14:17, 256
Rom 15:16, 12
Rom 15:6, 108
Rom 16:1-2, 151
Rom 16:17, 62
Rom 16:20, 223
Rom 16:25-26, 26
Rom 16:26, 226
Rom 16:6, 71
Rom 16:7, 66, 177
Rom 2:13-16, 191
Rom 2:16, 11, 253
Rom 2:5-10,13, 194
Rom 3:10-12, 224
Rom 3:20, 194
Rom 3:21-22, 196
Rom 3:28-30, 195
Rom 4:1, 152
Rom 4:16-18, 152
Rom 4:23-25, 142
Rom 4:25, 166
Rom 4:9, 195
Rom 4:9-12, 195

Rom 5:12, 31
Rom 5:14, 223
Rom 5:15, 29
Rom 5:18, 68
Rom 5:19, 199, 226
Rom 5:3, 260
Rom 6:12, 256
Rom 6:1-6, 142
Rom 6:17, 87
Rom 6:3-4, 192
Rom 7:22-23, 259
Rom 8:14-17, 65, 176
Rom 8:15, 255
Rom 8:15-16, 12
Rom 8:17, 194, 207
Rom 8:21, 256
Rom 8:28-30, 65
Rom 8:31-35, 122
Rom 8:34, 109
Rom 8:35-39, 80
Rom 8:9, 14, 66, 177
Rom 9:10-13, 132
Rom 9:21, 225
Rom 9:33, 94
Rom 9:5, 12, 16, 18
SACRAMENTS, 23, 25, 46, 64, 66, 113, 117, 119, 121, 127, 136, 155, 160, 190, 204, 222
Sadducees, 164, 168
saints, 12, 41, 48, 65, 75, 77, 78, 79, 81, 82, 83, 87, 90, 97, 103, 108, 111, 122, 126, 151, 163, 181, 183, 188, 196, 198, 207, 219, 238, 241, 248
Salvation, 12, 20, 22, 41, 46, 47, 48, 49, 52, 77, 81, 87, 92, 93, 98, 117, 120, 126, 136, 138, 140, 141, 143, 144, 146, 148, 150, 160, 189, 190, 191, 193, 196, 198, 200, 201, 202, 205, 206, 208, 210, 219, 222, 239, 241, 246
Samaritan, 24, 142

Samaritans, 98, 141, 142, 145
Scribes, 11, 34, 40, 97, 99, 102, 164, 198, 202
Septuagint, 35, 36, 37, 38, 39, 52, 100, 228, 230
Seraphim, 212
Sir 15:15, 193
Sir 2:1, 260
Sir 21:9-10, 216
Sir 22:15, 185
Sir 24:3-21, 9
Sir 26:1-4, 122
Sir 28:2, 259
Sir 28:2-6, 43
Sir 3:30, 194, 204
Sir 39:23, 185
Sir 39:26, 257
Sir 39:26-27, 186
Sir 39:33, 254
Sir 44:22, 67
Sir 5:1-7, 202
Sir 7:32-33, 212
sola scriptura, 34, 46, 47, 49, 50, 51, 52, 53, 54, 74, 93, 99, 205, 206, 232
Song 2:8-10, 121
Song 4:12, 229
Song 6:10, 235, 250
Song 8:7, 260
sphragis, 246
St. Cyprian, 147
Statues, 181, 183
steward, 89, 95, 124, 125, 138, 206, 214, 215, 239
Sub Tuum Praesidium, 235, 250
Talmud, 35, 36, 37, 103
Temporal Consequences, 209
Thomas, 19, 64, 74, 97, 139, 142, 164, 167, 243
Tit 1:13-14, 89
Tit 1:5, 150
Tit 1:7-11, 89

Tit 1:9, 71
Tit 2:11, 69
Tit 2:12, 256
Tit 2:13, 12, 17
Tit 2:15, 70, 89
Tit 3:5, 143
Tit 3:8-10, 89
Titus 1:7, 88
Tob 12:8, 194
Tob 13:7-8, 67
Tob 3:2, 252
Tob 4:7-11, 193
Tob 5:5, 45
Tob 6:2-8, 16-17, 45
Tob 7:11, 42
Tob 7:13, 105
Tob 7:9-14, 121
Tob 8:4-9, 121
Tradition, 35, 36, 37, 38, 46, 49, 50, 53, 54, 96, 97, 99, 100, 101, 102, 103, 147
TRINITY, 8, 14, 120, 225, 238, 250
Wis 10:7, 185
Wis 11:15-16, 29
Wis 11:26, 81
Wis 12:12-13, 67
Wis 13:1-9, 190
Wis 16:10-12, 43, 67
Wis 16:20, 162
Wis 2:12-20, 44
Wis 2:23, 64
Wis 3:14, 153
Wis 3:1-5, 81
Wis 3:1-8, 213
Wis 3:5-6, 43
Wis 5:16, 235
Wis 5:17-20, 43
Wis 7:1-2, 250
Wis 7:26-27, 43
Wis 9:15, 259
Wis 9:17, 148
Wis 9:5, 237
Wis 9:8, 104
Women's Ordination, 150, 151

works of the Law, 101, 102, 163
Zech 1:3, 191, 257
Zech 10:2-3, 96
Zech 12:10, 13:1, 142
Zech 3:1, 19
Zech 7:9-10, 135
Zeph 2:9, 185

Check out our:
- doctrinal holy cards,
- Catholic calendars,
- books,
- MP3s
- Catholic posters,

and all our other great Catholic stuff at:

www.BridegroomPress.com
or
www.BestCatholicPosters.com

A Small Selection of Our Posters

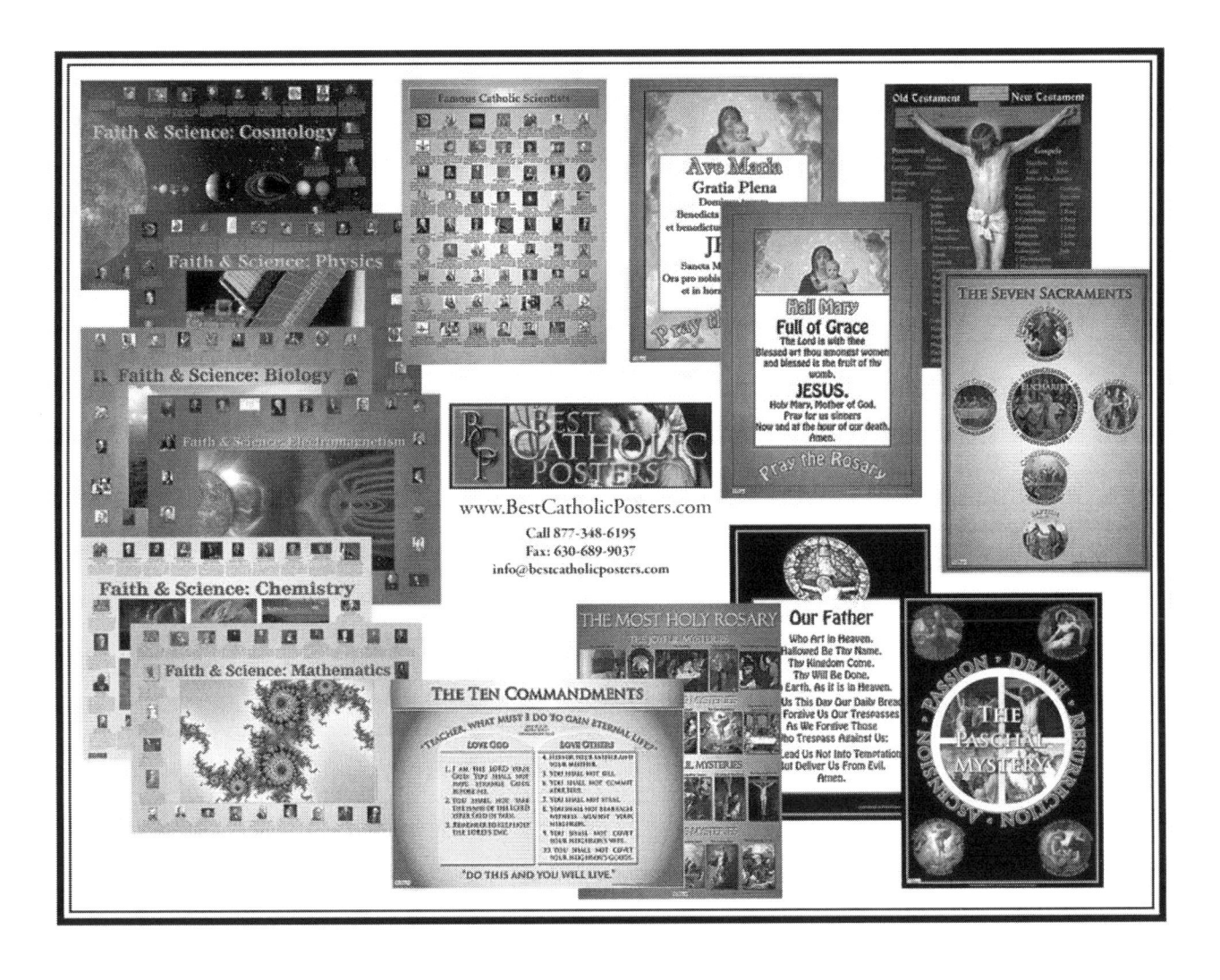

Printed in Great Britain
by Amazon